Amphibians and Reptiles
of Pennsylvania
and the Northeast

COMSTOCK BOOKS IN HERPETOLOGY
Aaron M. Bauer, Consulting Editor

Amphibians and Reptiles of Pennsylvania and the Northeast

Arthur C. Hulse,
C. J. McCoy, and Ellen Censky

Illustrated by Linda Witt Fries

COMSTOCK PUBLISHING ASSOCIATES
a division of

Cornell University Press

Ithaca and London

First published 2001 by Cornell University Press

Printed in the United States of America
Color plates printed in Hong Kong.

Library of Congress Cataloging-in-Publication Data

Hulse, Arthur C.
    Amphibians and reptiles of Pennsylvania and the Northeast / Arthur
C. Hulse, C. J. McCoy, and Ellen Censky; illustrations by Linda Witt
Fries.
        p.   cm.
    Includes bibliographical references (p.   ).
    ISBN 0-8014-3768-7 (cloth)
    1. Amphibians—Pennsylvania.   2. Reptiles—Pennsylvania.   3.
Amphibians—Northeastern States.   4. Reptiles—Northeastern States.   I.
McCoy, C. J. (Clarence J.)   II. Censky, Ellen J. (Ellen Joan), 1955–   .
III. Title.
    QL653.P4 H86 2001
    597.9′09748—dc21

                                                        00-011715

Cornell University Press strives to use environmentally responsible suppliers and materials to the fullest extent possible in the publishing of its books. Such materials include vegetable-based, low-VOC inks and acid-free papers that are recycled, totally chlorine-free, or partly composed of nonwood fibers. Books that bear the logo of the FSC (Forest Stewardship Council) use paper taken from forests that have been inspected and certified as meeting the highest standards for environmental and social responsibility. For further information, visit our website at www.cornellpress.cornell.edu.

Cloth printing   10 9 8 7 6 5 4 3 2 1

To Caleb Hulse
for his help and companionship
and
to the memory of Jack McCoy,
whose presence is greatly missed

Contents

Preface

It is with profound regret that we must compose the preface to this book by ourselves. Jack McCoy, our friend and co-author, died at his home on July 7, 1993. He is sorely missed, and his passing leaves a void in the study of herpetology. The present work had its origin in a previous publication of Jack's *Amphibians and Reptiles in Pennsylvania: Checklist, Bibliography, and Atlas of Distribution* (1982).

The very completeness of the atlas illustrated just how little information was available concerning Pennsylvania's herpetofauna. As a result, in the fall of 1988, one of us (ACH) suggested to Jack a collaborative effort in which we would augment the distributional information available in the checklist and expand the species accounts. We decided that what was needed for the state was not a field guide to the herpetofauna per se but rather a volume dealing with the natural history of Pennsylvania's amphibians and reptiles. This approach is different from that of most field guides, which give a brief description of typical specimens and a thumbnail sketch of the species as a biological entity.

Initially it was our intent to restrict the book to Pennsylvania; however, during the development of the manuscript, it was suggested that the scope of the book be increased to include the entire northeastern United States, with the distributional emphasis still being placed on Pennsylvania.

We intend the book for a wide audience, including both professional and amateur herpetologists, students, and those individuals who have a love of the out-of-doors and an abiding passion to learn more about the organisms that they encounter on their excursions into the field. Attempting to satisfy such a diverse audience is difficult, and we have probably not succeeded in every case. The book is intended to go beyond the normal scope of a field guide and present more detailed information on a wide range of natural history and ecological topics along with the necessary references to allow the reader to delve in greater detail into the topics discussed. Some of the information presented in the Habitat and Habits and Reproduction sections may be familiar to professional or experienced amateur herpetologists who are familiar with the fauna of the northeastern United States. However, this information will give the interested non-herpetologist or herpetologist from other regions of the country a clearer picture of each species discussed as a total biological entity rather than merely a series of key characters, photographs, and distribution maps. We did not intend, however, for the book to be a mere compilation or review of existing information. Much of the data presented herein is the result of our work both in the field and in the museum and contributes new information, especially pertaining to those species found in Pennsylvania.

This book is also intended to show clearly where our knowledge of the distribution and biology of the region's herpetofauna is incomplete or lacking. It is our hope that this work will stimulate readers, both professional and amateur, to delve more deeply into the study of the herpetofauna of the northeastern United States and thus begin to fill some of the gaps in our knowledge that are so noticeable in the species accounts.

Acknowledgments

We thank Thomas Pauley, Howard Reinert, Margaret Stewart, and Aaron Bauer for their careful and constructive reviews of the manuscript. Their comments greatly improved the text. A special debt of gratitude is owed to Aaron Bauer for bringing the manuscript to the attention of the editors at Cornell University Press. Steve Rogers helped greatly with procuring specimens and providing locality information from the collection of the Carnegie Museum of Natural History. R. Wayne Van Devender generously provided many of the photographs used within the text, and his exquisite photographic skills have added greatly to this work. Tom Diez provided critical photographs of some species and his contributions are gratefully acknowledged here.

Permits to collect and study amphibians and reptiles throughout Pennsylvania were provided to ACH by the Pennsylvania Fish and Boat Commission (PFBC). We thank Andrew Shiels, Endangered Species Coordinator of the PFBC, for the help he provided throughout much of this project. We thank the many volunteers of the Pennsylvania Herpetological Atlas Project (PHAP) for providing critical observations on many of the less common amphibians and reptiles of Pennsylvania. While all volunteers are thanked, a special thanks goes to Rick Koval, Stan and Alice Kotal, Skip Conant, Tom Diez, Terry Laux, Brian Gray, Mark Lethaby, and Tom Pluto. We also thank Frank Felbaum of the Wild Resources Conservation Fund for his unfailing support of the study of the herpetology of Pennsylvania.

A special debt of gratitude is extended to Peter Prescott, our editor at Cornell University Press, for working with us through the numerous stages in the process of converting a first draft manuscript into a finished book.Without his help, encouragement, and patience this book would have never been completed. Margo Quinto ably copy edited the final draft and provided many valuable suggestions and comments that greatly improved the text. We thank her for her assistance. Linda Witt Fries produced the drawings used in association with the keys.

Finally, one of us (ACH) owes a particular debt of gratitude to his son Caleb for help and companionship in both the field and the laboratory. We hope he will have many fond memories of this project in the years to come.

Introduction

Landform Patterns

The U.S. Northeast exhibits a diverse series of landform patterns. The major physiographic provinces of the region are the Coastal Plain, the Piedmont, the Valley and Ridge Province, the Appalachian Plateau, the Central Lowlands, the Adirondack Upland, and the New England Province. The mountains of the Northeast were created primarily during the Alleghenian Orogeny (mountain building), 260 million years ago. There has been little in the way of mountain building or uplifting since then, so for many millions of years the opposing forces of leveling (erosion, slide, and creep) have been at work shaping the landscape of Pennsylvania and the northeastern United States.

The different landforms and varied topographic relief of the Northeast are due to the different degrees of resistance to weathering and erosion of the rocks that make up the region. Sedimentary rocks, such as limestone and shale, weather rapidly and are carried away as fine sediments in streams and rivers. Other sedimentary rock, such as sandstone, as well as igneous rocks, such as granite, resist weathering and remain behind after the less resistant material has been removed.

The Coastal Plain is a low, level region of sand and gravel with generally poorly developed soils. The Coastal Plain extends from extreme southeastern Pennsylvania through southern and central New Jersey and through Staten Island and Long Island, New York. Cape Cod, Massachusetts, is a northern isolated segment of the Coastal Plain. In Pennsylvania, this landform is obscured by the city of Philadelphia and the heavily developed regions of Bucks and Delaware counties.

Interior to the Coastal Plain is the Piedmont. This is composed of relatively low ridges separating valleys of varying widths. The Piedmont extends diagonally in a narrow band from southeastern Pennsylvania to north-central New Jersey. A small northern extension of the Piedmont extends into southeastern New York.

The Valley and Ridge Province is bordered on the west by the Appalachian Plateau and to the east by the Piedmont and the New England physiographic provinces. As the name implies, it is made up of a series of parallel ridges and intervening valleys. The general orientation of these valleys and ridges is from the southwest to the northeast. The Valley and Ridge Province extends from south-central Pennsylvania in Bedford, Fulton, and Franklin counties northeastward into extreme northwestern

New Jersey. This province then extends northward in a narrow band along the Hudson River in New York. In general, the Valley and Ridge is a narrow landform, varying from about 80 miles (129 km) wide in south-central Pennsylvania to less than 14 miles (22 km) wide in the vicinity of High Point, New Jersey.

The most extensive landform (i.e., physiographic province) in Pennsylvania and New York is the Allegheny Plateau, which covers most of the western and northern portions of Pennsylvania and almost all of southern and central New York. This name, however, is somewhat deceptive. One usually thinks of a plateau as a flat elevated tableland. In the Allegheny Plateau, it is the rocks that are flat rather than the land-form itself. The rocks of the plateau are mainly a mixture of sandstone, shale, and limestone, all of which are found in relatively flat layers. As a result of differential weathering, streams have cut deep channels in the softer shale and limestone, forming steep-sided valleys, ravines, and hollows. In the process, they have left behind hills, ridges, and knobs of the harder, more resistant sandstone. The Allegheny Plateau is often referred to as a dissected plateau, alluding to the deep cuts made in the landscape by the processes of leveling. The deeply dissected areas of the plateau offer some of the most rugged landscape in the region.

The Central Lowlands occur in a narrow strip (5–30 miles, or 8–48 km, wide) bordering Lake Erie, Lake Ontario, and the St. Lawrence River in New York.

The Adirondack Upland of northern New York is characterized by tall rugged mountains. Some of the highest peaks in the region occur in the Adirondack Uplands. Among these are Mount Marcy at 5,344 feet (1,629 m) and Algonquin Peak at 5,114 feet (1,559 m).

The New England Province occupies almost all of the New England states. It is a complex landform, shaped largely by glacial activity. Most of the northern section (Vermont, New Hampshire, and the interior of Maine) is an irregular glacially dissected highland. Scattered low moun-tains and monadnocks occur in the region. This area is also characterized by relatively high mountain ranges such as the Green Mountains of Vermont and the White Mountains of New Hampshire. The southern section of the New England Province has been more eroded than the northern section and, as a consequence, is lower in elevation. The region gradually descends through a series of low mountains and plateaus to the coastal region. Most of the New England coastline is rocky owing to recent glacial scour activity.

Some amphibians and reptiles are restricted primarily to one or another of these landform regions. For example, the southern leopard frog, eastern mud turtle, northern pine snake, northern scarlet snake and ground skink are found only in the Coastal Plain. The mudpuppy, ravine salamander, seal salamander, mountain chorus frog, soft-shelled turtle, and shorthead garter snake are found only in the western section of the Allegheny Plateau.

Climate

Temperature in the northeastern United States, as elsewhere, is primarily determined by latitude and elevation. In general, annual average temperature tends to decline gradually from south to north. For example, the average annual temperature in Philadelphia is about 52°F (10°C), whereas the average annual temperature in northern Maine is only 40°–42°F (4–5°C). This relationship, however, does not hold all across the region. For example, as one travels from either the east or the west to the central portion of Pennsylvania along any given latitude, temperature tends to decrease. This decrease is due to elevational changes. Elevation increases in the eastern section of the Allegheny Plateau and the western Valley and Ridge Province. For example, in Somerset County along the mountainous south-central border of the state the annual temperature is similar to that of Pike County in the northeast or Erie County in the northwest. The lower latitude of Somerset County is compensated for by its higher average elevation.

These differences are even more pronounced in mountainous regions of New York and New England. In the Adirondack Mountains, Green Mountains, and White Mountains, mean annual temperatures can be as low as 38°F (3°C). Yet, at similar latitudes, Erie, Pennsylvania, and Buffalo, New York, have annual mean temperatures of about 48°F (9°C). They are, of course, at a lower elevation and near Lake Erie.

Another, and possibly biologically more meaningful, way of measuring temperature regimes in a region is by growing season. Growing season may be defined as the average number of days between the last killing frost in the spring and the first killing frost in the fall. In northern Maine, the growing season may be as short as 100 days. Growing seasons of as little as 80 days have been reported for some areas in the White, Green, and Adirondack mountains. Growing season increases along the coast. Coastal Maine has a growing season of up to 160 days. The growing season in coastal southern New England may be as long as 180 days, and in southeastern New Jersey a growing season of as much as 250 days has been reported. Inland, at similar latitudes, the growing season is shorter. For example, in southwestern Pennsylvania the growing season seldom exceeds 180 days and is often as short as 150 days.

These differences in temperature will affect many aspects of the biology of reptiles and amphibians, including the length of their annual activity period as well as their dates of emergence from and entrance into hibernation, their life history characteristics, and their geographic distribution. Most species with a regionwide distribution emerge from their winter inactivity earlier in the southeastern portion of the region than in the northern sections. They also tend to remain active later in the fall than do animals from the north. Reproductive activity can also be greatly affected by temperature. The timber rattlesnake *(Crotalus horridus)* at the northern edge of its range in New York is a quadrennial breeder (W. Brown 1991), whereas populations from central Pennsylvania appear to be biennial (Galligan and Dunson 1979). Individuals of the common musk turtle *(Sternotherus odoratus)* from southern populations mature at a smaller size and a younger age than do northern congenerics (Tinkle 1961). A review of the range maps will show that some species range farther north along the coast than in the interior, and some species that are widespread throughout the rest of New York are conspicuously absent from the Adirondack highlands.

Average July temperatures in Pennsylvania range from 74°F (23°C) in the southeast to 68°F (20°C) in the north-central portion of the state. Mean July temperatures in New England range from a low of 66.4°F (18°C) in Maine to a high of 71.2°F (22°C) in Rhode Island.

Annual precipitation in the northeastern portion of Pennsylvania varies from 44 in. (110 cm) to 38 in. (96.5 cm). The distribution of precipitation is more complex than is that of temperature. Most precipitation-producing weather enters the state from the west, and precipitation gradually increases to a maximum along the Allegheny high plateau. It then decreases owing to a slight rain shadow effect in the center of the state. Moist air coming off the Atlantic Ocean increases average rainfall to 42 in. (105 cm). and 44 in. (110 cm) in places along the eastern border. As this moist air moves westward there is a slight drying trend as moisture is lost through precipitation along the route.

The above discussion of precipitation and temperature is based on long-term averages, but climatic conditions can fluctuate drastically from year to year. For example, between 1931 and 1984 annual precipitation in Pennsylvania ranged from a low of about 31 in. (78.5 cm) in 1964 to a high of 52 in. (130 cm) in 1972.

Vegetation

Little of the original vegetation of the northeastern United States remains today. Virtually all plant communities that we see in the area are at some stage of recovery from logging, mining, agriculture, and a host of other activities. Deforestation along coastal areas began shortly after European colonization of the area and expanded inland with the western expansion in the late 1700s. By the early 1900s most of Pennsylvania's timber had fallen victim to the ax or the saw. The magnitude of this activity was so great in the 1920s that the entire northern section of the Allegheny Plateau (an area greater than 8,600 mi^2, or 23,000 km^2) was known as the berry patch because the entire region had been clear-cut and most was in the early stages of secondary succession, with brambles and wild berries being the dominant vegetation.

Despite this massive destruction of vegetation, the northeastern United States has a great variety of plant communities. Today, forests cover over 60% of the total land area within the northeastern United States. Most of the following discussion is based on Kuchler's *Potential Natural Vegetation of the Conterminous United States*, published by the American

Geographical Society in 1964. Kuchler recognized eight major forest types within the region.

The Appalachian oak forest is the major forest type in the region. It is dominated by red and white oaks, with hickory as a subdominant, and is sometimes referred to as oak-hickory forest. In addition to the oaks and hickories, this forest type harbors a variety of other tree species. This assemblage occupies most of southern and central Pennsylvania, southwestern and northeastern New Jersey, most of Connecticut, Rhode Island, and eastern Massachusetts and the region around the Finger Lakes of New York.

The second largest natural vegetation type is the northern hardwood forest, which occupies most of northern Pennsylvania, northwestern New Jersey, southern and central New York, northern and western Massachusetts, and low to intermediate elevations in Vermont, New Hampshire, and eastern Maine. Dominant species are sugar maple, hemlock, yellow birch, beech, and, in times past (before clear-cutting), white pine.

The northern hardwood spruce forest is the third largest assemblage in the region. It occurs throughout most of the Adirondacks, in the more mountainous regions of Vermont and New Hampshire, and in northern and western Maine. It is characterized by birch, beech, sugar maples, and a variety of conifers. In drier and warmer areas the dominant conifer is the hemlock, but in poorly drained areas and in the cooler regions hemlock is replaced by spruce and fir.

At higher elevations and in colder regions of northern New England and the Adirondacks, the northern hardwood spruce forest is replaced by the spruce-fir forest. The major trees is this assemblage are balsam fir and red spruce, with black spruce being restricted to bogs and other areas of poor drainage.

Four additional forest types occupy smaller areas within the northeastern United States, but they contribute much to the overall diversity of the region. The largest, in area, of these is the beech-maple forest. It occurs along the southern border of Lake Erie and Lake Ontario and along the banks of the St. Lawrence. As the name implies, this assemblage is dominated by beech and a variety of maples. In extreme southwestern Pennsylvania mixed mesophytic forest is the dominant form. This is a broadleaf deciduous forest type occupied by numerous codominant species such as tulip poplar, basswood, sugar maple, white and red oak, and beech. Oak-hickory-pine forest occurs along the lower Susquehanna River and in the Potomac drainage of Pennsylvania and in extreme southern New Jersey. It includes Virginia and pitch pine; black, chestnut, white, and scarlet oak; and hickory. Perhaps the most distinctive forest assemblage within the northeastern United States is the northeastern oak-pine forest. This assemblage occupies most of southeastern New Jersey (i.e., the Pine Barrens) as well as most of Long Island and portions of coastal Connecticut.

Human activity has greatly altered the natural vegetation of the northeastern United States. Most of the forested land in the region has been cleared at one time or another for a variety of reasons including but not limited to lumber, agriculture, charcoal production, mineral and fossil fuel extraction, and the wood chemical industry. As the forests recover from these activities species assemblages are often altered from the original forest composition. White pine was an important climax species in much of the northern hardwood forest but is virtually absent from it today, being replaced by a variety of hardwoods such as cherry. In addition, the introduction of exotic organisms has had a major impact on the species composition of much of the forested region of the northeastern United States. Two of the most destructive and best documented introductions are the gypsy moth and the chestnut blight.

These are only the major assemblages found within the region. Many smaller assemblages occur within or adjacent to these major forest types. The Pennsylvania Natural Diversity Inventory recognizes over 90 distinct vegetational habitats within the state. Many of these more specialized habitats are wetlands that often support rich assemblages of reptiles and amphibians. Among these habitats are quaking bogs, boreal swamps, hardwood swamps, shrub swamps, seeps, and calcareous fens. Readers interested in a more detailed account of Pennsylvania vegetation are referred to *The Atlas of Pennsylvania*.

Explanations

FAMILY AND GENUS ACCOUNTS

The 83 species of amphibians and reptiles historically known to occur in the Northeast represent 17 families and 49 genera. The family and genus accounts precede the accounts of the northeastern species contained within those families and genera. These short accounts are designed simply to acquaint the reader with the general characteristics shared by all members of the family or genus and the overall distribution and diversity of the group. They are not intended to be comprehensive in nature. Generic accounts are not presented for genera that have only a single species.

SPECIES ACCOUNTS

For each species, the standard common name, current scientific name, and etymology are given. Each species account is divided into a series of topics, which are explained below.

Standard Common Name, Current Scientific Name, and Etymology

The common names used in the accounts follow the usage of Conant and Collins (1991), but local common names for species of amphibians and reptiles often differ from the standard common names given here. An attempt should be made to introduce the standard common names into general usage, as has been done with birds. Scientific names are also those used by Conant and Collins (1991). For species that have one described subspecies in the region, the trinomial is used. If more than one subspecies has been reported, the account refers to the species in general and the Remarks section deals with pertinent subspecific differences, unless the subspecies have disjunct distributions in the region (e.g., *Virginia valeriae*, the earth snakes), in which case, each subspecies has its own species account.

The name of the author of the species (the individual who formally described the species) appears after the scientific name. If the current genus for the species is different from that to which it was originally assigned, the original author's name appears in parentheses.

Description

This section provides a general description of body shape and coloration that will aid the reader in identifying specimens. Variations in color and pattern are discussed when appropriate. When life history stages differ markedly in appearance, the individual stages are described. External characters useful in distinguishing between sexes are discussed for species that exhibit sexual dimorphism.

Sizes are given in metric and English units. Salamanders, lizards, and snakes have two measurements. The first is the snout-vent length (SVL), measured from the tip of the snout to the proximal (anterior) margin of the vent. The second measure is total length (ToL), measured from the tip of the snout to the tip of the tail. Total lengths are based only on animals with complete unregenerated tails. The length of frogs and toads is reproted as snout-urostyle length (SUL), the straight-line distance from the tip of the snout to the end of the body. For turtles, the medial straight-line carapace length (CL) is given. When sexual size dimorphism is great, separate sizes are given for males and females. A maximum size record for each species is given when available. See also the mensural data in the Appendix.

Confusing Species

This section is particularly important in those accounts where incorrect identification due to similarity with other forms is likely to occur. Confusing species are listed, and the necessary diagnostic characteristics for proper identification are given. In some cases, confusing species occupy different habitats or are found in different geographic locations, so detailed information on collecting locality and habitat is often helpful in making a correct identification. Because it is assumed that this book will generally be used to identify field-caught or field-observed specimens, diagnostic characters are those apparent in live animals. As a consequence, this section may not always adequately distinguish between similar species if they have been preserved.

Habitat and Habits

This section provides information on the habitats of the species and on daily and annual activity patterns, feeding, behavior, and other natural history information such as home range, density, and movement. The studies cited in this section were chosen on the same basis as the studies cited in the reproduction section.

Reproduction

This section deals with various aspects of the reproductive biology of the species. It includes such topics as size or age at maturity, breeding season, courtship behavior, habitat preference during courtship and mating, egg number and size, oviposition site, parental behavior, rate of development and size and ecology of neonates. See also the reproductive data in the Appendix.

Studies pertaining to the species' biology in the Northeast are cited. If no studies have been conducted within this area, then studies from other parts of the species' range are referenced. Information that has no citation associated with it comes from our personal observations or studies of the species. We rely as much as possible on our experiences.

Remarks

This section covers such topics as taxonomic status; unusual reports on the natural history, behavior, or appearance of the species; and the conservation status of species within the region, where appropriate.

Distribution

This section deals with the general range of the species or subspecies within the United States and the specific range within Pennsylvania and the rest of the Northeast. General ranges are taken from Conant and Collins (1991) or from specific works dealing with the overall distribution of the individual species. Detailed information on the range of the species in Pennsylvania comes both from voucher specimens in museums and from our fieldwork. The reader should refer to McCoy 1982 for a list of museums from which locality records for Pennsylvania specimens were obtained. A spot distribution map is presented for each Pennsylvania species on a base map showing Pennsylvania county boundaries. Each spot is centered on the exact locality but covers an area of approximately 5 mi (8 km) in diameter. Unless otherwise noted, the three types of symbols used on the maps represent the following. Solid circles indicate either that a voucher specimen is available or that one of us has observed specimens.

Half-solid circles indicate localities where specimens have been collected in the past but where their continued occurrence is questionable owing to habitat modification or pollution. Open circles indicate selected records reported by volunteers involved with the Pennsylvania Herpetological Atlas Project. Many of the latter records do not have voucher specimens associated with them, but we are confident of their validity.

APPENDIX

The appendix, "Pennsylvania Species Mensural and Reproductive Data," provides statistical data for individual species. Mensural data include mean length (plus or minus one standard error of the mean) for sexually mature individuals and some neonates, range, sample size, statistical comparison between male and female, and size at maturity.

Reproductive data include mean clutch size (plus or minus one standard error of the mean), range, sample size, and statistical ratios.

Observing and Collecting Amphibians and Reptiles

Readers should keep in mind that amphibians and reptiles are living organisms and should be treated with care and respect. Unlike birds, amphibians and reptiles can be and usually are actually captured for positive identification. Be sure that you handle the animals gently and return any amphibian or reptile that is temporarily collected to the site of capture; do not simply release it near your house. Unless there is a problem with identification, animals should not be removed from their place of capture. It is best to retain them in captivity for as short a time as possible (no more than a week). The majority of animals (especially snakes and salamanders) will be found only by actually moving cover objects in the animal's environment. This activity, although necessary, should be done carefully. Be sure that you return all cover objects to their original positions. If the animal was found under a rock or other cover object it should be replaced next to, rather than directly under, the cover object, to avoid inadvertently crushing the animal while replacing a cover object. In all cases, treat the environment with utmost respect.

Be sure to ask permission before entering posted land. If land is not physically posted, however, you may assume that you can enter at will. Never leave litter behind.

The classes Amphibia and Reptilia contain extremely variable groups of animals and as a consequence no single technique will work in locating all herps. In general, amphibians and reptiles tend to be secretive. Although looking for herps between April and October is likely to yield some specimens, maximum success is achieved during specific times of the year (e.g., mating season) and under specific environmental conditions (usually high humidity and rainfall). Techniques for observing or collecting each group of amphibian and reptile will be discussed separately.

SALAMANDERS

Salamanders are most active during early spring and fall. Because high humidity and rainfall tend to stimulate salamander activity, searching for salamanders is generally successful after any warm, soaking rain. They can most reliably be found by looking under cover objects such as rocks, logs, bark, and vegetation. Some aquatic forms can be observed swimming or floating in ponds or along the weedy shallow margins of lakes. Other aquatic forms can occasionally be located by lifting submerged cover objects.

Salamanders are most active on the land surface at night. Any area that is likely to yield salamanders during the day, including spring seeps, stream margins, and wooded ravines, is also a good area to locate the animals at night. Driving slowly along back roads and little-used highways after dark or by walking about in appropriate habitat with flashlight or lantern often proves very successful, especially under wet conditions.

TOADS AND FROGS

The fact that male toads and frogs are highly vocal during early spring and summer breeding seasons makes them most likely to be located at this time. Driving about at night and listening for choruses is the most effective method of collecting or observing frogs and toads. When not calling, frogs can most frequently be encountered by searching the margins of streams, rivers, lakes, and ponds at night with a lantern or a flashlight.

LIZARDS

Lizards are uncommon in the northeastern United States. They may be active anytime from early April to late September and are especially likely to be encountered on exposed rocky areas in forested regions. Most skinks are also located in open rocky spots in forested areas, usually in the vicinity of streams.

TURTLES

With the exception of terrestrial species such as the wood turtle and box turtle, turtles are probably the most difficult group of reptiles for the casual observer to encounter, primarily because of their aquatic habitats. Many species of turtle, however, bask either at the surface of the water (e.g., snapping turtles) or on emergent objects such as rocks, logs, and sandbars (e.g., painted turtles, map turtles, redbellied turtles, softshell turtles). As a result, careful and quiet observation of suitable bodies of water with binoculars or spotting scopes often reveals the presence of turtles. Terrestrial turtles are most active from mid-April through June. During the late spring and early summer egg-laying season, aquatic species can occasionally be found moving about on land in search of nesting sites.

Nesting turtles are especially likely to be spotted along the edge of roads near streams and bridges. In addition, otherwise aquatic species often move about on land after a heavy summer rain.

SNAKES

Snakes are most active from mid-April to mid-June and again in late August and early September. In general, the best places to look for snakes are along the margins of streams and lakes (especially for water and queen snakes), around human habitation and in regions where debris such as boards and other building material lies about, and in open rocky areas and on slopes (especially in early spring in areas that have a southern exposure). Small to medium-sized species of terrestrial snakes are most likely to be found by looking under cover objects, whereas large species are more frequently encountered in the open.

Keys to the Amphibians and Reptiles of Pennsylvania and the Northeastern United States

A taxonomic key is a device designed to identify an unknown biological specimen. The keys presented here are intended for use in the identification of all northeastern amphibians and reptiles, including larval salamanders, frogs, and toads. Taxonomic keys are generally designed for specific groups of organisms. As a result, there are seven keys in this section, one each for adults of the major groups of amphibians and reptiles in the Northeast and one each for larval salamanders, frogs, and toads.

The keys are presented as a series of numbered couplets. At the end of each part of the couplet is either a number directing the user to the next appropriate couplet of the name of the species. Keys use a process of elimination to arrive at an identification. Each couplet contains a contrasting set of characters (e.g., 1a, gill slits, and 1b, no gill slits). Select the set of characters that corresponds to your specimen. Look at the right-hand side of that couplet for a number indicating the couplet to which you should proceed. Continue from couplet to couplet until you arrive at a species name rather than a number. This should be the identity of your specimen. Using keys correctly requires some practice. We suggest that you first try to identify several specimens whose identity you know. The illustrations accompanying these keys will aid in the identification of certain characters that might not be immediately apparent from their description in the couplet. The following keys are intended for use in the identification of living specimens; internal characters are absent from the keys, and many of the characters may not be visible or readily seen in some preserved specimens. Keys are generally designed to identify "typical" specimens of a species. Individuals with aberrant patterns, colors, scale counts, and so on may not key correctly.

Key to the Adult Salamanders of Pennsylvania and the Northeastern United States

1a. Adults large, completely aquatic; either gill slits or external gills present.. 2
1b. Adults smaller, generally terrestrial; if aquatic, neither gill slits nor external gills present.. 3
2a. Body strongly compressed dorsoventrally; two small gill slits present, but gills absent; five toes on hind feet...
....eastern hellbender
(Cryptobranchus alleganiensis alleganiensis)
2b. Body rounded in cross section; feathery external gills present (Fig. 1); four toes on hind feet...
....mudpuppy *(Necturus maculosus maculosus)*

Figure 1. Dorsal view of *Necturus*, showing feathery external gills.

3a. Costal grooves absent...
..............red-spotted newt *(Notophthalmus viridescens viridescens)*
3b. Costal grooves present (Fig. 2)... 4
4a. Nasolabial groove absent 5
4b. Nasolabial groove present (Fig. 3)... 8
5a. Body fairly uniform in color, without conspicuous pattern.................
..........................Jefferson salamander *(Ambystoma jeffersonianum)*
5b. Body with noticeable pattern of bars or spots.................................... 6

Figure 2. Lateral view of salamander, showing costal grooves.

Figure 3. Frontal-lateral view of salamander, showing nasolabial groove.

6a. Pattern lacking spots, but with silvery gray to white crossbars on a black background.........marbled salamander *(Ambystoma opacum)*
6b. Pattern of spots or bars other than silvery gray.................................. 7
7a. Pattern of spots... 8a
7b. Pattern of irregular bars on blotches..
................eastern tiger salamander *(Ambystoma tigrinum tigrinum)*
8a. Pattern of several large dorsal spots that are bright yellow or yellowish orange on a dark background..
....................................spotted salamander *(Ambystoma maculatum)*
8b. Pattern of numerous blue or blue-gray spots on a black background
...................................blue-spotted salamander *(Ambystoma laterale)*
9a. Ventral surface of body enamel-white with dark spots (Fig. 4); tail with noticeable constriction at the base; all feet with four toes
.............................four-toed salamander *(Hemidactylium scutatum)*

Figure 4. Ventral surface of *Hemidactylium*, showing pattern and proximal tail constriction.

9b. Not as above.. 10

10a. Light line present from posterior margin of eye to angle of jaw
     (Fig. 5)... 11

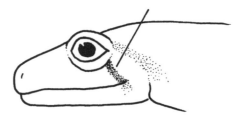

Figure 5. Lateral view of *Desmognathus*, showing diagonal light line running from eye to gape of mouth.

10b. Light line absent from eye to angle of jaw.. 12

11a. Tail round in cross section (Fig. 6); belly dark; light dorsal stripe
     usually present and straight edged; usually, dark chevrons within
     dorsal stripe (Fig. 7)..
     ....mountain dusky salamander *(Desmognathus ochrophaeus)*

Figure 6. *Desmognathus* tails in cross section.

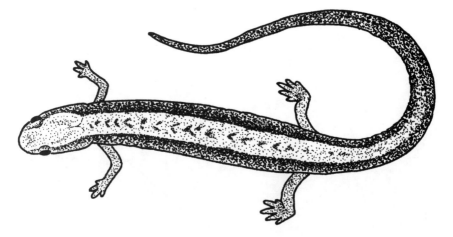

Figure 7. Dorsal view, showing pattern of *Desmognathus ochrophaeus.*

11b. Tail with a distinct dorsal keel (Fig. 6); belly light in color; dorsal stripe, if present, with a wavy edge.. 12

12a. Dorsal stripe never present; dorsum of adults usually patterned with black or brown markings; dorsal pattern of young consists of four or five pairs of orange or reddish orange spots......................................
....seal salamander *(Desmognathus monticola)*

12b. Dorsal stripe generally present, with a wavy edge (Fig. 8).................
................northern dusky salamander *(Desmognathus fuscus fuscus)*

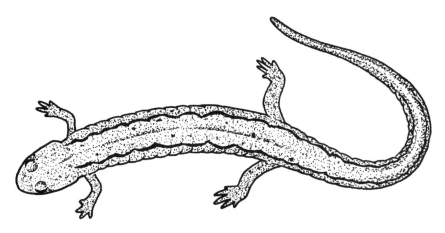

Figure 8. Dorsal view, showing pattern of *Desmognathus fuscus*.

13a. Entire margin of tongue is free, attached to floor of mouth by a central stalk (Fig. 9); basic body color red, orange, yellow, or purple
.... 14

13b. Margin of tongue free on sides and back but attached in the front; basic body color brown, black, or mottled green........................... 18

14a. Large salamander with a well-defined canthus rostralis (Fig. 10)
....northern spring salamander
....*(Gyrinophilus porphyriticus porphyriticus)*

Figure 9. Tongue.

Figure 10. Canthus rostralis.

14b. Canthus rostralis not well defined or absent.................................... 15
15a. Body stout; tail short; background color red or reddish purple with
     black spots.. 16
15b. Body slender; tail long... 17
16a. Large dark spots on body; eyes brown......................................
     ....eastern mud salamander *(Pseudotriton montanus montanus)*
16b. Small, numerous dark spots on body; eyes yellow...............................
     ....northern red salamander *(Pseudotriton ruber ruber)*
17a. Background color yellow to red with numerous dark spots; tail long
     and slender (Fig. 11), at least twice as long as body.............................
     ....longtail salamander *(Eurycea longicauda longicauda)*
17b. Background color yellowish green to yellow; two dorsolateral stripes
     extending from posterior margin of eyes to base of tail......................
     ....northern two-lined salamander *(Eurycea bislineata)*
18a. Body dorsoventrally compressed; coloration mottled green and
     yellow; tips of toes laterally expanded (Fig. 12)....................................
     ....green salamander *(Aneides aeneus)*

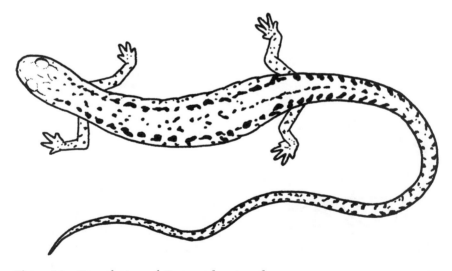

Figure 11. Dorsal view of *Eurycea longicauda.*

Figure 12. Expanded toes of *Aneides*.

18b. Not as above; basic body color brown or black; toes rounded......... 19
19a. Body robust with well-developed limbs; white or silvery white spots generally present on body.. 20
19b. Body slender; limbs thin and delicate in appearance; background color black or dark brown, with or without a reddish dorsal stripe but never with white or silvery white spots... 21
20a. Dorsal and lateral surfaces of body with numerous white or silvery white spots; throat dark; secretes large amounts of mucus when handled................northern slimy salamander *(Plethodon glutinosus)*
20b. White or silvery spots restricted to sides of body; a red spot may be present at the shoulder; throat light in color.......................................
....Wehrle's salamander *(Plethodon wehrlei)*
21a. Red or reddish dorsal stripe usually present; belly mottled salt-and-pepper (Fig. 13)...................redback salamander *(Plethodon cinereus)*
21b. Red stripe absent from back; belly uniformly dark or with fine mottling, never coarsely mottled.. 22

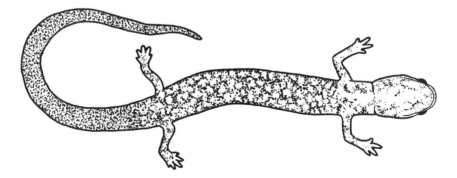

Figure 13. Ventral view of *Plethodon cinereus*.

22a. Throat and chin whitish; belly gray-black with some fine white mottling (Fig. 14)........valley and ridge salamander *(Plethodon hoffmani)*
22b. Throat, chin, and belly all a uniform grayish black without any mottling...........................ravine salamander *(Plethodon richmondi)*

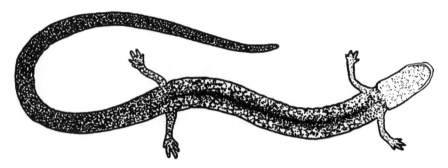

Figure 14.   Ventral view of *Plethodon hoffmani.*

Key to the Larval Salamanders of Pennsylvania and the Northeastern United States

1a. Body strongly depressed dorsoventrally; tail laterally compressed; gills transparent; head broad and flat...
......eastern hellbender *(Cryptobranchus alleganiensis alleganiensis)*
1b. Not as above... 2
2a. Four toes on hind foot.. 3
2b. Five toes on hind foot... 4
3a. Small, seldom over 35 mm ($1\frac{3}{8}$ in.) ToL; dorsal tail fin extends onto body; white or pale stripes absent from body...
.............................four-toed salamander *(Hemidactylium scutatum)*
3b. Generally larger than 35 mm ($1\frac{3}{8}$ in.) ToL; dorsal tail fin does not extend onto body; white or pale stripe present on each side of body
....mudpuppy *(Necturus maculosus maculosus)*
4a. Found almost exclusively in standing water (ponds and lakes)
.... 5
4b. Found almost exclusively in running water or spring seeps................ 8
5a. Body slender; head pointed when viewed from above, not broadly rounded; costal grooves absent...
.............red-spotted newt *(Notophthalmus viridescens viridescens)*
5b. Heavy and deep bodied, not slender; head short, broad and bluntly rounded when viewed from above; costal grooves generally present... 6
6a. Region of chin and throat darkly pigmented or mottled with dark pigment..........................marbled salamander *(Ambystoma opacum)*
6b. Region of chin and throat immaculate and pale................................. 7

7a. Dark spots absent from dorsum..
.....................................spotted salamander *(Ambystoma maculatum)*
7b. Dark spots present on dorsum...
.....................................jefferson salamander *(Ambystoma jef-fersonianum)* or blue-spotted salamander *(A. laterale)*
8a. Three pairs of gill slits associated with external gills...................... 9
8b. Four pairs of gill slits associated with external gills...................... 13
9a. From 13 to 16 costal grooves; body slender; dorsal pattern consists of either a middorsal light stripe or a series of paired spots............... 10
9b. From 16 to 19 costal grooves; body robust for the animal's size; pattern, if present, never consists of a middorsal light stripe or a series of paired spots.. 11
10a. Dorsal pattern a series of paired spots; from 14 to 16 costal grooves ....northern two-lined salamander *(Eurycea bislineata)*
10b. Dorsal pattern consists of a light middorsal stripe; 13 or 14 costal grooves...........longtail salamander *(Eurycea longicauda longicauda)*
11a. Dorsum without a distinct pattern of small or large dark dots or spots; snout upturned, often with a distinct canthus rostralis......................
....northern spring salamander *(Gyrinophilus porphyriticus porphyriticus)*
11b. Dorsum with a distinct pattern of small or large dark spots of dots; snout not upturned, bluntly rounded; canthus rostralis never present 12
12a. Dorsal pattern consisting of small dark spots on a pale background ....northern red salamander *(Pseudotriton ruber ruber)*
12b. Dorsal pattern consisting of relatively few large, dark spots on a brown to reddish brown background...
...........eastern mud salamander *(Pseudotriton montanus montanus)*
13a. Tail with poorly developed dorsal fin; dorsal pattern absent, except for two dark dorsal lateral lines..
..............mountain dusky salamander *(Desmognathus ochrophaeus)*
13b. Tail with well-developed dorsal fin; pattern consists of a series of paired dorsal spots.. 14
14a. Dorsal body pattern consists of four pairs of chestnut dots ....seal salamander *(Desmognathus monticola)*
14b. Dorsal body pattern consists of a series of 5–8 pairs of yellowish dorsal spots, separated by a pale middorsal stripe.................................
................northern dusky salamander *(Desmognathus fuscus fuscus)*

Key to the Adult Toads and Frogs of Pennsylvania and the Northeastern United States

1a. A single sharp-edged black spade on the hind foot (Fig. 15); skin smooth, not warty; pupils elliptical rather than round......................
.......................eastern spadefoot *(Scaphiopus holbrookii holbrookii)*
1b. Hind foot either without spade, or, if spade is present, skin is warty; pupils never elliptical.. 2

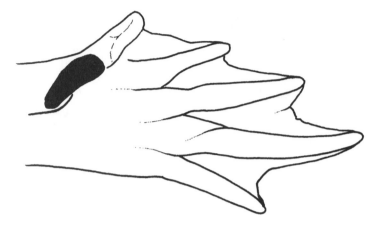

Figure 15.   Spade of *Scaphiopus.*

2a. Skin dry and warty; large parotoid glands present at back of head
    (Fig. 16a,b) 3
2b. Skin smooth and moist; paratoid glands absent................................... 4
3a. Large dorsal spots with only one or two warts per spot; chest gener-
    ally with dark maculations; parotoid glands either separated from
    the cranial crests or connected by a short spur (Fig. 16a).....................
    ....eastern American toad *(Bufo americanus americanus)*
3b. Large dorsal spots, usually with three or more warts per spot; chest
    generally immaculate; parotoid glands in broad contact with the
    cranial crests (Fig. 16b).........Fowler's toad *(Bufo woodhousii fowleri)*

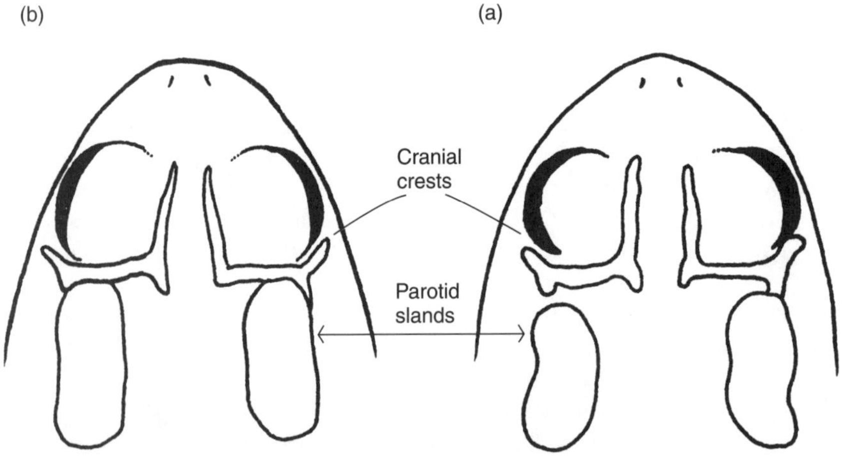

(b)   (a)

Cranial
crests

Parotid
slands

Figure 16.   Relationship of paratoid glands to cranial crest in (a) *Bufo americanus* and (b) *Bufo woodhousii.*

4a. Hind feet with very well-developed webbing (Fig. 17); toepads or discs never present.. 5

4b. Hind feet with moderate to slight webbing (Fig. 18); toes generally terminating in discs or pads; waist narrow..................................... 12

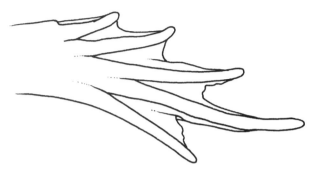

Figure 17. Hind foot of *Rana*.

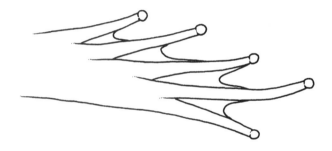

Figure 18. Hind foot of *Pseudacris*.

5a. Dorsolateral fold absent... 6

5b. Dorsolateral fold present... 7

6a. Small, seldom more than 65 mm ($2\frac{1}{2}$ in.) long; a pair of golden-brown dorsolateral stripes present..............carpenter frog *(Rana virgatipes)*

6b. Large, usually greater than 100 mm (4 in.) long; golden brown dorsal lateral stripes absent..............................bullfrog *(Rana catesbeiana)*

7a. Dorsolateral fold incomplete or broken, does not reach end of body (Fig. 19) 8

7b. Dorsolateral fold continues to the end of the body (Fig. 20)............... 9

8a. Small dark spots generally present on dorsal surface of body; hind legs with a pattern of dark cross-bands...
....green frog *(Rana clamitans melanota)*

8b. Dorsal pattern generally of medium to large blotches, giving a mottled appearance; dark elongate markings on hind legs somewhat irregular in shape, generally oriented with the long axis of the legs ....mink frog *(Rana septentrionalis)*

Figure 19. Dorsal view of *Rana clamitans,* showing dorsolateral fold terminating before end of body.

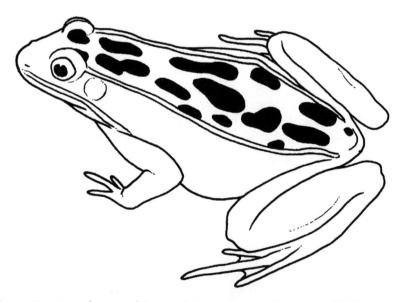

Figure 20. Dorsal view of *Rana pipiens,* showing dorsolateral fold continuing to end of body.

9a. Tympanum with a distinctive central white spot (Fig. 21).....................
.....................................southern leopard frog *(Rana sphenocephala)*
9b. Tympanum without a central white spot... 10
10a. With a dark mask running through the eye (Fig. 22); body without spots..wood frog *(Rana sylvatica)*

Figure 21. Lateral view of *Rana sphenocephala*, showing tympanum with white spot in center.

Figure 22. Lateral view of *Rana sylvatica*, showing mask on side of head.

10b. Without a dark mask; spots present on dorsum............................... 11
11a. Dorsal spots squarish and arranged in two rows (Fig. 23); inside of thighs bright yellow..............................pickerel frog *(Rana palustris)*
11b. Dorsal spots rounded, not arranged in definite rows (Fig. 20); inside of thighs white or cream-colored..
.....................................northern leopard frog *(Rana pipiens)*
12a. Toepads virtually absent; a rough-edged dark stripe (Fig. 24) extending along inside of thigh...
.....................................northern cricket frog *(Acris crepitans crepitans)*
12b. Toepads present... 13
13a. Webbing between toes of hind feet greatly reduced or, if not reduced, with a distinct X on middle of the back of the frog....................... 14
13b. Webbing between toes at least half the length of longest toe; X absent from middle of back.. 16
14a. Dorsal pattern a series of longitudinal stripes or broken stripes
.....................................chorus frog *(Pseudacris triseriata)*
14b. Dorsal pattern X-shaped crossbars or parentheses-shaped stripes... 15
15a. Dorsal pattern X-shaped...
.....................................northern spring peeper *(Pseudacris crucifer crucifer)*

Figure 23. Dorsal view of *Rana palustris*, showing pattern of squarish blotches.

Figure 24. Inside of thigh of *Acris*.

15b. Dorsal pattern not X-shaped..
.................................mountain chorus frog *(Pseudacris brachyphona)*
16a. Inner surface of thighs usually bright yellow or orange; white dot
generally present under eye; skin on back rough, somewhat warty
....gray treefrog *(Hyla versicolor)*
and Cope's gray treefrog *(H. chrysoscelis)*

16b. General background color usually bright green, with purplish stripes along sides of body, separated from green dorsal coloration by thin whitish stripes; dorsal surface smooth...
....Pine Barrens treefrog *(Hyla andersonii)*

Key to the Larval Toads and Frogs of Pennsylvania and the Northeastern United States

Most keys to larval toads and frogs (tadpoles) rely heavily on descriptions of mouthparts (e.g., beaks, labial tooth row formulas, and shape and size of papillae). It is virtually impossible to see these characters without the aid of a microscope, and the tadpole must be killed or chemically immobilized to see the characters. This key is based exclusively on external characters, primarily of color and pattern. In cases in which it is impossible to distinguish between two closely related species in the tadpole state, both species are listed at the end of the appropriate couplet.

1a. Anal opening located near tail, along ventral midline...................... 2
1b. Anal opening located near tail but to right side of ventral midline... 3
2a. Body black with some bright metallic spots....................................
.......................eastern American toad *(Bufo americanus americanus)*
or Fowler's toad *(B. woodhousii fowleri)*
2b. Body dark brown or bronze..
.......................eastern spadefoot *(Scaphiopus holbrookii holbrookii)*
3a. Tip of tail (up to distal one-third) black..
.................................northern cricket frog *(Acris crepitans crepitans)*
3b. Tail not tipped with black.. 4
4a. Body brownish above and bronze below; small, seldom exceeding 30 mm (1$\frac{1}{4}$ in.) ToL...........................mountain chorus frog *(Pseudacris brachyphona)* or Western chorus frog *(P. triseriata triseriata)*
4b. Body usually some shade of green or, if brownish, usually much larger than 30 mm (1$\frac{1}{4}$ in.) ToL.. 5
5a. Body brown, to 85 mm (3$\frac{3}{8}$ in.) ToL...
......................................northern leopard frog (in part) *(Rana pipiens)*
5b. Body some shade of green.. 6
6a. Dorsal tail crest high (1.5 times depth of tail muscle), extending onto head; tail muscle with distinct reddish coloration..........gray treefrog *(Hyla versicolor)* and Cope's gray treefrog *(H. chrysoscelis)*
6b. Dorsal tail crest moderate to low or, if high, tail muscle lacking reddish pigmentation.. 7
7a. Ventral surface pigmented with yellow.. 8
7b. Ventral surface white or cream-colored... 9
8a. Dorsal tail crest moderate (height equal to tail muscle depth); dorsal surfaces green with diffuse dark spots; both tail muscle and tail crest densely covered with dark spots..
....green frog *(Rana clamitans melanota)*

8b. Dorsal tail crest low *(*height of crest less than depth of tail muscle*)*; dorsal surfaces green with sharply defined dark spots; tail crests translucent or cloudy, lacking sharply defined dark spots ....bullfrog *(Rana catesbeiana)*

9a. Small, less than 34 mm ($1\frac{1}{4}$ in.) long; dorsal crest moderate; body green flecked with gold; belly white or cream-colored, but throat mottled with diffuse dark pigment...northern spring peeper *(Pseudacris crucifer crucifer)*

9b. Moderate to large; dorsal crest low to moderate; body some shade of green, lacking golden spots; belly and throat white or cream-colored, immaculate 10

10a. Moderate, to 45 mm ($1\frac{3}{4}$ in.) ToL; dorsal crest moderate; dorsal coloration dark green; tail muscle lighter than body and flecked with black..wood frog *(Rana sylvatica)*

10b. Large, to 85 mm ($3\frac{3}{8}$ in.) long; dorsal crest low; dorsal coloration yellow-green to olive-green; tail muscle generally not lighter than body 11

11a. Dorsal coloration green or olive-green with small dark spots; tail muscle and crests with large dark blotches or pigmented uniformly dark...pickerel frog *(Rana palustris)*

11b. Dorsal coloration green or yellowish green; tail cloudy or translucent but lacking large dark blotches or uniformly dark pigmentation ....northern leopard frog *(Rana pipiens)* or southern leopard frog *(R. sphenocephala)*

Key to the Turtles of Pennsylvania and the Northeastern United States

1a. Carapace comprising a series of horny scutes................................... 3

1b. Carapace without horny scutes.. 2

2a. Carapace with spines and tubercles; nasal septa with a distinct ridge ....eastern spiny softshell *(Apalone spinifera spinifera)*

2b. Carapace smooth; nasal septa without noticeable ridge........................ ....midland smooth softshell *(Apalone mutica mutica)*

3a. Gular scute of plastron (Fig. 25a) undivided.................................... 4

3b. Gular scute of plastron longitudinally divided (Fig. 25b)..................... 5

4a. Plastron small, not covering appendages; pectoral scute squarish or rectangular (Fig. 26a)... ....common musk turtle *(Sternotherus odoratus)*

4b. Plastron large and hinged, covering most of the body; pectoral scute triangular (Fig. 26b)... ....eastern mud turtle *(Kinosternon subrubrum subrubrum)*

5a. Plastron small and cruciform (Fig. 27); head large; tail long, with triangular plates on dorsal surface.. ....common snapping turtle *(Chelydra serpentina serpentina)*

5b. Not as above.. 6

6a. Carapace dome-shaped; plastron hinged so that it can be completely closed........................eastern box turtle *(Terrapene carolina carolina)*

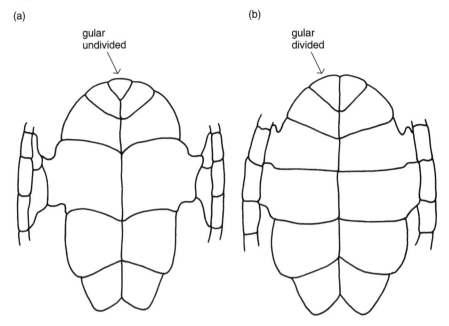

Figure 25. Plastron of (a) nonkinosternid turtle and (b) kinosternid turtle.

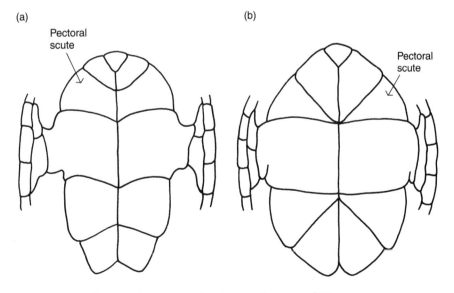

Figure 26. Plastral view comparing *Sternotherus* and *Kinosternon*.

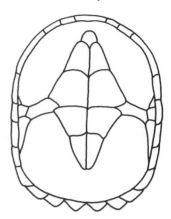

Figure 27. Plastron of *Chelydra.*

6b. Not as above.. 7
7a. Carapace jet black with one or two yellow spots per scute....................
....spotted turtle *(Clemmys guttata)*
7b. Not as above.. 8
8a. Body size small; large bright orange blotch (Fig. 28) behind eye...........
....bog turtle *(Clemmys muhlenbergii)*
8b. Medium to large; orange spot absent.. 9
9a. Carapace appears to be carved from wood; underside of chin and legs
bright orange....................................wood turtle *(Clemmys insculpta)*
9b. Not as above.. 10
10a. Head and legs with dark spots on a grayish background; restricted to
saltwater and brackish water...........................northern diamondback
terrapin *(Malaclemys terrapin terrapin)*
10b. Head and legs either unmarked or with stripes; if spots present, they
are yellow.. 11
11a. Medial carapacial scutes with weak midline bumps or spines (Fig. 29)
.....................................common map turtle *(Graptemys geographica)*
11b. Medial carapacial scutes smooth... 12

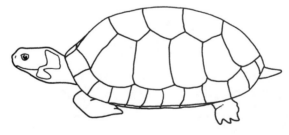

Figure 28. Lateral view of *Clemmys muhlenbergii,* showing blotch behind eye.

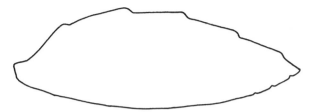

Figure 29. Lateral view of *Graptemys geographica*, showing outline of carapace.

12a. Carapacial pattern of numerous small yellow spots or short streaks; throat and chin bright yellow..
....Blanding's turtle *(Emydoidea blandingii)*
12b. Carapacial pattern not as above.. 13
13a. Reddish markings present on costal scutes; plastron usually with gray smudges..............................redbelly turtle *(Pseudemys rubriventris)*
13b. Costal scutes lack reddish markings; plastron either immaculate or with a large central blotch..
....painted turtle *(Chrysemys picta)*

Key to the Lizards of Pennsylvania and the Northeastern United States

1a. Body scales keeled (Fig. 30a), not smooth and shiny.............................
...............northern fence lizard *(Sceloporus undulatus hyacinthinus)*
1b. Body scales smooth (Fig. 30b), highly polished.................................... 2
2a. Lower eyelid with a translucent window in it; body slender; no light stripes on body................................ground skink *(Scincella lateralis)*
2b. Lower eyelid lacks a translucent window; body usually with four or five light stripes; if stripes absent, individuals are large and robust 3

(a)   (b)

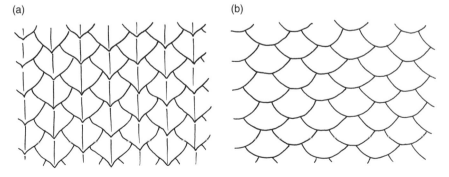

Figure 30. (a) Keeled scales of *Sceloporus* and (b) smooth scales of *Eumeces*.

3a. Postmental scale single (Fig. 31a), not divided; body pattern composed of four light lateral stripes...
...................northern coal skink *(Eumeces anthracinus anthracinus)*
3b. Postmental scale transversely divided (Fig. 31b); either five or no body stripes 4
4a. Four supralabial scales before the subocular scale (Fig. 32a); two small postlabial scales present just anterior to the tympanic opening
....five-lined skink *(Eumeces fasciatus)*
4b. Five supralabial (Fig. 32b) scales anterior to the subocular scale; postlabial scales absent..............broadhead skink *(Eumeces laticeps)*

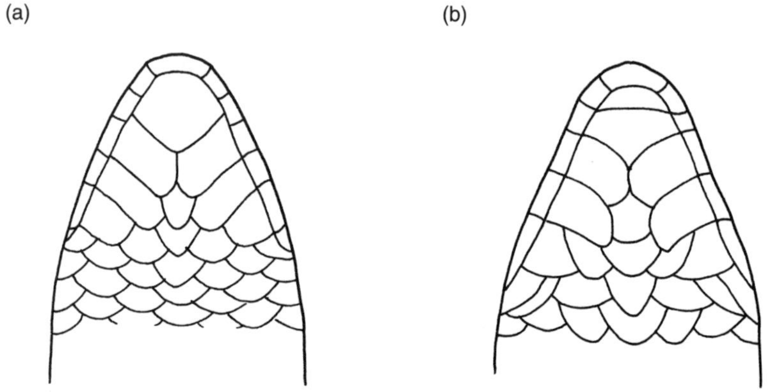

(a)   (b)

Figure 31. (a) Undivided postmental scale of *Eumeces anthracinus* and (b) divided postmental scale of *E. fasciatus*.

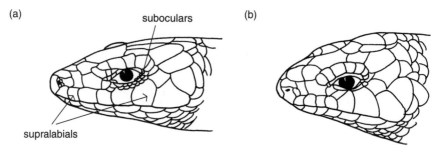

Figure 32. Supralabial scales of (a) *Eumeces fasciatus* and (b) *E. laticeps*.

Key to the Snakes of Pennsylvania and the Northeastern United States

1a. A single row of subcaudal scales (Fig. 33a); loreal pit present between eyes and nares (Fig. 34a); pupil of eye elliptical............................... 2

(a)

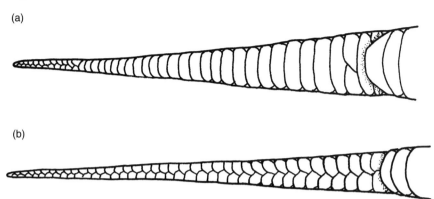

(b)

Figure 33. (a) Single row and (b) double rows of subcaudal scales.

(a)   (b)

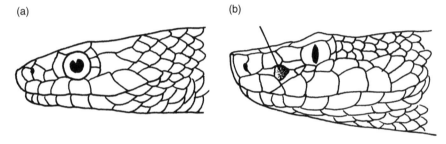

Figure 34. Lateral view of head of (a) venomous snake, with loreal pit, and (b) nonvenomous snake.

1b. Two rows of subcaudal scales (Fig. 33b); loreal pit absent; pupil of eye circular (Fig. 34b)... 4

2a. Tail terminates in horny rattle or, if individual is very small, horny button (Fig. 35).. 3

2b. Tail tapers gradually to a tip, no rattle present; if individual is very small tip of tail is bright yellow... ....northern copperhead *(Agkistrodon contortrix mokasen)*

3a. Top of head covered with numerous small scales.................................. ....timber rattlesnake *(Crotalus horridus)*

3b. Top of head covered by nine large scales (Fig. 36)............................... ....eastern massasauga *(Sistrurus catenatus catenatus)*

4a. Dorsal body scales smooth, without a central elevated ridge (Fig. 37a)... 5

4b. Dorsal body scales keeled, a central elevated ridge present (Fig. 37b).. 13

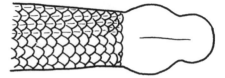

Figure 35. Horny button of neonate rattlesnake.

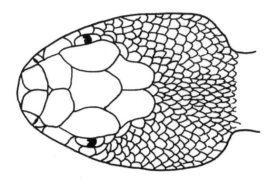

Figure 36. Dorsal view of *Sistrurus*, showing nine large head scales.

(a)   (b)

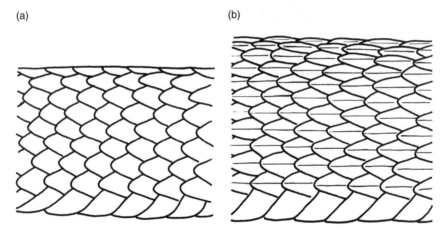

Figure 37. (a) Smooth and (b) keeled body scales.

5a. Dorsum with a distinct pattern.. 6
5b. Dorsum basically solid-colored and patternless................................ 9
6a. Dorsal background coloration black with thin white to yellow lines
     forming a chainlike pattern on dorsum...
     ....eastern kingsnake *(Lampropeltis getula getula)*

6b. Pattern not as above.. 7

7a. Venter has a strong checkerboard pattern; dorsal pattern consists of 30 to 47 squarish blotches..
................eastern milk snake *(Lampropeltis triangulum triangulum)*

7b. Venter immaculate, patternless... 8

8a. Dorsal pattern consists of a series of 48 to 70 narrow body blotches; venter without noticeable pattern..
........northern black racer (juvenile) *(Coluber constrictor constrictor)*

8b. Dorsal pattern consists of a series of bright red saddles or bands bordered by black; red/black sequences separated by pale yellow or white bands...
...........................northern scarlet snake *(Cemophora coccinea copei)*

9a. Dorsal coloration solid velvety black....................................
............northern black racer (adult) *(Coluber constrictor constrictor)*

9b. Dorsal coloration other than black.................................... 10

10a. Dorsal coloration brownish...11

10b. Dorsal coloration other than brown................................. 12

11a. Dorsal scales occur in 13 rows at midbody (Fig. 38 shows the technique used to count scale rows but does not represent the eastern worm snake's scale count); eye very small; short tail terminates in a sharp spine...
.......................eastern worm snake *(Carphophis amoenus amoenus)*

11b. Dorsal scales occur in 15 rows at midbody; eye of normal size; spine absent from tip of tail..
...................................eastern earth snake *(Virginia valeriae valeriae)*

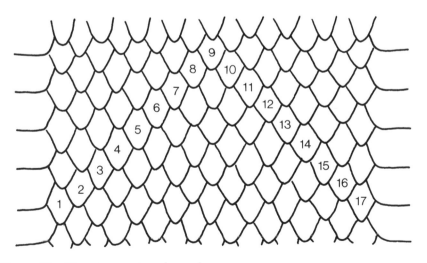

Figure 38. How to count snake scale rows.

12a. Body color uniform bright green, except for hatchlings, which are dark olive-gray; tail long, at least 40% of SVL; distinct ring absent from neck...........................smooth green snake *(Opheodrys vernalis)*

12b. Dorsal coloration slate-gray to bluish gray; tail less than 40% of SVL; distinct yellow or orange ring present on neck....................................
....................eastern ringneck snake *(Diadophis punctatus edwardsii)*

13a. Anal plate entire (Fig. 39a).. 14

13b. Anal plate divided (Fig. 39b)... 17

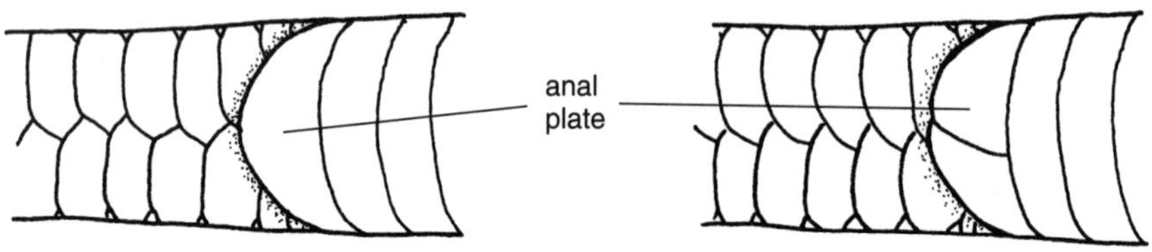

(a)   (b)

Figure 39.   (a) Undivided (entire) and (b) divided anal plate.

14a. Body pattern contains lateral stripes; pattern never black and white 15

14b. Body pattern lacks lateral stripes, generally consists of black to brown blotches on a whitish background; scales strongly keeled......
...........northern pine snake *(Pituophis melanoleucus melanoleucus)*

15a. Lateral body stripe involves scale rows 3 and 4 (never row 2); tail long and slender, at least 45% of SVL..
........................eastern ribbon snake *(Thamnophis sauritus sauritus)*
or northern ribbon snake *(T. s. septentrionalis)*

15b. Lateral body stripe involves scale rows 2 and 3 (rarely row 4); tail not as long as above (less than 35% of SVL).. 16

16a. Head indistinct from neck, appears to be too small for body..............
....shorthead garter snake
(Thamnophis brachystoma)

16b. Head separated from body by a distinct neck; head appears to be of normal size for body..
....eastern garter snake *(Thamnophis sirtalis)*

17a. Rostral scale modified to form upturned snout (Fig. 40)......................
....................................eastern hognose snake *(Heterodon platirhinos)*

17b. Snout not modified as above.. 18

18a. Body color uniform bright green, except for neonates, which are greenish gray.........................rough green snake *(Opheodrys aestivus)*

18b. Body color not green... 19

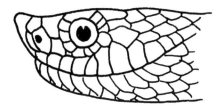

Figure 40. Lateral view of head of *Heterodon platirhinos*, showing upturned snout.

19a. Dorsal scales occur in more than 20 scale rows at midbody........... 20
19b. Dorsal scales occur in fewer than 20 scale rows at midbody............. 22
20a. Dorsal scales occur in 21 to 23 scale rows at midbody and are strongly keeled; body pattern, when present, consists of a series of reddish brown to dark brown saddles and tends to break up into distinct dorsal and lateral blotches posteriorly..
...............................northern water snake *(Nerodia sipedon sipedon)*
20b. More than 23 dorsal scale rows at midbody; scales weakly keeled 21
21a. Pattern in adults solid black; pattern in juveniles irregular black blotches on a gray background...
....black rat snake *(Elaphe obsoleta obsoleta)*
21b. V-shaped marking on head; dorsal pattern a series of red or orange blotches outlined in black...........corn snake *(Elaphe guttata guttata)*
22a. Ventral pattern two rows of black spots on a red background ....Kirtland's snake *(Clonophis kirtlandii)*
22b. Ventral pattern not as above.. 23
23a. Dorsal scales occur in 19 rows at midbody...
....queen snake *(Regina septemvittata)*
23b. Dorsal scales in either 15 or 17 rows at midbody............................. 24
24a. Ventral coloration usually bright red or orange, occasionally bluish black...northern redbelly snake
(Storeria occipitomaculata occipitomaculata)
24b. Ventral coloration other than above...25
25a. Dorsal scales weakly keeled; six supralabials (Fig. 41)........................
...............................mountain earth snake *(Virginia valeriae pulchra)*

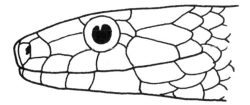

Figure 41. Lateral view of head of *Virginia*, showing six supralabials.

25b. Dorsal scales strongly keeled; seven supralabials (Fig. 42); white
      teardrop mark present under eye..
      ....northern brown snake *(Storeria dekayi dekayi)*

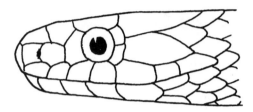

Figure 42. Lateral view of head of *Storeria dekayi,* showing seven
supralabials.

1. Eastern hellbender *(Cryptobranchus alleganiensis alleganiensis)*. Westmoreland County, Pa. Note the lack of external gills and the highly wrinkled skin. (R. W. Van Devender)

2. Mudpuppy *(Necturus maculosus maculosus)*. Crawford County, Pa. Note the presence of external gills. (R. W. Van Devender)

3. Mudpuppy *(Necturus maculosus maculosus)*, showing juvenile pattern. Indiana County, Pa. (A. C. Hulse)

4. Mudpuppy *(Necturus maculosus maculosus)* egg mass. Indiana County, Pa. (A. C. Hulse)

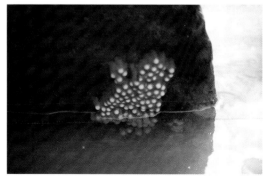

5. Blue-spotted salamander *(Ambystoma laterale).* Southwestern New Hampshire. (T. Diez)

6. Jefferson salamander *(Ambystoma jeffersonianum).* Erie County, Pa. (R. W. Van Devender)

7. Spotted salamander *(Ambystoma maculatum).* Indiana County, Pa. (A. C. Hulse)

8. Spotted salamander *(Ambystoma maculatum),* recently deposited egg mass. Indiana County, Pa. (A. C. Hulse)

9. Spotted salamander
(Ambystoma maculatum)
larva. Franklin County, Pa.
A typical pond-type larva.
(R. W. Van Devender)

10. Marbled salamander
(Ambystoma opacum).
Pike County, Pa. (A. C.
Hulse)

11. Marbled salamander
(Ambystoma opacum) lar-
vae. Union County, Pa.
(A. C. Hulse)

12. Tiger salamander
(Ambystoma tigrinum).
(T. Diez)

13. Adult female red-spotted newt *(Notophthalmus viridescens viridescens).* Franklin County, Pa. (R. W. Van Devender)

14. Terrestrial red eft stage of the red-spotted newt *(Notophthalmus viridescens viridescens).* Cameron County, Pa. Note the dry granular skin of this terrestrial form. (A. C. Hulse)

15. Red-spotted newts *(Notophthalmus viridescens viridescens)* in amplexus; male above and forward, female below and behind. Elk County, Pa. (A. C. Hulse)

16. Green salamander *(Aneides aeneus).* Fayette County, Pa. Note the square-tipped toes. (R. W. Van Devender)

17. Adult female northern dusky salamander *(Desmognathus fuscus fuscus)*. Cumberland County, Pa. (A. C. Hulse)

BELOW LEFT
18. Recently metamorphosed juvenile northern dusky salamander *(Desmognathus fuscus fuscus)*. Armstrong County, Pa. (A. C. Hulse)

ABOVE RIGHT
19. Northern dusky salamander *(Desmognathus fuscus fuscus)* female brooding eggs. Franklin County, Pa. (R. W. Van Devender)

20. Seal salamander *(Desmognathus monticola)*. Westmoreland County, Pa. Note the sharply keeled tail and the light stripe extending from the eye to the gape of the mouth. (R. W. Van Devender)

21. Mountain dusky salamander *(Desmognathus ochrophaeus)*. Armstrong County, Pa. Note the rounded tail and the straight-edged dorsal stripe. (A. C. Hulse)

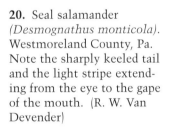
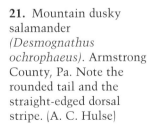

22. Northern two-lined salamander *(Eurycea bislineata)*. Crawford County, Pa. (R. W. Van Devender)

23. Recently metamorphosed northern two-lined salamander *(Eurycea bislineata)*. Armstrong County, Pa. (A. C. Hulse)

24. Longtail salamander *(Eurycea longicanda longicauda)*. Potter County, Pa. Note the long tail and herringbone pattern. (A. C. Hulse)

25. Northern spring salamander *(Gyrinophilus porpyriticus porphyriticus)*. Westmoreland County, Pa. Note the well-developed canthus rostralis extending from the eye to the nare. (R. W. Van Devender)

26. Northern spring salamander *(Gyrinophilus porphyriticus porphyriticus)* larva. A typical stream-type larva. (R. W. Van Devender)

27. Four-toed salamander *(Hemidactylium scutatum)*. Huntingdon County, Pa. Note the distinct constriction at the base of the tail. (A. C. Hulse)

28. Four-toed salamander *(Hemidactylium scutatum)*, ventral view. Huntingdon County, Pa. (A. C. Hulse)

29. Redback salamander *(Plethodon cinereus)*. Indiana County, Pa. (A. C. Hulse)

30. Redback salamanders *(Plethodon cinereus)*, illustrating the various color patterns. Franklin County, Pa. (R. W. Van Devender)

31. Redback salamander *(Plethodon cinereus)*, erythristic phase. Potter County, Pa. (A. C. Hulse)

32. Northern slimy salamander *(Plethodon glutinosus)*. Potter County, Pa. (A. C. Hulse)

33. Juvenile northern slimy salamander *(Plethodon glutinosus)*. Cumberland County, Pa. (A. C. Hulse)

34. Valley and ridge salamander *(Plethodon hoff-mani)*. Huntingdon County, Pa. Note the fine gold flecks on the body. (A. C. Hulse)

35. Ravine salamander *(Plethodon richmondi)*. Greene County, Pa. Note the fine silver flecks on the body. (A. C. Hulse)

36. Wehrle's salamander *(Plethodon wehrlei)*. Indiana County, Pa. (A. C. Hulse)

37. Comparison of Wehrle's salamander (upper right) and the slimy salamander (lower left). Potter County, Pa. (A. C. Hulse)

38. Eastern mud salamander *(Pseudotriton montanus montanus)*. Franklin County, Pa. (A. C. Hulse)

BELOW LEFT
39. Northern red salamander *(Pseudotriton ruber ruber)*. Adams County, Pa. (A. C. Hulse)

ABOVE RIGHT
40. Larval northern red salamander *(Pseudotriton ruber ruber)*. Franklin County, Pa. (R. W. Van Devender)

41. Eastern spadefoot *(Scaphiopus holbrookii holbrookii)*. Cumberland County, Pa. (T. Diez)

42. Eastern American toad *(Bufo americanus americanus)*. Armstrong County, Pa. (A. C. Hulse)

43. Eastern American toad *(Bufo americanus americanus)*. Huntingdon County, Pa. Calling male. (A. C. Hulse)

44. Eastern American toad *(Bufo americanus americanus)*. Huntingdon County, Pa. Pair in amplexus. (A. C. Hulse)

45. Recently laid egg strand of eastern American toad *(Bufo americanus americanus)*. Franklin County, Pa. (R. W. Van Devender)

46. Fowler's toad *(Bufo woodhousii fowleri)*. Franklin County, Pa. (R. W. Van Devender)

47. Northern cricket frog
(Acris crepitans crepitans).
Cumberland County, Pa.
(T. Diez)

48. Pine Barrens treefrog
(Hyla andersonii). New
Jersey. (T. Diez)

49. Gray treefrog/Cope's
gray treefrog (*Hyla versi-
color/chrysocelis* complex).
Franklin County, Pa.
(T. Diez)

50. Mountain chorus frog
(Pseudacris brachyphona).
Westmoreland County, Pa.
(T. Diez)

51. Northern spring peeper *(Pseudacris crucifer crucifer)*. Indiana County, Pa. (A. C. Hulse)

52. Northern spring peeper *(Pseudacris crucifer crucifer)*. Franklin County, Pa. Transforming larva. (R. W. Van Devender)

53. Northern spring peeper *(Pseudacris crucifer crucifer)*. Westmoreland County, Pa. Calling male. (R. W. Van Devender)

54. Western chorus frog *(Pseudacris triseriata triseriata)*. Pennsylvania. (T. Diez)

55. Upland chorus frog *(Pseudacris triseriata feriarum)*. Pennsylvania. (T. Diez)

56. Bullfrog *(Rana catesbeiana)*. Bucks County, Pa. Note the lack of a dorsolateral fold. This individual is a female. Notice that the tympanic membrane is equal in size to the eye, rather than being much larger than the eye. (A. C. Hulse)

57. Green frog *(Rana clamitans melanota)*. Bucks County, Pa. Note the interrupted dorsal lateral fold. This specimen is a male. Notice that the tympanic membrane is much larger than the eye. (R. W. Van Devender)

58. Egg raft of the green frog *(Rana clamitans melanota)*. Elk County, Pa. (A. C. Hulse)

59. Pickerel frog *(Rana palustris)*. Forest County, Pa. (A. C. Hulse)

60. Northern leopard frog *(Rana pipiens)*. Erie County, Pa. (R. W. Van Devender)

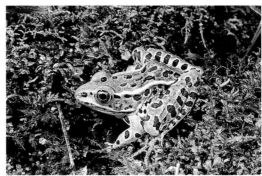

61. Southern leopard frog *(Rana utricularia)*. Bucks County, Pa. Note the central white spot in the tympanic membrane. (R. W. Van Devender)

62. Mink frog *(Rana septentrionalis)*. Ontario, Canada. (R. W. Van Devender)

63. Wood frog *(Rana sylvatica)*. Warren County, Pa. (A. C. Hulse)

64. Wood frog *(Rana sylvatica)*. Armstrong County, Pa. Pair in amplexus. (A. C. Hulse)

65. Carpenter frog *(Rana virgatipes)*. New Jersey. (T. Diez)

66. Common snapping turtle *(Chelydra serpentina serpentina)*. Westmoreland County, Pa. (R. W. Van Devender)

67. Common snapping turtle *(Chelydra serpentina serpentina)*. Greene County, Pa. Note the reduced plastron. (A. C. Hulse)

BELOW LEFT
68. Eastern mud turtle *(Kinosternon subrubrum subrubrum)*. Delaware County, Pa. (T. Diez)

ABOVE RIGHT
69. Common musk turtle *(Sternotherus odoratus)*. Crawford County, Pa. Note the growth of algae on the carapace. (R. W. Van Devender)

70. Common musk turtle *(Sternotherus odoratus)*. Huntingdon County, Pa. Note the reduced plastron. (A. C. Hulse)

71. Painted turtle *(Chrysemys picta)*. Huntingdon County, Pa. (A. C. Hulse)

72. Painted turtle *(Chrysemys picta)*. Indiana County, Pa. The plastron of this specimen is heavily stained with iron deposits. (A. C. Hulse)

73. Painted turtle *(Chrysemys picta)*. Cameron County, Pa. Dorsal view of hatchling. (A. C. Hulse)

74. Painted turtle *(Chrysemys picta)*. Cameron County, Pa. Ventral view of hatchling. (A. C. Hulse)

75. Spotted turtle *(Clemmys guttata)*. (R. W. Van Devender)

76. Wood turtle *(Clemmys insculpta).* Fulton County, Pa. (A. C. Hulse)

77. Plastron of a young wood turtle *(Clemmys insculpta).* Fulton County, Pa. (A. C. Hulse)

78. Bog turtle *(Clemmys muhlenbergii).* Adams County, Pa. (R. W. Van Devender)

79. Bog turtle *(Clemmys muhlenbergii).* Adams County, Pa. Note the large orange-yellow blotch behind the eye. (R. W. Van Devender)

80. Northern diamond-back terrapin *(Malaclemys terrapin terrapin)*. (T. Diez)

81. Northern diamond-back terrapin *(Malaclemys terrapin terrapin)*. (T. Diez)

82. Blanding's turtle *(Emydoidea blandingii)*. (C. H. Ernst)

83. Common map turtle *(Graptemys geographica)*. Bucks County, Pa. (R. W. Van Devender)

84. Redbelly turtle *(Pseudemys rubiventris)*. Bucks County, Pa. (R. W. Van Devender)

85. Redbelly turtle *(Pseudemys rubiventris)*. Bucks County, Pa. (R. W. Van Devender)

86. Eastern box turtle *(Terrapene carolina carolina)*. Armstrong County, Pa. (A. C. Hulse)

87. Eastern box turtle *(Terrapene carolina carolina)*. Armstrong County, Pa. Ventral view. (A. C. Hulse)

88. Midland smooth softshell *(Apalone mutica mutica)*. (T. Diez)

BELOW LEFT
89. Eastern spiny softshell *(Apalone spinifera. spinifera)*. Bucks County, Pa. Female. (T. Diez)

ABOVE RIGHT
90. Eastern spiny softshell *(Apalone spinifera. spinifera)*. Male. (T. Diez)

91. Northern fence lizards *(Sceloporus undulatus hyacinthinus)*. Westmoreland County, Pa. Male on the left and female on the right. (A. C. Hulse)

92. Northern coal skink *(Eumeces anthracinus anthracinus)*. Elk County, Pa. (A. C. Hulse)

93. Recently hatched northern coal skink *(Eumeces anthracinus anthracinus)*. Union County, Pa. (A. C. Hulse)

94. Melanistic northern coal skink *(Eumeces anthracinus anthracinus)*. Warren County, Pa. (A. C. Hulse)

95. Clutch of northern coal skink *(Eumeces anthracinus anthracinus)* eggs. Union County, Pa. (A. C. Hulse)

96. Female five-lined skink *(Eumeces fasciatus)*. Perry County, Pa. (A. C. Hulse)

97. Male five-lined skink *(Eumeces fasciatus)*. Franklin County, Pa. (R. W. Van Devender)

98. Broadhead skink *(Eumeces laticeps)*. Virginia. Male. (A. C. Hulse)

99. Ground skink *(Scincella lateralis)*. Chambers County, Tx. (R. W. Van Devender)

100. Eastern worm snake *(Carphophis amoenus amoenus)*. Huntingdon County, Pa. (A. C. Hulse)

101. Northern scarlet snake *(Cemophora coccinea copei)*. New Hanover County, N.C. (R. W. Van Devender)

102. Kirtland's snake *(Clonophis kirtlandii)*. Illinois. (R. W. Van Devender)

103. Kirtland's snake *(Clonophis kirtlandii)*. Effingham County, Ill. Note the distinct ventral pattern. (R. W. Van Devender)

104. Northern black racer *(Coluber constrictor constrictor)*. Elk County, Pa. Adult. (A. C. Hulse)

105. Northern black racer *(Coluber constrictor constrictor)*. Indiana County, Pa. Juvenile. (A. C. Hulse)

106. Northern ringneck snake *(Diadophis punctatus edwardsii)*. Elk County, Pa. (A. C. Hulse)

107. Corn snake *(Elaphe guttata guttata)*. Charleston County, S.C. (R. W. Van Devender)

108. Black rat snake *(Elaphe obsoleta obsoleta)*. Fayette County, Pa. Adult. (A. C. Hulse)

109. Recently hatched black rat snake *(Elaphe obsoleta obsoleta)*. Clarion County, Pa. (A. C. Hulse)

BELOW LEFT
110. Black rat snake eggs *(Elaphe obsoleta obsoleta)*. Union County, Pa. (A. C. Hulse)

ABOVE RIGHT
111. Eastern hognose snake *(Heterodon platirhinos)*. Luzerne County, Pa. (A. C. Hulse)

112. Melanistic phase of the eastern hognose snake *(Heterodon platirhinos)*. Pike County, Pa. (R. W. Van Devender)

113. Eastern hognose snake *(Heterodon platirhinos)* feigning death. Pike County, Pa. (R. W. Van Devender)

114. Eastern hognose snake *(Heterodon platirhinos)* emerging from its egg. Pike County, Pa. (R. W. Van Devender)

115. Eastern kingsnake *(Lampropeltis getula getula)*. Virginia. (R. W. Van Devender)

116. Eastern milk snake *(Lampropeltis triangulum triangulum)*. Clearfield County, Pa. (A. C. Hulse)

117. Northern water snake *(Nerodia sipedon sipedon)*. Elk County, Pa. (A. C. Hulse)

118. Rough green snake *(Opheodrys aestivus)*. Virginia. (A. C. Hulse)

119. Smooth green snake *(Opheodrys vernalis)*. Warren County, Pa. (R. W. Van Devender)

120. Clutch of smooth green snake eggs *(Opheodrys vernalis)*. Warren County, Pa. (A. C. Hulse)

121. Northern pine snake *(Pituophis melanoleucus melanoleucus)*. (T. Diez)

122. Queen snake *(Regina septemvittata).* Westmoreland County, Pa. (R. W. Van Devender)

123. Northern brown snake *(Storeria dekayi dekayi).* Forest County, Pa. (A. C. Hulse)

124. Northern redbelly snake *(Storeria occipitomaculata occipitomaculata).* Union County, Pa. Black phase. (R. W. Van Devender)

125. Northern redbelly snakes *(Storeria occipitomaculata occipitomaculata).* Warren County, Pa. Two common color variations. (A. C. Hulse)

126. Shorthead garter snakes *(Thamnophis brachystoma)*. Warren County, Pa. The two color patterns. (A. C. Hulse)

127. Eastern ribbon snake *(Thamnophis sauritus sauritus)*. Chester County, Pa. (R. W. Van Devender)

128. Eastern garter snake *(Thamnophis sirtalis sirtalis)*. Butler County, Pa. (R. W. Van Devender)

129. Mountain earth snake *(Virginia valeriae pulchra)*. Warren County, Pa. (A. C. Hulse)

130. Northern copperhead *(Agkistrodon contortrix mokasen)*. Westmoreland County, Pa. (R. W. Van Devender)

131. Timber rattlesnake *(Crotalus horridus)*. Elk County, Pa. Yellow phase. (A. C. Hulse)

132. Timber rattlesnake *(Crotalus horridus)*. Carbon County, Pa. Black phase. (A. C. Hulse)

133. Eastern massasauga *(Sistrurus catenatus catenatus)*. Butler County, Pa. (R. W. Van Devender)

Amphibia

The class Amphibia is represented by three living orders and an additional six orders that are known exclusively from the fossil record. There are over 3,900 described species of living amphibians. Species are found on all continents but Antarctica and on most of the major islands of the world. Amphibians occupy all major terrestrial and freshwater environments but, with rare exceptions, are absent from brackish and saltwater environments.

They are an extremely diverse group and as such are difficult to characterize with unqualified statements. The following applies to most amphibians. Amphibians have naked skin, with no covering such as scales, feathers, or hair. Their skin is moist and highly glandular. Skin glands are of two types: mucous glands that function to keep the skin moist and poison glands that aid in defense. Although all amphibians have poison glands, the degree of toxicity varies greatly; most species possess an exceedingly mild poison that poses no threat to people or pets. Some tropical species, however, secrete highly toxic poisons and must be handled with the greatest of care. Amphibians lack true claws and nails on their toes and fingers, although some species have horny toe tips. They exhibit a complex life history; most have an aquatic larval stage and develop into terrestrial adults. They breathe through gills or lungs or both and through their skin. All adult amphibians are carnivorous, but larvae exhibit more diverse feeding strategies. Like fishes, amphibians have only 10 cranial nerves, and, like reptiles, they possess a heart with three chambers.

Salamanders

Salamanders belong to the amphibian order Caudata. There are approximately 415 described species of salamander contained within 10 families. Salamanders are found in North America, Central America, South America, Europe, northern Africa, and parts of Asia. There are 148 species of salamander in the United States. Nine families are found in the United States, and four of them are found nowhere else in the world. The eastern United States, in particular, is home to a large percentage of the known species of salamander. Five families, 11 genera, and 23 species of salamander are native to the northeastern United States.

Salamanders are generally characterized by a long tail, a discernible neck, and two pairs of well-developed legs of approximately equal size.

Salamanders occupy a wide range of habitats, but all are fairly moist; moisture helps prevent their skin from drying out. The need to maintain a moist skin greatly affects their behavior and activity. Except for a few totally aquatic species, salamanders are seldom seen moving about during the day. Surface activity is more common at night, when temperatures are lower and humidity is higher. However, even at night most individuals remain under cover.

All salamanders are carnivorous, and the composition of their diet varies mainly as a function of their size and habitat. With the exception of the hellbender (which tends to specialize on crayfish), salamanders are opportunistic feeders utilizing any abundant and easily captured prey.

Salamander courtship occurs either on land or in the water, depending on the species. It generally involves the male's touching his chin along the female's body and head. If the female is receptive, she follows the male. He deposits on the ground a structure called a spermatophore, composed of a gelatinous base that supports a packet of sperm. The receptive female picks up the sperm packet with the lips of her cloaca. Fertilization generally does not occur immediately, but rather the sperm is stored in a special structure called a spermatheca until the eggs are ready to be laid. As the eggs are being extruded from the oviduct, sperm is released from the spermatotheca and fertilization occurs. Therefore, fertilization is indirect, but internal. All northeastern salamanders have internal fertilization, except for the hellbender, whose fertilization is external. Depending upon the species, mating may occur in the spring, summer, or fall. Females can store sperm for long periods of time, and egg laying is not necessarily closely timed with courtship.

Eggs may be laid singly, in small or large masses, or in long strands. They may be attached to vegetation in the water or to the undersurface of logs, rocks, and other cover objects on land or in water. Eggs may also be deposited in loose piles under rocks or in small groups in cracks and crevices. Although most eggs hatch into gilled larvae that have an obligatory aquatic stage, the eggs of the green salamander (*Aneides aeneus*) and the woodland salamanders (genus *Plethodon*) develop directly and hatch as miniature replicas of adults. For a detailed discussion of many northeastern salamanders, see *The Salamanders of New York* (Bishop 1941).

CRYPTOBRANCHIDAE (GIANT SALAMANDERS)

The family Cryptobranchidae contains two genera and three species. There is a disjunct distribution, with one genus (*Cryptobranchus*) occurring in the eastern United States and the other (*Andrias*) found in China and Japan.

All members of the family are permanently aquatic and inhabit large streams and rivers. They are dorsoventrally flattened, have small eyes that lack lids, and possess loose folds of skin along their sides that function in gas exchange with the aquatic environment. Adults lack external gills but retain a single pair of gill slits. As their common name, giant salamanders, implies, they are among the largest salamanders alive today. One species of *Andrias* attains a maximum length of about 1.5 m (almost 5 ft). Unlike most other North American salamanders, *Cryptobranchus* has external fertilization.

Eastern Hellbender *Cryptobranchus alleganiensis alleganiensis* (Daudin)
Gr. *kryptos*, hidden; Gr. *branchia*, gill; *alleganiensis*, a place name meaning "in the Allegheny"
Description. The eastern hellbender (Plate 1) is the largest of the Northeast salamanders and one of the largest species of salamander in the world. Its basic background coloration varies from yellowish or greenish brown to blackish brown. Ventral coloration is similar to dorsal background color. The dorsum is generally patterned with irregular dark blotches that tend to be darker and more conspicuous in younger animals. Recently transformed individuals have maculations on the tail and limbs. The venter of mature larvae is considerably lighter than the dorsum. Fine dark maculations occur on the dorsal and lateral surfaces of the larvae as well as on their appendages. An albino specimen has been reported from Missouri (Dyrkacz 1981).

The eastern hellbender is a stout animal of bizarre appearance. Adults are strongly compressed dorsoventrally. The neck and body are encased in flabby wrinkled folds of skin. The tail is laterally compressed and has a well-developed dorsal caudal fin that originates on the back just anterior to the insertion of the hind limbs. The legs have posterior projecting folds of skin and are short and squat. The fingers and toes are thick and blunt. The head is large, almost as broad as it is long, and is set off from the body by a slightly distinct neck. The eyes, located on the top of the head, are small and lack lids. The mouth is huge and extends along the side of the head to a point well behind the eyes. The skin of the chin is extremely wrinkled, and a well-developed gular fold is present. Although larvae have well-developed external gills, all that remains of the gills in adults is a pair of gill slits on the sides of the head.

Adults exhibit significant sexual dimorphism in size but not in relative tail length. The average mature male measures 426.4 mm (17 in.) ToL, whereas the average mature female is 540 mm (21 in.) ToL. There is great variation in average size and size distribution in both males and females from population to population. Record size for the species is 740 mm (29½ in.) ToL for a specimen collected near Gatlinburg, Tennessee (Fitch 1947). Tail length of both sexes averages about 51% of SVL.

Confusing Species. The only other large aquatic salamander in Pennsylvania and the northeastern United States is the mudpuppy. The mudpuppy retains external gills as an adult, whereas hellbenders lose their gills during their partial metamorphosis. Young mudpuppies are boldly striped, but larval hellbenders lack stripes.

Habitat and Habits. Eastern hellbenders are inhabitants of flowing waters that range from medium-sized streams to large rivers such as the

Allegheny and the Susquehanna. Preferred habitats are cold, shallow, moderate to fast-flowing areas with a gravel or sandy bottom and an abundance of large flat rock slabs. Such slabs serve as both shelter and foraging sites for the salamanders. Hillis and Bellis (1971), working in French Creek, Crawford County, found that eastern hellbenders preferred water between 20 and 50 cm (8–20 in.) deep and rock slabs that ranged from 56 to 109 cm ($22\frac{1}{2}$–$40\frac{1}{2}$ in.) in greatest diameter. We have found the same to be true in several other streams. Ultsch and Duke (1990) demonstrated that the hellbender's preference for cold, fast-flowing water is based on physiological requirements. Hellbenders have limited gas exchange ability and as a consequence are restricted to aquatic habitats where the oxygen content of the water is high. Surprisingly though, they can survive for relatively long periods of time in warm water, probably by occasionally rising to the surface to gulp air.

Eastern hellbenders are probably active throughout the year. Specimens have been collected in every month but January, and there is no reason to believe that this entirely aquatic species should be inactive in the middle of winter.

On a diel basis, activity is predominantly nocturnal. Several authors speak of hellbenders moving actively about streams at night (Hillis and Bellis 1971, Swanson 1948). Our observations indicate that they are exceedingly sedentary, and at most only a small percentage of the population is active on any specific night. Bishop (1941) reported that this nocturnal pattern is disrupted during the breeding season, when individuals may be found moving about at all hours. We also have noted a dramatic increase in diurnal activity during the height of the mating season in late August and early September.

For such large animals, eastern hellbenders have exceedingly small home ranges. In Pennsylvania, their home range has been estimated to average 346 m^2 (3,200 ft^2) (Hillis and Bellis 1971) and may be even smaller than that. We have found animals repeatedly under the same cover object over a period of several months. Whether they make occasional forays to search for food is not known. Eastern hellbenders can achieve high densities in suitable habitat; we have noted densities as great as one animal per linear meter of stream, with biomass estimates as high as 500 kg/ha (ca. 400 lb/acre) of suitable stream.

Hillis and Bellis (1971) reported a skewed sex ratio favoring males (1.58:1) in a population from western Pennsylvania, but in some populations the sex ratio does not vary significantly from 1:1.

Several authors have commented on the exceedingly uneven age distribution in populations of this species. We too have found age distribution to be uneven. The majority of animals collected are reproductively mature. This age distribution may be real or merely an artifact of collecting techniques in which adults are favored over other size and age categories. It is also possible that larvae occupy a different habitat than the adults. In a long-lived species such as the hellbender, however, it is probable that larval and juvenile mortality are high and that recruitment into the adult population is very low. If this is the case, it has significant implications for management of the species (see Remarks).

Except during the breeding season, hellbenders are solitary creatures, with each individual occupying its own shelter. Individuals are virtually never found together under rocks, and there is considerable evidence that the occupant of a specific shelter site will actively defend the area against intruders (Hillis and Bellis 1971). However, during the fall mating season as many as four individuals have been found under a single rock.

Hellbenders feed predominantly on crayfish. In a Pennsylvania sample ($N = 27$) from the Carnegie Museum, 100% of the individuals that contained food had fed on crayfish. One animal had also eaten an unidentified cyprinid (minnow) fish. The stomachs of some specimens were packed with five or more large crayfish. Swanson (1948) suggested that in winter, when crayfish are less active, hellbenders feed more on fishes but that during the rest of the year crayfish constitute the majority of their diet. Because of this heavy reliance on crayfish for food, hellbenders are not found in streams that lack substantial crayfish populations. Hellbenders have often been unjustly accused by anglers of preying upon trout, trout eggs, and other gamefish. These accusations are unfounded. The few fish remains that have been reported are those of "rough" fish, with the majority being either minnows or suckers. We have also found hellbenders to occasionally consume the following items: adult mudpuppies, northern water snakes, brook lampreys, and the larvae of dobsonflies (hellgrammites). Hellbenders consume eggs of their own species during the reproductive season. On several occasions, we have seen individuals regurgitate eggs that had recently been ingested.

Reproduction.   Courtship and mating occur in late August and early September. Activity, both day and night, increases greatly at this time of year. Animals are almost never found in the open during the day at other times of the year.

Males construct shallow nest depressions under large, partially or completely embedded slabs of rock for the deposition of eggs. These depressions can be up to 30 cm by 50 cm (12 in. by 20 in.) in size. We have also noted large cracks and crevices in boulders being used as nest locations. In some streams, most nests are located in cracks or in depressions under large boulders and rocky outcrops bordering the streams. When a receptive female enters the nest chamber, egg laying begins. Hellbenders have external fertilization, and the eggs are fertilized as the female deposits them. They are laid in long, rosary-like strands. The eggs are pale yellow, about 6–7 mm (about $\frac{1}{4}$ in.) in diameter, but with accessory envelopes they vary from 18 to 20 mm ($\frac{3}{4}-\frac{7}{8}$ in.) in diameter. Once oviposition is complete, the male chases the female away from the nest site and remains with the eggs. Males will occasionally consume some of the eggs, but the extent of this behavior and its impact on the percentage of hatching success remain unknown.

The female reproductive cycle of hellbenders from Pennsylvania is apparently annual. Vitellogenesis begins shortly after egg deposition in the fall. Yolk deposition slowly occurs throughout the winter, spring, and early summer, and eggs are ovulated in August. Egg deposition occurs in late August and early September. Clutch size for a Pennsylvania population ranged from 235 to 478 eggs and was significantly correlated with female body size. The extremely large clutches, more than 1,000 eggs, reported by Swanson (1948) are in error because he counted both mature follicles and small immature follicles that would not develop into mature eggs until the following year.

Incubation varies from 60 to 87 days, and larvae hatch at about 30 mm ($1\frac{1}{4}$ in.) ToL. Larvae at hatching possess well-developed external gills, and forelimb and hind limb buds are present. The larval period lasts approximately 2 years. Transformation is complete when external gills are completely resorbed (Bishop 1941), at about 135 mm ($5\frac{3}{8}$ in.) ToL.

Females mature at ToLs of 370–400 mm ($14\frac{5}{8}$–16 in.), and males at ToLs of 300–330 mm (12–$13\frac{1}{4}$ in.). Bishop (1941) suggested that both sexes mature at 5 to 6 years of age, but this estimate has not been verified.

Remarks. Merkle and colleagues (1977), in a genetic analysis of hellbenders, noted an extremely interesting and somewhat confounding condition. The genetic diversity of individuals and entire populations was exceedingly low. Most populations exhibited zero genetic diversity (i.e., for all intents and purposes, all individuals were genetically identical), and in those populations where diversity did exist it was extremely low (about 2%). Typically in vertebrates, individuals exhibit about 6% genetic diversity and populations from 10% to 20% diversity as determined by standard electrophoretic techniques. Merkle and co-workers suggested that this remarkably low diversity might be a side effect of paedomorphosis (exhibiting sexual maturity while still retaining larval characteristics). They based this suggestion on the fact that the mudpuppy (another paedomorphic aquatic salamander) also has very low genetic diversity. Extremely low levels of divergence in mitochondrial DNA lead Routman and colleagues (1994) to propose a recent invasion from the Ozarks into the Ohio River drainage. They suggest that Pleistocene glaciation eliminated hellbender populations north of the Ohio and, as the glaciers receded, the newly created rivers were colonized from northern Ozark populations.

The microdistribution of the hellbender has been dramatically affected during the past two centuries by habitat destruction and modification, with many local populations being driven to extinction. D. Williams and co-workers (1981) suggested for this reason that there is a need to manage this species. We concur with them, but before meaningful management practices can be instituted it will be necessary to gain much more information on the basic ecology of this species, especially in the areas of reproduction and age distribution.

Distribution. The hellbender ranges from southern New York southward through central and western Pennsylvania along the western edge of the Appalachians to northern Georgia and Alabama. Its western range extends northward to southern Indiana and Ohio. Disjunct populations occur in central Missouri.

The eastern hellbender reaches the northern limit of its distribution in the Allegheny and Susquehanna drainages of southern New York. In Pennsylvania, hellbenders are absent from the eastern third of the state (primarily the Delaware River drainage). Localities in the rest of the state encompass the three major rivers (Susquehanna, Allegheny, and Ohio) and their tributaries. Most of the records of specimens from Pennsylvania are old, and it is probable that many of the areas have experienced local extirpation due to either habitat destruction or pollution.

In 1990, a single large individual was captured in an eel weir set in the middle of the Delaware River in northeastern Pennsylvania. This specimen probably represents an accidental or intentional introduction, but small populations may exist in the upper Delaware River drainage. Surveys are needed in the region to determine the actual status of hellbenders in this area.

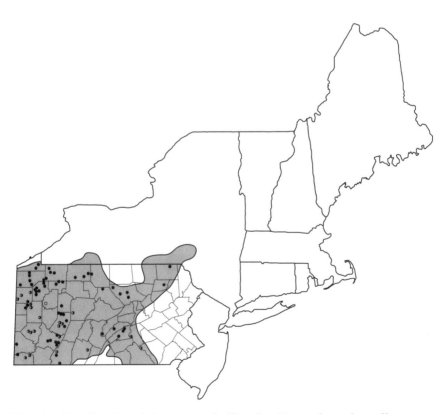

Map 1. Distribution of the eastern hellbender *(Cryptobranchus alleganiensis alleganiensis)*. Open triangle indicates recent specimen captured in an eel weir in the Delaware River.

PROTEIDAE (MUDPUPPIES AND WATERDOGS)

Proteidae is a small family (two extant genera and six species) of aquatic salamanders. The family has a disjunct geographic distribution, with one genus (*Proteus*) restricted to Italy and Yugoslavia. The European species is cavernicolus and blind and lacks pigmentation. The second genus (*Necturus*) contains five species and occurs only in North America. Most members of the family are large (300–400 mm, or 12–16 in.) and possess well-developed gills throughout their life.

Necturus
Gr. *nekton*, swimming

The genus *Necturus* contains the waterdogs and the mudpuppy. The five species in this strictly North American genus range from southern Quebec to the Gulf of Mexico in the east and from eastern Texas to southeastern Manitoba in the west.

Mudpuppies and waterdogs are medium-sized to large aquatic salamanders that have external gills. They never leave the water. They are found in standing water and in streams and rivers.

Mudpuppies and waterdogs are carnivorous and feed on a broad range of aquatic invertebrates and vertebrates including snails, clams, crayfish, fish, and aquatic insects. They lay their eggs on the undersurface of cover objects such as logs and stones. Females tend the nest until the eggs hatch.

Mudpuppy *Necturus maculosus maculosus* (Rafinesque)
L. *macula*, spotted
Description. The mudpuppy is a large, permanently aquatic salamander. The dorsal background coloration varies from grayish brown to reddish brown to black. This coloration becomes lighter on the sides but generally extends onto the lateral margins of the venter. The central portion of the belly varies from beige or cream to pinkish gray or sooty gray. The pattern on the dorsal and lateral surfaces consists of a series of small to large irregular black blotches. Smaller blotches generally extend onto the posterior dorsal surface of the head. The venter is most often immaculate or sometimes is covered with small blotches. A dark stripe on each side of the head extends from the nares, passes through the eyes, and ends at the gills.

The body is stout and somewhat dorsoventrally compressed. The head is flat, broadest just behind the eyes, and rapidly tapers to a truncated snout. The eyes are small, dark, and lidless. Three pairs of bushy external gills occur at the junction of the head and neck and may be held fully extended or flattened against the neck (Plate 2). Mudpuppies from cold, well-oxygenated water tend to have less developed gills, whereas those that occur in habitats where the water is frequently warm and low in dissolved oxygen have larger gills. For their size, their legs are small and not well developed. Both the hind feet and the forefeet have four toes. The tail is short and strongly compressed laterally and has a distinct caudal fin. The body proportions of young individuals are similar to those of the adults, except that juveniles have a slightly longer tail. The mean tail length is 48% of SVL in juveniles; it is only 43% of SVL in adults.

The average size of mature males in Pennsylvania is 266 mm ± 10.9 mm (10$\frac{3}{8}$ in.) ToL. Females are considerably larger, with an average of 291 mm ± 3.6 mm (11$\frac{1}{2}$ in.) ToL. These sizes, however, fall far short of the record ToL of 486 mm (19$\frac{3}{8}$ in.) reported by Conant and Collins (1991).

In characters other than size, mudpuppies exhibit little sexual dimorphism. Mature males, however, can generally be distinguished from females by the condition of the cloaca. The cloaca of females is a simple longitudinal slit. That of males is expanded, wrinkled along the edge, and usually bordered along the posterior margin by a distinct groove. These differences are most apparent during the breeding season.

The juvenile pattern is distinctly different from that of the adult (Plate 3). Juveniles have obvious dark dorsal and lateral stripes that are separated by pale yellowish cream to light greenish stripes. These stripes extend onto the head and tail. The ventral surfaces are immaculate cream-colored or beige. The dark lateral stripes break up and become mottled with cream or beige as they approach the venter.

Confusing Species. Its large size and the presence of gills at all life history stages distinguishes the adult mudpuppy from all other northeastern salamanders. The distinct stripes of the juvenile further distinguish it from all other species.

Habitat and Habits. Although mudpuppies are large, their secretive nature and aquatic habits have greatly hampered the study of them. As a consequence, surprisingly little is known about the biology of this interesting salamander.

Mudpuppies are habitual inhabitants of aquatic situations, but the nature of the aquatic environment is exceedingly variable. They may be found in both standing and flowing water. In standing water, they occur in clear open lakes with sandy bottoms, in weed-choked ponds, and in the vegetated littoral zone of large lakes. In flowing water, their habitat varies from sluggish warm-water streams to fast-flowing rock-strewn creeks and large rivers. We have noted, however, that in fast-flowing streams they tend to inhabit less turbulent backwaters and pools. In all habitats, they are generally associated with some form of submerged cover (e.g., rocks, logs, brush piles, or human debris). In clear-water situations, mudpuppies are primarily nocturnal, but in areas where turbidity is high they may be active at any time of the day or night.

Little detail is known about peaks and depressions of annual activity, but individuals have been collected in all months of the year. They are occasionally observed swimming under ice in the middle of winter, so it seems reasonable to conclude that they are active all year. A population from an oligotrophic lake in Michigan apparently migrates into shallow water during early spring then returns to deeper water for the rest of the year (Gibbons and Nelson 1968).

We have found mudpuppies to feed on crayfish, fish, and aquatic insects such as dobsonflies (hellgrammites). Published additions to this list include fish eggs, amphibians, worms, snails, and amphipods (Bishop 1941), but no recent analysis of their diet has been published. The most complete summary of food and feeding habits is that of J. Harris (1959). Mudpuppies are occasionally caught by anglers using live bait. They are occasionally preyed upon by hellbenders and the northern water snake.

Reproduction.   Reproduction has been briefly described by Bishop (1926). After courtship and mating in the fall, sperm are retained in the female mudpuppy's spermatheca over winter for use in late spring. Oviposition time varies from one geographic location to another. In the southern portion of its range, oviposition may occur as early as the end of April and is completed by the middle of May (Shoop 1965). Farther north (New York and Pennsylvania) oviposition does not begin until the end of May and extends through the first half of June. At any given location oviposition for the entire population occurs over a short period of time (Bishop 1941). When ready to lay eggs, females excavate a depression under a suitable cover object (usually a rock, but occasionally a log or a board). Water depth at the nest site may vary from as little as 25 cm (10 in.) to over 2 m (6 ft). In a population from Little Mahoning and Mahoning creeks, nest placement occurred primarily under rocks located within 3 m (10 ft) of shore and in water less than 40 cm (16 in.) deep.

Each egg is laid singly and attached to the underside of the cover object by a mucilaginous stalk (Plate 4). Egg yolks range from 5 to 6 mm ($\frac{1}{4}$ in.) in diameter; with all associated membranes and envelopes the eggs are about 14 mm ($\frac{5}{8}$ in.) in diameter. Females remain with the eggs throughout the incubation period. There is some evidence that they may even remain with the young for a period of time after they hatch (Cochran and Lyons 1985). Nothing is known of the behavior of the females while they are tending eggs, but if they are like most other species of salamander, they feed no more than opportunistically on suitable items that enter the egg refuge and defend the eggs from potential predators. Bishop (1941) reported an average clutch of 107 eggs. Average clutch size at Little Mahoning and Mahoning creeks was 108.6 eggs. Dissection studies indicate that mudpuppies in Pennsylvania are biennial in clutch production. Approximately half of the females examined from times of the year when vitellogenesis should have been occurring possessed small flaccid ovaries with tiny white follicles and small oviducts; the rest contained yolking follicles.

Incubation time varies from about 38 to over 70 days depending on the temperature of the water. Hatching generally occurs from early August through early September. The SVL of hatchlings varies from 11 to 15 mm ($\frac{3}{8}$–$\frac{1}{2}$ in.), and the ToL ranges from 21 to 25 mm ($\frac{7}{8}$–1 in.). Little is known about the larval ecology of this species. Cochran and Lyons (1985) found a female apparently tending 30–40 young that were considered, on the basis of size, to be about 25 days old. We have observed females and recently hatched young under the same shelter rock on at least 10 occasions. We do not know if these observations represent additional parental care on the part of the females or if females simply have a high degree of site fidelity. We have also found on several occasions (ca. 13) large numbers of young under a single rock but without a female in attendance. Presumably these young were litter mates that had not yet dispersed. All individuals were about 40 mm ($1\frac{5}{8}$ in.) ToL, so presumably they had not hatched recently.

In the southern portion of the mudpuppy's range males and females mature at about 130 mm ($5\frac{1}{4}$ in.) SVL (Shoop 1965). In Pennsylvania, males mature at about 130 mm, but dissections indicate that females do not become reproductive until they are about 150 mm (6 in.) SVL.

Distribution. The mudpuppy ranges from southern Quebec west to southeastern Manitoba and south to the northwestern tip of South Carolina, northern Georgia, Alabama, and Mississippi and westward to eastern Iowa and Missouri. It is absent from most of northern Minnesota and southwestern Wisconsin.

In the Northeast, it occurs from western Vermont through New York, excluding the Adirondacks and the southeastern portion of New York, south through western Pennsylvania. The mudpuppy has a disjunct distribution throughout New England (Klemens 1993). This distribution is, in all likelihood, due to the establishment of breeding populations by released individuals. Mudpuppies are known from the Connecticut River; the earliest observation from the river was made in 1875. A second population has been reported from Great Pond in Kennebec County, Maine (Crocker 1960). A third isolated population has been reported from Scituate Reservoir in Rhode Island (Vinegar and Friedman 1967). In Pennsylvania, the mudpuppy is restricted to the western third of the state, where it has been reported primarily from the Allegheny and Shenango rivers and their tributaries, as well as from Lake Erie. Until recently, it had not been collected in the extreme southwestern portion of the state, but recent surveys have revealed that mudpuppies are present in several tributaries of the Monongahela and the Youghiogheny rivers. It is probably more widespread in the southwestern corner of the state than was previously presumed, especially considering the fact that mudpuppies have been reported from the Monongahela River in adjacent West Virginia (Bond 1931).

The single record from the Delaware River in Delaware County is in all likelihood based either on a mislabeled specimen or on an escaped individual, but McCoy (1982) cited the possibility of dispersal through the Delaware and Hudson Canal. Literature records from Blair (Yoder 1940) and Dauphin (Surface 1913) counties are almost certainly in error, because

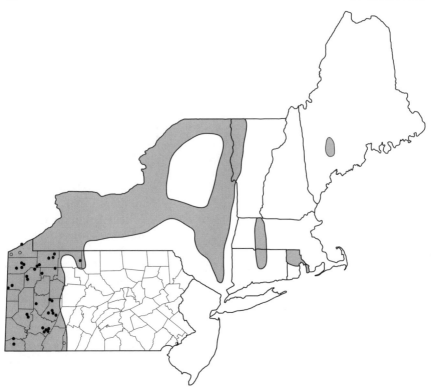

Map 2. Distribution of the mudpuppy *(Necturus maculosus maculosus)*. Half-open circle in the southeast represents capture of an introduced specimen.

mudpuppies have never been reported from any other section of the Susquehanna River or its tributaries. Further collecting is required in the Potomac River drainage of the state to determine whether mudpuppies occur in those streams.

AMBYSTOMATIDAE (MOLE SALAMANDERS)

The salamander family Ambystomatidae contains one extant genus *(Ambystoma)* and 30 species. They range throughout most of the United States and adjacent Canada southward onto the Mexican Plateau. Ambystomatids are moderate-sized, stout-bodied animals with relatively few costal grooves. Nasolabial grooves are absent. Fertilization is internal, and the eggs are commonly laid in thick gelatinous masses in ponds or lakes. The larvae of most species are typical pond-type, with a broad head, well-developed caudal and dorsal fins, and balancers during the early stages of development.

Ambystoma
Gr. *ambyx*, the rounded top of a cup; Gr. *stoma*, a mouth

The genus *Ambystoma* consists of the mole salamanders. Thirty species are contained in this exclusively North American genus.

Mole salamanders are medium-sized animals. Most are stout-bodied and have a short tail, but a few, such as the Jefferson salamander (*Ambystoma jeffersonianum*), are relatively slender. They differ from plethodontid salamanders by the lack of nasolabial grooves and from the salamandrids by the possession of costal grooves. Adults are generally terrestrial and fossorial (hence the common name mole salamander), emerging only for short periods of time to engage in reproductive activity. Most species are found in forested regions.

During reproduction, they generally congregate in large numbers at woodland ponds. Eggs are laid in either floating or submergent masses. Most species breed in late winter or early spring, but some reproduce in the fall. They feed on a wide variety of terrestrial invertebrates including worms, beetle larvae, sowbugs, and spiders.

Blue-Spotted Salamander *Ambystoma laterale* Hallowell

Description.   The blue-spotted salamander (Plate 5) is a medium-sized mole salamander, growing to 122 mm (ca. 5 in.) ToL and 67 mm ($2\frac{1}{2}$ in.) SVL in the Northeast. The maximum ToL recorded is 160 mm (ca. 6 in.), but this individual was probably a hybrid (Conant and Collins 1991). There does not appear to be sexual dimorphism in size.

The background color is black or bluish black with bright blue to bluish white flecks that are heaviest on the sides, legs, and venter. The ventral coloration is black to gray-black with black around the vent. The blue-spotted salamander has a narrow head when compared with the Jefferson salamander.

The larvae are very similar to Jefferson salamander larvae. They have large bushy gills and a variably marbled pattern on the caudal fin.

Confusing Species.   The blue-spotted salamander is often confused with the Jefferson salamander, especially juveniles. They differ in that the blue-spotted salamander has a narrower head, larger blue markings, and more costal grooves. The venter of the Jefferson salamander is gray-brown and is always lighter than the dorsum. The blue-spotted salamander might also be confused with the slimy salamander, but the slimy salamander has a groove from the nostril to the lip. The blue-spotted salamander also has fewer costal grooves (13) than the slimy salamander (16).

Habitat and Habits.   The blue-spotted salamander has been found in a variety of habitats, including wooded, swampy, or moist areas (Minton 1954). In Connecticut and adjacent areas, Klemens (1993) reported them from wooded swamps with soils ranging from water-soaked loam to sand. He also reported them to have a greater tolerance for disturbed areas than the Jefferson salamander has. Some populations of blue-spotted salamanders have been found in suburban areas and heavily distressed areas. Hunter et al. (1992) report their preferred habitat in Maine to be damp deciduous or mixed forests.

Surface activity appears to be concentrated in the breeding season during March and April; however, individuals can be found under logs and debris near the soil surface throughout the year. Activity is highest on wet nights (Klemens 1993).

Edgren (1949) reported an aggregation of 33 recently metamorphosed individuals under debris in the fall in Wisconsin. He attributed the aggregation to young individuals seeking refuge from unseasonably cold weather. In Canada, the larvae occasionally overwinter (Bleakney 1952).

The blue-spotted salamander adult is reported to feed on invertebrates, including larval and adult insects, spiders, annelids, and centipedes (DeGraaf and Rudis 1983, Hunter et al. 1992). Larvae feed on planktonic animals when small and shift to aquatic worms, insect larvae, and small crustaceans as they grow (Hunter et al. 1992). The eastern garter snake has been known to prey on the blue-spotted salamander (Klemens 1993).

Reproduction.   Courtship and mating of the blue-spotted salamander occur in early spring. Eggs are deposited from as early as late February in the southern part of the range to late April in the northern part of the range (Kumpf and Yeaton 1932, Hunter et al. 1992, Klemens 1993).

Klemens (1993) observed that blue-spotted salamanders prefer grassy, floodplain wetlands for breeding. Others have found them breeding in ponds on the edges of open fields and in floodplain pools, swamps, abandoned beaver flowages, and highway ditches (J. Anderson and Giacosie 1967, Hunter et al. 1992, Nyman et al. 1988). Kumpf and Yeaton (1932) described courtship behavior in detail.

Eggs are deposited either singly or in loose clumps of 2–8 eggs (Hunter et al. 1992), which either fall freely to the bottom sediment (Landre 1980) or are attached to litter and bottom detritus (Stille 1954), twigs (Uzzell 1967), or grass blades (Klemens 1993). Individual females may lay as many as 500 eggs (Gilhen 1984). Eggs hatch in about a month (P. Smith 1961), and the larval phase is brief. Newly transformed individuals measure about 50 mm ($1\frac{3}{16}$ in.) ToL in Maine (Hunter et al. 1992) and 65 mm ($2\frac{1}{2}$ in.) ToL (Gilhen 1984) in Nova Scotia.

Females mature at approximately 84 mm ($3\frac{3}{8}$ in.) ToL and 51 mm (2 in.) SVL, and males mature at about 71 mm ($2\frac{3}{4}$ in.) ToL and 42 mm ($1\frac{3}{4}$ in.) SVL (Uzzell 1967).

Remarks.   Hybrid blends of *Ambystoma jeffersonianum* and *A. laterale* are found throughout the Northeast. In southern New England, hybrid forms are more numerous than either parental species (Klemens 1993). Klemens (1993) has done an excellent job of summarizing and describing hybridization in northeastern populations.

Distribution.   The blue-spotted salamander occurs from the Canadian maritime provinces and Labrador south along the Atlantic coast to

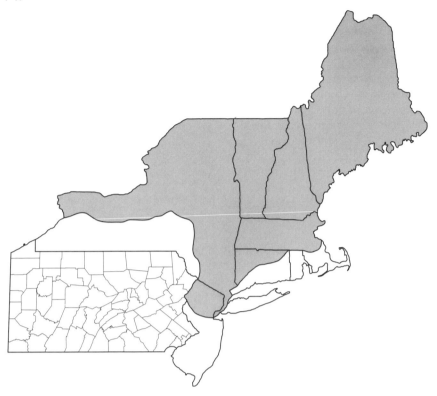

Map 3.   Distribution of the blue-spotted salamander *(Ambystoma laterale).*

northern New Jersey. Its range extends westward through northern Indiana and northeastern Illinois, through most of Wisconsin, eastern Minnesota and the southern half of Ontario.

In the Northeast, it is found in scattered localities throughout northern and eastern New York, including Long Island, and in New England. Hybrid populations of the blue-spotted and Jefferson salamanders may occur in several locations in Pennsylvania, but additional genetic analysis needs to be conducted to clarify this issue (Klemens, pers. comm.).

Jefferson Salamander *Ambystoma jeffersonianum* (Green)
Named after the type locality at Jefferson College, Pennsylvania
Description.   The Jefferson salamander (Plate 6) is a moderate-sized, relatively slender mole salamander. The color pattern varies with age. Older individuals are a uniform brownish black. Younger animals have a grayish black background coloration that becomes lighter on the sides and ventral surfaces. The dorsum and sides are covered with pale blue flecks that tend to be both larger and more numerous on the sides than on the back. These blue flecks also extend onto the dorsal surfaces of the head

and appendages. As an individual ages, the spots begin to disappear and the background color gradually darkens until it is brownish black. Albino specimens have been reported from Ohio and Maryland (Dyrkacz 1981).

The Jefferson salamander has strong, well-developed legs and long slender toes. The head is only slightly distinct from the neck. The tail is heavy, oval in cross section, and usually tapered to a point. Dermal glands are located over the entire dorsal surface and are concentrated on the tail. There are 12 costal grooves.

Sexual dimorphism occurs in size but not in relative tail length. Mature males are smaller than mature females. Pennsylvania males average 65.2 mm ($2\frac{5}{8}$ in.) SVL and 129.2 mm ($5\frac{1}{8}$ in.) ToL. The larger females average 81.0 mm ($3\frac{1}{4}$ in.) SVL and 158.2 mm ($6\frac{3}{8}$ in.) ToL. Maximum ToL for this species is 210 mm ($8\frac{3}{8}$ in.) (Conant and Collins 1991). The tail of both sexes averages 101% of SVL. During the breeding season, males can easily be distinguished from females by their greatly enlarged cloacal lips.

Larvae vary in size from 10 mm ($\frac{1}{3}$ in.) at hatching to approximately 80 mm ($3\frac{1}{4}$ in.) at transformation. The larvae are characterized as typical pond-type larvae, with large, well-developed dorsal and caudal fins. The head is large and broad. The limbs, once developed, are long and thin. The body is greenish gray or brown and may have some yellow mottling. The belly is pale.

Recently transformed individuals tend to be brownish dorsally and somewhat lighter ventrally. The blue flecks characteristic of the young adult are absent, but occasionally the brown background color may be flecked with yellow. Adult coloration develops during the spring following transformation. Size at transformation ranges from 48 to 90 mm ($1\frac{1}{2}$–$3\frac{1}{2}$ in.) ToL.

Confusing Species.   The large size, blue-flecked to uniform coloration, and low number of costal grooves distinguish the Jefferson salamander from any other found in the Northeast, with the exception of the blue-spotted salamander. The blue markings of Jefferson salamanders tend to be smaller than those of the blue-spotted. In addition, the venter of the Jefferson salamander is much lighter than the dorsum, and it has a broader head.

Habitat and Habits.   The Jefferson salamander is primarily an inhabitant of deciduous or mixed hardwood-coniferous forests that contain either temporary or permanent ponds. Although found in both bottom-land and upland forests, it is more common in upland forests (Thompson et al. 1980).

Like other mole salamanders, Jefferson salamanders are not frequently encountered except during the reproductive season (March to early April), at which time they are usually active on the surface. During the rest of the year, they are found only sporadically, usually under cover of rocks, logs, bark, and leaf litter. Apparently in some areas of its range the species is very abundant at times outside the breeding season, especially in the fall. Bishop (1941) reported finding several hundred in a few hours of collecting in the fall in western New York. Judd (1957) also considered them to be very common in southern Ontario in the fall.

Bishop (1941) reported aggregations of 20 or more recently transformed individuals and those nearing maturity under logs and bark in the fall and spring. He also stated that in loose soil they will burrow 30 cm (ca. 12 in.) or more below the surface to hibernate.

Nothing is known of their dietary habits in the Northeast. In Ontario, adults have been found to eat a wide variety of foods, including slugs, snails, worms, isopods, centipedes, spiders, roaches, collembolans, and ants (Judd 1957). In general, prey items reflect the invertebrate community found under the salamander's cover. C. Smith and Petranka (1987) reported larvae feeding on cladocerans, copepods, and chironomid (fly) larvae.

When threatened, Jefferson salamanders may exhibit defensive behavior typical of *Ambystoma*. They spread and brace their hind legs, thus elevating the posterior half of their body. They hold their tail in an arc or raise it vertically and thrash it about while exuding copious quantities of a milky white secretion (Rand 1954).

Reproduction.   Courtship and mating of Jefferson salamanders occur in early spring after the salamanders have migrated to their breeding ponds. Kumpf and Yeaton (1932) discussed courtship behavior in detail.

Vernal migration to breeding pools is stimulated by environmental cues. In Kentucky, Douglas (1979) showed that evening rains associated with moderate temperatures (greater than 7.0°C during the day and 4.4°C at night; 44.6°F and 40°F) initiate salamander migrations. In Pennsylvania, migrations can occur as early as the end of February and as late as the beginning of April depending upon location and climatic conditions. Males tend to move under less favorable conditions of temperature than do females and, as a result, usually arrive at breeding ponds before the females. Sex ratio in the ponds is skewed significantly in favor of males. Douglas (1979) reported mating pool sex ratios of 2.7:1 and 2.3:1. Horne and Dunson (1994) and Rowe and Dunson (1993) studied the relationship between abiotic parameters (e.g., pH, aluminum, sulfate) in pond water and egg mass deposition. Among other things, they found that ponds with low pH, high aluminum, and high sulfate had fewer egg masses than did ponds with higher pH and lower concentrations of aluminum and sulfate.

At the time of mating, females contain ovarian follicles of ovulatory size, and they begin egg deposition shortly after mating. Eggs are deposited in small groups (usually 10 to 25) in a jelly mass on slender branches or stems of vegetation in the water. After the jelly coat absorbs water and swells, the masses are usually cylindrical and about 25–40 mm (1–1½ in.) in diameter and about twice that size in length. A series of such small masses, totaling 150–300 eggs, may be deposited. The eggs vary from 2 to 2.5 mm (⅛ in.) in diameter and with their associated capsules are about 4–4.5 mm (¼ in.) in diameter.

Incubation time varies from 30 to 45 days depending upon temperature. Recent hatchlings vary from 10 to 14 mm (¼–½ in.) ToL and have well-developed balancers. Transformation can begin as early as the first week of July, but it may extend into the middle of August. Size at transformation is variable, ranging from about 50 to 80 mm (2–3¼ in.) ToL.

Females mature at about 70–75 mm (2¾–3 in.) SVL; males mature at about 55 mm (2¼ in.) SVL.

Remarks. As is the spotted salamander, the Jefferson salamander appears to be threatened by acid precipitation. Freda and Dunson (1986) showed that embryonic mortality increased as the pH of the water decreased, and in the laboratory they noted that no hatching occurred at a pH lower than 4.5. They further demonstrated that in central Pennsylvania pools containing Jefferson salamanders had significantly higher pH values than did pools that contained no Jefferson salamanders.

Distribution. The Jefferson salamander ranges from western New England through southern New York, northern New Jersey, and most of Pennsylvania into Ohio and southern Indiana. The range extends southward into Kentucky, West Virginia, and Virginia.

In the Northeast, it occurs from western Vermont to the uplands of Massachusetts and Connecticut west of the Connecticut River (it

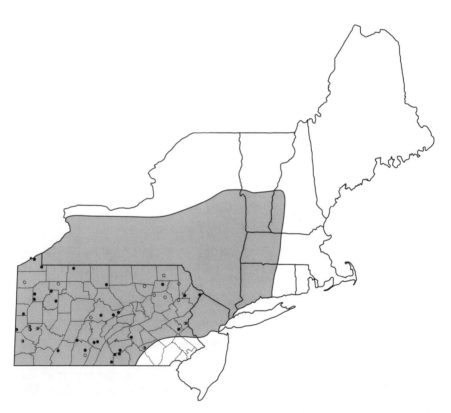

Map 4. Distribution of the Jefferson salamander *(Ambystoma jeffersonianum)*.

just crosses the river in extreme northern Massachusetts and extreme southwestern New Hampshire) through southeastern New York and northern New Jersey. In the rest of New England and New York, it is known to hybridize with *Ambystoma laterale*.

Its known distribution in Pennsylvania is spotty but widespread. Specific collecting around temporary ponds in early spring would probably produce more localities for this species in the state. There are numerous literature records from the southeastern Coastal Plain and Piedmont but no voucher specimens to substantiate them (Baldauf 1943). Additional surveys are necessary to determine the actual status of the animal.

Spotted Salamander *Ambystoma maculatum* (Shaw)
Gr. *maculatus,* spotted
Description.   Adult spotted salamanders (Plate 7) are large and have a dark lustrous black dorsum, which becomes slate gray on the lower sides and ventral surfaces. Brilliant large yellow or yellowish orange spots are distributed in a variety of patterns on the head, back, and tail. The lower surfaces have no pattern. Albinos are known for this species (Hensley 1959, Lowcock 1985).

It is a heavy-bodied animal with strong, well-developed legs. The head is broad, somewhat depressed, and set off from the body by a distinct neck. The tail is fairly short, is oval in cross section, and rapidly tapers to the tip. Costal grooves usually number 12 but range from 11 to 13. Dermal glands are present on the dorsal surfaces and are best developed along the dorsal surface of the tail.

Sexual size dimorphism does not occur in spotted salamanders from Pennsylvania and the Northeast. The average SVL of mature individuals is 88.8 mm ($3\frac{1}{2}$ in.), and the average ToL is 172.8 mm (7 in.). The maximum size is 248 mm (10 in.) ToL (Conant and Collins 1991). The mean tail length is slightly less than the SVL. Males can easily be distinguished from females during the breeding season by the noticeable swelling of the cloacal lips.

Recently transformed individuals have a uniform unpatterned brown dorsum grading to light tan on the belly. This color phase, however, is very transient, and within a few weeks the coloration blackens and spots become well developed. Size at transformation is variable, ranging from 35 to 70 mm ($1\frac{3}{8}$ to $2\frac{3}{4}$ in.) ToL, depending upon environmental conditions.

Confusing Species.   The spotted salamander may be confused with the northern slimy salamander, but the combination of bright yellow spots and lustrous black background color and the lack of nasolabial grooves distinguish the spotted salamander from any other found in Pennsylvania and the Northeast.

Habitat and Habits.   The spotted salamander is most frequently encountered in deciduous forests or mixed hardwood-coniferous forests that have either temporary vernal or permanent woodland ponds. Although they may occasionally be found in coniferous forests, they are not common in that habitat. They are found both in lowland woods and on upland ridges. Gibbs (1998) examined amphibian distribution along a forest fragmentation gradient in southern Connecticut. He found that spotted salamanders are absent from portions of the gradient where forest cover was below 70%.

Although they may be abundant in a given habitat, the probability of finding them outside of the breeding season is low because they have a very short surface activity period. Spotted salamanders are active on the surface and in ponds during the second half of March and the first few weeks of April. During the rest of the year they live underground, providing the general name of the senus (mole salamander). Between the end of April and October individuals may occasionally be found at the mouth of their burrow, which is usually located under a rock or a log. Presumably, the animals hibernate in their underground retreat.

No detailed studies of the diet of this species have been conducted. Animals we have examined contained snails, worms, adult and larval beetles, spiders, isopods, and crickets. Bishop (1941) suggested that they do not eat while engaged in migratory and reproductive activity. Feeding may be reduced at this time, but it certainly does not cease. We found that approximately 33% of adults taken at breeding ponds contained food.

Unlike marbled salamanders, spotted salamanders actively attempt to escape into their retreats when discovered. If they cannot escape, they assume a typical defensive posture in which they extend and stiffen their hind limbs, thus raising the posterior part of their body and arching the tail. The tail contains a dorsal ridge of well-developed glandular tissue that may secrete a white milky substance. Brodie and colleagues (1979) have shown that this is an effective antipredator mechanism, repelling even repeated advances of the highly predatory short-tailed shrew.

Reproduction.   Courtship and mating occur in early spring (15 March to approximately 10 April) in the woodland ponds where the eggs will be laid. In extremely cold years, courtship may extend to the end of April. Courtship has been described in detail by Breder (1927). At the time of mating, females contain eggs of ovulatory size, and they deposit their eggs shortly after courtship terminates.

Salamander migration to the breeding ponds is initiated by the first rains of early spring, associated with increasing temperature. Males often arrive at the ponds before the females, but occasionally they arrive together (Baldauf 1952).

Individuals tend to return to the same pond year after year (Sexton et al. 1986, Whitford and Vinegar 1966). McGregor and Teska (1989) have shown that individuals can distinguish by means of olfactory substances water from their pond as opposed to water from nearby ponds. They postulate that migrating individuals follow the olfactory cues from their own pond based on seepage out of the pond into the surrounding area. Ponds most frequently used for reproduction tend to be shallow with heavy leaf litter on the bottom and ample emergent vegetation (i.e., shrubs and weeds) to allow for the attachment of the eggs and to provide refuge for the larvae. The heavy reliance on temporary ponds is probably due to the fact that they never contain fish, which would prey on both larvae and adults. Survival in fishless ponds is about four times as great as survival in ponds that contain fish (Ireland 1989).

Sex ratios are highly skewed in favor of males at breeding ponds. Whitford and Vinegar (1966) reported sex ratios of 3.5 males per female in Rhode Island. It is not known if this bias toward males is a function of higher female mortality or if females breed every other year or at more irregular intervals (Woodward 1982).

Egg masses (Plate 8) are generally laid attached to emergent or submergent vegetation. In the absence of vegetation, the egg masses are found resting on the bottom. When first laid, the egg masses are small (2.5 cm [1 in.] or less in diameter), but the jelly coat surrounding the eggs rapidly absorbs water and swells to four or five times the initial size of the mass. Individual masses contain from 60 to 200 eggs, and a single female may lay two or three masses (Bishop 1941). The thick jelly coat greatly reduces the chance that the egg mass will dry out, even if it becomes temporarily stranded on shore or above the water on sticks when the pond level drops. The salamander's tendency to lay eggs communally further reduces the chance of desiccation of stranded eggs owing to the increased surface-area-to-volume ratio of clumped egg masses (Nyman 1987). The heavy jelly coat also acts as an effective antipredator device. In the laboratory, the jelly coat even protected the eggs from large voracious predators such as sunfish. Egg masses may be either clear or opaque after swelling. It has been demonstrated that the opaque masses result from the presence of a glycoprotein located in the walls of the oviduct (L. Hardy and Lucas 1991). The opacity of the masses does not appear to affect development.

Egg masses tend to develop a greenish color over time as they become infiltrated with single-celled green algae (*Oophilia ambystomatis*). Eggs with algal associations have a higher level of oxygen than the outside environment, even when the surrounding water is oxygen depleted (Bachman et al. 1986). In fact, Pinder and Friel (1994) demonstrated that simple diffusion alone is inadequate to supply late-stage embryos at the center of masses with sufficient oxygen to meet their metabolic demands. Masses with algal symbionts, however, have more than enough oxygen at the center to meet the demands of the embryos. Both incubation time and time to transformation are variable depending upon environmental temperature. Incubation time usually lasts 30–50 days, with larvae hatching from mid-May to early June. At hatching, larvae range from 11 to 13 mm ($\frac{1}{4}$–$\frac{1}{2}$ in.) ToL and possess well-developed balancers (Plate 9). Transformation usually occurs in August, but it may be extended into September if temperatures are low. In exceedingly low water temperatures larvae have been reported to overwinter before transforming (Stangel 1988, Whitford and Vinegar 1966).

The larvae are carnivorous and feed on a variety of benthic and plank-tonic organisms. Their diet includes, but is not restricted to, fly larvae (chironomids and culicids), beetles, and cladocerans.

As do other *Ambystoma* larvae, the larvae of the spotted salaman-der make daily vertical migrations from the bottom of the pond to the top. This migration is presumably in response either to changing light conditions or to the daily migrations of their microcrustacean prey items.

Size at transformation varies greatly both within and between popu-lations, ranging from 40 to 70 mm ($1\frac{1}{2}$–$2\frac{3}{4}$ in.) ToL (Bishop 1941). Most recently transformed animals that we examined were about 50 mm (2 in.) ToL.

Remarks.   If at all possible, populations of spotted salamanders, as well as other temporary pond–breeding amphibians, should be closely moni-tored over time for population changes. Several recent studies have sug-gested that increased acidification of ponds due to acid precipitation is adversely affecting survivorship of spotted salamanders. Increased acidity has been shown to reduce hatching success, increase larval mortality, increase hatching time, cause egg membranes to thicken and toughen, cause curvature of the spine of embryos, and stunt gill development (K. Clark 1986, Portnoy 1990, Robb and Toews 1977). Blem and Blem (1989) predicted that if acidification continues there will be a dramatic decrease in spotted salamander populations in Virginia. The entire state of Penn-sylvania receives precipitation of an acidity that is potentially dangerous to spotted salamanders as well as other temporary pond fauna. Temporary pond fauna is especially vulnerable to acidification because temporary ponds are, in general, poorly buffered and often have associated with them a variety of organic acids resulting from the decomposition of vegetation.

Concern has also been expressed about the effects of forest clear-cutting on salamander populations (Messere and Ducey 1998), but little attention has been paid to the effects beyond the edge of the clear-cut. Demagnadier and Hunter (1998) demonstrated that several amphibian species in Maine were negatively affected by clear-cutting at depths of 25–35 m (80–115 ft) inside forests adjacent to clear-cuts. Among the species affected were spotted salamanders, redback salamanders, blue-spotted salamanders, and wood frogs. Their findings may have a significant impact on determining the size and distribution of clear-cut sites.

Distribution.   The spotted salamander is widespread, occurring in the eastern third of North America from southern Quebec to Ontario and south through Georgia, west to central Wisconsin, southern Missouri, and extreme eastern Oklahoma and Texas. It is absent from Florida, south-eastern Georgia, eastern North Carolina, and extreme southeastern Virginia.

It is widespread throughout the Northeast, though it is absent from many New England islands (Klemens 1993) and from the western and northwestern portions of Maine (Hunter et al. 1992).

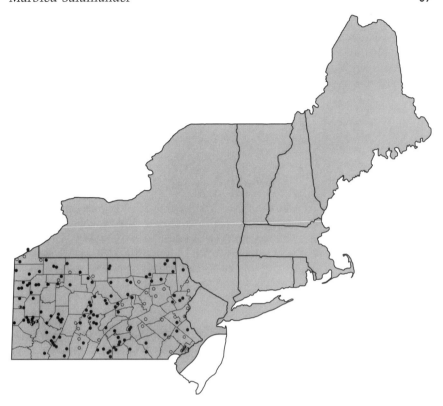

Map 5. Distribution of the spotted salamander *(Ambystoma maculatum).*

This species is widely distributed throughout the state of Pennsylvania, although the distribution is spotty.

Marbled Salamander *Ambystoma opacum* (Gravenhorst)
Gr. *opacum,* shaded or dark
Description. The marbled salamander (Plate 10) is a small, stout-bodied species. The dorsal background coloration is rich black, becoming bluish black on the lower sides. The dorsal pattern consists of a series of whitish to silvery gray transverse bands that are usually narrowest dorsally and widest laterally, giving them a roughly hourglass shape. These bands stop midway down the sides of the body. Sometimes the bands are interrupted along the midline and the individual exhibits two dorsolateral stripes with irregular margins. The transverse bands continue on the tail, giving it a ringed appearance from above, but they stop midway down the sides. The silvery gray to white markings usually extend onto, and completely border, the head, leaving a black oval spot in the center. In some cases, however, the markings are interrupted at the back of the head and, as a consequence, form a V-shaped pattern rather than a circular one. The

ventral surfaces of the body are immaculate bluish black. The dorsal markings of the male tend to be lighter than those of the female, especially
during the breeding season (Bishop 1941). Albino specimens have been
reported from Maryland and Mississippi (Dyrkacz 1981).

The head is broad and rounded, not distinctly set off from the body. The
limbs are short and thick, and the tail is short, averaging only 60% of SVL
in adults. The marbled salamander is the smallest of the mole salamanders found in Pennsylvania and the Northeast. The average Pennsylvania specimen is 61.9 mm ($2\frac{1}{2}$ in.) SVL and 102.7 mm (4 in.) ToL. Females
tend to be larger than males, but the difference is not significant. The
maximum size for the species is 127 mm (5 in.) ToL (Green and Pauley
1987).

The larvae (Plate 11) range in size from about 15 mm ($\frac{1}{2}$ in.) at hatching
to 70 mm ($3\frac{3}{4}$ in.) ToL at transformation. Larvae of all sizes generally have
a brownish olive dorsal background coloration, and a series of light dorsolateral spots runs along the length of the body. The ventral surfaces are
mottled brownish beige. The larvae are typical pond-type, with a short
broad head and somewhat triangular body. The dorsal caudal fin is well
developed and extends forward to the middle of the back. At transformation, the dorsal background coloration varies from brown to black, becoming lighter ventrally. The dorsal surface is covered with scattered light
flecks and spots, and the light dorsolateral spots of the larvae are still
present. The length of time for the development of the adult color pattern
varies, ranging from 2 weeks to several months (Bishop 1941).

Confusing Species.   The adult marbled salamander is difficult to
confuse with any other member of Pennsylvania or northeastern herpetofauna. Recently transformed individuals could be mistaken for the
northern slimy salamander, except that the marbled salamander lacks a
nasolabial groove and has only 11 or 12 costal grooves.

Habitat and Habits.   Owing to the infrequent collection of this species
in Pennsylvania, most of this discussion relies on studies conducted in
other parts of its range. Marbled salamanders are predominantly inhabitants of upland forests supporting temporary ponds that fill with water
during the winter and spring. In Ohio, these are characterized as "swamp
forests" (W. King 1935). Within this general habitat, marbled salamanders
are occasionally encountered under rocks, logs, and other surface debris,
but they tend to be uncommon except during the reproductive season.
When found on land outside of the reproductive season, they tend to
occupy drier situations than other species of mole salamander (Bishop
1941).

In Pennsylvania, marbled salamanders are most often found during the
fall, which corresponds to the reproductive season for the species. At all
other times of the year their occurrence on the surface and under surface
cover is rare. They apparently spend most of their time in subterranean
retreats.

No detailed studies of feeding have been conducted on adults. Bishop
(1941) reported that they eat snails and slugs, beetles, ants, worms, and

orthopterans (grasshoppers and crickets). Specimens we examined contained spiders, earthworms, grasshoppers, beetles, wasps, millipedes, centipedes, and isopods. Unlike many species of salamanders that prey on relatively small food items, marbled salamanders tend to consume prey that is large compared with their size.

Marbled salamanders are exceedingly lethargic. When first encountered, they usually remain motionless or slowly attempt to move away. If continuously annoyed, they assume a defensive position in which they stiffen their hind legs and elevate their tail. If the body is touched, the tail will lash in the direction of the stimulus (Brodie 1977). If molestation continues a milky secretion is released from specialized glands located predominantly on the dorsal surface of the tail. It has been demonstrated that these secretions function as an effective antipredator device and can repel an attack by short-tailed shrews (DiGiovanni and Brodie 1981).

Reproduction.   Courtship and mating occur in early fall in the northern portion of the range (J. Anderson and Williamson 1973, W. King 1935). Noble and Brady (1933) described courtship in detail.

At the time of mating, females contain eggs of ovulatory size, and they oviposit shortly after mating has been completed. Egg laying occurs earlier (September) in the northern part of the range than in the southern portion, where eggs are usually laid in November. Oviposition appears to be initiated by temperature rather than moisture or other environmental factors. The marbled salamander is unique among mole salamanders in that the eggs are laid in terrestrial situations and are attended by the female. Females construct, then lay their eggs in, an oblong or ovoid nest that averages 9.7 cm by 8.2 cm ($3\frac{3}{4}$ in. by $3\frac{1}{4}$ in.) and is about 2 cm ($\frac{4}{5}$ in.) deep (Petranka and Petranka 1981b). Nests are primarily constructed under vegetation or leaf litter or, to a lesser extent, under cover objects such as logs and rocks. Nests are constructed in areas that will later fill with water from winter rainfall or early spring snowmelt. These sites are predominately woodland vernal pools, but they may also occur in dry streambeds and along the sides of permanent ponds that have shrunk in size owing to drying. Nest site position along the banks of these areas is not random. Females tend to select sites that maximize the probability of hatching but minimize the possibility of the pond's drying before development has been completed. Because the optimal conditions vary from region to region, the locations of nest sites also vary (M. Jackson et al. 1989, Petranka and Petranka 1981a).

Females generally tend the nest, but, because they do not feed at this time (late fall or winter), there is no energetic cost associated with this behavior (Kaplan and Crump 1978). Female nest attendance has been positively associated with hatching success (W. King 1935). Embryonic development begins in the nest and continues to a point just before hatching. When the nest is inundated, the eggs immediately hatch and the larvae enter the pond.

The average diameter of eggs is 2.7 mm ($\frac{1}{8}$ in.), and the average size of the eggs plus associated capsules is 4.7 mm ($\frac{1}{4}$ in.) (Bishop 1941). Clutch size has been reported to vary between 48 and 200 eggs, with a mean of about 100. Clutch size may or may not be positively correlated with female body size (Petranka and Petranka 1981b, Walls and Altig 1986). The average size of mature females has been reported at 62.5 mm ($2\frac{1}{2}$ in.) SVL.

Incubation time is variable, being dependent upon nest site inundation. Hatchlings range from 14 to 22 mm ($\frac{1}{2}$–1 in.) ToL (Hassinger et al. 1970).

Larvae are carnivorous and feed on a variety of prey, predominantly microcrustacean zooplankton such as copepods and cladocerans (Branch and Altig 1981, Petranka and Petranka 1980). Stenhouse and co-workers (1983) demonstrated that in some areas, at least, marbled salamanders prey upon the larvae of the closely related spotted salamander. In a sample of individuals near transformation size from central Pennsylvania, we found a predominance of adult aquatic beetles in the animals' diet.

It has frequently been noted that the larvae tend to make vertical migrations in the water column on a daily basis. At night, they tend to be near the surface and during the day in the litter and vegetation at the bottom (Hassinger et al. 1970). It has been suggested that this migration is in response to the daily movement of prey items.

Time to transformation is about 135 days but varies somewhat depending upon environmental temperature. In central Pennsylvania, transformation occurs from about the middle of June to early July. The average size at transformation for a sample ($N = 6$) from Pennsylvania was 31.5 mm SVL (range: 30–33 mm; $1\frac{1}{5}$–$1\frac{3}{10}$ in.) and 54.0 mm ToL (range: 50–56 mm; 2–$2\frac{1}{4}$ in.). Recently transformed young tend to remain in the vicinity of the ponds from which they emerged for several weeks before dispersing into the surrounding woods.

Few data are available on size at sexual maturity, although the marbled salamander has been studied intensively with regard to other aspects of its reproductive biology. In a small sample from Pennsylvania, mature females averaged 64.4 mm SVL (range: 60–72 mm; $2\frac{2}{5}$–3 in.), and mature males averaged 58 mm SVL (range: 54–60 mm; $2\frac{1}{5}$–$2\frac{2}{5}$ in.; $N = 6$).

Distribution. The range of the marbled salamander extends from southern New England to the Florida panhandle and westward to eastern Texas, southeastern Oklahoma, Missouri, and southern Illinois. Disjunct populations border the Great Lakes from Pennsylvania to Indiana.

In the Northeast, it occurs as far north as extreme southern New Hampshire and is widespread throughout Massachusetts, Rhode Island, and Connecticut, where it occurs below 3,609 m (1,100 ft) in elevation (Klemens 1993). In New York, it is known from Long Island, "the extreme southeastern portion of the state" (Klemens 1993).

The marbled salamander has a spotty range in Pennsylvania that extends diagonally from the northeast to the southwest. The species' secretive habits and short fall activity season make it unlikely to be observed even in areas where it may be common. The most effective way to determine its presence in an area is to search temporary ponds in the spring for larvae and then to return in the fall to look for the adults.

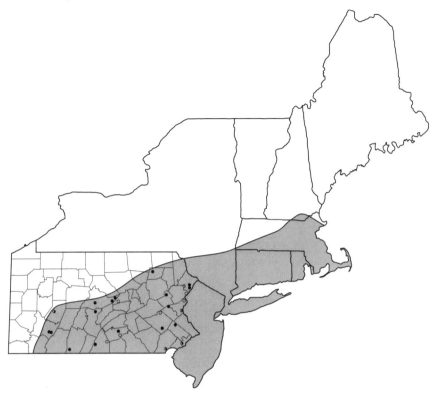

Map 6. Distribution of the marbled salamander *(Ambystoma opacum)*.

Eastern Tiger Salamander *Ambystoma tigrinum tigrinum* (Green)
L. *tigrin,* striped like a tiger
Description. The eastern tiger salamander (Plate 12) is a large species of mole salamander. The dorsal background color ranges from brown to brownish black. Eastern tiger salamanders are boldly patterned with large olive to olive-yellow spots and bars forming a pattern on the sides and dorsum of the body and on the tail, head, and legs. The ventral surfaces are yellowish olive and are marked with darker blotches.

It is a heavy-bodied salamander. The head is short and broad, with a bluntly rounded snout. Tiger salamanders are well adapted for a fossorial existence. The limbs are strong and well developed, and the digits are short and broad and terminate with dark brown cornified tips used for digging in the soil.

In western Ohio, males average 103 mm $(4\frac{1}{8}$ in.) SVL and 204 mm (8 in.) ToL. Females average 106.5 mm $(4\frac{1}{4}$ in.) SVL and 199.7 mm $(7\frac{7}{8}$ in.) ToL (Pfingsten and Downs 1989). The maximum size for the subspecies is 330 mm $(13\frac{1}{8}$ in.) ToL (Conant and Collins 1991). Only a single specimen exists from Pennsylvania.

Confusing Species.   The eastern tiger salamander could be mistaken for the spotted salamander, but it differs in pattern. The tiger salamander pattern is a series of spots and more elongate marks on both the dorsum and sides of the body. The spotted salamander pattern consists of well-formed rounded spots restricted to the dorsal surfaces. In addition, the spots of the tiger salamander tend to be olive or olive yellow, whereas those of the spotted salamander are usually yellow or yellowish orange.

Habitat and Habits.   Eastern tiger salamanders generally inhabit woodland situations where the soil is suitable for their burrowing activity, but they can also survive in old fields and open meadows having soil conditions permitting burrowing. Eastern tiger salamanders, which have a longer breeding season than other mole salamanders, may be active on the surface from late fall to early spring.

Reproduction.   Unlike other species of mole salamander, which generally breed in temporary ponds, tiger salamanders reproduce in ponds that seldom, if ever, dry up. The larval period is generally longer (in some cases well over 100 days) than that of other mole salamanders, and at metamorphosis the young are almost reproductive size. Therefore, they can generally breed the following reproductive season, rather than having to spend one or two years growing before achieving reproductive maturity.

Remarks.   Populations of eastern tiger salamanders still exist in southern New Jersey and on Long Island, New York. There is only one verified locality for the eastern tiger salamander in Pennsylvania. This is for a single specimen collected in the mid-1800s from London Grove in Chester County. Reports of the species in several other localities in Pennsylvania have been published, but, in a thorough review of the reports, Netting (1938) concluded that all records except for those in London Grove and in Wexford and Pittsburgh in Allegheny County were erroneous. Allegheny County is one of the most thoroughly collected counties within the state, yet the species has not been reported since two specimens were collected in Wexford in the early 1900s. Furthermore, Allegheny County is located in the middle of a large hiatus in the distribution of the eastern tiger salamander, with the nearest verified localities more than 241.4 km (150 mi) away in any direction. Therefore, it is our opinion that the species was never native to Allegheny County. The fact that larvae of tiger salamanders were in the past commonly sold as fish bait under the name of waterdogs may explain the Allegheny County record.

We consider the eastern tiger salamander to be extirpated from the state. The area around London Grove in southern Chester County has undergone dramatic alterations over the years, with most of the land having been cleared either for agriculture or for residential or light industrial use. Tiger salamanders generally breed in permanent ponds that lack populations of fish. The nature of habitat alteration in Chester County destroyed most of the potential breeding sites that had been available to the salamanders.

Map 7. Distribution of the eastern tiger salamander *(Ambystoma tigrinum tigrinum)*.

In the event that eastern tiger salamanders still occur in Chester County, adults should be sought at potential breeding ponds between late fall and early spring (November to March), and larvae from early spring to early summer (March to June).

Distribution. The range of the eastern tiger salamander extends along the Coastal Plain and Piedmont from Long Island, New York, and southern New Jersey southward to northern Florida and the Gulf of Mexico. In the west, it extends from Minnesota in the north to eastern Texas in the south. It is absent from the Appalachian Mountains as well as all of West Virginia and the eastern half of Ohio.

The only valid record from Pennsylvania is from southern Chester County (see Remarks).

SALAMANDRIDAE (NEWTS)

The family Salamandridae contains 15 genera and approximately 53 recognized species. It is primarily an Old World group, with only two genera occurring in North America. The eastern newts (*Notophthalmus*) are found throughout the eastern half of the United States and adjacent Canada and Mexico. The Pacific newts (*Taricha*), as the name implies, occur along the Pacific coast from southern Alaska to extreme southern California.

Members of the family lack costal grooves and nasolabial grooves. They have well-developed lungs. Reproduction varies from eggs laid in the water to retention of eggs and live birth to direct development of terrestrial eggs. Some species have an additional life history stage, the eft, between the larva and the adult. All species in the family produce toxic skin secretions, and many species have bright warning (aposematic) coloration.

Notophthalmus
Gr. *notos*, the back; Gr. *ophthalmos*, the eye

The genus *Notophthalmus* (the eastern newts) includes three species. It is a small but widespread genus, ranging from southern Canada to southern Florida in the east and from Minnesota to northern Veracruz in Mexico in the west.

Eastern newts are small, stocky animals with a tail about as long as the body. Adult and larval newts are aquatic, but there is often an intermediate life history stage called the eft that is terrestrial. Efts, when present, are brightly colored and are generally found in the leaf litter of forests. Adults and larvae are found in a variety of standing water situations, but usually in areas where fish are absent or at low population levels. Unlike the skin of most salamanders, that of the newt is rough and granular rather than smooth and slippery.

Newts are carnivorous, feeding on a variety of aquatic organisms including clams, snails, amphibian eggs, aquatic crustacea (e.g., water fleas and amphipods), and aquatic insects.

Newts, unlike most salamanders, lay their eggs singly rather than in clumps. The eggs are laid attached to strands of aquatic vegetation and are often wrapped in the leaves of plants. Egg laying is frequently prolonged, occurring over a period of several weeks.

Red-Spotted Newt *Notophthalmus viridescens viridescens* (Rafinesque)
L. *viridescens*, greenish
Description.   The red-spotted newt (Plate 13) is a moderate-sized species that has a complex life history involving an aquatic larva, an intermediate terrestrial form, and an aquatic adult. The stages are all distinct in appearance and will be discussed separately.

Adults are strongly two-toned, with the dorsal half of the body brownish green and the belly and lower sides lemon yellow to orange. The belly is patterned with distinct, sharp-edged black spots of varying sizes and intensities. The dorsal and lateral surfaces also have black markings, but these tend to be less distinct and, as a result, have rather irregular outlines. Two series of bright red dots, each dot bordered by black, extend from the neck to the base of the tail along the upper sides of the body. The dots vary greatly in number (usually 3 to 8) and size as well as exact placement. Some individuals have a few red spots along the lower sides. The spotting pattern is so variable that some workers have been able to recognize individual animals in their study populations solely on the basis of the pattern of spots. An enduring misconception is that the age of a red-spotted newt can be determined by counting the number of spots on the animal.

The body of the adult is somewhat rounded, and the limbs are short but well developed. The head is barely distinct from the neck. The tail is compressed laterally and has a variably developed caudal fin.

Males and female red-spotted newts are similar in body size and proportion, although the hind legs of males are larger than those of females of similar size. The average size for a large sample from Pennsylvania was 48.5 mm ($1\frac{5}{8}$ in.) SVL and 90.2 mm ($3\frac{5}{8}$ in.) ToL. The maximum size has been reported as 140 mm ($5\frac{5}{8}$ in.) ToL (Conant and Collins 1991). The tail length averages 102% of SVL.

During the reproductive season the sexes are strongly dimorphic. The changes primarily affect the males in the following ways: the caudal fin becomes greatly enlarged; the parietal and temporal regions of the head swell and develop hedonic pits; horny nuptial excrescences develop on the insides of the thighs; and the cloacal lips become greatly swollen with cloacal papillae developed to a point at which they protrude from the cloacal opening.

The terrestrial subadult, or red eft (Plate 14), differs dramatically from the adult. The background coloration varies from light orange to brilliant brick red, becoming lighter ventrally. The venter is either immaculate or patterned with small black spots. Two series of light reddish spots bordered with black run along the dorsolateral surfaces. Small black spots may also be scattered along the dorsolateral surfaces. As the final transformation to adult approaches, the dorsal color begins to become yellowish green; however, transforming adults often enter the water while still possessing an orange brown coloration.

The body of the eft is slightly more rounded than that of the adult. The tail is round in cross section rather than laterally compressed. The legs are somewhat longer and better developed. Efts vary from 15 to 44 mm ($\frac{5}{8}$–$1\frac{7}{8}$ in.) SVL and from 29 to 84 mm ($1\frac{1}{4}$–$3\frac{3}{8}$ in.) ToL ($N = 67$). The tail is slightly shorter than that of the adult, being only 91% of SVL. The skin of the eft is thick and granular, whereas the skin of adults is somewhat smoother.

Red-spotted newt larvae vary in size from 8 to 10 mm ($\frac{3}{16}$–$\frac{3}{8}$ in.) at hatching to about 35 or 36 mm ($1\frac{3}{8}$ in.) ToL at transformation. When first hatched, the larvae have balancers, and their forelimb buds are developed. Older larvae are rather elongate and thin, with well-developed but shallow dorsal and caudal fins. The gills are well developed. The body is triangular in cross section. The general dorsal coloration is grayish yellow, becoming lighter ventrally. Scattered black spots are located all over the body.

Confusing Species.   Adult red-spotted newts are difficult to confuse with any other species found in the Northeast. It is, however, possible to mistake the red efts for immature red salamanders. Efts can be readily distinguished from northern red salamanders by the lack of a nasolabial groove, the absence of costal grooves, and the fact that their skin is dry and granular rather than smooth and moist.

Habitat and Habits.   Red-spotted newts occupy a wide variety of aquatic habitats, including (but not restricted to) ponds, both temporary and permanent; lakes; and slowly moving streams and creeks. They tend to be most common in small ponds with either abundant aquatic vegetation or a substrate heavily covered with leaf litter. This dense cover provides the animals with a place to both hide and forage for food. Aquatic habitats occupied by red-spotted newts are generally in or near woods, but occasionally they will be as much as a kilometer (0.62 mi) away from forested areas. Beaver ponds along small streams often produce ideal habitat for all stages in the life history of red-spotted newts. However, they will also occupy the margins of larger bodies of water, usually being found in the vicinity of dense submergent vegetation. George and co-workers (1977) reported them from a depth of 13 m (40 ft) in Lake George, New York. Efts are usually found in forested regions, frequently in small clearings.

In permanent water habitats, the adults are active throughout the year, although they occasionally burrow into the substrate during the middle of winter. Individuals that occupy temporary pools burrow into the muddy bottom when the waters dry. In Virginia, Gill (1978) reported that the entire adult population exits the pond in the fall and hibernates in terrestrial situations, returning to the ponds in March. Efts tend to initiate surface activity in early April and remain active until early or mid-October, provided that the environment remains moist enough. During periods of hot, dry weather they aestivate.

Neither adults nor efts show any strong tendency toward being either primarily diurnal or nocturnal. Adults can be found swimming about or floating motionless both day and night. During the day, however, they may be closer to the bottom or in dense vegetation.

Active movement on the part of the efts seems to be controlled by rainfall and moisture rather than light intensity. Efts are generally active during and shortly after periods of rainfall when the ground is wet. At other times, they may be found under cover objects or in the leaf litter.

Red-spotted newt adults feed on a wide variety of aquatic organisms, including, but not restricted to, ostracods, cladocerans, midge larvae, snails, pill clams, mosquito larvae, and amphibian eggs and larvae. In some habitats, they feed throughout the year (Morgan and Grierson 1932). Hamilton (1940) showed that the larvae feed on small prey items such as microcrustaceans and insect larvae in proportion to the prey items' abundance in the environment. Efts feed primarily on leaf litter invertebrates, especially colembollans, mites, fly larvae, land snails, and slugs.

The red eft, with its brilliant coloration, is an excellent example of aposematic (warning) coloration. The eft, when attacked, releases toxic secretions from its glandular skin. These are neurotoxins similar to, if not identical with, the toxins produced by puffer fish and some brightly colored poisonous frogs (such as the poison dart frogs of tropical South America). The brilliant coloration warns potential predators of the eft's unsuitable nature as a prey item. It has also been suggested that efts and newts also produce chemical secretions that have antileech properties (Pough 1971), although we have found up to 5% of some red-spotted newt populations parasitized by an amphibian leech of the genus *Batrachobdella*.

Reproduction.   Most mating occurs in the spring (March through June); however, occasional courting pairs may be seen in fall and early winter. Courtship and mating are aquatic. The males are unique among northeastern salamanders in that their courtship behavior differs depending upon the initial reaction of the female. If the female is responsive to a male's initial advances contact between the two is minimal; however, if the female is initially unresponsive the male will grasp the female around the neck with its hind legs (amplexus). They may remain in this position for several hours before mating is again attempted (Plate 15).

Eggs are deposited singly. They are usually attached to aquatic vegetation, but if vegetation is absent they may be attached to objects on the bottom of the pond or stream. Each female lays from 200 to more than 350 eggs (Bishop 1941). The eggs have a diameter of about 1.5 mm ($\frac{1}{16}$ in.) and are surrounded by an elliptical jelly capsule. Hatching time depends on temperature, but eggs usually hatch 3–5 weeks after deposition.

The larvae are typical pond-type animals. Hatchlings vary from 7 to 10 mm ($\frac{1}{8}$–$\frac{1}{4}$ in.) ToL, possess well-developed but unbranched gills, and have balancers and forelimb buds. Transformation occurs about 3 months after hatching. Transforming larvae generally range from 30 to 40 mm ($1\frac{1}{4}$–$1\frac{5}{8}$ in.) ToL.

The duration of the eft stage is variable. Bishop (1941) considered the terrestrial stage to last for 2 or 3 years, but Healy (1974) in Massachusetts determined that the eft stage lasted from 3 to 7 years. The length of the eft stage in the rest of the Northeast remains unknown but probably varies from location to location. Transforming efts generally enter ponds in late summer and early fall.

Not all populations of red-spotted newts have the eft stage. The above description of the life history of this species is generally true for upland populations. Some coastal populations lack the eft stage (Healy 1974). In some cases, coastal populations retain the eft stage but omit the typical aquatic adult stage. In these populations, sexually mature efts migrate to breeding ponds to mate and lay eggs and then return to a terrestrial habitat to feed (Noble 1926).

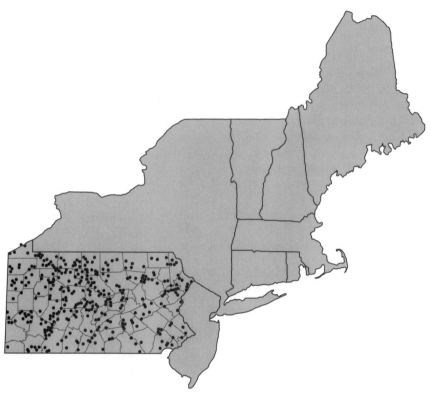

Map 8. Distribution of the red-spotted newt *(Notophthalmus viridescens viridescens)*.

In Pennsylvania both males and females mature at 40–42 mm (1$\frac{5}{8}$ in.) SVL.

Distribution. The red-spotted newt ranges throughout much of the eastern United States and adjacent Canada. Its range extends west to central Indiana and south to central Alabama and Georgia.

It is widely distributed throughout the Northeast, being most common in upland areas.

PLETHODONTIDAE (LUNGLESS SALAMANDERS)

Plethodontidae is the largest family of salamander (27 genera and about 221 species) in the world and is also the best represented in the northeastern United States. Plethodontids are found throughout the eastern United States and adjacent Canada as well as along the West Coast. Their range also extends from central Mexico to the Amazon. A few species occur in Italy and France. There are 7 genera and 15 species of plethondontids in the Northeast. New species of plethodontids are being described all the time in the United States. Most of the new species descriptions are based on biochemical analysis.

Plethodontids are small to medium-sized salamanders that range in body form from slender to stout. All members of the family lack lungs (gas exchange occurs through the skin) and can be distinguished from all other families by the presence of a nasolabial groove.

They occupy a wide variety of habitats, ranging from dry terrestrial situations (e.g., talus slopes) to completely aquatic environments such as streams and rivers. Some species live exclusively in caves deep beneath the surface; other species reside in mountainous regions at elevations in excess of 3,600 m (11,500 ft). Some species lay eggs on land and have direct development. Others lay their eggs in or near water, and the larvae are aquatic. A few species are neotenic (i.e., retaining larval characteristics in the adult stage).

Aneides
Gr. *aneides,* shapeless

The genus *Aneides* contains the climbing salamanders. There are five species in the genus. One species (*A. aeneus*) ranges throughout the southern Appalachian Mountains. The other four are found in the West. One species (*A. hardii*) is restricted to a three mountain ranges in New Mexico, and the other three (*A. ferreus, flavipunctatus,* and *lugubris*) are located along the West Coast from southern British Columbia southward into northern Baja California, Mexico.

Climbing salamanders are small to moderate-sized species with a build varying from slender to robust. These salamanders are partly arboreal, climbing about on rock faces and trees. The western species tend to live in rocky and arid areas; the eastern species is found in forested areas (albeit often with numerous rock faces in the area).

Aneides eat a wide variety of terrestrial invertebrates. Females lay small clutches of large eggs in cracks and crevices and tend the eggs until they hatch. Development is direct.

Green Salamander *Aneides aeneus* (Cope and Packard)
L. *aeneus,* bronze or coppery
Description. The green salamander (Plate 16) is a small to medium-sized terrestrial species, which varies in dorsal background coloration from brownish black to black. The dorsal pattern is made up of a series of irregular yellowish green lichenlike blotches. These blotches extend onto the appendages as well as the sides of the body. The venter is typically immaculate and varies in color from light yellow to gray. The chin is similar to the venter in background color but is frequently covered with numerous small light spots.

The body is strongly compressed dorsoventrally. The limbs and digits are long, and the terminal phalanges of the digits are expanded laterally.

The tail is as long as or slightly longer than the body, rounded in cross section, and gradually tapered toward the tip. Costal grooves number 14 or 15. On older individuals, especially males, the temporal region of the head is greatly enlarged owing to hypertrophy of the jaw muscles. In addition to the size of the temporal region, males and females exhibit sexual dimorphism in tooth morphology and cloacal anatomy. The maxillary teeth of males are enlarged and spikelike. During the reproductive season, the cloacal area of the males becomes greatly swollen and contains numerous visible papillae.

The green salamander is not sexually dimorphic in size. The mean size for Pennsylvania specimens is 50.6 mm (2 in.) SVL and 110.1 mm ($4\frac{3}{8}$ in.) ToL. This is only slightly smaller than the specieswide mean SVL of 53 mm ($2\frac{1}{8}$ in.) reported by R. Gordon (1967). The maximum size for the species is 140 mm ($5\frac{5}{8}$ in.) ToL (Conant and Collins 1991).

Green salamanders have direct development, and the young are essentially miniature adults, although C. Walker and Goodpaster (1941) stated that the light dorsal pattern of young is duller and more yellowish than that of the adult.

Confusing Species.   The combination of expanded toe tips and yellowish green lichenlike pattern distinguishes the green salamander from all other species found in Pennsylvania.

Habitat and Habits.   Little is known about the biology of the green salamander in Pennsylvania, so the following discussion relies heavily on studies carried out in other portions of its range.

Green salamanders have specific and restrictive habitat requirements. They are found either under the bark of fallen or standing dead timber (Pope 1928) or in cracks and crevices or solution pockets of sandstone, limestone, or granite outcrops (R. Gordon 1952, Richmond 1952, Walker and Goodpaster 1941). The cracks and crevices must be moist but not wet, generally receiving no direct surface runoff. Rocky outcroppings used by the green salamanders are usually located in hemlock or mixed mesophytic hardwood forests and are heavily shaded. Mushinsky (1976) demonstrated that habitat selection in this species appears to be highly innate and not subject to modification. Cliburn and Porter (1987), studying a northern Mississippi population, showed that these salamanders do not use cracks and crevices near the base of outcrops. The height of crevices used ranged from 30.5 to 396 cm (14 in. to 13 ft.). This avoidance of lower crevices may be due to excessive moisture in such microhabitats. Some southern populations do not appear to be as tied to rocky situations as those in the north. Pope (1928) studied a population in North Carolina that was mainly associated with standing and fallen dead timber rather than with rock. In Pennsylvania, green salamanders are restricted to sandstone outcrops of the Pottsville Formation.

The annual activity of the green salamander is strongly bimodal. In northern Maryland near the Pennsylvania border, individuals emerge from hibernation in late March or early April. Activity increases to an initial peak in late May and early June. It then drops off for most of June, July, and August and begins to increase again in early September, reaching a second peak in late September and early October. After this, activity rapidly declines, and animals enter hibernation by the beginning of November (Thompson and Taylor 1985). The June peak is most likely a result of courtship and mating activity; the fall peak probably results from the emergence of newly hatched young in conjunction with adults aggregating near suitable hibernation sites. Green salamanders appear to exhibit no strong diel pattern of activity, since animals have been reported active both day and night. At night, however, they tend to be closer to the opening of their crevice. During daylight, they retreat farther back in the crevices. R. Gordon (1952) reported that crevices were not used if sunlight could reach the back at any time of the day.

Gordon (1952) determined that, in general, green salamanders do not have a very large home range. The maximum distance that any animal moved in his study was about 98 m (321 ft), and most moved much shorter distances (the minimum distance was 4 m; 13 ft). Cupp (1971) demonstrated that males at least will defend a crevice from male intruders.

Green salamanders are almost entirely insectivorous. Lee and Norden (1973), studying a population from Monogalia County, West Virginia, determined that major prey items were small beetles, ants, and mosquitoes.

Several authors, including Netting and Richmond (1932) and Thompson and Taylor (1985), have reported on the green salamander's tendency to become limp and "play dead" when captured.

Reproduction. Courtship and mating have been observed in both the spring (R. Gordon 1952) and the fall (Cupp 1971). In central West Virginia, Canterbury and Pauley (1994) found mating pairs in late May and early June. Courtship occurs in the rock crevices where the salamanders live. Mating pairs have been observed remaining together for as long as 7 days (Canterbury and Pauley 1994).

Females emerge from hibernation with well-developed ovarian eggs. The eggs are laid in early June throughout the range of the species (R. Gordon 1952, Thompson and Taylor 1985). The latter two authors suggested that, in Maryland, individual females might be biennial breeders. Likewise, Canterbury and Pauley (1994) believe that West Virginia females exhibit a biennial cycle.

The eggs are deposited in rock crevices. Both Gordon and Thompson and Taylor suggested that "breeding crevices" differ from crevices that are not used for reproductive activities, but they did not adequately discuss the supposed differences between the two types. When the female is ready to oviposit, she turns over on her back and presses her ventral surface to the roof. The eggs are then attached by mucous threads to the roof of the crevice.

Clutch size varies from 10 to 26 eggs, and the average egg diameter is 4.5 mm ($\frac{3}{16}$ in.). Females remain with the eggs until hatching occurs. Brooding females actively guard the eggs and will lunge at and attempt to bite intruders (Gordon 1952). Development is direct, and there is some evidence that the young remain with the female for a period of time after hatching (Walker and Goodpaster 1941). Hatching occurs in September. Gordon stated that the mean incubation time is 86 days but ranged from 84 to 91 days. Neonates average 19.7 mm ($\frac{3}{4}$ in.) ToL and 12.9 mm ($\frac{1}{2}$ in.) SVL.

Thompson and Taylor (1985) indicated that both sexes mature at about 52 mm (2 in.) SVL. This may be an overestimate because it was based solely on external characteristics. In Pennsylvania, males with a SVL of 49 mm ($1\frac{7}{8}$ in.) were mature, and the smallest female with enlarged ovarian follicles had a SVL of 43 mm ($1\frac{3}{4}$ in.).

Remarks.   The restricted geographic range in Pennsylvania and stringent habitat requirements make green salamanders extremely vulnerable to local extinction. They have been granted protection as a threatened species by the state of Pennsylvania. The biggest dangers are habitat destruction from lumbering, followed by possible exploitation by overzealous collectors. Clear-cut lumbering exposes the rocky outcrops that they occupy to the sun and consequently causes excessive drying of the habitat.

Map 9.   Distribution of the green salamander *(Aneides aeneus).*

Distribution. The range of the green salamander extends from southwestern Pennsylvania to northern Alabama and extreme northeastern Mississippi in the Allegheny and Cumberland mountains. Disjunct populations also occur in the southern Blue Ridge Mountains of North Carolina, South Carolina, and Georgia, along the Ohio River in southwestern Ohio, and in central Tennessee and northeastern West Virginia.

In Pennsylvania, the species occurs in only a few localities in Fayette County, where it is restricted to suitable sandstone outcrops of the Pottsville Formation.

Desmognathus
Gr. *desma*, band or ligament; Gr. *gnathos,* jaw

The genus *Demognathus* (the dusky salamanders) contains 12 species, which are distributed throughout the eastern United States.

Dusky salamanders are small to moderate-sized species with a tail about as long as the body. Members of this genus are recognized by the presence of a white or pale diagonal line extending from the posterior margin of the eye to the angle of the jaw. Dusky salamanders are semi-aquatic and are usually found under cover objects near spring seeps, runs, and small streams. They tend to be less common or absent from larger streams where predatory fish are common.

Dusky salamanders feed on a variety of small aquatic and terrestrial invertebrates. Females construct nest cavities under streamside cover or in stream banks. The female lays her eggs in the cavity and tends them until they hatch. The newly hatched larvae make their way to the water.

Northern Dusky Salamander *Desmognathus fuscus fuscus* (Rafinesque)
L. *fuscus,* brown
Description. The northern dusky salamander (Plate 17) is a small to moderate-sized salamander. The background coloration of adults is yellowish to grayish brown or, occasionally, dark brown. The dorsal pattern of adults consists primarily of a broad dorsal stripe that is light brown and contains variable dark markings. This stripe is bordered by dark wavy lines. The sides of the body are mottled, and the venter is lighter, with gray or brown mottling that is usually light but may occasionally be very heavy. On old adults, the dorsal stripe often becomes obscure, and the dorsum takes on a uniform grayish brown coloration. Xanthic (yellow) individuals have been reported for this species (Tyning 1977). True albinos have also been reported (Dyrkacz 1981).

Young individuals are more vividly patterned than adults (Plate 18). Their dorsal pattern consists of five to eight pairs of yellowish spots connected by a dark wavy band. This pattern of dorsal spotting continues onto the dorsal surface of the tail.

The northern dusky salamander is a well-proportioned species, with strong well-developed limbs. The tail is laterally compressed and has a distinct dorsal keel. Mature males are larger than mature females. The mean size of males is 51.2 mm (2 in.) SVL; females average 46.2 mm (1¾ in.) SVL. Males average 94 mm (3¾ in.) ToL, and females average 86.3 mm (3½ in.) ToL. The tail in both sexes ranges from 83% to 100% of SVL. The above measurements represent values obtained from populations throughout Pennsylvania, but northern dusky salamanders in Pennsylvania exhibit significant interpopulation variation in size (Davic 1983). The maximum size for the species appears to be 142 mm (5⅝ in.) ToL for a specimen from Adams County, Ohio (Pfingsten and Downs 1989).

The larvae have a rounded body and well-developed limbs. The tail is laterally compressed and has a caudal fin. The head is large and distinct from the body.

Confusing Species. The northern dusky salamander can be distinguished from the mountain dusky salamander by the presence of a keeled tail and wavy margins along the dorsal stripe. The pale venter of the seal salamander in conjunction with its stronger dorsal pattern will usually distinguish it from the northern dusky, although the potential for confusion between the two species is high.

Habitat and Habits. Northern dusky salamanders are rarely encountered far from flowing water. They are found near streams, seepage areas, and springs but are most commonly encountered around small woodland streams with abundant cover objects. A stable streamside habitat appears to be necessary for the continued existence of this species. In Georgia, Orser and Shure (1975) demonstrated that streams affected by development were not occupied by northern dusky salamanders, whereas unmodified nearby streams supported large viable populations of the animals. They attributed the lack of salamanders in the disturbed streams to a loss of cover vegetation and the concomitant increase in erosion and reduction in streamside stability.

Northern dusky salamanders are generally found within a meter or two (1.3–6.5 ft) of the streambed, but in areas where they are sympatric with seal salamanders they tend to disperse farther away from the stream. Where seal salamanders are abundant, northern dusky salamanders are often absent. Preferred cover for this species consists primarily of medium to large rocks, but they will occasionally be found under smaller rocks, logs, bark, moss, and other vegetation along the stream bank.

In suitable locations (i.e., those where open water remains all winter), northern dusky salamanders are active year-round, although peak activity tends to occur in spring and early summer. In extremely cold weather, they burrow in rocky or gravelly ground below the frostline. Hamilton (1943) reported finding active individuals below the surface in a shale bank associated with a seepage area. Individuals moved vertically through this area in response to temperature, moving nearer the surface during relatively warm weather and deeper below the surface during cold periods. Salamanders continued to feed within their subterranean retreats in the winter. Females are inactive during late July, August, and early September, when they are brooding eggs.

This species is active primarily at night. They can be found under cover during the day, but they come out to forage for food at night. Keen and Sharp (1984) reported that most activity occurred shortly after sunset during periods of dry weather, but on moist nights activity was continuous from dusk to dawn. In periods of heavy rain they may occasionally be found out and about during the day.

The home range is usually small. Ashton (1975) determined that individuals in an Ohio population had an average home range of only 1.4 m^2 (15 ft^2), but Barbour and co-workers (1969a) determined an average home range of 48.4 m^2 (521 ft^2) in Kentucky. Hall (1977), studying a population from Tioga County, Pennsylvania, determined an average density of 1 animal/0.8 m (1 animal/32 in.) of stream bank.

Northern dusky salamanders are carnivorous. We found them to prey on flies and fly larvae (including horse flies), ants, centipedes, mayflies, beetles and beetle larvae, amphipods, and snails. Most specimens that we examined also contained worms. Krzysik (1979) found that the northern dusky salamanders in Westmoreland County, Pennsylvania, fed primarily on the adults and larvae of flies and moths. Diet apparently varies greatly from location to location and reflects the availability of prey items of suitable size. In other words, northern dusky salamanders are opportunists, feeding on abundant prey.

Northern dusky salamanders exhibit caudal autotomy and a substantial percentage (56% of males, $N = 46$, and 48% of females, $N = 36$) of adults have either newly broken or regenerated tails.

Reproduction.   Courtship in the northern dusky salamander occurs in both spring and fall, as described by Bishop (1941) and Organ (1961b). Vitellogenesis begins in late fall and continues through the spring. Follicles reach a mature size of 2–2.5 mm ($\frac{1}{8}$ in.) in late June, and oviposition occurs almost exclusively in July. Clutch size, based on follicular complement in Pennsylvania, averages 28.6 eggs (range 18–51) and is positively correlated with female SVL. Females construct a shallow nest depression in mud or sand under a suitable cover object near the water. In Pennsylvania, these egg depressions are generally constructed under rocks (Krzysik 1979), but in other parts of the species' range mosses are frequently used (Hom 1987). Eggs and their associated membranes are about 4–4.5 mm ($\frac{1}{4}$ in.) in diameter. After egg deposition, the female generally coils around the nest and tends the eggs until they hatch (Plate 19). This female role, although not well understood, is important. For example, Juterbock (1987) showed that untended nests in Ohio suffered 100% mortality. Females do not feed while tending the nest, but they apparently can gain sufficient resources afterward to be able to successfully yolk a new complement of eggs for the next reproductive season. As a result, this species reproduces annually despite providing parental care. Part of this ability might be due to their remaining active and feeding during the winter.

The duration of incubation depends on temperature and varies from about 40 to more than 60 days. Larvae first begin to emerge in late August, and emergence continues until the beginning of October. Upon emergence, hatchlings wriggle into the nearby water. Hatchlings vary from 10.5 to 12 mm ($\frac{3}{8}$ to $\frac{1}{2}$ in.) SVL and have a well-developed large reserve of yolk. It takes a larva up to 70 days to use all of the yolk (Montague 1987). Little is known about the larval biology of this species. Transformation occurs at a SVL of between 14 and 20 mm ($\frac{1}{2}$–$\frac{3}{4}$ in.) (Juterbock 1990), from the end of May to early July of the following summer.

Sexual maturity is achieved at 2 to 3 years of age at a SVL of 38–40 mm ($1\frac{1}{2}$–$1\frac{5}{8}$ in.) for males and 42–45 mm ($1\frac{5}{8}$–$1\frac{3}{4}$ in.) for females.

Remarks.   An analysis of the genetic makeup of sympatric populations of the northern dusky salamander and the mountain dusky salamander found that hybridization occasionally occurs (Karlin and Guttman 1981). Hybridization has occurred in the population near Greenwood, Mercer County, Pennsylvania.

Distribution.   The northern dusky salamander occurs from southern Quebec and New Brunswick southward to northwestern South Carolina. Its range extends westward through eastern and southern Ohio and southeastern Indiana to western Kentucky and central Tennessee.

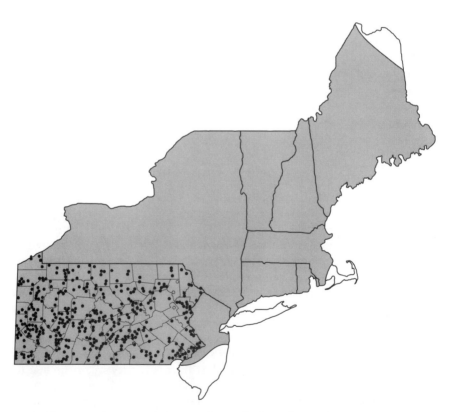

Map 10. Distribution of the northern dusky salamander *(Desmognathus fuscus fuscus).*

In the Northeast, the northern dusky salamander is widely distributed in upland areas, with scattered coastal localities mostly associated with bedrock outcrops. It is common and widely distributed throughout Pennsylvania.

Seal Salamander *Desmognathus monticola* Dunn

L. *mons,* mountain; L. *cola,* inhabit

Description.   The seal salamander (Plate 20) is a medium-sized, heavy-bodied animal. Seal salamanders are usually strongly patterned. The pattern exhibits significant ontogenetic variation. Larvae and recently transformed individuals have four or five pairs of staggered spots on the back between the insertion of the forelimbs and that of the hind limbs. These spots vary from orange to reddish orange and are set in a dark background. The dorsal portion of the tail is also spotted. The dark background coloration becomes mottled along the sides. The undersides of the body, chin, and appendages are pale. With age, the dorsal spots become larger and coalesce to form an irregularly shaped light brown dorsal area surrounded by darker markings. The dorsal surface of the head is mottled brown and black. An albino specimen has been reported from Kentucky (Houtcooper 1981).

The tail of this species is strongly compressed laterally and has a sharply defined knifelike dorsal keel. The head is large, bluntly rounded, and wider than the body. A distinct gular fold is present, and the temporal and mastoid regions of the head are hypertrophied (especially in large adults).

In a sample (N = 93) from Pennsylvania, there was no sexual dimorphism in body size, but females did have a longer tail than males. The mean size was 58.7 mm ($2\frac{3}{8}$ in.) SVL for mature individuals and 110.3 mm ($4\frac{3}{8}$ in.) ToL. The tail length of males was only 88% of SVL; that of females was 97% of SVL. Seal salamanders apparently do not grow as large in Pennsylvania as they do in other parts of their range (Bruce and Hairston 1990). The record size for the species is 149 mm (6 in.) ToL (Conant and Collins 1991).

Confusing Species.   Seal salamanders can be distinguished from all other salamanders except congenerics by the presence of a light diagonal line extending from the corner of the eye to the angle of the mouth. Compared with congenerics, the seal salamander's tail is more distinctly keeled than the northern dusky salamander's, and the dorsal pattern is not bordered by a wavy lateral line. The mountain dusky salamander is much smaller than the seal salamander, and its tail is round in cross section.

Habitat and Habits.   Seal salamanders are found close to small to medium-sized mountain streams, either in the stream or along the stream bank. They are more closely associated with this habitat than is any other species of dusky salamander in Pennsylvania. During the day, seal salamanders can be located under rocks in and adjacent to streams. They exhibit a strong preference for large rocks and are only rarely found under smaller stones or other streamside cover such as logs, bark, and vegetation. They are infrequently found in streams that have a bottom of either fine gravel or sand (Krzysik 1979). Seal salamanders are less abundant within their range than either the mountain dusky salamander or the northern dusky salamander, both of which have less stringent habitat requirements. Southerland (1986) demonstrated that the density of seal salamanders in North Carolina was determined by cover availability. As cover was artificially increased, the abundance of seal salamanders increased.

The seal salamander's annual activity is bimodal, with a peak in the spring, reduced activity in midsummer (July and August), and a second peak of activity in late summer and fall. Annual activity for adults begins in mid to late March and ceases in late October or early November. On a diel basis, the species is primarily nocturnal. During the day, it can be found under cover objects, but at night it is frequently seen sitting atop rocks in or near streams or at the entrance to burrows along the stream bank.

Hibernacula have not been found for this species, but presumably they hibernate either in crayfish burrows or below the surface in the interstitial spaces produced by the large gravel substrate that they prefer.

Seal salamanders have restricted home ranges, but home range size increases as the density of the population increases (Kleeberger 1985). Apparently, this increase is in response to increased competition for trophic resources and the resultant need to forage farther afield to gather food. Seal salamanders are also territorial in that they will actively defend specific cover sites from both conspecific and congeneric intruders (Keen and Sharp 1984). The degree of defense is directly related to food availability at the cover site. Sites that provide appropriate prey are defended more vigorously than are sites that offer few or no prey items (Keen and Reed 1985).

Little information is available about the diet of this species. Krzysik (1979) noted that seal salamanders eat a variety of invertebrate prey items, most of which are insects. The majority of food items in a sample ($N = 36$) of animals from Pennsylvania were insects. However, 15% of the salamanders in our sample had fed on other salamanders (*Desmognathus* or *Eurycea*), indicating that in some areas seal salamanders may be significant predators on other salamanders.

Seal salamanders exhibit a very high percentage of tail loss and regeneration. In a sample ($N = 92$) of all size classes from Pennsylvania, 45.6% had a regenerated tail. Tail loss increases with age: 57% of adults had a regenerated tail. Tail loss is often associated with predation and is considered to be an indication of predation intensity on a species. In seal salamanders, it is more likely that the high incidence of tail loss is a result of territorial defense. Seal salamanders are highly territorial, and Keen and Sharp (1984) observed that seal salamanders defend territories by attacking an invader and biting its tail. It is this behavior that is probably most responsible for the high incidence of tail loss in this species.

Reproduction. We have not observed courtship in Pennsylvania, but Organ (1961b) described it in detail for specimens from North Carolina. Mating occurs in both spring and fall. Females oviposit in June and early July. Clutch size in field records from North Carolina varied from 16 to 39 eggs (Organ 1961b). Clutch size in Pennsylvania, based on ovarian complement from gravid females, is similar. Insufficient data are available to determine if clutch size is correlated with body size.

Females oviposit in cracks and crevices under stones and rocks or between rocks and tree roots. The eggs are attached singly to the under-surface of the rocks. Nests are located close to, but not in, streams. Eggs have a total diameter of 4.5–5 mm ($\frac{1}{4}$ in.). Females tend the nest until the eggs hatch. Hatchlings first appear in mid-August and probably continue to emerge until the end of September. The average SVL of hatchlings is 11.7 mm ($\frac{1}{2}$ in.) (Bruce 1990) in North Carolina. Transformation occurs in the spring following hatching. At transformation, the SVL varies from 15 to 17 mm ($\frac{5}{8}$ in.).

Females exhibit a biennial rather than an annual reproductive cycle, as is often the case for species that tend the nest and provide parental care.

Males mature at about 49 mm (2 in.) SVL; females mature at about 52 or 53 mm ($2\frac{1}{2}$ in.).

Distribution. The range of the seal salamander extends along the Appalachian Mountains and foothills from southwestern Pennsylvania to extreme northern South Carolina and Georgia and east-central Alabama. Disjunct populations exist in southern Alabama and the Florida panhandle.

Within Pennsylvania, the majority of records for this species occur along Laurel Hill and Chestnut Ridge. To the west of Chestnut Ridge, it is found in and around isolated mountain streams that are located in steep-sided, well-shaded ravines. The records in eastern Somerset County bear careful examination to determine their validity. Yoder (1940) incorrectly reported this species from Blair and Clearfield counties. Neither of those records is valid, and in all likelihood both were based on misidentified northern dusky salamanders.

Mountain Dusky Salamander *Desmognathus ochrophaeus* Cope
Gr. *ochra*, yellow; *phaeios*, dusky or dark
Description. The mountain dusky salamander (Plate 21) is a small species. The dorsal pattern usually consists of a broad, straight-edged, vertebral stripe that extends from the back of the head over the entire body and onto the tail. This stripe varies greatly in color. It can be yellow, orange, red, or various shades of brown or gray. A medial row of dark, often chevron-shaped, spots generally, but not always, occurs within the stripe. Bordering the vertebral stripe on each side is a dark brown or black pig-mented stripe that becomes lighter and more mottled near the venter. The ventral surfaces are pale and usually immaculate or very lightly mottled. As is typical of *Desmognathus*, a pale stripe extends diagonally from the posterior margin of the eye to the gape of the mouth. On old individuals,

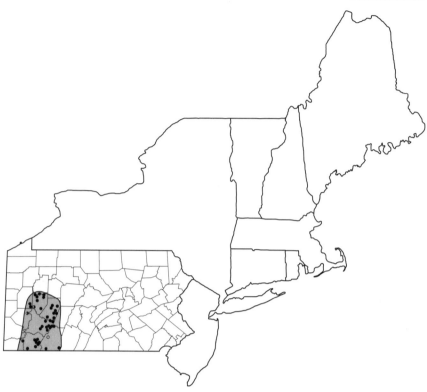

Map 11. Distribution of the seal salamander *(Desmognathus monticola)*.

the dorsal pattern tends to become obscure, and dorsal coloration is uniformly dark brown or brownish black. Often the diagonal stripe from the gape to the eye is also obscured. Larvae and recently transformed young are patterned similarly to adults, although the dorsal stripe of young animals is sometimes more vivid.

The mountain dusky salamander is well proportioned. The limbs are strong, and the hind limbs are about twice the size of the forelimbs. The tail (at least the proximal half) is round in cross section. In both sexes, the tail is approximately as long as the body. This is one of our smallest salamanders. The average size of mature individuals is 38.2 mm ($1\frac{1}{2}$ in.) SVL and 76.7 mm (3 in.) ToL. Males tend to be slightly larger than females on the average, but size overlap between the sexes is almost complete. The maximum size for the species is 111 mm ($1\frac{3}{8}$ in.) ToL (Conant and Collins 1991).

The larvae have a rounded body, and the limbs, once they form, are well developed. The tail is weakly keeled, and the distal two-thirds of the tail is laterally compressed. The head is large and distinctly set off from the body by a constricted neck region. The gills are short and slender and may possess short terminal branches.

A recent analysis of genetic distance data in the *Desmognathus ochrophaeus* complex revealed that the populations from the Northeast through southeastern Kentucky form one homogeneous and well-differentiated form (Tilley and Mahoney 1996).

Confusing Species.   The presence of a diagonal light stripe from the eye to the gape is sufficient to separate the mountain dusky salamander from all other salamanders except congenerics. The mountain dusky salamander can be distinguished from both the seal and the northern dusky salamanders by its rounded tail in cross section.

Habitat and Habits.   The mountain dusky salamander is the most terrestrial of the *Desmognathus* species in the Northeast. It is often encountered hundreds of meters from water in moist deciduous or mixed hardwood-coniferous forests, where it may be found under rocks, logs, bark, and other natural cover objects. Terrestrial activity is most common in the warmer months. During cold weather (early spring, winter, and late fall) mountain dusky salamanders migrate to small streams, springs, and hillside seeps and are found under cover, especially mosses and rocks, where the soil is saturated.

In areas where surface water does not freeze, mountain dusky salamanders are active all winter long. In areas where the surface water does freeze, they generally congregate in cracks and crevices below the surface. Often these hibernacula are associated with shale banks in seepage areas or in the cobble occurring along small to intermediate-sized streams. In Ohio, Keen (1979) found that dusky salamanders occupying seepage areas were more active in winter than were conspecifics found along streams. The reasons for this difference remain unclear. At other times of the year, activity tends to be correlated with moisture. Activity decreases or ceases entirely during periods of extended drought.

As is typical of salamanders in general, surface activity is usually nocturnal and tends to be stimulated by high humidity or rainfall. Individuals seldom venture far from their diurnal retreats during these nocturnal forays.

Mountain dusky salamanders do not move over large areas except when migrating to and from water. The home range for individuals in an Ohio population has been estimated to be approximately $1\,m^2$ ($10.8\,ft^2$) in streamside habitat (Holomuzski 1982). In certain favorable habitats, mountain dusky salamanders can attain astounding densities. Huheey and Brandon (1973) reported densities of 25 animals/m^2 (2.5 animals/ft^2) of rock face habitat in the Blue Ridge Mountains of North Carolina. It is obvious that these salamanders play an important role in the community-level processes of energy transfer and nutrient cycling.

Mountain dusky salamanders feed on a wide variety of small invertebrates. Our samples from Pennsylvania contained beetles and beetle larvae, worms, fly larvae, sowbugs, snails, and ants. Additional dietary items include mites, springtails (collembolans), spiders, and caterpillars (Keen 1979).

Reproduction. Mating apparently takes place in either spring or fall. No adequate description of courtship and mating exists for this species.

Virtually nothing is known about the reproductive cycle of the mountain dusky salamander in the Northeast, so this discussion relies heavily on work done in other parts of the species' range. Females have a more complex reproductive cycle than most other northeastern salamanders. Because the cycle is not synchronous, not all females breed at the same time of the year. In both North Carolina (Tilley 1973) and Ohio (Keen and Orr 1980) oviposition has two annual peaks. In North Carolina, females lay eggs either in early summer or in the winter. Early summer eggs hatch in late summer and winter eggs hatch in the spring. In Ohio, eggs are laid either in early spring (March and April) or in late summer. Pennsylvania specimens seem to have a cycle similar to those from Ohio. Although females do tend the nest, the energetic cost must be fairly low since the female reproductive cycle is basically annual rather than the biennial cycle common in species of salamander whose females attend the eggs. However, in West Virginia, mountain dusky salamanders exhibit a biennial cycle (Pauley, pers. comm.).

Clutch size, based on ovarian complement for a sample ($N = 26$) from Pennsylvania, ranges from 12 to 24 ($X = 19.1$) eggs and is positively correlated with female body size. Females construct nest chambers under rocks, moss, and logs and in stream banks. After the eggs are deposited the female remains with the nest and tends the eggs. Forester (1977, 1981) has shown that females seek potential nest sites several weeks before oviposition and return to the same general area to lay eggs in subsequent years. Female nest attendance is extremely important to the eggs. Mortality is much higher for unattended eggs than for those tended by the female. Increased mortality results from a combination of factors including desiccation, increased susceptibility to fungal infections, and predation (Forester 1979, 1984).

The incubation period is temperature dependent. Incubation varies from 50 to 74 days. Hatchlings have a SVL of approximately 10 mm ($\frac{3}{8}$ in.) and a ToL of approximately 17 mm ($\frac{5}{8}$ in.). In North Carolina, Bruce (1989) determined that the larval period is 9 to 10 months. However, Bishop (1941) reported individuals' losing gills shortly after hatching in New York. Little growth occurs during the larval period, and individuals transform at ToLs that are only a millimeter or two greater than their size at hatching.

The smallest reproductive males mature at approximately 32 mm ($1\frac{1}{4}$ in.) SVL and females at about 35 mm ($1\frac{3}{8}$ in.) SVL. It is probable that both sexes mature in their second year following transformation.

Distribution. The range of the mountain dusky salamander extends from northern New York, southward through Pennsylvania, then south along the Appalachian Mountains to extreme northern Georgia and Alabama.

The mountain dusky salamander is absent from most of the northeastern states, except New York and Pennsylvania. There is one record from Vermont (Lazell 1976b), but that record has not been confirmed by subsequent fieldwork (Tilley and Mahoney 1996). In Pennsylvania, mountain dusky salamanders are widely distributed in the Allegheny Plateau region, but they are absent from most of the Valley and Ridge Province as well as from the Piedmont and Coastal Plains areas. The few records from the Valley and Ridge Province need to be investigated, and the whole area needs to be carefully collected to determine the actual distribution of the species. The population in Delaware County, if it still exists, is undoubtedly the result of either an intentional or an accidental introduction. The range in New York is concentrated in the western and central portions of the state, with scattered localities in the east and north.

Eurycea
Gr. *eurys,* wide

The genus *Eurycea* (the brook salamanders) contains 13 species. Brook salamanders range throughout the eastern United States and adjacent Canada. In addition, three species occur in central Texas.

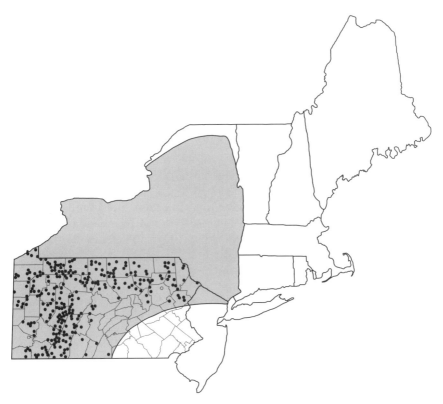

Map 12. Distribution of the mountain dusky salamander *(Desmognathus ochrophaeus).*

Brook salamanders are small to moderate-sized, slender-bodied animals. The tail length varies from about as long as the body to more than twice the body length. Brook salamanders inhabit small streams, springs, spring seeps, and caves.

Brook salamanders feed on a variety of small aquatic and terrestrial invertebrates. Eggs, in those species studied, are attached to the roof of rocks and other cover objects. Eggs hatch into larvae.

Northern Two-Lined Salamander *Eurycea bislineata* (Green)
L. *bis*, twice; L. *lineola*, a line
Description.   The northern two-lined salamander (Plate 22) is a small, slender species of streambank salamander. The dorsal coloration varies from greenish to yellowish brown. A dark brown or black dorsolateral stripe extends along each side of the body from the posterior margin of the eye to the base of the tail. The vertebral band between the stripes usually contains a series of small dark brown or black spots that vary in both intensity and position. On some individuals, the spots form a median broken stripe, but on others they are randomly scattered along the back. Below the dorsolateral stripes, the sides of the body are maculated with small irregular black spots. This pattern continues along the sides of the tail and onto the dorsal surfaces of the limbs. The ventral surfaces are immaculate pale to lemon yellow. Albinos have been reported (Rubin 1963).

Adults are slender and have thin but well-developed limbs. The tail is laterally compressed and has a moderately developed keel. The head is long and slender and, in front of the eyes, rapidly tapers to a rounded snout. Mature individuals of both sexes measure 40.6 mm ($1\frac{5}{8}$ in.) mean SVL and 85.3 mm ($3\frac{3}{8}$ in.) mean ToL. The record size for the species is 121 mm ($4\frac{7}{8}$ in.) ToL (Conant and Collins 1991). The tail length of both sexes averages about 110% of SVL.

The larvae are typical stream-type animals, with elongate and slender bodies and thin but fairly well-developed limbs. The caudal fin is moderate and begins at a point just above the hind legs. The head of recently hatched larvae is disproportionally long (30% of SVL) and broad, but with growth the head becomes relatively short (20% of SVL) and narrow. Gills tend to be small and only moderately branched.

Recently hatched individuals have a grayish or brownish netlike pattern on a yellowish green background. Ventral surfaces are immaculate whitish yellow. As the larvae grow, they gradually develop the pattern typical of the transformed individual.

Confusing Species.   The northern two-lined salamander may be distinguished from the mountain dusky salamander by the yellow venter; the absence of a diagonal stripe extending from the eye to the gape of the mouth; and the laterally compressed, rather than rounded, tail.

Habitat and Habits.   The northern two-lined salamander is primarily a streamside species, living in small and medium-sized streams with sandy to gravel substrates. It is most commonly found under rocky cover within a meter of streams but may occasionally be found as much as 50 m (164 ft) farther from water or in springs and hillside seeps. During most of the year, transformed individuals are seldom found in the water but rather along the margin at the water's edge. Northern two-lined salamanders are commonly found with northern dusky salamanders.

In suitable locations, northern two-lined salamanders are active throughout the year, with winter activity restricted to streams and seeps. Ashton and Ashton (1978) reported winter aggregations of as many as 27 individuals under rocky cover in unfrozen springs and seeps.

Northern two-lined salamanders are usually found under cover. When surface activity occurs, it is almost exclusively nocturnal and tends to be associated with periods of high humidity and heavy rain, especially in the spring. At these times, individuals are occasionally found as far as 90–100 m (280–330 ft) from water.

In suitable habitat, northern two-lined salamanders can reach exceedingly high densities. Burton and Likens (1975) estimated densities of 1 larva/2 m (0.5 larva/ft) stream bank in a New Hampshire forest and densities 10 times as high for larvae in the stream. M. Stewart (1968) also found exceedingly high densities (11 animals/m^2) (1.1 animals/ft^2) of adults and larvae in small, shale-bottomed streams in northern New York.

In New Hampshire, northern two-lined salamanders feed mainly on snails and small ground-dwelling insects such as springtails (collembolans), beetles, and fly larvae (Burton 1976). We have found adults to feed on beetles, spiders, isopods, and snails. No other data exist.

Reproduction.   Courtship occurs in the fall but may also take place in early spring. Vitellogenesis begins in the fall and continues until late spring, when the follicles are of ovulatory size. Oviposition generally occurs from May until July throughout the geographic range of the species (Baumann and Huels 1982, Bruce 1982, Wood and Duellman 1951); however, Green and Pauley (1987) reported oviposition as early as the end of March in West Virginia. The eggs are laid under cover in small streams and springs. Rocks are the preferred cover; it has been suggested that lack of suitable rocky cover might either restrict population size in a given area or be responsible for an increased incidence of communal nesting. The eggs are attached by gelatinous stalks to the roof of the cover. They are pale yellow and 2.5–3 mm ($\frac{1}{8}$ in.) in diameter, but with the associated envelopes and jelly coats the total size of the eggs is about 5 mm ($\frac{1}{4}$ in.). Females generally attend the eggs until they hatch. Incubation takes 30 to more than 70 days (Bishop 1941, Wilder 1924), depending on temperature.

Clutch size in Pennsylvania, based on ovarian complement, varies from 30 to 74 eggs and is positively correlated with female body size. Baumann and Huels (1982), using natural nests, gave a range of 15 to 110 eggs, but most clutches varied from 25 to 40 eggs. The very large clutches they reported might have resulted from communal nesting. Data from Pennsylvania indicate that the reproductive cycle of females is annual rather than biennial, even though they attend the nest.

Larvae are 11–13 mm ($\frac{1}{2}$ in.) ToL at hatching. Eggs hatch from late June to late July. Young larvae are primarily nocturnal and may be found foraging about the stream bottom. Hudson (1955), however, reported that larvae become progressively more diurnal as they age.

A considerable literature has arisen concerning northern two-lined salamander larvae as a component of stream drift (Bruce 1986, J. Johnson and Goldberg 1975, Stoneburner 1978). Drift is the passive downstream movement of organisms carried by the current. Most drift of northern two-lined salamanders occurs in early to midsummer and involves recently hatched individuals (i.e., those that still lack an adequate ability to swim or to move about in the current). Drift of the salamanders also occurs most frequently at night, reflecting their nocturnal behavior. Bruce (1986) noted that the net effect of drift was to move young animals downstream, away from their point of origin, since individuals do little to counterbalance the drift; they make no attempt to swim back upstream.

Larvae feed on a wide variety of aquatic invertebrates including, but not restricted to, nymphs of mayflies and stoneflies; larvae of caddisflies, dobsonflies (hellgrammites), beetles, and true flies (dipterans); gastropods; and small crustaceans such as ostracods and copepods. Petranka and co-workers (1987) demonstrated that larvae use olfaction to locate prey.

The length of the larval period is exceedingly variable, ranging from 1 year for some southern populations (Bruce 1982) to 3 years for some individuals of northern regions (Hudson 1955). Most individuals in most populations, however, transform at 2 years of age (Plate 23). Two-year-olds usually transform when they are between 34 and 43 mm ($1\frac{3}{8}$–$1\frac{3}{4}$ in.) ToL. Three-year-olds may transform at ToLs of 67 or 68 mm ($2\frac{5}{8}$ in.).

In Pennsylvania, males reach maturity at about 33 mm ($1\frac{3}{8}$ in.) SVL, and females at 35–36 mm ($1\frac{1}{2}$ in.) SVL. Both sexes, regardless of the age at which they transform, mature in their third year.

Distribution.   The range of the northern two-lined salamander extends from New England and adjacent Canada southward to northern Virginia, northern West Virginia, and western Ohio. Northern two-lined salamanders are common and widely distributed throughout the northeastern states.

Longtail Salamander *Eurycea longicauda longicauda* (Green)
L. *longus*, long; L. *cauda*, tail
Description.   The longtail salamander (Plate 24) is moderately long and slender and is highly variable in color and pattern. The dorsal coloration varies from light straw yellow to orange to deep brick red.

The body pattern usually consists of abundant black irregular spots covering both the dorsum and the sides of the body. The spots are largest dorsally and get smaller nearer the ventral surface of the body. The top of the head has a few round spots. Dense spotting occurs along the sides of the head, often forming a distinct line from the neck to the posterior margin of the eye.

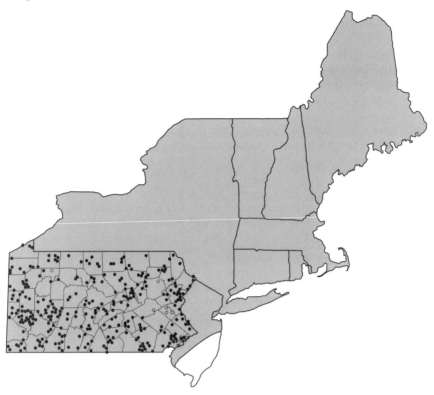

Map 13. Distribution of the northern two-lined salamander *(Eurycea bislineata).*

A second, less common, body pattern consists of abundant black irregular spots covering the sides but only a single medial row of dorsal spots. The top of the head is immaculate, but spotting occurs on the sides of the head.

In the third and least common pattern, the body is covered with fine black specks rather than irregular black spots. Spots are absent from the top of the head, and the spots along the sides are smaller and fewer than in the other two patterns.

In all pattern types, the ventral surfaces are light yellow and immaculate. However, the chin, throat, and upper chest regions occasionally contain some dark maculations. Although these maculations do not usually occur on juveniles, their occurrence does not appear to be truly ontogenetic in that large and small adults exhibit the spotting in similar proportions.

The distinctive tail pattern consists of a series of black herringbone markings running the entire length of the tail along each side. The dorsal surface of the tail is usually mottled with black, but it is occasionally free of markings.

The longtail salamander is an exceedingly slender species. The head is distinctly set off from the body, somewhat depressed dorsoventrally, and tends to be widest just behind the eyes. The eyes are large and protrude on either side of the head. The limbs are well developed and strong. As the common name implies, the tail is very long, averaging about 130% SVL of adults of both sexes. The larval tail is much shorter. The tail of recently transformed individuals averages about 100% of the SVL. The early growth of transformed individuals is strongly allometric, with the tail growing at a much faster rate than the body. As a result, by the time the animals are second-year juveniles, the tail/body length proportion is similar to that of adults. The tail of all individuals is laterally compressed and has a well-developed knifelike dorsal keel.

In Pennsylvania, males are slightly smaller than females. Mature males average 51.8 mm (2 in.) SVL and 131.5 mm ($5\frac{1}{4}$ in.) ToL. The slightly larger females average 54.9 mm ($2\frac{1}{8}$ in.) SVL and 140.0 mm ($5\frac{5}{8}$ in.) ToL. The maximum size has been recorded as 197 mm ($7\frac{7}{8}$ in.) ToL (Conant and Collins 1991).

Larvae have a well-developed caudal fin that does not extend onto the body but, rather, terminates at a point directly above the insertion of the hind legs. The gills are short and branch slightly. The ventral surface is immaculate white. Numerous small dark flecks cover the lateral and dorsal surfaces of the head and body. Later in development, the dorsum develops a medial row of spots on a clear yellowish background. At this time, the sides are heavily flecked with dark reticulations. The pattern of individuals beginning to transform is very similar to the second pattern described above for the adults. J. Anderson and Martino (1966) completely described the larval stages from recent hatchling to individuals just before transformation.

Confusing Species.   The combination of long tail and distinctive herringbone pattern on the sides of the tail distinguishes the longtail salamander from any other species in Pennsylvania and the northeastern United States.

Habitat and Habits.   The longtail salamander is primarily a terrestrial species, and it occupies a wide variety of habitats. At various times of the year it may be found in upland deciduous and mixed hardwood-conifer forests; in meadows at the edge of woods; in open shale banks and road cuts; around ponds, streams, and springs; and in caves and mines. J. Anderson and Martino (1966) noted that in New Jersey the species tends to be found farther away from water (streams and ponds) early in the season but that as summer progresses they can be found closer to water, although they are still basically terrestrial. In times of extreme drought, most are found under cover at the edges of streams and ponds.

Annual activity is unimodal. The longtail salamander emerges in late April or early May, one of the last species to do so in the spring in Pennsylvania. Initial activity is high and tends to remain at a constant high level through August. Activity sharply declines beginning in September, with all surface activity ceasing by the end of October. Anderson and

Martino (1966) suggested that, in the glaciated limestone region of northern New Jersey, when surface activity has ceased the salamanders continue activity in subterranean retreats.

Longtail salamanders have been found hibernating in shale banks in central Pennsylvania (Bell 1955). It is also possible that many individuals remain somewhat active throughout much of the winter in caves and mines. We have found large numbers of longtail salamanders active in caves at times of the year (late winter and early spring) when they are not active on the surface. Activity in caves has also been noted by other workers (Franz 1964, Mohr 1943).

Longtail salamanders are primarily nocturnal. During the day, they are normally found under a variety of cover objects, such as rocks, logs, bark, and human-made debris. Surface activity is fairly common at night, and they can frequently be seen foraging. Activity is highest on rainy or very humid nights, but it is not necessarily restricted to those climatic conditions. Anderson and Martino (1966) reported that longtail salamanders occasionally climb on herbaceous vegetation and trunks of trees. We have never observed this behavior in Pennsylvania.

No detailed study of the food habits of this species has been conducted in the northeast. A sample of 82 Pennsylvania specimens contained a varied diet, consisting predominantly of noninsect arthropods, especially isopods, spiders, and centipedes. Food items of secondary importance are beetles and beetle larvae, leafhoppers, ants, land snails, crickets and grasshoppers, and the larvae of lepidoptera and flies. This is slightly different from the diet reported by Anderson and Martino (1967) for a population from northern New Jersey. They noted that beetle larvae and spiders were the dominant food items in specimens that had been collected on the surface, while specimens from a mine ate primarily isopods, crickets, and spiders.

When first encountered, longtail salamanders will frequently coil their body so that the head is near the cloaca. They then simultaneously elevate and undulate their tail. This is presumably an adaptation to divert a predator's attention away from the more vulnerable body toward the easily autotomized tail. The tail, if autotomized, will regenerate. This behavior results in a substantial proportion of a given population having a recently broken or regenerated tail. Bell (1960) reported 33% regenerated tails for adult males and 23.5% for adult females for a population from central Pennsylvania. This is slightly higher than the percentage in a sample ($N = 105$) of animals from the Carnegie Museum. In the Carnegie Museum sample, 26.9% of males and 15% of females had regenerated tails.

Reproduction. The time of courtship and mating in this species is unknown, but they are assumed to occur in late fall or early winter while individuals are in their subterranean retreats. In Pennsylvania, females emerge from hibernation with small white nonyolked follicles. Follicular growth begins in late May or early June and continues throughout the summer and early fall. By late September and early

October, females contain yolked follicles of nearly ovulatory size (2.5–3 mm; $\frac{1}{8}$ in.). Ovarian complement in a sample ($N = 15$) of Pennsylvania specimens with near ovulatory-size follicles ranged from 33 to 92 eggs. Clutch size is strongly correlated with body size. The female cycle appears to be annual since virtually all mature females examined from August through October contained yolked follicles rather than small inactive ovaries.

Eggs are apparently laid sometime during the winter hibernation period. The only reports of oviposition sites for this species are those of Mohr (1943) and Franz (1964). Both were in subterranean habitats. Mohr found eggs attached singly, but generally in contact with each other, in running water 51–356 mm (2–14 in.) deep. Most were attached to the tops of submerged objects; a few eggs were attached to the undersides of rocks. Franz found a female attending a group of five eggs that were attached just above the water's surface. The ova themselves were from 2.5 to 3 mm ($\frac{1}{8}$ in.) in diameter, but with all of the associated membranes and jelly capsules the size of the eggs was about 8 mm ($\frac{3}{8}$ in.).

Eggs hatch in March and April (J. Anderson and Martino 1966, Bruce 1982). Recently hatched individuals are about 12 mm ($\frac{1}{2}$ in.) SVL and 17–19 mm ($\frac{5}{8}$–$\frac{3}{4}$ in.) ToL (Mohr 1943). Few studies have been conducted on the larvae, and little is known of their biology. Larvae may occur in both flowing and standing water. Anderson and Martino (1966) noted that larvae were more common in fish-free ponds. Larvae are generally found in the shallow areas of ponds and tend to hide in leaf litter. Their food habits are unknown. The larval period is 4 to 5 months, and transformation occurs in June and July. There is some evidence, however, that individuals may occasionally overwinter as larvae and transform the following year (Bishop 1941). Transformation occurs at SVLs of between 20 and 30 mm ($\frac{3}{4}$–$1\frac{1}{4}$ in.) and ToLs of 38–55 mm ($1\frac{1}{2}$–$2\frac{1}{4}$ in.) (Anderson and Martino 1966, Franz and Harris 1965). Recently transformed individuals remain near water for a few weeks and then move into the surrounding area.

In Pennsylvania, males mature at approximately 45 mm ($1\frac{3}{4}$ in.) SVL and at approximately 110 mm ($4\frac{3}{8}$ in.) ToL. Females mature at a slightly larger size of 48 mm ($1\frac{7}{8}$ in.) SVL and 118 mm ($4\frac{3}{4}$ in.) ToL. This is similar to the size at maturity for individuals from New Jersey.

Distribution.   The longtail salamander occurs from southern New York and northern New Jersey southwestward through Pennsylvania, West Virginia, and the western quarter of Virginia; through parts of Ohio and Maryland; in all of Kentucky and most of Tennessee; and into the extreme northern portions of Alabama and Georgia.

Longtail salamanders are absent from most states in the Northeast, reaching their northern distribution in southern New York and northern New Jersey. They are widespread throughout most of Pennsylvania. The extremely high concentration of localities in Indiana, Westmoreland, Allegheny, and Butler counties reflects collecting intensity rather than areas of specialized or ideal habitat for the salamander.

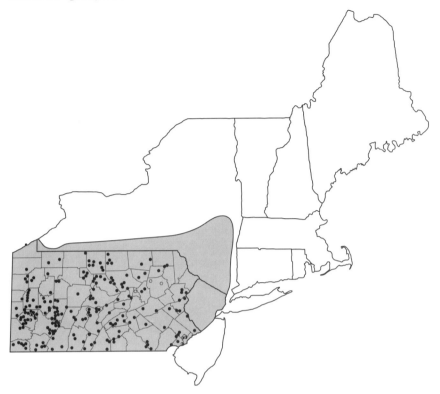

Map 14. Distribution of the longtail salamander *(Eurycea longicauda longicauda)*.

Gyrinophilus
Gr. *gyrinos*, tadpole; Gr. *philos*, loving

The genus *Gyrinophilus* (the spring salamanders) contains three species. All three are found in the eastern United States and range from Maine southward to northern Alabama and Georgia.

These are moderately large species with a well-developed tail, approximately the length of the body. The body is robust. Two species (*G. palleucus* and *G. subterraneus*) are cave dwellers; the third and most widely distributed species (*G. porphyriticus*) lives primarily in springs and small streams.

Spring salamanders feed on a variety of aquatic invertebrates and on other species of salamander. The eggs are attached to the roof of rocks and other cover objects. The eggs hatch into larvae.

Northern Spring Salamander *Gyrinophilus porphyriticus porphyriticus*
(Green)
Gr. *porphyros*, purple
Description. The northern spring salamander (Plate 25) is a large, robust species. As is often the case in salamanders, color pattern differs

with age as well as with life history stage. Recently transformed individuals have a background coloration of salmon red and a pattern of faint, irregular markings and reticulations. With age, the background coloration changes to reddish brown, and the pattern darkens. With increasing age the background color further changes to a deep purplish brown, and the pattern tends to disappear. In all age classes, the sides are lighter than the back and are usually mottled. The lower sides and ventral surfaces in all but the largest adults are immaculate pale pink or beige. Small black dots may be scattered on the belly of very large adults.

The northern spring salamander has a moderately heavy body and well-developed limbs. The tail is short in both sexes, averaging only 65.3% of SVL. It is compressed laterally, especially at the distal end, and is strongly keeled with a knifelike dorsal edge. The head is large and well-developed and is widest just behind the eyes. A noticeable light canthus rostralis extends from the eye to the posterior border of the nares. Adults do not exhibit sexual dimorphism in either size or body proportion. Adult northern spring salamanders from Pennsylvania average 92.6 mm ($3\frac{3}{4}$ in.) SVL and 149.5 mm (6 in.) ToL. The record size for the species is 232 mm ($9\frac{3}{8}$ in.) ToL (Conant and Collins 1991).

Larvae (Plate 26) have body proportions similar to those of adults, although the head of the larva is somewhat larger than that of the adult and the tailfin is more laterally compressed. Larvae range in size from about 25 mm to 120 mm ($1–4\frac{3}{8}$ in.) ToL.

The dorsal surfaces of young larvae are patterned with purplish brown reticulations or dark maculations. The ground color within the reticulations is yellowish white. A well-developed vertebral stripe is present on young larvae but not on older larvae. The yellowish white background coloration extends down the sides and onto the ventral surfaces, which are immaculate. The pattern and coloration of older larvae are similar to those of recently transformed animals.

Confusing Species.   Although adults may bear a superficial resemblance to the northern red salamander, the presence of a well-developed, highly visible canthus rostralis is sufficient to distinguish the adult northern spring salamander from all other species found in the Northeast.

Habitat and Habits.   The northern spring salamander is primarily a salamander of cool springs, spring seeps, and fast-flowing mountain or piedmont streams. They are, however, occasionally found in larger, slower-flowing streams, but in all cases a rocky substrate is present. They are sometimes found in caves, both in Pennsylvania and in other parts of their range (Dearolf 1956). The larvae are entirely aquatic and are usually found under cover objects (usually rocks, but occasionally logs) in both riffle and pool habitats. Both the larvae and the adults swim with quick eel-like movements. Adults are generally found under cover objects in streams or along the margins of streams and springs. In aquatic settings that do not freeze, adults and larvae are active all year long. Terrestrial activity is most common in late spring and early summer, but adults are seldom found far from suitable aquatic habitat.

Northern spring salamanders may occasionally be found moving about on the surface during and immediately after heavy spring and summer rains. When active on the surface they are primarily nocturnal.

The food of adults consists of both invertebrate and vertebrate prey items including, but not restricted to, salamanders (northern dusky, two-lined, and woodland species), fish (sculpins and darters), beetles, worms, centipedes, spiders, and lepidopteran larvae. Larval northern spring salamanders feed on aquatic invertebrates, with stonefly nymphs, mayfly nymphs, and caddisfly larvae making up the bulk of the diet. The diet of the larvae suggests that they forage for food primarily under stones and other cover objects. Both adults and larvae feed throughout the year.

This is an exceedingly difficult species to capture. Adults are usually close to their complex burrow system, into which they can retreat if disturbed. When grabbed, they wriggle violently, and their wriggling combined with their extremely slimy skin make them difficult to hold.

Reproduction.   We have not observed mating in this species, but the condition of testes and vas deferentia suggests that it occurs in the fall. Bishop (1941) gave the only description of courtship for northern spring salamanders. Courtship occurs in the water and involves more physical contact than is generally observed in plethodontid salamanders.

The reproductive cycle for female northern spring salamanders is biennial. Ovarian follicles begin vitellogenesis the summer following oviposition, and vitellogenesis continues throughout the fall and winter. Eggs of ovulatory size were present in females collected in April and May.

Egg laying occurs over an extended period, beginning in early April and continuing until mid-July. Oviposition occurs in the water, where eggs are attached singly to the undersides of large, flat stones. The eggs are 3.5–4 mm ($\frac{1}{8}$ in.) in diameter and measure 10 mm ($\frac{3}{8}$ in.) when all associated membranes and jelly coats are included. Clutch size varies from 44 to 132 eggs. Available data are insufficient to determine if clutch size is positively correlated with female body size, although a trend in that direction seems to be present. The female remains in attendance until hatching occurs. Hatchlings first appear in late July and early August, but they continue to emerge until early fall (September). Recently hatched individuals range from 23 to 27 mm (1–1$\frac{1}{8}$ in.) ToL and from 14 to 17 mm ($\frac{1}{2}$–$\frac{5}{8}$ in.) SVL (Bruce 1980, Organ 1961a).

Very little is known about the larval biology of this species. In North Carolina, the larval period is 3 to 5 years (Bruce 1980). We assume that the larval period is at least that long in Pennsylvania and the rest of the Northeast. However, Bishop (1941) reported a larval period of only 3 years for a New York population. Size at transformation is exceedingly variable and may be a function of local environmental conditions. The smallest transformed individual that we examined in a sample of 37 individuals was 100 mm (4 in.) ToL; the largest larva with well developed gills was 126 mm (5 in.) ToL.

Males mature at 77–80 mm (3$\frac{1}{8}$–3$\frac{1}{4}$ in.) SVL and females at 82–85 mm (3$\frac{3}{8}$ in.) SVL.

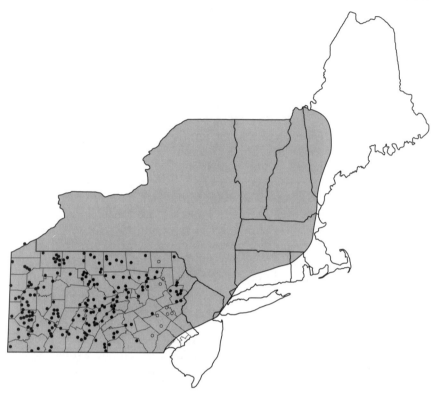

Map 15. Distribution of the northern spring salamander *(Gyrinophilus porphyriticus porphyriticus).*

Distribution.   Northern spring salamanders range from west central Maine and extreme southeastern Quebec westward to Ohio and south-ward to central Alabama and northern Georgia. Throughout most of their range in the southern and central United States they are limited to the Appalachian Mountains and adjacent Piedmont region.

Northern spring salamanders are common in Maine, New Hampshire, and Vermont but are rare in most of southern New England (Hunter et al. 1992, Klemens 1993) and are absent from eastern Massachusetts, Rhode Island, and coastal Maine. They have been found throughout most of New York and throughout all but southeastern Pennsylvania. They are absent from southern and central New Jersey.

Four-Toed Salamander *Hemidactylium scutatum* (Schlegel)
Gr. *hemi*, half; Gr. *daktylos*, finger or toe; L. *scutum*, scale-like
Description.   The four-toed salamander (Plate 27), a moderately slender species, is one of the smallest salamanders found in the Northeast. The dorsal surface of the head and body is reddish brown, and the back is often

mottled with black markings that may extend onto the dorsal surface of the tail. The upper surfaces of the limbs and the tail are a bright reddish orange with brown maculations occurring on the limbs. Laterally, the coloration becomes grayish. The ventral surfaces are bright enamel white with scattered large irregular black blotches (Plate 28).

The legs are fairly long and slender. Four toes occur on both the forefeet and hind feet. The body is cylindrical, and the head is somewhat flattened. The snout of females is rounded, and that of males is short and truncated. The tail is moderately long, oval in cross section, and bears a distinct constriction at the base (1–2 mm posterior to the cloaca; $\frac{1}{16}$ in.) that functions as the autotomy plane.

Males are smaller than females, averaging 27.9 mm ($1\frac{1}{8}$ in.) SVL and 61.5 mm ($2\frac{3}{8}$ in.) ToL. Females average 34.5 mm ($1\frac{3}{8}$ in.) SVL and 73.6 mm ($2\frac{7}{8}$ in.) ToL. Four-toed salamanders do not demonstrate sexual dimorphism in tail length. The tail varies from 96% to 141% of the SVL of adults, but it is significantly shorter in immature individuals. The maximum size for this species is 102 mm (4 in.) ToL (Conant and Collins 1991).

The larvae range in size from about 12 to 24 mm ($\frac{1}{2}$–1 in.) ToL. The head of young larvae is broad and short, and the body is distinctly triangular in cross section. A well-developed caudal fin extends from the posterior half of the body to the tip of the tail. Ventrally, it extends from the tail tip to the posterior margin of the cloaca. The gills are well developed and feathery. The limbs are poorly developed at hatching. The dorsal and lateral surfaces of the body are mottled greenish yellow on a brownish gray background. The ventral surfaces are immaculate.

Confusing Species.   The combination of an enamel-white belly with black spots, constriction of the tail, and the presence of only four toes on the hind feet separate this species from all other salamanders found in the Northeast.

Habitat and Habits.   Except during the time of egg deposition and incubation, adults are found in forested areas (either hardwood, conifer, or mixed) associated with mesic environments such as bogs, marshes, or woodland ponds. They may occasionally be found in open meadows or on dry wooded hillsides. In all of the above habitats, they are almost invariably located under rocks, logs, bark, and other natural cover. They may move about on nights with rain or high humidity. Bishop (1941) reported that surface activity is most frequent during the early spring "migrations" to breeding sites.

Four-toed salamanders begin to emerge from hibernation in April and late March or occasionally mid-March in the milder regions of the Northeast. Activity increases in April, gradually declines in October, and ceases by early November. Females tend to be more active in May (prime time for oviposition) than males, but at other times of the year male and female activity is similar. This activity pattern, in part, contradicts the findings of Blanchard (1933b) for Michigan, where females predominated in the spring and males were the most common sex encountered in the fall.

Four-toed salamanders have been found hibernating buried in a shale bank in central Pennsylvania (Bell 1955). Blanchard (1933b) reported that, in Michigan, individuals often congregate in large numbers (more than 200 animals) in late fall. He felt they were preparing to enter hibernation in nearby animal burrows and the tunnels and channels produced by rotting roots associated with old trees and stumps.

With the exception of breeding migrations, nothing is known concerning the movements or home range of this species.

No detailed studies of food habits have been conducted on four-toed salamanders, but Surface (1913) reported that they eat spiders, springtails (collembolans), drosophilid flies, and small leafhoppers. The stomach contents in 17 specimens from Pennsylvania contained colembollans, ants, and the larvae of small dipterans. Spiders and beetles were a minor component of their diet. Virtually all specimens that contained food held only a single prey taxon, although several individuals of the taxon might have been consumed.

Four-toed salamanders exhibit several antipredator adaptations. When initially encountered, they form a tight body coil and remain motionless. They will occasionally, however, while remaining in a tight body coil, elevate their tail and move it back and forth, thus exposing the white and black ventral surface of the tail (Brodie 1977). This behavior functions to draw the attention of a potential predator away from the body and toward the tail. If grabbed, the tail separates from the body at the autotomy plane and wriggles about violently. This action distracts the predator, giving the salamander a chance to escape. In some cases, the tail does not have to be grabbed to be autotomized. Bishop (1941) showed that a single violent shake of the body can be sufficient to cause tail separation. The tail is eventually regenerated.

Reproduction.   Courtship and mating usually occur in the fall (September and October) but may begin as early as August (Bishop 1941, Blanchard 1933c). Noble and Brady (1930) described courtship in this species.

Females begin to develop follicles in June or July. Vitellogenesis continues throughout the summer and fall, and females enter hibernation with follicles near ovulatory size. Shortly after emergence from hibernation, eggs reach ovulatory size, 2.5–3 mm ($\frac{1}{8}$ in.) in diameter. Ovarian complement in a sample of individuals from Pennsylvania ranged from 8 to 38 eggs ($X = 22.4$). This is similar to clutch size reported for New York ($X = 24.4$; Gilbert 1941). Clutch size is positively correlated with female body size. The female cycle appears to be biennial. Forty-two percent of a sample ($N = 27$) of mature females that we examined showed no sign of vitellogenic activity during the reproductive season. This finding strongly suggests that reproduction does not occur on an annual basis. A biennial pattern of reproduction is further supported by the fact that the number of days a female spens brooding is significantly positively correlated with weight loss (R. Harris et al. 1995). Presumably weight loss is due to lack of feeding while in the brood chamber and recovery might require an entire year.

Egg deposition occurs from early April through late May. Females deposit eggs in cavities made in sphagnum or similar types of moss, although eggs may occasionally be deposited in other types of vegetation such as grass, grass roots, and pine needles (Bishop 1941). Nests are usually located within a few centimeters of suitable water (bogs, marshes, woodland ponds, and meandering, slow-moving streams). The eggs with associated envelopes and jelly coats average about 5 mm ($\frac{1}{4}$ in.) in total diameter. They are deposited singly in the nest cavity and adhere both to each other and to the vegetation lining the cavity. Nests may be used communally. Blanchard (1934) found as many as 1,110 eggs in a single nest, but this huge number is the exception rather than the rule. The degree of communal nesting within a population is highly variable, being common in some populations and rare or nonexistent in others (Breitenbach 1982, R. Harris and Gill 1980). Breitenbach suggested that the incidence of communal nesting in an area is a function of habitat. In areas where suitable nest sites are rare communal nesting is common, and where there is an abundance of suitable habitat the frequency of communal nesting is very low. R. Harris and co-workers (1995), however, could demonstrate no relationship between the density of salamanders and the proportion of joint nests within a population. They did, however, note that at high-density sites joint nests "tended" to contain eggs of more females.

As is often the case with plethondontids, female four-toed salamanders exhibit a high degree of parental care, remaining with their eggs for varying periods of time after deposition. In communal nests, only a single female usually remains in attendance (R. Harris and Gill 1980). Hatching success has been shown to be positively correlated with the degree of female nest attendance.

The incubation time for eggs depends upon environmental conditions and the location of the nest. It may vary from 35 to 60 days in the field but may be as short as 25 days in the laboratory (Bishop 1941). Most hatching occurs in early June. When larvae emerge, they range from 11 to 14 mm ($\frac{3}{8}$–$\frac{1}{2}$ in.) ToL. They actively wriggle out of the nest until they fall into the nearby water. Little is known about the biology of the larvae. The larval period lasts approximately 6 weeks, and transformed young vary from 18 to 22 mm ($\frac{3}{4}$–$\frac{7}{8}$ in.) ToL. Recently transformed individuals can be readily recognized by the presence of a small black patch at either side of the neck where the gills have been reabsorbed.

In Pennsylvania, males mature at about 22 mm ($\frac{7}{8}$ in.) SVL and 45 mm ($1\frac{3}{4}$ in.) ToL. Females mature at a slightly larger size: 29 mm ($1\frac{1}{8}$ in.) SVL and 56 mm ($2\frac{1}{4}$ in.) ToL. These sizes are similar to the sizes reported for males and females from New York: 49 and 60 mm (2 and $2\frac{3}{8}$ in.) ToL, respectively (Bishop 1941).

Remarks.   The four-toed salamander's specialized habitat requirements (i.e., bogs or woodland ponds) make it vulnerable to localized extirpation due to habitat modification or destruction associated with agriculture, industrialization, and suburban sprawl. Minton (1972) mentioned that populations in Indiana disappear rapidly in areas of human modification.

Protection of wetlands is necessary to preserve the species' remaining habitat in the Northeast.

Distribution.   Four-toed salamanders occur from Nova Scotia westward through central New England and southern Ontario to Wisconsin. From New England, their range extends southward to western South Carolina and northern Georgia and Alabama. Disjunct populations occur in Missouri, Arkansas, Louisiana, and several other states.

The species is absent from most of northern New England. In southern New England, it is widespread but localized (Klemens 1993). In Pennsylvania, New Jersey, and New York, the species has a wide but spotty distribution that is due, in part, to the animal's narrow habitat requirements. In addition, the distribution may appear spotty because these secretive animals often go unnoticed by the casual observer. It is likely that several of the historical populations recorded from the eastern portion of Pennsylvania and in Allegheny and Beaver counties in the west are no longer extant due to habitat modification and destruction.

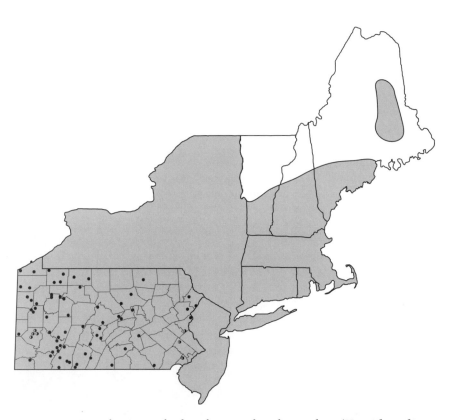

Map 16. Distribution of the four-toed salamander *(Hemidactylium scutatum)*.

Plethodon
Gr. *pleth*, to be full; L. *dont*, teeth

The genus *Plethodon* (the woodland salamanders), the largest genus of salamander in the United States, contains 43 species. Woodland salamanders range throughout the eastern United States and adjacent Canada. They are absent from the Great Plains and Rocky Mountain states but have a second center of diversity in the Pacific Northwest, from northern California to southern British Columbia. Disjunct populations occur in Idaho, Montana, and New Mexico.

Woodland salamanders are small to moderate-sized species with a tail 1 to 1.5 times the length of the body. In body proportions, they vary from slender to moderately robust. They are restricted to forested regions and are active when humidity is high. They can often be found wandering about on the surface. At other times they can be located by turning cover objects such as rocks and logs. When the weather is exceedingly dry, they move deep beneath the surface.

Woodland salamanders feed on many types of small forest-floor invertebrates, including worms, mites, spiders, sowbugs, and insects. The female constructs a nest under a cover object or in a subterranean cavity, where she lays a small clutch of relatively large eggs. The female guards the eggs until they hatch. Development is direct.

Redback Salamander *Plethodon cinereus* (Green)
L. *cinic*, ashes or ash-colored
Description.   The redback salamander (Plate 29) is a small, relatively slender woodland salamander. The color pattern is variable (Plate 30). The most common pattern is the striped morph, in which a middorsal, straight-edged, bright red stripe extends from the nape of the neck along the entire length of the body and onto at least the proximal half of the tail. Black pigment spots often occur in the red dorsal stripe, and occasionally the middorsal stripe is some color other than red (beige, cream, or gray). The middorsal stripe is bordered by black that becomes mottled with white along the lower half of the sides. The venter is coarsely mottled black and white, giving the belly a distinctive salt-and-pepper appearance.

A second, less common morph is the lead-back phase. In this form, the dorsal stripe is absent, and the back is a uniform dark grayish black, occasionally flecked with minute white or brassy flecks. As in the striped morph, the ventral surfaces are mottled salt-and-pepper.

The final form is the least common. In Pennsylvania, it has been found only in southern Potter County. This is the red, or erythristic, morph (Plate 31), in which the dorsal and lateral surfaces are bright red and the red pigment extends onto the sides of the belly.

In all of the above forms, recently hatched young resemble the adults. An albino individual has been reported from Maryland (Dyrkacz 1981).

Redback salamanders are slender animals. The body is somewhat rounded, and the head is only slightly set off from the body. The snout is short and truncated. The tail is about the same length as the body and remains fairly thick to just before its termination, where it rapidly tapers to a point. The limbs are small and spindly. Mature females are slightly, but significantly, larger than males. Males average 42.3 mm ($3\frac{1}{4}$ in.) SVL and 80.5 mm ($2\frac{1}{2}$–$3\frac{3}{4}$ in.) ToL. Females average 44 mm ($1\frac{3}{4}$ in.) SVL and 83 mm ($3\frac{3}{8}$ in.) ToL. The record size for this species is 127 mm ($5\frac{1}{8}$ in.) ToL (Conant and Collins 1991).

Confusing Species.   The red morph is readily distinguished from most other species found the Northeast. The lead-back phase, however, could easily be confused with either the ravine salamander or the valley and ridge salamander. Although all three species have a mottled venter, the ventral pattern of the redback salamander contains more white than the pattern of the other two, and the redback salamander is the only one that has the salt-and-pepper appearance. In addition, the dorsal flecks on the redback salamander are not as well developed as dorsal flecks on either of the other two species. Redback salamanders have 18 or 19 costal grooves. Valley and ridge salamanders have 20 or 21, and ravine salamanders have 19 or 20.

Habitat and Habits.   The redback salamander is primarily a woodland species that inhabits deciduous, mixed hardwood-conifer, and coniferous forests. They are also found in disturbed areas at the borders of forests, especially along rocky road cuts and railroad rights-of-way. In forested areas, they generally prefer upland habitat that is not too dry or exposed. As a consequence, they are not usually found along wooded, exposed, sandy ridges, nor are they usually found near streams and creeks. Their preferred microhabitat varies with climatic conditions. During moist periods, they are found under a wide variety of cover objects, varying from leaf litter and bark to large rocks and fallen timber. With increased drying, they tend to occupy cover that provides a moist retreat (especially large rocks and partially decayed logs). Wyman and Hawksley-Lescault (1987) found that redback salamanders avoid areas of low soil pH (less than 3.7). Pough and co-workers (1987) demonstrated that light forest utilization, such as cutting select timber for firewood, had little effect on redback salamander populations but that more extensive cutting severely affected their population size.

The redback salamander has one of the longest surface activity periods of any terrestrial salamander in the Northeast. Activity can begin as early as the end of January and extend to the beginning of December. Even during the two months of relative inactivity, several days of unusually warm weather may initiate surface activity. We have even found individuals active under rocks when there was 75 mm (3 in.) of snow on the ground. During the rest of the year, surface activity appears to be controlled by rainfall and reproductive state. At any time of the activity season, decreased moisture in the environment will curtail redback salamander activity, and during periods of drought all surface activity ceases.

Females are inactive in the summer when they are brooding eggs. Daily activity is decidedly nocturnal and is associated with humidity and rainfall. When conditions are too dry, animals tend to remain in their diurnal retreats and to shift to retreats that afford greater protection from desiccation (Jaeger 1980).

Presumably, redback salamanders hibernate in subterranean shelters such as cracks and crevices where they remain secure from freezing and drying. Other hibernacula have been reported as follows: in abandoned ant mounds (R. Caldwell 1975), under rocks in streams (J. Cooper 1956), and in channels of partly rotted roots (Hoff 1977).

Redback salamanders are usually solitary, but in the spring they may often be found with other individuals. In prime habitat they can reach astounding population densities. Heatwole (1962) reported a density of approximately 1 animal/m^2 (0.1 animal/ft^2) in Michigan.

Studies of forest ecosystems have shown that redback salamanders are very important components of the trophic structure in some forests because of their high densities, their ability to harvest small consumers that are not preyed upon by other carnivores, and their high efficiency (60%) in converting consumed energy into salamander biomass (Burton and Likens 1975). In a New Hampshire forest, Burton and Likens found that the biomass of redback salamanders equaled that of mice and shrews and was twice that of nonraptor forest birds.

Redback salamanders feed on a variety of small soil and leaf litter invertebrates. Prey items include, but are not restricted to, mites, springtails, millipedes, fly and beetle larvae, worms, flies, ants, and beetles. On rainy nights, redback salamanders have been seen climbing vegetation in search of food (Jaeger 1978). During periods of drought, salamander movement is severely curtailed and dietary intake drops to a low level, with the diet primarily limited to prey animals of appropriate size that stray into the retreat.

Redback salamanders are highly territorial and will vigorously defend their territory against intruders. Territorial defense involves threat postures in which the legs are extended and the body, except for the distal portion of the tail, is elevated off the ground. This behavior is followed by a lunge at the intruder and often a bite to the nose or tail. The degree of territorial defense increases with length of occupancy (Nunes and Jaeger 1989). In 74% of territorial disputes, the original owner won (Jaeger et al. 1982), suggesting a higher level of motivation on the part of the site owner than on that of the intruder. Jaeger (1981) observed a phenomenon that he called Dear Enemy, in which territorial owners were less likely to attack salamanders that possessed neighboring territories than they were to attack salamanders that were strangers. Recognition of intruders and territorial boundaries involved olfaction and pheromones produced by the salamanders.

Reproduction.   Noble and Brady (1930) described the courtship of this species. The mating season is prolonged. Over much of the redback salamander's range, mating may occur anytime from the middle of fall

(October) until the following February and March (Bishop 1941, Blanchard 1928). Gergits and Jaeger (1990) reported that courtship occurred as early as August. They also demonstrated that males locate mates on the basis of sex pheromones secreted by the female.

Vitellogenesis is initiated the fall before oviposition. By late May and early June, eggs are fully yolked and of ovulatory size (3–3.5 mm; $\frac{1}{8}$ in.).

Oviposition generally occurs in June, but egg laying has been reported to extend into August for Michigan populations (J. Werner 1971).

Oviposition sites vary depending on the structural makeup of the habitat. Test and Heatwole (1962) reported that, in northern Michigan, where conifer logs are abundant, most nests were located in cracks and crevices in the logs. Even in areas where hardwood logs predominated, conifers were selected. In southern Michigan, where conifers are rare, redback salamanders select burrows constructed by other animals as sites for egg laying. Little is known of the oviposition sites for the northeastern redback salamanders, but in West Virginia many nests are located under flat rocks (Pauley, pers. comm.)

Clutch size for Pennsylvania specimens varies from 3 to 11 eggs (X = 6.0, N = 34) and is positively correlated with female body size. The frequency of oviposition is variable. An annual cycle is suggested because most females in spring samples contained large, yolked eggs, which would be oviposited in June. Annual cycles have also been reported for a Michigan population (J. Werner 1971) and a Tennessee population (Nagel 1977). Other workers, however, have reported a biennial cycle (Bishop 1941, for New York; Sayler 1966, for Maryland; Vogt 1981b, for Wisconsin). Lotter (1978) suggested that older and larger individuals have an annual cycle, whereas younger and smaller individuals have a biennial cycle in Connecticut.

Females remain at the nest site and defend the eggs from predators. Highton and Savage (1961) showed that female nest attendance significantly increases the likelihood that the eggs will hatch. Development is direct; therefore, there is no larval stage. Hatching begins in August and neonates become more common as the fall progresses.

Females have been reported to mature at SVLs ranging from 33 to 39 mm ($1\frac{3}{8}$–$1\frac{1}{2}$ in.) (Lotter 1978, Sayler 1966). The smallest mature female from Pennsylvania was 40 mm ($1\frac{1}{2}$ in.) SVL. The smallest mature male was 35 mm ($1\frac{3}{8}$ in.) SVL. The average size of mature females from Pennsylvania is 44.1 mm ($1\frac{3}{4}$ in.) SVL and of mature males 42.3 mm ($1\frac{5}{8}$ in.) SVL. These average sizes are very similar to those reported by Werner (1971) for a Michigan population, where the average female SVL was 44 mm ($1\frac{3}{4}$ in.) (N = 56), and the average male SVL was 42 mm ($1\frac{5}{8}$ in.).

Remarks.   The frequency of occurrence of the lead-back, or black, morph in the Northeast needs to be studied in greater detail. It appears that the black morph is often absent from populations in Pennsylvania or occurs at very low frequencies. However, this conclusion is based primarily on the results of casual rather than systematic collecting of redback salamanders. In Ohio, Pfingsten and Walker (1978) noted that, except in the south and the east, most populations contained at least some black morphs, and in the areas around western Lake Erie they made up 70% or more of the populations. In New England, Lotter and Scott (1977) showed that morph frequency is correlated with environmental temperatures, with the black morph fairly common in warmer regions. In these warmer locations, the frequency of the black morph ranges from 5% to 33% ($X =$ 18.2%). In colder areas of New England, the black morph is generally absent or, when present, occurs at very low frequencies. Moreno (1989) demonstrated differential mortality of the black and striped morphs and correlated it with environmental temperatures. The black morph has a higher mortality rate at low temperatures, whereas the striped morph experiences higher mortalities in warmer climates. J. Brown (1965) showed that the frequencies of the morphs remain stable over time. It appears, then, that the benefits gained by differential survival are offset by some other selective factor or factors; otherwise, one would expect a gradual increase in one or the other morph.

Although in Pennsylvania the erythristic form has been reported only from Potter County, it may occur in other areas as well. Pfingsten and

Map 17. Distribution of the redback salamander *(Plethodon cinereus).*

Downs (1989) reported this morph from northeastern Ohio. Tilley and co-workers (1982) suggested that the red morph may be an example of Batesian mimicry, in which individuals possessing the color pattern achieve a degree of safety from avian predators by resembling the distasteful and toxic red eft stage of the red-spotted newt. This may be possible, but, since the redback salamander occurs sympatrically with red efts over a wide geographic range, Batesian mimicry does not explain why only scattered, northern populations contain the red morph.

Distribution.   The redback salamander's range extends over much of the northeastern United States and adjacent Canada, as well as the north-central portion of the United States. Its range extends southward to southern Indiana, Ohio, and North Carolina. A number of disjunct populations occur.

The redback salamander occurs throughout the northeastern states.

Northern Slimy Salamander *Plethodon glutinosus* (Green)
L. *gluten*, sticky
Description.   The northern slimy salamander (Plate 32) is a moderately large species. The color and pattern remain constant in all size and age classes of this species. The back and sides are jet black with white to silvery spots. The degree of dorsal spotting varies from very dense to almost absent, but spots always occur along the sides of the body. The ventral surfaces are slate gray and are generally immaculate. The gular fold is light brown. Northern slimy salamanders have direct development, and neonates (Plate 33) resemble adults in color and pattern. Albinos have been reported for this species (Piatt 1931).

Northern slimy salamanders are robust but not exceedingly heavy bodied, except when compared with other woodland salamanders. The head is moderately large, square, and slightly set off from the body. The snout is sharply truncated. The limbs are muscular and terminate in well-developed fingers and toes. The tail is circular in cross section and gradually tapers to a point.

In Pennsylvania, females attain sizes larger than males. Males average 68.6 mm ($2\frac{3}{4}$ in.) SVL and 136.4 mm ($5\frac{3}{8}$ in.) ToL. Females average 73.5 mm ($2\frac{7}{8}$ in.) SVL and 150.3 mm (6 in.) ToL. In Ohio, however, males attain sizes larger than females. The record size for this species is 206 mm ($8\frac{1}{4}$ in.) ToL (Conant 1975). The relative tail length averages 102% of SVL for both sexes.

During the breeding season, mature males can be readily distinguished from females by the presence of a noticeable hedonic gland located on the anterior portion of the chin. In addition, the male's cloacal lips are greatly enlarged at this time and cloacal papillae are present.

Confusing Species.   The combination of its large size, black body with white spots, and copious production of slime when handled help distinguish the northern slimy salamander from all others found in the Northeast.

Habitat and Habits.   The northern slimy salamander is found in heavily forested areas or in open shale-covered embankments and hillsides adjacent to dense forest. The species tends to reach its greatest abundance in mature woodlands where there is an abundance of rocks and fallen logs to provide cover and protection.

Surface activity begins in mid-March and is associated with rising ambient temperatures and spring rains. Northern slimy salamanders remain active above ground until late October or early November, depending upon local climatic conditions. Activity may continue throughout most of the winter in subterranean retreats. Between March and November, surface activity can be dramatically curtailed if climatic conditions become adverse. During drought, all surface activity ceases.

When active outside their retreats, northern slimy salamanders are decidedly nocturnal. They can frequently be found foraging among the leaf litter or at the entrance to their burrows at night. Nocturnal activity is greatest during and shortly after rain.

Presumably, hibernation occurs in moderately deep subterranean refugia, especially in areas of tumbled cobble and glacial debris and in areas rich in shale that have numerous crevices affording the animals easy access to deep frost-free retreats. Bishop (1941) suggested that northern slimy salamanders may remain active in their hibernacula and reported that some had been found 1.2–1.5 m (4–5 ft) deep in shale banks in central New York.

Under normal climatic conditions, northern slimy salamanders are primarily solitary. Animals aggregate, however, during periods of courtship and climatic stress. Under drought conditions, we have found as many as 13 adults occupying a single cavity in a decaying log. Wells and Wells (1976) noted the same tendency to aggregate during drought in North Carolina. Wells (1980) further noted a tendency for males and females to aggregate during the mating season.

In prime habitat, northern slimy salamanders can reach high population densities, although their secretive nature often belies their numbers. Semlitsch (1980) estimated a density of 1 individual/m^2 (0.1 individuals/ft^2) in suitable habitat, and Merchant (1972) estimated a density of about 1 individual/4 m^2 (1 individual/40 ft^2) in suitable habitat.

Northern slimy salamanders feed on a wide variety of invertebrates including millipedes, centipedes, worms, beetles, insect larvae, ants, and snails (Davidson 1956, Powders and Tietjen 1974). We found that millipedes and beetles were the most common prey, and isopods, ants, worms, and snails were of secondary importance.

Northern slimy salamanders have two antipredator defense mechanisms. As is typical of many plethondontids, they exhibit caudal autotomy and can shed their tail when captured. In addition, they secrete copious quantities of a very slippery, whitish mucus that becomes sticky as it dries. This secretion is sufficient to repel most predators.

Reproduction.   Organ (1960) described the courtship of the northern slimy salamander. Courtship time varies geographically. The condition of vas deferentia indicates that courtship occurs either in fall or in early spring in Pennsylvania, shortly after emergence from hibernation.

Vitellogenesis begins in the fall and continues through the next spring. By late May or early June, follicles of ovulatory size (3.5–4 mm; $\frac{1}{6}$ in.) are present in the ovaries, and oviposition occurs. The females guard the eggs. Little is known of the oviposition site or the behavior of the females during nest attendance. Nests with attendant females have been reported from caves and from cavities in rotting logs (Fowler 1940, Noble and Marshall 1929). Probably, most oviposition and nest attendance occur in underground retreats.

Clutch size is positively correlated with female body size and ranges from 12 to 34 eggs. Oviposition is biennial, probably owing to the energetic costs of nest attendance during the summer. In the southern portion of the species' range, where annual activity is longer, reproduction occurs annually. The length of incubation is not known.

Semlitsch (1980) noted significant interpopulation variation in size at maturity for female northern slimy salamanders in southern Pennsylvania and adjacent Maryland. The size at maturity ranged from 63 to 70 mm ($2\frac{1}{2}$–$2\frac{3}{4}$ in.) SVL. In our statewide Pennsylvania sample, we found females to mature at about 65 mm ($2\frac{5}{8}$ in.) SVL and males to mature at between 55 and 65 mm ($2\frac{1}{4}$ in.) SVL. Females from Bedford County mature at a SVL of about 50 mm (2 in.) (Highton 1962). Both sexes mature at 4 years of age, but they may not reproduce until their fifth year (Highton 1962).

Remarks. An electrophoretic analysis (Highton 1989) suggests that *Plethodon glutinosus* is actually a complex of several species that share similar characteristics and have a common ancestry. We recognize Highton's revision. All specimens from Pennsylvania, however, are the nominate species.

Distribution. In the East, the northern slimy salamander ranges from central New York to Maryland and then southwest along the Blue Ridge Mountains to central Alabama and Georgia. In the Midwest it ranges from Alabama northward through most of Tennessee and Kentucky to southern Illinois, Indiana, and Ohio.

In the Northeast, northern slimy salamanders are found in extreme southwestern Connecticut and southwestern New Hampshire. Specimens from southwestern New Hampshire are considered suspect (Klemens 1993). The species is uncommon and localized east of the Hudson River (Klemens 1993). It is found throughout the state of Pennsylvania but appears to be less common along the Coastal Plain and in the Piedmont region than elsewhere in the state.

Valley and Ridge Salamander *Plethodon hoffmani* Highton
Named for Richard L. Hoffman, who collected the first specimens
Description. The valley and ridge salamander (Plate 34) is a small to medium sized, slender species, with small, thin legs. Background coloration is brownish black to black. Silvery white to brassy spots and flecks may occur on the back and sides, giving the animals a metallic sheen at times. The brassy flecks tend to be restricted to the dorsal surface, whereas the white flecks and larger spots are more numerous on the sides. Ventral

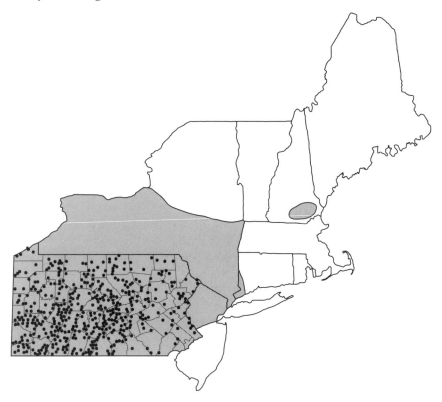

Map 18. Distribution of the northern slimy salamander *(Plethodon glutinosus)*.

coloration is black with a fine pattern of white maculations. The throat is lighter than the belly. In hatchlings, the dorsal coloration is similar to that of the adults, but the ventral surface is not as dark, being more lightly mottled in appearance.

The body of this species is very elongate and wormlike. The legs are short and slender. The tail is relatively long, rounded, and tapered. The head is distinct from the body and widest at a point just behind the eyes. Females are slightly, but significantly, larger than males. Mature males average 48.2 mm ($1\frac{7}{8}$ in.) SVL and 98 mm (4 in.) ToL. Mature females average 51.8 mm (2 in.) SVL and 106.5 mm ($4\frac{1}{4}$ in.) ToL. Maximum size for the species is 137 mm ($5\frac{1}{2}$ in.) ToL (Conant and Collins 1991). Tail length is similar for both sexes; it averages 104.6% of SVL in adults. Juveniles have much shorter tails than do adults. Average tail length for small individuals (less than 30 mm; $1\frac{1}{5}$ in.) is 76.6% of SVL.

Confusing Species. Redback salamanders generally have a distinctive middorsal red stripe, but this may occasionally be absent. If absent, their belly is significantly more mottled than that of the valley and ridge salamander. The valley and ridge salamander has a lighter throat and a slightly more mottled belly than does the ravine salamander.

Habitat and Habits.   The valley and ridge salamander occurs in deciduous forest or mixed conifer-hardwood habitat on hillsides and ridge tops and on exposed, sparsely vegetated, talus slopes. They are occasionally found near stream beds and on valley floors. Their habitat always contains an abundance of surface rocks that provide cover and foraging areas. The soils where they occur in Pennsylvania are generally sandy or rocky and, as a consequence, are well drained and fairly dry. Within their range, they tend to be replaced in more poorly drained or clay soils by their relative the redback salamander. P. Brown and colleagues (1977) demonstrated that the valley and ridge salamander is physiologically better adapted to dry soil conditions than either redback or northern slimy salamanders.

If climatic conditions are suitable, valley and ridge salamanders will commence surface activity as early as the first week of March, but consistently predictable surface activity does not occur until the beginning of April. Surface activity remains high during May and early June, but by the end of June activity ceases and generally does not resume until the middle of September. Falling temperatures and increasing rainfall initiate a second activity period that continues through October. Hibernation, or at least inactivity, occurs from November to February.

When not in hibernation or aestivation they can be found almost exclusively under rocks. They do, however, make occasional nocturnal forays into the open during periods of rainy weather and high humidity.

In Pennsylvania, the valley and ridge salamander feeds primarily on ants. Beetles and insect larvae contribute to the diet but are of secondary importance. They also feed on a variety of other invertebrates including, but not restricted to, termites, spiders, worms, sowbugs, slugs, pseudoscorpions, crickets, and wood roaches.

Reproduction.   Courtship and mating have not been observed for this species. Indirect evidence suggests that they occur in April and May, because it is at this time of the year that males produce spermatophores.

The reproductive cycle in females is biennial, as indicated by the presence of yolked follicles in about half of the mature females in a population at times of the year when reproduction occurs. In reproductively active females, the cycle begins in the fall with initiation of vitellogenesis. As a result, females enter hibernation with partially yolked follicles. Upon emergence from hibernation, follicle diameter varies between 2 and 2.5 mm ($\frac{1}{10}$ in.). Follicular growth in the spring is rapid, and by the end of May follicles have reached ovulatory size (4.5–5 mm; $\frac{1}{5}$ in.). Oviposition presumably occurs underground at the end of May or beginning of June.

In Pennsylvania, clutch size varies from 4 to 9 eggs and is not correlated with female SVL. Angle (1969) reported a clutch size of 4.7 eggs (range 3–8) for a population near the Maryland-Pennsylvania border.

It is assumed that females tend the nests for at least part of the developmental period as has been observed in many species of *Plethodon*. Hatching presumably occurs in late summer as small (16 mm SVL; $\frac{5}{8}$ in.) neonates are first observed on the surface at that time (Angle 1969).

Males mature at approximately 41 mm ($1\frac{5}{8}$ in.) SVL; females do not mature until they reach a SVL of 50 mm (2 in.). Angle (1969) reported that females mature between 40 and 46 mm ($1\frac{5}{8}$–$1\frac{3}{4}$ in.) SVL. This smaller size for females may also account for the smaller average clutch size reported by him.

Remarks.   Until 1972 the valley and ridge salamander was thought to be conspecific with the ravine salamander (Highton 1971). As a result, references to the ravine salamander before 1972 from Pennsylvania refer to or involve a composite of both species. Since their ranges do not overlap in Pennsylvania, they can be separated in these earlier works on the basis of locality.

Distribution.   The range of the valley and ridge salamander extends from central Pennsylvania southward to southeastern West Virginia and western Virginia in a narrow band along the Appalachian Mountains. In

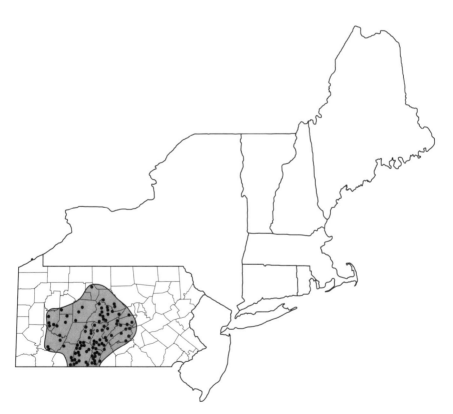

Map 19. Distribution of the valley and ridge salamander *(Plethodon hoffmani)*.

Pennsylvania, the majority of records come from the southern half of the Valley and Ridge Province, with a sharp western border formed at the Allegheny Front. Several scattered records for the species do, however, exist for counties west of the front. McCoy (1982) suggested that this species penetrated the Allegheny Front by means of the West Branch of the Susquehanna River and subsequently moved south and west from there.

Ravine Salamander *Plethodon richmondi* Netting and Mittleman
Named in honor of Neil Richmond, who collected the holotype
Description.   The ravine salamander (Plate 35) is a small, thin, elongate species of woodland salamander. The general dorsal background coloration (including head and tail) is brownish black to black. The entire dorsal surface is maculated with fine silvery white or gold spots. Ventral background coloration is similar to that of the dorsum and is finely mottled with whitish spots, giving it an overall grayish appearance. The subcaudal region is similar to, or slightly darker than, the belly. The background coloration of the dorsum of hatchlings is lighter brown than that of adults, but it too is maculated with fine silvery white or gold spots. Occasionally these maculations are interspersed with larger (2 or 3 times as large) spots, giving the dorsum a slightly patterned appearance. The eyes and eyelids of neonates are black, and because of their relatively large size and protuberant shape they stand out vividly on the head. The ventral surface of the neonate is a finely mottled light brown.

The body of this species is elongate and wormlike. The legs are short and slender. The head is moderately distinct from the body, and the tail is relatively long and rounded and tapers to a point. The average size of adults for a sample from southwestern Pennsylvania was 46.1 mm ($1\frac{3}{4}$ in.) SVL and 91 mm ($3\frac{5}{8}$ in.) ToL. The maximum size reported for the species is 143 mm ($5\frac{3}{4}$ in.) ToL (Conant and Collins 1991). Adults have from 19 to 22 costal grooves, with most specimens having 20 or 21.

The ravine salamander exhibits a significant level of ontogenetic variation in proportions of body parts, due to allometric growth. The legs of hatchlings and juveniles are relatively much longer than those of adults. As few as 5 costal grooves occur between the toes of the forelegs and hind legs when they are pressed along the side of the body. In adults, 12 costal grooves are generally present between the adpressed limbs. Whereas the legs become relatively shorter with age, the opposite happens with the tail. The tail of hatchlings is only 60% to 70% of SVL, but the tail length of adults ranges from 110% to 125% of SVL.

Confusing Species.   The ravine salamander may be confused with the redback salamander, which usually has a distinct middorsal red stripe. However, this is occasionally absent. Ravine salamanders may be distinguished from redback salamanders by having more costal grooves (20 or 21 versus 19) and by the finely mottled ventral pattern versus "salt and pepper." The valley and ridge salamander has slightly coarser mottling on the belly.

Habitat and Habits.   As the common name implies, this species is primarily an inhabitant of steep, fairly heavily wooded ravines with small to
medium-sized streams. Within this habitat they are most common on
wooded talus slopes, with abundant flat limestone rocks serving as passageways to their underground retreats. Petranka (1979) suggested that
this habitat requirement is due to the poor burrowing ability of the
species. In the absence of such microhabitat, ravine salamanders are not
able to survive because they cannot retreat deep enough to escape the
effects of prolonged inclement weather (cold or hot and dry). As a result,
their distribution within the geographic range of the species is localized
and spotty. Even when other cover objects are available in the environment, ravine salamanders are invariably found under rocks. They occur
more frequently on the slopes of ravines rather than on the floor or along
the top.

The limited sample (N = 27) of ravine salamanders from Pennsylvania
suggests that they are most active in April and May and again in September and October. Annual activity begins in March and continues
through late November. Surface activity is virtually nonexistent during
June, July, and August. This same type of bimodal annual activity cycle
has been reported for the species in other parts of its range (Duellman
1954, Wallace and Barbour 1957). In southern Ohio, they occasionally are
active throughout the winter, especially during periods of thaw (Duellman
1954).

Terrestrial surface activity is uncommon in this species. When it does
occur it tends to be restricted to nocturnal forays during and after heavy
rains.

Presumably, both hibernation and aestivation occur deep in cracks and
crevices on rocky hillsides. The only record of hibernation for ravine salamanders is that of Duellman (1954). He found an aggregation of 12 individuals buried in clay soil beneath a large piece of limestone.

Apparently, energy reserves for hibernation and aestivation are stored
in the tail. Salamanders collected just before a period of inactivity tend to
have a large swollen tail, whereas those collected shortly after emergence
have a thin tail. Energy reserves stored in the tail are mobilized during
inactivity, and the tail diminishes in size accordingly.

Duellman (1954) commented that ants and sowbugs (terrestrial isopods)
made up the bulk of the animal's diet in southern Ohio. We have found
that in southwestern Pennsylvania ants and small ground-dwelling beetles
predominate in the diet of ravine salamanders, with spiders and fly larvae
of secondary importance. No Pennsylvania specimens were found to
contain isopods.

Reproduction.   Courtship and mating have never been observed in this
species, but they are presumably similar to courtship and mating in other
species of *Plethodon* salamanders such as the redback salamander. Mating
occurs over a prolonged time period, from November until February
or March. In Tennessee, Nagel (1979) found a gradual increase in
percentage of gravid females with sperm in their spermatotheca from 4%

in November to 100% in February. He also noted that females had fresh spermatophores in their cloacas in November, December, January, and March.

Females emerge from summer aestivation with small (less than 1 mm) ovarian follicles. Follicular growth is slow but steady, and, by March or April, heavily yolked follicles measure about 3 mm ($\frac{1}{8}$ in.) in diameter. By late May or early June, follicles are of ovulatory size (about 4 mm; $\frac{1}{8}$ in.) and are apparently deposited in subterranean retreats in late May or June. Eggs are probably attended by the female, although brooding females and eggs have rarely been found in the wild. Wallace and Barbour (1957) once found two adults (one female and one of unknown sex that escaped) under a flat stone that also harbored two hatchlings and two eggs that hatched upon being touched.

Ovarian complement has been reported as ranging from 5 to 17 eggs and is not correlated with female body size (Nagel 1979, Wood 1945). Duellman (1954) mentioned a clutch of 12 eggs found under a rock in a shallow depression. The eggs were unpigmented, approximately 5 mm ($\frac{1}{5}$ in.) in diameter, and not attached to the substrate. A female was not present, but Duellman assumed that the nest was probably that of a ravine salamander since it was the only woodland species commonly found in the area.

Ravine salamanders, like other woodland salamanders, have direct development. Hatching occurs around September, and hatchling size is reported to be 23–24 mm (1 in.) ToL, with a SVL of 14–15 mm ($\frac{5}{8}$ in.) (Wallace and Barbour 1957). Little growth occurs between hatching and the next spring. Two specimens from Pennsylvania collected in late April had ToLs of 25 and 27 mm (1 and $1\frac{1}{8}$ in.), and Duellman (1954) reported the average SVL of spring-collected juveniles in Ohio as 17.8 mm ($\frac{5}{8}$ in.).

Both males and females mature at about 40 mm ($1\frac{5}{8}$ in.) SVL. Nagel (1979) suggested that after first reproduction, reproductive cycles might be biennial. This appears to be the case in Pennsylvania, where less than 50% of a sample of reproductive-sized females were gravid during the reproductive season.

Remarks.   Highton (1999) used electrophoresis to examine several populations of the ravine salamander from across its range. From his analysis of 24 loci (gene locations), he concluded that the ravine salamander as currently recognized actually represents two sibling species whose ranges abut each other but do not overlap. He has placed all of the Pennsylvania populations into a new species, *Plethodon electromorphus*, and has given them the common name of northern ravine salamander. The range of this species extends from southwestern and west-central Pennsylvania and adjacent northwestern West Virginia westward through Ohio and northern Kentucky to eastern Indiana.

Distribution.   The ravine salamander occurs from western Pennsylvania westward throughout most of Ohio and southward through eastern Kentucky and western West Virginia. Its range terminates in western Virginia and adjacent Tennessee and North Carolina.

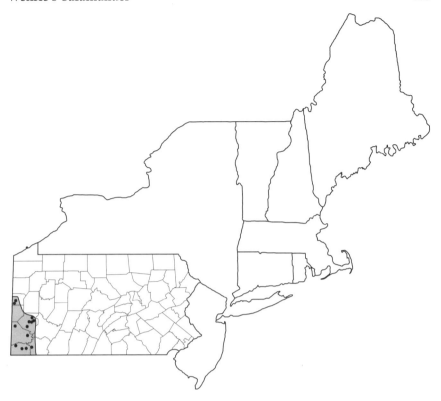

Map 20. Distribution of the ravine salamander *(Plethodon richmondi).*

In Pennsylvania, it is restricted to the extreme west-central and southwestern corner of the state.

Wehrle's Salamander *Plethodon wehrlei* Fowler and Dunn

Named in honor of R. W. Wehrle, who collected the first specimens

Description. Wehrle's salamander (Plate 36) is a moderate-sized woodland species. The dorsal background coloration varies from brownish black to dark bluish black. This background coloration continues onto the head and lightens along the upper region of the jaws. The sides of the body are patterned with numerous irregular white blotches that often extend onto the head in the region behind the angle of the jaws. The dorsum is either unmarked or has small white flecks that are much smaller than the lateral blotches. Distinct red blotches are occasionally located behind the shoulders. These are more common on juveniles than on adults. The chin is whitish, and the belly and undersurface of the tail are slate-gray. Juveniles resemble adults in general color and pattern.

Wehrle's salamander is a slender species with a tendency to become more robust with increasing size and age. The legs are short but well developed. The tail of adults is as long as, or slightly longer than, the body. It is stout and circular in cross section and tapers to a point. The head is flattened and moderately distinct from the body. Adults average 66 mm ($2\frac{5}{8}$ in.) SVL, and males and females do not differ in size in northern Pennsylvania (Hall and Stafford 1972). Pauley and England (1969), however, reported significant size differences between the sexes for Wehrle's salamanders from northern West Virginia, with females longer than males. Conant and Collins (1991) reported a maximum size of 152 mm (6 in.) ToL. Tail length is similar for both sexes and averages 102.1% of SVL. As is frequently the case in salamanders, juveniles have relatively shorter tails than adults.

Confusing Species. Wehrle's salamander may be mistaken for the northern slimy salamander (Plate 37), but it differs from it in that the white blotches are restricted to the sides and that the chin is pale rather than black. Wehrle's salamander can be distinguished from both the valley and ridge salamander and the ravine salamander by the presence of large irregular blotches along the sides of the body rather than small whitish or silvery flecks.

Habitat and Habits. Wehrle's salamander is primarily an inhabitant of mature forest communities, including mixed deciduous, mixed hardwood-conifer, and conifer forests. Mature forests have a closed canopy and reduced herbaceous ground cover, both of which appear to be requirements for Wehrle's salamander. An additional requirement of large populations is an abundance of rocks on the surface or rocky outcrops associated with surface rocks. Although Wehrle's salamander may occasionally be found under bark or logs, the majority of individuals are found under rocks. When environmental conditions are appropriate, this species can reach very high population numbers. A Tioga County, Pennsylvania, population had an estimated density of about 1,000 animals/ha (412 animals/acre), with a biomass of between 1.5 and 3 kg/ha (0.9–2 lb/acre) (Hall and Stafford 1972). The population was located in a woodlot and therefore may not be representative of populations found in mature forest.

Wehrle's salamander tends to be found in upland habitats rather than in forested areas near streams or other bodies of water. Soils in these areas tend to be rocky or sandy and have reduced water-holding capacity. Pauley (1978b) demonstrated that Wehrle's salamander is better adapted than the closely related redback salamander to dry environments. Wehrle's salamanders were able to lose a higher percentage of body weight due to dehydration and survive than were redback salamanders. They also lost water at a lower rate than the redback salamanders.

In Pennsylvania, surface activity begins in early April and ceases around the middle of November. Unusually warm weather can, however, extend the season at either end. Wehrle's salamander appears to be less affected by summer climatic conditions than are many other species of woodland salamander (e.g., ravine salamander and valley and ridge salamander). Specimens can be found under cover objects even in July and August. As a result, the species exhibits a unimodal annual activity cycle. Wehrle's salamander will occasionally be found active at night, especially on cold evenings after a rainstorm.

We have never found the hibernation site for this species, but they probably seek refuge from cold weather underground in cracks and crevices of rocky areas.

Although no specific studies on the movement patterns of Wehrle's salamander have been performed, Hall and Stafford (1972) suggested that movement during the activity season is very limited. They base this conclusion on the fact that three marked animals that were recaptured a total of eight times were, in every instance, found under the same rock where they had originally been captured.

Wehrle's salamander may not have as varied a diet as some woodland salamanders. In a sample of 17 individuals, food items were primarily ants, beetles, and insect larvae. This is similar to the findings of Pauley (1978a) for a sample from West Virginia. He did, however, find a marked dietary shift with age. Springtails constituted almost 25% of the diet of juveniles but were absent from the diet of adults. Hall (1976) reported a remarkable degree of specialization in the diet of this species in north-central Pennsylvania. Fifty percent of the summer prey items found in a sample from Tioga County, Pennsylvania, was made up exclusively of an introduced insect, the European strawberry weevil. The remaining prey items were a wide range of invertebrates, none of which made up a significant contribution to the total diet of the population.

Reproduction. Courtship and mating have not been observed or reported for this species. The timing of mating appears to vary from region to region. In West Virginia, mating occurs in March and April (Pauley and England 1969), whereas in northern Pennsylvania Hall and Stafford (1972) suggested that mating is in the fall. These basic differences are also reflected in the vitellogenic cycle of the female. Northern Pennsylvania females begin vitellogenesis in late May or early June, and by the end of October the follicles are of ovulatory size (4 mm; $\frac{1}{8}$ in.). Hall and Stafford reported egg laying during hibernation. In West Virginia, vitellogenesis apparently begins in the fall. Individuals emerge from hibernation with large (2.5 mm; $\frac{1}{10}$ in.) ovarian follicles, which complete the vitellogenic process by the end of March or the beginning of April. Oviposition occurs in late March or April (Pauley and England 1969). It is not known whether the population of Wehrle's salamander from southern Pennsylvania has a reproductive cycle similar to that reported for the northern Pennsylvania populations or to that of West Virginia populations.

Clutch size ranges from 7 to 24 eggs and is positively correlated with female SVL (Hall and Stafford 1972).

Eggs are apparently laid in subterranean retreats and are presumably tended by females, as is commonly the case in woodland salamanders. Wehrle's salamander exhibits direct development and lacks a free-living larval stage. Hall and Stafford reported hatchlings emerging in March. Hatchlings are about 16 mm ($\frac{5}{8}$ in.) SVL.

Hall and Stafford (1972) reported an annual reproductive cycle for females from Pennsylvania. This is rather unusual for woodland salamanders, as most members of the genus exhibit a biennial cycle, especially in the northern portion of their ranges. The annual cycle might be a function of the timing of oviposition. Most woodland species lay their eggs in either spring or summer, when metabolic demands are fairly high and the females are prevented from foraging for food at a time optimal for most prey items found in their diet. This timing presumably results in a reduction in nutritional intake and the necessity of an additional year to recover before the next cycle. Wehrle's salamander, on the other hand, lays eggs in the winter, when metabolic costs are at their lowest and when salamanders would not normally be foraging for food. As a consequence, they have the entire activity season to obtain sufficient resources to reproduce every year.

Males from the southern portion of Pennsylvania mature at a SVL of about 50 mm (2 in.), whereas animals from the north mature at about 60–62 mm ($2\frac{3}{8}$ in.) SVL. Females statewide appear to mature at about 60 mm ($2\frac{3}{8}$ in.) SVL.

Remarks. Several literature records of this species from Pennsylvania are incorrect. In the original description (H. Fowler and Dunn 1917), it was reported from Juniata County. This report was based on a misidentified northern slimy salamander. Wehrle's salamander does not occur east of the Allegheny Front. Lachner (1942) reported Wehrle's salamander from Mercer County; this report, too, was based on a misidentified northern slimy salamander. Wehrle's salamander is absent from most of the western portion of the Allegheny Plateau.

Distribution. Wehrle's salamander ranges from extreme southwestern New York southward through central western Pennsylvania and extreme southeastern Ohio through most of West Virginia and the extreme western section of the Maryland panhandle. Its range terminates in North Carolina just south of the Virginia border.

In Pennsylvania, Wehrle's salamander primarily occurs in the fairly mountainous eastern and northern segment of the Allegheny Plateau. It is found outside the Allegheny Mountains in northwestern Greene County along Tenmile Creek near the town of Jefferson.

Pseudotriton
Gr. *pseudes*, false; Gr. *triton*, newt

The genus *Pseudotriton* (red and mud salamanders) contains two species. *Pseudotriton* is found exclusively in the United States. It ranges from northern Pennsylvania and southern New York southward to the Gulf of Mexico.

Mud and red salamanders are moderate to large, stout-bodied animals. When young, they are a brilliant red, but they tend to darken with age. They are semiaquatic species that inhabit both muddy and clear-flowing water and nearby terrestrial habitats.

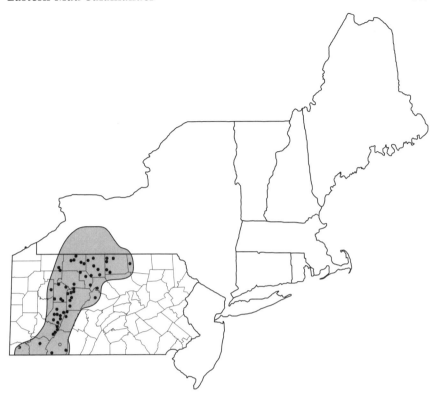

Map 21.   Distribution of Wehrle's salamander *(Plethodon wehrlei).*

Both species feed on a variety of aquatic and terrestrial invertebrates. Eggs are laid in the water, and there is a larval stage.

Eastern Mud Salamander *Pseudotriton montanus montanus* Baird

L. *mont,* belonging to a mountain

Description.   The eastern mud salamander (Plate 38) is a moderate to large species. It exhibits considerable ontogenetic color variation. Recently transformed individuals and young adults have a dorsal background color of bright coral red, but with age the dorsum become suffused with brown so that the overall color changes to muddy red. The ventral surfaces of the throat, body, and appendages are orange with a tinge of red. All dorsal surfaces are patterned with scattered distinct black spots, some of which may be as large as the eye. The ventral surfaces are immaculate in young individuals, but with age they develop scattered black flecks.

This is a stout-bodied species, with small but well-developed limbs. The tail, although circular in cross section at the base, rapidly becomes laterally compressed and keeled distally. Bruce (1975) reported the mean

SVL of mature females from South Carolina as 72.4 mm (3 in.). Mature males from the same area averaged 61.0 mm (2¼ in.). Conant and Collins (1991) reported the maximum size for this species as 207 mm (8¼ in.) ToL.

Confusing Species.   The eastern mud salamander bears a superficial resemblance to the red eft stage of the red-spotted newt, but the eft's dry skin and lack of costal grooves are sufficient to distinguish the two. Eastern mud salamanders and northern red salamanders are very similar, but they may be distinguished by the brown iris of the eastern mud salamander versus the bright yellow iris of the northern red salamander. In addition, eastern mud salamanders have fewer, but larger, dorsal spots, with little tendency for the spots to fuse, even in older individuals.

Habitat and Habits.   Virtually nothing is known about the biology of eastern mud salamanders in the Northeast. As a result, this section and the one on reproduction rely heavily on the few literature reports from other portions of its range.

This species is found in or near muddy floodplain streams, muddy seeps and springs, streams in swamps, and forested areas in the vicinity of the above habitats. In Pennsylvania, the species has been found only in hemlock-mountain laurel habitat in the vicinity of streams.

Nothing is known about the length of the activity period or about the diet of this species. Presumably, they are similar to the activity period and diet of the northern red salamander.

Reproduction.   Little is known about the reproductive biology of this species, and what is known pertains to southern, rather than northern, populations.

T. Robinson and Reichard (1965) provide the only description of a possible mating for this species. A pair was found clasping each other under a small piece of limestone in a Kentucky stream in late September. Bruce (1975) suggested a fall mating season, noting that males from South Carolina had vas deferens packed with sperm from August through November. He noted that females oviposit in autumn and winter but was unable to locate specific oviposition sites. On the basis of dissection, he determined that clutch size ranged from 77 to 192 eggs and was positively correlated with female body size.

South Carolina females mature at 4 to 5 years of age and reproduce at irregular intervals thereafter (Bruce 1975).

Remarks.   Controversy exists concerning the significance of the red body coloration in the eastern mud salamander. Brandon and colleagues (1979) suggested that these salamanders are moderately distasteful and that the red coloration acts as a warning to potential predators. However, Pough (1974) and Brodie (1976) suggested that eastern mud salamanders are Batesian mimics of the highly noxious red eft stage of the red-spotted newt.

Distribution.   The eastern mud salamander inhabits the Coastal plain and Piedmont from southern New Jersey to central Georgia and southern South Carolina.

Map 22. Distribution of the eastern mud salamander *(Pseudotriton montanus montanus)*.

Until recently, the only record of the species from Pennsylvania was the type-locality of "South Mountain near Carlisle (Cumberland County) Pennsylvania." A specimen was recently collected from Caledonia State Park, Franklin County (McCoy 1992).

Northern Red Salamander *Pseudotriton ruber ruber* (Latreille)
L. *rubeo,* to be red
Description.   The northern red salamander (Plate 39) is a moderately large species with stout body proportions. As is typical of many salamander species, northern red salamanders exhibit significant ontogenetic change in color and pattern. In recently transformed individuals and young adults, dorsal and lateral coloration is a brilliant coral to scarlet red, and the lower sides and venter are apricot (pinkish beige). The head, back, and proximal half of the tail are profusely covered with round to slightly irregular black spots. On young individuals, spots tend to be absent from the lower sides and ventral surfaces, although the chin usually bears a margin of fine black flecks. With age, the coloration undergoes a general darkening, and dorsal and lateral spots enlarge and fuse, producing a murky pur-

plish brown coloration. The sides and venter darken and become salmon red. Along with this change in color, numerous black spots appear on the venter and lower sides of most individuals. Spotting also occurs on the distal half of the tail. The basic ground color of larvae is brownish with dark mottling (Plate 40). As larvae age, the background color begins to take on a reddish tinge, but the brilliant red color does not develop until after transformation.

The northern red salamander is stout, with proportionately small, but strongly developed, limbs. The head is moderately large and slightly distinct from the body. The tail is laterally compressed and possesses a distinct dorsal keel. Males are significantly smaller than females, averaging 77.2 mm ($2\frac{7}{8}$ in.) SVL and 124 mm (5 in.) ToL. Females average 83.5 mm ($3\frac{3}{8}$ in.) SVL and 131.7 mm ($5\frac{1}{4}$ in.) ToL. The maximum size for the species is a female from Maryland that measured 180 mm ($7\frac{1}{4}$ in.) ToL (J. Hardy and Mork 1950). Pennsylvania specimens have a short tail. In both sexes, tail length is approximately 60% of SVL.

Confusing Species.   Northern red salamanders differ from the red eft of the red-spotted newt in that the skin is moist and smooth rather than dry and granular, and they have costal grooves and nasolabial grooves. The northern red salamander is very similar in appearance to the eastern mud salamander, but it differs in having a yellow iris, whereas the eastern mud salamander's iris is brown. Northern red salamanders can be distinguished from spring salamanders by the lack of a well-developed canthus rostralis.

Habitat and Habits.   Northern red salamanders require clear, cool streams and springs that are fairly shallow, with rock-strewn bottoms. These may vary from tiny permanent springs to moderate and large-sized streams and creeks. Usually they are found in forested regions of considerable topographic relief, but they may occasionally occur in flatland swampy areas or open marshy regions.

Except during very cold weather, adults are generally not found in the water but are usually under rocks and other cover items such as bark, logs, and moss. Individuals remain under cover, except during and shortly after periods of heavy rain, when they may be encountered on the surface, often in large numbers. Surface activity is most frequent at night.

Although most often found in the vicinity of streams, northern red salamanders may occasionally occur as much as 300 or more meters (>930 ft) from the nearest suitable water.

In streams that do not freeze, adults are active all year, returning to water during the cold months and resuming terrestrial activity during the rest of the year. Collection records suggest that adults are most active in April and May and again in August.

Adults feed on a wide variety of invertebrates as well as on other salamanders. The main items in the diet of adults include isopods, worms, and beetle larvae. The larvae feed on a number of invertebrates typical of stream habitats, including chironomid fly larvae, seed clams (*Pisidium*), mayfly nymphs, stonefly nymphs, and caddisfly larvae. The nature of the prey suggests that the larvae forage primarily under and around large rocks and cobble in the stream.

Some controversy has arisen concerning the function and evolutionary significance of the brilliant red coloration of this species. Brandon and colleagues (1979) suggested that the species is moderately distasteful and that the red coloration functions to warn potential predators of its unpalatable nature. Other workers (Brodie 1976, Pough 1974) suggested that northern red salamanders are mimics of the highly noxious red eft of the eastern newt and, as such, gain a degree of protection from predators that have learned to avoid efts. Pough based his conclusion on the fact that northern red salamanders living in areas where red efts are absent never possess the brilliant coloration typical of the species. In addition, he noted that as animals get significantly larger than efts, their coloration darkens and becomes more cryptic.

Reproduction. Little is known about the reproductive biology of this species, especially in the northern portion of its range. Organ and Organ (1968) described courtship. Both courtship and oviposition occur over an extended period of time. In the southern United States, courtship occurs throughout much of the summer (Bruce 1978). Bruce also reported a sex ratio skewed in favor of males, but samples from Pennsylvania do not differ significantly from 1:1.

Reproduction is annual. Vitellogenesis appears to begin either in the fall or in early spring, and by late July females possess yolked follicles of ovulatory size. In the Northeast, oviposition takes place from August to late October. Eggs are placed on the underside of rocks in springs and streams, fastened by narrow gelatinous stalks. Eggs vary from 3.5 to 4 mm ($\frac{1}{8}$ in.) in diameter, and with associated membranes and envelopes measure between 6 and 7 mm ($\frac{1}{4}$ in.). The yolk is pale yellow. Ovarian complement indicates that clutch size in Pennsylvania varies between 50 and 102 eggs ($X = 78.8 \pm 7.7$; $N = 8$) and is positively correlated with female body size. This is similar to the clutch size (70 eggs) reported by Bruce (1978) for a population from the Blue Ridge Mountains.

Larvae hatch in late fall or early winter. Hatchlings measure 11–13 mm (ca. $\frac{1}{2}$ in.) SVL and 20–24 mm ($\frac{7}{8}$–1 in.) ToL (Martof 1975). Little is known about the larval ecology of this species. The number of distinct size classes of larvae in large samples suggests that larval life ranges from 3 years in the South to 3 or 4 years in the North. The size at transformation in this species is exceedingly variable. Recently transformed individuals may be as small as 43 mm (1$\frac{3}{4}$ in.) SVL. We have, however, seen some larvae with well-developed gills that have SVLs in excess of 60 mm (2$\frac{3}{8}$ in.) and ToLs of more than 105 mm (4$\frac{1}{4}$ in.). The reason for this great variation in size at transformation remains unclear.

The smallest reproductive female in Pennsylvania measured 75 mm (3 in.) SVL; males mature at 60–65 mm (2$\frac{3}{8}$–2$\frac{5}{8}$ in.) SVL. This is larger than the size for southern populations; in the South, males mature at about 53 mm (2$\frac{1}{8}$ in.), and females achieve maturity at sizes ranging from 55 to 65 mm (2$\frac{1}{4}$–2$\frac{5}{8}$ in.) (Bruce 1978).

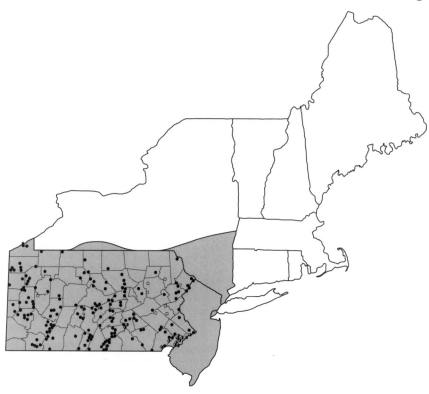

Map 23. Distribution of the northern red salamander *(Pseudotriton ruber ruber)*.

Distribution. The range of the northern red salamander extends from southern New York and eastern Ohio southward to northern South Carolina and northern Georgia and Alabama.

Northern red salamanders reach their northern distributional limit in extreme southern New York. They barely enter the southern-tier counties of western and central New York. However, the species occurs throughout southeastern New York exclusive of Long Island. It ranges to east-central New York along the Hudson River valley. It occurs throughout the states of Pennsylvania and New Jersey.

Toads and Frogs

Toads and frogs belong to the amphibian order Anura. This is the largest order of amphibians, with over 4,100 described species divided among 20 to 27 families, depending on what scheme of classification is used. Anurans have a cosmopolitan distribution; they are found on all the continents except Antarctica and on most of the major islands and island groups of the world. They reach their greatest abundance and diversity in the tropical regions of Africa, Asia, and the New World. There are 8 families and approximately 88 species in the United States, with 4 families and 18 species occurring in the northeastern United States.

All anurans have the same basic body plan. They have a shortened body and a vertebral column that allows for very little dorsoventral or lateral movement of the body. A neck is not apparent. The head is broad and flat and terminates in a large mouth. As adults, frogs lack a tail. Two pairs of legs are present, with the hind legs more strongly developed than the forelegs. Jumping is the primary means of locomotion, although squat species (such as toads) with short hind legs tend to either hop or walk. Toads (Family Bufonidae) are a subset of anurans. They differ from most other anurans by possessing a dry skin, pronounced parotoid glands behind the eyes, and numerour "warts" on the dorsal surface of the body and appendages.

Anurans occupy a very wide range of habitats and are found from tropical to boreal forest and from swamps and marshes to deserts. They occur at elevations of greater than 4,500 m (14,000 ft). Although many are associated with permanent bodies of water, others utilize temporary water or are found in the vicinity of water only during the reproductive season.

Anurans tend to be generalized carnivores, feeding on any animal of appropriate size. A few species, however, have a more specialized diet. The larvae exhibit a greater diversity of feeding regimes, with many of them being herbivores, omnivores, or detritivores.

Courtship usually occurs in or near water. Males vocalize to attract females. Fertilization is external (except in a few rare cases), and the eggs are usually laid in an aquatic situation. Most species have indirect development with an aquatic larval stage, but several species exhibit direct development with the larval stage occurring within the egg.

PELOBATIDAE (SPADEFOOTS)

The family Pelobatidae is a small group (10 genera and 95 species) of primitive frogs with a relictual distribution in North America, Eurasia, and Southeast Asia. There are six North American species, all members of the genus *Scaphiopus*. They are primarily distributed in the arid and semiarid portions of the western United States and the Mexican Plateau, but one species ranges into the eastern states. All are burrowing frogs that spend most of their adult lives underground. They are explosive breeders, responding to torrential rains by assembling en masse to breed in temporary pools. The larval period is characteristically short, and transformation may be accelerated by drying of the breeding pools.

Scaphiopus
Gr. *scaphan,* a spade; Gr. *pus,* foot

The genus *Scaphiopus* (the spadefoots) has six species. Spadefoots are found throughout most of the United States and adjacent south-central Canada; their range extends southward to southern Mexico.

Spadefoots are small to moderate-sized frogs with a squat, stout body, short but powerful hind legs, and a single well-developed metatarsal spade. They have vertically elliptical pupils and smooth skin with either no or poorly developed parotoid glands. Spadefoots tend to inhabit arid or semi-arid habitats. Even in the more humid eastern United States, they are found primarily in sandy or gravelly soil. They use their well-developed metatarsal spade to burrow vertically down in the soil, where they spend most of their time.

Spadefoots are generalized carnivores, feeding on most invertebrates found in the vicinity of their breeding ponds. Spadefoots are explosive breeders, emerging from their subterranean retreats in response to heavy rainstorms. They breed in temporary ponds, but within one to three days after emergence, all reproductive activity ceases. Development is rapid; the time between laying and transformation is as little as 8 days for some desert species.

Skin secretions can cause allergic reactions (sneezing and nasal discharge) in humans. These secretions can also irritate mucous membranes, so it is wise to wash one's hands after handling them.

Eastern Spadefoot *Scaphiopus holbrookii holbrookii* (Harlan)
Named for John E. Holbrook, an early nineteenth-century herpetologist, author of *Herpetology of North America* (1842)
Description.   The eastern spadefoot (Plate 41) is a stout-bodied frog. The dorsal ground color varies from dark brown or gray to almost sooty black. Two irregular, light dorsal stripes extend from the eyes to the sacrum. These stripes are closest together in the middle of the back, like reversed parentheses. The sides of the body and legs are mottled with spots of light pigment, as are the sides of the head. The venter is dirty gray or white.

The body is squat and stout. Both forelegs and hind legs are short and heavy. The head is short and broad, and the snout is round when viewed from above. The eyes are large and protuberant and are placed high on the sides of the head. The pupil, when expanded, is circular. When it contracts, it becomes vertically elliptical. The iris of the eye is a striking greenish yellow. The skin of the head is fused to the underlying cranial bones. Cranial crests are lacking. Parotoid glands are present, but they are small, round, and inconspicuous. The dorsal skin contains scattered small warts, and the ventral skin is smooth. The toes of the hind feet are webbed, and webbing extends almost to the tip of the longest toe. The inner metatarsal tubercle is a wide, sharp, and heavily cornified black "spade," hence the common name.

Sexual dimorphism in the eastern spadefoot is minimal. The single, median vocal sac is visible only when males are calling. During the breeding season, males develop black cornifications on the first three fingers of the forefeet.

In Pennsylvania, Cumberland and Northumberland county individuals average 54.3 mm ($2\frac{1}{2}$ in.) SUL. A sample of 10 mature males from Connecticut ranged in size from 52 to 64 mm SUL (X = 59.1 mm), and 6 females ranged from 55 to 67 mm SUL (X = 61.0) (Klemens 1993). The record size is 73 mm ($2\frac{7}{8}$ in.) SUL (Conant and Collins 1991).

Tadpoles of the eastern spadefoot are small, seldom if ever exceeding 30 mm ($1\frac{1}{2}$ in.) ToL. The eyes are located on the top of the head and are close together. Coloration varies from dark brown to bronze. The nonmuscular portions of the tail (i.e., tail crest or fin) are translucent and moderately well developed.

Confusing Species. Because of its toadlike shape, the eastern spadefoot might be confused with the true toads (*Bufo*) that occur in the Northeast. It can be distinguished from true toads by its vertically elliptical pupil, indistinct parotoid glands, and smooth ventral skin.

Habitat and Habits. The unpredictable nature and extremely short duration of this frog's surface activity make this an exceedingly difficult species to study. As a consequence, even though it is widely distributed in the eastern United States, very little information is available about its biology and virtually nothing is known about its natural history in the Northeast.

In the Northeast, the eastern spadefoot is an inhabitant of sandy soils along the floodplains of streams and rivers and in agricultural fields. Seasonal activity is variable and is dependent upon the frequency and intensity of rainfall. Eastern spadefoots initiate surface activity only after heavy rains (Pearson 1955). In Pennsylvania, they have been found on the surface in April, May, July, and August. This is similar to the activity periods reported by Klemens (1993) for Connecticut. In all cases, heavy rainstorms immediately preceded these bouts of activity. Pearson (1955) reported that individuals in Florida were active only 8% of the year, with the remaining time being spent in underground retreats. He recorded the longest period of inactivity as 109 days. In the Northeast, it is possible that animals remain inactive for more than 200 days. The eastern spadefoot is almost exclusively nocturnal. Individuals are only rarely found active during the daylight.

Presumably, eastern spadefoots hibernate in their subterranean retreats. Eastern spadefoots possess an interesting mechanism for burrowing in the soft soils they inhabit. They shuffle their hind legs back and forth while sitting on the substrate. The large spades on their feet scrape the soil away from under them and move it up on the sides. As a result, they simply sink out of sight as they burrow straight down. The depth of burrows in the Northeast is unknown, but Pearson (1955) reported a maximum depth of 300 mm (12 in.) in a population from Florida. Pearson (1955) also reported an average home range of about 12 m^2 (14 yd^2).

Eastern spadefoots are insectivorous, feeding primarily on the caterpillars of butterflies and moths and on adult beetles (Whitaker et al. 1977). Punzo (1992) in Florida reported a high degree of dietary overlap between eastern spadefoots and the southern toad. The same high degree of dietary overlap occurs, in all probability, between eastern spadefoots and American and Fowler's toads.

Reproduction. Eastern spadefoots have no definitive season for courtship, mating, and egg laying. The timing of these activities is dependent upon heavy rains. Reproductive activity has been reported in April, July, and August in Pennsylvania. In the southern portion of this species' range, reproduction can occur at almost any time of the year. Pearson (1955) reported mating in September, February, April, and August in northern Florida. Raithel (in Klemens 1993) stated that to the best of his knowledge Rhode Island eastern spadefoots bred in only two years between 1979 and 1991.

When reproduction occurs, it is explosive, usually lasting one or two nights. Reproductive activity occurs in small rain-filled ponds, often along the edge of streams and rivers or in agricultural fields. Mating choruses within a given area will develop more than once a year if climatic conditions are appropriate. It is not known, however, if individual eastern spadefoots engage in reproductive activity more than once a year.

Males call while floating spread-legged in the water. Freyburger (1941) reported up to 200 males calling from a single pond in central Pennsylvania. When a receptive female approaches, the male grasps her around the waist, rather than around the chest, as is typical of other Pennsylvania frogs. Once in amplexus, the female swims with the male to a suitable oviposition site. Eggs are generally laid in shallow water and are attached to either emergent or submergent vegetation. The eggs are laid in bands 25–50 mm (1–2 in.) wide and up to 300 mm (12 in.) long (Wright and Wright 1949). The eggs are small, only 1.4–2 mm ($\frac{1}{16}-\frac{1}{8}$ in.) in diameter.

Developmental time is temperature dependent, with length of time decreasing as temperature increases. Hatching can occur in as little as 24 hours, or it can take as long as 7 days (Richmond 1947). The time from hatching to metamorphosis ranges from 28 to 63 days (Drivers 1936, Richmond 1947). Richmond suggested that most spring reproduction in eastern spadefoots from West Virginia is unsuccessful because ponds dry before development proceeds to metamorphosis.

Tadpoles often form large aggregations. The function of these aggregations is not known, but they may involve thermoregulation. Toadlets transform at an average size of 12.5 mm ($\frac{1}{2}$ in.) (Rubin 1965). Unlike adults, newly transformed young are active during the daytime. They spend one or more weeks in the vicinity of their larval ponds foraging for insects and other small invertebrates attracted to the margins of the ponds.

Both males and females reach maturity at about 50 mm (2 in.) SUL (Wright and Wright 1949).

Remarks. Klemens (1993) considered the eastern spadefoot to be the rarest anuran in southern New England. It is one of the least common anuran species in Pennsylvania; however, it may be more commonly distributed within Pennsylvania than is apparent. Its infrequent and unpredictable surface activity, however, make it a species that is unlikely to be encountered. The best time to see this species is during and immediately after extremely heavy rains in the late spring and summer.

Distribution. The eastern spadefoot is widely distributed in the southern and eastern United States, ranging from Florida to the Mississippi Valley, northward to southern Illinois and southern Ohio, and along the Atlantic Coastal Plain northward to Cape Cod.

In the Northeast, the eastern spadefoot is found in coastal and lowland areas of Connecticut, Rhode Island, Massachusetts, New York, and New Jersey. There is a disjunct population in east-central New York along the Hudson River valley. In Pennsylvania, a few scattered and localized populations have been recorded in the Cumberland and Susquehanna valleys (to Northumberland County). The species has been reported, without voucher specimens, in the Delaware Valley from the Philadelphia area northward into Monroe County. If eastern spadefoots did actually occur in this region in times past, they have probably been extirpated owing to urban development and industrialization.

BUFONIDAE (TRUE TOADS)

The true toads occur on all major land masses within the range of amphibians, although their presence in New Guinea and Australia is due to the

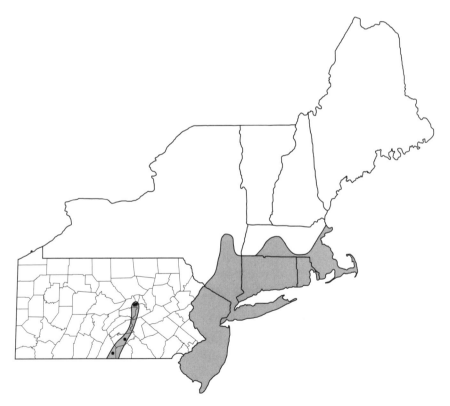

Map 24. Distribution of the eastern spadefoot *(Scaphiopus holbrooki holbrooki)*.

introduction of the cane toad (*Bufo marinus*, a large species native to South America) as a possible biological control for insect pests in sugar cane fields. This attempt was unsuccessful.

Although most members of the family are contained in the genus *Bufo* (with over 200 species), there are radiations of specialized genera (about 32 genera and 180 species) in the highlands of South America, in eastern and western Africa, and in Southeast Asia. These specialized genera often look decidedly un-toadlike. Some are long and slender and are brightly colored, with smooth, nonwarty skin.

Toads typically lay very large complements (thousands) of small eggs in a great variety of aquatic habitats. The larvae are small, toxic, and unpalatable and have relatively short developmental times. Some species, however, have direct development so that miniatures of the adult hatch out of the eggs. Some toads even have internal fertilization (a great rarity in anurans) and give birth to young rather than lay eggs.

Bufo
L. *bufonis*, a toad

The genus *Bufo* (toad) has approximately 206 species. Toads are one of the most widely distributed genera of anurans in the world. They occur throughout North and South America, Africa, Europe, and Asia as well as on numerous islands in the Caribbean and Indian Ocean.

Toads range in size from small (less than 20 mm [$\frac{3}{4}$ in.]; for example, the oak toad, *Bufo quercus*) to huge (more than 200 mm [8 in.]; for example, the cane toad, *Bufo marinus*). Whether large or small, toads are squat, robust animals, with short, thick legs, far better designed for hopping or walking than for jumping. Although a few are brightly colored, most have subdued coloration. Many species have a heavily cornified, thick epidermis that allows them to carry out a more terrestrial existence than is usual for an anuran. As might be expected in such a large genus, toads occupy a wide variety of environments. Some species are found in lush tropical rain forests, while others are common in hot, dry deserts where rain may occur no more then once every two years.

Toads primarily feed on insects and other invertebrates. Mating occurs in both temporary and permanent bodies of water. Most species lay large numbers of small eggs that are packaged in long strands. The eggs hatch rapidly, and developmental time is fairly short. Tadpoles are small, dark brown or black, and toxic.

Eastern American Toad *Bufo americanus americanus* Holbrook
Named for America, alluding to the geographic location of the species
Description.   The eastern American toad (Plate 42) is the toad familiar to most people. The dorsal ground color is extremely variable, ranging from bright yellow to almost black, but the most common hues are warm reddish browns. The color of individuals can also vary depending upon the temperature and light intensity of the environment. There are three or

four pairs of large, black spots on either side of the midline of the back. Each spot contains one or two large warts. A middorsal stripe, if present, is indistinct, not sharp edged. The sides of the body are lighter than the dorsum and exhibit dark mottling. The venter is dirty cream-colored and is marked with numerous black spots on the chest and throat.

The body is squat and stout, and the legs short and heavy. The head is broad, and the eyes are prominent with a circular pupil that may appear horizontal owing to darker pigmentation of the golden iris in front of and behind the pupil. Cranial crests are well developed and have postorbital branches in front of the parotoid glands. The parotids are prominent, elongate, and parallel and are separated from the postorbital crests or touch them only by a spur. The skin of the back, the sides, and the dorsal surfaces of the legs is covered with cornified warts of all sizes. The ventral skin is coarsely granular but not warty. The toes of the hind feet are moderately webbed, and there are prominent inner and outer metatarsal tubercles.

Sexual size dimorphism in the eastern American toad is extreme, with females larger than males. At one breeding pond, calling males averaged 59.0 mm ($2\frac{3}{8}$ in.) SUL, and gravid females averaged 78.0 ± 2.1 mm ($3\frac{1}{8}$ in.) SUL. The record size for the species is 111 mm ($4\frac{3}{8}$ in.) SUL (Conant and Collins 1991). In addition to the size difference, males can usually be distinguished from females by darker pigmentation on the throat.

Tadpoles are small, seldom exceeding 30 mm ($1\frac{1}{4}$ in.) ToL. The body and muscular portion of the tail are black or dark brown. The nonmuscular tail fin is generally translucent and somewhat smoky in color. The tail fin is rounded, and the tail is short.

Confusing Species. The eastern American toad and Fowler's toad are easily confused, and the sporadic occurrence of hybrids between the species adds to the confusion. The eastern American toad has one or two large warts in each dark spot on the dorsum, a spotted chest, and parotoid glands that are either separated from the cranial crests or connected to them by a spur. The eastern spadefoot is similar in form, but the eastern American toad has round pupils, distinct parotoid glands, and a rough venter.

Habitat and Habits. The eastern American toad and its close relative, Fowler's toad, are the most terrestrial of our anurans. Except during the breeding season, eastern American toads usually are not found in the vicinity of water and can be found up to several kilometers away from the nearest source of water. They are habitat generalists. Out of the breeding season, they can be found in fairly open, upland habitats such as fields, meadows, and rocky hillsides. They are also common on agricultural land and in suburban backyards. These toads are less frequently encountered in forests.

Eastern American toads emerge from hibernation in early March, stimulated by the first "warm" rains of spring. Activity rapidly reaches a peak at breeding sites in late March and early April. After breeding, adults disperse into the surrounding countryside, where they maintain a high level of activity throughout the summer. Prolonged periods of drought, however, will dramatically reduce surface activity, and toads may occasionally be found huddled in small depressions that they construct under rocks. Activity remains high into September and early October, when animals begin to enter their winter retreats. They hibernate in subterranean retreats, often of their own construction.

Eastern American toads are active both day and night. Diurnal activity is more common during cooler temperatures but may occasionally occur on hot days. Nocturnal activity tends to occur throughout the animal's activity season, with reduced activity during periods of extreme cold early in the year. Precipitation greatly increases the level of surface activity.

Eastern American toads employ both active and sit-and-wait foraging techniques. They can often be observed moving about the habitat apparently searching for food. If a toad encounters a large concentration of food, however, it will remain stationary and catch prey using short lunges and rapid flicks of the tongue. It is very common to find one or more eastern American toads sitting at the base of a lighted utility pole or underneath a camp lantern gorging on insects attracted by the light. Some toads return night after night to the same light to forage.

Eastern American toads are generalized carnivores, feeding mainly on insects. In a sample ($N = 34$) of adults from Pennsylvania, the major food items were ants and beetles, with grasshoppers, millipedes, isopods, and spiders making up a smaller percentage. Around human habitation and in agricultural areas, eastern American toads eat cucumber beetles, potato beetles, and the caterpillars of a variety of butterflies and moths that feed on crops. Recently hatched juveniles also have a varied diet, but, as one would expect, it is composed of smaller animals. They feed on the following items in descending order of importance: fly larvae, mites, ants, beetles, thrips, and springtails (Hamilton 1930).

Both males and females reduce their dietary intake during the spring reproductive season. It is rare to find a gravid female with food in her stomach, and calling males usually have few food items.

Reproduction.   Eastern American toads begin reproductive activity shortly after emergence from hibernation in March, and April is the month with the greatest intensity of reproductive activity. Males usually begin to call within a day or two of emerging (Plate 43). The reproductive season is extended. It is not unusual to find some animals still engaged in calling and egg laying in the middle of May.

Males select a wide array of habitats from which to call. They utilize both temporary and permanent bodies of water. Temporary water includes roadside ditches and small to medium-sized ponds and pools in woodlands and fields. In permanent situations, they call from marshes, swamps and small ponds as well as the margins of large lakes. In coastal areas, they have been reported to occasionally utilize brackish water habitats (Kivat and Stapleton 1983, Klemens 1993). Some individuals also utilize the slow-moving sections and quiet backwaters of streams and rivers. Males generally call while in the water, close to shore, and usually facing away from the shoreline.

The call is a long trill. Males clasp virtually anything of sufficient diameter that enters their vicinity. If another male is grasped, it will struggle and emit a low rapid "release call" that causes its body to strongly vibrate. This is a signal to the clasping male to cease amplexus. Nonreceptive females also give a release call if clasped. When a receptive female is grasped, she moves off with the male clasped firmly around her chest (Plate 44). The female extrudes a long, double strand of eggs, which are fertilized as they are laid (Plate 45). The female may move slowly around while laying her eggs or remain relatively stationary. If she remains stationary, the egg strands form a large tangled mass at the bottom. Oviposition usually occurs in shallow water.

Hatching is temperature dependent and may occur in as little as 2 days. Developmental time is fairly short, and toadlets begin to emerge at the end of May or the beginning of June. Emergence may continue until the middle of July.

Eastern American toad tadpoles are gregarious, often found in very large aggregations. In some cases, these aggregations engage in feeding activity in which a large group of tadpoles swims slowly near the bottom, stirring up the sediments and suspending food particles in the water column. Tadpoles, before transformation, often congregate in large groups in shallow water, presumably giving them a thermal advantage over single individuals and accelerating the developmental process (Beiswenger 1975).

Newly transformed eastern American toadlets are predominately diurnal in activity and can frequently be seen hopping around the borders of ponds and streams or hiding in cracks and crevices in drying mud or among the vegetation along the water's edge. Heinen (1985) demonstrated that toadlets prefer habitats such as dark soil and vegetated regions where they are difficult to see.

Females attain sexual maturity at about 68 mm ($2\frac{5}{8}$ in.) SUL; males mature at about 50 mm (2 in.). Both males and females are mature by the beginning of their second full growing season.

Remarks.   The eastern American toad and Fowler's toad frequently mate with each other. The hybrid offspring are intermediate in appearance. Hybrids tend to be scattered geographically, but some regions show consistent levels of hybridization. In Indiana, hybrids have been observed in the same area for at least 30 years (J. Jones 1973). Hybridization stops with the first generation of hybrids. They apparently either are sterile or lack the ability to attract mates. This tendency to hybridize can, however, make identification in some areas exceedingly difficult.

Distribution.   The eastern American toad ranges from eastern Canada (Nova Scotia and Labrador) westward to the edge of the Great Plains and southward to northern Georgia, Alabama, Mississippi, and Louisiana.

The eastern American toad is widespread throughout the Northeast. It is, however, absent from Long island and central and southern New jersey, where it is replaced by Fowler's toad. The eastern American toad has been

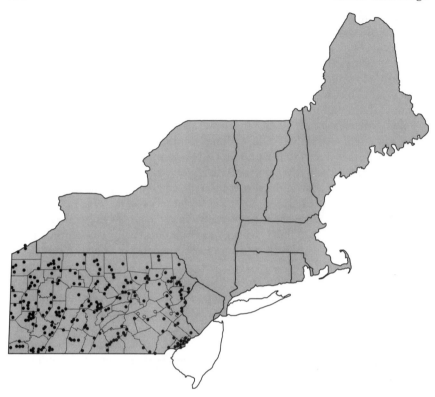

Map 25. Distribution of the eastern American toad *(Bufo americanus americanus).*

recorded in every county in Pennsylvania and is the most commonly encountered anuran in the state.

Fowler's Toad *Bufo woodhousii fowleri* Hinckley
Named for the nineteenth-century naturalists S. W. Woodhouse and
Samuel P. Fowler
Description. Fowler's toad (Plate 46) lacks striking recognition characters. The dorsal ground color is light brown or gray, sometimes with a greenish cast. A series of irregular, paired dark spots occurs on either side of the middorsal line of the back. Each spot contains several (usually four to six) large warts. Frequently there is a thin, light middorsal stripe. The sides are spotted with dark pigment on a light background. The ventral color is dirty cream-colored, usually without spotting or with a single dark spot on the center of the chest.

Fowler's toads, as is typical of the genus, have a squat, stout body, broad head, prominent eyes, and short heavy legs. The cranial crests are well developed, with postorbital branches behind the eyes. The parotoid glands are prominent, elongate, slightly divergent posteriorly, and in broad contact with the postorbital crests. The dorsal skin is covered with various-sized warts, and the ventral skin is rough and granular. The toes of the hind feet are moderately webbed, and the feet possess enlarged inner and outer metatarsal tubercles that are used for digging.

Fowler's toads exhibit sexual dimorphism in several characters. Males have a chin that is noticeably darker than the chest and rest of the ventral surfaces, whereas the chin of females is similar in color to their chest. In addition, males, especially during the reproductive season, have greatly enlarged and cornified patches on the thumb and first finger that are used to clasp females during amplexus. Females are much larger than males. A sample of males from Pennsylvania had a mean 55.7 mm ($2\frac{1}{4}$ in.) SUL, whereas mature females averaged 71.5 mm ($2\frac{7}{8}$ in.) SUL. The maximum size for this species is 95 mm ($3\frac{3}{4}$ in.) (Conant and Collins 1991).

Tadpoles of Fowler's toads are virtually indistinguishable in appearance from those of the eastern American toad.

Confusing Species. Fowler's toad and the eastern American toad may be mistaken for each other. Fowler's toad is usually recognized by the following characters: three or more warts in the largest of the dorsal spots, an unmarked chest, and parotoid glands in contact with the postocular cranial crests. The eastern spadefoot is of similar size and shape, but Fowler's toad can be distinguished from it by the round pupil, distinct parotoid glands, and rough ventral skin.

Habitat and Habits. In the Northeast, Fowler's toad is primarily an inhabitant of lowland areas and is generally found in open habitat where the soil is sandy or gravelly and well drained. As a consequence, most Fowler's toads are found in the vicinity of streams and rivers. It is unusual to find them in either upland habitat or in densely wooded areas.

Unlike the eastern American toad, Fowler's toad does not emerge early in the season. In Pennsylvania, it is unusual to find this species active before the end of April or beginning of May. Activity remains fairly constant from May to the end of summer but drops precipitously in September, and by early October Fowler's toads have entered hibernation. This pattern of seasonal activity in Pennsylvania corresponds closely to the annual activity pattern found in Connecticut (Clarke 1974a). We have not been able to locate specific hibernation sites for this species, but they presumably hibernate buried in sand and loose soil.

Fowler's toad is primarily a nocturnal species, and activity is greatest during and immediately after rainstorms. During the day, it may be encountered in shallow pits constructed in the sand or in depressions dug under cover objects such as logs and rocks.

Fowler's toads are sit-and-wait predators that feed on insects. Studies conducted to determine the food habits of Fowler's toad indicate that they feed primarily on ants and beetles (Bush and Menhinick 1962, Clarke 1974b).

The home range size for Fowler's toad in Connecticut varies from $521\,m^2$ to $2,500\,m^2$ (571–$2,750\,yd^2$). Connecticut individuals tend to occupy the same home range year after year (Clarke 1974c).

Reproduction. In keeping with their late spring emergence, Fowler's toad reproductive activity does not begin until mid-May and usually extends into the latter part of June. Most reproduction occurs in ponds in the vicinity of streams and rivers. Males generally call from the margins of ponds in open water. As does the eastern American toad, Fowler's toads will clasp and enter into amplexus with any animal that comes within their immediate vicinity. As a result, males often enter into amplexus other males. The male being clasped delivers a low-frequency call referred to as a release call, indicating to the clasping male that he is not a receptive female. The release call results in the release of the grasped individual.

Females emerge from hibernation with a well-developed complement of ovarian follicles of ovulatory size. After a receptive female is grasped, she releases eggs in the form of a long double strand. The female and clasping male often swim slowly about while releasing the eggs and sperm so that the egg strands of a single female may twist and turn over a large area of the pond. Amplexus may last for several hours, and up to 8,000 eggs may be laid.

The eggs are small and black. The eggs of Fowler's toad differ from eastern American toad eggs in that they lack an inner envelope and individual eggs are not separated from each other by partitions. Unless the water is unusually cold, hatching occurs in two or three days.

The tadpoles are small and dark and are virtually impossible to distinguish from the tadpoles of eastern American toads. The tadpoles generally form large aggregations of tadpoles of similar size, even if two or more size classes are present in the pond (Breden et al. 1982). A study by Woodward (1987) might explain this size segregation. In the laboratory, he found that the presence of other tadpoles of similar size did not affect the rate of growth or survivorship of the tadpoles, but when small and large tadpoles were placed together, the small individuals grew at a slower rate and experienced a higher rate of mortality than the large tadpoles. Transformation generally occurs in 40–55 days. Recently transformed individuals average $10.7\,mm$ ($\frac{3}{8}$ in.) SUL (Labanick and Schlueter 1976).

Unlike adults, recently transformed toadlets are generally active during the day and spend most of their time foraging along the margins of the pond for food items, especially small flies. During periods of inactivity they take shelter under cover objects and in the cracks and crevices produced by drying mud. They become nocturnal within a few weeks.

The growth of transformed individuals is very rapid. Labanick and Schlueter (1976) noted that transformed animals grew from an average of $10.7\,mm$ ($\frac{3}{8}$ in.) SUL at the end of June to an average of $31.3\,mm$ ($1\frac{1}{4}$ in.) by August 6, a daily average growth of $0.36\,mm$ (0.01 in.). Clarke (1974c) noted that males and females matured by July or August of the year following their metamorphosis. He calculated this to be a 6.5-fold increase in size in a single year. Growth rate decreases dramatically after maturation.

In a Connecticut population, survivorship ranged from 11% to 30% in different years, but within a year it appeared to be fairly constant among all age classes of animals (Clarke 1977). In Pennsylvania, males mature at a SUL that ranges from 48 to 50 mm (2 in.), and females mature between 57 and 60 mm ($2\frac{1}{4}$–$2\frac{3}{8}$ in.) SUL.

Remarks. Fowler's toad and the eastern American toad are closely related and occasionally hybridize. For a more detailed discussion of their hybridization, see the remarks section of the eastern American toad account.

Distribution. Fowler's toad has a broad distribution in eastern North America. Its range largely overlaps that of the eastern American toad, though it does not range as far north. Fowler's toads occur from southern New England westward to Iowa, and throughout the south, with the exception of the southeastern Coastal Plain and Florida.

Fowler's toad is generally found along coasts and rivers and in the lowland areas of the northeastern states from southern New Hampshire

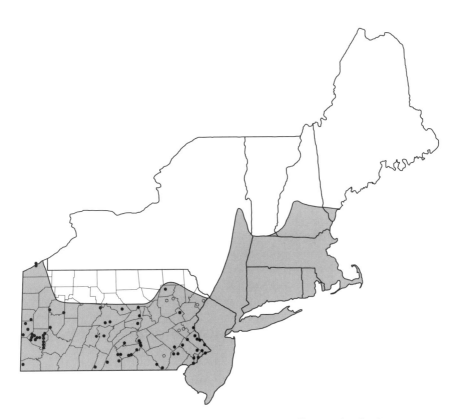

Map 26. Distribution of Fowler's toad *(Bufo woodhousii fowleri)*.

through Rhode Island, Massachusetts, and Connecticut. It is found in southeastern and east-central New York, including Long Island and all of New Jersey. The distribution of Fowler's toad in Pennsylvania is more localized than that of the eastern American toad since it is a habitat specialist, restricted to sandy soils. It has been collected from the Ohio River valley and the Lake Erie shore, scattered lowland sites in the Valley and Ridge Province, and in southeastern Pennsylvania.

HYLIDAE (TREEFROGS, CHORUS FROGS, AND CRICKET FROGS)

The family Hylidae (treefrogs) is found throughout North and South America, northern Africa, temperate Europe and Asia, New Guinea, and Australia. The main centers of diversity in the family are in tropical America and Australia. It is a large group with over 740 described species, contained in approximately 38 genera.

Most treefrogs are adapted to an arboreal existence. They are moderately slender, with long, thin legs. The fingers and toes are long and terminate in discs of varying sizes that aid in adhering to tree trunks and other vertical substrates. An extra element, the intercalary disc, is present between the ultimate and penultimate phalanges of the fingers and toes. This allows for better contact between the toepads and the substrate. The dorsal skin is usually smooth, but the ventral skin tends to be granular and very loose. This design allows for the ventral skin to closely adhere and mold itself to such things as the bark of trees or the surface of rocks. Some species of treefrog, however, are terrestrial or fossorial, and these species lack many aspects of the typical treefrog form. Hylids range in size from 18 mm to over 140 mm ($\frac{3}{4}$–$5\frac{1}{2}$ in.) SUL.

Hylid frogs exhibit an incredible degree of reproductive variation.

Acris
Gr. *akris*, a cricket

The genus *Acris* (cricket frogs) has two species. It is found throughout much of the eastern (exclusive of New England) and central United States, to Mexico just south of the Rio Grande.

Cricket frogs are small (maximum size 38 mm; $1\frac{1}{2}$ in.) and are the least arboreal of all of the treefrogs found in the eastern United States. Their skin is decidedly warty. They are found in a variety of permanent aquatic situations but most often occupy open grassy or reedy habitats at the margins of ponds, lakes, streams, and marshes. They are often active during the day and, at the least indication of danger, make a series of long (for their size) and erratic leaps to elude capture.

Northern Cricket Frog *Acris crepitans crepitans* Baird
L. *crepito*, to rattle
Description. The northern cricket frog (Plate 47) is a diminutive species. The dorsal body color is gray, brown, or light green, usually with

a diffuse middorsal stripe that is either bright green or chestnut brown. Dark spots are scattered over the back. A well-defined triangular dark spot occurs between the eyes, with the apex pointing backward. The upper lip is marked with alternating light and dark spots, and a light bar extends from the eye to the base of the foreleg. The dorsal surfaces of the hind legs have dark crossbars, and there is a longitudinal dark stripe on a light background along the back of the thighs. Large diffuse dark spots occur on the sides of the body. The ventral surface of the body is white, sometimes tinged with yellow in the region of the groin and around the base of the forelegs.

The head is long and pointed, and the upper jaw extends well in front of the lower jaw. The body is slender. The forelegs are of normal size, and the fingers are not webbed. The hind legs are extremely long, and the toes are long and fully webbed. Both fingers and toes terminate in discs, but these are very small, often no greater in diameter than the width of the digit. The dorsal skin is granular with scattered warts. The ventral skin on the chest is smooth but becomes granular posteriorly.

This is the smallest species of frog found in the northeastern United States. Pennsylvania females are slightly larger than males. The average male measures 21.3 mm ($\frac{7}{8}$ in.) SUL, and the average female is 22.7 mm ($\frac{7}{8}$ in.) SUL. During the breeding season, the enlarged, yellowish vocal sac of males distinguishes them from females. The vocal sac is less noticeable in nonbreeding males but can usually be seen as a series of folds or wrinkles on the throat. The maximum size for the species is 35 mm ($1\frac{3}{8}$ in.) (Conant and Collins 1991).

For such a small frog, tadpoles are remarkably large, reaching a maximum ToL of about 50 mm (2 in.). The dorsal surface of the tadpoles is olive green, mottled with black. The ventral surface is much lighter and somewhat iridescent in appearance. The muscular portion of the tail is similar in color to the body, and the end of the tail is tipped with black. The tail crests are relatively low and translucent with scattered dark spots.

Confusing Species.   The northern cricket frog can be confused with recently transformed individuals of *Rana* or adults of the chorus frog. They can be distinguished from all of these, however, by the presence of a dark longitudinal stripe on the back of each thigh.

Habitat and Habits.   Little is known about the biology of the northern cricket frog, either in the Northeast or in other parts of its range. Far more information is available on the biology of Blanchard's cricket frog (*Acris crepitans blanchardi*), a subspecies that occurs in the central states. Most of the information presented here has been extracted from reports on Blanchard's cricket frog, but in general it should also apply to the northern cricket frog.

Northern cricket frogs, unlike the other small species of frogs found in the Northeast, do not leave the vicinity of water after the reproductive season has ended. Rather, they remain in the vicinity of water throughout the year. They also differ from the other small species in that their preferred habitat is permanent water rather than temporary situations.

They are usually found along the edges of slow-moving streams in open habitat and along the margins of lakes and ponds, both in and out of the water and in the vicinity of springs and marshy areas. They avoid dense vegetation and are absent from heavily wooded regions. These are the least arboreal of the treefrogs found in the Northeast. When disturbed, they escape by making surprisingly long and erratic leaps into the water.

Seasonal activity is variable, depending upon geographic area and local climatic conditions. In the southern portion of the range, northern cricket frogs are active throughout the year. Even in the north, they may remain active throughout the year if the water in their habitat remains unfrozen. In Kansas, Linsdale (1927) found specimens that inhabited a spring to be active year round. Gray (1971) found active animals in a spring in January in central Illinois. Given the moderate climate of southeastern Pennsylvania, it is likely that some northern cricket frogs remain active throughout the year. Northern cricket frogs are active both day and night, throughout the season.

Northern cricket frogs, when they hibernate, do so in terrestrial rather than aquatic sites. They have been reported hibernating in the cracks and crevices formed in drying mud at the margins of ponds (Gray 1971), in coarse gravel at the edge of ponds (Walker 1946), and under rocks and other cover objects (Pope 1944).

They are generalized carnivores, eating a wide variety of arthropods. The major food items include ants, springtails, beetles, true bugs, spiders, and leafhoppers. Most of their food is terrestrial; only 3.2% of all prey consumed were aquatic in a study by Labanick (1976).

Reproduction.   Although northern cricket frogs emerge from hibernation early in the season, reproductive activity does not begin until much later in most parts of its range. Males chorus from May to late July or early August. They call from both floating mats of vegetation and from the banks of ponds and streams, predominantly using permanent bodies of water. They chorus from fairly open areas and are relatively easy to approach. Calling males usually are least a meter apart (Perrill and Shepherd 1989). As in some other species, an alternative reproductive tactic is employed by some males, known as satellite males (Perrill and Magier 1988). Satellite males maintain a very low profile relative to the calling male, remain silent, and are usually within 40 cm ($15\frac{3}{4}$ in.) of a calling male. The satellite male achieves reproductive success by intercepting females as they move toward a specific calling male. It is not known whether this strategy occurs in the Northeast.

Females emerge from hibernation with well-developed ovarian follicles, and by late April the follicles have reached ovulatory size. In Illinois, some females are still noticeably gravid in early August (Gray 1983). In Ohio, amplexus begins in early May and continues throughout most of June. Gravid females were still present in late July in a Pennsylvania population. Females swim to calling males and enter into amplexus. Once in amplexus, the female swims to an appropriate oviposition site. The eggs are laid singly and attached to submergent vegetation, or they are laid in small masses on the bottom. Eggs are larger than those of the northern spring peeper (the other northeastern anuran that lays eggs singly rather than in groups). The eggs (including envelopes and jelly coats) of northern cricket frogs may be as large as 5 mm ($\frac{1}{5}$ in.) in diameter (Walker 1946), whereas those of the northern spring peeper are seldom more than 2.5 or 3 mm ($\frac{1}{10}$ in.) in diameter. Northern cricket frog females may produce up to 250 eggs. Although the breeding season is long, there is no evidence to suggest that females lay more than one clutch of eggs.

Development takes from 40 to 90 days depending upon environmental temperature (Dundee and Rossman 1989). In Ohio, transformed individuals begin to emerge in late July, and emergence continues into the first week of September (Walker 1946). Tadpoles reach a maximum size of 46 mm ($1\frac{3}{4}$ in.). Tadpoles of the northern cricket frog can be distinguished from those of the northern spring peeper by the presence of a black tail tip. Northern cricket frogs are extremely large at transformation, considering the small size of adults. Recently transformed individuals range from 13.5 to 15 mm ($\frac{1}{2}$–$\frac{3}{5}$ in.) in Ohio (Walker 1946).

Both male and female northern cricket frogs mature the spring after transformation, at about 20 mm ($\frac{4}{5}$ in.) SUL. Mortality during this period is very heavy. This is an annual species, as determined by the fact that few, if any, animals survive to reproduce a second year.

Remarks. Northern cricket frogs were collected from five locations in central Allegheny County, Pennsylvania, over a period of several years in the early 1900s. To our knowledge, however, no specimens have been collected in the county since then.

Allegheny County is more than 195 km (120 mi) west of the westernmost known locality for the species (Franklin County, Pennsylvania). Apparently, individuals were introduced, either accidentally or intentionally, sometime in the late 1800s and managed to establish short-term reproducing populations before going extinct.

Distribution. The northern cricket frog occurs along the Coastal Plain from southern New York and Long Island through southeastern Pennsylvania to the Gulf Coast states westward to eastern Texas.

In the Northeast, it has been found in southeastern New York, including Long Island and New Jersey. In Pennsylvania, northern cricket frogs have been reported to occur in the southeastern Coastal Plain and Piedmont as well as the extreme eastern portion of the Valley and Ridge Province.

Hyla
Gr. *hyla,* wood

The genus *Hyla* (treefrogs) is large, with over 260 species. *Hyla* are distributed throughout North and South America, Europe, and northern Africa.

Treefrogs are small (less than 25 mm; 1 in.) to large (more than 150 mm; 6 in.) anurans. They tend to be slender, with a narrow waist. The legs are

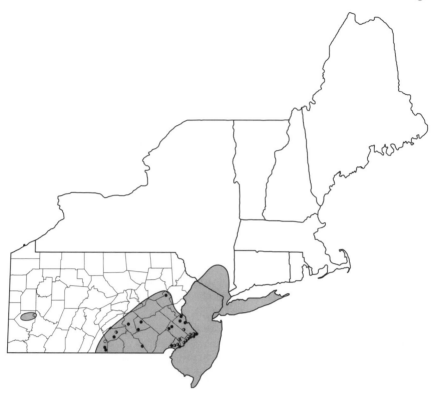

Map 27.   Distribution of the northern cricket frog *(Acris crepitans crepitans).*

long and slender and terminate in long, flexible fingers and toes that have large, well-developed toepads. Treefrogs occupy a wide variety of habitats, from temperate swamps to tropical forests and from marshes and ponds to desert streams. Most species are adapted for an arboreal existence, but several seldom venture far from the ground. Some spend most of their time on rocks and cliff faces.

Treefrogs are generalist carnivores that feed on a broad spectrum of invertebrates. All species possess aquatic tadpoles that emerge from eggs laid variously in ponds, lakes, streams, and water-filled depressions in trees and bromeliads. Males call from many different locations.

Pine Barrens Treefrog *Hyla andersonii* Baird
andersonii, the species is named in honor of John Anderson, a nineteenth-century naturalist.

Description.   A medium-sized frog, the Pine Barrens treefrog (Plate 48) is easily identified. It ranges in size from 28 to 44 mm ($1\frac{1}{8}$–$1\frac{3}{4}$) (Conant and Collins 1991). Females are larger than males (Gosner and Black 1967,

Wright 1932). The Pine Barrens treefrog is distinguished from other treefrogs in the Northeast by its green dorsum color and lavender stripes that extend from the nose through the eye and laterally on the body. These stripes are bordered by a white to yellowish stripe. The underside of the legs of these frogs can have a considerable amount of bright orange with numerous spots. The chin of males is dark purplish drab; that of females is white, gray, or with a slight purplish drab (Wright 1932). Breeding males have a median, subgular vocal sac. Newly metamorphosed juveniles resemble adults in pattern and coloration.

Confusing Species.   There are no species that can be confused with the Pine Barrens treefrog in the northeastern states.

Habitat and Habits.   The species is not well studied. It is known from the Pine Barrens of New Jersey and South Carolina and the upper coastal plain of South Carolina, where it is a resident of swamps, bogs, and brown acid water (Conant and Collins 1991, Martof et al. 1980). Its has been found in cedars, magnolias, oaks, blueberry bushes, pitch pines, and gum trees (Martof et al. 1980, Wright 1932). Gosner and Black (1957) reported that the embryos of Pine Barrens treefrogs were extremely tolerant of the highly acidic conditions of the Pine Barrens, and that tolerance might explain their distribution.

Pine Barrens treefrogs are active from April to September. They are agile climbers, having been recorded 2.7 m (8 ft) off the ground (Wright 1932). They feed on insects, including grasshoppers, beetles, ants, and flies (Noble and Noble 1923, Wright 1932).

Water snakes are known predators on the adult frogs (Kauffeld 1957). Research by Lawler (1989) on predation on tadpoles found that, in an artificial environment, tadpoles tended to be fairly active and to position themselves at an intermediate level between pelagic and benthic. They reduced their activity and moved to a more benthic position when predators were present. Predators included the red-spotted newt *(Notophthalmus viridescens)*, the black-banded sunfish *(Enneacanthus obesus)*, and dragonfly naiads *(Pantala)*.

Reproduction.   The breeding season of the Pine Barrens treefrog is prolonged, lasting from late April to mid-July in New Jersey (Morin et al. 1990). Eggs are laid singly (Gosner and Black 1967) in shallow water, and each female lays a clutch of about 500 eggs (Martof 1980). Noble and Noble (1923) stated that females may lay as many as 800–1,000 eggs, but they could not verify that number in the laboratory. Eggs hatch in three to four days in North and South Carolina but may take longer in New Jersey. Morin and colleagues (1990) reported that breeding late in the season reduced the growth and survival of offspring.

Distribution.   The Pine Barrens treefrog has a disjunct distribution. It occurs in the western Florida panhandle and adjacent Alabama, the string bogs of south-central North Carolina and adjacent South Carolina, and in southern New Jersey.

Map 28.   Distribution of the Pine Barrens treefrog *(Hyla andersonii)*.

Cope's Gray Treefrog/Gray Treefrog *Hyla chrysoscelis*
Cope/*H. versicolor* LeConte
Gr. *chryso,* gold; Gr. *celi,* spot; L. *versi,* various; L. *color,* color
Description.   Cope's Gray treefrog and the gray treefrog (Plate 49) form
a complex of species that are morphologically indistinguishable from each
other and can be distinguished in the field only by their calls. This
complex is discussed in more detail in the Remarks section. In view of
their morphologically identical appearance, both species will be referred
to by the single name gray treefrog.
Gray treefrogs are moderate-sized frogs. The dorsal background coloration is generally light gray, but they may rapidly change their background color from light gray to dark gray to green or greenish gray. The
dorsal pattern consists of a dark central blotch with projecting branches
extending in all directions. The branches may be wavy or straight edged
and are often broken into separate segments. The dorsal pattern is highly
individual, with no two animals having an identical pattern. The top of
the head and the eyelids are patterned with dark spots. The dorsal surfaces of the legs are patterned with a series of dark crossbars. The sides of

the head are darker than the top, and there is a vivid white spot, bordered with black, below each eye. The ventral surfaces of the chest and belly are cream-colored, but the groin and undersides and back of the thighs have a pattern of black reticulated lines on a background of bright orange or yellow. These act as a flash pattern or distraction when the animals leap to escape a predator.

The gray treefrog has the typical treefrog form of flexible body, long legs, and long, flexible toes with large adhesive pads at the tips. The head is broad with a blunt snout. The eyes are large and positioned on the sides of the head for maximum peripheral vision. The tympana are smaller than the eyes and rather inconspicuous. The dorsal skin is covered with small warts, giving it a rough appearance and texture. The ventral skin is granular. The toepads are approximately twice the width of the toes, and the toes of the hind feet are webbed.

Sexual dimorphism, other than in size, is not well developed in this species. Males have a dark gray throat due primarily to the coloration of the vocal sac. Males are smaller than females. Males from Pennsylvania average 43 mm ($1\frac{3}{4}$ in.) SUL; females average 49 mm ($1\frac{15}{16}$ in.) SUL. The maximum size for the species is 60 mm ($2\frac{3}{8}$ in.) SUL (Conant and Collins 1991).

Tadpoles are moderate sized, reaching a maximum ToL of 50 mm (2 in.). The eyes are located along the sides of the head, rather than on the top. The dorsum and sides of the body are greenish and flecked with gold. The belly is iridescent cream. The muscular portion of the tail is usually distinctly reddish, while the tail crest is somewhat translucent and patterned with large dark blotches. The tail crest is very high.

Confusing Species. Recently transformed individuals of the gray treefrog could be mistaken for northern spring peepers. The distinct cross on the dorsum of the northern spring peeper should be sufficient to distinguish it from the gray treefrog.

Habitat and Habits. As the name implies, this is an arboreal species that is usually found in deciduous woodlands, but during the breeding season, it may occur in the lower vegetation of old fields, meadows, and ecotonal habitats. Gray treefrogs are generally found in the vicinity of pools, ponds, or roadside ditches.

They are one of the last anurans to emerge from hibernation in Pennsylvania and the rest of the Northeast, with activity generally beginning in early to mid-April, increasing in May, and peaking in June. Activity declines in July and then remains at a low level until hibernation in October. Surface activity is controlled by temperature and moisture. In mid and late summer, surface activity is correlated strongly with periods of rainfall and high humidity.

Gray treefrogs are primarily nocturnal animals, with little, if any, activity during daylight hours.

Nothing is known of the hibernation activity of gray treefrogs. They are, however, freeze tolerant (Layne and Lee 1989), so it is likely that they hibernate on land rather than in the water.

Gray treefrogs feed predominantly on terrestrial and aerial insects (Ralin 1968), but no detailed study of their diet has been conducted.

Reproduction. Gray treefrogs are one of the last species to begin reproductive activity in the Northeast. Calling seldom begins before the first week or two of May. The reproductive season of gray treefrogs is lengthy, and reproductive activity often extends into the first half of August. Although the reproductive season is long, choruses are not continuous throughout the season; rather, choruses form at irregular intervals. Warm weather and high moisture levels stimulate chorusing behavior. As a result, although the reproductive season may extend over 90 days, actual reproductive activity occurs on far fewer days during the season.

Call sites are not very specific for gray treefrogs. Males may call from the ground or from heights of a meter (3 ft) or more above the ground in bushes and trees. They may call at the water's edge or up to several meters from the nearest water.

Gray treefrogs use both temporary and permanent bodies of water for reproduction, but they have a greater tendency to breed in temporary situations. They most commonly utilize woodland pools, ditches, cattle tanks, and the margins of small ponds and lakes.

Females are attracted to the calls of and move toward the male. Once in amplexus, the female moves to the water and swims about with the male on her back while she locates an oviposition site. A female may contain as many as 2,000 eggs, but they are not all laid in a single location. Rather, they are laid in small masses of fewer than 50 eggs (Wright and Wright 1949). The masses may either be free floating or attached to emergent and submergent vegetation in the water. Eggs are about 1.2 mm ($\frac{1}{16}$ in.) in diameter and, including the jelly coats, have a total diameter of 4–8 mm ($\frac{1}{8}$–$\frac{1}{4}$ in.) (Wright and Wright 1949).

Because of their late reproductive start, water temperatures are usually high when eggs are laid. As a result, developmental time is short, with transformation occurring within 45–65 days of oviposition. Tadpoles achieve a maximum size of about 50 mm (2 in.), and recently transformed individuals range in size from 17 to 20 mm ($\frac{5}{8}$–$\frac{7}{8}$ in.) SUL.

Males mature at about 39 mm ($1\frac{5}{8}$ in.) SUL. The smallest mature female from Pennsylvania was 47 mm ($1\frac{7}{8}$ in.) SUL. It is possible that they mature at a smaller size, however. Ritke and Colleagues (1990) found that the minimum size for mature female gray treefrogs from Tennessee was 45 mm ($1\frac{3}{4}$ in.) SUL.

Remarks. The gray treefrog and Cope's gray treefrog are impossible to distinguish on the basis of external characteristics. However, they are reproductively isolated and as a consequence represent separate species. The two species can be separated by call characteristics (Blair 1958). The call of both species is a trill. The gray treefrog has a trill rate that is much slower (16–35 notes per second) than that of Cope's gray treefrog (29–64 notes per second). In addition, Cope's gray treefrog is a diploid species (has two sets of chromosomes per cell), whereas the gray treefrog is a tetraploid species (has four sets of chromosomes per cell) (Bogart and Wasserman 1972). The two species can also be distinguished from each other by the size of their cells and the nuclei within their cells. Because the gray treefrog is tetraploid, it has twice the genetic material in each cell as the diploid Cope's gray treefrog. As a consequence, when microscopically examined, the cells of gray treefrogs are about 1.3 times as large as comparable cells from Cope's gray treefrog, and the nuclei of the gray treefrog are about 1.4 times the diameter of the nuclei of Cope's gray treefrog.

Although it is now possible to accurately determine the species, little work has been carried out to attempt to determine the exact range of the two species. As a result, most works dealing with the two species show a composite range. It was previously thought that only the gray treefrog occurred in Pennsylvania (McCoy 1982), but a study by Little and colleagues (1989) suggests the possible existence of Cope's gray treefrog in southwestern Pennsylvania.

Distribution. Gray treefrogs range throughout the eastern United States, from Maine to the Gulf of Mexico and westward into the eastern Great Plains. They are, however, absent from peninsular Florida.

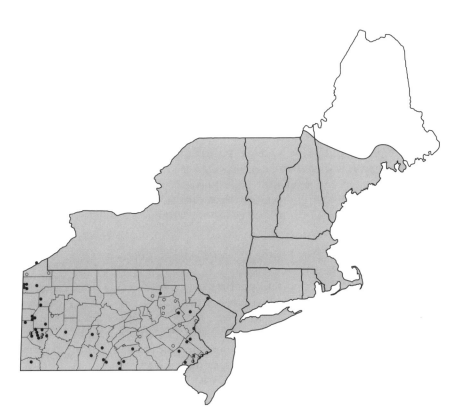

Map 29. Distribution of the gray treefrog complex *(Hyla versicolor* and *H. chrysoscelis)*.

The gray treefrogs' northeastern distribution extends from southern and central portions of Maine southward throughout the rest of New England, New York, and New Jersey. In Pennsylvania, gray treefrogs have a wide, but very spotty, distribution and appear to be most common in the southeast and southwest.

Pseudacris
Gr. *pseudis,* false; Gr. *akris,* a locust

The genus *Pseudacris* (chorus frogs) contains nine species and is exclusively North American. In the East, members of the genus range from central Ontario and Quebec to the Gulf Coast. In the West, they range from near the Arctic Circle in Canada and Alaska to the mountains of central Arizona.

Chorus frogs and spring peepers are all small, moderate to slender species. The smallest species of frog found in the United States is in this genus (the little grass frog, *Pseudacris ocularis,* with a maximum SUL of 17 mm; $\frac{11}{16}$ in.). In general, chorus frogs and peepers have small terminal discs on their toes and fingers. They are not accomplished climbers and are seldom found more than a few feet off the ground, in grass and shrubs. Chorus frogs and spring peepers occupy a wide variety of habitats, ranging from lowland swamps to upland forests and from small temporary ponds to the margins of large lakes. These frogs are seldom encountered, except during the breeding season when males are conspicuous because of their callings.

Chorus frogs and peepers are generalized carnivores, feeding on a wide variety of small invertebrates.

Chorus frogs and peepers are early spring breeders in the northern part of their range and winter and early spring breeders in the southern part of their range. Reproduction may take place in a variety of habitats but usually occurs in shallow ponds or swampy areas. Males generally call from clumps of grass or other types of vegetation.

Mountain Chorus Frog *Pseudacris brachyphona* (Cope)
Gr. *brachis,* short; Gr. *phone,* sound
Description. The mountain chorus frog (Plate 50) is a small species. The dorsal ground color varies from tan to light brown and is patterned with dark brown to black markings. Although somewhat variable in appearance, these markings are usually shaped like a pair of inverted parentheses, and they extend from the back of the head to the groin along each side of the body. They may touch or occasionally fuse on the midline of the body. A dark triangular blotch with its apex pointed backward is located on the head, between the eyes. The dorsal surfaces of the legs are patterned with dark bars. The ventral surfaces are immaculate cream-colored. Skin texture varies from slightly rough on the dorsal surfaces to coarsely granular on the chest and belly.

For its size, the mountain chorus frog has a robust body form. The head is broad and flat, and the snout is rounded in dorsal view. The forelegs are small and thin, and the hind legs are long and slender. The tip of each toe has a small but well-developed disc. Webbing between the toes is minimal.

The mountain chorus frog exhibits sexual dimorphism in size. Females are significantly larger than males. In a sample from a breeding chorus located in Westmoreland County, Pennsylvania, males averaged 24.6 mm (1 in.) SUL. In the same chorus, females averaged 30.3 mm ($1\frac{1}{4}$ in.) SUL. The record size for this species is 38 mm ($1\frac{1}{2}$ in.) (Conant and Collins 1991). Males may also be distinguished from females during the breeding season by the presence of a noticeable vocal sac that is usually yellowish. Outside of the breeding season the vocal sac is not as noticeable but may still be seen as a series of folds along the underside of the throat.

Tadpoles are small, never exceeding 30 mm ($1\frac{1}{4}$ in.) ToL. The dorsum and sides of the body are dark brown and may be flecked with metallic bronze. The ventral surfaces are bronze and iridescent. The tail crest is moderately developed and translucent, with a pattern of small dark spots and flecks.

Confusing Species.   The mountain chorus frog might be mistaken for either the striped chorus frog or the northern spring peeper. It can readily be distinguished from the striped chorus frog by the fact that only the former has two longitudinal stripes on its back, with the stripes curving inward to form a pair of reversed parentheses. The striped chorus frog has three dorsal stripes (a middorsal stripe and two that are dorsal-lateral).

Distinguishing between the mountain chorus frog and the northern spring peeper can be considerably more difficult. In most cases, the two can be told apart by the dorsal pattern. The northern spring peeper has two dorsal stripes that intersect each other and form a very visible X-shaped cross, whereas they form a pair of reversed parentheses in the mountain chorus frog. Unfortunately, in about 30% of mountain chorus frogs the dorsal stripes converge at the midline to form an X-shaped cross. The mountain chorus frog has a white stripe running along its upper lip and a large, well-developed backward-pointing triangle on its head. When present in the northern spring peeper, the triangle is much smaller than in the mountain chorus frog. In addition, mountain chorus frogs have webbing extending only a quarter of the length of the toes of the hind foot, whereas the webbing of the northern spring peeper extends halfway up the toes of the hind foot.

Habitat and Habits.   The mountain chorus frog is one of the least known species of frog in Pennsylvania and one of the least studied frogs in the United States. It is an upland species and is not associated with streams, ponds, or lakes. Its primary habitat is deciduous woodlands. Except for the breeding season, mountain chorus frogs are not associated with any form of water. They are distributed through the woods and may be found under surface cover objects or seen moving about in the open after heavy summer rains.

Mountain chorus frogs begin to emerge from hibernation in late March. Activity peaks in April and remains high throughout May. Once reproduction is over, activity drops off dramatically and remains at a very low frequency until the fall, when frogs enter hibernation. It is unlikely that the frogs actually cease most activity in the summer. More likely, they are seldom seen because they are no longer active on the surface.

Green and Pauley (1987) reported that mountain chorus frogs feed on a variety of small forest-floor invertebrates, including, but not limited to, beetles, spiders, and true bugs.

Reproduction.   The only published information on reproduction in this species is that of Green (1938) and Barbour and Walters (1941). Most of the following information is from those sources. In Pennsylvania, males have been heard calling as early as 7 April and as late as 16 May. In Kentucky, they call as early as late February. Calling activity appears to be temperature dependent, with males calling only when air temperatures are above 5°C (41°F). Males generally call from near the water's edge and may be found either in the water or on land along the shore. In all cases, calling males face the water. Unlike northern spring peepers, male mountain chorus frogs do not hide in vegetation or call from concealed sites in shrubs and low-growing trees. Rather, mountain chorus frogs call in the open and are readily visible. Calling sites include roadside ditches, small, temporary woodland ponds, and pools associated with seepage springs. Ponds may be shallow and as small as $2\,m^2$ ($22\,ft^2$) in area.

Females emerge from hibernation with follicular eggs of ovulatory size. Upon emergence, females proceed to the breeding sites, attracted by the call of the males. Receptive females will swim up to males and usually touch them before being grasped in amplexus. Once in amplexus, the female swims to a suitable oviposition site, where she begins to lay her eggs. Eggs are laid in small masses, composed of 10–50 eggs, and are attached in midwater to vegetation. Eggs are about 1.5 mm ($\frac{1}{10}$ in.) in diameter and with all associated membranes and jelly envelopes range in size from 6 to 8.5 mm ($\frac{1}{4}$–$\frac{3}{8}$ in.). A single female will deposit numerous egg masses; the number of eggs varies from 300 to 1,500 eggs, with an average of about 950 eggs.

All reproductive activities (i.e., calling, amplexus, and oviposition) can occur during either the day or the night.

Both hatching and transformation are temperature dependent. Eggs hatch in 4–10 days, and transformation occurs in 40–65 days. At transformation, froglets have a SUL of 8–9 mm ($\frac{3}{8}$ in.). Frogs mature in the spring after their transformation. Males mature at about 22 mm ($\frac{7}{8}$ in.) SUL, and females at around 28 mm SUL ($1\frac{1}{8}$ in.).

Distribution.   The distribution of the mountain chorus frog is disjunct, with the main portion of its range from southwestern Pennsylvania and adjacent Ohio southward into northern Tennessee. Another population

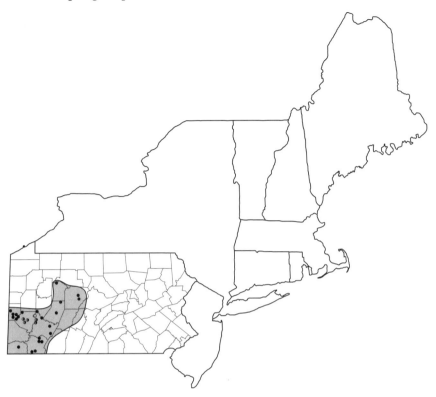

Map 30.   Distribution of the mountain chorus frog *(Pseudacris brachyphona).*

occurs in Alabama, and a third population in northern Georgia and southern Tennessee.

In the Northeast, the mountain chorus frog occurs only in Pennsylvania, where populations have been reported from most of the counties located west of the Allegheny Front, as far north as Jefferson County. However, all of the reports of it in the state are historical. No specimens have been reported in the past 20 years or so.

Northern Spring Peeper *Pseudacris crucifer crucifer* (Wied)
L. *crux*, cross; L. *fer*, bearing
Description.   The northern spring peeper (Plate 51), a small species, is the most widely and commonly encountered treefrog in the Northeast. The dorsal coloration is some shade of brown, usually a medium to dark tan, but it may occasionally be darker (almost black) or lighter (pinkish tan). Coloration in this species can change dramatically to match the animal's background. On light backgrounds, the frog's color rapidly lightens, and the converse is true for dark backgrounds (Kats and Van Dragt 1986). The dorsum has a large, X-shaped mark; hence, its scientific name.

The arms of the X extend from the back of the head to the groin on each side of the body. Additional markings may occasionally be present on the back, but the X is a constant character. There is a dark bar present on the top of the head that usually runs from one eye to the other. A dark bar generally extends along the side of the head from the nose through the eye. Behind the eye this bar becomes wider and ends in the vicinity of the tympanum. Crossbars occur on the dorsal surfaces of the forelegs and hind legs. With the exception of the chin in males, the undersurfaces are cream-colored and immaculate. In males, the throat is yellow to yellowish green. The concealed skin in the area of the groin is yellow.

The body is moderately robust, and the head is short and broad, with a slightly pointed snout. The legs are well developed, and the tips of the toes have a well-developed terminal disc that is wider than the toe. The toes of the hind feet exhibit moderate webbing. The dorsal skin is finely granular, and the ventral skin is coarsely granular.

Females are larger than males. Adult males in Pennsylvania average 25.2 mm (1 in.) SUL. Mature females average 31.8 mm ($1\frac{1}{4}$ in.) SUL. Breeding choruses often contain two distinct size classes of males: newly matured individuals in their first breeding season and older males. For example, in an Allegheny County, Pennsylvania, chorus, young males averaged 22.1 mm ($\frac{7}{8}$ in.) SUL, whereas second-year and older males averaged 26.4 mm (1 in.) SUL. The maximum size for the species is 37 mm ($1\frac{1}{2}$ in.) SUL (Conant and Collins 1991).

Tadpoles (Plate 52) of this species are small, never exceeding 35 mm ($1\frac{3}{8}$ in.) ToL. The eyes are located on the sides of the head, rather than on the top. The dorsum and sides of the body are greenish and may exhibit gold flecks. The belly is immaculate white or cream-colored and is iridescent. The tail crests are translucent and are patterned with dark maculations, especially along the dorsal margin and near the tip. The tail crests are moderately developed.

Confusing Species.   The northern spring peeper might be confused with the mountain chorus frog. The northern spring peeper has larger toepads and more extensive webbing between the toes of the hind feet than does the mountain chorus frog.

Habitat and Habits.   The northern spring peeper is primarily an inhabitant of deciduous woodlands and swamps and adjacent marshy fields and meadows. It is most frequently seen in open (i.e., nonwooded) areas early in the season during reproductive activity. After breeding has been completed, the frogs move back into wooded areas. They are found either on the ground or climbing in low herbaceous and woody vegetation, but not in trees. As a consequence, they are less arboreal than treefrogs, but more so than the chorus frogs.

One of the first species to appear, northern spring peepers begin calling in middle to late March (March 15–25). However, during years with short warm winters, they may emerge and begin to call in February. Activity in Pennsylvania rapidly peaks in early April and remains fairly high through late May and early June. Dropping precipitously by the end of June, activity remains low until the animals enter hibernation in the fall. This apparent sudden drop in activity, however, might not be real. In June, the frogs move away from the breeding ponds, and calling virtually ceases. As a consequence, the animals are much more difficult to locate. It is possible that they are still very active but in areas (e.g., leaf litter) where they are not likely to be seen. Klemens (1993) suggests a second activity peak, for Connecticut, in September and October just before hibernation. The frogs are freeze tolerant, but their survival is inversely proportional to the duration of the freeze episode, with full recovery if the freeze period is a few days (Layne and Kefauver 1997).

Northern spring peepers are active during daylight hours and at night. Diurnal activity, however, is most frequent among adults during the reproductive season. As the season progresses, diurnal activity becomes more concentrated nearer to dusk. After reproduction, adult activity is primarily nocturnal. Diurnal activity is common among recently transformed individuals, even in the middle of the summer.

Northern spring peepers are generalized carnivores that feed on a variety of small invertebrates. Both sexes curtail feeding during the spring breeding season (Oplinger 1967).

Northern spring peeper populations tend to exhibit a distinct size structure, with three size classes of individuals present in most populations. There is usually a group of small immature frogs that represent the previous season's transformed individuals. A second group of medium-sized individuals represent 2-year-old animals that are breeding for the first time. A third group of larger individuals represents 3- and 4-year-olds (Lykens and Forester 1987). This general pattern is seen in males and females.

Reproduction.   The northern spring peeper is one of the earliest frogs to initiate calling in the Northeast. Shortly after emerging from hibernation, males migrate to breeding areas. Northern spring peepers breed in swamps, marshes, and small woodland ponds and along the swampy margins of larger ponds and lakes. Males call from sites where they have established calling stations (Plate 53). Chorusing occurs during both the day and the night. Males often call in tandem, with one male calling immediately after another male stops. Up to four or five males may engage in this behavior (M. Rosen and Lemon 1974). However, if calling males get too close to one another, aggressive interactions may occur. The male possessing the calling station gives a nonsexual aggressive call, warning the intruder away. If the intruder fails to respond, the resident male attacks and a wrestling match ensues. The winner remains at the calling station. Rosen and Lemon (1974) noted that, in most cases, the nearest calling neighbors were 80–106 cm (32–41 in.) apart, and aggressive interactions occurred when an intruder came within 30 cm (12 in.). Most populations of northern spring peepers also have "satellite" males. These are noncalling males that station themselves close to calling males, but, because they remain quiet, they are undetected by the resident calling male. Satellite males achieve a degree of reproductive success by intercepting receptive females as they move toward a calling male. Satellite males are smaller than calling males and would probably be at a disadvantage in obtaining a quality calling station (Forester and Lykens 1986).

Females respond to calling males by swimming toward them. Once the female is in contact with the male, amplexus occurs. The female then moves with the male to an oviposition site. Northern spring peepers, unlike most northeastern frogs and toads, lay eggs singly rather than in masses or strands. The eggs are attached to submergent vegetation in the water. Egg size is variable both within and between clutches, with egg diameter ranging between 1.03 and 1.48 mm (ca. $\frac{1}{25}$ in.) (Crump 1984). The number of eggs is positively correlated with the size of the female and ranges from 200 to over 1,200 (Oplinger 1966).

Little is known about the incubation time or larval ecology of the northern spring peeper. Hatching occurs in 6 days to 2 weeks, depending upon temperature. C. Walker (1946) reported a total developmental time of 90–100 days for northern spring peepers from Ohio.

Sex ratio varies dramatically as a function of where and when the populations are sampled. Oplinger (1966) reported a sex ratio dramatically skewed in favor of males (9.2 : 1) from a breeding chorus of northern spring peepers. This is the result of females' constantly moving in and out of the ponds while males remain in the ponds most of the time while they call to attract mates. Immature northern spring peepers sampled in the fall before entering hibernation exhibited a sex ratio of nearly 1 : 1.

Pennsylvania females mature at about 27 mm ($1\frac{1}{8}$ in.) SUL, and males at about 21 mm ($\frac{7}{8}$ in.) SUL.

Remarks.   The northern spring peeper was long regarded as a member of the treefrog genus *Hyla*. Hedges (1986) used an analysis of proteins to demonstrate that it is more closely related to the chorus frogs (genus *Pseudacris*). Ecologically, the northern spring peeper is also more similar to *Pseudacris* than to *Hyla* in that it breeds early in the spring and is far more terrestrial than the typical treefrog.

Distribution.   The northern spring peeper has an enormous geographic range in North America. It extends from Nova Scotia westward to the edge of the Great Plains in Minnesota and southward to central Georgia and east Texas.

The species is widespread and common in the Northeast. In Pennsylvania, the relatively few collecting localities on the state distribution map reflect the tendency of herpetologists to not collect those species that are extremely common and widespread.

Western Chorus Frog/Upland Chorus Frog/New Jersey Chorus Frog
Pseudacris triseriata triseriata (Wied)/*Pseudacris triseriata feriarum*/*Pseudacris triseriata kalmi*
L. *tri*, three; L. *seri*, a series or row; L. *feria*, festive; *Kalmi*, in honor of Pehr Kalm, an eighteenth-century naturalist
Description.   The species *Pseudacris triseriata* is referred to as the striped chorus frog. Three subspecies of this widespread species occur in

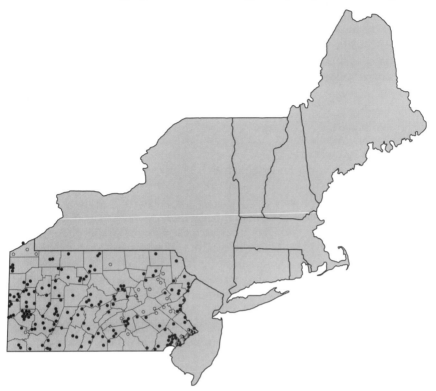

Map 31. Distribution of the northern spring peeper *(Pseudacris crucifer crucifer)*.

the Northeast: the western chorus frog *(Pseudacris triseriata triseriata)* (Plate 54), the upland chorus frog *(Pseudacris triseriata feriarum)* (Plate 55), and the New Jersey chorus frog *(Pseudacris triseriata kalmi)*. The three subspecies are somewhat different in color pattern and size. These differences are discussed in the Remarks section.

The striped chorus frog is a small species. The dorsal ground color varies from gray to tan to greenish brown. A dark stripe on each side of the body runs from the snout, through the eye, and extends to the groin. On the head, a bright white stripe occurs just below this dark stripe. The dorsal body pattern usually consists of three longitudinal stripes (a middorsal stripe and a pair of dorsolateral dark stripes), hence the common name of the species. These stripes may be complete, occasionally broken, or broken into a series of spots. There is a triangular dark spot between the eyes that may connect with the middorsal body stripe. The dorsal surfaces of the legs are patterned with dark spots or bars. The ventral surfaces are cream-colored to white, with occasional black flecks.

The striped chorus frog has a body of moderate proportions, with a narrow, pointed head. The dorsal skin is slightly rough, and the ventral skin is coarsely granular. The forelegs are short, but the hind legs are moderately long. The hind toes are elongate and webbed only at the base. The toepads are small, not wider than the toes.

Sexual size dimorphism occurs in this species. Females are significantly larger than males. Males average 24.9 mm (1 in.) SUL. Females average 28.7 mm ($1\frac{1}{8}$ in.) SUL. The record size for this species is 38 mm ($1\frac{1}{2}$ in.) (Conant and Collins 1991). During the breeding season, males may also be distinguished from females by the presence of a dark yellow vocal sac.

Tadpoles of the chorus frog are indistinguishable from those of the mountain chorus frog.

Confusing Species. The striped chorus frog might be confused with either the mountain chorus frog or the northern spring peeper. However, it differs from both species in that the dorsal pattern consists of three stripes or rows of spots that do not cross, whereas both of the other species possess only a pair of longitudinal stripes that invariably cross in the peeper and frequently cross in the mountain chorus frog.

Habitat and Habits. The chorus frog is an inhabitant of dense vegetation in wooded areas or in marshes and meadows. Although it is a member of the treefrog family, it is not arboreal. Specimens are almost always found on the ground, although Walker (1946) reported occasionally finding juveniles by sweeping vegetation with an insect net. Except in the breeding season, western chorus frogs are not necessarily associated with water. During the reproductive season, they are found in a variety of temporary and permanent bodies of water. Later in the year they may be long distances from water.

Emergence from hibernation is temperature dependent but usually occurs in mid-March. During exceptionally short or long winters, however, emergence may be as early as mid-February or as late as the end of March or the beginning of April. Activity peaks in April at breeding ponds and rapidly drops off by the end of May. Throughout the rest of the year western chorus frogs are exceedingly elusive, so the actual level of activity is not known. The latest record for them in Pennsylvania is 6 October. There is no information available on hibernation sites; however, it is likely that they hibernate on land since they are freeze tolerant (Storey and Storey 1987). Freeze tolerance is found in species that hibernate in terrestrial retreats where there is a high possibility that temperatures will fall below freezing. It is seldom if ever seen in species that hibernate in aquatic situations.

As are the mountain chorus frogs, these three subspecies are active day and night during the reproductive season. After reproduction is over, the animals become extremely secretive and little is known of their daily activity.

For such small animals, striped chorus frogs move considerable distances. Kramer (1974) found that their home range outside of the reproductive season varied from 641 m^2 to 6,024 m^2 (705–6,626 yd^2).

The most detailed study of food habits in this species is from a population in west-central Indiana (Whitaker 1971). He found that recently metamorphosed individuals fed mainly on mites and springtails, both very common at pond's edge. Adults, terrestrial after the end of the reproductive season, fed on spiders, ants, slugs, beetles, and other invertebrates. Individuals found in or near breeding areas during the reproductive season fed primarily on spiders, snails, and, to a lesser extent, caterpillars and fly larvae. This is in sharp contrast to northern spring peepers, which fast during the reproductive season (Oplinger 1967). Whitaker (1971) noted predation on adult western chorus frogs by northern water snakes and by eastern ribbon snakes.

Reproduction. The striped chorus frog is one of the earliest frogs to begin calling in the spring in Pennsylvania. Chorusing males have been heard as early as 3 March and as late as 11 May. Chorusing, however, may begin earlier if there is sufficient warm weather. Whitaker (1971) noted calling as early as mid-February during an unusually warm winter in Indiana. Farther south, they often chorus in late fall and throughout the winter into early spring (Dundee and Rossman 1989).

Mating takes place in temporary pools and flooded areas in forests, old fields, meadows, and marshes as well as in roadside ditches. Calling occurs both during the day and at night. Males call from anywhere in the breeding pond but are usually associated with emergent vegetation. "Satellite" males (see Northern Spring Peeper, Reproduction) have been found in some populations of western chorus frogs (Roble 1985).

The female responds to a calling male by swimming toward him. Once the two are in contact, amplexus occurs. Although the calling season may extend over a period of 6–10 weeks, females do not enter the pond continuously through the entire calling season. Rather, they usually enter the breeding ponds in relatively large numbers on only a few nights each year (Whitaker 1971). The total egg complement for chorus frogs ranges from 500 to 1,500 eggs (Wright and Wright 1949). The eggs are laid in small groups. The egg masses are irregular clusters generally less than 2.5 cm (1 in.) in diameter and contain from 12 to 245 eggs. The egg masses are attached to submergent vegetation at a depth of 50–200 mm (2–8 in.).

Eggs hatch in 3 to 13 days, depending upon environmental temperatures (Dickerson 1920, Whitaker 1971). Larval development is also variable and takes between 35 and 55 days. Most individuals transform by the beginning of June. The size at transformation averaged 11.54 mm ($\frac{1}{2}$ in.) SUL in a population from Isle Royale, Michigan (D. Smith 1983). Smith noted that larger individuals of both sexes reached sexual maturity in the spring following their transformation, whereas smaller individuals needed a second year to reach maturity.

Remarks. The three subspecies of this frog are distinguished by dorsal pattern and average differences in body proportions. However, the upland and western chorus frogs are often exceedingly difficult to separate on the basis of appearance. The western chorus frog has a dorsal pattern of three broad, longitudinal dorsal stripes, and the upland chorus frog has a pattern of three thin, longitudinal dorsal stripes that are often broken into a series of shorter lines or spots. Unfortunately, the pattern of the western chorus frog occasionally varies, and longitudinal stripes may be very thin, or in some cases even broken. The New Jersey chorus frog's pattern is similar to that of the western chorus frog, but it is more robustly built. The three longitudinal dorsal stripes on it are almost always broad and well defined. In Pennsylvania, subspecies can be identified if the geographic location of the individuals is known. (See Distribution.)

Various authors have suggested that these subspecies are separate species, on the basis of differences in biochemical patterns (Hedges 1986) and differences in mating calls and morphological characters (Platz 1989, Platz and Forester 1988). A final decision cannot be made until studies have been conducted throughout the species' range, especially in areas where the ranges of subspecies overlap.

Distribution.   The striped chorus frog is widespread in North America, ranging over most of the eastern, boreal, and higher-altitude western regions.

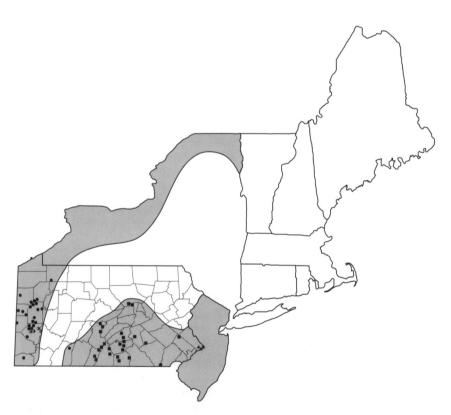

Map 32. Distribution of the three subspecies of the striped chorus frog. Closed circles and half-open circles represent the western chorus frog *(Pseudacris triseriata triseriata)*; closed squares represent the upland chorus frog *(Pseudacris triseriata feriarum)*; closed triangles represent the New Jersey chorus frog *(Pseudacris triseriata kalmi)*.

In Pennsylvania, the three subspecies are geographically separated. The New Jersey chorus frog is restricted to the coastal plain in extreme southeastern Pennsylvania. The upland chorus frog ranges from the piedmont of Chester and Montgomery counties into the southern and central Valley and Ridge Province. The western chorus frog occupies the westernmost counties of the state, all within the Allegheny Plateau. The western chorus frog also occurs in western and extreme northern New York and Vermont in the Lake Champlain area.

RANIDAE (TRUE FROGS)

The family Ranidae includes the "true frogs" and contains over 700 species in about 46 genera. The family is nearly cosmopolitan in distribution, being absent only from southern parts of South America, Australia south of the Cape York Peninsula, and New Zealand. There are radiations of specialized genera in Africa and Southeast Asia, but more than 279 of the species in the family are in the widespread genus *Rana*. Despite the large number of described species, most ranids are not very diverse in body shape or color. They are typically medium-sized to large, aquatic frogs with long hind legs and strongly webbed toes. They are superior leapers and proficient swimmers. Throughout temperate zones of the world, ranids are the most characteristic amphibians found in permanent water. They lay moderate-sized to large clutches of small to medium-sized eggs in either temporary or permanent waters. Some are explosive breeders (e.g., the wood frog), but most have prolonged breeding seasons. Larvae may transform within a few months, or the larval stage may be extended (two or three years).

Rana
L. *rana*, a frog

The genus *Rana* (true frogs) has more than 270 species. True frogs are distributed on all continents except Antarctica; however, their distribution is restricted in Australia and South America, with one native species found on each of those continents.

Rana range in size from small to very large. They tend to be rather long-limbed, with slender fingers and toes. The toes are strongly webbed. *Rana* are primarily aquatic and occupy most types of permanent water habitats.

All species are generalized carnivores. Males possess either paired vocal sacs or a single sac, depending upon the species. If the vocal sacs are paired, they may be located either on the sides of the neck or under the throat. Eggs are laid in the water in a variety of types of masses.

Bullfrog *Rana catesbeiana* Shaw
Named For Mark Catesby, an eighteenth-century naturalist
Description.   The bullfrog (Plate 56) is the Northeast's largest frog. The dorsal color varies from bright leaf-green to olive, olive-brown, or brown.

There is no regular dorsal pattern, but the back and sides may be mottled or marbled with dark brown or black pigment. Recently metamorphosed and subadult individuals are greenish gray, with scattered small, intense black spots. The belly is white to dirty white, often with extensive black mottling. The legs may have indistinct bars of darker pigment. Albino specimens have been reported (Dyrkacz 1981).

The bullfrog is a robust species, with strong forelegs and long, muscular hind legs. The snout is rounded and blunt, and the eyes are set high on top of the large, broad head. The tympanum is large and obvious. A short glandular fold begins at the corner of the eye, curves around the top and back of the tympanum, and ends in front of the foreleg. There is no dorsolateral fold. The dorsal skin is smooth to pebbled in texture, sometimes with scattered small warts. The ventral skin is smooth. The toe tips are pointed, not expanded, and toes of the hind feet are webbed nearly to the tip of the longest toe.

Sexual size dimorphism is absent in this species. The average size for mature bullfrogs in Pennsylvania is 119.3 mm ($4\frac{3}{4}$ in.) SUL. The maximum size for the species is 203 mm ($8\frac{1}{8}$ in.) (Conant and Collins 1991).

Adult male bullfrogs may have yellow suffusion on the throat during the breeding season, and the first toe of the forefoot may be enlarged. The tympanum of males is larger than the eye, but that of females is equal to or smaller than the diameter of the eye.

Tadpoles of the bullfrog are very large, usually reaching 130–140 mm ($5\frac{1}{4}$–$5\frac{5}{8}$ in.) ToL, and are occasionally much larger. The eyes are positioned high on the head. The dorsum of the body and head is dark green with numerous dark spots and dots. The dark dorsal color lightens laterally, and the ventral surfaces are yellowish. The muscular portion of the tail is lighter in color than the body. The tail crests are translucent and patterned with numerous small black dots. The tail crest is low to moderate in height.

Confusing Species.   The bullfrog could be confused with the green frog, which also has green pigment on the head and is a large aquatic species. The bullfrog can be distinguished from the green frog by the complete lack of a dorsolateral fold.

Habitat and Habits.   Bullfrogs are our most aquatic species of frog and require permanent bodies of water. They may be found in a wide variety of habitats, from small farm ponds to the margins of large lakes. They are also found in small streams and large rivers. However, they inhabit only slow-moving creeks, streams, and rivers or quiet backwaters of faster-flowing streams. They are generally found on or within a few feet of the shore, but in weed-choked ponds and lakes they often occur far from shore among the weeds and water lilies. Most of the time, bullfrogs are very wary animals. During the breeding season, however, males become far more visible and are more easily approached.

Bullfrogs generally emerge from hibernation in early to mid-April, but they have been reported as being active as early as 28 February, when it was unusually warm. Activity rapidly increases from April into May, then remains at a fairly constant level throughout the summer. Activity begins to decline in September, and animals enter hibernation by the middle of October. Surface activity is controlled by temperature. In the warmer, more southerly portion of its range, the bullfrog is often active throughout the year.

Bullfrogs hibernate in mud and litter at the bottom of the body of water where they resided during the summer activity season. Stinner and Colleagues (1994) discussed the overwintering behavior of Ohio bullfrogs in detail.

The daily activity of bullfrogs usually begins around sunset and continues until sunrise. Periods of heavy rains will occasionally stimulate daylight activity.

Raney (1940) and Ingram and Raney (1943) studied the movement of the bullfrog. The extent of movement varies greatly from individual to individual and also by time of year. Little significant movement of individuals occurs during the reproductive season, but afterward some individuals may move distances of up to a kilometer (0.62 mi) while others remain in the vicinity. Similar results were found for the movement of individuals between years. Some individuals were located in the same place year after year; others moved as much as 1,400 m (ca. 1 mi) from their point of initial capture.

Bullfrogs are generally sit-and-wait carnivores, although they will occasionally actively forage for food, especially in water. The diet is distinctly different between immature and mature individuals. Young animals feed primarily on insects, gastropods (snails), spiders, beetles, flies, and dragonflies. Adults capture much larger prey. Prey taken include crayfish, other frogs (especially other members of the genus *Rana*), reptiles (e.g., box turtles, baby snapping turtles, young water snakes and garter snakes, and young painted turtles), mammals (e.g., bats, moles, and voles), and an occasional bird. The most common prey among adults are other frogs and crayfish. Bullfrogs are opportunistic feeders. Korschgen and Baskett (1963) reported that bullfrogs will often feed extensively on prey items when they are locally abundant and not utilize them at times of the year when they are not plentiful. Grasshoppers and cicadas constituted a major dietary item when they were extremely abundant in the environment but were not consumed at all when their populations returned to normal levels.

The bullfrog can gorge on extremely large meals. One was recorded consuming a hairytail mole weighing 33% of the frog's body mass, and another was reported to have consumed a green frog that was 80 mm ($3\frac{1}{4}$ in.) SUL (Raney and Ingram 1941). These huge meals occasionally prove fatal as bullfrogs have been found dead with large prey lodged in their throat.

Reproduction.   Reproductive activity does not commence with emergence from hibernation. Males seldom begin to call before the end of April, and actual choruses are rarely heard before the latter part of May. The reproductive season is long, extending to the middle or end of July. Males arrive at breeding sites two to three weeks before females. Males are highly territorial and actively defend their territory from intruders. Although male bullfrogs usually keep a low profile in the water, with just their eyes and nostrils above the surface, their position changes when they are in their territory in the reproductive season. At this time, they maintain a very high posture by keeping their lungs filled with air. This posture advertises their possession of the territory to other males. If another male approaches too closely, the territory holder turns, faces the male, and gives a sharp warning call. As the intruder continues to approach, the territory holder continues to give warning calls. When the intruder approaches within a few inches, one of two actions occurs: either the territorial holder jumps on the intruder, or both individuals charge and grab each other around the body with their forearms. In the latter case, a wrestling match ensues. These matches usually last for 15–20 seconds, but they may continue for as long as 5 minutes (Emlen 1968). Eventually one individual, usually the intruder, is defeated and leaves the territory to the victor. The establishment of a quality territory is very important to the male because it has been shown that females select males on the basis of the quality of the territory (Howard 1978).

Females emerge from hibernation with well-developed ovarian follicles. They enter the breeding areas over an extended time period, rather than en masse as is the case for many species of frogs. Once a female has selected a male, they enter into amplexus. The eggs are deposited within the territory of the male. Howard (1978) showed that embryo mortality is related to the quality of the male territory. Larger males control oviposition sites that experience reduced rates of embryonic mortality.

The eggs are small, averaging about 1.3 mm ($\frac{1}{16}$ in.) in diameter. Clutch size varies from about 6,000 eggs to over 20,000 eggs. There is a positive correlation between the size of the female and the size of the clutch. Both Emlen (1977) and Howard (1978) reported on the production of a second clutch of eggs by some females. Only older females who produced their first clutch early in the season produce a second clutch. Howard showed that the second clutch contains fewer and smaller eggs than the first clutch.

The eggs are laid in a large floating raft that is a single egg layer deep. The rafts of eggs are roughly circular and may be as much as 60 cm (2 ft) in diameter. Ryan (1980) reported an average egg mass area of 3,208 cm² (541 in.²) for a population of bullfrogs from New Jersey. The rafts of eggs are deposited amid low emergent vegetation. Ryan (1978) noted that eggs in rafts tended to remain about 0.8°C (1.5°F) cooler than the surrounding water. He speculated that this temperature difference was advantageous because bullfrog eggs are usually deposited in unshaded areas of water, so the potential is high for the eggs to become very warm. It has been shown that elevated temperatures lead to developmental abnormalities in bullfrog larvae.

Hatching usually occurs within 4 days. The time to metamorphosis is exceedingly variable. The minimum time from hatching to metamorphosis is 79 days, and the maximum time is in excess of 3 years. Both growing season and food availability appear to influence time to metamorphosis. As growing season decreases, time to metamorphosis increases. Bullfrogs from southern states usually metamorphose within 6 or 7 months, whereas some populations from northern New York may spend 3 years as larvae. In Pennsylvania, tadpoles overwinter and metamorphose the following summer (June, July, and August). A superabundance of food can dramatically speed up the developmental process. Corse and Metter (1980) found that tadpoles living in a Missouri fish hatchery and feeding on fish and fish chow underwent metamorphosis in as little as 79 days. In the colder areas of the Northeast (northeastern New York, Vermont, New Hampshire, and Maine), it is probable that bullfrogs do not metamorphose until sometime during their third year.

Cecil and Just (1979) examined aspects of the population biology of bullfrog tadpoles in northern Kentucky. Tadpole survival to metamorphosis was fairly high, ranging from 11.8% to 17.6%, depending upon the year. Population densities reached a high of 13.2 tadpoles/m^2 (12.9 tadpoles/yd^2) and a maximum biomass of 103 g/m^2 ($\frac{1}{4}$lb/yd^2). The size at metamorphosis is as variable as the time to metamorphosis. The SUL of recently transformed individuals ranges from 29 to 57 mm ($1\frac{1}{8}$–$2\frac{1}{4}$ in.).

Remarks. Bullfrogs can have a pronounced economic impact on certain activities. In fish hatcheries, bullfrogs can have a strong negative economic effect by consuming the fish. Corse and Metter (1980) estimated that each bullfrog residing in ponds at a goldfish hatchery in Missouri consumed an average of $12 (in 1980 dollars) of fish per year, for a total loss to the hatchery of $42,000 dollars a year. In addition, they found that the tadpoles competed with the goldfish for food.

A far more profound and disturbing negative impact of bullfrogs is associated with their introduction into bodies of water where other amphibians are present, as has occurred in many areas of the western United States. In these situations, native populations of amphibians often decline owing to competition with bullfrogs for resources and predation by bullfrogs. Hecnar and M'Closkey (1997) documented a fourfold increase in green frog numbers at Point Pelee National Park, Ontario, Canada, after the apparently natural extinction of bullfrogs within the park between 1990 and 1991. They suggest that this population explosion might have been due to the ecological release caused by the removal of a dietary competitor. It might also have been due to the removal of a predator on green frogs. Bullfrogs have been documented feeding on juvenile green frogs (E. Werner et al. 1995).

Distribution. The original geographic range of the bullfrog will probably never be known because of widespread stocking of the species. It now occurs throughout eastern North America, from Nova Scotia and the Great Lakes westward onto the Great Plains and south to the Gulf Coast. It has been widely introduced, both within this area and farther west, including Hawaii and numerous foreign countries.

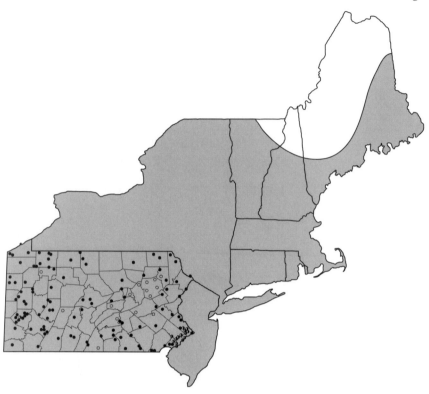

Map 33. Distribution of the bullfrog *(Rana catesbeiana)*.

Bullfrogs are absent from northern Maine, northern New Hampshire and northeastern Vermont. They are common in Pennsylvania and potentially occur in every county. This distribution may not reflect the original range in the Commonwealth, however, as the Pennsylvania Fish and Boat Commission distributed bullfrog tadpoles for many years.

Green Frog *Rana clamitans melanota* (Rafinesque)
L. *clamitantis,* loud calling; Gr. *melina,* black; Gr. *nota,* back
Description.   The green frog (Plate 57) is a moderate to large species. The basic background coloration varies from bright to dark green or occasionally greenish brown. The dorsum is either immaculate or has a pattern of small dark maculations. The sides of the head are bright green. The ventral coloration varies from white to cream and may be immaculate or exhibit a reticulate pattern of dark lines.

The head is broad and fairly short, and the snout is rounded. The eyes are large. Distinct dorsolateral folds occur on the body, but they fail to reach the end of the urostyle. The forelegs are short and heavy, and the toes lack webbing. The hind legs are long and muscular. The toes of the hind legs are long and webbed. The dorsal skin is somewhat rough and granular, and the skin of the ventral surface is smooth.

Pennsylvania adult green frogs ($N = 49$) average 85.8 ± 0.6 mm ($3\frac{3}{8}$ in.) SUL. This is much larger than the size reported for a sample from Connecticut, where the average SUL was 66 mm ($2\frac{3}{4}$ in.) and the range was 52–94 mm (1–$3\frac{7}{8}$ in.) (Klemens 1993). The maximum size for the species is 108 mm ($4\frac{1}{4}$ in.) (Conant and Collins 1991).

No sexual size dimorphism is evident. However, males and females differ in several other physical characteristics. Females have a tympanum that is equal to or slightly smaller than the diameter of the eye. The tympanum in males greatly exceeds the diameter of the eye. During the reproductive season, the chin of males tends to be bright lemon yellow, whereas the female's chin remains pale white or cream. The thumb of the male becomes greatly swollen at this time and is used in the process of amplexus. The forearms of males are hypertrophied.

Tadpoles of the green frog are moderately large, reaching a ToL of 90–100 mm ($3\frac{5}{8}$–4 in.) The eye is located in a dorsal position. The dorsum of the body and head is dark green with black maculations. The ventral surfaces are yellowish. Both the muscular portion of the tail and the tail crest are heavily spotted with black blotches. The tail crest is moderately developed.

Confusing Species.   The length of the dorsolateral fold should be sufficient to distinguish the green frog from all other members of the genus *Rana* in the Northeast. The bullfrog, with which it is most likely to be confused, lacks a dorsolateral fold.

Habitat and Habits.   With the exception of requiring water, the green frog is a habitat generalist. It may be found in small ponds, in marshes and swamps, and along the borders of large lakes. In flowing water, green frogs occur from tiny streams to the banks of large rivers, although they tend to avoid areas where the current is exceedingly fast. Adults sit in or at the edge of the water or float among aquatic vegetation with just the top of the head exposed. When in the water or at the water's edge, they sit facing the water. They are very wary and will dive beneath the surface at the slightest disturbance. They usually swim to the bottom and take refuge in vegetation or under soft sediments in situations where vegetation is lacking. Recently metamorphosed individuals frequently hide under rocks and other cover objects along the banks of both standing and flowing water.

Seasonal activity extends from mid-March to the end of October or the beginning of November. Green frogs usually hibernate buried in soft sediments under water, but they have, on rare occasion, been found in cavities on land (Bohnsack 1951).

Green frogs are active day and night. Diurnal activity is usually greatest early and late in the activity season. Terrestrial foraging tends to occur on rainy nights. At these times, green frogs may be seen, often hundreds of meters from water, moving about in the woods and crossing roads.

Green frogs are carnivores that employ several foraging techniques. They sit motionless until a prey item comes within striking distance, then they rapidly lunge forward to capture the prey. If motion is detected at a distance greater than their striking distance, the frogs will occasionally slowly stalk the prey until they get close enough to capture it with a quick lunge. Their prey consists of terrestrial and aerial invertebrates such as beetles, caterpillars, dragonflies, snails, flies, and spiders. Jenssen and Klimstra (1966) noted that food consumption varied with season and that green frogs ate the most in the spring. They further noted that during the breeding season females feed more than males. Hamilton (1948) reported an ontogenetic shift in diet for a New York population: only larger individuals fed on other frogs (recently metamorphosed and juvenile animals); they also ate proportionately more caterpillars and grasshoppers than smaller individuals.

Reproduction.   Although green frogs commence activity in March and early April, reproductive activity does not begin until the end of April or the beginning of May. The reproductive season often extends well into August. We have found freshly laid eggs as late as 11 August.

Males have been reported to migrate from streams and rivers to standing water for reproduction (Martof 1956). Male green frogs are territorial, as studied by Wells (1977) in populations of green frogs from New York. Males defend their territory from other males by chasing or jumping on intruders. Individuals occasionally get into wrestling matches over territorial disputes. This activity may account for the hypertrophied forearms of males. Territories are usually centered around some type of sheltered site and have fairly heavy stands of vegetation in the form of reeds, sedges, or submergent vegetation. Wells (1977) determined that an optimal territory has shallow water, dense emergent vegetation, and an abundance of submergent weeds. Reproductive success is associated with the quality of the territory. High-quality territories often support "satellite" males. These are males that occupy another individual's territory but remain unnoticed by remaining low in the water. When the owner of the territory acquires a mate, the satellite male takes his place.

Females emerge from hibernation with well-developed ovarian follicles. Wells (1976) noted that in a New York population all females that laid their first clutch of eggs before 21 July were able to produce a second clutch of eggs before the breeding season ended in late August. At the beginning of the breeding season the ovaries contain two distinct size classes of follicles. One set of follicles is of ovulatory size; the other set is made up of eggs about a third that size.

Females cruise around the pond, maintaining a low profile in the water until they find a suitable mate, at which time they make their presence known to the male. Once a female has selected a mate and is in amplexus, she moves to an oviposition site. The oviposition site may or may not be in the male's territory. The preferred sites for oviposition are shallow backwaters.

The eggs are laid in a broad, shallow raft that is usually one egg layer thick (Plate 58). Individual egg masses may contain 3,000 to 5,000 eggs and can cover an area 15–20 cm ($3\frac{3}{4}$–5 in.) on a side. Hatching is temperature dependent but usually occurs in 3 to 5 days. Recently hatched tadpoles remain near the egg raft, but within a day or so they disperse into the surrounding vegetation. Warkentin (1992) studied tadpole behavior and noted that young tadpoles spend all of their time foraging in dense vegetation where they can remain hidden from many potential predators. As tadpoles increase in size, a minority of them begin to forage in the open water column. Eggs and tadpoles are preyed upon by a variety of aquatic insects such as giant water bugs, water scorpions, the larvae of predaceous diving beetles, and the nymphs of dragonflies.

The period for development from hatchling to metamorphosis is variable (70–360 days) and depends primarily on when the eggs are laid in the breeding season. In Michigan, eggs laid before 25 June metamorphosed in the same year, while those laid later than 10 July overwintered as tadpoles and metamorphosed the following summer (Martof 1956). It is likely that in warmer climates a greater proportion of tadpoles metamorphose in the same year that they are laid.

Some tadpoles begin to develop limb buds at lengths between 60 and 65 mm ($2\frac{3}{8}$–$2\frac{5}{8}$ in.), but others attain sizes as large as 90 mm ($3\frac{1}{2}$ in.) before showing any sign of metamorphosis. Recently metamorphosed individuals (those showing a small remnant of tail) average 29.7 mm ($1\frac{1}{8}$ in.) SUL.

Females attain sexual maturity at about 70 mm ($2\frac{3}{4}$ in.) SUL; males mature at the slightly smaller size of 60–63 mm ($2\frac{1}{2}$ in.) SUL. Green frogs mature by the beginning of their second full growing season.

Distribution.   The green frog ranges from Newfoundland, Maine, and Nova Scotia to northern South Carolina, Georgia, and Alabama in the East and from Minnesota and southern Manitoba southward into Oklahoma and Arkansas in the West.

The green frog is widespread throughout the Northeast. It is the most common frog observed in Pennsylvania.

Pickerel Frog *Rana palustris* LeConte
L. *paluster*, marshy
Description.   The pickerel frog (Plate 59) is a medium-sized species. The dorsal coloration is usually some shade of brown, often light tan. There are two rows of dark brown or black blotches between the dorsolateral folds on the back. The blotches are squarish or rectangular, and, although sharply set off from the background, they lack a light border or margin. A single dark blotch is usually found on the head. There are one or two rows of dark blotches along the sides of the body. These blotches are often more irregular in outline than are those on the back. The dorsal surfaces of the limbs are patterned with dark crossbars (on the hind limbs) or more irregular blotches (on the forelimbs). A fine light line extends along the side of the head from the nares to behind and below the

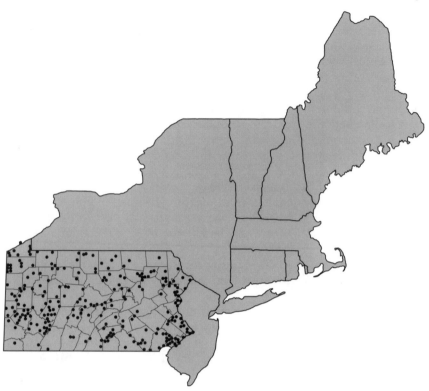

Map 34.   Distribution of the green frog *(Rana clamitans melanota)*.

tympanum. The anterior ventral surfaces are usually white, although the chin may be mottled. The posterior section of the body and the insides of the thighs are yellow.

The pickerel frog is a moderately built species. The head is fairly broad, and the snout is either rounded or slightly pointed. The eyes are large but are not located high on the side of the head. The tympana of both sexes are smaller than the eye. The forelegs are strongly developed, and the fingers are short, and blunt and lack webbing. The hind legs are long and muscular, and the toes are long and moderately webbed. The dorsolateral folds are well developed and uninterrupted. The skin between the dorsolateral folds is smooth, but often is formed into short longitudinal ridges along the posterior half of the back. The ventral skin is smooth, except on the posterior section of the thighs, where it is granular.

During the breeding season, males can be distinguished from females by the presence of greatly enlarged thumbs. Males have paired vocal sacs, but they are visible only when a male is calling. Females are significantly larger than males. In Pennsylvania, mature males average 53.0 mm $(2\frac{1}{8}$ in.)

SUL, and mature females average 66.4 mm ($2\frac{1}{2}$ in.) SUL. The maximum size for the species is 87 mm ($3\frac{1}{2}$ in.) SUL (Conant and Collins 1991).

Tadpoles of the pickerel frog are moderately large, reaching a maximum size of about 80 mm ($3\frac{1}{8}$ in.). The eyes are located on the top of the head. The body varies from green to olive-green and is covered with numerous small black dots. The ventral surface is white and shiny. The muscular portion of the tail is similar in color to the body. The entire tail (both muscular portion and tail crests) is covered with large dark maculations. The tail crest is low in profile.

Confusing Species.   The pickerel frog can be distinguished from the northern leopard frog by the presence of yellow pigmentation on the inner thighs and in the area of the groin and from the southern leopard frog by the lack of a white spot in the center of the tympanic membrane.

Habitat and Habits.   The pickerel frog is a semiaquatic species and as such will vary its habitat with season. During the spring mating season, pickerel frogs are found in the vicinity of water. They may be found in habitats such as temporary woodland and pasture ponds and pools, the borders of streams and rivers, overflow ponds associated with rivers and large streams, and the shallow, often weedy, areas of ponds and lakes. After breeding, frogs disperse into surrounding terrestrial habitats. Although not intimately associated with water at this time of the year, they do tend to occupy fairly mesic habitats. They are found in deciduous and mixed deciduous coniferous forests, wooded ravines, low-lying open fields, and meadows. When encountered in the open, they escape by making a series of long-distance leaps. Even when water is nearby, they are not extremely likely to escape into it; they are just as likely to leap along the bank or to move away from the water.

Pickerel frogs have a long annual activity period. They emerge from hibernation in early to late March, or in early April in exceptionally cold years. Their peak activity (due to reproduction) occurs from mid-April to the beginning of May. Pickerel frogs maintain a steady level of activity throughout the summer into the early fall before entering into hibernation in October and early November. It is not known whether pickerel frogs hibernate in terrestrial habitats or in aquatic situations. They are, however, frequently encountered in caves during the late fall and winter.

In the spring, pickerel frogs are active both during the day and at night, although chorusing generally occurs after dark. In late spring and early summer, when the frogs have moved away from water, surface activity is controlled by moisture availability rather than by time of day. Pickerel frogs are most frequently active when humidity is high. It is common to find large numbers crossing or resting on roads in forested areas during and immediately after heavy summer rains. At other times, they are often found in shallow excavations under rocks, logs, and other cover objects.

Pickerel frogs are generalized carnivores, feeding on a variety of terrestrial invertebrates.

Reproduction.   Although pickerel frogs often emerge from hibernation in March, significant reproductive activity seldom begins before the middle of April. Reproduction extends over a period of 4–6 weeks, usually ending in late May. Reproduction occurs in both temporary and permanent water but is generally restricted either to standing water (i.e., ponds, lakes, and pools) or to the quiet backwaters of streams. Males congregate in relatively small areas to engage in chorusing. Calling males are usually located in the water near the shore or in clumps of sedges and other emergent vegetation in the shallows.

Females emerge from hibernation with well-developed ovarian follicles. They enter breeding ponds singly over an extended period of time, rather than en masse. As a consequence, males far outnumber females in breeding ponds. Once a female selects a male, they enter amplexus and the female (carrying the male) swims to an appropriate oviposition site. Eggs are usually laid in shallow (less than 30 cm; 12 in.) water and are attached to submergent or emergent vegetation. Masses may be laid singly or communally. Wright and Wright (1949) reported as many as 31 masses deposited in an area less than $1 m^2$ ($30 yd^2$). Masses are almost spherical, rather than flattened as are the egg masses of leopard frogs. They resemble the masses of wood frogs but are laid later in the season. Egg masses contain from 2,000 to 3,000 eggs. The eggs are distinctly bicolored, with the dorsal surface dark brown and the ventral surface yellow.

Hatching occurs in about a week. Metamorphosis occurs within 70–90 days of hatching. The maximum size for tadpoles is 80 mm ($3\frac{1}{8}$ in.) ToL. Newly transformed individuals range from 19 to 27 mm ($\frac{3}{4}$–$1\frac{1}{8}$ in.) SUL (Wright and Wright 1949).

Males mature at about 44 mm ($1\frac{3}{4}$ in.) SUL, and females at around 50–55 mm (2–$2\frac{1}{4}$ in.) SUL. Immature individuals are very common in the spring, indicating that both sexes probably mature in the second spring after transformation.

Distribution.   The pickerel frog ranges throughout much of eastern North America, from New England and adjacent Canada southward to northern Georgia and westward into Minnesota, Missouri, southeastern Oklahoma, and eastern Texas.

The pickerel frog is widely distributed throughout the Northeast.

Northern Leopard Frog *Rana pipiens* Schreber
L. *pipiens*, to peep
Description.   The northern leopard frog (Plate 60) is a medium-sized to large species. The dorsal background coloration ranges from bright green to dark greenish brown or brown. The dorsal and lateral surfaces of the body, head, and appendages are covered with numerous circular to elliptical spots. The spots are dark brown or black and are bordered by a thin white or yellow margin. The dorsal spots are seldom, if ever, arranged in rows; rather, they are usually randomly distributed over the back of the frog. A light or white line generally runs along the margin of the snout,

Map 35. Distribution of the pickerel frog *(Rana palustris).*

to a point just above the shoulder, behind the tympanic membrane. The ventral surfaces are immaculate white, except for the edge of the lower jaw, which is sometimes dusky.

The body is moderately slender. The head is elongate, and the snout is slightly pointed. The eyes are large and sit high on the sides of the head. In both sexes, the tympanum is smaller than the eye. The legs are muscular, and the toes and fingers are pointed. The fingers lack any webbing, but the toes are extensively webbed. The dorsal skin is smooth, with a few scattered glandular ridges. The ventral skin is completely smooth.

During the breeding season, males possess enlarged and darkened thumbs. Their forearms are more strongly developed than are those of females. Females are significantly larger than males. In a sample from western Pennsylvania, males averaged 69.8 mm ($2\frac{7}{8}$ in.) SUL, and females averaged 78.6 mm ($3\frac{1}{8}$ in.) SUL. The maximum size for the species is 111 mm ($4\frac{3}{8}$ in.) SUL (Conant and Collins 1991).

The tadpoles of the northern leopard frog are moderately large, up to 85 mm ($3\frac{3}{8}$ in.) ToL. The dorsum varies in color from olive green to brown, and the ventral surfaces are iridescent white. The muscular portion of the

tail is slightly lighter in color than the body. The tail crests are translucent. Both the crests and the muscular portion of the tail are profusely
covered with spots and lines of dark pigment. The tail crest is moderately
low.

Confusing Species.   The northern leopard frog may be confused with
the other two "spotted" species of *Rana* in the northeast. It differs from
the pickerel frog by having round, rather than squarish or rectangular,
dorsal spots and by possessing no yellow coloration in the region of the
groin and inner thighs. It differs from the southern leopard frog in lacking
a distinct white spot in the center of the tympanum. In addition, the vocal
sacs of male northern leopard frogs are not visible externally, except when
the males are actually in the process of calling.

Habitat and Habits.   The northern leopard frog is a semiaquatic species
that occupies a wide variety of habitats. It is found primarily along the
vegetated margins of ponds, lakes, and slow-flowing rivers and streams as
well as in marshes and swampy situations. Reproduction often occurs in
less permanent habitats (see Reproduction). During the summer, some
individuals venture far from the nearest permanent water. It is not
unusual to find adult northern leopard frogs in fields, meadows, and woodlands during the warmer months of the year. Northern leopard frogs are
wary animals, and if near water they will dive in at the slightest disturbance. If in a more terrestrial situation, they often remain immobile until
closely approached and then escape by making a series of quick leaps,
often changing direction while jumping.

The earliest and latest dates for northern leopard frog activity in Pennsylvania are 16 March and 27 October. Without doubt, the season, at
times, extends beyond these dates owing to more moderate climatic conditions. For example, C. Walker (1946) reported occasionally finding
leopard frogs active as early as the middle of February during unusually
warm winters and as late as November in Ohio. More information is available on hibernation in the northern leopard frog than for most other
species of anurans. Northern leopard frogs overwinter at the bottom of
streams and lakes. Merrell (1977) noted that it is not true hibernation but
rather a quiescent state, with the animals making occasional movements
during the winter. He observed them simply resting on the bottom,
usually in the vicinity of aquatic vegetation. Emery and colleagues (1972)
found that a Quebec population constructed small pits in the bottom of
ponds or streams, where they spent the winter. These pits were in water
as much as 3 m (10 ft) deep. Pits ranged from 8 to 13 cm ($3\frac{1}{4}$–$5\frac{1}{4}$ in.) in diameter and from 2.5 to 8 cm (1–$3\frac{1}{4}$ in.) deep.

Northern leopard frogs may be active either during the day or at night.
Dole (1965) noted that during the summer most frogs made a single, relatively short, movement each day that might occur at any time during the
24-hour period. Extensive movement, however, occurred only after moderate to heavy rains and mostly at night.

The only detailed study of the diet of northern leopard frogs is that of
Linzey (1967) for a population from central New York. Terrestrial insects

made up the majority of the diet in both adults and recently transformed young. Lesser quantities of worms, spiders, snails and slugs, millipedes, and centipedes were also consumed.

Reproduction. Although northern leopard frogs hibernate in water and tend to emerge early in the season, reproduction is usually delayed until April. Part of the reason is that northern leopard frogs often do not breed in the same bodies of water in which they hibernate. Merrell (1977) and Walker (1946) both reported that the frogs make extensive migrations to breeding ponds. Many of the breeding ponds are temporary, rather than permanent, and are found in open meadows and fields.

The most detailed discussion of reproduction in the northern leopard frog is that of Merrell (1977) for populations from Minnesota. Unless otherwise cited, information in this section is from that work. Males do not establish calling stations all over breeding ponds, but rather tend to congregate in fairly small areas. Areas apparently are selected on the basis of thermal properties; that is, males select the sections where the water is warmest. In general, these are sites where the water is shallow, has good exposure, and contains submergent aquatic vegetation. The selection of calling sites by males affects the rest of mating as well, since all reproductive activity takes place in the region where calling occurs.

Males are extremely indiscriminate in reproduction and will attempt to engage in amplexus with anything in their environment that is of an appropriate size and diameter. Females maintain a low profile until ready to move toward a calling male, at which time they swim toward the male of their choice. Once he has detected a female in his vicinity, a male will immediately grasp her. If she is not receptive or has already oviposited, she will give a brief release call. Males that are inadvertently grasped also utter a release call.

Eggs are laid in flattened masses and are oval rather than spherical. They are generally attached to submerged vegetation but may lie freely on the bottom. Egg masses are often in close association with each other, although this may not necessarily represent communal nesting. Egg masses contain from 2,000 to 6,000 eggs. Eggs are darkly pigmented and average 1.7 mm ($\frac{1}{16}$ in.) in diameter (Walker 1946).

The time to hatching and metamorphosis is temperature dependent. Hatching usually occurs within 10 days, and most individuals transform by the middle of July. The size at transformation is apparently variable. Leclair and Castanet (1987) reported an average size of 25 mm (1 in.) SUL for recently metamorphosed froglets from Quebec, which is similar to that for Ohio populations (Walker 1946). Merrell (1977), however, reported the normal metamorphic size for Minnesota populations as 35–40 mm ($1\frac{3}{8}$–$1\frac{5}{8}$ in.) SUL and stated that in an uncrowded environment they do not metamorphose until 48–59 mm ($1\frac{7}{8}$–$2\frac{3}{8}$ in.) SUL. What accounts for this dramatic difference remains unknown.

Distribution. The northern leopard frog, as the name implies, has a primarily northern distribution, ranging over most of the northern portion of North America. Its distribution extends from Nova Scotia to the

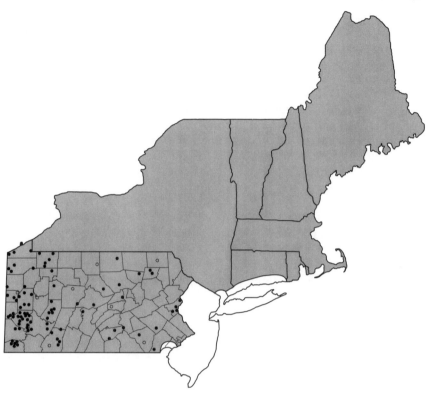

Map 36.   Distribution of the northern leopard frog *(Rana pipiens).*

Northwest Territories, throughout the northern Great Plains and Rocky Mountains southward into northern New Mexico and the mountains of Arizona. In the East, it extends south to northwestern Virginia and Ohio.

In the Northeast, the northern leopard frog is found throughout New England, except for eastern and southwestern Connecticut. It is absent from much of eastern and western New York. It does not occur in New Jersey. In Pennsylvania, it is primarily found in the western third of the state and throughout much of the Valley and Ridge Province. It is absent from the southeastern and south-central sections of the state as well as from the north-central and northeastern sections.

Southern Leopard Frog *Rana sphenocephala* Cope
Gr. *sphen,* a wedge; Gr. *cephal,* the head
Description.   The southern leopard frog (Plate 61) is a moderate-sized species. The dorsal coloration ranges from bright green to dark brown and is often a combination of both. In the latter case, frogs appear to be mottled green on a brown background. The dorsal and lateral surfaces of the body

and appendages are covered with a series of medium to large rounded or elliptical dark spots. The ventral surfaces are white. A white stripe extends along each side of the head from the snout to a point just behind the insertion of the foreleg. This line runs below both the eye and the tympanum. The tympanum contains a white or light-colored central spot. The dorsolateral folds are well developed and white.

The southern leopard frog is similar in shape and size to the northern leopard frog. The body is moderately slender. The head is elongate, and the snout is slightly pointed. The eyes are large and sit high on the sides of the head. The tympanum is smaller than the eye in both sexes. The legs are muscular. The toes are pointed at the tips rather than expanded, and the toes of the hind feet are strongly webbed. The dorsal skin is generally smooth, with a few scattered glandular ridges, and the ventral skin is entirely smooth.

Males can be distinguished from females by the presence of large external vocal sacs located on either side of the head. These sacs are visible at all times, not just when the males are calling. Females are significantly larger than males. In a sample from southeastern Pennsylvania, mature males averaged 55.8 mm ($2\frac{1}{4}$ in.) SUL, and mature females averaged 63.7 mm ($2\frac{1}{2}$ in.) SUL. The maximum size for the species is 127 mm ($5\frac{1}{16}$ in.) SUL (Conant and Collins 1991).

Southern leopard tadpoles are virtually indistinguishable from those of the northern leopard frog.

Confusing Species.   The southern leopard frog is very similar in appearance to the northern leopard frog. It differs from the northern leopard frog in the following characters: it has a white spot on the tympanum; it rarely has dark spots on the tip of the snout; and the vocal sacs of males are visible externally even when the frog is not calling. It differs from the pickerel frog in that the dorsal spots are more rounded and that the inside of the thighs are white rather than yellow.

Habitat and Habits.   Very little is known concerning the biology of the southern leopard frog in the Northeast. As a consequence, most of the discussion in this section and in the one on reproduction will draw on data collected in other parts of the frog's range.

The southern leopard frog is a semiaquatic species that inhabits a variety of habitats. It is found in marshes, in ponds, and along the margins of slow-moving rivers and streams. Farther south, the species occupies a broader range of aquatic habitats and even enters brackish water in Florida (Christman 1974). It does not, however, occupy fast-flowing water, so it is found only in slow-moving streams and rivers or in the quiet backwaters of fast-flowing streams. Southern leopard frogs are wary animals and will usually jump into the water at the least disturbance. At times, individuals will jump into dense vegetation instead of into the water. Frogs are even more difficult to approach during the reproductive season, a time when many other species can readily be captured.

The earliest and latest records for southern leopard frogs in Pennsylvania are 20 March and 5 October. In all likelihood the season is longer, probably extending from late February or early March to early November. Farther south, from the coastal plain of North Carolina to the Gulf Coast states, southern leopard frogs are active year round (Brandt 1936). Presumably, in the Northeast they hibernate at or just below the mud-water interface in the same bodies of water that they occupy during the active season.

Southern leopard frogs are primarily nocturnal. Pechmann and Semlitsch (1986) found that all movement to breeding ponds occurred at night, even on those days when rain fell during daylight hours.

No systematic study of diet has been conducted for this species, but it has been reported to feed on insects, arthropods, snails, and anurans (Duellman and Schwartz 1958).

Reproduction. Reproductive activity appears to occur primarily in April in southeastern Pennsylvania. Females collected in March contained ripe ovaries with well-developed follicles, whereas females collected in May had all laid their eggs. Females from April represent a mixture of gravid and spent individuals, indicating that oviposition occurs during that month. It is probable that females from New Jersey and New York exhibit a similar pattern. The breeding season occurs progressively earlier with decreasing latitude. Southern leopard frogs from North Carolina breed in January and February (Brandt 1936); those from farther south in South Carolina and along the Gulf Coast have two separate seasons: one in late fall (October and November) and the other in midwinter (January and February) (J. Caldwell 1986).

Males call to females while floating in the water. Their usual posture during calling is sprawled out, floating at the surface with both external vocal sacs inflated. The eggs are laid in flattened masses about 4 cm ($1\frac{1}{2}$ in.) thick and 10 cm (4 in.) wide. The masses are usually attached to aquatic vegetation at varying depths below the surface. Masses may be laid singly or communally. This variation in oviposition behavior appears to be dependent upon water temperature. At colder temperatures, egg masses tend to be located in shallow exposed areas and communal nesting is common, with as many as 126 egg masses laid together. At warmer temperatures, egg masses tend to be located in deeper water in more shaded regions, and communal nesting is absent. The mean water temperature during communal nesting in South Carolina was 15°C (59°F), whereas the mean water temperature during individual nesting was 27.5°C (80°F) (Caldwell 1986). The behaviors associated with low water temperatures are all designed to increase the temperature of the egg masses and therefore reduce developmental time. Single masses may contain as many as 1,500 eggs.

The time to hatching is temperature dependent, but hatching generally occurs within 7 days. In Louisiana, the larval period lasts from 50 to 75 days, and the young transform at a SUL of 22–25 mm ($\frac{7}{8}$–1 in.) (Dundee and Rossman 1989). The only information on development in Pennsylvania is a transforming tadpole that was collected on 10 June. The individual had well-developed limbs but still possessed a large tail. On the assumption of a mid-April oviposition date, it would appear that developmental time is similar to that reported for tadpoles from Louisiana.

Females and males mature at a SUL of about 50 mm (2 in.).

Remarks. In older literature, the southern leopard frog was usually referred to as *Rana pipiens sphenocephala* or *Rana sphenocephala*. Pace (1974) demonstrated that the southern leopard frog is a distinct species and resurrected the name *Rana utricularia*. In 1992 the International Commission on Zoological Nomenclature ruled that the name of the species will be *Rana sphenocephala*. However, most of the literature dealing with the species between 1974 and 1992 refers to it as *Rana utricularia*.

Distribution. This ecological counterpart of the northern leopard frog ranges from Long Island, extreme southeastern New York and New Jersey, southward throughout Florida and the Gulf States, and west to eastern Texas and Oklahoma. The ranges of the two species are largely complementary (i.e., they have adjacent, but no overlapping, ranges).

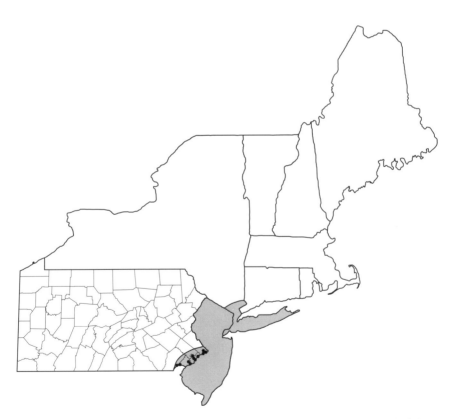

Map 37. Distribution of the southern leopard frog *(Rana sphenocephala)*.

The southern leopard frog was unknown from Pennsylvania until discovered in the vicinity of Bristol, Bucks County, in 1952 (Hudson 1956). In Pennsylvania, the southern leopard frog is found only in the lower Delaware Valley of the southeastern portion of the state. In this area, it is restricted to the Coastal Plain from Chadd's Ford, Chester County, in the west to Tullytown, Bucks County, in the east. Because of severe environmental threats (habitat destruction and manipulation) in this heavily urbanized and ecologically altered area, the Pennsylvania Fish and Boat Commission lists the species as endangered in the Commonwealth.

Mink Frog *Rana septentrionalis* Baird

L. septentrionalis, northern

Description.   The mink frog (Plate 62) is a small to medium-sized frog, with adults ranging in size from 45 to 76 mm ($1\frac{7}{8}$–3 in.). The dorsum may be mottled or spotted with dark brown reticulations. The spots are variable in size and often are round. Females have a greater asymptotic size than males, which appears to be the result of more rapid growth (Shirose and Brooks 1994). However, the maximum size of males and females does not differ. Females have more dark pigmentation than males, especially large females (SVL > 55 mm; $2\frac{1}{8}$ in.) (Kramek and Stewart 1980). Large females have a dark reticulate pattern not seen in males. The venter is yellow-white and unmarked. The hind legs have dark markings that form irregular blotches that parallel the long axis of the leg.

The dorsolateral ridges are highly variable between individuals, varying from very prominent to partially developed to absent. The toes on the hind feet have webbing to the last joint of the fourth toe and to the tip of the fifth toe.

The skin of the mink frog is smooth and may produce a scent similar to that of a mink (or rotten onions) when the frog is handled.

The tadpole of the mink frog is yellowish to dark olive green, with small dark spots. The belly is yellow and opaque, and the tail has pinkish spots (Logier 1952).

Confusing Species.   The mink frog is often confused with the green frog, which occurs over much of the range of the mink frog. The green frog can be distinguished from the mink frog by toe webbing that barely reaches the beyond the second joint of the fourth toe and that does not reach the tip of the fifth toe. In addition, the green frog has cross-banding on the hind legs.

Habitat and Habits.   The mink frog is an aquatic frog, inhabiting permanent or semipermanent lakes and rivers. It prefers the vicinity of outlets and inlets where there is a slight current (Logier 1952). It is also found in streams, pools, puddles, and ditches. In Canada, it was found to prefer a riparian habitat with a medium to high density of emergent vegetation or areas with extensive floating vegetation (Courtois et al. 1995). In open waters, it can be found basking and foraging among lily pads. The species is sometimes found in northern bogs. It breeds and hibernates only in permanent waters (DeGraaf and Rudis 1983). It is rarely found more than a few feet from water (Logier 1952).

The terrestrial activity of mink frogs has been reported from Ontario (Schueler 1987) and Minnesota (Hedeen 1986). It appears to be associated with precipitation and most often occurs late in the season, suggesting overland movement to reach hibernating sites.

Mink frogs feed mainly on insects, particularly aphids and chrysomelid beetles (Kramek 1972). However, it has been known to feed on minnows, leeches, snails, and spiders. Feeding behavior appears variable, possibly relating to changes in the level of hunger. These frogs have shown both sit-and-wait feeding and active searching behavior (Kramek 1976). Prey is taken primarily from the water surface (DeGraaf and Rudis 1983). Breeding behavior does not appear to affect feeding behavior (Kramek 1976).

Several theories have been put forward explaining the southern limit of the mink frog distribution. These include limitation due to predation by bullfrogs (Moore 1952) and by northern water snakes (Schueler 1975) and the need for cool, oxygen-rich waters for egg development (Hedeen 1986).

Reproduction.   The breeding season for the mink frog extends from the first week of June through the first week of August, with a peak in July (Bleakney 1958, Hedeen 1972, Wright and Wright 1949).

Eggs are laid in a globular jellylike mass that is attached to submergent vegetation that drops to the bottom of the body of water, where the eggs develop (DeGraaf and Rudis 1983). As many as 500 eggs may be laid in a clutch (Hedeen 1972). The egg size for a New York population was 1.60–1.68 mm ($\frac{1}{8}$–$\frac{1}{10}$ in.) (Moore 1952).

Metamorphosis occurs during the summer when the tadpole is at least 1 year old (DeGraaf and Rudis 1983, Logier 1952). The mean size of the mink frog at transformation varies among sites; an Ontario population averaged 42.6 mm ($1\frac{3}{4}$ in.) (Shirose and Brooks 1995), and a Minnesota population averaged 37.2 mm ($1\frac{1}{2}$ in.) (Hedeen 1972).

Distribution. The mink frog occurs from southern Labrador and the Maritime Provinces to southeastern Manitoba in Canada, south to northern New York and northern Wisconsin and into northern Minnesota. There are isolated populations in northern Quebec and Labrador.

In the Northeast, this species is found from the northern third of Maine through the northern half of New Hampshire and Vermont.

Wood Frog *Rana sylvatica* LeConte

L. *sylva*, a wood or forest

Description.   The wood frog (Plate 63) is a moderate-sized species. The dorsal coloration varies from gray brown to dark brown but is often reddish brown. A dark chocolate brown line forms a mask extending from the snout, through the eye, and terminating at a point posterior to the tympanum. The line acts to hide the distinct dark pupil of the eye, which otherwise would be extremely visible. Dark crossbars occur on the hind legs. The ventral surfaces are generally white or cream-colored.

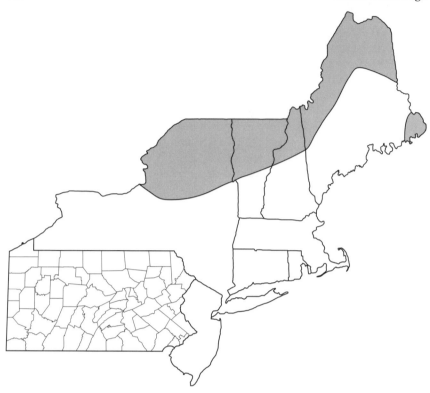

Map 38. Distribution of the mink frog *(Rana septentrionalis).*

The head is wide, and the snout is rounded. The tympanic membrane is smaller than the eye. Well-developed dorsolateral folds are present and extend to the end of the body. The forelimbs are short and moderately developed. The fingers are short and well-developed and lack webbing. The hind legs are long and slender. The toes of the hind foot are long and thin and distinctly webbed. The dorsal skin usually exhibits a slight rugosity; the ventral skin is smooth.

Wood frogs exhibit sexual dimorphism in size and in coloration. R. King and King (1991) demonstrated that male wood frogs are darker and less reflective than female wood frogs. Males are significantly smaller than females. The average size for males is 53.6 mm ($2\frac{1}{8}$ in.) SUL, and females average 61.1 mm ($2\frac{3}{8}$ in.) SUL. The maximum size for the species is 83 mm ($3\frac{3}{8}$ in.) (Conant and Collins 1991). In addition to size and color, males also differ from females in having the thumb greatly swollen. The characteristic is most prominent during the breeding season, and the thumb tends to diminish in size after reproduction. Occasionally, the paired vocal sacs of the male may be visible at the sides of the throat.

Tadpoles are of moderate size, usually attaining a length of about 50 mm (2 in.). The eyes are located high, but on the sides of, the head.

The dorsum and sides of the body are dark green and flecked with fine gold spots. The belly is pale and iridescent. The muscular portion of the tail is lighter than the body, and the tail crests are spotted with black. The tail crest is moderately high, especially for a *Rana*.

Confusing Species. The distinct pattern and facial mask of wood frogs preclude confusing these with any other species of *Rana* found in the Northeast. Juvenile wood frogs might be confused with adult mountain chorus frogs. The presence of distinct dorsolateral folds in wood frogs and their absence in mountain chorus frogs is sufficient to distinguish the two.

Habitat and Habits. As its common name implies, the wood frog is primarily an inhabitant of forested regions. It is found primarily in moist or lowland deciduous forests and is rarely, if ever, encountered in pure coniferous forests, although it is found in hemlock-northern hardwood-white pine communities in the northern portion of Pennsylvania. During the breeding season, wood frogs are observed in or near standing bodies of water, either temporary or permanent, that are located either in forests or adjacent to them in ecotonal areas. Throughout the rest of the year, they tend to be located away from water in the forest floor litter.

Wood frogs have the longest activity period of any northeastern anuran. They generally emerge from hibernation in early March but will emerge as early as mid to late February if climatic conditions are suitable. Peak activity occurs immediately after emergence from hibernation and corresponds with reproduction. After reproduction, the frogs disperse into the surrounding woodland, where they are less frequently encountered. Most individuals enter hibernation by the beginning of October. Occasionally, individuals may be found active on the surface as late as the end of November or early December.

Wood frogs are active diurnally and nocturnally during late winter and spring, with temperature tending to control activity time. When the weather is warm, frogs are active day and night, but on days when temperature remains low (less than 12°C; 53°F) activity is restricted to daylight hours. Surface activity in the summer is dependent upon moisture availability rather than on temperature. Frogs move about most frequently when humidity is high, usually at night and during and immediately after rainstorms.

Wood frogs generally hibernate in shallow burrows in deciduous forests. These burrows are seldom deep enough to be below the frostline of the soil. As a consequence, wood frogs face the possibility of freezing during the winter. The frogs have a freeze tolerance and withstand temperatures as low as −7°C (20°F) before freezing. They withstand such cold temperatures by producing glucose through metabolic activity of the liver. Increased glucose levels lower the freezing point of the body. The production of the cryoprotectant glucose is dependent upon the amount of glycogen (animal starch) present in the liver. As a result, wood frogs are more susceptible to freezing in the spring, when liver glycogen has been depleted (Costanzo and Lee 1993). Wood frog juveniles can survive freezes for 7–14 days (Layne 1995).

Little information is available concerning either movement or home range in this species. C. Walker (1946) reported movements of wood frogs to breeding ponds in open areas near woodlands. Bellis (1965) reported an average home range size of $70\,m^2$ ($77.2\,yd^2$) for a population of wood frogs from Minnesota.

Reproduction.   Wood frogs are the earliest species of anuran to mate and reproduce in Pennsylvania. Shortly after emergence from hibernation males move to breeding ponds and begin calling. The earliest that we have recorded calling activity is 4 March. Reproduction in this species is explosive and in any given area seldom lasts for more than a week. In some cases, calling activity is interrupted by freezing weather conditions. Although at any specific site the reproductive season is short, it can be spread out over a long time areawide. It is not unusual for calling to still occur in the colder northern sections of Pennsylvania at the end of April and beginning of May.

Petranka and Thomas (1995) demonstrated that synchronous breeding, and therefore synchronous emergence of larvae, is adaptive in this species. Larvae of a similar size do not prey on each other. However, large wood frog larvae will readily consume the eggs and smaller larvae of conspecifics. In an experiment, they added fresh egg masses to a pond a week after all reproduction had ceased in the pond. Upon hatching, all of the larvae from the introduced eggs were eaten by older wood frog larvae within 19 hours.

Wood frogs use both temporary and permanent bodies of water for reproduction. We have found them breeding in temporary and permanent woodland ponds, beaver ponds, roadside ditches, unused canals, and flooded borrow pits. Substrate within these various habitats varies from bare rock and dirt to heavy leaf litter. In some cases, ponds contain moderate to dense stands of emergent vegetation such as cattails and sedges, grasses, shrubs, and sapling trees. In general, the ponds are free of vertebrate predators.

Females emerge from hibernation with ovarian follicles of ovulatory size. Once in amplexus, females move to communal oviposition sites (Plate 64). Most females in a pond or other breeding aggregation will utilize one or at most two communal nesting sites. We have found as many as 78 individual masses clumped together into a single large aggregate mass. Seale (1982) reported an incredible 963 individual masses all deposited together. Waldman (1982) and Waldman and Ryan (1983) investigated the benefits of such communal deposition sites. They found that large masses of eggs were warmer than individual masses and that masses in the center were warmer than those along the periphery. Central masses also showed a more rapid development (as would be expected with the higher temperatures) and a higher hatching success than peripheral masses. All masses in communal aggregations exhibited higher survival and shorter hatching times than did eggs masses laid singly. Waldman (1982) felt that the explosive breeding in this species is due to their communal nesting behavior. Since central nests are laid first and have a developmental advantage, selection favors those individuals that lay their eggs early. Overall, this advantage leads to a shortened breeding season.

The large communal masses tend to be laid in the same site year after year. At one pond we examined, a large aggregate mass was laid in the same location in four successive years. This tendency to lay eggs in the same place year after year has been mentioned by others (Seale 1982, C. Walker 1946).

The eggs are embedded in spherical masses of crystal-clear jelly. Masses vary in size from 75 to about 100 mm (3–4 in.). Egg diameter ranges from 1.7 to 2.1 mm ($\frac{1}{16}$ in.). Berven (1988) studied clutch characteristics in several Maryland ponds. He found that mean clutch size varied from year to year, with a high average clutch of 745 eggs and a low average clutch of 572 eggs. Berven also noted no relationship between egg number and female body size, but he did observe a positive correlation between female body size and size of eggs.

The time from deposition to hatching is variable and dependent upon temperature. We have found recently hatched individuals as early as 2 April and as late as 23 May. D. Meeks and Nagel (1973) reported an incubation period of 20 days at an average temperature of 8.3°C (45°F). At hatching, larvae are about 8 mm ($\frac{1}{3}$ in.) long. Recently hatched larvae remain in the vicinity of the nest for 1 to 2 days before moving off to feed on the bottom. Berven (1988) reported the tadpole stage as lasting from 80 to 113 days in Maryland. Tadpoles of wood frogs achieve a maximum size of about 66 mm ($2\frac{1}{2}$ in.) and generally average 60 mm ($2\frac{1}{4}$ in.) in Tennessee (D. Meeks and Nagel 1973). At metamorphosis, froglets range in size from 17 to 20 mm ($\frac{5}{8}$–$\frac{7}{8}$ in.) SUL.

Distribution. The wood frog has a primarily northern distribution, ranging from Labrador in the East to Alaska in the West. It is found throughout much of the northeastern and north-central United States and extends southward into northern Georgia and South Carolina in the Appalachian Mountains.

The wood frog is widely distributed throughout the Northeast.

Carpenter Frog *Rana virgatipes* Cope
L. *virga* or *virgatus*, striped; L. *pes*, foot
Description. The carpenter frog (Plate 65) is a medium-sized frog ranging in size from 41 to 67 mm ($1\frac{5}{8}$–$3\frac{1}{2}$ in.) (Conant and Collins 1991). Its dorsal color ranges from brown to olive brown. There are four yellowish to golden-brown lateral stripes, two dorsolateral and two lateral. Carpenter frogs have no dorsolateral ridges. The ventral surfaces are white to pale yellow, sometimes with light to dark markings. The webbing on their feet is moderate, with the tip of the fourth toe exposed well beyond the web. There is sexual dimorphism in the tympanum size: the tympanum of males is larger than the eye, and that of females is either the same size as or smaller than the eye. Tadpoles are large, attaining a length of up to 92 mm ($3\frac{5}{8}$ in.). They are dark brown ith some darker spotting. Their tails are lighter than the body and have a rim of large spots on the upper half.

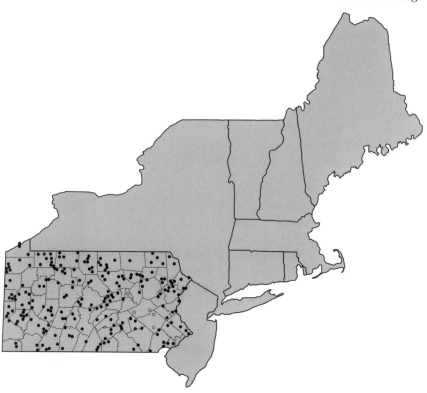

Map 39.   Distribution of the wood frog *(Rana sylvatica).*

Confusing Species.   Within its range in the Northeast, the carpenter frog cannot be confused with any other species.

Habitat and Habits.   Little recent research has been done on this species other than work by Given (see Reproduction). The carpenter frog is active from April to September (Wright 1932). This species thrives in sphagnum bogs and quiet streams with emergent grasslike vegetation. Gosner and Black (1957) reported that carpenter frog embryos are extremely tolerant of highly acidic conditions, and that acid tolerance might explain their distribution.

This species is known to feed on insects and worms (Wright 1932). Known predators include the northern water snake and the banded water snake (Gosner and Black 1968, Kauffeld 1957).

Reproduction.   This North American ranid has a prolonged breeding season. In New Jersey, the calling season begins in late April and continues through late July or early August (Given 1987). Calling begins after sunset and intensifies between 11:00 P.M. and 1:00 A.M. Calls resemble a repetitive hammerlike sound. Male carpenter frogs have a complex vocal repertoire consisting of a 1- to 10-note advertisement call, a single-note and multinote aggressive call, and a growl that is given during wrestling (Given 1987).

The frequency and intensity of male calls are strongly correlated with body size (Given 1987). Females also have a courtship call that elicits a single-note aggressive call from males (Given 1993). It has been suggested that this signal aids the female in determining the territory owner.

Male carpenter frogs are territorial and use physical interactions and vocalizations to defend their calling site. Males prefer calling sites near high densities of calling conspecifics (Given 1988) and may be found in mixed-species aggregations along lake perimeters (Given 1990). Females always approach the males in their territory, although either sex may initiate coupling (Given 1987).

Females attach eggs to underwater vegetation near the male's calling territory. Eggs are laid in subspherical or elongate globular masses that may be as large as 65 × 100 mm ($2\frac{5}{8}$ × 4 in.) (Gosner and Black 1968).

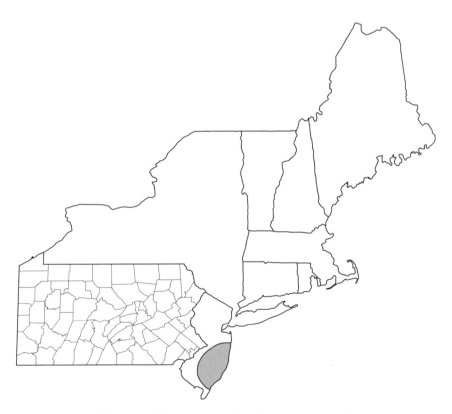

Map 40. Distribution of the carpenter frog *(Rana virgatipes)*.

Clutches contain 200 to 600 eggs. The tadpole stage lasts for one year (Martof et al. 1980).

Distribution.   The carpenter frog occurs in the mid-Atlantic Coastal Plain from the New Jersey Pine Barrens to the Okefinokee Swamp of Georgia and adjacent Florida. There is a disjunct population in Virginia.

Reptilia

The class Reptilia is represented by four living orders (Testudines, Squamata, Crocodylia, Rhynchocephalia). There are over 7,800 species of extant reptiles. Living species are found on all continents except Antarctica and on most of the major islands of the world. They occupy all major terrestrial and freshwater environments. They have also successfully invaded the marine environment and, as a result, representatives are found in all tropical and temperate oceans and seas of the world.

Reptiles are an extremely diverse group in appearance, but they do have a series of characters in common. All possess a dry, relatively gland-free skin that is covered by either epidermal scales (snakes and lizards) or scutes (turtles and crocodilians). Fertilization is internal, and development is direct (i.e., there is no larval stage). Females either lay eggs or give birth to live young. Reptiles have either claws or nails on their fingers and toes. Their lungs are well developed, and most gas exchange occurs through the lungs. Reptiles have 12 cranial nerves and, with the exception of crocodilians, have a three-chambered heart.

Although most species of reptile are carnivorous, some turtles and lizards are either omnivores or herbivores.

Turtles

Turtles belong to the order Testudines. There are approximately 275 species of turtle, divided among 12 families. They have a cosmopolitan distribution, being found on all major land masses with the exception of Antarctica. Turtles also occur in the Pacific, Indian, and Atlantic oceans. There are 7 families and 50 species of turtle in the United States, with 4 families and 14 species occurring in the northeastern United States.

Turtles are one of the most readily recognized groups of animals because of their unique appearance, with their body being generally encased in a hard inflexible shell. The upper shell is called the carapace, and the lower shell, the plastron. These two parts are generally connected by a pair of bony bridges along the sides of the animal. Most turtles can retract their head and appendages within this shell. Turtles lack teeth; instead, they have a horny beak. Their legs are modified, depending upon the environment in which they live. Terrestrial species tend to have large heavy, stumplike legs, whereas marine turtles have flippers for swimming. The toes of most freshwater turtles are strongly webbed for swimming.

Turtles occupy a wide range of environments, from the open oceans to the middle of harsh deserts. Most species are aquatic, but some are semi-aquatic and others (especially the tortoises) are terrestrial. Turtles are popular pets, and there is an active trade in species from all over the world. Occasionally, some of these pets either escape or are intentionally released, and as a consequence species of turtle can often be found far from their normal habitats and geographic ranges.

Turtles may be carnivorous, omnivorous, or herbivorous, and their diet often changes with size.

Courtship in turtles varies from exceedingly elaborate to virtually nonexistent. All turtles have internal fertilization and lay eggs. Turtle eggs may be soft and flexible or hard and brittle like birds' eggs, and they vary in shape from spherical to elliptical.

CHELYDRIDAE (SNAPPING TURTLES)

The family Chelydridae includes two species of snapping turtle, in two genera. These are the largest freshwater turtles in North America. The alligator snapping turtle of the southeastern United States is the larger of the two and reaches a maximum size of 66 cm (27 in.) carapace length and a maximum weight of 91 kg (200 lb). The common snapping turtle is smaller; it reaches a maximum size of 47 cm ($18\frac{3}{4}$ in.) carapace length and a maximum weight of 34 kg (75 lb). Snapping turtles are found in a wide variety of freshwater habitats. Their diet is highly variable.

Common Snapping Turtle *Chelydra serpentina serpentina* (Linnaeus)
Gr. *chelys*, tortoise; L. *serpens*, a serpent
Description. The common snapping turtle (Plate 66) is the largest species of turtle found in the Northeast and the second largest freshwater turtle in North America.

The carapace varies in color from light brown to olive brown to almost black. Carapacial scutes often exhibit a pattern of dark radiating lines running from the center to the edges. These are most readily observed on small to medium-sized individuals, as the pattern is usually obscured in adults. Often, much of the carapace is hidden under a heavy growth of algae. The plastron varies from off-white to yellowish gray. The skin of the head, neck, legs, and tail varies from brownish gray to brown-black above, but ventrally it is generally whitish. In some populations where the iron content of the water is high, the skin has a strong overtone of orange. The head of the common snapping turtle is free of markings, but the jaws are often streaked with dark lines.

The carapace is somewhat oblong and very heavy. The costal and vertebral scutes have raised keels that are most noticeable in hatchlings and juveniles but that tend to become smaller with age. Old individuals usually lose all trace of these keels and have a smooth carapace. The posterior margin of the carapace is strongly serrated. As is the keeling, this serration is accentuated in hatchlings and juveniles. In sharp contrast to the carapace, the plastron is relatively small and cruciform and is connected to the carapace by a pair of long, narrow bridges (Plate 67).

The head is massive, and the neck is extremely long and thick. The jaws are heavy, and the upper jaw has a hooked tip. The eyes are located high on the side of the head so that a submerged turtle can see above the surface with only a minimum of the head exposed. A small pair of barbels occur under the chin. The skin of the rest of the head and neck is covered with numerous tuberosities.

The legs are large and powerful, and the feet have thick, strong claws. The tail is long and thick at the base and rapidly tapers to a point. A row of enlarged medial plates occurs on the dorsal surface of the tail, giving it a sawlike appearance.

The common snapping turtle exhibits sexual dimorphism in overall size, weight, and tail length. Males grow much larger than females. In a population of common snapping turtles from Lake Wilhelm, Crawford County, Pennsylvania, 70 adult males averaged 351 mm (14 in.) CL, whereas a sample of 42 adult females averaged 284 mm ($11\frac{3}{8}$ in.) CL. Males averaged 22 kg (48 lb) live weight, and females averaged 11.4 kg (24 lb) live weight. The average length of the tail is 104% of CL in males and 97% of CL in females. When the tail is fully extended in males, the vent is located even with or posterior to the edge of the carapace. In females, the vent never reaches the edge of the carapace. The record size of the common snapping turtle is 494 mm ($19\frac{3}{4}$ in.) CL (Conant and Collins 1991).

Confusing Species. It is impossible to mistake an adult common snapping turtle for any other turtle found in the Northeast. The young, however, could conceivably be mistaken for small wood turtles or musk turtles. The long, keeled tail of the common snapping turtle is sufficient to distinguish it from either of those.

Habitat and Habits. The common snapping turtle is a habitat generalist. It is found in virtually every freshwater habitat, from pools in small streams (less than 1 m [3 ft] wide) to the main stream of large rivers such as the Delaware or Ohio. In standing water, common snapping turtles occur from small woodland ponds and marshes to large lakes such as Erie and Ontario. They are most common, however, in shallow standing water with a muddy substrate and an abundance of vegetation.

Although the common snapping turtle is primarily an aquatic species, some individuals do make occasional forays onto the land. Many individuals found out of the water are gravid females looking for a nest site, but a surprising number of individuals not engaged in egg-laying activities are also found moving about on land. Indeed, it is not unusual to see a common snapping turtle crawling along the side of a highway, especially during rainy weather.

Examination of records from the Carnegie Museum suggests a seasonal activity pattern that begins from late March to mid-April and ends in mid-October. Seasonal activity peaks in June and July and begins to taper off in August. This pattern is similar to that reported by Obbard and

Brooks (1981) for a population from Ontario. The pattern was unimodal, with a peak of activity in June and July, as in Pennsylvania.

It is generally assumed that common snapping turtles are active both day and night, and we have had equal success in trapping turtles both during the day and at night. A study in Ontario, Canada, involving turtles fitted with radio transmitters indicated that peak activity was in the morning, with a lesser peak in late afternoon and early evening (Obbard and Brooks 1981).

Hibernation behavior is better known for common snapping turtles than for most other species of turtle. R. Meeks and Ultsch (1990) give a good summary of hibernation for animals from Ohio. Turtles generally move into shallow water, where weeds and cattails are often common. In these areas, they burrow into the mud in water that is shallow enough so that the submerged turtle can occasionally extend its head and break the surface for air without disturbing its position under the mud. Other preferred hibernation sites are in the vicinity of muskrat houses and in shallow muddy channels of streams feeding into lakes. Common snapping turtles often hibernate in groups, and as many as 22 animals have been collected from a single hibernation site. G. Brown and Brooks (1994) found that snapping turtles in Ontario exhibited a high degree of fidelity to hibernacula. Ten of 13 individuals returned to within 1 m ($3\frac{1}{4}$ ft) of their previous hibernation site. Hibernation sites were very similar to those reported by Meeks and Ultsch (1990).

Obbard and Brooks (1981) found that common snapping turtles in an Ontario population had a mean home range of 3.4 ha (8.5 acres). The home range size in this population was not affected by either size or sex. The size of the home range probably varies greatly from population to population, depending upon the quality of the habitat, with home range size decreasing as habitat quality increases. The density of common snapping turtles follows the same pattern. Major (1975) found a density of 60.5 animals/ha (25.2 animals/acre) in some small ponds in western West Virginia where habitat was ideal. Lagler (1943) determined a density of only 5 animals/ha (2.1 animals/acre) in the less suitable habitat of a deep-water lake.

Common snapping turtles have an extremely varied diet that tends to change somewhat from location to location. They feed on aquatic insects, snails, clams, worms, fish, amphibians, reptiles, birds, and mammals. In most cases, invertebrates or fish constitute the major components of their diet. Common snapping turtles generally employ a sit-and-wait foraging technique in which they remain motionless on the bottom until a suitable prey item comes within striking distance. The turtle then rapidly lunges forward and simultaneously opens its mouth and expands its throat, thus causing water and the prey item to be drawn into the mouth.

On land, common snapping turtles are extremely aggressive and will strike repeatedly and with great force (sometimes actually lifting themselves off of the ground) at anything that threatens them. Their long neck and powerful jaws make them a truly formidable animal. Their aggressiveness tends to disappear when they are in the water. Small common snapping turtles can be safely carried by the tail, but this technique should not be employed with larger individuals because of the potential damage that may be done to their caudal and sacral vertebrae by dangling them by the tail. Large individuals can be carried by firmly grasping the posterior margin of the carapace with both hands and holding the animal well away from your body.

Common snapping turtles are preyed upon by a variety of animals, but predation tends to decrease dramatically with age. Hatchlings and young turtles are eaten by largemouth bass, northern pike, herons, raccoons, and mink. As adults, common snapping turtles have few predators other than people. They are, however, apparently vulnerable during hibernation to predation by other animals. Brooks and colleagues (1991) reported heavy mortality in a Canadian population of communally hibernating turtles that were attacked by otters.

Reproduction.   Mating may occur during any month of the activity season and takes place in the water.

Females emerge from hibernation with well-developed ovarian follicles that are ovulated by mid to late May. Egg laying generally occurs over a 2- to 3-week period, but its onset is variable. The time of oviposition varies both geographically and within a single population from year to year. Southern populations begin egg laying earlier than northern populations; egg laying appears to be temperature dependent. The initiation of egg laying is dependent upon the total heat available to the animals since emergence from hibernation (Congdon et al. 1987). Obbard and Brooks (1987) were able to predict within a day the start of egg laying over four consecutive years by measuring total heat units.

Eggs are generally laid in vegetation-free sandy soil, but occasionally they are deposited in areas where plants are growing. Suitable habitat for oviposition is not uniformly or commonly found in most common snapping turtle habitats. As a consequence, females often have to travel considerable distances away from water before an appropriate nesting site is found. Congdon and colleagues (1987) reported that one female from a Michigan population traveled 1,625 m (ca. 1 mi) from the water before nesting. Females construct their nests by digging with their hind feet. If no obstructions are encountered the nest cavity takes on a flask shape. However, if an obstruction is met the nest tends to become flattened. Once the nest has been dug, the eggs are deposited. After all eggs have been laid, the cavity is filled with soil and packed down by the plastron. In many areas of Pennsylvania, common snapping turtles use levated railroad bed rights-of-way as nesting sites, especially in areas where railroads traverse swampy or marshy regions, as in the northwestern portion of the state.

Predation on nests is extremely high, and, indeed, in some years at some sites all nests are destroyed (Congdon et al. 1987). The principal predators on turtle nests vary from area to area, but they include at least some of the following: gray foxes, red foxes, skunks, raccoons, and mink. Predation is highest shortly after the eggs are laid, then tapers off (C. Robinson and Bider 1988).

Common snapping turtle eggs are spherical and range from 20 to 28 mm ($\frac{3}{4}$–$1\frac{1}{8}$ in.) in diameter. For nine gravid females from Pennsylvania, clutch size ranged from 28 to 60 eggs and was positively correlated with female body size. Only a single clutch of eggs is laid each year.

Hatchlings in Pennsylvania have been reported from as early as 31 August to as late as 8 October. This is similar to the emergence times reported by Congdon and colleagues (1987) for hatchlings from Michigan. At hatching, young common snapping turtles are almost circular in outline. Their CL ranges from 25 to 31 mm (1–$1\frac{1}{4}$ in.), and their carapace width from 24–29 mm (1–$1\frac{1}{8}$ in.). Baby common snapping turtles, like baby sea turtles, appear to orient toward water by following the increased albedo produced by the water.

In a large sample of adults from western Pennsylvania, the smallest mature female was 208 mm ($8\frac{1}{4}$ in.) CL, and the smallest mature male was 256 mm ($10\frac{1}{4}$ in.) CL. The age at maturity in Pennsylvania is not known, but in Michigan females mature at a minimum age of 12 years.

Remarks.   There is a long history of people hunting common snapping turtles for use as food. At present, the Pennsylvania Fish and Boat Commission has neither a bag limit or possession limit nor a season for the taking of these turtles. The lack of regulation is probably due to the presumed abundance of the species. Its close relative, the alligator snapping turtle, has been hunted to the point that it is threatened or endangered over most of its range (Pritchard 1989). There is a real danger, if hunting pressure increases, that extreme damage could be done to populations of common snapping turtles in Pennsylvania, as well as in other states and Canadian provinces. Long-lived species with low reproductive rate (and therefore recruitment) can give the illusion of maintaining healthy populations for years after the real harm has been inflicted on the population. In such cases, the population eventually undergoes a dramatic and extremely sudden crash. Turtle populations should be managed to ensure adequate replacement of mature individuals removed from the population. Management often requires the taking of far fewer individuals than might be considered reasonable by trappers. R. Brooks and colleagues (1991) documented a significant negative impact on a Canadian population of common snapping turtles due to a sudden increase in otter predation on hibernating individuals. Recovery from increased predation is extremely slow.

Distribution.   The common snapping turtle is widely distributed in the eastern two-thirds of North America. In the East, its range extends from southern Canada southward into the panhandle of Florida and extends westward to the foothills of the Rocky Mountains.

It is common throughout the Northeast. In Pennsylvania it is distributed throughout the state. Counties where it has not been reported probably reflect a lack of surveying rather than an actual absence of the turtle from the county.

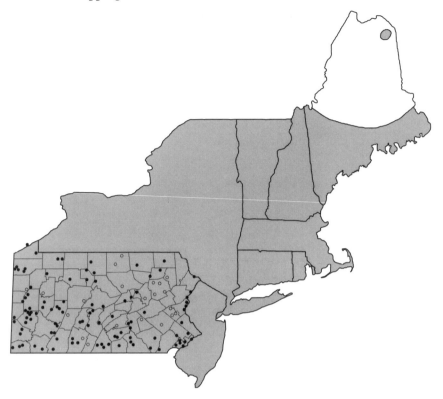

Map 41.   Distribution of the common snapping turtle *(Chelydra serpentina serpentina)*.

KINOSTERNIDAE (MUSK TURTLES AND MUD TURTLES)

The family Kinosternidae contains the mud and musk turtles. There are four genera and 22 species in the family. Kinosternidae is a strictly New World group, ranging from southern Canada to northern Argentina. They possess plastrons with fewer than 12 scutes, and all but one (the Mexican giant musk turtle) are small to medium-sized species. They are aquatic, emerging from the water only to lay eggs or to move to another area if their habitat is drying out. Most of their activity time is spent walking about on the bottom, foraging for food.

Kinosternon
Gr. *kino,* moveable; Gr. *sternon,* breast

The genus *Kinosternon* contains the mud turtles. There are 15 species within the genus. Mud turtles have a wide geographic distribution, occurring in most of the eastern three-quarters of the United States. Their range extends through Mexico and Central America into South America and terminates in northern Argentina.

They are small to medium-sized turtles. The plastron is large and well developed, with two transverse hinges that allow it to close tightly against the underside of the carapace. The genus is highly aquatic. Mud turtles generally prefer still or slow-moving water and are found in ponds, lakes, swamps, marshes, streams, and rivers. A few species occupy temporary bodies of water. Those that live in temporary habitats bury themselves in the mud until rain refills their habitat.

Mud turtles feed on a wide variety of aquatic plants and animals. Some species are highly carnivorous; other species exhibit a broadly omnivorous diet. All mud turtles lay elongate eggs with white, brittle shells.

Eastern Mud Turtle *Kinosternon subrubrum subrubrum* (Lacepede)
Gr. *sub-*, beneath, under; Gr. *rubra*, red

Description.   The eastern mud turtle (Plate 68) is a small aquatic turtle. The carapace varies in color from yellowish brown, to olive-brown, to almost black, and is without pattern. The plastron is an immaculate yellow or yellowish brown. The skin on all appendages varies in color from olive to olive-brown. The skin on the top of the head is olive-brown, becoming yellowish or mottled with yellow along the sides and on the jaws and chin. In profile, the carapace is low and lacks keels. When viewed from above, it is oblong, with smooth margins. The plastron is large, covering most of the underside of the turtle. There are two well-developed transverse hinges on the plastron (one on each side of the abdominal scutes) that allow the turtle to tightly seal itself within the shell. The legs are short but well developed. All four feet exhibit webbing between the toes.

There are too few specimens of the eastern mud turtle from Pennsylvania in collections to generate meaningful measurements of size. However, a sample of 100 adult males from Virginia had an average CL of 93.7 mm ± 7.2 ($3\frac{7}{8}$ in.), and 98 adult females had an average CL of 92.8 ± 8.4 mm ($3\frac{7}{8}$ in.) (Mitchell 1994).

Sexual dimorphism occurs in the eastern mud turtle. Males have a thicker and longer tail than females. The posterior margin of the male is deeply notched, whereas that of females is only slightly indented. Males have two patches of enlarged coarse scales on the inside of each hind leg.

Confusing Species.   The eastern mud turtle could be mistaken for a common musk turtle. The plastron of the eastern mud turtle, however, is much larger than that of the common musk turtle, and the eastern mud turtle lacks the yellow head stripes that are so noticeable on the musk turtle.

Habitat and Habits.   Virtually no information is available on the biology of the eastern mud turtle in the Northeast, so the following information relies upon our experience with the eastern mud turtle in other areas of its range and upon the literature.

The eastern mud turtle is an aquatic species that prefers slow-moving or standing water with a soft mud bottom and abundant aquatic vegetation.

The length of the activity season is extremely variable depending upon geographic locality. In the South, the turtles are active throughout the year; farther north, activity is shortened. Nichols (1947), reporting on a population from Long Island, New York, noted that the earliest and latest dates for turtle activity were 11 April and 11 November. It is probable that turtles in other parts of the Northeast have an activity schedule similar to that of animals from Long Island. Eastern mud turtles are primarily diurnal. During the summer, there are generally two activity periods, one centered around the early morning and a second in the late afternoon and early evening (Ernst and Barbour 1972). Eastern mud turtles hibernate buried in the soft sediments on the bottom or occasionally in burrows constructed by the turtles on land (Bennett 1972).

Virtually nothing is known about the home range size or movement patterns of the eastern mud turtle. In some populations in Illinois (Skorepa and Ozment 1968) and South Carolina (Bennett 1972), turtles apparently spend a considerable portion of their time out of water, but in most areas they appear to be completely aquatic, leaving the water only to lay eggs or to make rare overland migrations.

Eastern mud turtles actively forage for food on the bottom. They move slowly along the bottom with their neck partially extended. When a suitable food item is seen, it is stalked until the turtle is within striking distance, at which time the turtle lunges forward with mouth open. Eastern mud turtles are opportunistic omnivores, feeding on aquatic insects, crustaceans, mollusks, aquatic plants, and carrion.

Reproduction. Mating in the eastern mud turtle has been reported to occur from mid-March through May (Ernst and Barbour 1972). Mating takes place under water. Vitellogenesis begins before females enter hibernation. As a consequence, they emerge from hibernation with well-developed ovarian follicles. The follicles continue to yolk until they reach ovulatory size, usually in May, but earlier in southern populations (Iverson 1979). Throughout the range of the species, egg laying occurs from late April to late July. As is often the case with kinosternids, females do not necessarily dig a nest. At times, eggs are laid in piles of debris, under cover objects, or even in the open. Some females dig a nest in sandy or loose loamy soil and lay the eggs in the nest. An attempt may or may not be made to cover the nest after the eggs have been deposited (Ernst and Barbour 1972).

The eggs of eastern mud turtles are elliptical and have a white, brittle shell. The size of eggs varies from 22 to 30.5 mm ($\frac{7}{8}$–$1\frac{1}{8}$ in.) in length and from 13 to 17 mm ($\frac{1}{2}$–$\frac{5}{8}$ in.) in diameter (Iverson 1979). The clutch size ranges from 1 to 8 eggs and tends to increase with increasing latitude (Gibbons 1983). Anywhere from one to four clutches may be laid in a single season. The number of clutches tends to increase with decreasing latitude (Iverson 1979).

Hatchlings may begin to emerge as early as mid-July in some southern locations, but Nichols (1947) suggested that, in New York, hatchlings overwintered in the nest and emerged the following spring. Hatchlings range in size from 17 to 27 mm ($\frac{5}{8}$–$1\frac{1}{8}$ in.) CL. The minimum incubation time recorded is 76 days (Lynn and Von Brand 1945), but an incubation period of around 90–110 days appears to be more normal.

Both males and females mature at CLs between 70 and 80 mm ($2\frac{7}{8}$–$3\frac{1}{4}$ in.) throughout their range (Gibbons 1983).

Remarks. There have been numerous published reports of the eastern mud turtle from locations in the Piedmont, southern Valley and Ridge Province, and western Allegheny Plateau (Baldauf 1943, Iverson 1986, Netting 1935). These reports are in error and are most likely based either on specimens with erroneous locality data or on misidentified musk turtles.

Distribution. The eastern mud turtle occurs from Long Island, New York, southward along the Coastal Plain and Piedmont to northern Florida. Its range extends westward along the Gulf Coast to western Mississippi and then northward to southern Indiana and Illinois.

In Pennsylvania, the eastern mud turtle is historically restricted to the Coastal Plain in Philadelphia, Delaware, and Bucks counties, where it has been reported from the backwaters and marshes along the Delaware River and some of the coastal streams entering the Delaware River. Recent intensive sampling in the Coastal Plain, however, has failed to produce any mud turtles (Van Devender, pers. comm.). The most recent report of the species was from Tinicum Marsh, Delaware County, in 1986 (Groves, pers. comm.). It is possible that the species may have been recently extirpated from the state. Additional surveys in the southeastern portion of the state are needed to resolve the status of the eastern mud turtle in Pennsylvania.

Sternotherus
Gr. *sternon*, breast; Gr. *thairos*, hinge

The genus *Sternotherus* contains the musk turtles. There are five species in this strictly North American genus. Musk turtles occur throughout most of the eastern United States and adjacent southern Ontario in Canada.

Musk turtles are small and have a reduced plastron. The carapace is often covered with a luxuriant growth of algae, attesting to their highly aquatic nature. Although they are aquatic, they are not powerful swimmers and spend much of their time crawling about on the bottom foraging for food. Musk turtles inhabit a wide variety of aquatic situations.

Musk turtles are carnivorous, feeding on snails and clams, aquatic insects, worms, crustaceans, and carrion. All species lay elongate eggs with a brittle, white shell.

Common Musk Turtle *Sternotherus odoratus* (Laterille)
L. *odorus*, odorous
Description. The common musk turtle (Plate 69) is one of the smallest turtles in the world. The carapace varies in color from dark olive-brown to almost black. In adults, it generally lacks any type of pattern, although

Map 42. Distribution of the eastern mud turtle *(Kinosternon subrubrum subrubrum)*.

a series of small black smudges may at times be seen. In juveniles and subadults, these smudges are more pronounced and tend to form a series of short black streaks, occurring in an apparent random pattern over the entire carapace. The plastron is immaculate and varies in color from yellow to dark brown. The skin of the legs and tail is dark gray to black and is generally unmarked, but it may occasionally exhibit a series of small black spots against the light background, especially on the forelegs. The lateral edge of the foreleg is sometimes marked with a faint pale yellow stripe. The skin of the head and neck is of the same general color as the appendages. The head, however, is boldly patterned on each side with a pair of white or yellow stripes. These stripes originate on the snout and diverge as they go back, with one occurring just above and the other just below the eyes.

The carapace is oblong in outline when viewed from above. It is high and rounded in profile. Three dorsal keels are present in juveniles and subadults. The shell of the adult, however, tends to be smooth, with just a hint of a medial keel along the anterior vertebral scute. The plastron is reduced in size, exposing much of the undersides of the legs (Plate 70). The plastral seams are extremely wide. The neck is long, and the head is large for the size of the animal. Barbels are present on both the chin and the underside of the throat. The legs are moderately well developed, and the feet exhibit some webbing.

Although some workers (Ernst 1986a, Mitchell 1988, Tinkle 1961) have reported no difference in size between males and females, a sample of individuals in the collection of the Carnegie Museum exhibited significant sexual dimorphism for size. Males averaged 107.0 mm ($4\frac{1}{4}$ in.) CL, and females averaged 98.6 mm (4 in.) CL. Males and females also differ in the size and shape of the tail. The tail of females is tiny and does not extend beyond the posterior margin of the carapace. The tail of males is very broad at the base, extends well beyond the posterior margin of the carapace, and has a strongly curved and pointed tip. Males also have a pair of roughened patches of skin on the inside of the hind legs. One of the patches is just above the knee joint, and the other is just below it. The record size for the species is 137 mm ($5\frac{1}{2}$ in.) CL (Conant and Collins 1991).

Confusing Species.   Although the common musk turtle is a rather distinctive species, it could be mistaken for either a common mud turtle or a juvenile snapping turtle. It can be distinguished from the common mud turtle by its much smaller plastron and the light stripes on the sides of the head. The long, strongly keeled tail of the snapping turtle is enough to distinguish it from the musk turtle.

Habitat and Habits.   The common musk turtle is primarily an aquatic species. Individuals seldom leave the water except to lay eggs, although heavy rains and flooding will on occasion cause them to seek shelter away from streams. At such times, they may be found along the sides of roads.

Common musk turtles do not exhibit much preference in aquatic habitat, but they do tend to avoid areas with fast currents. In the Northeast, they have been found in marshes, swamps, abandoned canals, small ponds, and large lakes (e.g., Erie and Ontario) and from small streams to large rivers (e.g., Delaware and Susquehanna). In large bodies of water, they are generally found in quiet backwaters or embayments.

Capture records from the Carnegie Museum indicate that turtles first become active in mid-April and enter hibernation in late September and early October. This cycle corresponds closely to the annual activity cycle reported by Ernst (1986a) in the White Oak Bird Sanctuary in Lancaster County, Pennsylvania. We have never found hibernating individuals, but Ernst has located them hibernating in soft mud beneath cover objects and in the vicinity of muskrat houses. They occasionally congregate in large numbers during hibernation. Thomas and Trautman (1937) found about 450 individuals buried in the mud in less than 26 m² (270 ft²) of the bottom of a drained canal in Ohio.

During the summer, we have found common musk turtles to be active both day and night. It is possible that with the cooler temperatures of spring and fall activity shifts more toward the daylight hours. This shift has been noted for other populations of common musk turtles (Mahmoud 1969).

The abundance of this species varies dramatically from one population to another. Ernst (1986a) estimated a density of only 24 animals/ha (10 animals/acre) in south-central Pennsylvania, whereas Dodd (1989) estimated a density of 148.5 animals/ha (64.1 animals/acre) in a small lake in northern Alabama.

Virtually nothing is known about the home range size or movement patterns of these turtles. As mentioned earlier, they do come out on land to lay eggs and to escape flooding conditions.

Common musk turtles, unlike most aquatic species, seldom engage in aerial basking, but they will float at the surface of the water to absorb heat from the sun. At times, they can be found just under floating vegetation. This aquatic rather than aerial basking has a major consequence for the turtles. They tend to develop luxuriant growths of algae on their carapace. It is unusual to find a common musk turtle that does not have at least some algae. The major algae found on these and other aquatic turtles is a filamentous green algae called *Basicladia*. *Basicladia* is a habitat specialist and is found exclusively on the shell of turtles. Musk turtles are often parasitized by the leech *Placobdella parasitica*. Ernst (1986a) found that 37% of the musk turtles at the White Oak Sanctuary harbored leeches.

Common musk turtles actively forage for food on the bottom. They slowly walk along the bottom while foraging, usually with their neck partially extended. When a prey item is sighted, the turtle lunges forward with its mouth open. Common musk turtles are opportunistic feeders and have been reported to eat worms, snails, small clams, aquatic insects, crayfish and other crustaceans, small vertebrates such as tadpoles and fish, and carrion (Ernst 1986a). Although some vegetation is eaten, most of it is probably ingested incidentally to the capture of animal prey.

Reproduction.   We have never observed mating in this species, but it apparently may occur at any time during the annual activity season. Most matings, however, occur in spring and fall (Ernst 1986a). Mating takes place in the water, on the bottom.

Reproductive patterns are dramatically affected by temperature. As a consequence, more southerly populations tend to exhibit the various aspects of their reproductive cycle earlier than the northern populations discussed here. Females emerge from hibernation with well-developed ovarian follicles. These rapidly mature and reach ovulatory size by May. Egg laying in Pennsylvania occurs from late May to early July. Female common musk turtles tend to have a more cavalier attitude to laying their eggs than do most species of turtle. They do not necessarily dig a nest; rather, some simply lay their eggs under objects or bury them under surface debris. For example, Cagle (1937) found 16 nests under a single small log. With this haphazard method of egg laying, females seldom travel far from water to lay their eggs. Ernst (1986a) reported a maximum distance of 11 m (36 ft) from water and an average of 6.6 m (23 ft) traveled to lay eggs.

The eggs of common musk turtles are elliptical and have a brittle shell. The average size of eggs for a Pennsylvania population was 26.2 mm ($1\frac{1}{16}$ in.) long and 14.6 mm ($\frac{5}{8}$ in.) wide (Ernst 1986a).

Clutch size in this species is extremely variable. Ernst (1986a) reported an average clutch of 3.2 eggs, with clutch size ranging from 2 to 4 eggs, whereas Tinkle (1961) reported an average clutch size of 4.6 eggs and a range of 2–7 eggs for northern common musk turtle populations.

Hatchlings emerge from August through September after an incubation period of 75–82 days (Ernst 1986a). Hatchlings are tiny and can easily fit on a quarter. Ernst reported that 78% of all nests at White Oak Bird Sanctuary were destroyed by predators. Presumably, the major predators are raccoons and skunks.

The size at maturity is variable. In a Virginia population, males matured at 2 years of age and had a plastron length of 51 mm (2 in.), and females matured at 4 years, with a plastron length of 66 mm ($2\frac{5}{8}$ in.) (Mitchell 1988). Tinkle (1961) gave 63 mm ($2\frac{1}{2}$ in.) CL as the size for maturity of males and 80–88 mm ($3\frac{1}{4}$–$3\frac{1}{2}$ in.) CL as the size for maturity of females.

Distribution.   In the East, the common musk turtle ranges from southern Canada to the Gulf of Mexico and the southern tip of Florida. Its range extends westward to Kansas, Oklahoma, and eastern Texas.

In the Northeast, the common musk turtle occurs from southern Maine and New Hampshire to western Vermont through Massachusetts and Connecticut. It also has a disjunct range in New York, occurring in the extreme southeastern and northwestern portions of the state and along the Hudson River valley to the Vermont border. In Pennsylvania, it also has a disjunct distribution. It is found in most of the Valley and Ridge Province as well as in the Piedmont and Coastal Plain, but it is absent from the vast majority of the Allegheny Plateau. It is also found in extreme northern Pennsylvania in Erie, Crawford, and Mercer counties, but only in the Lake Erie and Ohio river drainages. It has apparently never gotten into streams that drain into the Allegheny River or those that enter the Ohio River in Pennsylvania.

EMYDIDAE (WATER TURTLES AND BOX TURTLES)

The members of the family Emydidae have been given the common names water turtles and box turtles. Emydidae is the largest and most diverse turtle family and contains 33 genera and 91 species. The family ranges throughout North America and the Caribbean; in parts of South America, Europe, northern Africa, and southern Asia; and on offshore islands. Emydids have a well-developed shell. They range in CL from 114 mm ($4\frac{1}{2}$ in.) for the little bog turtle from the northeastern United States to 800 mm ($31\frac{1}{2}$ in.) for the Malaysian giant turtle. Most species are aquatic, but a few are either semiaquatic or terrestrial. Their diet is extremely varied; species range from specialized carnivores to generalized omnivores. Some species are herbivorous.

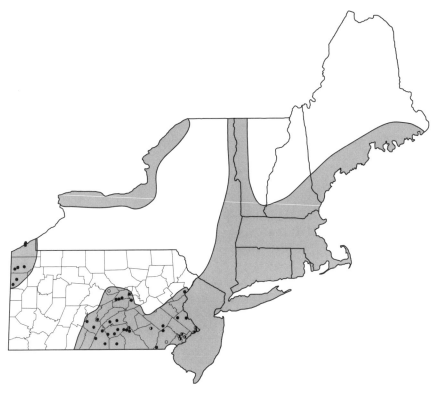

Map 43. Distribution of the common musk turtle *(Sternotherus odoratus)*.

Painted Turtle *Chrysemys picta* (Schneider)

Gr. *chrysos*, gold; Gr. *emys*, a freshwater turtle; L. *pictus*, painted

Description. The painted turtle (Plate 71) is a small aquatic species. The carapace ranges from dark olive-green to black. The margins of the carapacial scutes are bordered by a thin margin of lighter olive-green. The dorsal surfaces of the marginals are marked with red lines in the form of semicircles and curlicues, and the undersides of the marginals are marked with red bars. The plastron varies from beige to yellow and generally has a dark central blotch that varies in both size and outline. A purplish color often develops on the plastron of turtles that inhabit water high in dissolved iron (Plate 72). This is due to some of the iron's accumulating on the shell of the turtle. The accumulation is most obvious on the plastron, since that section of the shell is light in color. The background color of the head, neck, limbs, and tail is black. The skin of the head, neck, limbs, and tail is patterned with narrow red or yellow stripes or both.

The carapace is keel-less and low when viewed in profile. When viewed from above, the carapace is elongate, with slightly flaring, but unserrated, posterior marginals. The plastron is large and connected to the carapace by a broad bridge. Both plastral and carapacial scutes are shed whole each year, so the shell usually has a smooth, shiny appearance.

The legs are small and thin, but the hind feet are broad and fully webbed. The neck is short, and the head is fairly small. The tail is short.

The painted turtle exhibits considerable sexual dimorphism in both size and body proportions. A sample of mature males from Pennsylvania averaged 119 mm (4¾ in.) CL, and the females averaged 140.9 mm (5⅝ in.) CL. The record size for the painted turtle is 251 mm (10 in.) for the western subspecies (Conant and Collins 1991). Males have a longer and much thicker tail than do females. The claws of the forefeet of males are much longer than are the claws of the forefeet of females. These claws are used during courtship.

Hatchlings differ somewhat in appearance from adults (Plates 73 and 74). The shell is more circular in outline, and a slight central keel is present. The margins of the scutes are not set off by thin olive lines, and the tail is disproportionately long.

Confusing Species.   At a distance, the painted turtle could be confused with the common map turtle or the redbelly turtle. It differs from the map turtle in having a very smooth and low-profile carapace and lacking any serration of the posterior marginals. Redbelly turtles lack the light borders that are so visible along the seams of the carapacial scutes of the painted turtle.

Habitat and Habits.   The painted turtle is an aquatic species. It is a habitat generalist, found in almost every aquatic habitat in the Northeast, except for bogs. It is also absent from small, swift-flowing streams that lack quiet pools or backwaters and from standing water that lacks aquatic vegetation. The optimal habitat occurs in the form of small, slow-flowing streams and ditches, small weed-filled ponds, and the open waters of marshes. Within these habitats, painted turtles will usually be found concentrated around basking sites such as logs, stumps, rocks, or muskrat houses.

In Pennsylvania, painted turtles have been observed active in every month except February. They usually emerge from hibernation at the end of March or the beginning of April. Activity increases to a peak in late May. High levels of activity are sustained throughout the summer and early fall. Toward the end of September or the beginning of October, activity declines, and most turtles have entered hibernation by the end of October or the beginning of November. The level of activity is strongly influenced by water temperature. Below 10°C (50°F) turtles remain in an inactive state. Activity begins to increase at water temperatures above 10°C (50°F), but feeding and most sexual behavior are not initiated until the water has reached 20°C (68°F). As long as the water remains above 20°C, activity remains high (Ernst 1971).

Painted turtles are diurnal; the only exception is that a female already in the process of laying eggs will continue after sunset. Daily activity varies with season and local climatic conditions. In the summer, turtles generally begin their daily activity by basking, spend the middle of the morning foraging, bask during much of the middle of the day, and resume foraging later in the afternoon. However, on very cool days, most of their time is spent basking, and during periods of cloudy weather basking ceases (Ernst 1971). In spring and fall, painted turtles forage in the middle of the day.

Painted turtles often exhibit aggressive behavior while basking. This behavior involves primarily biting and pushing other turtles so as to displace them from preferred or optimal basking sites. The degree of aggressive behavior increases with an increase in the number of turtles attempting to use a specific basking location (Lovich 1988).

Painted turtles can be incredibly common in aquatic habitats, but abundance varies dramatically from one habitat to another. In a marshy location in Lancaster County, Pennsylvania, painted turtles had a density of 573 animals/ha, (238.7 animals/acre) (Ernst 1971), whereas in a pond habitat in northeastern New York, density was only 24 animals/ha (10 animals/acre) (Bayless 1975). Painted turtles generally have a sex ratio that does not differ significantly from 1:1 (Ernst 1971, Mitchell 1988). This normal sex ratio in painted turtles is rather unusual in light of the sex determination mechanism in the species (Schwartzkopf and Brooks 1985). Sex in painted turtles is determined during embryonic development and is dependent upon incubation temperature. At temperatures above 30°C (86°F) all females are produced; temperatures below 27°C (81°F) produce all males. Both males and females are produced at intermediate temperatures. In most species with this type of sex determination, the sex ratio is skewed in favor of one or the other sex on the basis of prevalent nest temperatures (Janzen 1994).

Painted turtles generally hibernate buried in the mud at the bottom of ponds, streams, and marshes or buried in the muddy banks of streams. It is likely that many hatchlings spend their first winter hibernating in their nest.

Painted turtles are opportunistic omnivores. No detailed studies have been carried out on the diet of painted turtles from Pennsylvania, but the species has been studied in other portions of its range. Raney and Lachner (1942) noted that plant and animal material were equally represented in the diet of a lake population of turtles from southwestern New York. Gibbons (1967) and Knight and Gibbons (1968) noted differences based on habitat in the diet of Michigan painted turtles. In a polluted river where pollution-tolerant invertebrates were abundant, the turtles were mainly carnivores, but in habitats where invertebrate prey were less abundant turtles exhibited a primarily herbivorous diet. Painted turtles feed on a wide array of animals, including snails, fish, small crustaceans, aquatic insects, worms, and crayfish. They also consume plants in the form of filamentous algae, duckweed, water lily seeds and leaves, and the leafy vegetation of other submergent flowering plants. Diet tends to change with the availability of food.

Diet can have a dramatic effect on the growth rate of turtles and the maximum size that turtles reach. Gibbons (1967) demonstrated that both

growth rate and the average size of painted turtles in Michigan were associated with dietary composition. Growth rate was slowest in a pond where
the turtles were primarily herbivorous and was greatest in a polluted river
where animal food was abundant. The largest turtles also came from the
polluted river, and the smallest came from the pond. A third habitat, intermediate in availability of animal prey, contained turtles intermediate in
growth rate and average adult size.

The painted turtle, like many aquatic turtles, is parasitized by the
common turtle leech *(Placobdella parasitica)*. Leeches are most frequently found on turtles early in the season, before they begin to engage
in extensive aerial basking. Leeches most commonly occupy the axillary
and inguinal pockets, but they may be anywhere on the turtle's body,
including the shell. It is not known whether leech infestations have any
adverse effect on the turtles.

Reproduction. Mating in painted turtles occurs exclusively in the
water. Males actively search for females. When a female is located, the
male initiates courtship by chasing the female. When the female is over-
taken, the male swims in front, turns to face her, and then strokes the
sides of her head with the elongated claws of his forefeet. This courtship
behavior may last for as long as 15 or 20 minutes before the female makes
a definitive response. If the female is receptive, she remains motionless
and begins to sink to the bottom. At this time, the male mounts and
copulation occurs.

Painted turtles have been observed courting in spring (April to early
June) and fall (September and October). Gist and colleagues (1990) suggested that effective courtship (i.e., where sperm transfer actually occurs)
takes place only in the fall, because they found that females from an Ohio
population contained fresh sperm only in the fall.

The ovarian cycle begins in late summer after oviposition has been
completed. Ovarian follicles begin to grow, and by the time the female
enters hibernation they are quite large. After the female emerges from
hibernation in spring, follicular growth continues, and follicles reach ovulatory size by the middle of May. Oviducal eggs are present from the end
of May to the beginning of July. In general, when the first set of follicles
are ovulated a second set of intermediate size are already present in the
ovaries. It is likely that this second set can grow and be ovulated in
the same year. As a consequence, it is possible that two clutches of eggs
are laid each year in the warmer regions of the Northeast.

Nesting occurs from late May to early July. During the nesting season,
females are often encountered on land as they move to and from nesting
sites. During this period, many individuals are killed by vehicular traffic
as they attempt to cross roads. This carnage can be extremely high if a
road happens to be constructed so as to separate a population of turtles
from their preferred nesting site. Carr (1952) reported finding between 200
and 400 road-killed turtles along a 90-m (300-yd) section of road cutting
through a New Jersey marsh. The preferred nesting sites usually are
located on gentle slopes that have little vegetation and have a good angle

of exposure to the sun. The soil at nest sites tends to be sandy and is always well drained. Painted turtles travel up to 620 m (ca. 2,000 ft) from water to nest (Christens and Bider 1987), but most nests are located within 100 m (330 ft) of water (Congdon and Gatten 1989). Hatching success can be very low. Christens and Bider (1987) reported a hatching success in Quebec of only 24%. Predation accounted for almost 75% of the mortality, while flooding was responsible for the rest of the deaths.

The eggs of the painted turtle are white, elliptical, flexible, and leathery to the touch. In a sample from Pennsylvania, the average egg dimensions were as follows: egg length, 28.4 mm ($1\frac{1}{8}$ in.); egg width, 17.5 mm ($\frac{5}{8}$ in.); egg weight, 5.9 g ($\frac{1}{5}$ oz). Only one study of reproduction has been conducted on Pennsylvania painted turtles (Ernst 1971). In that study, clutch size varied from four to six eggs. The average clutch size, however, varies greatly (from 4.1 to 19.8 eggs) throughout the range of the painted turtle (Iverson and Smith 1993). As a result, it is possible that other populations of painted turtles in Pennsylvania have significantly different clutch sizes. Pennsylvania painted turtles may lay two clutches a year, although Ernst (1971) recorded only a single clutch each year for a Lancaster County population.

Incubation time is difficult to determine in most painted turtle populations because the hatchlings generally overwinter in the nest site and emerge the following April or May. Overwintering hatchlings exhibit a remarkable ability to resist freezing. They have been shown to be able to survive nest temperatures of −6.2°C (22°F), a temperature that would kill most turtles (Packard et al. 1989). This amazing tolerance appears to be due to the ability of the turtles to undergo supercooling rather than to the production of a substance that depresses the freezing point of the body (Paukstis et al. 1989). The survival of neonates if frozen is very low. In one study, the freezing of body fluids for as little as 2 days resulted in 56% mortality, and no hatchlings survived freezing for greater than 54 hours (Attaway et al. 1998).

Hatchlings range in size from 25 to 27.8 mm ($1–1\frac{1}{16}$ in.) CL.

Remarks.   The painted turtle is a polytypic species that contains four distinct subspecies. Painted turtles in the Northeast are members of either the subspecies *Chrysemys picta marginata* (the midland painted turtle) or the subspecies *C. picta picta* (the eastern painted turtle), or they are intergrades (i.e., hybrids) between those two subspecies.

Ernst (1971) studied the geographic variation of painted turtles in Pennsylvania. He demonstrated that populations of turtles in the Lake Erie and Ohio River drainages were midland painted turtles, and populations in the Susquehanna, Potomac, and Delaware drainages were intergrades between the midland and eastern subspecies. The midland painted turtle has the following characters: the seams of the costal and vertebral scutes on the carapace are misaligned; there is a large dark blotch on the center of the plastron; and there are dark narrow borders on the marginal seams. The eastern painted turtle has the costal and vertebral seams in alignment, has no dark plastral blotch on its yellow plastron, and has wide borders on the marginal seams. Hybrids exhibit intermediate states with regard to these characters. Ernst and Ernst (1971) noted that the genetic influence of the midland painted turtle declined going from west to east.

Distribution.   The painted turtle is one of the most widely distributed turtles in North America. Its range extends from southern Maine and adjacent Canada across the country to Vancouver Island, British Columbia. In the East, it extends southward into South Carolina and northern Georgia to extreme northeastern Texas; in the central portion of the United States it extends into eastern Colorado, Kansas, and southern Missouri.

In the Northeast, the painted turtle is found from southern Maine, through the southern two-thirds of New Hampshire, throughout Vermont, and south and east through Massachusetts, Connecticut, New York, and New Jersey. It is widely and commonly distributed throughout most of Pennsylvania. Gaps in its distribution on the range map are most likely due to lack of surveying rather than an actual absence of the turtle.

The eastern painted turtle occurs throughout Maine, southwestern New Hampshire, eastern Massachusetts, Connecticut, Rhode Island, extreme southeastern New York and Long Island, and New Jersey. The midland painted turtle occurs in western Pennsylvania, most of New York, and Vermont. A broad band of intergradation between the two subspecies has been documented that includes central and eastern Pennsylvania, northwestern New Jersey, most of southern New York, western Massachusetts, and most of New Hampshire.

Clemmys
Gr. *klemmys*, a tortoise

The genus *Clemmys* contains four species of pond turtle. *Clemmys* is a strictly North American genus, occurring throughout most of the eastern United States and along the west coast from southern British Columbia to northwestern Baja California.

Members of the genus *Clemmys* are small to medium-sized turtles. There are no readily discernible external characters that unite them and at the same time separate them from all other turtles. They vary in habitat from semiaquatic to aquatic and occur in a wide variety of habitats, including bogs, marshes, streams, ponds, and moist woodlands.

The genus is omnivorous, feeding on a wide variety of plant and animal material. All members of the genus lay elliptical, white eggs with a flexible shell.

Spotted Turtle *Clemmys guttata* (Schneider)
L. *gutta*, spotted or speckled
Description.   The spotted turtle (Plate 75) is a small aquatic species. The background coloration of the carapace is jet black. Scattered about on this black background is a series of small bright yellow spots. The number

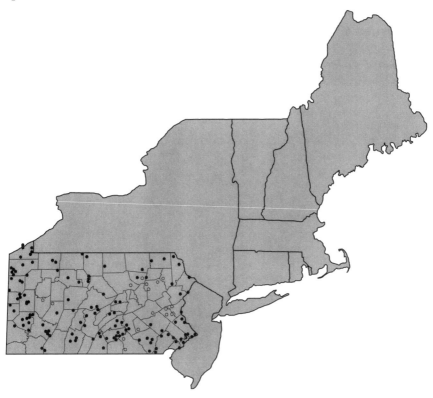

Map 44. Distribution of the painted turtle *(Chrysemys picta).*

and placement of these spots are variable, but generally every carapacial scute contains at least one spot. The plastron and the ventral surface of the marginals have a background color of yellow. In young individuals, each plastral scute contains a squarish black patch located on its pos-teriolateral corner. In older individuals, these patches tend to increase in size and coalesce, so that they sometimes cover almost the entire plastron. The legs, tail, head, and neck are black above, becoming lighter ventrally. Yellow dots occur on the head and neck but are absent from the tail and legs. The jaws are yellowish brown.

The carapace is low in profile and oblong or oval in outline when viewed from above. The surface and margins of the carapace are smooth. The plastron is very large, and the bridge that connects it to the carapace is wide. The legs and feet are slender, and webbing is absent from the toes. The head is small, and the neck is short.

Males and females do not differ in size; however, they do exhibit other sexually dimorphic traits. The average carapace size for 98 mature spotted turtles in the collection of the Carnegie Museum was 104.7 mm (4¼ in.) CL. The record size for the species is 127 mm (5 in.) (Conant and Collins 1991). Males have a concave plastron; that of the female is flat. Males have a longer and thicker tail than females, and the cloacal opening extends beyond the posterior margin of the carapace, whereas in females the cloacal opening barely reaches the posterior margin of the carapace.

Hatchlings and young turtles differ somewhat in appearance from adults. Hatchlings generally have only a single spot on each carapacial scute (additional spots develop with age), and the carapace is almost circular in outline when viewed from above.

Confusing Species.   The spotted turtle could be confused with the bog turtle, which is similar in size and overall appearance and often occupies a similar habitat. The spotted turtle, however, lacks a large, orange spot behind the eye and generally has yellow spots on the carapace. The shell of the spotted turtle is lower in profile than the shell of the bog turtle.

Habitat and Habits.   The spotted turtle is an aquatic species that inhabits marshes, wet meadows, swamps, bogs, and the shallow borders of ponds, lakes, and streams. Although it is the most aquatic of the northeastern species of *Clemmys*, it is not a powerful swimmer and is generally found crawling about on the bottom in shallow water or walking on submerged vegetation.

Spotted turtles tend to prefer cooler temperatures, as reflected in their annual activity cycle. In Lancaster County, Pennsylvania, activity begins in March and increases slightly until it reaches a peak in May and remains fairly high in June. Activity drops off precipitously by the end of June and for all intents and purposes ceases for the year by the middle of July (Ernst 1976). In Ohio, activity also begins in March, but the increase to a peak in May is steeper and activity falls off dramatically in June rather than July (Conant 1951). This difference is reflective of the continental climate of Ohio and western Pennsylvania where it is slower to warm in the spring but rapidly reaches high temperatures in late spring and early summer. Presumably, seasonal activity in western Pennsylvania is more similar to that of Ohio spotted turtles than to that of spotted turtles from eastern Pennsylvania.

Although spotted turtles are exclusively diurnal animals (Ernst 1976), their activity period during the day does change with season. Early in their annual activity cycle, turtles are most active during the early afternoon, but as the season progresses and daytime temperatures rise they become active earlier in the day. By May and June, the majority of activity occurs before 11:00 A.M.

During the summer, spotted turtles tend to aestivate, burrowed in the soil and leaf litter of deciduous woodlands adjacent to their spring aquatic habitat (Ward et al. 1976). In the winter, they hibernate in muskrat burrows and lodges and in the bottom mud of pools in flowing water situations (Ernst 1976).

The average body temperature for a Lancaster County population of spotted turtles was 20.1°C (68°F) (Ernst 1982). However, spotted turtles will engage in many different activities at much lower temperatures. Feeding is initiated when water temperatures reach 14°C (57°F), and reproductive behavior occurs at water temperatures as low as 8°C (46°F).

Little work has been conducted on population structure or density in this species. Ernst (1976) reported a population density that varied from 32 to 77 turtles per hectare (16–32/acre) over a 7-year period in Lancaster County, Pennsylvania.

Ernst (1970a) found that home range size averages about 0.6 ha (1.3 acre) and that home range size is not significantly different for males and females. Home ranges often overlapped broadly, but individuals showed no signs of territorial aggression. Individuals do exhibit homing ability. Twenty-eight percent of the turtles that Ernst (1968) displaced 850 m (ca. $\frac{1}{2}$ mi) from their point of capture were able to return to their own home range.

Spotted turtles actively forage for food by slowly walking along the bottom with the head and neck partially extended. When a potential food item is located, the turtle lunges at the prey with its mouth open. Spotted turtles are generalized carnivores, feeding on a wide variety of aquatic invertebrates and carrion. Dietary items include aquatic insects, crayfish, mollusks, the tadpoles of the American toad, and a variety of carrion, such as dead fish and ducks.

Spotted turtles are subject to leech infestation, and Ernst (1976) found that about 25% of all individuals harbored leeches. The number of leeches on each animal ranged from 1 to 11, with a mean of about 2.5 leeches per turtle. Filamentous green algae *(Basicladia)* was growing on about 50% of the turtles from Lancaster County, Pennsylvania.

Reproduction.   Mating activity begins immediately after emergence from hibernation in March. Ernst (1976) observed what he thought was a "mating aggregation" of spotted turtles in Lancaster, Pennsylvania. He found 16 turtles in a small pool on 19 March. Four pairs of turtles were copulating, and a fifth pair was clasping but had not yet copulated. Ernst observed no mating activity after 15 April. All copulation and courtship occurred in the water. Spotted turtles nest in June, and most egg laying occurs in the afternoon and early evening. The preferred nesting sites are in open areas where the soil is well drained. Females dig the nest with alternate strokes of their hind feet, and the nest is about 50 mm (2 in.) deep.

A study of a northern population (Georgian Bay, Ontario, Canada) revealed significantly different reproductive characteristics (Litzgus and Brooks 1998b). Litzgus and Brooks reported that oviposition was primarily a nocturnal activity. Clutch size in this population was significantly larger (X = 5.3 eggs) than that reported by Ernst (see below). In addition, females in this population appeared to have either a biennial or a triennial egg-laying cycle rather than the annual cycle typical of more southern populations.

Body size also appears to be strongly affected by geography and subsequent climatic differences (Litzgus and Brooks 1998a). Litzgus and Brooks demonstrated that individuals from cold climates mature later and at a larger size than do spotted turtles from the southern portion of the species' range. Indeed, the minimum size for sexual maturity in their study was equal to the mean size of mature spotted turtles from Pennsylvania.

The average clutch size in Lancaster County, Pennsylvania, was 3.5 eggs (range: 3–5 eggs) (Earnst 1970b). The eggs are elliptical and have a white, flexible shell. On average, eggs were 32.9 mm ($1\frac{3}{8}$ in.) long and 16.7 mm ($\frac{5}{8}$ in.) wide. A single clutch of eggs is laid each year (Ernst 1970b).

Hatchlings begin to emerge in mid-August after an average incubation time of 76 days (range: 70–83 days). Hatchlings average 29.8 mm ($1\frac{1}{4}$ in.) CL (range: 28–31.2 mm; $1\frac{1}{8}$–$1\frac{3}{8}$ in.). Both males and females mature in about 10 years at a plastral length of about 80 mm ($3\frac{1}{5}$ in.) (Ernst 1970b).

Remarks.   Ernst (1983) reported on a hybrid individual that resulted from a cross with a bog turtle. The hybrid resembled the spotted turtle in general pattern and coloration, but its shell morphology was like that of a bog turtle, with a more domed shell than would be expected in the spotted turtle and a serrated posterior margin rather than the smooth margin found in spotted turtles. The head pattern contained elements of both the spotted turtle and the bog turtle, having a series of small yellow dots on the head and a large broad orange blotch behind the eye. The hybrid came from Baltimore County, Maryland.

Distribution.   The spotted turtle ranges from extreme southern Maine to northern Florida. In the North, it ranges westward into southeastern Wisconsin and northeastern Indiana. South of Pennsylvania its westward range is restricted to the Coastal Plain and Piedmont.

In the Northeast, it can be found from extreme southern Maine, southern New Hampshire and Vermont, through Massachusetts, Rhode Island, and Connecticut and from the southern half of New York. There are also a number of records from western and central New York. In Pennsylvania, spotted turtles occur both in the southeastern Coastal Plain and Piedmont and in the west. They are absent from most of the Valley and Ridge Province and north-central and northeastern portion of the state, although a specimen has been reported from McKean County (Pauley, pers. comm.).

Wood Turtle *Clemmys insculpta* (LeConte)

L. *insculpta,* engraved

Description.   The wood turtle (Plate 76) is a medium-sized species. The carapace is grayish brown to brown in background coloration. A series of yellow and black radiating lines often occur on each of the carapacial scutes. These lines are often obscure and can best be observed by wetting the carapace. The plastron is yellow and is patterned with a squarish, black blotch on the posteriolateral margin of each plastral scute. The dorsal surfaces of the head, neck, legs, and tail range in color from dark brown to almost black. The ventral skin of the neck and legs, especially that skin which is usually hidden, is bright red or reddish orange.

The carapace is low in profile, and a distinct middorsal keel is present. When viewed from above, the carapace is elongate in outline, with strongly flaring posterior marginals. The carapace of this species is strik-

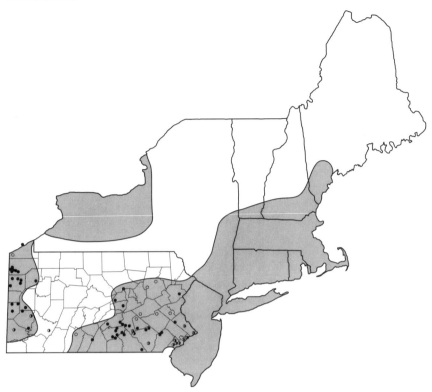

Map 45. Distribution of the spotted turtle *(Clemmys guttata)*.

ingly distinctive. Each scute is heavily sculpted with deeply incised growth lines, causing the formation of a pyramidal projection. The plastron is large and smooth and is attached to the carapace by a broad bridge. The neck is long, and the head is large and flat. The upper jaw is strongly notched at the tip. The legs are well developed and strong.

Wood turtles exhibit sexual dimorphism in several characters. Males have a concave plastron, and females have a flat one. The tail is much longer and thicker in males than in females. Males are significantly larger than females. A sample of males from Pennsylvania had an average CL of 176 mm (7 in.), whereas a sample of females had an average CL of 158 mm (6$\frac{3}{8}$ in.). The record size for the species is 234 mm (9$\frac{3}{8}$ in.) (Conant and Collins 1991).

Hatchlings and juveniles (Plate 77) differ somewhat in appearance from the adults. The carapace is low in profile and almost circular in outline. Juveniles lack the rough carapacial scutes that are associated with the deeply incised growth rings. The tail is extremely long, and in some cases may be as long as the carapace. In addition, the bright orange or red coloration of the underside of the head and appendages, so characteristic of the adult wood turtle, is absent from the hatchlings.

Confusing Species.   With its distinctively sculpted carapace, it is difficult to mistake a wood turtle for any other species found in the Northeast.

Habitat and Habits.   The wood turtle is a semiaquatic species, but few
people see wood turtles except when they are on land. Wood turtles are
habitat generalists, being found in a wide variety of terrestrial habitats
including open meadows, bogs, deciduous and coniferous forests, and old
fields. Kaufmann (1992a) conducted a detailed study of habitat use by
wood turtles from central Pennsylvania. He found that they spent most
of their terrestrial activity in alder thickets, open meadows, and corn
fields. Aquatic activity occurs almost exclusively in flowing water. We
have found wood turtles in aquatic habitats varying in size from medium-
sized rivers (e.g., Shenango River) to small second-order streams. They are
found in both slow-moving and fast-flowing streams. In streams with a
high current velocity, they are usually encountered only in slower-moving
sections.

Seasonal activity begins in late March or early April. The turtles remain
fairly active throughout the spring and summer and enter hibernation
from late September to early October. It has often been assumed that wood
turtles are primarily aquatic during the very early and late portions of their
activity period and highly terrestrial during the months of June, July, and
August (Ernst 1986b). This is not really the case. Throughout their activity season, wood turtles spend a considerable portion of their time in the
water (Kaufmann 1992a). In the cool months of spring and fall, the turtles
are primarily aquatic and make only occasional forays onto land. They
are most frequently observed during the spring because they are actively
moving about and herbaceous vegetation has not begun to grow so that
cover is less dense. With the approach of summer, they become more terrestrial, but even then they generally return to the water at night; they
also enter the water during the day during periods of prolonged unseasonably cold weather or during periods of drought. In the fall, they again
become predominantly aquatic.

Wood turtles are diurnal, but we have too few observations to be able
to determine if they are more active at one time of the day than another
or if time of activity changes with season. During the night, they rest
either in shallow depressions on the land or in the water along the edges
in the vicinity of overhangs or vegetation where they may remain out of
sight.

Hibernation occurs in the water. Typical hibernation sites are beneath
cut banks, where they often wedge themselves in among the semiexposed
roots of trees and other streamside vegetation. They often bury themselves
in the muddy bottom of slow-moving streams. Ernst (1986b) reported that
the depth of streams used for hibernation in a Lancaster County, Pennsylvania, population ranged from 100 to 230 cm (3–7 ft). It is doubtful that
turtles actually require water that deep for hibernation. Wood turtles have
been reported to hibernate in large aggregations. Twenty-eight animals of
all sizes were found at a single hibernation site in northern New Jersey
(Farrell and Graham 1991).

Ernst (1986b) determined a density of approximately 7 turtles/ha (2.9 turtles/acre) in a Lancaster County marsh. Farrell and Graham (1991) estimated an average population density of 10.6 animals/ha (4.4 animals/acre) for a northern New Jersey population. Adults usually outnumber juveniles, and females tend to outnumber males, occasionally by ratios as high as 2.5 females per male (R. Brooks et al. 1992).

Home range sizes vary considerably. The home range size for central Pennsylvania turtles averages 4.3 ha (10.3 acres) (Kaufmann 1995). The home ranges of southern New Hampshire turtles average 3.9–5.8 ha (9.3–13.9 acres) (Tuttle and Carroll 1997). The home ranges of Wisconsin turtles average only 0.1–0.9 ha (0.24–2.3 acres) (Ross et al. 1991), but the home range recorded for turtles in Ontario was 24.3 ha (58 acres) (Quinn and Tate 1991). Carroll and Ehrenfeld (1978) reported a highly developed homing ability in wood turtles. Eighty-three percent of the turtles displaced as much as 2 km (1.2 mi) from their point of capture were able to return to their original area. The homing ability fell sharply at distances greater than 2 km.

Little is known about the specific diet of wood turtles. They are opportunistic omnivores and have been observed feeding on a variety of items in the wild. During the spring, they feed on the leaves and flowers of wild strawberries, and later in the year they eat the fruits of strawberries, blackberries, and wild raspberries (Farrell and Graham 1991). They also feed on mushrooms, earthworms, snails, insects, and a variety of dead animals. In captivity, they readily feed on fruits, vegetables, and meat, including canned dog food.

The wood turtle is frequently parasitized by the common turtle leech, *Placobdella parasitica*. Infestations may be very heavy, especially during the spring and fall, when the turtles are more aquatic. Farrell and Graham (1991) found that 90% of all turtles collected during the spring and fall harbored at least some leeches. Leech infestations can be extremely heavy, with as many as 39 adults being found on a single turtle. Gravid leeches often attach to turtles during the fall and brood their eggs on the turtle over the winter. It is not unusual in the spring to find turtles with clusters of 50 or more baby leeches. Leeches generally occupy the more inaccessible areas of the animal's skin, such as the inguinal and axillary pockets and the area where the neck connects to the body. The impact of leech infestation on the turtles is not known.

Kaufmann (1991) observed what he termed a cleaning symbiosis between the turtles and minnows in a central Pennsylvania stream. The turtles remained motionless with their neck and legs fully extended while small minnows nipped at them. Presumably, the fish were feeding on bits of skin and ectoparasites that are attached to the turtle.

Wood turtles from some populations exhibit significant numbers of injuries involving any or all of the following: loss of portions of the tail, toes and parts of feet missing, sections of the carapace missing, and partial and complete amputations of forefeet and hind feet. These injuries appear to occur at frequencies much higher than those generally found for populations of other turtle species. They are probably due to attacks by potential predators such as raccoons, foxes, and skunks, but some may be due to aggressive courtship activity or male–male combat during the mating season (see Reproduction).

Reproduction.   Courtship and mating occur in the water, primarily in the spring and fall, but they may occur at any time of the year when the turtles are active. In Pennsylvania, most mating activity occurs in the fall from mid-September through October (Kaufmann 1992b). Male wood turtles are aggressive and force females into mating by biting, herding, and butting them. Males also exhibit aggression toward other males and will bite and snap at them. Aggression between males reflects dominance structure rather than territoriality (Kaufmann 1992b). This extreme aggressiveness may account for some of the injuries noted in wood turtle populations. Actual copulation occurs in the water, with the male holding onto the underside of the female's carapace with the claws of all four feet. If one male encounters another during copulation, a fight will often ensue, the winner of which mates with the female.

Females emerge from hibernation with well-developed ovarian follicles. Eggs are generally laid over a relatively short period in the middle of June. Nest sites are located in well-drained soil, with little vegetation and a good exposure to the sun. Railroad rights-of-way, shale banks, exposed hillsides, and sandy patches all make good oviposition sites. Nesting is one of the few activities of wood turtles that occasionally lasts into the night. The female begins nesting by constructing a shallow depression with her forefeet. Once this depression has been completed, the female enters it and then begins to construct the actual nest cavity with her hind feet. Nest predation may be very high. Brooks and colleagues (1992) reported over 90% predation for a population of wood turtles from Ontario, Canada.

Clutch size averages about 8.5 eggs and ranges from 3 to 13 eggs. Clutch size is positively correlated with female body size (Brooks et al. 1992, Farrell and Graham 1991). Only a single clutch of eggs is laid a year. The average egg measures 36.2 mm ($1\frac{3}{8}$ in.) in length, 23.3 mm ($\frac{7}{8}$ in.) in width, and 11.7 g ($\frac{1}{2}$ oz) in mass.

The incubation time is about 70 days (Farrell and Graham 1991), and hatchlings emerge in late August or early September. Hatchlings average 33.9 mm ($1\frac{3}{8}$ in.) CL and 8.9 g ($\frac{1}{3}$ oz) in mass.

The size at maturity appears to increase in more northern populations. Farrell and Graham (1991) reported that both males and females mature at 14 years of age at CLs of about 160 mm ($6\frac{3}{8}$ in.) in northern New Jersey. In Ontario, females mature at about 185 mm ($7\frac{3}{8}$ in.) CL and an age of about 18 years, whereas males do not mature until 22 years of age at a CL of about 199 mm ($7\frac{7}{8}$ in.) (Brooks et al. 1992).

Remarks.   Although the wood turtle is not considered to be in any immediate danger in Pennsylvania, the potential for extirpation in the state does exist. Populations are declining in many areas of the species' range, and several states have listed it as a threatened or an endangered species. The two greatest dangers to wood turtles in Pennsylvania come from highway fatalities as they wander about, especially in the spring, and from collecting. Wood turtles make excellent pets. They are alert, active, and intelligent and readily adapt to a captive existence. As a consequence, there is considerable demand for them in the pet trade, both in the United States and in other countries. Populations in Pennsylvania, especially in the south-central portion of the state, should be monitored closely to determine if commercial exploitation is occurring.

Saumure and Bider (1998) examined the effects of agricultural activity on wood turtle populations in Quebec. They found fewer young and old animals in agricultural areas than in less disturbed wooded regions. They also noted a 2.7-fold increase in shell injuries within the agricultural population.

Distribution.   The wood turtle has a decidedly northern distribution. It occurs from Nova Scotia westward to eastern Minnesota. In the East, it ranges southward to the mountains of northern Virginia. In the western part of its range, its distribution is spotty to northeastern Iowa.

The wood turtle is found throughout the Northeast. It is found throughout Pennsylvania, except in the southwestern corner of the state. In all likelihood, this distribution is an artifact of surveying rather than an actual absence of the turtle from the southwestern corner. Wood turtles tend to be most commonly encountered in the more mountainous counties of the Valley and Ridge Province.

Bog Turtle *Clemmys muhlenbergii* (Schoepff)
Named for Gottholf H. E. Muhlenberg, a late eighteenth- and early nineteenth-century botanist

Description.   Along with the musk turtle, the bog turtle (Plate 78) is Pennsylvania's smallest turtle. The carapace, plastron, and upper surfaces of the head, legs, and tail range from brown to brownish black. The undersides of the legs are lighter and mottled with yellow, and the plastron may contain some lighter markings. On each side of the head, behind the eye and above the tympanum, is a large bright orange blotch, somewhat variable in size but always larger than the eye (Plate 79).

The carapace is slightly domed in profile and has a middorsal keel. Growth rings are distinct and deeply etched into the carapace, giving the shell a rough appearance. When viewed from above, the carapace is elongate and fairly straight sided. The posterior marginals flare slightly and are weakly serrated. The plastron is large and is attached to the carapace by a broad bridge. The head and neck are moderate in size. The legs are short and well developed.

Sexual dimorphism occurs in several characters. Barton and Price (1955) demonstrated that females have a significantly higher-domed carapace. The plastron of males is convex, whereas that of females is flat. The tail is broader and much longer in males than in females. A sample of specimens from the Carnegie Museum showed no sexual dimorphism in size. The average size was 87.9 mm ($3\frac{1}{2}$ in.) CL. The record size for this species is 114 mm ($4\frac{1}{2}$ in.) CL (Conant and Collins 1991). However, Lovich and

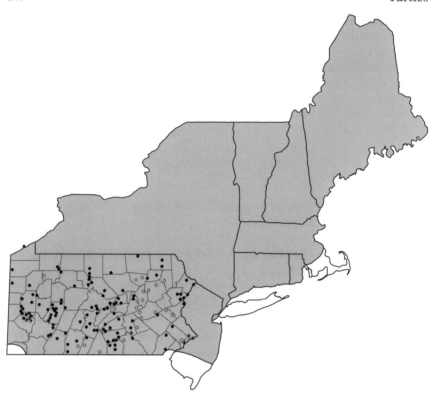

Map 46.   Distribution of the wood turtle *(Clemmys insculpta).*

colleagues (1998) noted sexual dimorphism in carapace length in a sample of individuals from Pennsylvania and New Jersey. In their sample, males had a significantly longer carapace than did females.

Confusing Species.   The bog turtle could be confused with spotted turtles (e.g., those that lack or have reduced dorsal spots). The bog turtle, however, can be readily distinguished from spotted turtles by the presence of a large orange spot on each side of the head, just behind the eyes. In addition, the posterior margin of the carapace flares in the bog turtle and exhibits a slight degree of serration. The posterior margin of the carapace of the spotted turtle does not flare and is smooth.

Habitat and Habits.   The bog turtle is an extreme habitat specialist. Populations occur in bogs and wet meadows where tussocks of grass provide basking sites and water is available for thermoregulation and for foraging for food. Both a muddy substrate and abundant grassy or mossy cover are universal characters of bog turtle habitats. Chase and colleagues (1989) carried out an extensive study of bog turtle populations in Maryland and determined the following characters common to prime bog turtle habitats: (1) the habitat occurs in a circular basin with spring-fed pockets of shallow water; (2) the bottom substrate is a mixture of soft mud and rocks; (3) low grasses and sedges dominate as vegetation; and (4) the meadow has both wet and dry pockets. If any of the specific conditions required by bog turtles changes, the turtle population goes into decline (sometimes slowly, sometimes rapidly) and eventually disappears.

Chase and colleagues further noted that virtually all the turtles they located were either found in standing water (62%) or within 20 cm ($7\frac{7}{8}$ in.) of water (23%). Bog turtles prefer very shallow (less than 8 cm [$3\frac{1}{4}$ in.] deep) water.

Seasonal activity generally begins in mid to late March, peaks in April, declines in May and June, and then remains at a very low level until all turtles have entered hibernation in October (Ernst 1977). Ernst (1977) found that, in Lancaster County, Pennsylvania, bog turtles became active at a water temperature of 13.5°C (56°F), but they did not begin to feed until the water temperature was 17°C (63°F).

Bog turtles are diurnal, but little information is available as to specific times of the day when they are most or least active. Ernst (1977) has observed them active from 7:30 A.M. to 6:30 P.M. in Lancaster County. Some of this time is spent basking.

Hibernation sites apparently change in response to the environment. In a Lancaster County, Pennsylvania, population where muskrats were common, the majority of turtles went into hibernation in the mud in the bottom of muskrat burrows from 1 to 1.8 m (3–6 ft) from the mouth of the burrow. The rest of the turtles were found hibernating under soft mud in the bottom of slow-flowing waterways. In New Jersey, at a site where muskrats were absent, all hibernating turtles were found burrowed in soft mud in the bottom of slow-flowing waterways. The turtles were generally under 20–25 cm (8–10 in.) of water in the waterways and under 3–7.5 cm ($1\frac{1}{4}$–3 in.) of mud (Ernst et al. 1989).

Population density in this species varies greatly. Chase and colleagues (1989) found turtle density to range from 9 to 213 individuals per hectare (3.8–84.5 individuals/acre) depending upon the habitat. The sex ratio in all populations did not vary significantly from 1:1.

In Lancaster County, Pennsylvania, males have a mean home range of 1.33 ha (3.3 acres), and females, 1.26 ha (3.1 acres) (Ernst 1977). This is much larger than for a Maryland population studied by Chase and colleagues (1989), where male home range was 0.176 ha (0.7 acre) and female home range was 0.06 ha (0.1 acre). Bog turtles do not appear to be territorial. Both Ernst (1977) and Chase and colleagues (1989) noted a large overlap in the home ranges of individuals and often noted individuals in the immediate vicinity of each other with no sign of aggressive interactions.

The diet of bog turtles consists principally of insects but also includes carrion and some vegetation. Surface (1908) found that the two specimens he examined contained 80% insects and 20% berries. Barton and Price (1955) found that two Lancaster County, Pennsylvania, specimens had eaten the following items (in decreasing order of abundance): caterpillars, beetles, pondweed and sedge seeds, caddisfly larvae, insect cocoons, snails, and millipedes. Other reported food of the bog turtle includes earthworms, crayfish, tadpoles, crickets, frogs watercress, and skunk cabbage (Bury 1979).

Reproduction.   Mating occurs from late April to early June (Barton and Price 1955). Courtship is aggressive. The male subdues the female by biting at the head and forelimbs to immobilize her, then mounts and hooks the claws of all four feet under the edge of her carapace. Mating may occur on land or in shallow water.

Clutch size ranges from 1 to 5 eggs (Bury 1979). The eggs, which are white and elliptical and have a flexible shell, average 29.7 mm ($1\frac{1}{4}$ in.) in length and are about 15 mm ($\frac{5}{8}$ in.) wide. Nests are constructed in moss or in sedge tussocks (Barton and Price 1955). Hatching occurs from late August to early October.

Hatchling bog turtles range from 24 to 30 mm ($1–1\frac{1}{4}$ in.) CL.

Growth is rapid during the first 2 years of life, but it slows dramatically as maturity approaches. Both males and females mature at a CL of about 75 mm (3 in.) and at an age of at least 6 years.

Remarks.   Bog turtles are considered endangered throughout their range for a variety of reasons, both natural and anthropogenic. The habitat that they live in is often an intermediate seral stage in ecological succession and as such has a short life expectancy. If similar habitats are not developing in the vicinity, a population can become extinct because it has no place to move to as the present habitat changes. Bog turtle habitat (i.e., "wetlands") has until recently been considered valueless land and was commonly drained to make it suitable for other more "useful" purposes such as agriculture or development. Finally, because of its rarity and appealing looks, the bog turtle is much sought after by the pet trade. There is, unfortunately, an active illegal market in bog turtles, and unscrupulous collectors will go to known bog turtle localities and collect as many animals as possible, sometimes doing irreversible damage to the populations.

Bog turtle sanctuaries have been established in Pennsylvania. The Nature Conservancy has been in the forefront of establishing such sanctuaries. Chase and colleagues (1989), after extensive study in Maryland, recommended that conservation efforts should focus on the development of a wetlands network (i.e., corridors), thereby allowing for movement between populations so as to maintain a normal flow of individuals from one population to another.

Distribution.   The bog turtle has an extremely fragmented and limited distribution. The largest portion of its range extends from the Hudson River valley of New York to adjacent states, southward to extreme southern New Jersey and eastern Pennsylvania and adjacent Maryland. It is also found in western New York, western Pennsylvania, and the southern Appalachian Mountains.

In Pennsylvania, the bog turtle's range extends from Franklin and Cumberland counties eastward to the Delaware River. Literature records extend their range northward to the Pocono Plateau in the east, but these have not been verified. The western populations in Crawford and Mercer counties have probably been extirpated. Recent intense survey efforts have failed to produce any animals from these historical locations.

Because of its extreme habitat specialization and resultant spotty distribution throughout the state, the Pennsylvania Fish and Boat Commission has listed the bog turtle as an endangered species within Pennsylvania.

Northern Diamondback Terrapin *Malaclemys terrapin terrapin* (Schoepff)
G. *malakos*, soft; G. *klemmys*, a tortoise terrapin, variant on *terrapene*,
the Algonquin name for turtle

Description.   The northern diamondback terrapin (Plates 80 and 81) is a small to medium-sized turtle of brackish waters. Its carapace varies from light brown to black and is oblong. The posterior marginals may be slightly serrated. The vertebral keel lacks knobs. There are concentric grooves on the vertebral and plastral scutes. The plastron is orangish to green-gray. The skin of the head and legs is usually light-colored with dark spots or

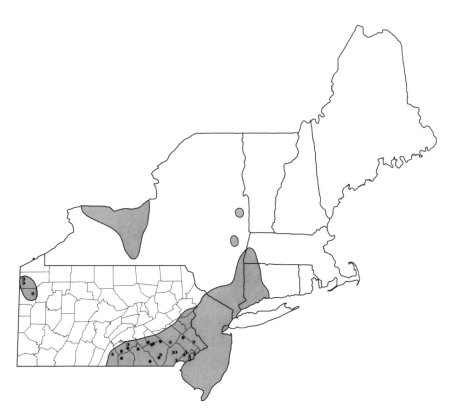

Map 47.   Distribution of the bog turtle *(Clemmys muhlenbergii).*

other markings, but the limbs may be uniformly gray. There is often a dark mustachelike marking on the light-colored upper jaw. The feet are strongly webbed, and the hind feet are large (Ernst et al. 1994, Klemens 1993).

This species exhibits sexual dimorphism in body size with females attaining larger sizes than males. Females are 150–230 mm ($6\frac{1}{2}$–$9\frac{5}{8}$ in.) long, and males are 100–140 mm ($4\frac{1}{4}$–$5\frac{7}{8}$ in.) long. Females also have a wider head, deeper shell, and shorter tail than males (Ernst et al. 1994).

Hatchlings resemble adults in appearance, except that the pattern of concentric rings on the carapace scutes is usually more prominent.

Confusing Species.   The northern diamondback terrapin is not easily confused with other turtles in the same habitat. The wood turtle has a shell with concentric rings that superficially resembles that of the terrapin; however, wood turtles do not have webbed hind feet and they never enter brackish water. Snapping turtles may enter brackish water, but they have a long tail that is saw-toothed and a small plastron.

Habitat and Habits.   The northern diamondback terrapin is found only in saltwater or brackish waters, such as coastal salt marshes, estuaries, and tidal creeks. Living in saline waters, northern diamondback terrapins are apparently capable of discriminating among different levels of salinity. They drink little water at high salinity and progressively more water as the salinity level decreases (G. Robinson and Dunson 1976).

In the Northeast, this species does not become active until late April or early May (Klemens 1993), and it ceases activity in November. It has been known to hibernate singly or in groups buried in the mud near the high-tide line, beneath undercut banks, and resting on the bottom in water. Terrapins in the Northeast remain dormant throughout the winter (Yearicks et al. 1981).

Males and females grow at the same rate for the first 2 years of life. Their growth rates and age at maturity are probably affected by the length of the active season (Ernst et al. 1994). In Florida, males reach maturity at about 3 years, at which time their growth slows. Females do not reach maturity until at least 4 years of age, when growth slows considerably (Seigel 1984). Data on growth rates are not available for northern populations.

Diamondback terrapins feed on a variety of prey, including hard-shelled gastropods (especially *Littorina*), crabs, and bivalves. Other prey taken are carrion, fish, and marine annelids (Ernst et al. 1994).

Reproduction.   In the Northeast, nesting begins in June and continues through July (Klemens 1993). The peak nesting time during the day is at high tide, ensuring that the nests are placed above the tidal zone (Burger and Montevecchi 1975). A complete description of nest site excavation is provided by Burger (1977), and nest dimensions are provided by Montevecchi and Burger (1975).

The clutch size for this species ranges from 4 to 18 eggs, with females in the northern part of the range producing more and smaller eggs than females in the south (Seigel 1980). Klemens (1993) reported that females in southern New England and New York produce clutches of 11–18 eggs. The eggs are pinkish white and leathery. Egg dimensions vary geographically (Ernst et al. 1994, Seigel 1980). Incubation time varies with temperature and ranges between 61 and 104 days (Burger 1977, Klemens 1993). Hatching takes place between June and late September in Connecticut (Klemens 1993) and in September through autumn in Massachusetts (Lazell 1979).

Remarks.   Although many populations of the diamondback terrapin are considered to be declining, those in the Northeast, except in Connecticut, are thought to be stable (Seigel and Gibbons 1995). The Connecticut population, especially nesting females, appears to be affected by incidental drowning in crab traps and by habitat loss and road mortality (Seigel and Gibbons 1995).

Distribution.   The diamondback terrapin occurs coastally from Cape Cod, Massachusetts, to Texas, and into the Florida keys.

In the Northeast, it is found along the coastline from Cape Cod, Massachusetts, to Long Island, New York, and southern New Jersey.

Map 48.   Distribution of the northern diamondback terrapin *(Malaclemys terrapin terrapin)*.

Blanding's Turtle *Emydoidea blandingii* (Helbrook)

Gr. *emys*, a freshwater tortoise; Gr. *-oidea*, like or similar to; named for William Blanding, an early nineteenth-century naturalist

Description.   Blanding's turtle (Plate 82) is a medium-sized species. The background coloration of the carapace ranges from dull black to blue-black. The carapace is covered with many small yellow circular or elongate spots. The background plastral coloration is yellow, and the plastron is boldly patterned with large black blotches originating on the posterior lateral surface of each scute. At times, these blotches can become so extensive that they obliterate the yellow plastral coloration. The skin of the tail and legs is blue-gray to blue-black, and an occasional scale contains yellow pigment. The skin on the top and sides of the head is also blue-black with occasional brownish streaks. The chin and throat are bright lemon-yellow.

The shell, when viewed from the side, is low in profile and lacks a keel. When viewed from above, the carapace is oblong and has smooth margins. The plastron is large and attached to the carapace by ligaments rather than by a pair of bony bridges, as is typical of most turtles (the box turtle is a notable exception). A single hinge between the pectoral and abdominal scutes allows the two lobes of the plastron to be drawn up toward the carapace. The legs are well developed, and the feet are webbed. The tail is short. The head is fairly large and very flat on the top. The neck is long.

Blanding's turtles do not exhibit much sexual dimorphism. The male's plastron is slightly concave when compared with the plastron of the female. The tail is slightly larger and thicker in males than in females, and the cloaca of the male extends beyond the posterior margin of the carapace. Ernst and Barbour (1972) reported Blanding's turtles to range from 125 to 260 mm ($7–10\frac{1}{4}$ in.) CL.

Juveniles look remarkably different from the adults. The shell is very low in profile and almost circular when viewed from above. The carapace is black and lacks spots. Distinct yellow dashes and short lines occur on the sides of the head and neck. The plastron tends to be yellow along the border and has a large dark central blotch. The tail is slender and almost as long as the plastron.

The following measurements are from a population of Blanding's turtles from Middlesex County, Massachusetts (Graham and Doyle 1978). Males had an average CL of 215.5 mm (9 in.), with a range of $7\frac{5}{8}–9\frac{3}{4}$ in., 182–235 mm and females averaged 204 mm ($8\frac{3}{4}$ in.), with a range of 179–217 mm ($7\frac{3}{4}–9\frac{1}{8}$ in.). The maximum size for the species is 268 mm ($10\frac{3}{4}$ in.) CL (Conant and Collins 1991).

Confusing Species.   Because of the hinged plastron, Blanding's turtle could be confused with the eastern box turtle. The eastern box turtle, however, lacks the brilliant yellow throat and chin coloration present in Blanding's turtle. It is also possible that smaller individuals could be mistaken for atypical spotted turtles, but the movable lobes of the plastron distinguish Blanding's turtle from that species.

Habitat and Habits.   Blanding's turtle is primarily an inhabitant of poorly drained lowlands. It is usually found in areas that are mosaics of marshes, wet meadows, ponds, and slow-moving streams. Although it has often been considered to be semiaquatic, recent studies indicate that it is primarily an aquatic species that makes occasional forays onto land (Ross and Anderson 1990, Rowe and Moll 1991). Ponds and other standing water are favored over streams.

In Illinois, Blanding's turtles initiate activity when the water temperature is about 10°C (50°F) (Rowe and Moll 1991). The water usually reaches that temperature in mid-March or early April. Activity reaches a peak in June, rapidly drops off in July, and then remains at a low level (Rowe and Moll 1991).

Blanding's turtles are diurnal and generally exhibit a bimodal activity pattern with, a peak occurring from mid to late morning and a second peak in the late afternoon (Rowe and Moll 1991). Although nesting may occasionally continue after sunset, virtually all nesting activity is initiated in the afternoon (Congdon et al. 1983).

Blanding's turtles enter hibernation between the middle of September and the middle of November, depending upon geographic area and local climatic conditions (Ross and Anderson 1990, Rowe and Moll 1991). Hibernation tends to occur in the same pond where summer activity takes place. During hibernation, turtles partially bury themselves in the soft bottom sediments of the ponds.

Most studies indicate a virtual absence of juvenile Blanding's turtles. Pappas and Brecke (1992) documented juvenile activity for a Minnesota population. They found that young turtles used shallow standing water in alder thickets and a shallow eutrophic pond that was bordered and invaded by tussocks of sedges. Some young turtles were seen either basking on the tussocks or actually perched in the branches of the alders, to a height of 90 cm ($3\frac{3}{4}$ in.). Most turtles were seen retreating into burrows, into holes at the base of sedge tussocks, or within the roots of the alders. Pappas and Brecke postulated that the habitat utilized by young turtles both provided them with protection from predators and reduced potential competition with adults.

Blanding's turtles are primarily aquatic carnivores (Rowe 1992). Rowe determined that only 12% of their diet was composed of aquatic vegetation, and much of that may have been ingested incidentally to the capture of animal prey. Mollusks, mostly snails, made up the majority of prey contained in their stomachs. Other major food categories were crayfish and aquatic insects. None of the food items recorded by Rowe (1992) were of terrestrial origin, giving added credence to the fact that these turtles are truly aquatic.

Reproduction.   Blanding's turtles apparently mate in the spring and summer in Massachusetts (Graham and Doyle 1978). Mating occurs in the water, and there is little in the way of courtship activity (Ernst and Barbour 1972).

Females emerge from hibernation with well-developed ovarian follicles. Ovulation occurs in late May or in June. In Michigan, over a 6-year period, the nesting season began between 23 May and 9 June and lasted from 16 to 30 days (Congdon et al. 1983). In Massachusetts, nesting occurred from late May to late June (Linck et al. 1989).

Females will move varying distances from their home pond to lay eggs. Nests have been located within 2 m (6 ft) of ponds and at distances of more than 1 km (0.62 mi) away from ponds (Congdon et al. 1983). Nesting activity generally begins in the mid to late afternoon and may continue after sunset (Congdon et al. 1983). Nests are located in sandy loam soil and tend to be in areas where grasses and sedge tussocks are common. However, a Massachusetts population showed a marked preference for laying eggs in a corn field (Linck et al. 1989).

Predation on nests in some populations is high. Congdon and colleagues (1983) reported that an average of 63% of all nests were destroyed by predators, with a maximum predation rate of 93% and a minimum rate of 42%. One hundred percent of the nests studied by Ross and Anderson (1990) in Wisconsin were destroyed before hatching.

There seems to be consensus among a number of workers that Blanding's turtles lay a single clutch a year. Clutch size varies from location to location. In Massachusetts, it ranged from 9 to 16 eggs (DePari et al. 1987). In Michigan, clutch sizes varied from 3 to 15 eggs (Congdon et al. 1983), and in Ontario clutch sizes ranged from 6 to 11 eggs (MacCulloch and Weller 1988). In Michigan, less than half of the females lay eggs each year. The percentage of females that laid eggs in a single season varied from 23% to 48%. Eggs averaged 38.2 mm ($1\frac{1}{2}$ in.) in length and 23.4 mm ($\frac{7}{8}$ in.) in width (MacCulloch and Weller 1988).

Incubation lasts 73 to 106 days in Michigan (Congdon et al. 1983).

Distribution.   Blanding's turtle has a northern distribution, extending from southern Ontario in the East and westward into Minnesota, Iowa, and Nebraska.

There are several disjunct populations in the Northeast. One disjunct population is found in southeastern New York (Klemens 1993), and another, larger, population occurs from southwestern Maine and southeastern New Hampshire to northeastern Massachusetts. No recent localities have been found in Connecticut (Klemens 1993). Blanding's turtle may very well be extirpated from Pennsylvania. Specimens were found in Conneaut Lake and in the nearby town of Linesville, both in Crawford County. Netting (1932) hypothesized that Blanding's turtle reached Conneaut Lake from Lake Erie via the Erie Canal. No specimens from those localities, however, have been reported since 1906. This area has undergone extensive environmental modification since the early 1930s. Among other things, the Shenango River was dammed and Pymatuning Swamp was flooded to produce Pymatuning Reservoir in 1935, dramatically modifying much of the wetlands in the area. Specimens are sporadically found along the Lake Erie shore, especially in Presque Isle State Park. It is likely that these occasional specimens represent waifs washed in from other populations rather than actual members of a small but viable population in northwestern Pennsylvania. Even if there were a viable natural population of Blanding's turtles in Presque Isle, the heavy vehicular traffic that the park experiences during the nesting season would rapidly reduce the population below a viable number of animals.

Graptemys
Gr. *graptos*, inscribed, painted; Gr. *emys*, a freshwater tortoise

The genus *Graptemys* contains the map and sawback turtles. There are 10 species within the genus. Map turtles range throughout most of the eastern and central United States and adjacent Canada.

Map turtles are medium to large turtles. The carapace bears a central ridge that is usually very well developed and has discrete protuberances arising from each of the vertebral scutes. The plastron is large. Map turtles are primarily riverine species, but a few species are also found in large lakes.

Map turtles are carnivorous, and several species have become specialized on a diet comprising snails and freshwater mussels. All species lay elliptical, white eggs with a flexible or parchmentlike shell.

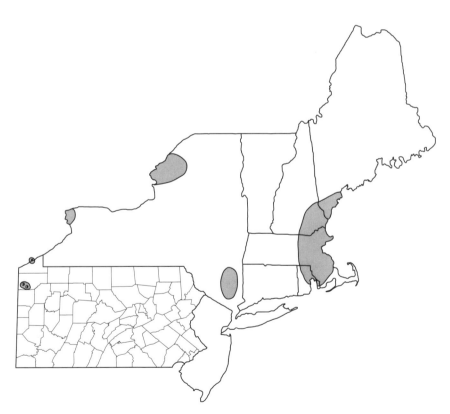

Map 49. Distribution of Blanding's turtle *(Emydoidea blandingii)*.

Common Map Turtle *Graptemys geographica* (LeSueur)

Gr. *geographica*, maplike lines

Description.   The common map turtle (Plate 83) is a medium-sized species of aquatic turtle. The overall background coloration is olive to olive-brown. The carapace is covered with a complex pattern of narrow yellow lines. The head, legs, and tail also have an olive-brown background color. The head, neck, and chin, are strongly patterned with a series of thin longitudinal lines. An elongate yellow blotch generally occurs on each side of the head, just above the ears. The legs exhibit a pattern of thin yellow longitudinal stripes. The plastron is generally pale yellow and immaculate.

In profile, the carapace is long, flattened, and relatively smooth. A slight keel usually occurs along the midline of the carapace and is produced by low blunt tuberosities on the anterior borders of the central scutes. This keel becomes less prominent with size and age. When viewed from above, the carapace is oval in outline and has smooth borders except for a slight serration along the posterior margin. The plastron is large and attached to the carapace by a wide bridge.

This species exhibits considerable sexual dimorphism. Sexually mature females are much larger than males. Males from Pennsylvania average 108 mm ($4\frac{1}{4}$ in.) CL, whereas females average 198 mm ($7\frac{7}{8}$ in.) CL. The maximum size for the species is 273 mm (11 in.) CL (Conant and Collins 1991). Relative to their size, females have a broader and heavier head than do males. Males, however, possess longer claws on their forefeet and have a larger and thicker tail than females.

Ontogenetic changes occur in this species. When viewed from above, the carapace of the young is almost circular. The midline keel of the carapace is more conspicuous than in the adult, and the carapace is more boldly patterned.

Confusing Species.   The common map turtle could be confused with the painted turtle, a species with which it may frequently be found basking. The larger size of the common map turtle, in conjunction with its slightly serrated posterior margin and keeled carapace, should be sufficient to distinguish it from the painted turtle.

Habitat and Habits.   The common map turtle is primarily a species of large bodies of water. In Pennsylvania, it is restricted to Lake Erie and rivers more than 50 m (170 ft) wide. Although an inhabitant of large water, it is not generally found far from shore. In Lake Erie, it frequents bays and backwaters. In rivers, it is mostly found in slow-flowing sections where snags, rocks, or downed trees emerge from the water and furnish suitable basking sites. In the Juniata River, a tributary of the Susquehanna River in central Pennsylvania, it prefers slow, deep (>1 m; 3 ft) sections, to either slow shallow areas or deeper regions where the flow increases (Pluto and Bellis 1986).

The annual activity cycle of the common map turtle is lengthy, extending from late March or early April into the early winter. Pluto and Bellis (1986) reported finding common map turtles active as late as 6 December.

In Canada, D. Gordon and MacCulloch (1980) even reported seeing common map turtles basking on ice flows in the early spring.

The common map turtle is a diurnal species and often spends a significant portion of its time basking, especially on days that are sunny or slightly overcast. Although these turtles will bask on almost any emergent object (e.g., log, rock, tree), large downed trees appear to be their favorite basking site. Pluto and Bellis (1986) have observed as many as 32 animals basking on the branches of a single large tree in the Juniata River. Presumably, they prefer trees because even when the water is high, the upper portions of the tree will still be available for basking; log or rock basking sites disappear during times of high water. Common map turtles are rather aggressive when basking. Pluto and Bellis have observed numerous occasions when larger turtles would physically displace smaller individuals from basking sites. Basking turtles are extremely wary and will slip into the water at the least disturbance. Communal basking by the species aids in their escape behavior. Turtles, when basking together, orient in different directions, so virtually no direction of approach to a basking site is not in view of at least one turtle. When a single turtle dives into the water, the rest follow. This shyness is also reflected in the choice of basking sites relative to distance from shore. Most sites used by common map turtles are located 20 or more meters (66 or more feet) from land (Pluto and Bellis 1986).

Virtually nothing is known about the home range in this species, but some observations have been made concerning their general movements. Pluto and Bellis (1988) noted that males tended to engage in greater movement than did females. Most males moved from deep water in spring and fall into shallower water in summer. Females had a tendency to remain in the same area throughout the entire activity season.

Little is known about common map turtle population size or structure. Pluto and Bellis (1988) reported a density of about 25 turtles/km (1 turtle/130 ft) of stream in the Juniata River, and D. Gordon and MacCulloch (1980) reported a density of 15 animals/km (1 turtle/220 ft) of lake shore in Canada. The sex ratio varies widely within this species. Vogt and Bull (1984) reported a sex ratio of 0.21 males per female in a Wisconsin population. In Pennsylvania, the sex ratio does not deviate significantly from 1:1 (Pluto and Bellis 1988); in Canada males outnumbered females by a ratio of 1.3:1 (Gordon and MacCulloch 1980). This great variation in sex ratio is probably explained by the mechanism of sex determination in the common map turtle. The sex of the individual is determined by the temperature at which the egg is incubated. Site-to-site variations in the incubation temperatures of nests could have profound effects on adult sex ratios.

Mollusks make up the majority of the diet of female common map turtles. The rest of their diet is composed of aquatic insects and fish (mostly carrion). Males, on the other hand, tend to consume fewer mollusks and more insects and other invertebrates (Vogt 1981a). This difference in diet is explained by the sexual dimorphism that occurs with regard to overall head width and size. Females have a larger head and, therefore, more powerful jaws for breaking the hard shells of mollusks. Moll (1976) reported that an Indiana population occasionally fed on floating terrestrial insects that had fallen into the water.

Reproduction.   Mating takes place in both fall and spring (Evermann and Clark 1916), although no detailed account of this process has ever been published.

Oviposition occurs from late May to early July, with the bulk of egg laying taking place in June. Females select sandy soil in the vicinity of water as their nesting sites. Most nesting occurs in the daytime rather than at night. The mortality of nesting turtles can be rather high. Cochran (1987a) reported finding the remains of 13 dead turtles in a nesting area in Minnesota but did not speculate as to the nature of the predator.

The clutch size in Missouri ranges from 6 to 16 eggs, and two clutches of eggs are laid each season (White and Moll 1991). Ernst and Barbour (1972) reported eggs as varying in length from 32 to 35 mm ($1\frac{1}{4}$–$1\frac{3}{8}$ in.) and in width from 21 to 22 mm ($\frac{7}{8}$ in.). Nothing is known about hatching time or hatchling behavior in this species.

Females reach reproductive maturity at a CL of about 190 mm ($7\frac{5}{8}$ in.).

Remarks.   Graham and colleagues (1997) reported leech infestations of map turtles from the Lamoille River, Vermont, during hibernation. Of seven turtles captured in March, all had leeches attached, and four of the seven supported from 9 to 52 young leeches.

Distribution.   The geographic distribution of the common map turtle is centered in the central Great Lakes region. From this core, its distribution radiates outward and extends as far south as central Alabama and southern Arkansas. It extends westward into eastern Kansas and Oklahoma and eastward to Lake Champlain.

The distribution of this species in the Northeast is from the Lake Champlain area southwestward along the northern border of New York. There are disjunct populations in southeastern New York and along Lake Ontario. The species also occurs along the Hudson River south to Orange County, New York. In Pennsylvania, it exhibits a disjunct distribution that corresponds to three of the drainage systems in the state: Lake Erie drainage, Susquehanna River drainage, and Delaware River drainage.

The Delaware River population was discovered only in 1972. Its origin is debatable. Arndt and Potter (1973) considered the population to have resulted from either an accidental or a deliberate introduction to the river. They based their conclusion on the assumption that it would be unlikely for such a conspicuous species of basking turtle to remain unobserved in the densely populated eastern portion of the state until 1972. Although the turtle may have reached the area via canals (McCoy 1982), we agree that the population probably was the result of human intervention rather than an isolated natural population.

Within the Susquehanna drainage, common map turtles have been reported only from the Susquehanna and one of its major tributaries (the Juniata). It is likely, however, that the species will also be found in several of the large creeks and streams that enter the Susquehanna.

Historical records exist for this species from the Allegheny River, but no specimens have been collected or reported in over 70 years. Old records indicate that it occurred around Cochrans Mill in Armstrong County and Verona in Allegheny County, Pennsylvania. This entire region has been severely affected by acid mine drainage and industrial pollution in general, and it is unlikely that common map turtles could have survived this habitat degradation. Common map turtles have been reported from the Monongahela and Cheat rivers in northern West Virginia, so it is possible that they occur in the lower reaches of the Monongahela in Fayette and Greene counties.

Pseudemys
Gr. *pseud*, false; Gr. *emys*, a freshwater tortoise

The genus *Pseudemys* contains the cooters and redbelly turtles. There are five species in the genus. The genus is primarily distributed within the southeastern and south-central United States, with a single species entering Pennsylvania and parts of southern New England.

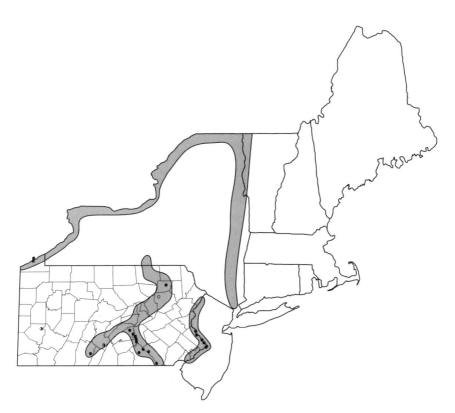

Map 50. Distribution of the common map turtle *(Graptemys geographica)*.

Cooters and redbelly turtles are large basking turtles with a smooth and moderately domed carapace. The posterior margin of the carapace is moderately serrated. The plastron is large. Cooters and redbelly turtles are aquatic and are found in a wide variety of water habitats, although some species show a distinct preference for large rivers. One necessity is an adequate number of basking sites, usually fallen logs, emergent stumps, and rocks.

Cooters and redbelly turtles range from carnivorous to herbivorous. Younger individuals tend to be carnivorous, whereas older, larger animals eat mostly or exclusively plant material.

All species lay moderately large clutches of soft, flexible eggs.

Redbelly Turtle *Pseudemys rubriventris* (LeConte)
L. *rubr*, red; L. *ventro*, belly
Description.   The redbelly turtle (Plates 84 and 85) is a large aquatic species. The carapacial background coloration varies from brown to black. Each marginal and costal scute generally contains a vertical reddish bar or line. Individuals darken with age, and melanism is not uncommon in old animals. The plastron in adults tends to be pink to salmon red and is generally immaculate. The skin of the head and appendages is dark brown. The head is patterned with a series of vivid yellow stripes, extending to the point where the neck merges with the body. Thin yellow lines are also present on the legs.

The carapace, when viewed in profile, is moderately domed and smooth. When viewed from above, it is oblong and has a relatively smooth margin. The plastron is large, covering most of the ventral surface, and is connected to the carapace by a broad bridge.

The legs are well developed, and the feet are strongly webbed.

Sexual dimorphism occurs in redbelly turtles, but it is not as extreme as in many species of turtle. Females are slightly larger than males. Iverson and Graham (1990) measured a large sample from across the species' range and found that males in the sample had a mean of 263.2 mm ($10\frac{1}{2}$ in.) CL. Females averaged 289.3 mm ($11\frac{5}{8}$ in.) CL. The tail of males is larger and thicker than that of females. The cloacal opening of both sexes is located behind the margin of the carapace. The maximum size reported for the species is 400 mm (16 in.) (Conant and Collins 1991).

The pattern of hatchlings is considerably different from that of adults. The carapacial background coloration in hatchlings and juveniles varies from brown to olive-brown and has a pattern of yellow lines that divide the carapace into a series of irregular geometric shapes. The plastron has a bold dark midline blotch that is somewhat irregular in shape and extends the entire length of the plastron. Lateral projections of the blotch occasionally extend along the plastral seams. This pattern fades with age.

Confusing Species.   The only species the redbelly turtle could be confused with is the painted turtle, a species with which it frequently basks. Redbelly turtles, however, lack the light borders along the carapace seams that are present in painted turtles.

Habitat and Habits.   The redbelly turtle is one of the least studied turtles in the United States, and little information is known about it.

The redbelly turtle is primarily an inhabitant of large bodies of water, including lakes and ponds, slow-moving rivers and creeks, and marshes. The presence of suitable basking sites such as logs and downed trees is requisite for the occurrence of this turtle. The bottom substrate is usually sandy or muddy, and aquatic vegetation is present.

Although this is an aquatic species, it does spend considerable time engaged in aerial basking. Redbelly turtles are extremely wary and will dive from basking sites into the water at the least disturbance. Basking sites are generally located near deep water.

Babcock (1971) reported that in New England the species is active at least from May until the middle of October, when the turtles enter hibernation in the soft, bottom mud of ponds.

No specific studies of the redbelly turtle's diet have been conducted, but general accounts (Babcock 1916, Ernst and Barbour 1972) indicate that it is an omnivorous feeder. The diet includes snails, crayfish, tadpoles, and aquatic vegetation. It is likely that adults are primarily herbivorous, since all other members of the genus are herbivores as adults. Indirect evidence for herbivory in this species comes from the fact that it is extremely difficult to trap in baited nets.

Reproduction.   Courtship and mating have not been observed in redbelly turtles. Eggs are laid in June and July, usually in sandy or loamy soil. Females may travel as much as 250 m (800 ft) from water to locate a suitable nest site (Mitchell 1974). Nests are typically flask-shaped and about 8–9 cm ($3\frac{1}{2}$–$3\frac{3}{4}$ in.) deep.

The eggs are elliptical, smooth, flexible, and white. The clutch size varies from 8 to as many as 35 eggs. Clutch size appears to be correlated with female body size (Babcock 1971).

The average length of a clutch of eggs from Massachusetts was 34.4 mm ($1\frac{3}{8}$ in.) and the average width was 24.5 mm (1 in.). The weight of the eggs averaged 11.9 g ($\frac{1}{2}$ oz) (Mitchell 1974). This clutch, when kept at a constant temperature of 26°C (79°F), hatched in 73 days. On the basis of this evidence, it would appear that hatching generally occurs from late August to early October. Mitchell (1974), however, presented evidence that hatchlings may overwinter in the nest. He observed three hatchlings emerging from the ground on 13 April. Excavation of the site revealed a nest with an additional 13 hatchlings.

Hatchlings are almost circular in outline. The average length for a sample from the Carnegie Museum was 30.8 mm ($1\frac{1}{4}$ in.) CL, with an average width of 29.7 mm ($1\frac{1}{8}$ in.). Mitchell reported an average 9.4 g ($\frac{1}{3}$ oz) mass for a nest from Virginia.

Remarks.   The redbelly turtle once ranged as far north as New York. In the late 1800s, heavy commercial pressure was placed on the redbelly turtle. As populations of diamondback terrapins were reduced in numbers by hunting, the hunters switched to redbelly turtles to supply the demand for edible turtles in the large metropolitan markets of the East (i.e., New

York, Philadelphia, Baltimore, and Washington). The redbelly turtle was apparently extirpated from its range north of southern New Jersey and was greatly reduced in numbers within the region of the Chesapeake Bay and the Delmarva Peninsula.

Distribution. The redbelly turtle occurs along the Atlantic Coastal Plain and parts of the Piedmont from southern New Jersey to central North Carolina. A disjunct population occurs in Plymouth County, Massachusetts. The current range disjunction between New Jersey and Massachusetts is probably of recent occurrence given that the Massachusetts population was found to have little allozymic differences from the New Jersey population (Browne et al. 1996).

In Pennsylvania, redbelly turtles occur in the eastern Coastal Plain, in the lower reaches of the Susquehanna River (e.g., south of Harrisburg), and in a few tributaries of the Potomac River in Adams and Franklin counties. Much of the range of the redbelly turtle in Pennsylvania is within the densely populated southeast, where the potential for an adverse impact on the turtle's habitat is high. Consequently, it is listed as a threatened species by the Pennsylvania Fish and Boat Commission.

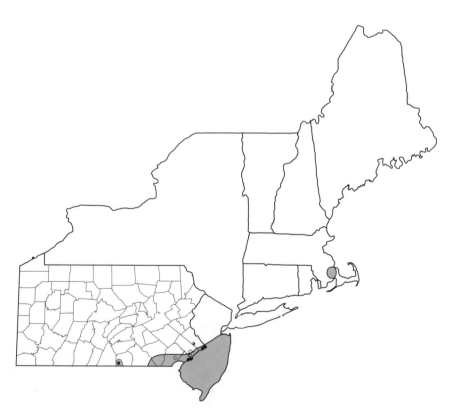

Map 51.   Distribution of the redbelly turtle *(Pseudemys rubriventris)*.

Terrapene
Terrapene, Algonquin name for turtle

The genus *Terrapene* contains the box turtles. There are four species in the genus. The range of the box turtles extends throughout much of the eastern and central United States and continues southward into the Yucatan Peninsula.

Box turtles are small to medium-sized species with a high-domed carapace. The plastron is large and has a single hinge between the pectoral and abdominal scutes that allows the two lobes of the plastron to be tightly drawn against the carapace. This action seals the turtle tightly inside its shell. Three species in this genus are terrestrial, and one is semiaquatic. Box turtles inhabit woodlands, prairies, and marshy environments.

All box turtles are omnivores and eat an extremely diverse diet of fruits, berries, leaves, and invertebrates. All lay soft, white, flexible eggs that are elliptical.

Eastern Box Turtle *Terrapene carolina carolina* (Linnaeus)
Named for the site of original collection
Description. The eastern box turtle (Plates 86 and 87) is a small species of terrestrial turtle. The background coloration of the carapace is brown or brownish black. The carapace is strongly patterned with numerous lines, blotches, and bars. These markings vary from pale yellow to bright orange. The plastron is variable in color, ranging from an immaculate yellow-brown to a dark brownish black or black. Often it is brownish black in the center, becoming yellowish brown along the margins. The head, neck, and legs are usually heavily patterned with yellow to orange (occasionally reddish) streaks, blotches, and bars arranged on a dark brown background.

When viewed from the side, the carapace is high, domed, and slightly keeled. From above, it appears oblong, with slightly flaring posterior marginals. The plastron is extremely broad and is not attached to the carapace by a bridge. The plastron is hinged, thus allowing independent motion of the anterior and posterior lobes. As a result, when disturbed, the turtle can fully retract its head and other appendages and completely close the shell by pulling the two lobes of the plastron tightly against the carapace. The fit is generally so tight that not even the thin blade of a knife can be inserted between the plastron and carapace when the shell is closed.

Sexual differences are present but somewhat subtle. The plastron of males is concave, whereas that of females is flat or slightly convex. Although the tail of both sexes is small, the cloacal opening of the male occurs behind the margin of the carapace rather than before. Males usually have a bright red iris; the iris of females is brown or dull reddish brown. Males and females do not differ in overall size. Males from Pennsylvania average 126.7 mm (5 in.) CL. Females average 124.6 mm (5 in.) CL. The maximum size for the eastern box turtle is 198 mm ($7\frac{7}{8}$ in.) CL (Conant and Collins 1991).

Hatchling eastern box turtles differ greatly from adults in appearance. The background carapace coloration is light brown, and each carapacial scute contains a single central yellow blotch. The plastron has a large central dark brown blotch and is bordered by a margin of yellow. The hatchlings cannot draw the plastron tightly against the carapace.

Confusing Species. The eastern box turtle's high-domed carapace; bold pattern of lines, blotches, and bars; terrestrial habits; and ability to completely seal its shell readily distinguish this species from all other turtles found in Pennsylvania and the Northeast.

Habitat and Habits. The eastern box turtle is the only truly terrestrial turtle found in the Northeast. It occurs in deciduous woodlands, old fields, pastures, and marshy areas, but it is most frequently found in deciduous forest and in ecotonal areas between forests and old fields. Within its general habitat, it tends to avoid steep slopes.

Eastern box turtles generally emerge from hibernation in April and remain active until mid to late October. Unusually warm weather at either end of the season will extend their activity. Turtles are most active in June and the early part of July.

The eastern box turtle is a diurnal species that adjusts its activity on the basis of season and temperature. During spring and fall, eastern box turtles are generally found active during the middle of the day, but with the onset of summer and warmer daytime temperatures, activity occurs earlier and earlier in the day. During hot dry spells the turtles often seek out damp or wet areas, where they remain for days or even weeks. During a dry spell in Pennsylvania, eight individuals were found partly buried in the muck at the base of a spring. If conditions become too dry, they actually burrow into the soil and aestivate. After rainfall, normal daily activity is resumed. During the summer, the best time to locate eastern box turtles is after heavy rainstorms, when they are actively walking about.

In Ohio, eastern box turtles hibernate in wooded areas and seldom burrow more than 14 cm ($5\frac{1}{2}$ in.) below the surface of the soil (Claussen et al. 1991). The soil in most hibernation sites is generally overlain with 6–8 cm ($2\frac{1}{2}$–$3\frac{1}{4}$ in.) of compacted leaf litter that acts as additional insulation. Claussen and colleagues noted an average hibernation period of 142 days. The shallow burrows that the turtles construct offer little protection from subfreezing temperatures. It has been shown that eastern box turtles can withstand temperatures below freezing for days or weeks. Under freezing temperatures, these turtles can dehydrate their body tissues and increase the tissue concentration of glucose by as much as 500%. The high concentration of glucose serves the same function as antifreeze in a water-cooled engine and depresses the freezing point of the tissue. Stickel (1989) noted that eastern box turtles within her study area in Maryland did not leave their summer home range to locate hibernation sites.

In bottomland forests in Maryland, the average home range diameter for male turtles was 100 m (330 ft), and that of females was 110 m (370 ft) (Stickel 1950). In Indiana, the home range size for both males and females averaged 174 m (565 ft) (Williams and Parker 1987). Stickel and E.

Williams and Parker noted a high degree of fidelity of the turtles to their home range areas, with most turtles retaining their home range area from year to year. Indeed, over a 13-year period, only 10% of the females and 15% of the males made significant shifts in home range area in Indiana. Turtles from Indiana also demonstrated a remarkable homing ability. All 11 turtles displaced (some up to 777 m; 2,525 ft) away from their home range returned within 32 days of being removed.

Eastern box turtles can live to extremely old ages. Stickel (1978) noted that 15% of the males and 11% of the females that were more than 20 years old when she originally marked them in 1945 were still alive in 1975. On the basis of carapacial condition at the time of initial marking, she assumed that some of the turtles were over 80 years of age in 1975. Similar survival has been demonstrated for an Indiana population (Williams and Parker 1987).

Although eastern box turtles exhibit great longevity, both Stickel (1978) and Williams and Parker (1987) noted a disturbing trend in the populations that they studied for long periods. They both noted a significant decrease in the density of turtles; that is, the populations were decreasing in number of individuals per unit area. In Indiana, the density in 1960 was 5.7 animals/ha (2.3 animals/acre); by 1970 it was 3.7 animals/ha (1.5 animals/acre); and it had dropped to 2.7 animals/ha (1.1 animals/acre) by 1983. Stickel also noted an overall decline in numbers, with the greatest decline being seen in juveniles. This trend indicates that new individuals are not being recruited into the population at the same rate as they previously were.

Eastern box turtles have extremely catholic tastes when it comes to diet. They are opportunistic omnivores, feeding on a wide variety of plant and animal material. Dietary items include snails, slugs, worms, insects, spiders, fungi, fruits and berries, and the meat of a variety of dead animals, including crows, skunks, snakes, frogs, and mice. Box turtles are apparently immune to the toxins contained in many mushrooms and can eat them with no ill effects. Humans have been known to become ill after ingesting the flesh of box turtles. Presumably, these were individuals that had recently fed on poisonous fungi and still contained some of the toxins in their bodies.

Hatchlings are undoubtedly preyed upon by a variety of animals, although the only actual predators recorded are copperheads and water moccasins. The biggest threat to box turtles comes from people. Untold thousands are killed on the highways of the Northeast each year, and, unfortunately, many of these are gravid females seeking a nesting site. Pauley (1992) noted that box turtles make up 70% of all reptiles that he found dead on West Virginia highways.

Reproduction.   Box turtles have been observed mating in almost every month in which they are active, but peak mating occurs in June, July, and October. Stickel (1989) noted that males do not wander from their home range in search of females but, rather, tend to mate with females that possess adjacent or overlapping home ranges.

Female box turtles have the ability to retain viable sperm for long periods after mating. As a consequence, mating does not have to occur near the time when eggs are ovulated, or even in the same year that eggs are ovulated. Ewing (1943) reported on a female maintained in captivity in the absence of other box turtles for 4 years that was still producing fertile eggs at the end of the 4-year period.

Ovulation occurs in May, and eggs are usually laid in June or early July. In Maryland, all turtles laid their eggs between 6 and 25 June (Stickel 1989). Box turtles seldom move far from their home range for other activities, but Stickel noted that females would travel as much as 700 m (2,275 ft) to locate a suitable nesting site. Her population was located in a moist bottomland, and the animals tended to move up to drier and more open slopes to oviposit. She noted that females returned to the same general vicinity year after year to lay their eggs, usually placing succeeding nests within 20 m (65 ft) of sites previously used. Nests are usually located in fairly open areas in loamy or sandy soil.

As is typical, the female constructs the nest using alternate strokes of the back feet. Nest construction is not as rapid as in some species and may take five or more hours to complete. After all of the eggs have been laid, the female covers the nest with dirt, tamps it down, and rubs her plastron over the nest. The female may void the contents of her bladder on the nest either during the construction process or after the eggs have been laid and the nest covered.

Clutch size varies from 1 to 8 eggs, with most females laying 4 or 5 eggs (Ernst and Barbour 1972). The eggs are elliptical, smooth, flexible and white when first laid. The egg size in two Pennsylvania clutches averaged 35 mm ($1\frac{3}{8}$ in.) in length and 22.2 ± 0.3 mm ($\frac{7}{8}$ in.) in width.

Incubation periods from 67 to 103 days have been reported (Ewing 1933). Incubation time is undoubtedly dependent in large part on nest temperature. Hatchlings may emerge anywhere from late August to the middle of October.

The carapace of hatchlings is virtually circular. A clutch of hatchlings from Pennsylvania averaged 27.7 mm ($1\frac{1}{8}$ in.) CL and 27.2 mm ($1\frac{1}{8}$ in.) in carapace width. A real mystery is what happens to eastern box turtles between the time they hatch and the time that they are about 80 mm ($3\frac{1}{4}$ in.) CL. Hatchlings and juveniles are almost never encountered, even in areas that support otherwise dense populations of eastern box turtles. Cahn (1937) noted that, immediately upon hatching, young turtles buried themselves in whatever substrate was available.

Distribution.   The eastern box turtle ranges along the eastern seaboard from Massachusetts to southern Georgia. Its range extends westward into Illinois, Kentucky, Tennessee, and northeastern Mississippi.

In the Northeast, the species occurs in coastal Massachusetts, Rhode Island, and Connecticut, through Long Island and into extreme southeastern New York and all of New Jersey. It is also found in the southern-tier counties of New York and along the Hudson River valley to Saratoga County. It also occurs from central Connecticut to mid-central Massachusetts in the Central Connecticut Lowland (Klemens 1993). In Pennsylvania, the species is widely distributed over the southern two-thirds of the state. In the west, in ranges into Erie County. It has also been reported from McKean County (Pauley, pers. comm.).

TRIONYCHIDAE (SOFTSHELL TURTLES)

The family Trionychidae contains the softshell turtles. There are 14 genera and 22 species in this family. Trionychids are distributed in North America, Africa, and southern Asia. Softshell turtles are medium to extremely large turtles (the largest species is *Pelochelys bibroni*, from Southeast Asia, with a carapace length of 129 cm; $51\frac{1}{2}$ in.). Softshell turtles have a smooth, leathery, scute-free shell. They are aquatic, and their feet are fully webbed and form well-developed flippers. The head is elongate and terminates in a long, thin snout that functions like a snorkel. All species in the family are carnivorous. Softshell turtles seldom leave the water except to lay eggs and occasionally to bask on thc shore.

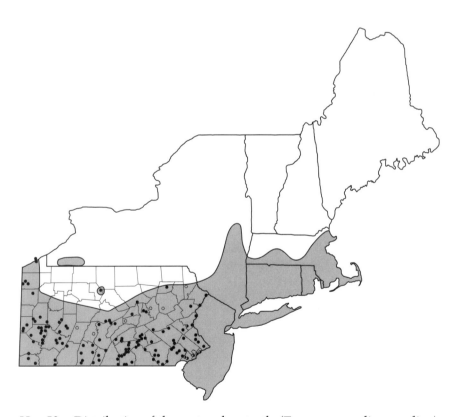

Map 52. Distribution of the eastern box turtle *(Terrapene carolina carolina).*

Apalone
Gr. *apalone,* soft

The genus *Apalone* contains the North American softshell turtles. There are three species in this genus. They are found throughout most of the Ohio and Mississippi drainages, as well as in Florida and those river systems draining into the Gulf of Mexico. The genus extends southward into the Mexican states of Coahuila, Tamulipas, and Nuevo Leon.

All softshell turtles are dorsoventrally flattened and are circular to oblong in outline when viewed from above. The carapace is soft and flexible, and scutes are absent from both it and the plastron. The feet are strongly webbed, and the head terminates in a sharply pointed snout. Softshell turtles are totally aquatic and are found in a wide variety of habitats, from small ponds to large lakes and from slow-moving creeks and streams to mainstream rivers such as the Mississippi.

Softshell turtles are carnivores, feeding on a wide variety of animals including crayfish, mollusks, fish, frogs, and aquatic insects. All three species lay spherical eggs with a white, brittle shell.

Midland Smooth Softshell *Apalone mutica mutica* LeSueur

L. *muticus,* unarmed

Description.   The midland smooth softshell (Plate 88) is a large aquatic turtle. The background coloration of the carapace varies from olive-brown to brown and may have a pattern of dark dots and short streaks or dashes. A light marginal band often occurs on the carapace and is bordered on the inside by a thin dark line. This band, when present, is generally broader along the posterior margin of the carapace and becomes thinner toward the anterior end. The plastron is immaculate and varies from white to grayish white. The dorsal surfaces of the appendages vary from greenish orange to olive-green above. Below, they range in color from white to gray. A wide white stripe bordered by thin black lines extends from the posterior margin of the eye onto the neck.

The carapace is extremely low in profile and round to slightly oblong in outline when viewed from above. The carapace is leathery and smooth. The plastron is somewhat reduced in size and cruciform in shape. Like the carapace, it is smooth and leathery to the touch.

Both forefeet and hind feet are strongly webbed. The head is long and narrow and terminates in a sharply pointed snout that acts like a snorkel. The nostrils are rounded in outline, and the septum separating them is smooth, lacking a ridge.

Midland smooth softshells exhibit considerable sexual dimorphism. The tail of the male is longer and much thicker than that of the female. Adult males are much smaller than adult females. Ernst and Barbour (1972) gave the range of carapace size for mature males as 110–175 mm $(4\frac{3}{8}-7$ in.) CL and that for mature females as 170–345 mm $(7-13\frac{3}{4}$ in.) CL. The maximum size for this species is 356 mm $(14\frac{1}{4}$ in.) CL (Conant and Collins 1991).

Confusing Species.   The smooth softshell could easily be confused with the spiny softshell. It differs from the spiny softshell in lacking the conical projections on the anterior portion of the carapace and in lacking the septal ridges in the nasal passageways.

Habitat and Habits.   Nothing is known about the biology of smooth softshells in the Northeast. Indeed, they may no longer be present in Pennsylvania (Distribution). As a consequence, all information in this section and the next on reproduction come from studies carried out in other parts of the animal's range, primarily Iowa and Kansas.

Midland smooth softshells are primarily inhabitants of large rivers. They seldom if ever venture into the shallower upstream sections of rivers and are not normally found in standing water. The only standing bodies of water that smooth softshells are associated with are those ponds that fill because of river flooding (T. Williams and Christiansen 1981).

Males, females, and juveniles all have different habitat preferences within the large rivers that they inhabit. Females are generally found in deep water; males usually reside in the vicinity of emergent sandbars; and hatchlings prefer shallow puddles that are produced by sandbars (Plummer 1977a). Smooth softshells bask but not to the extent that spiny softshells do.

In the Midwest, seasonal activity may begin as early as late March, but it usually does not start until the middle of April. Turtles remain active until October, when they presumably burrow into soft bottom substrates to hibernate.

Smooth softshells can, in appropriate habitat, reach very high population densities. Plummer (1977a) estimated a density of approximately one turtle for every 0.9 m (3 ft) of river along a 1.5-km (ca. 1 mi) stretch of the Kansas River.

There is considerable variation in the composition of the diet of this species as reported by different workers. Ernst and Barbour (1972) considered them to be very carnivorous and portrayed them as active agile predators able to catch fast-swimming fish. T. Williams and Christiansen (1981) found that an Iowa population fed mainly on aquatic insects (especially mayflies, caddisfly larvae, and fly larvae. Plummer and Farrar (1981) documented decided differences in the diet of the sexes. Females in their study fed predominately on aquatic animals, including fish, crayfish, and aquatic insects, but about 16% of their diet was made up of the fruit of mulberry trees. Males were decidedly omnivorous in their diet, feeding primarily on terrestrial insects that fell into the water and on mulberry fruits and the seeds of other plants, especially cottonwoods. In fact, over 40% of the diet of males was composed of mulberry fruits and cottonwood seeds.

Reproduction.   Plummer (1977b) documented courtship behavior in this species. Courtship may occur at anytime during the animal's annual activity season, but it is more concentrated in the spring and early summer. Males actively search for females. Males investigate all turtles encountered by probing at the underside of the body with their snout. If receptive, a female remains motionless, allowing the male to mount and mate. Unreceptive females usually attack and drive off investigating males.

Females emerge from hibernation with well-developed ovarian follicles. Eggs are generally ovulated in the second half of May or early in June, with most eggs being laid in June and the first week of July.

Smooth softshells lay their eggs on sandbars located within rivers. Within a sandbar, eggs are deposited in open areas on elevated ridges. The nesting success of this species is strongly associated with the position of the water table relative to the nest. Nests that are submerged below the water table during the incubation period suffer very high or complete egg mortality, whereas nests that remain above the water table generally have very low egg mortality (Plummer 1976). In general, nests of smooth soft-shells experience little destruction due to predators. The main reason is that eggs are generally laid on sandbars in rivers, with the river acting as a barrier to most mammalian predators (e.g., foxes and skunks).

Smooth softshells eggs are spherical and have a brittle, white shell. They range in size from 20 to 23 mm $(\frac{3}{4}-\frac{7}{8}$ in.) (Ernst and Barbour 1972). In a Kansas population, the clutch size ranged from 3 to 26 eggs and was significantly related to female body size (Plummer 1977c). In other areas, clutches as large as 33 eggs have been reported (Ernst and Barbour 1972). Females lay two, and possibly three, clutches in a single nesting season (Plummer 1977c).

Incubation has been reported as lasting from 65 to 77 days (Ernst and Barbour 1972). The shells of hatchlings are circular when viewed from above and have an average plastron length of 24.5 mm (1 in.) when the hatchings emerge from the nest (Plummer 1977c). After emergence, hatch-lings tend to remain in shallow pools and puddles associated with the sandbars. They double their size before entering hibernation (Plummer 1977c).

Plummer (1977c) determined that, in a Kansas population, males matured at a plastral length of 80 mm $(3\frac{1}{4}$ in.) and an age of 4 years, and females matured at a plastral length of 140 mm $(5\frac{3}{4}$ in.) and an age of 9 years.

Distribution.   The smooth softshells ranges from western Pennsylvania westward to eastern Kansas and South Dakota. Its range extends southward to the Gulf Coast of Texas in the West and to the western panhandle of Florida in the East.

The smooth softshells has been reported from only two localities in Pennsylvania: Neville Island, Ohio River, Allegheny County and Foxburg, Allegheny River/Clarion River. Both records are exceedingly old, the most recent being in 1901. It is doubtful that this species is still present within the state of Pennsylvania. All of the large rivers in the Ohio River drainage of Pennsylvania have experienced extreme pollution events that have dramatically altered the nature of the rivers. In addition, this species' ecological requirement for large rivers would preclude the possibility of remnant populations' taking refuge in smaller nonpolluted tributaries of the Ohio, Allegheny, or Clarion river and then reestablishing populations in the main rivers after recovery from pollution.

Eastern Spiny Softshell *Apalone spinifera spinifera* (LeSueur)
L. *spini*, a spine or thorn; L. *fer*, to bear
Description.   The eastern spiny softshell (Plates 89 and 90) is a large species of aquatic turtle. The background coloration of the carapace varies from olive to tan to olive-brown. A pattern of dark-ringed, somewhat irregularly shaped, ocelli (eyelike spots) are scattered over the carapace. The center of each ocellus is the same color as the background color of the carapace. The carapace is bordered by a light band that is widest at the posterior end and narrows anteriorly. This band is set off from the rest of the carapace by a thin black line. The plastron and the fleshy parts of the body in its vicinity are immaculate white to yellowish white. The dorsal surfaces of the legs are heavily mottled. Mottling also occurs on the ventral surfaces of the feet, but the rest of the ventral surfaces of the legs are immaculate white or cream-colored. The tail, especially of males, has two well-developed pairs of dark lines. One pair is dorsolateral in position, and the other is ventral-lateral. The head has a pair of light lines with

Map 53.   Distribution of the midland smooth softshell *(Apalone mutica mutica)*.

dark borders that extend from the snout to the anterior border of the eye. This line begins again on the posterior edge of the eye and continues onto the neck.

The carapace is flat and low in profile and appears round to oblong in outline when viewed from above. Eastern spiny softshells are unique among extant northeastern turtles in that their shell (both carapace and plastron) lacks horny scutes or plates. The carapace is leathery and extremely flexible around the edges. Except in old females, the shell is rough to the touch, having a sandpaper quality to it. A series of conical projections occurs along the anterior margin of the shell. The projections are most pronounced on large females. The plastron is slightly reduced in size and is soft, smooth, and leathery to the touch.

The feet of this species are strongly webbed. The neck is long, and the head is conical and terminates in a tubular snout. The septum that divides the nasal passages in the snout contains a septal ridge that projects laterally into each nasal passageway.

Sexual dimorphism in this species is pronounced. Females dwarf males in both size and weight. Pennsylvania males average 156 mm ($6\frac{1}{4}$ in.) CL, whereas females average 362 mm ($14\frac{1}{2}$ in.) CL. The record size for this species is 540 mm ($21\frac{3}{4}$ in.) CL for a specimen from Louisiana (Halk 1986). In a Tennessee population, males weighed an average of 130 g ($5\frac{1}{2}$ oz), and females averaged 1,500 g (3.3 lb). In addition to the much larger size, females tend to lose the pattern of carapacial ocelli, and the darker borders tend to suffuse inward, producing a series of irregular smudges on the carapace. The tail of the male is much longer and thicker than that of the female; the cloacal opening on the tail is nearly terminal on both sexes.

Confusing Species.   The only species the eastern spiny softshell could be confused with is the smooth softshell. The smooth softshell lacks the nasal septa and the conical projections on the anterior border of the carapace and has not been reported in our area since 1901.

Habitat and Habit.   The eastern spiny softshell inhabits a wide variety of aquatic environments, from large lakes and rivers to small ponds and slow-moving creeks. A sandy or muddy substrate is a necessary component of the habitat. Eastern spiny softshells may occasionally be found on rock or gravel substrate, but these are individuals in transit to more suitable habitat.

Although eastern spiny softshells are highly adapted for an aquatic existence, they frequently leave the water to bask, generally on sandy or muddy banks or on islands in rivers. When turtles are abundant in the aquatic environment, they may occasionally be seen basking in large numbers. While basking on land, the turtles generally face the water and will rush into the water at the slightest disturbance. When basking, they fully extend their limbs and spread their toes, thus extending to the fullest extent the webbing between their toes. While in this position, their appendages act like solar collectors and aid the animal in rapidly warming. Eastern spiny softshells can also be frequently found floating motionless at the water's surface.

In Pennsylvania, eastern spiny softshells have been collected from the beginning of May to the end of December. The peak activity, as measured by collecting records, occurs in August. Nothing is known about their hibernation, but they probably bury themselves in loose sediments in shallow water when the temperatures drop to a point that precludes normal activity.

In the Northeast, eastern spiny softshells are generally considered to be a diurnal species, but in other parts of the country (Texas and Arizona) we have had equal success trapping them during the day and at night.

Eastern spiny softshells are primarily carnivorous, but their diet differs from region to region. Their main foods include crayfish, aquatic insects (especially mayfly and dragonfly nymphs), and fish. In the upper Mississippi, they feed almost exclusively on aquatic insects (Cochran and McConville 1983), and several studies have indicated that crayfish and aquatic insects are of equal importance (P. Anderson 1965, Lagler 1943). T. Williams and Christiansen (1981) found that, in Iowa, fish constituted a significant component of the diet.

These turtles are benthic feeders that utilize a mixed foraging, strategy. They employ both an active foraging mode and a sit-and-wait technique. While actively foraging, they slowly move along the bottom, probing under rocks and into weeds and the substrate with their long snout. At other times, they will bury themselves in loose sediments (sand or mud), with just a portion of their head exposed above the substrate. When a suitable prey item comes within striking distance, the turtles lunge out to capture the prey.

Eastern spiny softshells undoubtedly have a number of predators, but there is no documentation of actual predation upon them.

Reproduction.   Mating has not been well documented, but apparently it occurs in April and May (Webb 1962). In Vermont, turtles leave their wintering grounds in the Lamoille River and descend into Lake Champlain for feeding and mating in late April (Graham and Graham 1997).

In Tennessee, females emerge from hibernation with well-developed ovarian follicles, occasionally of ovulatory size. Follicular growth continues until the eggs are ovulated in May (K. Robinson and Murphy 1978). Most egg laying occurs from mid-June to mid-July at northern latitudes. Surface (1908) reported eggs' being laid as early as May in Pennsylvania.

Eggs are generally laid within a few meters of the water on sandy or muddy banks or bars. Breckenridge (1944) provided the only detailed account of nesting behavior. In this case, a female pulled up onto a nesting site at 5:00 P.M. on 28 June and began digging a nest 2.6 m (8.5 ft) from the water. The nest was dug with alternate strokes of the hind feet and took about 15 minutes to construct. A clutch of 17 eggs was laid in 6 minutes, and an additional 5 minutes was spent in covering the nest. The first layer of eggs was located about 125 mm (5 in.) below the surface. Nesting banks or beaches are often utilized by numerous females. If the site is small and populations of turtles large, nests can occasionally overlap. Overlap has been reported by Neuman (1906) and Breckenridge (1944). Some of the sandbanks in the Allegheny River in Forest and Warren counties, Pennsylvania, receive heavy utilization by turtles as nesting sites.

Eastern spiny softshell eggs are spherical and range from 22 to 28 mm ($\frac{7}{8}$–$1\frac{1}{8}$ in.) in diameter (Breckenridge 1944). The eggs are white and brittle like those of a bird. Clutch size has been reported as varying from 7 to 32 eggs, with an average of about 17 eggs (Webb 1962). Little is known about clutch size in the Northeast. K. Robinson and Murphy (1978) presented some evidence that suggests that two clutches per year may be laid by some females from Tennessee.

The incubation period is not known for this species. Eastern spiny softshell hatchlings emerge as early as the beginning of August and as late as October (Ernst and Barbour 1972). Pennsylvania hatchlings average 30.2 mm ($1\frac{1}{4}$ in.) CL.

Males mature at an average CL of 120 mm ($4\frac{3}{4}$ in.), but females do not mature until a CL of about 225 mm (9 in.).

Remarks.   Eastern spiny softshells are quick and active animals. They will aggressively defend themselves if captured or otherwise molested. Their long neck and sharp jaws enable them to deliver a painful bite. These animals, especially large females, should be treated with caution.

Distribution.   The eastern spiny softshell is found from the Great Lakes region of the United States southward throughout Kentucky and Tennessee into the extreme northern region of Alabama and Mississippi.

The eastern spiny softshell's distribution reaches into the Northeast in western New York, and there is a disjunct population in eastern New York and northwestern Vermont. Disjunct populations occur in the vicinity of Lake Champlain and in the Maurice River system of southern New Jersey. This latter population is a well-established, but introduced, population (Conant and Collins 1991). In Pennsylvania, the eastern spiny softshell is restricted to Lake Erie and the Allegheny-Ohio drainage system. It has primarily been reported from large bodies of water (e.g., Lake Erie and the Allegheny, Ohio, and Clarion rivers). It does, however, occur in smaller streams such as French Creek. Although previously thought to be absent from the southwestern corner of the state, recent collecting has demonstrated its presence in the Wheeling Creek drainage. Individuals are occasionally seen in the lower Delaware River. These have undoubtedly been introduced to that system.

Marine Turtles

Three species of marine turtle are regularly found in the waters off the northeastern coast: the leatherback (*Dermochelys coriacea*; family Dermochelyidae), the loggerhead (*Caretta caretta*; family Cheloniidae), and the Atlantic ridley (*Lepidochelys kempii*; family Cheloniidae). Two other species, the green sea turtle (*Chelonia mydas*; family Cheloniidae) and the Atlantic hawksbill (*Eretmochelys imbricata imbricata*; family Cheloniidae) are less rarely seen. The Atlantic hawksbill is so infrequent that there is a question as to whether it should be considered part of the

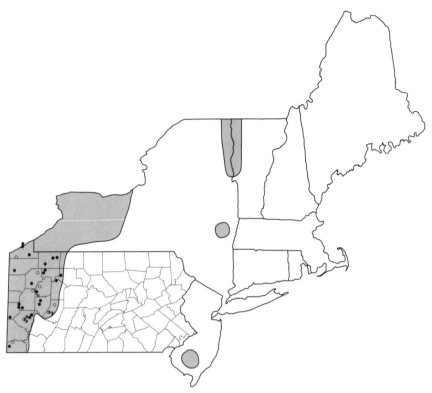

Map 54. Distribution of the eastern spiny softshell *(Apalone spinifera spinifera)*.

northeastern fauna (Klemens 1993). None of the sea turtles nests in the Northeast. Most of the sea turtles found in northeastern coastal waters have been immature individuals (Klemens 1993).

The leatherback is easily identified by its brown to black, leathery carapace that is divided by seven longitudinal ridges. This is the largest of the sea turtles, growing to 180 cm (75 in.) and 550 kg (1,210 lb). Leatherbacks migrate into the waters off the northeastern coast during the spring and leave the waters for southern localities in the autumn (Shoop 1987). They are found along the entire New England coast but rarely venture into Long Island Sound (Klemens 1993).

The loggerhead has a carapace that is reddish brown with yellow-bordered scutes. Five or more costal scutes flank each side of the carapace, with the first always in contact with the nuchal scute. The bridge usually has three scutes, and the plastron is reduced. Loggerheads grow to 115 cm (48 in.) long and weigh up to 160 kg (352 lb) (Klemens 1993). Shoop (1987) reported the loggerhead to be the most abundant sea turtle in New England waters, but Hunter and colleagues (1992) stated that, off the coast of Maine, leatherbacks were more common than loggerheads. Loggerheads do enter into Long Island Sound. Loggerheads follow the same pattern of migration as leatherbacks, with a northward migration in spring and a retreat south in autumn.

The Atlantic ridley is smaller (70 cm [29 in.] long and weighing 45 kg [99 lb]) than the loggerhead, which it superficially resembles. It has a gray to olive-colored carapace. There are five costal scutes on either side of the carapace, and the first costal scute is always in contact with the nuchal scute. There are usually four, sometimes five, scutes on the bridge and a reduced plastron. Though rare today, this species has been recorded from northeastern coastal waters, including Long Island Sound.

Both the green sea turtle and the Atlantic hawksbill have a carapace with four costal scutes on each side, and the first costal scute is not in contact with the nuchal scute. The green sea turtle is distinguished from the Atlantic hawksbill by having only one pair of prefrontal scutes on top of the head as opposed to two pairs in the hawksbill. The hawksbill also has thick, overlapping carapace scutes. Neither of these turtles is common in northeastern coastal waters. Green sea turtles have been reported from waters around Cape Cod, Massachusetts, and southward into Long Island Sound (Klemens 1993). Atlantic hawksbills have been reported only from Cape Cod, Massachusetts, and from Long Island Sound at Orient, New York (Klemens 1993).

Lizards

Lizards belong to the reptilian order Squamata (the same order that contains the snakes) and the suborder Lacertilia. There are 22 families and approximately 3,800 species of lizard. They have a cosmopolitan distribution, being found on all major land masses except Antarctica. Lizards have also invaded most islands, even small ones and those great distances from the continents. They have been able to invade islands because of the small size of many lizards and their ability to survive while adrift on vegetation. There are 11 families and 102 species of lizard in the United States. However, the Northeast's lizard fauna is exceedingly depauperate, with only 2 families and 5 species.

Lizards, generally, but not always, have two pairs of well-developed legs. Their head is distinctly set off from the body by a neck, and they have a moderate to long tail.

Lizards inhabit an incredible variety of terrestrial and semiaquatic habitats. However, with the exception of one species (the marine iguana of the Galapagos Islands), they have not entered the marine environment. Lizards range from the tropics to above the Arctic Circle. They may be found from below sea level to elevations in excess of 4,900 m (16,000 ft) in the Andes and the Himalayas. Lizards reach their greatest levels of abundance and diversity in tropical forests and deserts. They may be fossorial, terrestrial, arboreal, or semiaquatic.

As might be expected for such a diverse group, they exhibit a great range of diets. Most are insectivorous, but some are herbivores and others are carnivorous on vertebrates.

Courtship is often elaborate. Most species lay eggs, but some give birth to live young.

PHRYNOSOMATIDAE

There is no collective common name for the family Phrynosomatidae. It is a large family, with 10 genera and about 125 species. Phrynosomatids range throughout the United States and adjacent southwestern Canada southward to northern Panama.

All characteristics that unite these animals as a biological assemblage are internal. In external appearance they are a very diverse group, ranging from the short, squat, and extremely spiny horned lizards (*Phrynosoma*) of the American Southwest to the tree and rock-dwelling fence lizards (*Sceloporus*), which have long tails and elongate hind limbs. Ecologically, they are equally diverse, being inhabitants of desert scrub, sand dunes, deciduous forests, and tropical forests. Within these habitats, they may be saxicolous, arenicolous, terrestrial, or arboreal.

Most phrynosomatids are generalized carnivores that feed on a wide variety of invertebrate prey appropriate to their size. The only exception are the horned lizards (*Phrynosoma*), which are specialized to feed on ants.

Most male phrynosomatids exhibit complex sexual displays involving head-bobs and push-ups. These displays are intended both to attract sexually receptive females and to establish territory and warn off possible male competitors.

Some members of the family lay eggs; others are viviparous.

Sceloporus
Gr. *scelo*, leg; Gr. *porus*, pore

The genus *Sceloporus* contains the fence lizards and the spiny lizards. It is a large genus, containing approximately 95 species. They range from eastern New York, New Jersey, and Pennsylvania westward to the Pacific Northwest. The range of the genus extends south to northern Panama.

Spiny and fence lizards are small to medium-sized species. Their scales are strongly keeled and overlapping, giving them a very rough appearance. In many parts of their range, they are the dominant component of the herpetofauna. They are all active, diurnal lizards. Many species are arboreal or are found climbing about on rocks. Even the terrestrial species tend to use elevated perches to search for food.

They are alert, wary lizards and can be exceedingly difficult to capture. Some have powerful jaws and can give an unwary collector a painful bite. All members of the genus can autotomize their tail and then regenerate the lost portion. This is an effective antipredator adaptation.

Spiny and fence lizards are insectivorous but will also feed on an occasional spider or scorpion. Some members of the genus lay eggs; others are viviparous. The sexes are generally easy to distinguish because males have a brightly colored patch on each side of the belly and usually have a brightly colored chin as well.

Northern Fence Lizard *Sceloporus undulatus hyacinthinus* (Green)
L. *undulatus*, to rise in waves; Gr. *Hyacinthinus*, a mythological
character, the son of Amyclas, King of Laconia
Description.   The northern fence lizard (Plate 91) is a medium-sized species with well-developed limbs. In sharp contrast to the other northeastern lizards, northern fence lizards are not glossy in appearance. Their matte appearance is due to the nature of their scales, which are not highly polished but are overlapping and, except for those on the ventral surface of the body, strongly keeled and pointed at the posterior edge.

The overall ground color varies from grayish brown to brown. The dominant pattern on the dorsal portion of the body is a series of transverse wavy lines that may extend across the body unbroken or may be separated along the midline of the body. These bands vary from reddish brown to almost black and are bordered posteriorly by a thin pale line. In older males, these bands have a tendency to become indistinct or to disappear altogether. Similar transverse bands occur on the dorsal surface of the limbs and tail. A lateral stripe occurs on either side of the body and tends to be similar in color to the dorsal transverse bands, with which it generally connects. The head is covered with variable dark lines and bars associated with the eyes, temporal region, and supralabials. The ventral coloration is sexually dimorphic in this species. The ventral coloration of mature females and the young of both sexes is an immaculate beige or off-white. On males, however, the ventral surface is far more colorful. The chin generally sports a bright blue or blue-green central blotch. Large, bright blue to dark blue blotches occur on either side of the belly and are bordered medially by a black edge. The blue belly of the male is invisible when the individual is resting directly on the substrate, but it becomes highly visible when the body is lifted off of the ground.

Male northern fence lizards average 63.7 mm ($2\frac{1}{2}$ in.) SVL, and females average 66 mm ($2\frac{5}{8}$ in.) SVL. The tail of females is slightly shorter than that of males. The females' tail length averages 127% of SVL, and that of males averages 134% of SVL.

Confusing Species.   The strongly keeled scales of the northern fence lizard are sufficient to distinguish this lizard from all other species that occur in the Northeast.

Habitat and Habits.   In the Northeast, the northern fence lizard is generally found in open habitat within forests (e.g., rock slides, quarry faces, clearing due to clear-cutting or fire, rocky outcrops along waterways) and in the shale barrens of the south-central portion of Pennsylvania (Huntingdon, Bedford, and Fulton counties) and the Pine Barrens of New

Jersey. These locations provide them with ample basking sites as well as refuge sites in the form of surface cover objects or trees.

The northern fence lizard's seasonal activity may begin as early as mid-March during unusually warm years, but generally it does not begin until the end of March or early April. Adults usually cease activity by late August, but the young of the year remain active until late September or early October.

The northern fence lizard is a diurnally active species that may be readily observed. Unlike skinks, which spend much of their active time foraging under ground litter for food, the northern fence lizard spends most of its active time perched on elevated rocks or logs. Activity usually occurs from midmorning to late afternoon. During hot spells, activity may become bimodal, with a peak during midmorning and a second period of activity in late afternoon. At these times, midday activity is reduced because of excessive surface temperatures. Surface activity is dependent upon the lizards' being able to maintain adequate body temperature. As a result, northern fence lizards are seldom active on cool, cloudy days or when high winds greatly increase convective heat loss.

Hibernation apparently occurs in deep cracks and crevices or in caves within the area of their summer activity.

Northern fence lizards are sit-and-wait predators. Their primary mode of foraging is to perch immobile on a rock or log that has a clear view of the surrounding area. When an appropriate prey items comes within attack range, the lizard rushes from its perch to the prey and captures it. The attack range varies with the size of the individual, but it usually is within a few centimeters of the lizard. Northern fence lizards feed on a wide variety of actively moving prey, such as ants, beetles, spiders, caterpillars, butterflies, and grasshoppers.

Northern fence lizards are highly territorial. While animals are on their perches, they are also monitoring their territory. If another lizard intrudes upon a territory, the holder of the territory will display by doing a series of push-ups, lifting its body up and down off the ground by extending and flexing its forelegs. If this warning does not repel the intruder, the owner of the territory will advance while continuing to bob and do push-ups. If visual threats do not work, the individuals will engage in combat. The size of the territory has not been determined for northern fence lizards, but the territory of the northern prairie lizard (*Sceloporus undulatus garmani*, a similar subspecies from western Nebraska) has been reported as having a mean size of $121 \, \text{m}^2$ ($130 \, \text{yd}^2$) for males and $101 \, \text{m}^2$ ($110 \, \text{yd}^2$) for females (S. Jones and Droge 1980).

Northern fence lizards autotomize their tails, but not as readily or with the same frequency as skinks. Thirty-three percent of mature males and 28% of mature females ($N = 28$) in the collection of the Carnegie Museum exhibited broken tails. Tinkle and Ballinger (1972) found that 29% of the males and 39% of the females in an Ohio population exhibited broken tails. Nine percent of the juveniles in their population exhibited tail breakage. Less than 15% of immature individuals had broken tails. Broken tails rapidly regenerate, but the regenerated portion differs in appearance from the original tail. As a consequence, it is easy to distinguish between complete and regenerated tails.

Reproduction.   No detailed studies of reproduction have been carried out on northern fence lizards from the Northeast; however, Tinkle and Ballinger (1972) studied this species in Hocking County, Ohio.

In Ohio, courtship and mating occur shortly after animals emerge from hibernation in April. Males actively display to attract females and warn off other males from their territory. Their display consists of a series of push-ups and head-bobs. These movements display the bright blue color of the belly of the male. This bright ventral coloration allows the sexes to recognize each other. It has been demonstrated that males respond aggressively to other males and sexually to females owing to the presence or absence of ventral coloration (W. Cooper and Burns 1987).

Females emerge from hibernation with small ovarian follicles but with large deposits of fat stored in discrete fat bodies. Ovarian follicles yolk rapidly because of mobilization of fat from the fat bodies. By the middle of May, eggs have reached ovulatory size. Ohio females generally lay two clutches of eggs a season. The first is laid in mid to late May, and the second toward the end of June (Tinkle and Ballinger 1972).

In Ohio, the average clutch size was 11.8 eggs, but there was a significant difference in the size of first and second clutches. The average number of eggs in first clutches was 12.4, but it was only 10.1 eggs in the second clutch. Larger females had a tendency to lay larger clutches of eggs (Tinkle and Ballinger 1972).

Ohio hatchlings emerge from their eggs from the third week of August to the first week of October, after a natural incubation period of approximately 85 days. In a laboratory study, hatching occurred, on average, in 41 days when incubated at a constant temperature of 30°C (86°F) and in 68 days when incubated at a constant temperature of 25°C (77°F) (Sexton and Marion 1974). Natural incubation temperatures are exceedingly variable, and that variability accounts for the greater time until hatching in the field.

Hatchlings are about 25 mm (1 in.) SVL when they emerge from their eggs and average approximately 32 mm ($1\frac{1}{4}$ in.) SVL by the end of their first year (Tinkle and Ballinger 1972). Individuals that hatch late in the season exhibit little growth before they enter hibernation.

Females mature in their third year at a SVL of approximately 66 mm ($2\frac{3}{5}$ in.). The average size of females from Ohio was 75 mm (3 in.) SVL.

Remarks.   Most records for this species in Pennsylvania are more than 60 years old. It is possible that some of these historical populations may no longer be in existence. Much fieldwork is needed to accurately determine the present distribution of the northern fence lizard.

Distribution.   The northern fence lizard occurs from central New Jersey westward to eastern Nebraska. Its range extends south to central South Carolina in the East and to the Gulf Coast of Texas in the West.

In the Northeast, the species occurs in southeastern New York and southern and central New Jersey. In Pennsylvania, its range covers the southern third of the state, except in the Valley and Ridge Province, where populations extend into Clinton County. In addition, two isolated populations have been reported along the Delaware River in Pike and Wayne counties in the northeastern corner of the state.

SCINCIDAE (SKINKS)

The skink family is an enormous and diverse group of over 1,200 species of lizard that is found on all continents except Antarctica. Skinks are small to medium-sized (a few are large) lizards typified by an elongate, cylindrical body covered with overlapping cycloid scales. Osteoderms (small bony elements embedded in the skin) are well developed, giving skinks a characteristic hard feeling when handled. Skinks often have polished scales and appear to have been freshly lacquered. Most North American skinks belong to the cosmopolitan genus *Eumeces*, which includes about 60 species in North America, North Africa, the Middle East, and Asia.

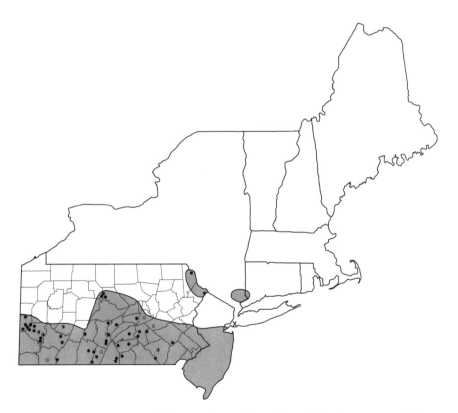

Map 55. Distribution of the northern fence lizard *(Sceloporus undulatus hyacinthinus)*.

Most skinks are secretive animals that live and forage under cover such as leaf litter, although they may emerge to bask. Some species are entirely terrestrial; others, such as the broadhead skink, may climb trees or rock faces. Still others are fossorial, and many of these exhibit some degree of limb reduction. All species are carnivores. Although most skinks lay soft-shelled, spherical to elongate eggs, some species are viviparous.

Eumeces
Gr. *eu*, good; Gr. *mekos*, length

The genus *Eumeces* contains the skinks. It is a large genus, with approximately 60 species. The genus is cosmopolitan in distribution, being found in the New World as well as in Africa, Europe, and parts of Asia.

Eumeces are small to moderately large lizards. They have a cylindrical body with highly polished scales. Their legs are short but well developed. The head is pointed, and adult males often have hypertrophied jaws.

Skinks are active diurnal animals. Most species are terrestrial, although some are semiarboreal. They are active foragers, often seen moving about in the leaf litter and vegetation in search of food. At other times, they can be located under rocks and logs. All members of the genus can readily autotomize their tail.

Skinks feed on a wide variety of invertebrates and the occasional vertebrate. *Eumeces* lay eggs. Parental care is well developed in the genus, and females may be found tending their eggs.

Northern Coal Skink *Eumeces anthracinus anthracinus* (Baird)
Gr. *anthrakon*, coal
Description.   The northern coal skink (Plate 92) is a small to medium-sized species with moderately well-developed limbs, for a skink. It has a glossy appearance owing to its smooth, highly polished cycloid scales.

Adults have a broad dorsal stripe that extends from the top of the head onto the dorsal surface of the tail. The stripe varies from light tan to olive-brown. Taylor (1935), however, reported seeing Pennsylvania specimens that were pea-green dorsally, but this coloration was without doubt due to color change in preservative. The dorsal stripe is bordered on both sides by a thin (about one-third of a scale wide) white to yellowish line that extends from the posterior margin of the eye to the anterior region of the tail. A series of fine black dots generally occurs along the medial sides of these white to yellowish lines. A second pair of thin white lines occurs along the ventral lateral margins of the body. They extend from the posterior margin of the ear to the anterior portion of the tail. A broad dark chocolate-brown to black band occupies the space between the dorsal lateral and ventral lateral lines and extends from the side of the head onto the tail. The ventral coloration from the chin to the tip of the tail is immaculate bluish gray to plain gray. The limbs are similar in color to the dorsal stripe.

Coloration varies somewhat with age and sex. Neonates have body colors similar to, but more intense than, adults (Plate 93). Their limbs tend to be almost black rather than brown, and the tail is a brilliant cobalt blue. The blue color of the tail is gradually lost as they mature. In adult males, the sides of the head turn an orange-reddish color during the breeding season, but breeding color change is not as pronounced as in some other members of the genus. Occasional melanistic individuals occur in some populations (Plate 94).

Northern coal skinks exhibit little sexual size dimorphism. Mature males from Pennsylvania average 54.1 mm ($2\frac{1}{8}$ in.) SVL. The average female SVL is 55.7 mm ($2\frac{1}{4}$ in.). This difference in size is not statistically significant. Taylor (1935) reported that the ratio of tail length to body length increased with age, with the tail being 1.4 times the SVL in young animals and increasing to 1.7 times the SVL in mature individuals. Too few northeastern specimens have entire tails, so it is impossible to determine tail lengths relative to SVL in the Northeast specimens. The maximum SVL for northern coal skinks has been reported as 70 mm ($2\frac{3}{4}$ in.) (Conant and Collins 1991).

Confusing Species.   The northern coal skink could be confused with both of the other species of skink of the genus *Eumeces* native to the Northeast, but it differs from both the five-lined skink and the broadhead skink in having only four, rather than five, longitudinal body stripes. The coal skink lacks the vertebral (midline) stripe present in both of the other species. Ontogenetic change in body pattern, however, occurs in both five-lined and broadhead skinks, so that older individuals of both species often lack one or more stripes. A foolproof way to distinguish the coal skink from either of the other species is to examine the postmental scale. In coal skinks, the postmental is entire, and in the other species it is transversely divided into two scales.

Habitat and Habits.   In the Northeast, northern coal skinks are generally found in fairly open habitat (less than 50% canopy cover by trees) where rocks and logs provide abundant cover. We have had most success in finding them along highway and powerline rights-of-way and in sections of clear-cut forest that have not yet gone into later stages of succession. They are generally found within 50 m (165 ft) of water, but not always. Populations occasionally occur many kilometers away from the nearest source of water.

Seasonal activity may commence as early as late March during unusually mild years, but it usually does not begin until the first week of April. The lizards remain active until the end of September or the beginning of October, depending upon temperature. No information is available on hibernation, but it is likely that northern coal skins simply move downward in the rocky substrate until they are deep enough beneath the surface to avoid freezing temperatures.

The northern coal skink is a diurnally active terrestrial species that is seldom observed, because most activity takes place under leaf litter or cover objects such as logs and rocks. Daily activity appears to occur from midmorning to late afternoon throughout the animal's activity season. There is no shift toward early morning or late afternoon activity during the hotter months. Surface activity within populations appears to be extremely unpredictable. Sites known to harbor skink populations may yield seven or eight skinks in a matter of minutes on one day and then produce no animals after hours of intensive searching on other days with similar climatic conditions.

Northern coal skinks are active, wide-foraging lizards that generally search for food under leaf litter, rocks, and logs. The diet reflects their foraging habits. The major food items are ground-dwelling beetles, spiders, crickets, isopods, and centipedes.

Coal skinks readily autotomize their tail. This defense mechanism presumably reduces their chance of being captured by predators. Damaged tails regenerate over a period of several months. The incidence of broken tails in Pennsylvania northern coal skinks is exceedingly high. Seventy percent of males and 80% of females in the collection at the Carnegie Museum of Natural History have a broken tail.

Reproduction.   Very little is known about reproduction in the northern coal skink. Mating apparently occurs in May and early June (R. Clausen 1938). At this time, the throat and lower region of the head of mature males develop an orange-reddish coloration. Females begin to yolk their follicles the preceding fall, since we have found females emerging from hibernation with large yolked ovarian follicles. Egg laying occurs in late June and possibly early July. The eggs are usually laid in a shallow depression constructed by the female under a cover object. All the nests we have found have been under medium to large slabs of rock, although other species in the genus have been reported to lay their eggs in rotting logs and under other types of surface debris. Females generally remain in attendance of the nest. R. Clausen (1938) reported that an attendant female held in captivity would attempt to bite his finger if he got too close to her eggs. We have not had the same experience with free-ranging coal skinks. Females we have observed remain motionless and coiled around the eggs. If disturbed too much, they attempt to escape but do not defend the eggs. Clausen reported that his captive female refused food while attending the eggs but fed readily after the eggs had hatched.

The eggs are white when first laid, but they become stained a light brown or tan from contact with the substrate. The eggs are oblong, being only slightly longer than they are wide. The average size of eggs ($N = 10$) for two nests from north-central Pennsylvania was 16 mm ($\frac{5}{8}$ in.) long and 12.2 mm ($\frac{1}{2}$ in.) wide. Clutch size in Pennsylvania varies from 5 to 11 eggs (Plate 95). The sample size from the region is too small to determine whether clutch size is correlated with the size of the female.

Hatching is dependent upon weather conditions. Eggs in nests discovered on 27 July 1990 had all hatched by 12 August. A nest of eggs located on 3 August 1992 did not hatch until 29 August. The summer of 1992 was unusually cool, cloudy, and rainy. These inclement conditions probably delayed development in 1992.

Neonates average 25.2 mm (1 in.) SVL and 26 mm (1 in.) tail length. Both males and females appear to reach maturity at a SVL of 50 mm (2 in.). The sex ratio of adults does not significantly differ from 1 : 1.

Remarks.   The northern coal skink is considered by the Pennsylvania Fish and Boat Commission to be a "secure" species within the state. However, populations of coal skinks are widely scattered, seem to be highly localized, and are composed of relatively few individuals. Populations of this sort (restricted in area and low in numbers of individuals) are exceedingly prone to localized extirpation due to habitat modification or destruction as well as to chance events. Before the true status of this species can be determined, detailed studies need to be conducted to determine its population dynamics and precise ecological requirements.

Distribution.   The northern coal skink has a fragmented distribution in the eastern United States. Its range extends intermittently from northwestern New York in the vicinity of Lake Ontario to the mountains of northern Georgia and Alabama. There is an isolated population in central Kentucky.

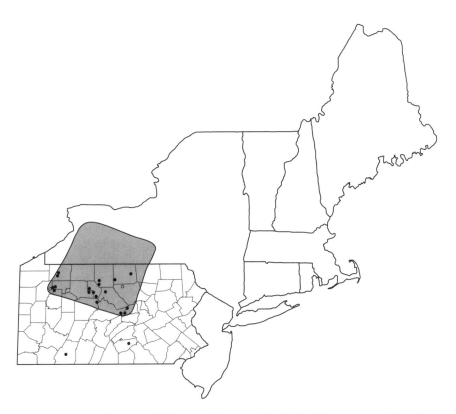

Map 56. Distribution of the northern coal skink *(Eumeces anthracinus anthracinus)*.

The species occurs as far north as Lake Ontario in western New York. In Pennsylvania, the northern coal skink is primarily found in the north-central and northwestern counties. A single locality for the species has been reported from Somerset County in south-central Pennsylvania. Recently, a specimen was observed in extreme southern south-central Pennsylvania in Adams County.

Five-Lined Skink *Eumeces fasciatus* (Linnaeus)
L. *fasciatus*, to envelope with bands
Description.   The five-lined skink (Plates 96 and 97) is a medium-sized lizard. As is typical of the genus, five-lined skinks have a polished appearance due to the smooth, shiny cycloid scales.

Young adults have a black background coloration with a pattern of five longitudinal stripes. The vertebral stripe is yellowish white, extends the length of the body and about halfway down the tail. At the posterior margin of the head, the vertebral stripe divides in two; both of these lines run along the top of the head and converge again on the snout. The dorsal lateral stripes are also yellowish white and originate on the supracilliary scales just above the eye and extend to the middle of the tail. The ventral lateral stripes are white and extend from the anterior supralabials to the midpoint of the tail. The stripes and background coloration blend to produce an overall brownish color on the distal half of the tail. The ventral surfaces of the chin and throat are beige; the rest of the ventral surfaces of the body are bluish gray.

As does the coal skink, the five-lined skink exhibits considerable sexual and ontogenetic variation in color and pattern. The background coloration of neonates and juveniles is intense black, and the tail is bright cobalt blue. By the time they reach sexual maturity, the background coloration has faded slightly, and the tail has lost all vestiges of the blue coloration.

As females age, their background coloration gradually changes from black to brown, and the longitudinal stripes become less distinct but do not disappear. As males age, the dorsal background coloration turns to a brownish tan, and the vertebral and dorsal lateral lines fade into oblivion. The lateral band also becomes brownish but remains darker than the dorsal stripes. The dorsal ventral stripes remain discernible, but they are less distinct than in the young individuals. During the breeding season, the head of males becomes a bright orange-red. This bright color fades after the end of the breeding season.

Males and females exhibit little sexual size dimorphism. In Pennsylvania, males are slightly larger than the females, but the difference is not significant. Males have an average SVL of 67.4 mm ($2\frac{5}{8}$ in.); females average 66 mm ($2\frac{5}{8}$ in.) SVL. Vitt and Cooper (1986b) reported mean SVLs of 63.1 mm ($2\frac{1}{2}$ in.) and 63.3 mm ($2\frac{1}{2}$ in.) for males and females, respectively. However, they documented a significant difference in head size between the sexes, with males having a broader head than females. The maximum size for the species is 86 mm ($3\frac{3}{8}$ in.) (Conant and Collins 1991). The tail, when complete, is long, about 1.5 times the SVL in adults but somewhat shorter (1.33–1.35 times the SVL) in neonates and juveniles.

Confusing Species.   Adult males might be mistaken for northern coal skinks, but the postmental scale in coal skinks is undivided, whereas in five-lined skinks the postmental is transversely divided into two scales. Five-lined skinks differ from broadhead skinks in having only four supralabials before the subocular scale. In broadhead skinks there are five supralabials before the subocular.

Habitat and Habits.   The five-lined skink is an infrequently encountered species in the northeastern United States, and as a result relatively little is known about its biology in the region. Five-lined skinks tend to be most often found in clearings in forested areas where surface cover objects are abundant. Cover objects might be fallen logs, rocks, or debris from human habitation (both occupied and unoccupied). They are frequently located in the vicinity of water, but water certainly is not a requirement, as they have been collected in open rock areas on mountain ridges miles away from the nearest surface water.

In Pennsylvania, five-lined skinks emerge from hibernation in early April and then remain active until mid to late September. This corresponds with the seasonal activity for populations from Kansas (H. Fitch 1954) and Connecticut (Klemens 1993), but it is shorter than the activity season reported from the Carolinas (Vitt and Cooper 1986b). Hibernation sites are unknown in the Northeast.

Five-lined skinks are diurnal, but their tendency to forage for food under cover objects and in leaf litter make it unlikely for them to be seen by the casual observer.

The home range size has not been determined for five-lined skinks in the Northeast. However, Gruner (in Klemens 1993) studied a Connecticut population in which 34 animals were marked in a 0.4-ha (1-acre) mountaintop. In Kansas, H. Fitch (1954) determined that males have a home range of approximately 30 m (90 ft) in diameter and that females have a home range of about 10 m (30 ft) in diameter. Individual home ranges tended to center on some structural feature of the environment that provided both food and shelter for the animal, such as a fallen log, tree stump, or large rock. Once established, lizards tended to use the same home range for life. Hecnar and M'Closkey (1998) demonstrated that skink populations declined where human activity in Point Pelee Park, Ontario, Canada, caused a reduction in woody debris (e.g., logs and boards).

Five-lined skinks are carnivorous and spend much of their activity time searching in leaf litter and under cover objects for food items hidden from view. Since the food is hidden, the primary sense used in prey location is olfaction. Burghardt (1973) demonstrated that newborn five-lined skinks were able to chemically distinguish between different potential prey items in their environment. In Kansas, the major food items included spiders, roaches, crickets, grasshoppers, and adult and larval beetles. This diet is in basic agreement with the few food records that we have for Pennsylvania specimens.

Five-lined skinks employ caudal autotomy as an escape mechanism. When a potential predator captures a skink the tail breaks; the predator tends to be distracted from the skink to the now-severed tail, thus allowing the skink an opportunity to escape while the predator is occupied with the tail. This is an exceedingly effective strategy. In controlled experimental interactions between predators and tailed and tail-less skinks, it was found that 56.4% of the tailed skinks escaped predatory attack (i.e., were not eaten) but that only 9% of the tail-less skinks survived an attack (Vitt and Cooper 1986c). After the tail has been broken, regeneration occurs rather rapidly. The regenerated tail is not a perfect replica of the original. Careful examination of the tail can tell where the regeneration began. Occasionally, skinks are found that exhibit multiple regenerations. Seventy-seven percent of the five-lined skinks in the collection of the Carnegie Museum have a broken or regenerated tail.

Reproduction. Reproduction has been studied in some detail by H. Fitch (1954) in Kansas and by Vitt and Cooper (1986b) in South Carolina. Much of the information in the following discussion is from those sources and is supplemented by what we have observed in Pennsylvania.

Mating has been reported to occur shortly after emergence from hibernation (April and May) in Kansas. No information is available for mating in the Northeast, but we have found males in early June in Pennsylvania that still possess bright red-orange heads. These mating colors usually fade rapidly after the breeding season ends. As a result, this coloration indicates that breeding is either more extended in Pennsylvania or is delayed until later in the year. Females generally oviposit from late May to the middle of June in Kansas and South Carolina, but they may be delayed by inclement weather.

Females usually deposit their eggs in cavities constructed beneath rocks or logs or in the rotted sections of hardwood logs and stumps. Hecnar (1994) found that females in Ontario, Canada, preferred large, moderately decayed logs where soil moisture content was likely to remain high throughout the incubation period. Clutch size varies geographically. Clutch size in Kansas ranges from 4 to 16 eggs, and in South Carolina from 3 to 8 eggs. Four gravid females from Pennsylvania contained from 8 to 11 eggs. Females remain in attendance of the eggs, and H. Fitch (1954) reported that they take a very active role in egg care: dampening the nest chamber when it is too dry, moving the eggs about so that they will not stick to the walls or the floor of the cavity, protecting the eggs from small predators, and even moving the eggs to a completely new nest site if conditions at the original nest become inappropriate for normal development.

The eggs are white when first laid, but they rapidly become tan or brown owing to exposure to the substrate. They are slightly oblong and rounded at both ends. They average 11 mm by 7.5 mm ($\frac{3}{8}$ in. by $\frac{1}{4}$ in.) when first laid (H. Fitch 1954). They increase in size after being laid, presumably because of the absorption of water. Incubation time is temperature dependent, and eggs hatch from 27 to 47 days after being laid.

Hatchlings from Pennsylvania have an average SVL of 25.7 mm (1 in.) and an average tail length of 35.4 mm ($1\frac{3}{8}$ in.). At hatching, the neonates have a brilliant blue tail.

Both males and females attain sexual maturity at SVLs between 52 and 55 mm ($2\frac{1}{16}$–$2\frac{1}{8}$ in.). This is similar to the size at maturity in other parts of the animal's range.

Remarks. Much discussion has centered around the function of the bright blue tail of juveniles of this and other species of *Eumeces* and why the tail color fades with maturity. Clark and Hall (1970) suggested that the bright blue tail functions as a social signal indicating to mature males that the individuals with the blue tail are too young to engage in any aspect of reproduction. Subsequent studies suggest that this is not the case. W. Cooper and Vitt (1986a) suggested that juveniles are more vulnerable to predation than adults because of differences in foraging behaviors and that they use the tail to distract predators away from the more vulnerable body.

Distribution. The five-lined skink is distributed throughout much of the eastern and east-central United States. Its range extends from eastern New York, western Vermont and central Pennsylvania, south to northern Florida, and west to eastern Nebraska and eastern Texas.

The species occurs in the Northeast as far north as central western Vermont and eastern New York north to Lake George. It occurs in western Connecticut, but is considered extirpated from Massachusetts (Klemens 1993). In Pennsylvania, it has a widely scattered distribution in the western portion of the Allegheny Plateau and the Valley and Ridge Province. A few populations have been reported from the Piedmont and Coastal Plains provinces.

Broadhead Skink *Eumeces laticeps* (Schneider)
L. *latos*, broad; L. *ceps*, head
Description. The broadhead skink (Plate 98) is a large species with well-developed limbs. As is typical of North American skinks, it has a glossy appearance due to the highly polished cycloid scales that cover its body.

Neonates and juveniles are boldly patterned, with five longitudinal stripes on a black background. The stripes include an unpaired vertebral stripe, a pair of dorsal lateral stripes, and a pair of ventral lateral stripes. All of the stripes are yellowish. The vertebral stripe bifurcates on the nuchal region of the head. The divided lines run along the medial boundary of the supraocular scales and again converge at the tip of the snout and extend approximately halfway down the length of the tail. The dorsal lateral stripes extend from the anterior margin of the eyes along the body and onto the proximal half of the tail. The ventral lateral lines extend from the supralabials posteriorly onto the proximal half of the tail. The tail is brilliant cobalt blue. The ventral surfaces of the body are white or bluish gray. As does that of other skinks, the appearance of the broadhead skink changes with sex and age.

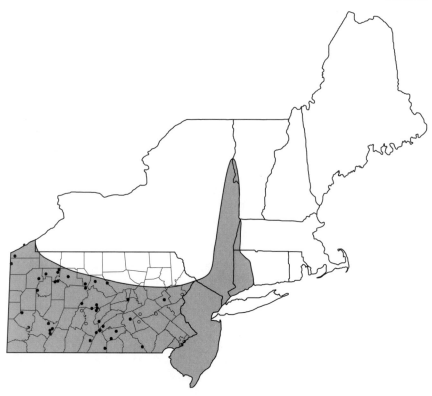

Map 57.   Distribution of the five-lined skink *(Eumeces fasciatus).*

In females, the stripes remain throughout life, although the vertebral stripe may become indistinct. The background coloration changes from black to some shade of brown. The dorsal coloration generally is light tannish brown. The background color between the dorsal and ventral lateral stripes remains uniformly dark brown, giving the appearance of broad dark bands running the length of the body. The blue tail color fades to brown by the time maturity is reached.

Adult males completely lose the longitudinal body stripes, and the body becomes uniformly light to olive brown. The tail loses all trace of blue pigmentation by the time maturity is reached.

Broadhead skinks exhibit considerable sexual dimorphism in size and coloration. This species is exceedingly rare in Pennsylvania, and only a single male (SVL 111 mm; $4\frac{1}{2}$ in.) and a single female (SVL 96 mm; $3\frac{7}{8}$ in.) have been collected in the state. As a consequence, data on size come from other populations. In South Carolina, males have an average SVL of 109.4 mm ($4\frac{3}{8}$ in.), whereas females average only 94.8 mm ($3\frac{3}{4}$ in.) SVL (Vitt and Cooper 1985). Males also have a much larger head than females (hence the common name broadhead skink) when measured either on an absolute basis or as a function of head size relative to body size. During the breeding season, the head of males becomes brightly colored with red or orange pigmentation. This color intensifies with the age of the animal. As a result, older males have a brighter head than younger males. The brilliant head color rapidly fades after the end of the breeding season.

The tail is about 1.5 times the length of the body, but most skinks have a broken or regenerated tail, so accurate measurements of tail length are very difficult to obtain. The maximum size for this species has been reported as 143 mm ($5\frac{3}{4}$ in.) SVL (Conant and Collins 1991).

Confusing Species.   The broadhead skink may be confused with either of the other skinks native to Pennsylvania. It may be differentiated from the northern coal skink by the fact that the postmental is transversely divided into two scales in the broadhead skink but is entire in the coal skink. Broadhead skinks have five supralabials in front of the suborbital scale as opposed to the four supralabials anterior to the suborbital scale in the five-lined skink (but see Plate 96).

Habitat and Habits.   The broadhead skink is so rare in Pennsylvania that nothing is known about its habits or reproduction in the state. As a consequence, the material in this section and the next relies on information published in studies in other parts of the skink's range.

There is strong consensus among herpetologists that the broadhead skink is the most arboreal of all the North American skinks. It is reported to frequent wooded areas where there is an abundance of dead standing timber and large stumps and hollow logs (Mount 1975). Broadhead skinks are often seen climbing high in trees (P. Smith 1961) and have been observed utilizing abandoned woodpecker holes (Collins 1974).

Seasonal activity generally begins in March at lower latitudes (Vitt and Cooper 1985). Surface activity extends into September and early October in northern Florida (Goin and Goin 1951). Broadhead skinks are diurnal.

No information is available concerning home range size. Males, for the most part, are nonterritorial. However, they will defend females during the reproductive season (Vitt and Cooper 1985).

Despite their arboreal tendencies, broadhead skinks spend much of their time foraging for food on the ground. The most detailed study of their diet and foraging behavior is that of Vitt and Cooper (1986a). Skinks move over and through the leaf litter. They rapidly move their head from side to side while moving about. They will occasionally stop, poke their head under the debris, and emerge with a prey item. They often burrow completely out of sight for several minutes before remerging. Apparently, both visual and olfactory cues are used in prey location. Their diet is extremely varied. They feed on crickets and grasshoppers, beetles and their larvae, caterpillars, earwigs, snails, isopods, spiders, lizards and lizard eggs, and other items. Apparently, they will feed on virtually any item of appropriate size. The only foods that they have been shown to avoid are millipedes and velvet ants.

Broadhead skinks will, if captured, defend themselves vigorously and can give a painful bite.

Reproduction. Vitt and Cooper (1985) published the most detailed account of reproduction in broadhead skinks. Unless otherwise noted, all information comes from their paper on a South Carolina population.

Mating generally occurs from May to early June. At this time, males have a brilliant orange-red head and are very aggressive. They will engage in combat with any other male that they encounter. Both aggressive behavior and head coloration are due to elevated levels of testosterone. After the breeding season, serum testosterone levels fall, and both aggressive behavior and bright head color fade (W. Cooper and Vitt 1987).

Females emerge from hibernation with small ovarian follicles. The follicles rapidly yolk, and by mid-May at least some of the females have eggs of ovulatory size. After breeding, males often remain with the female for 3–4 days, apparently to guard against the female's mating with another male before she begins nest construction and egg laying (W. Cooper and Vitt 1986b).

When ready to oviposit, the female constructs a nest chamber in the rotted wood of hardwood logs. Females tend their eggs, although they will emerge to forage for food, frequently enough during brooding to maintain their body weight.

Clutch size varies from 9 to 18 eggs and averages 13.7 eggs. Egg number is not significantly correlated with female body size in this species. On average, eggs weigh 1.07 g ($\frac{1}{25}$ oz) when laid and gain considerable mass during the course of incubation owing to the absorption of water.

Incubation averages 48.7 days, and neonates emerge from mid-July to early August. Hatchlings average 31.4 mm ($1\frac{1}{4}$ in.) SVL and weigh an average of 0.79 g (0.130 oz). The hatchlings of broadhead skinks have a brilliant blue tail.

Both males and females mature at about 85 mm ($3\frac{3}{8}$ in.) SVL.

Remarks. The broadhead skink is currently listed in Pennsylvania as a candidate species (i.e., a species "that could become endangered or threatened in the future"). We feel that its status should be elevated to at least threatened, and probably to endangered. Our reasons are as follows: the extreme limited range of the species in Pennsylvania, its apparent rarity (only two specimens reported from the state), and the fact that it occurs in a section of the state that is receiving heavy impact from agriculture as well as urban and suburban sprawl.

Distribution. Broadhead skinks range from southeastern Pennsylvania southward to northern Florida and west to eastern Texas and eastern Kansas.

In Pennsylvania, only two specimens have been recorded. One was collected in West Chester, Chester County, in the early 1900s. The other specimen was collected in 1985 from the southern Susquehanna River in York County. It is doubtful that the West Chester population is still in existence because of the extreme modification of the land in that area.

Map 58. Distribution of the broadhead skink *(Eumeces laticeps).*

Ground Skink (Say) *Scincella lateralis*

L. *scincela,* little skink; L. *lateralis,* refers to the dark dorsolateral stripes

Description. The smallest of the northeastern lizards, the ground skink (Plate 99) reaches a size of only 50 mm (2 in.) in males and 57 mm (2¼ in.) in females (G. Brooks 1975, Conant and Collins 1991). This lizard has smooth scales that vary from tan to dark brown or olive-brown, dorsally. There are sometimes scattered flecks of darker pigment, especially laterally. Dark dorsolateral stripes extend from the snout, through the eye, to the base of the tail. The ventral color varies from cream-colored to pale yellow. There is a transparent patch in the lower eyelid that may allow the lizard to see when the eye is closed.

Confusing Species. The ground skink cannot be confused with any other species within its range in the Northeast.

Habitat and Habits. Little comparative information is available for the ground skink in New Jersey, the only part of the Northeast in which it is found.

This lizard has been found in a wide variety of habitats, from mixed hardwood forests to open forest–grassland areas to subtropical hammocks.

It is most often found under leaf litter and surface soil. Ground skinks actively search for their prey, which consists of small invertebrates such as beetles, flies, roaches, and spiders (G. Brooks 1964, Hamilton and Pollack 1961, Mitchell 1994).

Ground skinks generally escape from predators by running and hiding under cover. Akin and Townsend (1998) reported that lizards escaped by diving into water and swimming. When captured, these lizards will readily autotomize their tail, increasing their chance of escaping. Ground skinks without tails are more likely to be captured and eaten than are those with intact tails (Dial and Fitzpatrick 1983, 1984). Animals with lower body temperatures flee earlier, with the predator more distant, than do warmer lizards, regardless of size or condition of tail (D. G. Smith 1998). Known predators of ground skinks are ringneck snakes, black racers, corn snakes, milk snakes, southern hognose snake, glass lizards, broadhead skinks, five-lined skinks, domestic cats, and armadillos (Beane, et al. 1998, G. Brooks 1967, Mitchell 1994).

The population ecology of this species was studied in Florida (G. Brooks 1967) and Louisiana (Akin 1998a, Turner 1960). In Florida, the home ranges of males were larger than those of females, and male home ranges overlapped considerably whereas female home ranges overlapped slightly. The density of lizards varied throughout the year, with the highest density recorded in late fall after the hatchlings appeared (G. Brooks 1967).

Akin (1998b) found that male ground skinks were more aggressive than female ground skinks, with a high degree of that aggression being directed toward females. He concluded that males may tolerate females only during the breeding season. During the remainder of the year, males compete with females for resources, and this aggression maintains spatial distance between the sexes.

Reproduction. Ground skinks have a characteristically small clutch of 1–7 eggs (H. Fitch 1970), which is laid in humus, rotten stumps, or logs (H. Smith 1967). In some populations, females lay multiple clutches of eggs each year (H. Fitch 1970). It is unknown whether the New Jersey population exhibits this characteristic. Unlike some other species of skink, female ground skinks do not remain in the nest with their eggs. Communal nesting sites were found in Virginia, with as many as 66 eggs deposited in one site (Mitchell 1994). Tail loss potentially influences the reproductive success of both male and female ground skinks by affecting the ability of males to perform courtship behavior and the ability of females to produce eggs (Dial and Fitzpatrick 1983).

Distribution. The ground skink is widespread in the southeastern United States. It occurs from southern New Jersey, west to eastern Kansas and most of Oklahoma, and south through Florida and into the Florida keys and through the western half of Texas.

In the Northeast, it is found only in southern New Jersey, where it is rare.

Map 59. Distribution of the ground skink *(Scincella lateralis)*.

Snakes

Snakes constitute the suborder Serpentes within the order Squamata. There are approximately 2,900 living species of snake known, and undoubtedly many more species have not yet been discovered. Snakes are found on all continents except Antarctica. They are also found on most major islands or island groups in temperate and tropical oceans and seas. The major exceptions are New Zealand, Ireland, and the Hawaiian Islands. The distribution of snakes extends from near the Arctic Circle to the southern tip of South America. They occur in all major terrestrial and estuarine habitats and can be found from below sea level to elevations in excess of 4,600 m (15,000 ft). Sea snakes occur in the warm waters of both the Indian and Pacific oceans and adjacent seas, but they are absent from the Atlantic.

The most recent classification of snakes recognizes 16 extant families (McDowell 1987). The Northeast's ophidian fauna consists of 25 species from two of those families.

Snakes are immediately recognizable by their elongate body and lack of limbs. In addition to these characters, snakes lack external ear openings. They also lack eyelids; the eyes, instead, are covered by immovable, transparent structures called brilles. The tongue is long, protrusible, and bifurcate and is used to collect odor particles from the environment and transfer them to specialized olfactory receptors (Jacobson's organs) located in the roof of the mouth. This is why snakes are normally seen flicking their tongues in and out. The ventral scales of most species (and of all northeastern species) are modified into large transverse plates called scutes that function in locomotion.

The skull and jaws of snakes are highly modified and specialized. The brain is firmly encased by dermal bones, and the rest of the bones of the head and upper jaws are loosely attached to each other. The articulation of the lower jaw to the cranium is also loose, and the two halves of the lower jaw are not fused as they are in most vertebrates; rather, they are attached by an elastic ligament. As a result, the entire skull is somewhat movable and highly flexible. This condition permits one of the most remarkable characteristics of snakes: that is, their ability to ingest food that is several times the diameter of their own head and body. The right and left sides of both upper and lower jaws can be independently moved. This feature enables the snake to literally walk the prey into the mouth.

All snakes are carnivores, and their prey is always swallowed whole. The diet of snakes varies greatly, and prey range in size from small insects to large mammals. Many species of snake are rather generalized feeders, utilizing a wide variety of food items, but a surprisingly large number of species are very specialized, feeding on only one or two types of food. Several species of northeastern snakes have extremely specialized diets.

Snakes, as is typical of most reptiles, exhibit indeterminate growth. That is, they continue to grow throughout their entire life, although growth rates tend to slow dramatically with age. To accommodate their growth, snakes periodically shed their skin. This process starts at the tip of the snout, where the old skin peels back. The snake then crawls out of its old skin, leaving behind a perfect cast of its body. It is often possible to identify a species of snake using characteristics of the shed skin.

All snakes have internal fertilization, and males have paired copulatory organs called hemipenes. Most species of snake lay eggs, but some give birth to live young. The percentage of live-bearing species tends to increase with increasing latitude. Indeed, 12 of the 25 species of snake found in the Northeast are viviparous. Clutch size varies from as few as one to as many as 100 eggs, although clutches from 4 to 16 eggs are the most common.

COLUBRIDAE (HARMLESS SNAKES)

The family Colubridae is the largest and most diverse family of snake. It contains approximately 270 genera and over 2,000 species. The colubrids are the predominant family of snakes on all continents and major islands with the exception of Australia, where their range is restricted to the northern border of the continent.

Colubrids occupy all major terrestrial and aquatic ecosystems within their geographic range. They have evolved specializations to fossorial, arboreal, aquatic, and arenicolous lifestyles. They vary in length from about 150 mm (6 in.) to over 4 m (13 ft).

Their teeth are located on the maxilla, pterygoid, palatine, and mandibular bones and in general are solid, smooth, and recurved. The posterior maxillary teeth of some species, however, are enlarged and grooved and may be attached to venom glands. Prey vary from insects, earthworms, and other invertebrates to most classes of vertebrate animals. Although most species are fairly generalized feeders, a considerable number of species are extremely specialized in their diet.

Most colubrids are oviparous, but some are viviparous. Clutch size varies from as few as 2 to as many as 100 eggs or young.

Carphophis

The genus *Carphophis* contains two species that are restricted to the eastern and central United States. Both species are small burrowing snakes that, because of their fossorial lifestyle, have been given the common name worm snake. Their bodies are cylindrical, and their dorsal scales are smooth. They are generally encountered under cover objects in regions of loose or sandy soil. They are inoffensive and never attempt to bite. Worm snakes feed primarily on earthworms. Both species lay eggs.

Eastern Worm Snake *Carphophis amoenus amoenus* (Say)
Gr. *carph*, a dry twig; Gr. *ophis*, serpent; L. *amoenus*, pleasing, lovely
Description.   The eastern worm snake (Plate 100) is a small, stout, cylindrical species. The dorsal coloration is uniform light to dark brown; however, the posterior tip of each scale is often darker than the rest of the scale and may give the body a slightly patterned appearance. The ventral scales are pinkish and translucent to the point that oviducal eggs can be seen through the scales and body wall. The ventral coloration extends from a half to two scale rows up on each side of the body. On the head, the dorsal color extends halfway down the supralabials. Allard (1945) reported on an adult female from Virginia on which the ventral pinkish coloration extended over the entire body. D. Clark (1970) reported an albino specimen from Montgomery County, Maryland.

The head is small and blunt and is not distinct from the body. The eyes are very small. The tail is short and terminates in a sharp spine. The dorsal scales are smooth and highly polished and give the animal a glossy appearance. In mature males, the dorsal scales in the anal region are often weakly keeled. Blanchard (1931) termed these weakly keeled scales "anal ridges." There are 13 scale rows at midbody, and the anal plate is divided. The subcaudals occur in two rows.

Eastern worm snakes exhibit significant sexual dimorphism in size, body proportions, and scale counts. The average SVL of adult males from Pennsylvania is 198.5 mm ($7\frac{3}{4}$ in.), and the average ToL is 241.7 mm ($9\frac{3}{4}$ in.). The females average 240.9 mm ($9\frac{5}{8}$ in.) SVL and 278.4 mm ($11\frac{7}{8}$ in.) ToL. The record size for the species is 322 mm ($12\frac{7}{8}$ in.) ToL (Conant and Collins 1991). Males have a significantly longer tail than females. Males have a mean tail length of 22% of SVL and 18.3% of ToL, whereas females have a mean tail length of 15.4% of SVL and 13.2% of ToL.

Confusing Species.   The combination of small size, small eyes, and highly polished scales that occur in 13 rows at midbody preclude confusing this species with any other snake found in the Northeast.

Habitat and Habits.   The eastern worm snake is a fossorial species and is morphologically, well adapted for that existence, with its small blunt head, reduced eyes, cylindrical body with highly polished scales, and short, sharply pointed tail. It is generally found in areas with soils suitable for burrowing. In Pennsylvania, it is usually found in rocky forested areas at the edge of woods where there is an abundance of rocky cover. Soils in most of these areas are moderately sandy. In other parts of its range, it has been reported from old fields, second-growth areas, and open pastureland, but it apparently occurs in these areas only if forested habitat is nearby (Barbour 1960). The eastern worm snake is a secretive species, seldom being found in the open. It is most commonly encountered under rocks and rotting logs and is occasionally plowed up in fields.

The earliest recorded date of collection in Pennsylvania is 12 April and the latest date is 30 September. D. Clark (1970) stated that, in Kansas, seasonal activity is strongly bimodal, with the greatest activity occurring in April and May, reduced activity in June and July, increased activity in August, and then a gradual decline in activity through September and October as the snakes enter hibernation. In Kentucky, Barbour and colleagues (1969b) found most daily activity to occur in midday and late afternoon, with activity decreasing after dark. There are too few records of the species from Pennsylvania to adequately discuss seasonal activity in the state. Most specimens collected by Klemens (1993) in Connecticut were obtained in late May and June.

Little is known about the hibernacula of eastern worm snakes. Grizzell (1949) found a small individual burrowed 60 cm (24 in.) below the surface in the vicinity of a groundhog burrow that he was excavating on 8 February in Maryland. In Georgia, eastern worm snakes hibernate in small tunnels, 30–60 cm (12–24 in.) below the surface of rocks (Neill 1948).

Eastern worm snakes from Kentucky have a mean home range size of 253 m^2 (280 yd^2) (Barbour et al. 1969b).

The eastern worm snake appears to be a solitary species. Only one instance of an aggregation has been reported in the literature. In this case, three individuals were found occupying the same rocky cover (Barbour et al. 1969b).

Eastern worm snakes feed almost exclusively on earthworms (Barbour 1960, D. Clark 1970, Hamilton and Pollack 1956), but one individual has been reported to have eaten a small salamander of the genus *Eurycea*. The only food found in the stomachs of Pennsylvania specimens has been earthworms.

Reproduction.   Mating occurs in both spring and fall. Females emerge from hibernation with small (ca. 6 mm; $\frac{1}{4}$ in.) ovarian eggs, and by late May or early June the eggs have enlarged and been ovulated. Egg laying occurs from mid-June to mid-July (Barbour 1960). Eggs are laid under stones and rotting logs and below ground. Clutch size varies from 1 to 5 eggs, with a mean of 3.1 eggs. Clutch size is positively correlated with female body size; larger females lay more eggs (D. Clark 1970). The eggs are elongate, cylindrical, and blunt at both ends. The average length of oviducal eggs for Pennsylvania specimens is 18.8 mm ($\frac{3}{4}$ in.), and the average width is 6.9 mm ($\frac{1}{4}$ in.). The incubation time is about 60 days, and hatchlings emerge from early August to mid-September (McCauley 1945, Simmons and Stine 1961). No data on hatching size are available for Pennsylvania or the rest of the Northeast, but McCauley (1945) reported a mean hatching size of 98.6 mm ($3\frac{7}{8}$ in.) ToL for animals from Maryland. Palmer and Braswell (1995) reported a mean ToL of 101.5 mm (4 in.) for hatchlings from North Carolina. There is no evidence of communal nesting in the eastern worm snake.

Females mature at a SVL of about 188 mm ($7\frac{1}{2}$ in.), and males at 177 mm ($7\frac{1}{16}$ in.) SVL (Barbour 1960, Clark 1970).

Remarks.   Eastern worm snakes are extremely docile and never attempt to bite. If held in the hand, a worm snake will attempt to escape by pushing its head through the fingers and pushing the tip of its tail against the skin as if it were burrowing. Unlike many species of snake, they do not discharge musk or feces upon capture.

Distribution.   The eastern worm snake occurs from southern Massachusetts and Rhode Island through southeastern New York and south through South Carolina, the northern half of Georgia and Alabama, and extreme northeastern Mississippi. The western border of its range then extends diagonally northeastward through eastern Tennessee and Kentucky into southeastern Ohio and Pennsylvania.

This species occurs in the Northeast in Connecticut, Rhode Island, south-central Massachusetts, southeastern New York, and New Jersey. Its distribution is poorly known in Massachusetts and Rhode Island (Klemens 1993).

In Pennsylvania, its distribution is spotty, but the majority of locality records occur in the central and south-central portions of the state. It is most commonly found on wooded hillsides in the Valley and Ridge Province and along the hillsides near the Susquehanna River. The only recent specimen from west of the Allegheny Front is one taken in Bolivar, Westmoreland County, near the hills overlooking the Conemaugh River. It is probable that it is more widely distributed in the southern and central Valley and Ridge Province, but its small size and secretive nature make it unlikely to be found by the casual observer.

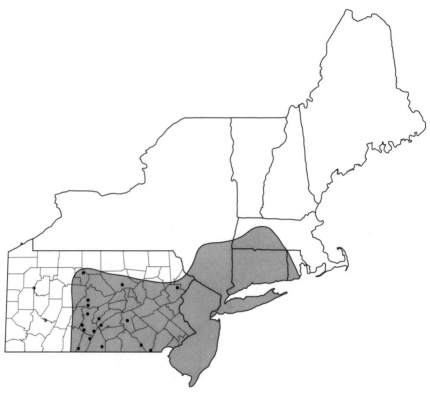

Map 60. Distribution of the eastern worm snake *(Carphophis amoenus amoenus)*.

Northern Scarlet Snake *Cemophora coccinea copei* Jan
Gr. *kemos*, muzzle; *phoreus*, bearer; L. *coccineus*, scarlet; *copei*, named for Edward Drinker Cope, a noted nineteenth-century herpetologist and paleontologist

Description.   The northern scarlet snake (Plate 101) is a boldly patterned species. The pattern consists of a series of red blotches on the dorsal surface of the body and tail. Each red blotch is outlined along the anterior and posterior borders with a black band. This band is less developed on, and occasionally absent from, the ventral borders of the blotches. The coloration between the blotches varies from white to yellowish. The snout is red, with a transverse black band extending from side to side and running through or just behind the eyes. The ventral surfaces of the head and body are immaculate white to cream-colored. Hatchlings resemble adults in general pattern, but the red blotches tend to be more pinkish (Woolcott 1959).

The rostral scale is strongly developed, resulting in a pointed snout that extends beyond the lower jaw. The head is slightly wider than the neck. The eyes are small. In a sample from Virginia (Mitchell 1994), males were significantly larger than females. Mature males ranged from 295 to 575 mm

$(11\frac{3}{4}-22\frac{3}{4}$ in.) long, with a mean of 450 mm $(17\frac{3}{4}$ in.). Females ranged from 260 to 483 mm $(10\frac{1}{4}-19$ in.) long, with a mean of 361 mm $(14\frac{1}{4}$ in.).

The scales are smooth and somewhat polished, occurring in 19 to 21 rows (usually 19) at midbody. The anal plate is entire, and the subcaudals occur in two rows.

Confusing Species.   The northern scarlet snake could be confused with intergrade individuals of the eastern milk snake × scarlet kingsnake because they have a similar dorsal pattern. The ventral surface of the scarlet snake, however, is immaculate white to cream-colored, whereas milk snake intergrades have numerous black blotches on the ventral scales.

Habitat and Habits.   In the Northeast, the scarlet snake is restricted to the Pine Barrens region of New Jersey. Very little information is available concerning this species in the Northeast; as a consequence, information in this section and the next comes from other areas of the species' range.

In general, scarlet snakes are found in areas where the soil is sandy and well drained. The scarlet snake is a fossorial species that uses its pointed snout to burrow through the loose soil. Observations on burrowing behavior in this species suggest that the snake thrusts its snout into the soil and then moves its head up and down or sideways to move the soil aside and compact it (Wilson 1951).

This species is generally not found under cover objects during the day. Most reports of the species indicate that it is occasionally active on the surface at night. Most individuals are found on the surface of roads at night (Palmer and Tregembo 1970). In South Carolina, Nelson and Gibbons (1972) reported considerable success in capturing scarlet snakes in pitfall traps associated with drift fences. They concluded that the species might be far more common than generally thought but that, owing to its nocturnal and fossorial habits, it eludes most collectors.

Scarlet snakes have been reported to be active from May through September in South Carolina, with peak activity occurring in June (Nelson and Gibbons 1972). In North Carolina, Palmer and Braswell (1995) reported the species to be found in every month of the year, with peak activity occurring in May, June, and July.

Scarlet snakes have been reported to feed on a variety of food items, but reptile eggs seem to be their staple diet, at least during the summer. Palmer and Tregembo (1970) reported that, although captive specimens were offered a variety of potential food items, the only one accepted was reptile eggs. The snakes feed on the eggs by first slitting the shell with their enlarged posterior teeth. They then place a body coil against or around the egg and squeeze the contents of the egg into the mouth.

Reproduction.   Little is known about reproduction in this species. Scarlet snakes are oviparous, and egg laying has been reported from July to August in captivity (Palmer and Braswell 1995). Only a few nests have been found in the wild. It appears that scarlet snakes lay their eggs under pine straw (Trauth 1982) and in moist humus (Woolcott 1959). One clutch of eggs laid in captivity on 4 July was deposited in sawdust. This clutch was incubated at 24°–26°C (75°–78°F), and all eggs hatched on 24 and 25 September (Braswell and Palmer 1984). The average ToL of hatchlings from this clutch was 176 mm, (7 in.), with a range of 168–183 mm ($6\frac{1}{2}$–$7\frac{1}{4}$ in.). Clutch size varies from 2 to 6 ($X = 3.58$) eggs. In one clutch, eggs averaged 28.9 mm ($1\frac{1}{4}$ in.) long and 13.1 mm ($\frac{1}{2}$ in.) wide (Braswell and Palmer 1984); in another clutch, the average egg size was 34.5 mm by 12.5 mm ($1\frac{3}{8}$ in. by $\frac{1}{2}$ in.) (Trauth 1982).

Distribution.   The northern scarlet snake ranges from Maryland southward to northern peninsular Florida. Its range extends westward to eastern Texas and Oklahoma. Disjunct populations occur in central Missouri and in southern New Jersey.

Kirtland's Snake *Clonophis kirtlandii* (Kennicott)
Gr. *klono*, twig; Gr. *ophis*, serpent; *kirtlandii*, named for Jared P.
Kirtland, a nineteenth-century naturalist
Description.   Kirtland's snake (Plate 102) is a small to medium-sized species. The head is short and not distinct from the body. The dorsal back-

Map 61.   Distribution of the northern scarlet snake *(Cemophora coccinea copei).*

ground coloration varies from gray to reddish brown. The dorsal pattern is composed of four rows of dark brown or black, squarish or rounded, alternating blotches that give the body a checkerboard appearance. In some specimens, these blotches may not be conspicuous as they tend to blend with the background coloration. In Pennsylvania, the number of blotches in each row varies from 44 to 51. The head is slightly darker than the body. Except for a narrow band at the top, the upper labials and the chin are cream-colored. The ventral coloration is bright red, tending to become pale orange on the anterior portion of the body. Each ventral scale has a pair of dark lateral spots so that two distinct rows of spots border the belly (Plate 103). These rows generally extend onto the proximal half of the tail.

The dorsal scales are strongly keeled and occur in 17 rows at midbody. The anal plate is divided, and the subcaudals are in two rows.

Kirtland's snake exhibits sexual dimorphism in both size and relative tail length. Adult males from Pennsylvania average 252 mm ($10\frac{1}{8}$ in.) SVL and 337 mm ($13\frac{1}{2}$ in.) ToL. Females average 321 mm ($12\frac{7}{8}$ in.) SVL and 411 mm ($16\frac{1}{2}$ in.) ToL. Males have a longer tail than females. The mean tail length of males is 33.3% of SVL and 25.1% of ToL. The mean tail length of females is 27.9% of SVL and 21.8% of ToL. The record size for the species is 622 mm ($24\frac{3}{4}$ in.) ToL (Rossman and Powell 1985).

Neonates and juveniles are darker than adults, and the dorsal blotches are often obscure. The ventral coloration of neonates tends to be brighter than that of adults.

Confusing Species.   The red venter of this species could cause initial confusion between it and the northern redbelly snake. However, northern redbelly snakes lack the rows of rounded black spots on each side of the venter.

Habitat and Habits.   This small semiaquatic species is one of the least-known snakes found in eastern North America. In natural environments, Kirtland's snake occurs primarily in moist, open situations such as the margins of streams and creeks, wet meadows and pastures, and woodland clearings where pools or ponds are present. Throughout its range, animals from such natural environments are only occasionally collected (Conant 1951, Minton 1972, P. Smith 1961). All of those authors commented on the much greater abundance of this species in urban and suburban environments than in rural or undeveloped areas; Kirtland's snakes have been collected in parks, vacant lots, wooded ravines, and wasteland. This pattern of distribution also holds true for Pennsylvania, where more than half of the collecting localities are in suburban Allegheny County. The remaining records from Pennsylvania are from either open swampy areas or near streams.

Specimens have been collected in Pennsylvania from May through September, but records are too few to determine annual activity patterns within the state. In Ohio, Kirtland's snakes emerge from hibernation in March and remain active through October, with peak activity in April and May (Conant 1938). In Indiana, Minton (1972) noted a second peak of activity in October. He also found them to be most active on mild days after rainstorms. Conant (1943) suggested that they are primarily nocturnal and spend the day resting under surface cover objects such as logs, stones, and debris from human activity.

In the wild, Kirtland's snake feeds on earthworms and slugs, but it has been induced to eat leeches and chopped fish in captivity. Tucker (1977) was unable to induce Kirtland's snakes to eat frogs, toads, or salamanders.

When first encountered, Kirtland's snake often becomes rigid and flattens its body so that it is thin and ribbonlike. Its behavior when handled is apparently variable. Conant (1951) stated that Kirtland snakes never attempt to bite when handled, but Ernst and Barbour (1989) remarked on their tendency to bite and chew when captured.

Reproduction.   Mating pairs have been found in early and mid-May (Minton 1972, P. Smith 1961). Gravid females of this viviparous species have been found in July and August. The dates of parturition are highly variable, ranging from late July (Minton 1972) to late September (H. Fitch 1970). Litter size varies from 4 to 15 young, with a mean litter size of 7.3 young (Tucker 1976). H. Fitch (1970) erroneously reported a maximum clutch size of 22 young, but that report was based on an aggregate of three litters.

Neonates born to two Pennsylvania females averaged 109 mm ($4\frac{3}{8}$ in.) SVL and 142.7 mm ($5\frac{3}{4}$ in.) ToL. The smallest mature male from Pennsylvania had a SVL of 228 mm ($9\frac{1}{8}$ in.), and the smallest mature female had a SVL of 303 mm ($12\frac{1}{8}$ in.). These represent the minimum size for reproductive maturity in the species.

Remarks.   Kirtland's snake is listed as endangered by the Pennsylvania Fish Commission owing primarily to the lack of recent specimens (the last one collected in Pennsylvania was in 1965) and the fact that most localities are in areas of Allegheny County that are rapidly being developed.

Distribution.   The range of Kirtland's snake is from central and eastern Illinois eastward through Indiana, southern Michigan, Ohio, and adjacent north-central Kentucky to west-central Pennsylvania. Two old records from the Delaware Valley in eastern Pennsylvania and New Jersey are in error (Conant 1943, McCoy 1982). Conant (1978) considered Kirtland's snake to be a member of the Prairie Peninsula fauna, which survives today in Pennsylvania as a relict from a time when prairie conditions were at their maximum. Several workers have anecdotally remarked upon the decline of the species in recent years (L. Brown et al. 1975, Ernst and Barbour 1989, Minton 1972, Rossman and Powell 1985). The primary reason these authors give for the decline is habitat destruction due to development.

With the exception of the doubtful specimen from the Delaware Valley mentioned above, Kirtland's snake has been reported in Pennsylvania only from Allegheny, Butler, Forest, and Westmoreland counties. Repeated attempts to recollect at known locations have consistently failed to produce additional specimens. If you should happen to encounter one of these rare snakes, please contact the section of Amphibians and Reptiles of the Carnegie Museum of Natural History.

An old record from Trenton, New Jersey (H. Fowler 1906), is obviously in error.

Coluber
L. *coluber*, a serpent

The genus *Coluber* contains the North American racers and other species distributed in southern Europe, northern Africa, and parts of Asia.

Members of the genus *Coluber* are large, snakes with smooth dorsal scales. Members of this genus are diurnal predators. They are extremely alert and usually escape undetected at the approach of a person. If captured, they will thrash about violently and defend themselves by repeatedly biting their attacker. Most of them are ground dwellers in open country, but they can climb well and may occasionally be found in bushes or shrubs.

Racers and their relatives feed on a wide variety of food, such as amphibians, insects, reptiles, birds, and small mammals. All species lay eggs.

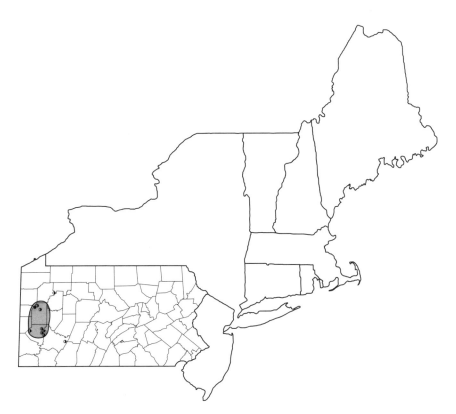

Map 62. Distribution of Kirtland's snake *(Clonophis kirtlandii).*

Northern Black Racer *Coluber constrictor constrictor* Linnaeus
L. *con*, with; L. *strictus*, draw tight

Description.   The northern black racer (Plate 104) is a large, slender species. The dorsal body coloration of adults is uniform matte black. The color of the dorsal surface of the head is similar to that of the body, but sometimes it becomes tannish brown on the internasal, prefrontal, and rostral scales. The lower portions of supralabials 1 to 5 or 6 are white. The ventral coloration varies from slate-gray to matte black. The chin is either immaculate white in small adults or white mottled with black in larger individuals. This light color pattern of the chin extends posteriorly for 3 to 15 ventrals. Albino specimens have been reported from Ohio and Maryland (Dyrkacz 1981).

The head of northern black racers is only slightly distinct from the body, and the eyes are very large. The dorsal scales are large and smooth and occur in 17 rows at midbody. The anal plate is divided, and the subcaudals occur in two rows.

Racers in Pennsylvania do not exhibit sexual dimorphism in either body size or body proportions. Adults average 974.5 mm (39 in.) SVL and 1,252 mm (50 in.) ToL. The slender tail averages 31.8% of the SVL and 24.5% of the ToL. The maximum size for the species is recorded as 1,886 mm (74 in.) ToL for a specimen from Allegheny County, Pennsylvania (Atkinson 1901).

The juvenile color pattern differs markedly from that of the adult and subadult (Plate 105). The dorsal background coloration varies from gray to grayish brown. The dorsal pattern consists of a series (48 to 70) of narrow body blotches that extend onto the sides. These blotches vary from dark gray to reddish brown and are edged with very dark gray or black. The blotches tend to become narrower and less distinct toward the tail. The tail is usually uniformly gray or brownish gray. Small dark spots alternate with the large blotches along the sides of the body. The dorsal head coloration is dark brown, becoming white on the supralabials. The ventral coloration is light, with numerous semicircular gray to black spots. The chin and throat are immaculate white. This juvenile pattern is gradually lost with age. By the time individuals reach a SVL of between 300 and 330 mm (12–13¼ in.), the juvenile pattern is completely replaced by that of the adult.

Confusing Species.   The only species likely to be mistaken for a northern black racer is the black rat snake. Black rat snakes have weakly keeled scales rather than smooth scales, and juveniles rat snakes have only 28–41 body blotches as opposed to the 48–70 body blotches typical of black racers.

Habitat and Habits.   The northern black racer in the Northeast is primarily an inhabitant of open country. It is most commonly found in meadows, old fields, utility rights-of-way, and farmland. Northern black racers are predominantly upland snakes and have no obvious ecological association with water.

In Pennsylvania, northern black racers are usually active from mid-April (although in warm years, activity may begin as early as late

March) to late October or early November. Klemens (1993) reported activity in Connecticut from mid-March to the end of October. Seasonal activity patterns are different for adults and juveniles. Juvenile activity is fairly constant throughout the entire season. Adults, in contrast, exhibit a strongly bimodal pattern of activity, with an initial peak in May followed by a steep decline in June and the virtual absence of individuals in July. A second, more sustained peak occurs in August and September and is followed by a gradual decline in activity in October.

The northern black racer is a diurnally active terrestrial species. It is generally encountered moving about in the open, rather than being found under cover as is typical for most species of terrestrial snake found in the Northeast. Klimstra (1959) noted that daily activity times varied with season. In spring and fall, snakes were typically active during the middle of the day, but with the approach of summer and associated hot weather daily activity became bimodal, with a peak in early morning and a second peak in late afternoon.

Northern black racers have been reported to hibernate in caves (Sexton and Hunt 1980), crevices in rocky hillsides (H. Fitch 1963b), and the burrows of small mammals such as voles (Cohen 1948). We have not collected hibernating northern black racers in Pennsylvania, but it is likely that they use all three of the above types of hibernacula. In many parts of the northern black racer's range, potential hibernation sites are rare and individuals have to travel considerable distances between denning areas and summer home ranges. In Utah, individuals traveled as much as 1.6 km (ca. 1 mi) between winter dens and summer home ranges (W. Brown and Parker 1976). Similar findings have been reported for snakes from Kansas (H. Fitch 1963b).

H. Fitch (1963b) showed that eastern yellowbelly racers (*Coluber constrictor flaviventris*) have well-defined home ranges that are often used year after year. He reported an average home range size of 10.8 ha (26 acres) for males and 10 ha (24 acres) for females. The northeastern subspecies is considerably larger than *C. c. flaviventris* and as a consequence may have a larger home range than that reported by Fitch.

For most of the year, northern black racers are solitary animals. During spring breeding season, however, it is common to find two or more individuals together. Northern black racers may also congregate just before entering hibernation.

Northern black racers rely primarily on sight for prey capture. It is not unusual to find one with its head held high off of the ground searching for prey. They exhibit the most varied diet of any northeastern snake. They feed on insects (e.g., crickets and grasshoppers), amphibians, lizards, snakes, snake and lizard eggs, birds, and small mammals. They occasionally exhibit true cannibalism (feeding on members of their own species). The specific epithet *constrictor* is a misnomer, since they do not kill prey by constriction. Once seized, small prey are consumed alive. Larger prey are pinned to the ground by the snake's body.

If encountered, northern black racers initially attempt to escape. If escape is impossible, they will turn, coil, rapidly vibrate their tail and strike repeatedly at their attacker. If picked up, they generally defend themselves vigorously by repeatedly striking at or biting their captor and releasing feces and musk as they writhe about.

Reproduction. Mating generally occurs in the spring, shortly after emergence from hibernation. Two or more males may actively court a female.

Females emerge from hibernation with well-developed ovarian follicles (8–10 mm; $\frac{3}{8}$–$\frac{1}{2}$ in.). Follicular growth is rapid, and eggs are ovulated by mid to late May. Oviposition occurs in June and early July. Eggs are generally laid under cover, in rotting wood or piles of vegetation and occasionally in the burrows of small mammals. Several authors (Foley 1971, Swain and Smith 1978) reported communal nesting by this species. This may be due to selection for nest sites with appropriate thermal properties where such sites are uncommon or rare in the habitat. Burger (1990) demonstrated that northern black racer eggs hatch more rapidly at higher temperatures. She found that eggs incubated at 28°C (82.4°F) hatch in 39–40 days, whereas those incubated at 22°C (7°F) take 62–65 days. In addition, hatchlings from 28°C exhibited behavioral differences that would tend to increase the ability to obtain prey and avoid predators. These include holding the head higher when foraging, having a greater striking distance, and striking higher.

It also appears that certain oviposition sites are used year after year, although it remains to be determined if individual females return to the same site in consecutive years.

The eggs are white and elliptical and have a granular leathery shell. In Pennsylvania, the average egg length is 31.9 mm ($1\frac{1}{4}$ in.), and the average egg diameter is 16.7 mm ($\frac{5}{8}$ in.).

Clutch size has been reported to range from 2 to 31 eggs (H. Fitch 1970). Clutch size in specimens from Pennsylvania ranges from 6 to 19 eggs and is significantly correlated with female SVL. This average clutch is very similar to the average of 15 reported by P. Rosen (1991) for a population of blue racers (*Coluber constrictor foxii*) from southern Michigan.

Hatchlings first emerge in mid to late August. Surface (1906) reported hatchlings emerging as late as the middle of October, although such late emergence is probably a rare event.

The average hatchling SVL is 209.0 mm ($8\frac{3}{8}$ in.), and the average ToL is 275.5 mm (11 in.). This is similar to hatchling size in other parts of the snake's range.

Both males and females mature at a SVL of around 700 mm (28 in.) and a ToL of about 850–900 mm (34–36 in.). In Michigan, females mature at a SVL of around 838 mm ($33\frac{1}{2}$ in.), and males at only 483 mm ($19\frac{1}{4}$ in.) (Rosen 1991). H. Fitch (1963b) noted a significant number of females of reproductive size that failed to reproduce on an annual basis. Data are too scant to determine if the same phenomenon occurs in Pennsylvania and the rest of the Northeast, but it would be extremely unlikely if this is the case since no other northeastern colubrid exhibits a true biennial reproductive cycle. In Michigan, *Coluber constrictor foxii* has an annual cycle (Rosen, 1991).

Remarks. Much has been written about the aggressive nature of the northern black racer (i.e., unprovoked attacks on humans), but in reality, when given the opportunity, northern black racers attempt to escape rather than attack.

Distribution. The range of the northern black racer extends from southern Maine and Newfoundland westward through central New York and eastern Ohio to extreme southwestern Ohio. From there, it extends southward through eastern Kentucky and Tennessee to the northern half of Alabama, Georgia, and South Carolina.

The northern black racer is widespread throughout southern New England, New York, and New Jersey, occurring from southwestern Maine (where it is considered endangered; Hunter et al. 1992) and southern Vermont and New Hampshire through the southern half of New York and all of New Jersey. It has a wide but scattered distribution throughout Pennsylvania.

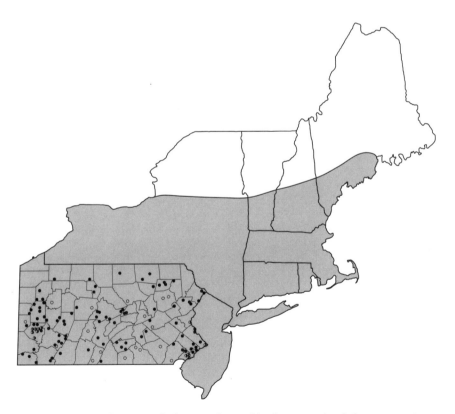

Map 63. Distribution of the northern black racer *(Coluber constrictor constrictor).*

Northern Ringneck Snake *Diadophis punctatus edwardsii* (Merrem)

Gr. *dia*, divided throughout; Gr. *ophis*, snake; L. *punctus*, spotted;

edwardsi, named for George Edwards, an eighteenth-century naturalist

Description.   The northern ringneck snake (Plate 106) is a slender, small to medium-sized species. The dorsal coloration of adults is a uniform slate-gray to bluish gray, sometimes with a brownish overtone, and it lacks any noticeable pattern. There is a yellow to orange neck ring that is generally 1.5–2 scales wide just posterior to the parietal scales. This ring is bordered both anteriorly and posteriorly by a narrow black band. The dorsal head coloration is the same as, or darker than, the body and extends onto the upper third of the supralabials. The remainder of the supralabials and chin are pale yellow. Neonates tend to be darker than adults. Albino specimens have been collected in New Jersey and West Virginia (Dyrkacz 1981).

The ventral coloration varies from pale yellow to deep orange. The ventral scales are generally immaculate but occasionally exhibit a variable pattern of black spots. This spotted pattern is usually restricted to the posterior half or two-thirds of the body. The spots, when present, are located in the middle of the ventral scales, are usually single (very rarely double), and form either a continuous or an interrupted row. There does not appear to be any correlation between ventral spotting and either locality or sex.

The dorsal scales are smooth and occur in 15 rows at midbody. The anal plate is divided, and the subcaudals occur in two rows.

Adult northern ringneck snakes average 283.4 mm ($11\frac{3}{8}$ in.) SVL and 379.2 mm ($15\frac{1}{8}$ in.) ToL. The record size for this subspecies is 568 mm ($22\frac{3}{4}$ in.) SVL and 706 mm ($28\frac{1}{4}$ in.) ToL (Freeman and Freeman 1982). Females tend to attain a larger size than males, but this difference is not statistically significant. Males, however, have a significantly longer tail than females. The mean tail length of males is 30% of the SVL and 24% of the ToL, whereas the mean tail length of females is 25% of SVL and 19.7% of ToL.

Confusing Species.   Adult northern ringneck snakes cannot be confused with any other species that occurs in the Northeast. Neonates, however, may be mistaken for young northern brown or northern redbelly snakes. Brown and redbelly snakes have keeled scales, whereas the scales of northern ringneck snakes are smooth.

Habitat and Habits.   With the possible exception of the eastern garter snake, northern ringneck snakes are one of the most commonly encountered snakes in Pennsylvania. They occur in a wide variety of habitats, including primary- and secondary-growth deciduous forests, old fields, rocky hillsides, grassy fields, and the borders of streams and rivers. No matter what their specific habitat is, they are generally found near deciduous woodlands. It is a secretive species, seldom being encountered in the open. Northern ringneck snakes may be found under a wide variety of cover types (e.g., rocks, logs, bark, human debris,) but are most frequently discovered under rocks. They appear to have two main habitat requirements to occur in large numbers: open areas where sunlight can reach and warm the surface and an abundance of rocky cover.

In the northern part of the region, annual activity begins in early April (usually the first week) and continues to the end of October. Presumably, in the milder southern portion of the Northeast annual activity extends from late March to early November. Seasonal activity is strongly bimodal. An initial peak of activity occurs in late May and June. Activity is reduced during July and August. This reduction is usually followed by increased activity in September, with a gradual decrease in October, before hibernation. Activity patterns, however, appear to be dependent upon weather, with bimodal activity being more pronounced during hot, dry summers. When summer is unseasonably cool and wet, as it was in 1992, northern ringneck snakes maintain a fairly constant level of activity throughout the summer. This activity may be due to increased and more prolonged surface activity by their principle prey (salamanders).

Northern ringneck snakes are often reported to be nocturnal, but the great majority of northern ringneck snakes we have collected have been found during the daylight hours. Individuals are occasionally seen crossing highways at night, usually after summer rainstorms. Their tendency to remain hidden under cover at all times probably precludes any strong preference on the part of the snakes for either nocturnal or diurnal activity.

We have not observed hibernacula for northern ringneck snakes in Pennsylvania, but Fitch (1975) reported that they hibernate in deep burrows and crevices in central Kansas.

It is common to find two or more northern ringneck snakes under the same cover object. The most that we have encountered under a rock was eight. Dundee and Miller (1968), in a study of the aggregating behavior of northern ringneck snakes in the Southeast, demonstrated that the snakes form aggregations by preference and that they appear to choose cover sites on the basis of soil water content. They select sites that are moist and avoid those that are either dry or saturated. Dundee and Miller also demonstrated that once a cover object has been used, it becomes "conditioned" so that the snakes continue to use it, apparently locating the appropriate cover on the basis of olfactory cues.

Over the geographic range of the species, northern ringneck snakes have been reported to eat a wide variety of food items, including salamanders, snakes, lizards, frogs, earthworms, slugs, and assorted insects. On a local level, however, diet appears to be much less varied. In Pennsylvania, salamanders of the genus *Plethodon* constitute the major food item eaten, with earthworms being the second most common food. One snake was found to contain an adult *Plethodon* (species unidentified) and 17 eggs that the adult *Plethodon* had apparently been attending when it was captured. Barbour (1950) reported the consumption of salamander eggs (*Aneides aeneus*) by ringneck snakes in Kentucky. In areas of the eastern United States where salamanders are common, they appear to be the major component of the diet of northern ringneck snakes. In regions where salamanders are either scarce or absent, earthworms are the major food item (E. Brown 1979b, H. Fitch 1975, Myers 1965).

Reproduction. Mating occurs in early spring, soon after emergence from hibernation. Females containing enlarged oviducal eggs are initially found in late May and continue in the population through early July. Egg laying occurs over a relatively short period of time, from the last week of June through the first week of July. Eggs may be laid under rocks, in rotting logs, in abandoned mammal burrows, or in cracks and crevices. Blanchard (1930) and H. Fitch (1975) presented evidence for communal nesting in this species. Fitch postulated that communal nesting was the rule in Kansas because large numbers of recently hatched young were found year after year at specific locations. Whether communal nesting occurs in the Northeast remains unclear.

Clutch size varies from 2 to 10 eggs and is positively correlated with female body size. Larger females tend to produce larger clutches, although the trend in Pennsylvania is not as obvious as that for a Kansas population studied by H. Fitch (1975). The eggs are white and elongate, with one end usually tapering more than the other. In a sample of 158 eggs, the average length was 22.1 mm ($\frac{7}{8}$ in.), and the average diameter was 5.4 mm ($\frac{1}{5}$ in.). Variation in egg size is not associated with female body size.

Incubation time is variable, depending upon the specific environmental conditions of the nest site. The earliest appearance of neonates in Pennsylvania is 7 August, and the latest appearance is 27 September. The average size of recently emerged neonates is 104 mm ($4\frac{1}{4}$ in.) SVL and 130 mm ($5\frac{1}{4}$ in.) ToL.

Males become sexually mature at a SVL of about 210 mm ($8\frac{3}{8}$ in.), and females at a SVL of about 230 mm ($9\frac{1}{4}$ in.). H. Fitch (1975) noted a bias for males in the Kansas population that he studied. In Pennsylvania, the overall sex ratio is 1:1, although sex ratio does differ seasonally. Males tend to be more common early (April and May) in the season, whereas females predominate during June and July. For example, at one location in mid-June, 55 of 56 animals observed in a single afternoon were female. This strong bias for females in June and July is probably associated with their reproductive state. Gravid females are frequently encountered in groups. Apparently, females at this time of the year are selecting cover sites with optimal conditions of moisture and temperature. The reproductive biology of males has not been studied in Pennsylvania, but Prieto (1975) studied male reproduction in New Jersey. Snakes in New Jersey emerge in spring with small testes. Testis growth is rapid from April through June, when sperm production is highest. Rapid regression of testes occurs in July, and testes remain small until the following spring. Mature sperm, however, was found in the reproductive tract at all times of the year.

Remarks. Northern ringneck snakes are inoffensive animals that do not bite upon capture. When disturbed, they release an offensive-smelling musk from glands at the base of the tail along with semiliquid feces. This vile-smelling mixture may be sufficiently distasteful to prevent some predators from further pursuing them.

Individuals in some populations of northern ringneck snakes, when disturbed, will expose the underside of their tail in a tight coil, presumably to startle a predator and to draw its attention away from the head. This behavior has been noted only in populations where the ventral coloration of the tail is red. Pennsylvania's northern ringneck snakes have a yellow tail and do not exhibit this behavior, although they thrash their tail about while discharging musk and feces. Gehlbach (1970) reported that snakes from Texas and California populations occasionally feigned death. This behavior has not been observed in Pennsylvania.

Because of the enlarged saberlike rear teeth of northern ringneck snakes, the chewing action associated with prey capture, and the subsequent death of prey released before ingestion, it has been suggested that northern ringneck snakes might be mildly venomous (Gehlbach 1970, Myers 1965). Even if they are venomous, their small size and inoffensive nature render them completely harmless to even the smallest of humans.

The northern ringneck snake may intergrade with the southern ringneck snake (*Diadophis punctatus punctatus*) in southern New Jersey. The southern ringneck snake differs from the northern in possessing an incomplete neck ring, in contrast with the complete ring of the northern subspecies. In addition, the southern subspecies has a series of large semicircular black spots forming a single central row on the ventral surface of the body. The ventral scales of the northern ringneck are either immaculate yellow or have scattered small black dots that do not form any definite pattern.

Distribution.   The northern ringneck snake occurs from Nova Scotia and Newfoundland westward to Wisconsin and southward to northeastern Alabama and northern Georgia.

The northern ringneck snake occurs throughout the Northeast.

Elaphe
Gr. *elaphos*, a deer

The genus *Elaphe* contains the rat snakes. At least 10 species are contained in the genus. The rat snakes range throughout the eastern and central United States, and southward through Mexico into Costa Rica. They are also found in the Old World from Europe into China.

Rat snakes are large, moderately built snakes that in cross section look like a loaf of bread (i.e., rounded on the top and straight along the sides and belly). The middorsal body scales are weakly keeled, but the rest of the scales are smooth. Rat snakes are found in a variety of upland habitats, from desert shrub to deciduous forest and tropical jungle. They are good climbers and are often found in trees. Rat snakes differ dramatically in demeanor. Some are extremely docile, but others will defend themselves vigorously at the least provocation.

Rat snakes are constrictors, suffocating their prey in their powerful body coils. They feed primarily on small to medium-sized mammals and

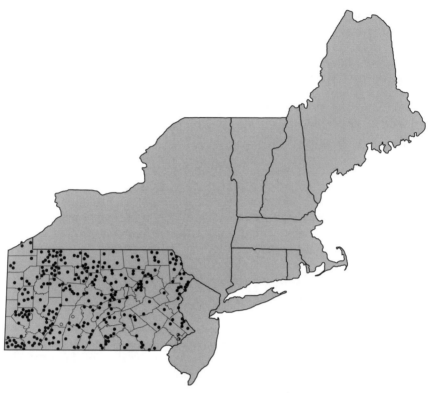

Map 64. Distribution of the northern ringneck snake *(Diadophis punctatus edwardsii).*

birds. Young individuals may take lizards, frogs, and earthworms. All rat snakes lay eggs.

Corn Snake *Elaphe guttata guttata* (Linnaeus)

L. *guttata,* spotted

Description.   The corn snake (Plate 107) is a medium to large snake of moderate build. The sides of this species are relatively straight so that the body, in cross section, resembles a loaf of bread.

This species is strongly patterned with a series of squarish blotches on the body and tail. The blotches tend to become more elongate and rectangular near the neck. The blotches vary from red to chestnut or brownish red and are bordered by black-pigmented scales. Smaller blotches may be present on the sides of the body but are frequently absent. The dorsal background coloration varies from red to gray. The ventral surface of the body is strongly patterned in a black-and-white checkerboard motif. A pair of dark, longitudinal stripes occurs on the ventral surface of the tail.

On the head, a black-bordered reddish stripe extends diagonally backward from the posterior margin of the eye to the neck just beyond the angle of the mouth. Extensions of the first dorsal body blotch extend forward and converge at the midline of the head just posterior to the eyes in a V-shaped pattern. The labial scales are white, edged with black. Juveniles resemble adults but have brownish rather than reddish blotches.

The dorsal scales are smooth or weakly keeled and generally occur in 27 (23–29) rows at midbody. The anal plate is divided, and the subcaudals occur in two rows.

Sexual dimorphism does not appear to occur in body size in this species. A sample of mature individuals from Virginia ranged in SVL from 525 to 1,245 mm $(20\frac{3}{4}$–$49\frac{1}{2}$ in.), with a mean of 869 mm $(34\frac{1}{4}$ in.). Males, however, have a slightly longer tail than do females (Mitchell 1994). The maximum ToL for this species has been reported as 1,829 mm (72 in.) (Conant and Collins 1991).

Confusing Species. The corn snake could be confused with the eastern milk snake. Milk snakes, however, have smooth dorsal scales, whereas at least some of the dorsal scales of the corn snake are weakly keeled.

Habitat and Habits. There is little information available about this species throughout its range, and virtually nothing is known about the species in the Northeast. Corn snakes are generally associated with either wooded habitats or agricultural lands where their rodent prey are abundant. They prefer dry sandy or otherwise loose unconsolidated soil. They are seldom found in bottomland forests, where the soil is generally moist or wet.

Corn snakes appear to be primarily nocturnal. Most reports of active snakes come from observations at night while the animals are crossing roads. Unfortunately, many of these observations involve snakes that have been killed by a passing car. Ernst and Barbour (1989), however, suggested that corn snakes may be more diurnal then generally thought. They reported finding most of their specimens in the morning or afternoon.

During the daytime, corn snakes can occasionally be found by searching under logs, debris, and other surface cover objects. Corn snakes are good climbers and are occasionally found in trees.

Palmer and Braswell (1995) reported that corn snakes have been found active in every month in North Carolina. The greatest activity in North Carolina occurs in May and June. Mitchell (1994) stated that their activity season extends from May to November farther north, in Virginia. Ernst and Barbour (1989) noted that, in Kentucky, corn snakes emerge from hibernation in late March or early April. In New Jersey, it is likely that they are active from May to late September or early October.

Corn snakes are constrictors, killing their prey by suffocation as the coils of the snake gradually tighten on the chest cavity of the prey. Corn snakes primarily feed on small rodents. They occasionally take young birds or bird eggs. Young corn snakes have been reported to feed on snakes, lizards, and frogs.

Reproduction. Courtship and mating behavior have been intensively studied in captivity in this species (see Gillingham 1979). Details of mating in the wild, however, are not available. Courtship has been observed in the wild in May (Palmer and Braswell 1995).

Natural nest sites have been found in sawdust piles and in rotting logs. Egg laying generally occurs from June to early July. The young emerge from their nests from mid-August to late September (Ernst and Barbour 1989, Palmer and Braswell 1995). In North Carolina, clutch size ranged from 6 to 31 eggs, with a mean of 12.7 eggs. The average dimensions of North Carolina corn snake eggs are 34.2 mm by 21.7 mm (1$\frac{3}{8}$ in. by $\frac{7}{8}$ in.). The eggs are white when first laid and have a tough leathery shell. They are highly adherent (they stick to each other). North Carolina hatchlings ranged in ToL from 286 to 357 mm (11$\frac{3}{8}$–14$\frac{1}{4}$ in.) with a mean ToL of 312.4 mm (12$\frac{1}{2}$ in.).

There have been reports of this species' laying two clutches in a single year in captivity (Tryon 1984). It is doubtful that they lay two clutches in nature, or, if they do, the eggs of the second clutch probably do not hatch before nest conditions became suboptimal for development.

Distribution. The main range of the corn snake extends from coastal North Carolina southward through the Florida keys. Its range extends westward to southeastern Louisiana and most of Mississippi and southern Tennessee. The corn snake also occurs in northern and central Virginia and adjacent Maryland and in disjunct populations in central Kentucky, in western Maryland, in the DelMar Peninsula in Virginia, and in southern New Jersey.

Black Rat Snake *Elaphe obsoleta obsoleta* (Say)
L. *obsoletus*, indistinct
Description. The black rat snake (Plate 108) is the largest serpent found in the Northeast. For its length, it is a moderately slender species. Unlike most other species of snake, on which the sides of the body are rounded, the sides of the black rat snake are straight. As a consequence, the body, in cross section, appears loaflike rather than circular.

The dorsal body coloration of adults is black, although there may be some light areas confined to the skin between scales, especially on smaller adults. The venter is mottled grayish black and white, becoming immaculate white in the region of the neck. The chin, lower labials, and upper labials are white. Albino specimens have frequently been reported in the literature (Hensley 1959).

The head is distinct from the body, and the snout is truncated rather than rounded. As a consequence, the head appears to be oblong or rectangular when viewed from above.

The dorsal scales are weakly keeled on the dorsum and smooth along the sides and occur in 23–27 rows at midbody. The anal plate is divided, and the subcaudals occur in two rows.

The black rat snake does not appear to exhibit significant sexual dimorphism in either size or tail length. Adults average 1,102 mm (45 in.) SVL and 1,335.9 mm (52$\frac{3}{4}$ in.) ToL. The maximum size for the species has been

Map 65. Distribution of the corn snake *(Elaphe guttata guttata).*

reported as 2,565 mm (103 in.) ToL (Ernst and Barbour 1989). The mean tail length is 19.4% of SVL and 16.6% of ToL.

The juvenile pattern (Plate 109) is in marked contrast to that of the adult. The dorsal background coloration is gray with a series of 28–41 somewhat irregular black blotches. On each side of this vertebral row of blotches is a series of smaller irregular black blotches. This pattern extends to the dorsal surface of the tail. The ventral background coloration is white, patterned with square or rectangular black maculations, whose density increases posteriorly. The chin and the most anterior ventrals are immaculate white. The background coloration of the head is gray to brownish gray and is strongly patterned in black. A diagonal stripe runs from just behind the eye to the posterior two supralabials; dorsally, the eyes are connected by a dark line that passes through the anterior edge of the supraorbitals and the posterior edge of the prefrontal. Dark blotches occur on a number of dorsal and lateral head shields. All infralabials and the fourth supralabial bear black posterior borders. Remnants of this juvenile pattern often persist well into the adult stage.

Confusing Species.   The black rat snake bears a superficial resemblance to the northern black racer in both adult and juvenile patterns. They can be distinguished from each other by their dorsal scales; the northern black racer has smooth dorsal scales, whereas the black rat snake has weakly keeled dorsals. Furthermore, the black rat snake has 23–27 scale rows at midbody, whereas the northern black racer has only 17 scale rows at midbody.

Habitat and Habits.   The habitat of the black rat snake in the Northeast ranges from dense forest to open fields and farm buildings. Most individuals, however, are encountered either in heavily forested regions or in ecotonal areas where forest and field environments intermingle. It is predominantly an upland species, seldom being found near water (with the possible exception of artificial impoundments). Using radiotelemetry on snakes from Ontario, Canada, Weatherhead and Charland (1985) noted that they had a marked preference for open fields and ecotonal areas during the bird breeding season (i.e., spring). McLeod and Gates (1998) found that, in Maryland, black rat snakes were more abundant in cut-over hardwood forests than in undisturbed hardwood forests. They postulated that the greater abundance of the snakes in the cut-over areas might be due to the fact that potential rodent prey (e.g., meadow voles and jumping mice) were more abundant in those areas than in undisturbed forests.

This species is semiarboreal, but the extent of its aboveground activity is unknown. Most individuals from Pennsylvania have been seen either actively crawling or sunning themselves on the ground, although nesting boxes set out to attract bluebirds occasionally contain black rat snakes. These boxes are set from 1.5 to 1.8 m (60–72 in.) above the ground on wooden posts. Stickel and colleagues (1980), studying a Maryland population, noted that solitary trees in open fields seemed to play an important role in the activity of rat snakes that they studied.

In Pennsylvania, black rat snakes are generally active from late April (earliest date, 20 April) to mid-October (latest date, 27 October), but they are most commonly encountered from May through September. This duration of annual activity is similar to that found by Weatherhead (1989) for Ontario black rat snakes and by Stickel and colleagues (1980) for a population from Maryland. It is, however, somewhat shorter than the annual activity pattern noted by H. Fitch (1963a) for a Kansas population that was under investigation for 15 years. Patterns of seasonal activity are fairly uniform for the two sexes throughout the year. Hatchlings, however, tend to be more active later in the year (September and October) than adults of either sex. This greater activity is a function of their dispersal from nest sites to winter hibernacula.

Hibernacula are generally located in rock crevices and caves. Around human habitation, black rat snakes occasionally hibernate in cellars, root cellars, cisterns, and wells. They often hibernate in mixed-species groups, especially with northern black racers, copperheads, and timber rattlesnakes (Galligan and Dunson 1979). Except when in the vicinity of the hibernacula and during the mating season, black rat snakes are basically solitary animals.

Both Stickel and colleagues (1980) and H. Fitch (1963a) demonstrated that black rat snakes have well-defined home ranges and that, once the home range has been established, it is occupied for many years. Home range size varies from about 10 ha (24 acres) (H. Fitch 1963a) to around 25 ha (62 acres) (Stickel et al. 1980) in different populations. In addition, it has been noted that males tend to have larger home ranges than females. Weatherhead and Hoysak (1989) determined that the home range of males was 3 times the size of the home range of females in Ontario.

Black rat snakes are constrictors, killing their prey by coiling about them and gradually suffocating them. They feed primarily on small mammals and birds and bird eggs. Surface (1906) noted that mammals and birds constituted the diet of black rat snakes from Pennsylvania when insects were excluded; Surface attributed any insects found in a natural population's diet to secondary ingestion along with birds. Similar findings have been reported by Stickel and colleagues (1980) for Maryland snakes. All the specimens that we have examined that contained food had the remains of mammals or birds.

Aggressiveness toward humans in black rat snakes is highly variable. Most individuals are exceedingly docile and never attempt to bite. A few, however, strike and bite at the slightest provocation.

Reproduction. Mating generally occurs in May and June, but fall matings have been observed in the field in Kansas (H. Fitch 1970). Courtship in this species has been discussed in detail by Gillingham (1979). Courtship involves primarily tactile and olfactory stimuli and consists of three basic stages: a tactile chase stage, in which the male locates and comes into contact with the female; a tactile alignment stage, which begins when the female stops moving and the male moves along the female's body in an attempt to copulate; and an intromission stage, in which copulation is accomplished.

In Pennsylvania, eggs are normally laid in late June and early July, but cold summer temperatures can delay the egg-laying process until early or middle August. The fate of eggs laid so late in the season remains unknown. Eggs are generally deposited in rotting logs and stumps or are laid in decaying vegetation. They are white and elliptical and have a smooth leathery shell (Plate 110).

The mean dimensions for 67 eggs from Pennsylvania specimens were 41.4 mm ($1\frac{5}{8}$ in.) long and 22.7 mm ($\frac{7}{8}$ in.) wide. The incubation period has been reported to range from 53 to more than 100 days (H. Fitch 1970). Hatchlings first appear in Pennsylvania around 20 August. If the earliest date of oviposition is assumed to be 15 June, the incubation time is 66 days. Actual incubation times are unknown for specimens from Pennsylvania. Clutch size has been reported to range from 5 to 44 eggs, but most specimens lay clutches of from 5 to 14 eggs (H. Fitch 1970). One instance of communal egg laying has been reported in which 76 eggs were found under debris in an abandoned lumber mill (Lynch 1966).

The average size within a week of hatching has been reported for males as 330 mm ($13\frac{1}{4}$ in.) ToL and for females as 320 mm ($12\frac{3}{4}$ in.) ToL

(Stickel et al. 1980). Too few specimens are available from Pennsylvania for comparison.

H. Fitch (1963a) determined that both males and females mature at 4 years of age at about 800 and 870 mm (32 and $34\frac{3}{4}$ in.) SVL, respectively. The smallest mature male from Pennsylvania had a SVL of 760 mm ($30\frac{1}{2}$ in.), and the smallest female had a SVL of 895 mm ($35\frac{3}{4}$ in.).

Remarks. Male–male agonistic behavior (i.e., combat) has been well documented for this species (Gillingham 1980, Rigley 1971).

The frequency of capture by humans relative to size in Pennsylvania black rat snakes is strongly bimodal. In a sample of 87 specimens, 47% were under 400 mm (16 in.) SVL, and 44% were longer than 800 mm (32 in.) SVL; only 9% fell within the 400–800 mm range. Stickel and colleagues (1980) noted the same tendency for specimens from Maryland. This bimodal frequency suggests that there might be behavioral differences between size classes that reduce the chances of encountering intermediate-sized individuals. It could be that intermediate-sized individuals have a greater tendency toward an arboreal existence than either hatchlings or adults.

Distribution. The black rat snake ranges from southwestern Vermont and central New York westward through extreme southern Ontario and central Michigan to southeastern Nebraska, eastern Kansas, and most of Oklahoma. In the East, its range extends south through South Carolina to central Georgia. It is replaced by another subspecies in the Lower Mississippi Valley and along the Gulf Coast.

The species invades the Northeast as far north as southwestern New England, occurring in southwestern Rhode Island, through much of Connecticut, and into the Connecticut River valley of Massachusetts. It has been recorded in extreme southwestern Vermont and in the southern half of New York and all of New Jersey. It also occurs in scattered localities in central and western New York and in the upper Hudson River valley to the Vermont border. The black rat snake is widely distributed throughout Pennsylvania, but it is less common in the northern-tier counties than elsewhere in the state.

Heterodon
Gr. *heteros*, different; *odous*, teeth

The genus *Heterodon* contains the hognose snakes. Three species make up this exclusively North American genus. They are widely distributed in the eastern and central United States.

Hognose snakes are medium-sized, heavy-bodied snakes with strongly keeled dorsal scales. They all exhibit a sharply upturned snout. All species exhibit a complex antipredator behavior involving spreading of a neck hood, hissing, and striking with closed mouth. If all these behaviors fail to frighten the potential attacker, hognose snakes roll over and play dead.

Hognose snakes are specialized feeders, taking almost exclusively toads and frogs as prey. All members of the genus lay eggs.

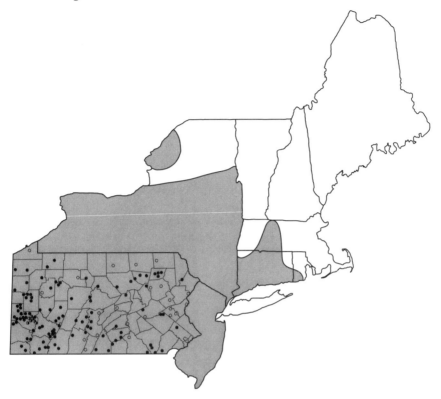

Map 66. Distribution of the black rat snake *(Elaphe obsoleta obsoleta)*.

Eastern Hognose Snake *Heterodon platirhinos* Latreille
Gr. *platy*, broad; Gr. *rhynchos*, snout

Description.   The eastern hognose snake (Plate 111) is a medium-sized, stout-bodied species. Its pointed, upturned rostral scale is unique in the Northeast's snake fauna. The head is broad and somewhat triangular owing to the hypertrophied muscles at the back of the head, and it is fairly distinct from the body.

Coloration and pattern are extremely variable. The background body color may be gray, tan, yellowish or reddish brown, brown, olive, or black. There are usually 20–30 brown squarish dorsal body blotches that are bordered by dark brown or black scales and are lighter brown inside. Along each side of the body is another row of smaller blotches that is staggered in position relative to the dorsal blotches. On the tail, dorsal and lateral blotches often fuse to become bands. The neck bears two elongate lateral blotches that often fuse in the region of the parietal to give a V-shaped appearance. A medial nuchal blotch may or may not be present. A dark bar runs across the top of the head between the eyes, and a dark diagonal stripe runs from the posterior margin of the eye to the corner of the mouth. The head scales are usually covered with small black spots, and the supralabials are lighter in color than the rest of the head. The chin is generally white, and the background coloration of the belly is yellowish white or gray, often mottled with darker gray or black. This mottling, if present, becomes heavier at the posterior portion of the body. The underside of the tail is generally lighter in color.

Some specimens lack the dorsal pattern and are a uniform olive-brown or black. Edgren (1957) reported on melanistic specimens of the eastern hognose snake (Plate 112). He reported a high frequency of the melanistic form from Pennsylvania (30.6% of his sample). The dark color phase does not appear to be sexually dimorphic, but he did suggest that it gradually develops with age, since he noted no young animals that were melanistic. Albino specimens have been reported from Alabama and New Hampshire (Hensley 1959).

The dorsal scales are keeled and generally occur in 25 rows at midbody (range: 21–27 rows). The anal plate is divided, and the subcaudals occur in two rows.

Eastern hognose snakes exhibit significant sexual dimorphism in both body size and relative tail length. In Pennsylvania, mature males average 435.8 mm ($17\frac{3}{8}$ in.) SVL and 546.8 mm (22 in.) ToL. Females average 611 mm ($24\frac{1}{2}$ in.) SVL and 722 mm ($28\frac{3}{4}$ in.) ToL. The maximum total length for the species is 1,156 mm ($46\frac{1}{4}$ in.) (Conant and Collins 1991). The mean tail length for females is 17.9% of SVL and 15.2% of ToL. The mean tail length of males is 24.5% of SVL and 19.6% of ToL.

Confusing Species.   Eastern hognose snakes with a blotched dorsal pattern might be confused with either the northern water snake or the eastern milk snake. The strongly upturned rostral scale, however, distinguishes the eastern hognose snake from either of those species.

Habitat and Habits.   Eastern hognose snakes are primarily inhabitants of grasslands and open forests near water and show a strong preference for dry, sandy soil where they can burrow, both for protection and in search of food. In Pennsylvania, eastern hognose snakes are primarily found along the beaches at Presque Isle, Erie County; along sandy river and stream bottoms; and on sand ridges in mountainous areas. Unlike many species of snake, they are seldom encountered under cover. When not active on the surface, eastern hognose snakes seek refuge in burrows, either in shallow ones (5–7 cm [2–3 in.] deep) they construct in loose, sandy soil or in those constructed by mammals (Platt 1969).

In the Northeast, eastern hognose snakes emerge from hibernation in late April and early May. Activity gradually increases to a peak in July and then slowly tapers off through August and September. Activity ceases in early or mid-October. This pattern of annual activity is similar to that reported by Platt (1969) for Kansas populations and by Conant (1938) for eastern hognose snakes from Ohio. It differs greatly, however, from South Carolina populations, where seasonal activity is strongly bimodal, with an initial peak of activity in late spring and a second peak in late summer (Gibbons and Semlitsch 1987). Individuals may occasionally be active at other times of the year if the weather is suitable. In Pennsylvania, one specimen was collected on 2 December in Union County and another on 21 January in Huntingdon County.

Eastern hognose snakes are diurnal. The greatest activity occurs in mid-morning and late afternoon. They generally hibernate individually. For hibernation, they construct burrows or use those of small mammals. Arndt (1980) found an individual burrowed 58 cm (23⅜ in.) below the surface in sandy soil, and P. Anderson (1965) found them to use the burrows of ground squirrels.

Eastern hognose snakes have been reported to feed on a wide variety of animals, including frogs, toads, salamanders, lizards, hatchling turtles, small mammals, earthworms, insects, and centipedes. Although the overall diet appears to be exceedingly diverse, the majority of food items taken by these snakes are frogs and toads. Platt (1969) reported that frogs and toads constituted 93% of the diet of this species in Kansas, and many other authors have remarked upon their preference for anurans. Weaver (1965) saw them actually excavate toads from their underground retreats.

Many authors have commented on the various adaptations of eastern hognose snakes to feeding on toads. H. Smith and White (1955) suggested that the hypertrophied adrenal glands are an adaptation to counteract the toxic secretions of the toads. Huheey (1958) noted that neonates are as immune to toad venom as are adults and thus concluded that the resistance to the venom is inherited rather than acquired. Toads, when disturbed or attacked, commonly inflate their lungs and swell to a large size, making them difficult to swallow. Several authors have suggested that the enlarged rear teeth of the eastern hognose snake are adaptations to puncture and deflate the lungs of toads, but Kroll (1976) demonstrated that the teeth are not long enough to puncture the lungs. However, the short, broad jaws of eastern hognose snakes are powerful enough to force the lungs to deflate even without puncturing them (Platt 1969).

The defensive behaviors of this species are impressive and involve some or all of the following activities in an escalating fashion. Upon initial approach, eastern hognose snakes often become immobile, relying upon cryptic coloration to protect them. If that strategy does not work, the snake will attempt flight or escape. If escape is prevented, it flattens its head and neck region, forming a slight hood, while at the same time gaping the mouth and making loud hissing noises. The snake will then strike repeatedly, with closed mouth, at the approaching object. If all of those efforts fail, the animal goes into violent contortions of the body, writhing about and releasing musk and fecal matter, which is spread over much of the body by the violent movement of the tail. The snake then turns belly-up, gapes its mouth, and becomes still and limp, as if dead (Plate 113). If a snake that is feigning death is righted, it immediately turns over again. This suite of behavioral defense mechanisms is rapidly lost in captivity.

The eastern hognose snake may be mildly venomous. Although it rarely bites, some people who have been bitten reported a stinging sensation along with localized swelling and pain. These symptoms disappeared within 24 hours (Grogan 1974, Kroll 1976). McAlister (1963) demonstrated that extracts of salivary glands, when injected into frogs, killed them within 24 hours, but they had little effect on mice.

Reproduction.   Mating probably occurs in the spring shortly after the snakes emerge from hibernation, but it may also occur in the fall (Platt 1969). Nichols (1982) observed copulation in this species in captivity.

Egg laying takes place from early June to mid-July. In the Northeast, it appears as if most eastern hognose snakes lay eggs in late June. Eggs are generally buried in loose soil at a depth of 10–15 cm (4–6 in.). Clutch size is variable, ranging from 4 to 61 eggs, with most females having clutches that range from 15 to 25 eggs. For specimens from Pennsylvania that we examined, the average clutch size was 14.8 eggs. Clutch size is correlated with female body size; larger females lay more eggs. Platt (1969) also noted an increase in egg size with increasing female body size.

Eggs are off-white and elliptical, with a thin parchmentlike shell that is nonadherent (the eggs do not stick to each other) (Edgren 1955). Platt (1969) reported the average egg length as 34.6 mm ($1\frac{3}{8}$ in.) and the average diameter as 22.6 mm ($\frac{7}{8}$ in.). Incubation periods have been reported to vary from 31 days (Edgren 1955) to 75 days (Nichols 1982), but normal incubation probably lasts from 45 to 64 days (Platt 1969).

Neonates (Plate 114) from Pennsylvania have a the mean SVL of 138.1 mm ($5\frac{1}{2}$ in.) and a mean ToL of 165.3 mm ($6\frac{5}{8}$ in.). This is significantly smaller the mean SVL of 194 mm ($7\frac{3}{4}$ in.) and mean ToL of 234 mm ($9\frac{3}{8}$ in.) for neonates from Kansas (Platt 1969). The sex ratio of hatchlings does not vary significantly from 1:1.

Platt considered that females generally mature in Kansas at a SVL of about 560 mm ($22\frac{1}{2}$ in.). The smallest mature female from Pennsylvania had a SVL of 464 mm ($18\frac{1}{2}$ in.). Nothing is known concerning the size at maturity for males.

Remarks.   The venomous nature of eastern hognose snakes remains conjectural, but care should be taken in handling them. This does not imply that they are a threat to either humans or pets, and they should not be killed.

The status of the eastern hognose snake in Pennsylvania is uncertain. It appears that it is not as common as it once was. Much fieldwork is needed to determine the present occurrence of this species within the state.

Distribution.   The eastern hognose snake ranges from southern New England south through Florida and westward to central Texas, Oklahoma, Kansas, Nebraska, and southern Iowa. The range extends into Michigan, Wisconsin, and eastern Minnesota.

In the Northeast, the eastern hognose snake occurs as far north as southern New Hampshire. It is widely distributed throughout Rhode Island and Connecticut, in most of Massachusetts, and in southeastern New York and New Jersey. In New York, it also occurs north along the Hudson River valley. It occurs in the southern and eastern half of Pennsylvania, with an outlier population on Presque Isle, Erie County. Within

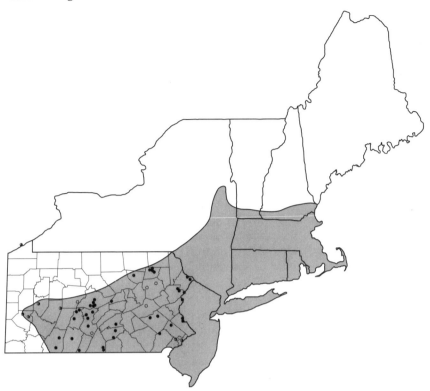

Map 67. Distribution of the eastern hognose snake *(Heterodon platyrhinos).*

its range in the state, the distribution of the eastern hognose snake is very localized, occurring in areas of suitable sandy soil. McCoy and Bianculli (1966) postulated three distinct stocks of these snakes in the state, with each stock having a different dispersal route. Those populations east of the Allegheny Front represent one stock that has dispersed northward through the broad river valleys of the east and intermountain valleys of the Valley and Ridge Province. A second stock, in southwestern Pennsylvania, has moved in along the Ohio and Allegheny rivers. The Presque Isle population represents a third stock of unknown origin. It is highly likely that the Presque Isle population has been extirpated because recent intensive collecting in the area has failed to produce any eastern hognose snakes (McKinstry 1987).

Lampropeltis
Gr. *lampros,* shining; Gr. *pelte,* shield

The genus *Lampropeltis* contains the kingsnakes and milk snakes. About 16 species are contained in the genus. The genus has an incredibly large geographic range. It extends from southeastern Canada westward to the

Pacific Coast in California and southward through the entire United States into Ecuador.

The kingsnakes and milk snakes are medium-sized to large snakes with smooth polished scales. They are powerfully built. Most are brightly colored. Kingsnakes and milk snakes are terrestrial species that range through a wide variety of habitats, from deciduous forests to hot deserts. Most individuals are found moving about, but some may be located by turning cover objects. These snakes vary widely in temperament but will often hiss and rapidly vibrate their tail if cornered. If captured, some species are extremely docile; others will vigorously defend themselves by thrashing about and biting.

Kingsnakes and milk snakes are constrictors, killing their prey by gradually suffocating them as they tighten their coils. Although they are notorious for feeding on other snakes, kingsnakes and milk snakes feed on many other prey items as well. They are known to eat snakes, lizards, rodents and other small mammals, and an occasional ground-nesting bird. All species of kingsnake and milk snake lay eggs.

Eastern Kingsnake *Lampropeltis getula getula* (Linnaeus)
Named for a North African people, the Getulans
Description.   The eastern kingsnake (Plate 115) is a large fairly stout species. It has a dorsal pattern of thin white to yellowish transverse lines that give the overall impression of a thin chain's having been placed on the back of the snake. The species epithet, *getula*, presumably refers to a chainlike pattern used by the North African Getulans that is similar in appearance to the dorsal pattern typically found on the eastern kingsnake. The overall background coloration varies from black to brownish black. White to yellowish marks occur on the head, and the labials are patterned in alternating black and white stripes. The venter is black with a variable pattern of white blotches. Young individuals resemble adults.

Mitchell (1994) noted sexual dimorphism in SVL for this species but did not notice a significant difference in relative tail length between the sexes. Virginia males ranged from 635 to 1,456 mm (25–57$\frac{1}{2}$ in.) SVL, with a mean SVL of 1,037 mm (41 in.) SVL. Females ranged from 660 to 1,291 mm (26–50$\frac{1}{2}$ in.) SVL, with a mean of 922 mm (36$\frac{1}{4}$ in.) SVL. Tail length was 12.1% of ToL in males and 11.4% of ToL in females. The maximum reported size for the species is 2,083 mm ToL (82 in.) (Conant and Collins 1991).

The scales are smooth and usually occur in 21 scale rows at midbody, but they may range from 20 to 23 rows. The anal plate is entire, and the subcaudals occur in two rows.

Confusing Species.   The black to dark brown background color of the eastern kingsnake combined with the vivid white to cream-colored chainlike dorsal pattern make it unlikely to be confused with other species. Northern pine snakes and black rat snakes, the two species most likely to be mistaken for an eastern kingsnake, both have keeled scales. The scales of the kingsnake are smooth.

Habitat and Habits.   When active on the surface, the eastern kingsnake is primarily a diurnal species. Individuals of this species are, however, most frequently found by looking under cover objects such as logs, rocks, and debris. Throughout their range, they are found in a variety of habitats, including deciduous forests, agricultural lands, mountainous regions, and often around swamps. In the Northeast, they occur only in southern New Jersey, where they are primarily associated with the Pine Barrens.

The portion of their biology that is best documented is feeding. Kingsnakes feed predominately on reptiles, especially snakes.

Reproduction.   For such a widespread and reasonably common species, surprisingly little is known about the reproductive biology of the eastern kingsnake. Virtually nothing is known of its reproductive biology in the northeastern portion of its range. The following information pertains to Virginia (Mitchell 1994) and North Carolina (Palmer and Braswell 1995) populations.

Mating appears to occur in the spring but has not been well documented.

The eastern kingsnake, like all other members of the genus, is oviparous. The eggs are generally laid from early June to the middle of July. The eggs are whitish and leathery and are very adherent so that all eggs within a clutch are usually attached to each other. Eggs have been found in a variety of situations, including in rotting logs and stumps, in piles of moist sawdust, and under leaf litter.

Palmer and Braswell (1995) gave the following dimensions for 93 eggs from North Carolina: 30.9–50.8 mm ($1\frac{1}{4}$–2 in.) long, with a mean of 38.9 mm ($1\frac{1}{2}$ in.), and 17.6–26.5 mm ($\frac{3}{5}$–1 in.) wide, with a mean of 21.8 mm ($\frac{7}{8}$ in). Clutch size in North Carolina ranged from 7 to 17 ($X = 10.7$) eggs. Slightly larger average clutches (12.6 eggs) have been reported for Virginia, although the range of clutch size is also 7 to 17.

Hatchlings range from 230 to 301 mm ($9\frac{1}{4}$–12 in.) ToL.

Distribution.   The range of the eastern kingsnake extends from southern New Jersey southward to northern peninsular Florida. It extends westward into Georgia, Alabama, and parts of Tennessee. Disjunct populations are found in extreme western Tennessee, west-central Kentucky, western Virginia, and southern New Jersey.

Eastern Milk Snake *Lampropeltis triangulum triangulum* (Lacepede)
L. *triangulum*, like a triangle
Description.   The eastern milk snake (Plate 116) is a medium-sized species. The dorsal background coloration varies from gray to beige. The body is strongly patterned; the pattern consists of a series of 30–47 large squarish dorsal blotches associated with one or two staggered rows of smaller, irregularly shaped ventrolateral blotches running along either side of the body. On adults, these blotches vary from light chocolate to rich chestnut brown and are bordered by black. On juveniles, the blotches often are bright reddish or orangish brown. The ventral background

Map 68.   Distribution of the eastern kingsnake *(Lampropeltis getula getula).*

coloration varies from white to cream, with variously positioned black square or rectangular markings forming a dense checkerboard pattern. The first dorsal body blotch extends anteriorly onto the head, forming a V-shaped or Y-shaped mark. A solid or (less commonly) interrupted diagonal line extends from the posterior margin of the eye to the angle of the mouth. A narrow black bar generally extends across the prefrontals. The ground color of the head varies from light tan to light brown, becoming lighter on the supralabials. Concentrations of dark pigment on some of the supralabials give these scales a barred appearance. The chin is white or cream-colored, with dark markings along the edges of the infralabials. The occurrence of albinos in this species is very common (Hensley 1959).

The head is small and only slightly distinct from the body. In Pennsylvania, males tend to be slightly larger than females and to have a slightly longer tail. Adult males average 725.8 mm (29 in.) SVL and 826 mm (33 in.) ToL. Females average 677.3 mm (27 in.) SVL and 768.2 mm (30¾ in.) ToL. The record length for this subspecies is 1,321 (53 in.) (Conant and Collins 1991). The tail length of males averages 15.1% of SVL and 13.2% of ToL. The tail length of females averages 14.4% of SVL and 12.7% of ToL.

The dorsal scales are smooth and generally occur in 21 rows (occasionally 19) at midbody. The anal plate is entire, and the subcaudals are in two rows.

Confusing Species.   The eastern milk snake may be mistaken for the northern water snake, the copperhead, a juvenile black rat snake, or a juvenile northern black racer. The smooth scales of the milk snake should be sufficient to separate it from all of those species except the northern black racer. The very short tail (less than 17% of SVL) of the eastern milk snake is in sharp contrast to the long tail (more than 25% of SVL) of the northern black racer.

Habitat and Habits.   Eastern milk snakes have been reported to occupy a wide variety of habitats throughout their range (K. Williams 1978). In Pennsylvania and the rest of the Northeast, they are primarily inhabitants of open country, ecotones, and areas around human habitations and other disturbed habitats, such as exposed roadcuts and powerline rights-of-way. They are also found in deciduous forests.

No matter what the habitat might be, eastern milk snakes are most frequently found by searching under cover objects, especially rocks and building debris. They are seldom encountered in the open. Several workers have reported them to be primarily nocturnal (e.g., Dyrkacz 1977, Green and Pauley 1987), although we have seen no evidence of their being nocturnal in Pennsylvania.

In Pennsylvania, eastern milk snakes are active from April (earliest date, 4 April) to October (latest date, 15 October) throughout most of the state. In the Coastal Plain, around Delaware and Chester counties in Pennsylvania and in southern New Jersey, they may have an extended annual activity season running from early March through the middle of November. The annual activity pattern is unimodal. Activity is initially low in April but begins to increase substantially in May. It reaches a peak in June, declines sharply during July, remains at a stable level in August and September, and then falls to zero by the middle of October as the last individuals enter hibernation. Eastern milk snakes from Pennsylvania have been reported to hibernate in shale banks (Lachner 1942) and wells (Hudson 1949).

These snakes are generally solitary, but occasionally two will be found sharing a cover object. They are more likely to be found with other eastern milk snakes earlier in the activity season (May) than later.

Eastern milk snakes are constrictors and kill their prey by suffocation due to constriction. Most studies of the diet of the eastern milk snake have reported that they feed primarily on small mammals (see K. Williams 1978 for a review). Green and Pauley (1987) specifically stated that the eastern milk snake is not as ophiophagus (snake eating) as other members of the genus *Lampropeltis*. An examination of Pennsylvania specimens showed that the diet of the eastern milk snake changes dramatically with age. Individuals under 300 mm (12 in.) SVL feed almost exclusively on other species of snake. The northern redbelly snake is the most commonly consumed prey item, but eastern garter snakes, northern ringneck snakes, and northern water snakes are also consumed. Adults, on the other hand, feed almost exclusively on small mammals, with birds making a slight contribution to the diet. We have never found the remains of snakes in the stomachs of adult eastern milk snakes.

When encountered, eastern milk snakes occasionally vibrate their tail (a sound that can be quite loud and startling if done in dry vegetation) and will strike if an intruder continues to approach. If captured, they often vigorously defend themselves by biting, retaining a grip, and chewing. Occasionally, they may release musk and feces upon capture and handling.

Reproduction. Mating has seldom been observed. Indeed, only two records of mating are available for the eastern milk snake. Wright and Wright (1957) found a mating pair on 11 June in New York, and McCauley (1945) encountered a mating pair on 2 June in Maryland. Presumably, Pennsylvania specimens mate at about the same time.

Females emerge from hibernation containing small (6–7 mm; $\frac{1}{4}$ in.) ovarian follicles. Follicular growth is rapid, and by the end of May the eggs are ready to be ovulated. Females containing shelled oviducal eggs are found during June, and by early July females have laid their eggs. Oviposition occurs from mid-June to early July. In Illinois, egg laying occurs from 30 June to 11 July (Dyrkacz 1977). Eggs are laid in and under a variety of materials including, but not restricted to, sawdust piles, rubbish heaps, rotting logs, rocks, boards, debris, and loose soil.

Clutch size ranges from 5 to 24 eggs and is correlated with body size (K. Williams 1978). Clutch size in Pennsylvania ranges from 6 to 14 eggs.

The eggs are white, smooth, and leathery. They are elliptical and tend to adhere to each other. Eggs vary from 24 to 41 mm (1–1$\frac{5}{8}$ in.) in length and from 11.5 to 17 mm ($\frac{3}{8}$–$\frac{5}{8}$ in.) in diameter (K. Williams 1978). For several specimens that we examined, egg size varied from 29.3 to 37 mm (1$\frac{1}{8}$–1$\frac{1}{2}$ in.) in length and from 14.1 to 17 mm (1/2–5/8 in.) in diameter.

Incubation time has been reported to vary from 49 to 61 days (Barton 1948, Dyrkacz 1977). Hatchlings first appear in Pennsylvania in mid-August. The average size of Pennsylvania hatchlings is 186.7 mm (7$\frac{1}{2}$ in.) SVL and 229 mm (9$\frac{1}{8}$ in.) ToL. This is somewhat smaller than the average size of 248 mm (9$\frac{7}{8}$ in.) ToL reported by Dyrkacz (1977) for an Illinois population. Hatchlings seem to frequently enter hibernation without feeding, because there often is virtually no difference between the size of hatchlings and the size of individuals that have emerged from their first hibernation.

Remarks. Specimens from southern New Jersey appear to be intergrades between the eastern milk snake and the scarlet kingsnake (*Lampropeltis triangulum elapsoides*) (see K. Williams 1978 for details).

Distribution. The eastern milk snake ranges from southeastern Maine westward through southern Quebec and Ontario, through all of Michigan, with the exception of most of the Upper Peninsula, and through the southern half of Wisconsin to southeastern Minnesota. Its range extends south through central New Jersey and southwestward to northern Georgia and Alabama along the Appalachians. In the Midwest, its range reaches south from Minnesota through eastern Iowa and northern Illinois into northern and central Indiana and eastern Kentucky.

The eastern milk snake occurs throughout the Northeast except for northeastern Vermont, northern New Hampshire, and most of Maine. It is widely and evenly distributed in Pennsylvania. This is the most common medium-sized snake encountered in urban and suburban areas of the state.

Nerodia
Gr. *neros,* a swimmer; Gr. *ode,* a thing like

The genus *Nerodia* contains the North American water snakes and salt marsh snakes. Nine species are contained in the genus. They are found in the eastern and central United States, in adjacent Mexico, and along the northern coast of Cuba. All nine species occur within the limits of the United States.

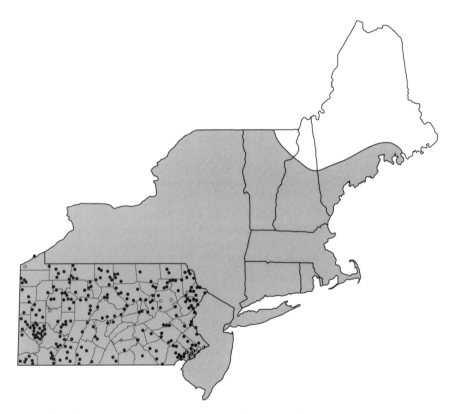

Map 69. Distribution of the eastern milk snake *(Lampropeltis triangulum triangulum).*

Water snakes are medium-sized to large, heavy-bodied animals. The dorsal body scales are strongly keeled, giving them a rough appearance. As the common name implies, these are semiaquatic snakes that are usually encountered in or at the edge of bodies of water. They may often be seen basking on rocks, fallen logs, or the branches of trees overhanging water. They are alert and dive into water at the slightest disturbance. If captured, they bite fiercely and discharge large amounts of foul-smelling musk, often mixed with feces.

Water snakes feed on a wide variety of aquatic and semiaquatic animals, including fish, frogs, salamanders, and crayfish. All water snakes are viviparous.

Northern Water Snake *Nerodia sipedon sipedon* (Linnaeus)
L. *siren*, a siren
Description. The northern water snake (Plate 117) is a medium-sized, heavy-bodied species. The dorsal background coloration varies from gray-brown to light brown. The dorsal pattern is composed of a series of saddles on the anterior third of the body that extend to the margins of the ventrals. The saddles are widest in the vertebral area and then narrow as they approach the ventrals. Posterior to this region, the saddles break up into separate dorsal and lateral blotches. The lateral blotches alternate in position with the dorsal markings, thereby giving a staggered pattern to the blotches. Both the saddles and the blotches vary from reddish brown to dark brown. Body blotches and saddles combined vary in number from 25 to 36. The dorsal head pattern consists of a grayish brown to brown background with variable dark markings. The supralabials are light beige to cream-colored with dark vertebral bars occurring along the sutures. The dorsal pattern of old individuals and individuals that are ready to shed is often obscure, and the animals appear a uniform brown.

The ventral coloration varies from cream to uniform yellow-brown, or occasionally, red. The venter is usually boldly patterned with posteriorly projecting blotches cut off square at the posterior margin of each ventral scute. These blotches vary from gray-brown to reddish brown and are bordered with black. The frequency of the blotches varies from individual to individual, but in all cases it increases on the posterior half of the body. This pattern continues onto the tail.

Several albino specimens of the northern water snake have been reported (Hensley 1959). Clay (1935) reported on a normal-colored female that gave birth to a litter of 23 individuals, 6 of which were albino.

The dorsal scales are strongly keeled and occur in 21 to 23 rows at midbody. The anal plate is divided, and the subcaudal scales are in two rows.

Northern water snakes exhibit significant sexual dimorphism in both size and body proportions. Adult males are much smaller than females, averaging 445 mm ($17\frac{3}{4}$ in.) SVL and 575 mm (23 in.) ToL. Females average 700 mm (28 in.) SVL and 907 mm ($36\frac{1}{4}$ in.) ToL. The record length for the species is 1,405 mm ($56\frac{1}{4}$ in.) ToL (Conant and Collins 1991). Males have a much longer tail than females. The mean tail length for males is 35% of SVL and 26% of ToL. The mean tail length for females is 27.7% of SVL and 21.7% of ToL.

Confusing Species.   The two species that northern water snakes could be confused with are the eastern milk snake and the northern copperhead. Eastern milk snakes have smooth glossy scales rather than strongly keeled scales, as in the northern water snake. Copperheads have a broad, triangular head and a narrow neck, whereas the head of northern water snakes is only moderately set off from the neck.

Habitat and Habits.   Northern water snakes are one of the most commonly encountered snakes in the Northeast. They occur in and around a wide variety of aquatic and semiaquatic habitats, including, but not restricted to, lakes, ponds, marshes, swamps, wet meadows, rivers, and slow- and fast-moving streams. Although northern water snakes are often found under cover objects (e.g., rocks, logs, boards) near water, they are also frequently found actively moving about, swimming or basking.

The annual activity cycle of northern water snakes from the Northeast is unimodal. They generally emerge from hibernation in early to mid-April, although they may emerge earlier during unusually warm weather (first week of March). Activity sharply increases in May and then remains high through July. In August and September, activity gradually decreases, and by the middle of October all animals have entered hibernation. This pattern is similar to that reported by Conant (1938) for northern water snakes from Ohio.

E. Brown (1958) suggested that northern water snakes are diurnal during spring and fall and become increasingly nocturnal in the warm months of summer. It has been our experience in Pennsylvania that northern water snakes are active both diurnally and nocturnally throughout their activity season. We have even seen them active at night in early March. Klemens (1993) has also observed nocturnal activity for this species in Connecticut. Swanson (1952) suggested that water snakes inhabiting cold-water streams may be restricted to diurnal activity because of the low temperature of the streams. He gave as evidence the fact that, although water snakes are common along Big Sandy Creek, Venango County, Pennsylvania, during the day, he never found them active at night, even though he spent much time in the stream at night hunting salamanders.

We have not found hibernating water snakes in Pennsylvania, but Carpenter (1953) in Michigan reported that they use ant mounds, meadow vole tunnels, and crayfish burrows as hibernation sites.

Several authors (Fraker 1970, Tiebout and Cary 1987) have commented on the tendency of northern water snakes to confine their movements to very small areas during most of the year. They have found the greatest tendency toward long-distance movement to occur during spring and fall, when the snakes are presumably moving either away from or back to their hibernation areas.

Northern water snakes often achieve very high population densities. Beatson (1976) recorded densities of from 34 to 41 animals/km

(54–68 animals/mi) of stream bank in Kansas, and King (1986), working around Lake Erie in Ohio, recorded an average density of 90 individuals (range: 22–381) per kilometer (145 individuals/mi; range: 35–614 individuals/mi) of shoreline. Northern water snakes often form small aggregations, especially in the vicinity of prime basking sites such as overhanging trees and large exposed rocks and ledges at the edge of streams and rivers.

Northern water snakes feed predominantly on fish and to a lesser extent on amphibians, especially frogs. Several studies have shown that fish constitute from 50% to 95% of the diet by volume (R. King 1986, Lagler and Salyer 1945, Raney and Roecker 1947). Although northern water snakes are often accused of feeding on game fish and pan fish, the vast majority of fish in their diet have no sport value and are generally considered by anglers to be "rough" fish. In Pennsylvania, all specimens that we examined that contained food had fed on either fish or frogs. Burghardt (1968) demonstrated that the northern water snake's predilection for fish and frogs is innate. When he presented newborn individuals with a variety of prey-odor choices, the only ones the young snakes struck at were fish and frog extracts.

When first encountered, these snakes generally attempt to escape into the water, where they dive to the bottom and hide in the mud and vegetation or among the rocks. However, if an escape route is blocked, they will defend themselves. They coil, flatten their body, and strike repeatedly. When successful in biting an intruder, they frequently hold on and chew. They also release feces and an unpleasant-smelling musk when captured or handled.

Reproduction.   Courtship and mating have been observed in Pennsylvania in early June (Mushinsky 1979). R. King (1986) reported that mating occurs in nearby Ohio between 11 May and 11 June. Follicles begin to enlarge in late summer, immediately after parturition. As a result, females emerge from hibernation with well-developed ovarian follicles. Follicular growth continues until ovulation in late May or early June of the next year. Northern water snakes are viviparous, and by early July gravid females contain well-developed embryos. Parturition occurs from 20 August to the middle of September in Pennsylvania. The litter size in Pennsylvania ranges from 11 to 36 young and is positively correlated with female body size. Neonates average 158.6 mm ($6\frac{1}{4}$ in.) SVL and 208.5 mm ($8\frac{1}{4}$ in.) ToL.

Males exhibit a typical temperate-zone type of reproductive cycle. They emerge from hibernation with small regressed testes. Testicular growth is rapid during late spring and early summer, and testes reach maximum size in July.

In Pennsylvania, males mature at a SVL of about 320 mm ($12\frac{3}{4}$ in.) and a ToL of 430 mm ($17\frac{1}{4}$ in.). Females mature at 514 mm ($20\frac{1}{2}$ in.) SVL and 770 mm ($30\frac{3}{4}$ in.) ToL. R. King (1986) noted that not all females are gravid every year. He determined that about 30% of the females of reproductive size were not gravid in any year around Lake Erie in Ohio. This same general tendency appears to occur in Pennsylvania. It is not known whether this phenomenon occurs in the rest of the Northeast. What factors determine whether a female will be reproductive remain to be determined. However, G. Brown and Weatherhead (1997) noted higher mortality among overwintering postpartum individuals than among individuals that had not had young. The higher mortality was likely due to their emaciated condition. Brown and Weatherhead suggested that the infrequent reproduction in small females might both reduce postpartum mortality and allow for increased size, which is associated with increased fecundity in this species.

Distribution.   The northern water snake ranges from southern Maine, southward to North Carolina and Tennessee, and west to Kansas and Nebraska, into eastern Colorado and eastern Oklahoma.

The species is common throughout southern New England, New York, and New Jersey and reaches north into southern Maine, southern New Hampshire, and most of Vermont. It is common and widely distributed throughout Pennsylvania.

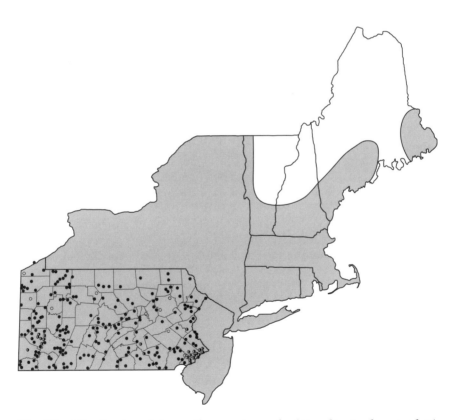

Map 70.   Distribution of the northern water snake *(Nerodia sipedon sipedon).*

Opheodrys
Gr. *ophis*, a serpent; L. *dryas*, an oak

The genus *Opheodrys* contains the green snakes. Two species are contained in the genus. Green snakes range from the Maritime Provinces of Canada westward to the Rocky Mountains. They range southward into northeastern Mexico.

Green snakes are small to moderately long, slender species with a very long tail. Scales are either smooth or keeled, depending upon the species. Green snakes are either terrestrial or arboreal. They are usually found in open habitat or in wooded areas near fields or streams. They are most frequently encountered while they are actively moving about. When captured, they may thrash about, but they never attempt to bite.

Green snakes feed on a variety of insects, including grasshoppers, caterpillars, and cicadas. Both species lay eggs.

Rough Green Snake *Opheodrys aestivus* (Linnaeus)
L. *aesta*, summer

Description. The rough green snake (Plate 118) is a moderately long, slender species. The dorsal coloration is a uniform light to pea green. The venter is without markings and may be cream-colored, yellow, or yellow-green. The supralabials and chin are usually white. Neonates are a uniform gray to greenish gray, but they take on the typical adult coloration after their first molt.

The head is moderately distinct from the body owing to the slender neck, and the eyes are large. Rough green snakes do not exhibit sexual dimorphism in body size or in relative tail length. Adults range in size from 285 to 650 mm ($11\frac{3}{8}$–26 in.) SVL and from 460 to 1,050 mm ($18\frac{3}{8}$–41 in.) ToL (Plummer 1987). The largest specimen from Pennsylvania had a SVL of 465 mm ($18\frac{1}{2}$ in.) and a ToL of 731 mm ($29\frac{1}{4}$ in.). The record size for this species is 1,159 mm ($46\frac{1}{2}$ in.) (Conant and Collins 1991). This species has a very long tail, averaging about 62% (range: 57.2% to 65.2%) of SVL and 38% (range: 36.3% to 39.4%) of ToL.

The dorsal scales are keeled and occur in 17 rows at midbody. The keels become less distinct laterally, and the two scale rows nearest the ventrals on each side are smooth. The anal plate is divided, and the subcaudals occur in two rows.

Confusing Species. The only species that the rough green snake could be mistaken for in the Northeast is the smooth green snake, but it is readily distinguishable from the smooth green snake by the presence of keels on the dorsal scales.

Habitat and Habits. The rough green snake is extremely uncommon in Pennsylvania and considered to be stable in New Jersey. The information presented here and in the reproductive section comes from studies in other portions of the animal's geographic range.

Rough green snakes are arboreal, usually being found in trees and shrubs at a height of from 1 to 3 m (3.3–10 ft) above the ground. Specimens are occasionally found on the ground. These may be females looking for oviposition sites. In Pennsylvania, all specimens have been collected in vegetation near streams. Plummer (1981), studying an Arkansas population, noted that 86% to 89% of all captures occurred within 3 meters (10 ft) of water and that 97% were captured within 5 m (16 ft) of water. Goldsmith (1984) also noted their tendency to be found along the edges of bodies of water (both standing and flowing). Both of the above authors mentioned that the species is also common along other edge habitats (e.g., forest vegetation bordering fields and pastures) and that rough green snakes prefer dense, highly branched vegetation. Juveniles appear to be less restricted to an arboreal environment and are often found on the ground (Goldsmith 1984).

The extent of seasonal activity is variable depending upon geographic location. In West Virginia, rough green snakes emerge in early May and cease activity by mid-October (Green and Pauley 1987).

Rough green snakes are diurnal and spend most of the day slowly moving through the vegetation foraging for food (Plummer 1981). They often forage with the head and anterior portion of the body elevated; they intermittently stop while foraging to rhythmically move their head from side to side. This type of behavior has been noted in other arboreal snakes. Collins (1974) suggested that it may be a form of cryptic behavior in that the snake's moving body would resemble a branch swaying in the breeze. Henderson and Nickerson (1975), however, suggested that the lateral movements of the head might enhance the animal's binocular vision for prey location.

Plummer (1981) noted that they are difficult to find in the daytime as their bright green color allows them to blend into their background. At night, however, when asleep, they are easily spotted from below because their pale venter reflects light, allowing them to be easily seen with the beam of a spotlight or powerful flashlight.

Rough green snakes have very restricted home ranges. Plummer (1981) noted a mean movement of only 62 m (190 ft) (range: 15–247 m; 50–775 ft) from the point of original capture. In high-quality habitat, rough green snakes can reach very high densities, with up to 714 animals/ha (295 animals/acre) (Plummer 1985a).

Rough green snakes are almost exclusively insectivorous (E. Brown 1979a, Plummer 1981). The main food items included in their diet are caterpillars, grasshoppers and crickets, spiders, and dragonflies and damselflies. A variety of other small insects are occasionally taken. In most species of snake, relatively few individuals are found to contain food (ca. 20%), and most individuals with food in the stomach have a single relatively large prey item. This is not the case with rough green snakes. Plummer (1981) found that 82.5% of the specimens he examined contained food and that the average number of food items per stomach was 3.1. This high incidence of food is probably a result of their preferred diet. Insects and spiders are generally small in relation to the size of the snake, and as a consequence the animals have to feed at frequent intervals and consume numerous prey items to meet their nutritional and energetic requirements.

Reproduction.   No data are available on reproduction in rough green snakes from the Northeast. Elsewhere, mating occurs in both spring and fall. Oviposition has been reported from as early as 17 June (Guidry 1953) to as late as 31 August (H. Fitch 1970), but most egg laying appears to occur in late June and July (Goldsmith 1984). Incubation time is highly variable (34–90 days) and may be a function of geographic location. It appears that northern populations have longer incubation periods (64–90 days) than southern populations (34–50 days). Females leave their arboreal environments to lay eggs on the ground or in specific nest trees. Eggs are laid in leaf litter, rotting logs and stumps, loose soil, and trash piles. Plummer and Snell (1988) demonstrated in the laboratory that females select nest sites on the basis of moisture content, preferring sites with high moisture content. Sites with a higher moisture content produced larger and heavier young but did not affect hatching success. Communal nesting is known to occur in this species, with as many as 74 eggs being found in a single oviposition site (Palmer and Braswell 1976).

Plummer (1989, 1990), using telemetry, showed that females leave their center of activity to search for a suitable nest site. Females that he observed selected nest sites in the cavities of living trees. They frequently nest in small chambers that are narrow vertical slits not much wider than the width of a single egg. The eggs are laid in these cavities end to end. Plummer suggested that the preponderance of reports of ground nesting may reflect the areas most commonly searched by herpetologists rather than the actual biology of the animals.

Clutch size varies from 3 to 12 eggs in Arkansas (Plummer 1990). The eggs are white and leathery. The mean egg length is 28.6 mm $(1\frac{1}{8}$ in.), and the mean width is 13.5 mm $(\frac{1}{2}$ in.) (Palmer and Braswell 1976). The mean total length of hatchlings is 203.5 mm $(8\frac{1}{8}$ in.). There is no sexual dimorphism in the size of neonates. The sex ratio of neonates is 1:1.

In Arkansas, males mature in 2 years at a SVL of about 300 mm (12 in.), and females mature in 2–3 years at a SVL ranging from 335 to 370 mm $(13\frac{3}{8}-14\frac{3}{4}$ in.) (Plummer 1985b). The time to maturity may be longer in the northern part of the species' range.

Remarks.   Rough green snakes are inoffensive animals that are not known to bite. Owing to their limited range in Pennsylvania, the Pennsylvania Fish and Boat Commission has listed them as a threatened species.

Distribution.   The rough green snake is widely distributed in the southeastern and south-central United States. It reaches the northern limit of its range in extreme southern Pennsylvania and the southern half of New Jersey.

In Pennsylvania, it is conclusively known to occur in only two isolated and widely separated localities: one in Greene County and the other in Chester County, near the Maryland border. The Chester County population appears to be viable, but no specimens have been collected at the Greene County site since 1924.

Several other localities have been cited in the literature but have not been verified by actual examination of specimens and may be based on misidentified smooth green snakes. Among these are Carnegie, Allegheny County (Atkinson 1901); Dauphin and Lancaster counties (Surface 1906); Pequea, Lancaster County (Roddy 1928); and Union County (Pawling 1939). A dead specimen was found, but unfortunately not preserved, near Waterford, Westmoreland County (Harwig, pers. comm.), and field notes deposited in the Carnegie Museum indicate that an individual was collected by H. D. Yoder between Scottdale and Dawson, Westmoreland County.

If you should encounter a rough green snake in any of the above localities or elsewhere in Pennsylvania, please contact the Section of Amphibians and Reptiles at the Carnegie Museum of Natural History in Pittsburgh.

Smooth Green Snake *Opheodrys vernalis* (Harlan)
L. *verno*, spring
Description.   The smooth green snake (Plate 119) is a moderately long, slender species with a long tapering tail. The dorsal coloration is a uniform

Map 71. Distribution of the rough green snake *(Opheodrys aestivus)*.

bright green. The venter is immaculate white to yellowish white. Occasionally, the lateral scales are tinged with blue. The supralabials and chin scales are usually white.

The head is only slightly distinct from the body, and the eyes are large. Unlike the rough green snake, the smooth green snake exhibits strong sexual dimorphism in body size and relative tail length. Adult males from Pennsylvania average 269.6 mm ($10\frac{3}{4}$ in.) SVL and 414.8 mm ($16\frac{1}{2}$ in.) ToL. Females average 323.8 mm (13 in.) SVL and 450.3 mm (18 in.) ToL. The record size for the species is 660 mm ($26\frac{1}{2}$ in.) ToL (Conant and Collins 1991). Males have a significantly longer tail than females. The mean tail length for males is 54.5% of SVL and 35.6% of ToL, whereas the mean tail length for females is only 43.4% of SVL and 30.2% of ToL.

The dorsal scales are smooth and occur in 15 rows at midbody. The anal plate is divided, and the subcaudals occur in two rows.

Newly hatched young are dark olive gray dorsally, becoming lighter on the sides. The venter is white. The young take on the typical adult coloration after their first molt.

Confusing Species.   The only species that the smooth green snake could be confused with is the rough green snake, but the absence of keeled scales on the smooth green snake readily distinguishes it from the rough.

Habitat and Habits.   Unlike the rough green snake, the smooth green snake is basically a terrestrial species, although it may occasionally be found moving about in low shrubby vegetation. Smooth green snakes are found in a variety of habitats, including old fields, pastures, farmland, and clearings in forested areas. Although they are occasionally encountered in the open, they are more commonly found under cover objects such as rocks and logs.

Annual activity begins in early April (earliest record, 7 April) and continues until late October or early November during years with mild fall temperatures. The annual activity pattern differs for males and females, although both exhibit bimodal patterns. The males' activity gradually increases to an initial peak in June, then drops dramatically in July, again begins to increase in August, and reaches a second peak in September. By early October, males have ceased activity for the year. The females' initial peak occurs in May; activity decreases in June, increases again in late July, and then becomes relatively constant through September, with a gradual decline in activity in October. These patterns of activity are similar to those reported by Siebert and Hagen (1947) for a population of smooth green snakes in northeastern Illinois and to the annual activity of May to November reported by Klemens (1993) for Connecticut. But they are of much longer duration than for smooth green snakes from Manitoba, Canada, where annual activity apparently stops in late August (Gregory 1977).

Like the rough green snake, the smooth green snake is primarily diurnal. The only record of hibernation in the species from Pennsylvania is that of Lachner (1942). He reported on two specimens that were taken from rocky soil in Mercer County at a depth of about 80 cm (31½ in.). Criddle (1937) and Carpenter (1953) both reported on smooth green snakes using ant mounds as hibernacula. Criddle found 148 individuals of all sizes in the lower chambers of an ant mound in Minnesota.

Smooth green snakes are insectivorous. They mostly feed on ground-dwelling spiders, caterpillars, grasshoppers, and crickets. Smooth green snakes have been reported to exhibit rhythmic lateral head movements while moving about (Cochran 1987b). These movements may aid the animals in locating food items as they forage along the ground.

Smooth green snakes are inoffensive animals and are not known to bite.

Reproduction. Mating has been reported as taking place in late summer and early fall (Drymond and Fry 1932, Wright and Wright 1957). We, however, have found mating individuals in early April.

In Pennsylvania, females emerge from hibernation with small ovarian follicles. Follicular growth is rapid, and by late May or early June females contain enlarged oviducal eggs. Oviposition occurs from mid-July to late August. Eggs are laid under cover objects such as rocks and boards in exposed locations. Sexton and Claypool (1978) reported finding clutches simply laid under clumps of weeds in open fields in southeastern Illinois. Oviposition sites may be used repeatedly year after year. We have found freshly deposited eggs under rocks in close association with egg shell fragments left from previous years. In some areas, smooth green snakes utilize communal egg-laying sites (Cook 1964, J. Fowler 1966).

Clutch size in Pennsylvania varies from 3 to 7 eggs (Plate 120). In other parts of the species' range, the clutch size is larger. Blanchard (1933a) reported clutches ranging from 3 to 11 eggs in southern Michigan. In Pennsylvania, clutch size is not correlated with female body size; however, Grobman (1989) reported a significant positive correlation between egg number and female body size for a large sample covering a broad geographic range.

Smooth green snake eggs are white, elongate, and cylindrical, with blunt rounded ends. Shelled oviducal eggs average 21.3 mm (⅞ in.) in length and 7.0 mm (¼ in.) in diameter. There is some indication that eggs increase in size while in the oviducts and, presumably, that once laid they increase further owing to the absorption of water. Incubation time ranges from 4 to 24 days (Blanchard 1933a). The reason for the short incubation period is that embryonic development begins while the eggs are still in the oviducts. Oviducal eggs from females collected in mid-August contain young that are fully developed (i.e., are of hatching size, are fully scaled, and have typical neonate coloration). This egg retention and egg laying at an advanced state of development is most likely an adaptation to colder climates in the northern portion of the species' distribution. Prolonged egg retention may allow the female to behaviorally select temperatures that are optimal for embryonic development.

Hatching occurs from early August to early September. In Pennsylvania, smooth green snake hatchlings average 92.8 mm (3¾ in.) SVL and

130.8 mm (5¼ in.) ToL. This is similar to the mean hatching size of 124.6 mm (5 in.) ToL from Michigan (Blanchard 1933a).

Remarks.   Smooth green snake populations seem to be declining, perhaps because of pesticide use on their main food items (caterpillars and grasshoppers). This trend should be carefully monitored. Klemens (1993) discussed this apparent decline in some detail for smooth green snakes from Connecticut. He attributed the decline to the use of DDT and other pesticides on the snakes' major prey and to the reverting of agricultural lands to forest.

Distribution.   The species ranges from eastern Nova Scotia to extreme southeastern Saskatchewan, southward through New England into Pennsylvania, West Virginia, and northern Virginia. It occurs in northeastern Ohio, Michigan, northeastern Illinois, and most of Wisconsin. Its distribution is spotty in the northern Plains States and Texas.

The smooth green snake occurs throughout the Northeast except in northern Maine, southern and central New Jersey, and the south-eastern Coastal Plain and Piedmont of Pennsylvania. It also appears to be absent from the mountains of the southern Poconos in eastern Pennsylvania.

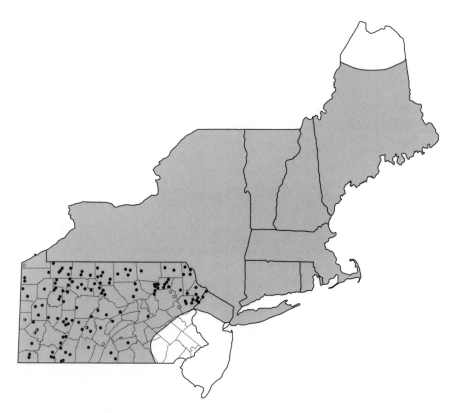

Map 72. Distribution of the smooth green snake *(Opheodrys vernalis)*.

Pituophis

The genus *Pituophis* contains two species. The range of the genus extends from southern Canada in the west southward through Mexico and central Guatamala. Both species of *Pituophis* are large, robust snakes that occupy a variety of habitats. They feed primarily on small mammals and ground-nesting birds. Once captured, prey are killed by constriction. Both species lay eggs.

Northern Pine Snake *Pituophis melanoleucus melanoleucus* (Daudin)
Gr. *pitys*, pine; Gr. *ophios*, snake; Gr. *melano*, black; Gr. *leukos*, white

Description.   The northern pine snake (Plate 121) is a large robust species. This species is boldly patterned with a series of black dorsal blotches on a white to cream-colored or yellowish background. These blotches become brownish on the posterior portion of the body. The head, which is only slightly distinct from the body, has a series of small black markings on a white to cream-colored background. The chin and labials are immaculate. The venter may be immaculate white or cream-colored or may have irregular dark markings scattered about. Hatchlings and juveniles resemble adults.

The dorsal body scales are strongly keeled and occur in 27–37 scale rows at midbody. The anal plate is entire, and the subcaudals occur in two rows.

Confusing Species.   Young black rat snakes bear a superficial resemblance to northern pine snakes and could be mistaken for them. The dorsal scales of the northern pine snake, however, are strongly keeled, whereas the scales of the black rat snake are either smooth or weakly keeled. In addition, black rat snakes have a divided anal plate, whereas the anal plate of the pine snake is entire.

Habitats and Habits. The northern pine snake is without doubt the best-studied snake in New Jersey and probably the entire Northeast, owing to the efforts of Burger and Colleagues, who have been intensively studying this species in the New Jersey Pine Barrens. Much of the information provided in this and the following section is derived from their efforts.

The northern pine snake is primarily an inhabitant of pine-oak woodlands and pine flatlands. These habitats are moderately xeric, and the soil is typically sandy or otherwise porous and dry (Burger and Zappalorti 1988). The species is fossorial, but when on the surface males show a distinct preference for logs and bark as cover objects. Females apparently have little or no microhabitat preference when on the surface (Burger and Zappalorti 1988).

Zappalorti and Colleagues (1983) stated that, in New Jersey, northern pine snake activity begins in April and extends into October. Surface activity is generally limited during hot dry weather (Burger et al. 1988). Burger and Colleagues (1988) have studied both hibernacula and aestivation den sites in great detail within the New Jersey Pine Barrens.

Dens appear to be primarily constructed by the snakes themselves. This behavior is unusual; most species of snake use either natural cavities or burrows constructed by other species. Entrances to northern pine snake hibernacula are generally located near fallen trees, and burrows initially follow the path of tree roots and rocks. The remainder of the site is constructed by the snake. The average length of all tunnels in a hibernacula is 642 cm (21 ft). Side tunnels, terminating in chambers, come off of the main tunnel. These are hibernation sites for individual snakes. The average hibernacula contains eight side chambers. The side chambers are located at depths ranging from 50 to 111 cm ($19\frac{3}{4}$–44 in.). Aestivation sites are shallower and of less complex construction.

Burger and Colleagues (1992) found evidence of predation on hibernating northern pine snakes. Predators included red foxes, striped skunks, and short-tailed shrews. The overall predation rate was low, approximately 2% of all hibernating animals. Short-tailed shrews surprisingly accounted for the most predation, but they attacked only hatchlings and small individuals. They killed the snakes by chewing through the back, vertebral column, and spinal cord.

The northern pine snake is a large constrictor and feeds primarily on mammalian prey and ground-nesting birds and their eggs (Palmer and Braswell 1995).

If cornered, northern pine snakes will engage in an impressive defensive display. This includes inflating their lungs and then forcibly exhaling, thus causing a loud hissing noise. This is usually accompanied by a rapid vibrating of the tail, which, if it occurs in dry vegetation, can produce a loud noise not unlike the sound produced by the rattle of a rattlesnake. They will also often strike repeatedly at their attacker.

Reproduction.   In New Jersey, mating has been observed in May (Zappalorti et al. 1983). Egg laying takes place from mid-June to mid-July. Nests are generally constructed in large clearings and may be used by single individuals or may be communal (Burger and Zappalorti 1986, 1991). Of 31 animals that Burger and Zappalorti (1986) observed, 16 nested singly while the remainder nested in groups of two, three, or four.

Nest tunnels are constructed by the snakes. Females dig by thrusting their head and neck forward into the soil and then curving the neck while retracting the body, thereby capturing the soil and dragging it out of the tunnel (Burger and Zappalorti 1991). Tunnels initially slant downward but then tend to move at an angle upward, possibly to prevent the flooding of the nest chamber that would likely occur if it were at the lowest part of the tunnel. Tunnels range in length from 39 to 228 cm ($15\frac{1}{2}$–89 in.), with a mean of 143 cm (56 in.). Tunnels terminate in a nest chamber. The average dimensions of nest chambers are 20 cm (8 in.) long, 11 cm $4\frac{3}{8}$ in.) wide, and 7 cm ($2\frac{3}{4}$ in.) high. Eggs may be laid communally, and old broken egg shells provide evidence that nest tunnels are used in successive years.

Burger and Zappalorti (1991) reported clutch sizes ranging from 4 to 16 ($X = 9.5$) eggs. Northern pine snake eggs are large. The dimensions of

16 eggs from North Carolina ranged from 54.1 to 81.2 mm ($2\frac{1}{8}$–$3\frac{1}{4}$ in.) in length and from 34.1 to 36.5 mm ($1\frac{3}{8}$ in.) in width; the mean length was 57 mm ($2\frac{1}{4}$ in.), and the mean width was (35.4 mm) ($1\frac{3}{8}$ in.) (Palmer and Braswell 1995). The egg shell is leathery and rough, and the eggs are very adherent (stick to each other). Burger and colleagues (1992) documented significant nest predation. Of 201 nests examined, 42 were destroyed by red foxes and 7 by striped skunks. In addition, in one nest they found a scarlet snake feeding on an egg. More disturbing than predation by these wild animals, however, is human disturbance. Twenty-three of 80 nests (29%) examined over a 3-year period had been raided by humans.

Hatching occurs in August and September. Palmer and Braswell (1995) reported that hatchlings range from 406 to 474 mm ($8\frac{1}{4}$–15 in.) ToL.

Distribution.   The northern pine snake has a fragmented distribution in the eastern United States. The main portion of the species' range extends from central South Carolina and southern North Carolina westward into Georgia, Alabama, and parts of Tennessee. Disjunct populations are found in extreme southwestern Kentucky, western Virginia, and southern New Jersey.

Map 73. Distribution of the northern pine snake *(Pituophis melanoleucus melanoleucus).*

Regina
L. *regina*, royal

The genus *Regina* contains the "crayfish" snakes. Four species are contained in the genus. The distribution of the genus is primarily the eastern United States.

The crayfish snakes are small to moderate-sized slender species. The dorsal body scales are keeled but not as strongly as those of their close relatives, the water snakes. Crayfish snakes are semiaquatic to aquatic species and live in and along the margins of a wide variety of aquatic habitats. The crayfish snakes do not bask with the same frequency as the water snakes and are more likely to be found by turning cover objects at the edge of water or by searching through aquatic vegetation. When captured, they release an unpleasant-smelling musk, but, unlike the water snakes, they do not generally attempt to bite their captor.

Crayfish snakes, as the name implies, feed predominately upon crayfish, although some species will occasionally take other prey items, such as fish and frogs. All four species give birth to young rather than lay eggs.

Queen Snake *Regina septemvittata* (Say)
L. *septem*, seven; L. *vitata*, band or stripe
Description. Queen snakes (Plate 122) are medium-sized, slender animals. The dorsal coloration is olive-brown to brown, with three black stripes (one dorsal and two lateral). These stripes may be obscured or absent in adults. The brown dorsal coloration is bordered below by a yellow stripe. The venter is yellowish and is patterned with four dark brown stripes, two located on either side of the midventral line and two along the lateral margins of the ventrals and extending onto the first row of dorsal scales. The dorsal surface of the head is dark brown and lacks a pattern. The labials (both upper and lower), chin, and anterior region of the neck are immaculate yellow. The pattern in this species generally is most noticeable and best developed in younger, rather than older, individuals. An albino specimen is known from Indiana (Dyrkacz 1981).

The dorsal scales are distinctly keeled and usually occur in 19 scale rows at midbody. The anal plate is divided.

Queen snakes exhibit significant sexual dimorphism in body size and proportions. Adult females are larger than males. Mature males average 405.5 mm ($16\frac{1}{4}$ in.) SVL and 539.6 mm ($21\frac{1}{2}$ in.) ToL. In contrast, females average 490.3 mm ($19\frac{1}{2}$ in.) SVL and 630.5 mm ($25\frac{1}{4}$ in.) ToL. The maximum size for the species has been reported as 975 mm (39 in.) ToL (Wright and Wright 1957). Males have a longer tail than females. The mean tail length for males is 33.6% of SVL and 25.1% of ToL. The mean tail length for females is 29.6% of SVL and 22.7% of ToL.

Confusing Species. Garter snakes have undivided anal plates as opposed to the divided anal plate of the queen snake. No other species in the Northeast could be mistaken for a queen snake.

Habitat and Habits.   Queen snakes are primarily inhabitants of moderate to fast-flowing streams, creeks, and small rivers, but they are occasionally found in slow-moving streams, ponds, and small lakes. The margins of the waters that they inhabit are usually bordered with shrubs and trees but have an open canopy so that sunlight can penetrate and provide ample basking sites for the snakes. Queen snakes are seldom encountered more than 1 or 2 m ($3\frac{1}{4}$–$6\frac{1}{2}$ ft) away from a stream bank or pond margin, perhaps because they have extremely permeable skin and as a result are very prone to desiccation (Stokes and Dunson 1982). No matter what the general habitat is, the one absolute requirement is that crayfish must be present and fairly abundant. In addition, ample cover objects must be present; if they are not, queen snakes will be rare or absent.

In Pennsylvania, annual activity generally begins in late April (rarely, individuals may be found as early as the end of March). Activity increases dramatically in May and reaches a seasonal high in June. Activity then drops in July and remains fairly constant through August. It then gradually tapers off in September. All activity in western Pennsylvania ceases by the middle of October. The activity season might be extended in populations from the warmer southeastern Coastal Plain and Piedmont. The annual pattern is similar to that found in other parts of the species' range, except that in climatically more moderate regions (e.g., Kentucky and Georgia) it has been shown to remain active into the middle of November (Branson and Baker 1974, Neill 1948).

Queen snakes are somewhat diurnal and may occasionally be found actively foraging for food or, more frequently, basking on rocks or in vegetation that overhangs stream banks. In slow-moving or standing water it is not unusual to see them floating in the water, with just the head and a small portion of the neck out of the water. Layne and Ford (1984) determined that escape behavior is correlated with temperature. As body temperature increases, basking queen snakes become increasingly wary and much more likely to flee an intruder (i.e., their minimum escape distance increases). Although Ernst and Barbour (1989) suggested that queen snakes are normally active on the surface, either basking or foraging, it has been our experience as well as that of Branson and Baker (1974) that most individuals are found under cover objects. Queen snakes are most commonly found during periods of drought, when stream levels are lowest.

We have not found the hibernacula of queen snakes, but Ernst and Barbour (1989) reported that they hibernate in muskrat burrows. In all likelihood, queen snakes hibernate in crayfish burrows and in deep cracks and crevices in rocky sections of streams.

It is common to find two or more queen snakes under a single cover object or basking close to each other. Extremely large aggregations have been observed during the fall. Wood (1944) found 32 individuals sunning on saplings along an Ohio stream on 27 October. Neill (1948) noted "dozens and dozens" basking along a small section of stream in Georgia in November.

Queen snakes are specialized feeders, utilizing almost nothing but crayfish as a food item. All quantitative feeding studies of queen snakes have shown that they consume crayfish to the virtual exclusion of all other food items (E. Brown 1979b, Godley et al. 1984, Raney and Roecker 1947). Almost all of the crayfish consumed are in the early molt stages, when the shell is soft and flexible. It would appear that this preference for crayfish and soft-shelled individuals in particular is innate. Burghardt (1968) demonstrated that naive neonate queen snakes presented with cotton swabs containing olfactory extracts of a wide variety of potential prey items (e.g., worms, salamanders, fish, slugs, and crayfish) responded only to those swabs with crayfish extract on them. In addition, he found that the response was strongest to extracts prepared from recently molted animals. We have seen queen snakes actively foraging among rocks on the bottom of streambeds. When a crayfish is dislodged from its hiding place, it is grabbed and generally is swallowed tail first.

Unlike their close relative the northern water snake, queen snakes are inoffensive and seldom attempt to bite when handled. They will, however, struggle violently when first captured and spray their captor with a mixture of musk and feces.

Reproduction.   Mating in the field has been observed only once (Minton 1972), but mating probably occurs in the spring. Follicles begin to enlarge in late summer or fall shortly after parturition. Females enter hibernation with 6–8 mm ($\frac{1}{4}$ in.) ovarian follicles. When the females emerge from hibernation, vitellogenesis resumes and ovulation occurs in very late May or the first two weeks of June. Queen snakes are viviparous, and by early July they contain developing embryos in the oviducts. Parturition occurs from about 1 August to 20 August. Litter size in Pennsylvania ranges from 4 to 15 young and is significantly correlated with female SVL. This is a little smaller than the litter size of a Kentucky population, in which it ranged from 7 to 17 young (Branson and Baker 1974). The maximum litter size has been reported as 23 young (H. Fitch 1970). Neonates average 177 mm (7 in.) SVL (Branson and Baker 1974).

In Pennsylvania, males mature at about 318 mm ($12\frac{5}{8}$ in.) SVL and 420 mm ($16\frac{3}{4}$ in.) ToL. Females mature at about 400 mm (16 in.) SVL and 520 mm ($20\frac{3}{4}$ in.) ToL.

Remarks.   Queen snakes are often found with conspicuous whitish blisters on their body. These tend to increase in frequency and size if the animals are kept in captivity. The blisters are caused by a parasitic fungus of the genus *Verticellium* (Branson and Baker 1974). Queen snakes are also occasionally parasitized by leeches of the genus *Placobdella*.

There is some concern that local populations of queen snakes are being reduced in number or completely extirpated owing to the adverse affects of pollution on populations of crayfish. At present, all the evidence is anecdotal, and careful monitoring of queen snake populations is severely needed to determine if they should be placed in a protected category.

Distribution.   The queen snake ranges from western Pennsylvania and New York westward through southern Ontario and Michigan to northeastern Illinois and southeastern Wisconsin. Its range extends south through Indiana into central Kentucky and Tennessee to the Gulf Coast of Alabama and Florida. In the East, it is absent from most of the Coastal Plain. Disjunct populations occur in northwestern Arkansas and possibly in southwestern Missouri (T. Johnson 1987).

The queen snake occurs in extreme western New York and much of Pennsylvania. In Pennsylvania, it exhibits a disjunct distribution. Queen snakes are found in the Allegheny Plateau area of the western third of the state and in the Piedmont and Coastal Plain sections of the southeastern corner of the state. It is highly likely that most of the populations in Philadelphia, Delaware, and southern Bucks counties have been extirpated owing to habitat destruction or pollution.

Storeria
Named for David H. Storer, a nineteenth-century herpetologist

The genus *Storeria* contains the brown snakes. The genus contains two species. The geographic distribution of the genus ranges from southern

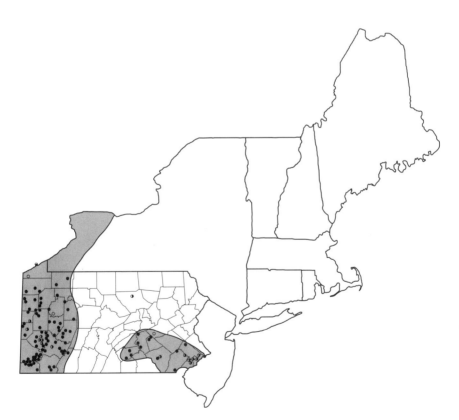

Map 74. Distribution of the queen snake *(Regina septemvittata).*

Canada southward throughout the eastern United States to central Honduras.

Brown snakes are small snakes with keeled scales. They are secretive and terrestrial snakes that are most likely to be found under cover objects such as rocks, logs, and debris. They are inoffensive and will not bite, but they do release an unpleasant musk if handled.

Brown snakes have a fairly specialized diet, feeding almost exclusively on slugs and earthworms and, perhaps, on snails. Both species give birth to live young.

Northern Brown Snake *Storeria dekayi dekayi* (Holbrook)
Named for James Edward DeKay, a nineteenth-century naturalist
Description.   The northern brown snake (Plate 123) is a small, moderately stout species. The dorsal background coloration varies from pale gray to grayish brown to medium brown, sometimes with a reddish tinge. The background coloration remains fairly constant along the length of the animal's body, although it may darken on the tail. A light medial dorsal stripe, three to four scales wide, is often present, bordered on either side by rows of dark brown to black blotches. Occasionally these blotches join to form crossbars. The skin between the scales on the side of the body is sometimes pigmented black, giving the sides a mottled appearance that often resembles additional rows of spots. The background color of the head is similar to that of the body but generally is mottled with minute black spots and becomes paler on the supralabials. Two dark marks are usually present under each eye, and there is a well-defined vertical bar extending from the temporals through the posterior two supralabials and ending on the posterior two infralabials. The ventral coloration varies from gray to yellowish brown. The venter is generally unmarked except for small black dots that may occur along the lateral margins of the ventrals. These dots are most common on the anterior ventrals and become less pronounced or absent on the posterior ventrals. Albino specimens have been reported (Groves 1984, Hensley 1959).

The dorsal scales are keeled and occur in 17 scale rows at midbody. The anal plate is divided, and the subcaudals occur in two rows.

The northern brown snake exhibits significant sexual dimorphism in body size and relative tail length. Adult males average 210.7 mm ($8\frac{5}{8}$ in.) SVL and 277.6 mm ($11\frac{1}{4}$ in.) ToL. Adult females average 254 mm ($10\frac{1}{8}$ in.) SVL and 315.8 mm ($12\frac{5}{8}$ in.) ToL. The record size for the subspecies is 491 mm ($15\frac{5}{8}$ in.) ToL (Conant and Collins 1991). The mean tail length of males is 32.5% of SVL and 24.1% of ToL. The mean tail length of females is 24.3% of SVL and 19.5% of ToL.

Neonates have a conspicuous yellow band or collar on the neck that is two or three scales wide and is bordered on either side by a thin dark brown or black line. The bodies of neonates are generally dark and unpatterned. H. Clausen (1936) reported that the young gradually take on the appearance of the adults with each successive shedding of their skin.

Confusing Species. Neonates can easily be confused with young ring-neck snakes, but northern brown snakes have keeled scales, whereas ring-neck snakes have smooth scales. Northern brown snakes differ from eastern earth snakes in having keeled scales and from mountain earth snakes in having seven supralabials rather than six.

Habitat and Habits. The northern brown snake is found in a wide variety of habitats in the Northeast, ranging from dense forests to open grasslands and vacant lots in urban environments and from dry hill sides to the marshy borders of ponds and lakes, provided that there are sufficient cover objects available for it to forage and take shelter under. It reaches its greatest densities in and around abandoned human habitation. Ernst and Barbour (1989) reported 603 individuals collected from an abandoned "shanty town" outside of Lancaster, Pennsylvania, in an area of about 2.1 ha (5 acres). Klemens (1993) stated that this species "thrives" in disturbed habitats in Connecticut.

In Pennsylvania, northern brown snakes have been found active in all months except January; however, normal activity does not begin until early April and usually ceases in mid-October. Males and females have somewhat different apparent annual activity patterns. Male activity is strongly bimodal, with an initial peak in April and May that corresponds with mating. Activity then sharply decreases in June and July and shows a second peak in August, with a gradual decline in September and October as they enter hibernation. Female activity gradually increases to an initial peak toward the end of May and then remains fairly constant until August, when annual activity increases to its highest level. As in the activity of males, there is a gradual decline in activity in September and October as the females enter hibernation. The August peak corresponds to parturition and probably postpartum foraging. This annual activity pattern is different from that reported by Gibbons and Semlitsch (1987) for brown snakes from South Carolina, where activity gradually increases throughout the spring and early summer, peaks in July, and then gradually declines through late summer and fall. This difference in activity patterns is most likely due to the overall more moderate climate of South Carolina. Annual activity appears to be of somewhat longer duration in Connecticut than in Pennsylvania; in Connecticut snakes emerge in March and enter hibernation in November (Klemens 1993).

Lachner (1942) reported finding five individuals burrowed 80 cm ($31\frac{1}{2}$ in.) deep in a gravel bank on 3 January in Mercer County, Pennsylvania. Bailey (1948) found a large number of individuals 20–50 cm (8–20 in.) below the surface in sandy loam soil on 22 March in Iowa. This den was composed of a series of small passageways in which the snakes were found. Those in the upper portion of the hibernaculum were dead, apparently the victims of freezing temperatures. Northern brown snakes utilize communal dens. H. Clausen (1936) reported that over 200 individuals were collected from four dens on Long Island. Noble and Clausen (1936) reported on groups of northern brown snakes that used rat burrows, ant mounds, and cracks and crevices as hibernating sites on Long Island. They reported that the snakes moved to these sites in October and November.

Northern brown snakes often share cover objects. Noble and Clausen (1936) reported finding as many as 12 individuals under a single cover object. However, gravid females, unlike gravid northern redbelly snakes (the other species in the genus), are apparently solitary. Burghardt (1983) noted aggregating behavior in neonate brown snakes and concurred with Noble and Clausen that visual stimuli appear to be more important in forming aggregations than olfactory stimuli.

Northern brown snakes feed almost exclusively on slugs and earthworms (Catling and Freedman 1980, Judd 1954). However, Surface (1906) and Atkinson (1901) reported that they eat insects and insect larvae in addition to slugs and earthworms in Pennsylvania. All specimens that we examined that contained food had fed on either slugs or worms. A report by Rossman and Myer (1990) documented the fact that brown snakes in captivity can extract snails from their shells. It is also possible that they do this in the wild and that some of the slugs in our feeding samples were actually shell-less snails.

Northern brown snakes are inoffensive animals that seldom if ever attempt to bite. Occasionally, an individual will assume a threatening position when discovered or handled. This generally involves forming a coil, depressing the body, expanding the head so that it becomes distinct from the neck and somewhat triangular in appearance, and striking repeatedly at any object that approaches it. Some individuals, when handled, curl their lips, thus exposing their teeth. This behavior is more common in northern redbelly snakes.

Reproduction. We have not observed mating or courtship in this species. H. Clausen (1936) and Noble and Clausen (1936) reported that mating occurs in March and April on Long Island, New York. This species is viviparous. Females emerge from hibernation with small ovarian follicles. Egg growth is rapid, and by mid-May most mature females contain enlarged oviducal eggs. Eggs at this time show no sign of embryonic development. By the end of June, embryonic development is well advanced, with the embryos exhibiting several body coils and having well-developed pigmented eyes. Parturition can occur as early as 11 July, but most females give birth in the first half of August. This schedule indicates an average gestation time of about 2.5 months. Ovarian eggs usually begin to enlarge shortly after parturition, and females enter hibernation with 3–4 mm eggs. The gestation period in Pennsylvania is similar to that of a population studied by Kofron (1979) in Louisiana. However, in Louisiana, ovulation and parturition occur about a month earlier than in Pennsylvania, reflecting the effects of the warmer climate on the timing of reproduction. In Pennsylvania, litter size varies from 5 to 25 young with a mean litter size of 14.2 ± 0.8 young $(N = 24)$. Litter size is correlated with the body size of the female; larger females have significantly larger litters. The mean litter size in Pennsylvania is virtually identical with the mean litter size in New York and Louisiana.

Neonates have a mean SVL of 74.5 mm (3 in.) and a mean ToL of 96.8 mm ($3\frac{7}{8}$ in.). This is similar to a mean ToL of 93.2 mm ($3\frac{3}{4}$ in.) for New York northern brown snakes (H. Clausen 1936).

Sexual maturity in females occurs at between 220 and 240 mm ($8\frac{3}{4}$–$9\frac{5}{8}$ in.) SVL in their second or third year, and in males at between 175 and 190 mm (7–$7\frac{3}{4}$ in.) SVL, probably in their second year. Reproductive maturity occurs at a much smaller size for females from southern populations. Kofron (1979) reported maturity at 170 mm ($6\frac{7}{8}$ in.) SVL. The sex ratio for males and females does not differ significantly from 1:1.

Remarks. Trapido (1944), in his review of the genus *Storeria*, described *Storeria dekayi wrightorum* partly on the basis of the dorsal spots' fusing to form crossbars, whereas in *S. d. dekayi* the spots remain separate and distinct. He suggested that populations of *S. dekayi* from extreme western Pennsylvania and eastern Ohio are intergrades between the two subspecies. Only 3.7% of a sample of 54 individuals from the western border counties of Pennsylvania exhibited any degree of crossbar pattern. In a sample of 184 specimens from statewide localities, 8.1% exhibited crossbar patterns. Although most of these were from the western half of the state, several specimens from Lancaster and Delaware counties also exhibited a crossbar pattern. As a result, it would appear that intergradation does not occur in Pennsylvania but that Pennsylvania *S. d. dekayi* generally exhibit a low frequency of crossbar pattern.

If one compares the statewide distribution of the northern brown snakes with that of the northern redbelly snake it becomes apparent that, for the most part, the two species have distributions that complement each other. The exceptions are the Allegheny Plateau in Forest, Venango, and Warren counties; northern Somerset County; and extreme eastern Westmoreland County. The northern brown snake appears to be mostly restricted to low elevations, whereas the northern redbelly snake is more commonly found in higher or more mountainous areas. Where they co-occur in Westmoreland and Somerset counties, most northern brown snakes are located in valleys and most northern redbelly snake are located on the ridges or in the mountains. Klemens (1993) noted the same pattern of distribution for northern brown snakes and northern redbelly snakes in Connecticut and adjacent Massachusetts.

Distribution. The northern brown snake occurs from southern Maine through most of New England, westward through southern Canada to Michigan, southward through South Carolina, and westward through eastern Kentucky and Ohio.

This snake is found throughout most of the Northeast, from southern Maine and the southern two-thirds of New Hampshire and Vermont south through New England, New York, and New Jersey. The northern brown snake exhibits a disjunct distribution pattern in Pennsylvania. It is widely distributed throughout the western third and the southeastern portion of the state. It is absent from the north-central and northeastern sections of the state. Its occurrence in the central portion of the state is scattered and is based largely on literature records that may not be accurate. Intensive searching in many areas where it is absent has failed to produce any specimens. Its range in the state may be restricted owing to competition with the northern redbelly snake.

Northern Redbelly Snake *Storeria occipitomaculata occipitomaculata* (Storer)

L. *occipito,* the back part of the head; L. *macula,* spot

Description.   The northern redbelly snake is a small, rather stout species whose coloration and pattern are extremely variable (Plates 124 and 125). The dorsal background coloration may be light tan to dark brown, reddish brown, gray, or black, although some shade of brown is most common. A midvertebral stripe generally three scale rows wide (occasionally four) is often, but not always, present. When present, it is lighter than the surrounding background coloration and is generally set off from it by lines of alternating white and dark spots. The skin between the scales is black and, as a result, if the body is distended by either food or embryos, individual scales may appear to be edged with black. The neck invariably has three light-colored spots (one medial and two lateral) that

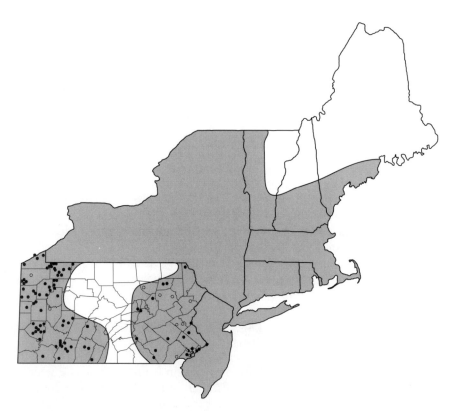

Map 75.   Distribution of the northern brown snake *(Storeria dekayi dekayi).*

vary in color from pale cream to yellow. Occasionally, these spots may fuse to form a pale-colored bar, which is usually separated from the light-colored ventrals by a band of dark pigment. The dorsal head coloration is similar to, but generally darker than, the dorsal body color. A light spot is present on the upper labials, just posterior to the eye.

The ventral color generally varies from yellow to light pink to dark red and extends to the tip of the tail. The intensity of the ventral coloration tends to decrease from midbody toward the throat. The general background coloration of the throat and chin is white. The dorsal body coloration extends onto the ventral scutes, suffusing this region with dark pigment spots, giving the general appearance of two dark stripes bordering the bright ventral pigmentation. Anteriorly, in the region of the throat and chin, these dark lateral stripes break up into a series of irregular dark spots. The width of the red belly stripe is variable, ranging from 20% to 80% of the width of the ventral scutes. Occasionally, the belly is gray to jet black.

The dorsal scales are keeled and occur in 15 rows at midbody. The anal plate is divided, and the subcaudals occur in two rows.

Northern redbelly snakes exhibit significant sexual dimorphism in size. Adult males average 213.1 mm ($8\frac{3}{5}$ in.) SVL and 283.3 mm ($11\frac{3}{5}$ in.) ToL. Females average 245.9 mm ($9\frac{4}{5}$ in.) SVL and 308.5 mm ($12\frac{1}{4}$ in.) ToL. The record size for the species is 406 mm ($8\frac{1}{4}$ in.) ToL (Conant 1975). Males have a significantly longer tail than females. The mean tail length for males is 31.7% of SVL and 24% of ToL. For females, it is 25.9% of SVL and 20.4% of ToL. Both males and females achieve a much greater size in the northern portion of their range than in the southern portion.

Confusing Species.   Neonate northern redbelly snakes could be confused with neonate northern ringneck snakes. The belly of the ringneck snake, however, is usually bright yellow, and the dorsal scales are smooth. Adult northern redbelly snakes might be confused with earth snakes or with the northern brown snake. Northern redbelly snakes always have three pale spots on their neck. These spots are absent from both earth and northern brown snakes.

Habitat and Habits.   The northern redbelly snake is primarily an inhabitant of deciduous hardwood forests and upland regions. It has, however, been reported from coastal Massachusetts (Lazell 1976b) and from Long Island, New York (Klemens 1993). Although often found in dense forest, northern redbelly snakes are most common in open canopy woodland and along ecotonal areas where woods merge with fields or streams and there is an abundance of open habitat near woods. Northern redbelly snakes are secretive and are seldom found crawling or basking on the surface. They are most frequently encountered under rocks, logs, bark, and other types of natural cover. Their specific microhabitat requirements remain unknown. In some areas, they are extremely abundant, whereas in other, apparently similar, environments they are completely absent.

In Pennsylvania, northern redbelly snakes first begin to emerge from hibernation around 15 April. Activity remains fairly constant from May through August, then begins to taper off in September. All surface activity stops around 15 October. This annual cycle is similar to that reported by Klemens (1993) for Connecticut populations and by Lang (1969) for populations from Minnesota, but it is much shorter than the annual activity cycle in the southern portion of the range (Semlitsch and Moran 1984). We have not found hibernacula for this species in Pennsylvania, but Lang (1969) and Criddle (1937) reported that northern redbelly snakes use abandoned ant nests as hibernacula. Lang reported an incredible 577 of these snakes from a single ant mound in Minnesota. In areas where northern redbelly snakes are abundant, they can be found under suitable cover both during the day and at night and thus appear to have no strongly developed daily activity preferences.

It is common to find two or more northern redbelly snakes, especially gravid females, using the same cover object. We have found as many as seven gravid females congregating under a single rock, when the majority of other cover objects in the area harbored no snakes. Whether individuals are attracted to each other or to specific environmental conditions of the cover object remains unknown.

Northern redbelly snakes in the Northeast feed almost exclusively on slugs. There are a few reports of their feeding on earthworms in addition to slugs in other portions of the range. Rossman and Myer (1990) demonstrated that individuals from the south can extract snails from their shells, so food identified as slugs may in fact be shell-less snails. Semlitsch and Moran (1984) noted pulses of activity associated with cycles of habitat drying. They suggested that the increased activity was the result of the snakes' tracking their food (slugs) along a moisture gradient. Differences in the abundance of slugs may be responsible for differences in the abundance of snakes in environments that otherwise appear to be very similar.

Northern redbelly snakes are inoffensive and are not known to bite. When handled, however, they will thrash about and discharge an unpleasant musk along with feces. Some specimens will, when disturbed, curl their lips, thereby exposing their teeth in what appears to be a sneer. The exact purpose of this behavior remains unclear, but it may be a defense behavior designed to frighten potential predators. If the head is drawn backward across the handler's skin while the teeth are exposed, an abrasion may result.

Reproduction.   We have not observed mating in this species, but literature accounts (Trapido 1940) suggest that it may occur at any time of the activity season and that females store sperm until ovulation of eggs in the spring. Enlarged oviducal eggs first appear in late May and early June in Pennsylvania. This species is viviparous, with the young developing within the mother's body. Parturition occurs from late July through early September, with the majority of females giving birth in mid to late August. In Pennsylvania, litter size varies from 4 to 21 young, which is higher than for populations from either Michigan (Blanchard 1937) or South Carolina (Semlitsch and Moran 1984). Litter size is positively correlated with female body size; larger females have larger litters. Litter size in Pennsylvania is much larger than that reported for more northern populations. Klemens (1993) reported a range of from 5 to 9 young from Connecticut, and Gilhen (1984) reported a range of from 3 to 12 for specimens from Nova Scotia, Canada. Neonates have a mean SVL of 73.8 mm ($2\frac{7}{8}$ in.) and a mean ToL of 96.7 mm ($3\frac{7}{8}$ in.).

Sexual maturity for both sexes is probably achieved in the third year of life at a SVL of about 185 mm ($7\frac{3}{8}$ in.) for females and about 170 mm ($6\frac{3}{4}$ in.) for males. The sex ratio for adults is skewed in favor of females. The sex ratio in neonates is about 1:1 in Pennsylvania. Blanchard (1937) noted a similar tendency in a Michigan population.

Remarks.   Jordan (1970) noted true death-feigning behavior in a gravid female from Georgia. Disturbance caused this animal to roll over, open its mouth, protrude its tongue, and contort its body. If righted, it would turn back to expose its ventral surface. This behavior continued for several weeks in captivity, but the response slowly diminished with time. We have not noted this behavior in the numerous individuals we have collected and handled. We have, however, frequently observed a different defensive behavior in this species. Upon capture, many individuals will flare their upper lips, thus exposing their maxillary teeth. This behavior is usually accompanied by the snake's attempting to rub the side of its head, with exposed teeth, against its captor's body.

Distribution.   The northern redbelly snake ranges from Maine and the Maritime Provinces of Canada westward to Manitoba and eastern North Dakota. The range extends southward to Oklahoma and Arkansas in the West and to South Carolina and northern Georgia in the East.

The species is widespread throughout the Northeast. In Pennsylvania, the northern redbelly snake is found primarily in the northern portion of the state, with its range extending southward in the Ridge and Valley Province. It is absent from most of the southern dissected plateau and from the southeastern lowlands.

Thamnophis
Gr. *thamnos*, bush; Gr. *ophis*, snake

The genus *Thamnophis* contains the garter snakes and the ribbon snakes. There are approximately 23 species of garter and ribbon snakes. The genus ranges from the Atlantic to Pacific oceans and from central Canada, throughout the United States, into central Costa Rica.

Garter snakes are small to medium-sized, slender to moderately built snakes. Their habitats range from completely terrestrial to semiaquatic. They may often be seen moving about or basking and are often the most frequently observed snake in an area. They frequently can also be found by looking under cover objects. When captured, they generally release an unpleasant musk. Their demeanor when captured is exceedingly variable, ranging from docile to extremely aggressive. Many species, when first approached, will flatten their head and body and hiss and strike at an intruder.

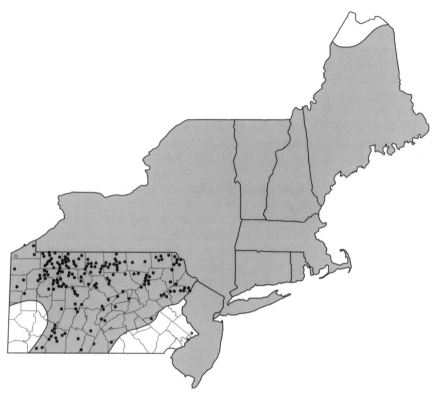

Map 76. Distribution of the northern redbelly snake *(Storeria occipitomac-ulata occipitomaculata).*

Garter snakes consume a wide variety of food items including worms, salamanders, fish, frogs and toads, tadpoles, small mammals, and small birds. Some species have a very specialized diet; others are generalized feeders. All species are viviparous.

Shorthead Garter Snake *Thamnophis brachystoma* (Cope)
Gr. *brachy,* wide; Gr. *stoma,* mouth
Description.   The shorthead garter snake (Plate 126) is a small to medium-sized species. The dorsal background coloration is usually olive to olive-brown. The dorsal pattern generally consists of one vertebral and two lateral stripes. The vertebral stripe varies from beige to yellowish and is very bright and distinct from the background coloration. The lateral stripes are dull buff and not as distinctly set off from the background as is the vertebral stripe. This is the dorsal pattern exhibited by about 98% of all individuals. Occasionally, individuals occur that have a greenish brown and indistinct vertebral stripe, but their lateral stripes are similar to those in the typical pattern. On these individuals, all of the stripes are bordered by a series of small black spots. On all specimens, the venter is

without markings and varies from tan to dark grayish green. The head is usually colored similarly to the body. The supralabials are separated by dark margins. The chin and throat vary from cream-colored to yellow and are immaculate.

The head is not distinct from the body and appears to be too small for the body. The dorsal scales are keeled and occur in 17 rows (occasionally 19) at midbody. The anal plate is entire, and the subcaudals are in two rows.

Shorthead garter snakes exhibit significant sexual dimorphism in both body size and body proportions. Adult males average 273.1 mm ($10\frac{7}{8}$ in.) SVL and 366.8 mm ($14\frac{5}{8}$ in.) ToL. Mature females average 325.3 mm (13 in.) SVL and 418 mm ($16\frac{3}{8}$ in.) ToL. The maximum size for the species is 559 mm ($22\frac{3}{8}$ in.) ToL (Conant and Collins 1991). Males have a significantly longer tail than females. The mean tail length for males is 34.8% of SVL and 25.6% of ToL. For females, the mean tail length is 29.7% of SVL and 23% of ToL. The tail proportions are similar to those reported by Pisani and Bothner (1970) for a population from the vicinity of Olean, New York. Adult SVLs for the Olean population, however, were much smaller than for Pennsylvania populations: the mean SVL of males was 256.2 mm ($10\frac{1}{4}$ in.), and that of females was 273.5 mm (11 in.).

Confusing Species. The only species that the shorthead garter snake could be confused with is the eastern garter snake. The shorthead garter snake differs from the eastern garter snake in that it lacks blotches or other markings between the vertebral and lateral stripes and has an extremely short head that is indistinct from the neck.

Habitat and Habits. The shorthead garter snake is primarily an inhabitant of open country, although it is occasionally found in dense woods. It most commonly occurs in old fields, meadows, and ecotonal areas between woods and fields. Often, but not always, it is found in the vicinity of streams or rivers (within a few hundred meters).

Shorthead garter snakes are occasionally found actively moving about or basking, especially in the spring, but are more frequently found under cover objects such as stones, logs, and debris (e.g., boards and shingles). Ernst and Barbour (1989) stated that during warm months these snakes frequently bask in the sun. This has not been our experience. During June, July, and August we have almost invariably found shorthead garter snakes under cover objects. The exception is during cool cloudy weather, when they are sometimes found actively crawling on the surface.

Seasonal activity in Pennsylvania begins as early as 7 April, but snakes do not become common until the second half of the month. Activity levels remain fairly constant through May, then reach a peak in mid-June. Activity declines dramatically in July, exhibits a second peak in August, probably as a function of parturition, then gradually declines through September and October. All snakes enter hibernation by the end of October or the beginning of November.

Hibernacula have not been reported from Pennsylvania, but Bothner (1963) reported a hibernaculum from adjacent Cattaraugus County, New

York. It was found on a west-facing shale bank located approximately 60 m (200 ft) from a stream. The entrance was a small (2.5 cm [1 in.] square) opening between two large pieces of shale about halfway up a 4-m (13-ft) bank. The hibernaculum did not contain an actual chamber; rather, the snakes were found "wedged" into cracks and crevices. The soil was saturated and had an ambient temperature that varied only at about 2.5°C (37°–38°F). A total of 12 individuals were found at depths varying from 50 to 115 cm (18–46 in.). The hibernaculum was shared with red-spotted newts, spotted salamanders, and northern redbelly snakes.

Individuals of this species are gregarious. It is common to find two or more sharing a single cover object. This gregarious behavior does not seem to be a function of either season or reproductive condition. Individuals have been found congregating at all times during the activity season, from April to September, and congregations have involved both males and females (both gravid and nongravid). Shorthead garter snakes are often found associated with ringneck snakes and less commonly with eastern garter snakes and northern redbelly snakes. Individuals, when displaced, rapidly return to their original cover object. On one occasion, a large (1.2 m²; 6 ft²) sheet of plywood was found to harbor 11 individuals.

Shorthead garter snakes feed exclusively on earthworms. In captivity, they feed readily on worms but refuse other potential foods (e.g., salamanders, young frogs, and fish).

Shorthead garter snakes never attempt to bite but will often thrash about violently and release feces and musk.

Reproduction.   Courtship and mating occur in the spring, shortly after emergence from hibernation. In Pennsylvania, females usually emerge from hibernation with moderately well-developed ovarian follicles. Follicular growth is rapid, and ovulation takes place from the end of May to early June. Shorthead garter snakes are viviparous, and by late June well-formed embryos are present in the oviducts. Parturition occurs in August. Litter size ranges from 5 to 14 young and is positively correlated with female body size. Neonates average 111.3 mm (4½ in.) SVL and 148.5 mm (5⅞ in.) ToL. Some of the above reproductive characters differ significantly from those observed by Pisani and Bothner (1970) for a population from Olean, New York. In that population, the average size of neonates was smaller, as was the litter size; however, females were smaller, too. Pisani and Bothner also suggested that the population had a biennial reproductive cycle. They based this suggestion on the fact that approximately 25% of the potentially reproductive females did not contain eggs or embryos during the breeding season. This is not the case in Pennsylvania, where virtually 100% of mature females examined were reproductively active each year.

Males exhibit a typical temperate-zone reproductive cycle. They emerge from hibernation with small testes. Testicular growth is rapid during the spring and early summer, and by mid-July the testes are at a maximum size. At this time, the testes begin to regress and are very small when the snakes enter hibernation. In late summer, while the testes are regressing, mature sperm are evacuated into the vas deferens, where they are stored through the winter for use in the spring mating season.

Males and females both mature in their second or third season. Males mature at about 200 mm (8 in.) SVL and 261 mm (10½ in.) ToL, and females mature at about 273 mm SVL (10⅞ in.) and 350 mm (14 in.) ToL.

Remarks.   Within its limited geographic range, the shorthead garter snake is extremely abundant, but its numbers drop off sharply along the edge of the range (Conant 1950). This sharp delineation of range would seem to indicate a species with very stringent ecological requirements that are met in only a small circumscribed area. This, however, appears not to be the case. When introduced outside of its normal range the species often becomes well established. Introduced populations have remained viable for more than 25 years in Pittsburgh, and other populations in Erie and Butler counties also appear to be well established.

Bothner (1976) expressed concern that the species might be declining, especially in the northern part of its range. He felt that the decline was due to expansion of the range of and subsequent replacement by the eastern garter snake. It is not clear whether replacement is occurring in Pennsylvania, but population numbers and community composition should be monitored for changes.

Distribution.   The shorthead garter snake has one of the most restricted ranges of any species of snake that occurs in the United States. It occurs primarily in the unglaciated portion of the Allegheny Plateau. Its natural range extends from the southern-tier counties of New York southward into the unglaciated area of Pennsylvania.

Its occurrence in basically urban areas of Allegheny, Butler, and Erie counties, Pennsylvania, is the result of human introductions (either intentional or unintentional). Netting (in Conant 1950) considered the records from eastern Mercer County, Pennsylvania, to be introductions. That area, however, is near the unglaciated area and probably represents a slight natural expansion of the species' range.

Eastern Ribbon Snake/Northern Ribbon Snake *Thamnophis sauritus sauritus* (Linnaeus)/*Thamnophis sauritus septentrionalis*

L. *septentrionalis*, northern. Gr. *sauros*, like a lizard

Description.   There are two subspecies of ribbon snake in the Northeast: eastern ribbon snake (*Thamnophis sauritus sauritus*) and northern ribbon snake (*Thamnophis sauritus septentrionalis*; see Remarks).

The eastern ribbon snake (Plate 127) is a moderately long, slender species. The dorsal pattern consists of three longitudinal stripes. The vertebral stripe involves the vertebral scale row plus the medial half of each adjacent row of scales and varies in color from golden yellow to yellowish brown. The lateral stripes involve scale rows 3 and 4 on each side of the body and are light yellow. The lateral stripes extend onto the tail but quickly grow indistinct, whereas the dorsal stripe extends to the tip of the tail. The region between the dorsal and lateral stripes varies from reddish

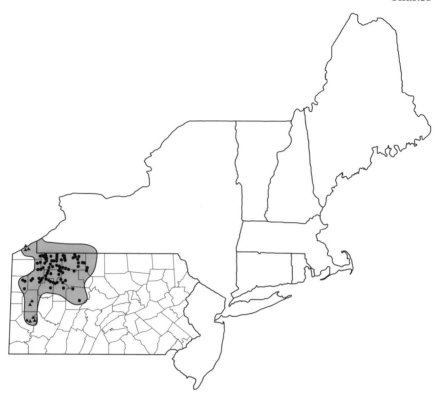

Map 77. Distribution of the shorthead garter snake *(Thamnophis brachys-toma)*. Triangles represent established introductions.

brown to black, while the ventrolateral regions are brownish. The venter is immaculate and varies from yellow to green. The dorsal surface of the head is brown and may have black maculations. Light spots are occasionally present on the parietals. The supralabials are mostly white and tend to be set off from the brown head by a thin black line. The preocular and first postocular tend to be white.

The head is moderately distinct from the body, and the eyes are large. The body is slender, and the tail is very long. The dorsal scales are keeled and occur in 19 rows at midbody. The anal plate is single, and the subcaudals occur in two rows.

The northern ribbon snake is similar but smaller and darker (see Remarks).

Pennsylvania's eastern ribbon snakes exhibit significant sexual dimorphism in both body size and relative tail length. Males average 400.5 mm (16 in.) SVL and 614.5 mm ($24\frac{1}{2}$ in.) ToL. Females average 459.3 mm ($18\frac{3}{8}$ in.) SVL and 682 mm ($27\frac{1}{4}$ in.) ToL. The maximum ToL is 965 mm ($38\frac{1}{2}$ in.) (Conant and Collins 1991). Males have a proportionately longer tail than females. The mean tail length for males is 53.3% of SVL and 34.2% of ToL, whereas in females the mean tail length is 48.6% of SVL and 32.6% of ToL.

Confusing Species.   The combination of the longitudinally striped body and extremely long tail distinguishes this species from all other snakes occurring in the Northeast.

Habitat and Habits.   Eastern ribbon snakes may be found in a wide variety of habitats, including, but not restricted to, rocky hillsides, grassy fields, deciduous forests, sandy beaches, and swamps, bogs, and other wetlands. Their main requirement, whatever the habitat may be, is proximity to a permanent water source. The permanent water can be either standing (e.g., lakes, ponds, bogs, or marshes) or flowing (streams, rivers, and springs). Eastern ribbon snakes are semiarboreal and are often found in bushes and shrubs. Carpenter (1952) reported that 61% of the animals he found in the summer were encountered in bushes, and Rossman (1963) reported it common to find them 60–120 cm (2–4 ft) off the ground. The slender body and long thin tail of the species are ideally suited to a partially arboreal existence.

On the basis of museum records for Pennsylvania, the sexes appear to have distinctly different seasonal activity patterns. Males may emerge as early as late March. Activity increases until a peak is reached in May, after which activity drops precipitously and remains very low throughout the summer. There is a second, but lesser, peak of activity in September. Female activity, in contrast, is not distinctly bimodal. Emergence occurs in April, and activity gradually increases in May. Activity remains fairly constant through June and July. It rapidly increases to a peak in August and sharply declines in September. The difference in male and female activity cycles is most likely due to different sexual schedules. Maximal male activity in May corresponds to the time of the year when courtship and mating occur. Peak female activity in August is correlated with the birth of young.

Eastern ribbon snakes are primarily diurnal in the Northeast; however, Rossman (1963) reported that in the south they are nocturnal, especially during the summer.

In Pennsylvania, eastern ribbon snakes have been found hibernating in shale banks at a depth of about 80 cm (32 in.) (Lachner 1942). In Michigan, they have been reported to use ant mounds, meadow vole tunnels, and rocky south-facing hillsides as hibernation sites (Carpenter 1952, 1953). In Connecticut, they have been reported to hibernate along trap rock ridges and in the old ties and beds of railroads (Klemens 1993).

There is virtually complete agreement that these snakes feed almost exclusively on amphibians, with anurans making up the bulk of the diet (E. Brown 1979a, 1979b; Carpenter 1952). Large specimens feed on larger species such as leopard frogs, green frogs, and American toads, whereas smaller individuals utilize predominantly small frogs such as cricket frogs, spring peepers, and chorus frogs. Hammerson (in Klemens 1993) reported the stomach contents of 16 specimens as follows: red spotted newt (in 6 specimens), northern spring peeper (8), green frog (3), and pickerel frog (1).

This amphibian diet closely agrees with the fact that, although they are found in a wide variety of habitats, eastern ribbon snakes are never found far from water.

When first encountered, eastern ribbon snakes attempt to escape, either into the water, where they rapidly swim away on the surface (seldom diving), or into dense vegetation. Their striped body pattern functions as a predator avoidance mechanism. It is difficult for a potential predator to determine either speed or direction of movement, since the continuous stripes allow for no visual reference point (see J. Jackson et al. 1976 for a detailed discussion of pattern and escape behavior). Eastern ribbon snakes seldom attempt to bite but will thrash about violently and discharge musk and feces when captured.

Reproduction.   Courtship and mating occur in April and May. Eggs are ovulated by the end of May. The eastern ribbon snake, like other members of the genus *Thamnophis*, is viviparous. By the end of June, embryos have two or three body coils and are easily recognized as young snakes. The embryos are fully developed (i.e., scaled and pigmented) by the end of July or the beginning of August. Birth generally occurs in August.

In a sample of Pennsylvania eastern ribbon snakes, litter size ranged from 8 to 13 young and was weakly correlated with female body size. Litter size over the entire range of the species varies from 3 to 26 young (Rossman 1963). It varies dramatically from one population to another but shows no distinct geographic trend.

Pennsylvania neonates have a mean SVL of 158.5 mm ($6\frac{3}{8}$ in.) and a mean ToL of 236 mm ($9\frac{1}{2}$ in.). This is similar to the size of neonates reported by Klemens (1993) in other parts of the Northeast. The tail length of juveniles is proportionately shorter than that of adults. The average tail length of juveniles is 47.5% of SVL and 32% of ToL.

Males from Pennsylvania mature at a SVL of about 330 mm ($13\frac{1}{4}$ in.) and a ToL of around 475 mm (19 in.). Females mature at a SVL of about 370 mm ($14\frac{3}{4}$ in.) and a ToL of about 540 mm (22 in.) and are probably 3 years old at that size. This is slightly smaller than the 420 mm ($16\frac{3}{4}$ in.) SVL reported by Carpenter (1952) for a Michigan population.

Remarks.   Rossman (1963) recognized four subspecies of eastern ribbon snake. The two that occur in the Northeast, the eastern ribbon snake and the northern ribbon snake, are primarily distinguished by relatively qualitative characters of color and by a difference in relative tail length. According to Rossman (1970) the eastern ribbon snake has a "relatively longer tail," whereas the northern ribbon snake's tail is "relatively short." The dorsum of the eastern ribbon snake is reddish brown with a golden-yellow vertebral stripe. That of the northern ribbon snake is velvety black or dark brown with a yellow vertebral stripe, often overlaid with brown. Tail lengths prove difficult to use because relative tail length varies with the size of the individual. Moreover, ribbon snakes exhibit a high percentage of broken tails. Therefore, the ranges of the two subspecies remain uncertain in Pennsylvania and will be resolved only with additional live material from critical areas.

As mentioned above, eastern ribbon snakes have a relatively long tail and have a tendency to exhibit tail loss. Tail loss presumably occurs as a result of unsuccessful attempts on the part of predators to capture the snakes. It has often been used as an indicator of predation pressure, with more frequent tail loss indicating greater predation (see Schoener 1979 for a critique of this assumption). Willis and colleagues (1982) noted a mean tail loss frequency of 7% for males and 12% for females in a Michigan population. The difference in frequency between sexes is significant and seems to indicate that females experience greater risk of predation than males. Tail loss frequency also increased with increasing size, suggesting that the probability of encountering a predator increases with age. A sample of specimens from Pennsylvania showed a much higher frequency of tail loss. Females had a tail loss frequency of 35.7%, and males 29.4%. As in the Michigan population, there was a significant increase in the frequency of tail loss with increasing size. The difference in frequency between the sexes might indicate that females are at greater risk of predation owing to viviparity, since the mass of the developing young may decrease female mobility.

Distribution. As its name implies, the eastern ribbon snake's range involves most of the eastern United States. Its range extends from southern Maine through New England to Florida. The range extends westward through southern Ontario and Michigan and southward through Indiana, Kentucky, and most of Tennessee and Mississippi.

In the Northeast, the northern ribbon snake occurs from western Pennsylvania through New York, excluding the southeastern part of that state, and into central Vermont and New Hampshire and southwestern Maine. The eastern ribbon snake ranges from eastern Pennsylvania and New Jersey into southeastern New York and throughout the southern New England states to southern Vermont, New Hampshire, and extreme southern Maine.

The precise distribution of the two subspecies of ribbon snake in Pennsylvania are not known. The eastern ribbon snake occurs throughout the Coastal Plain and Piedmont provinces as well as most of the Valley and Ridge Province. Northwestern populations (i.e., Erie, Crawford, and Mercer counties) are northern ribbon snakes. The remaining populations that occur in the northeastern and south-central portions of the state are of undetermined status. It is especially in these areas where additional surveys need to be made to elucidate the precise distribution of the subspecies in the state.

Eastern Garter Snake/Maritime Garter Snake *Thamnophis sirtalis sirtalis* (Linnaeus)/*Thamnophis sirtalis pallidulus*

L. *pallidula*, pale L. *sirtalis*, like a garter

Description. There are two subspecies of garter snake in the Northeast: eastern garter snake (*Thamnophis sirtalis sirtalis*) and maritime garter snake (*Thamnophis sirtalis pallidulus*; see Remarks).

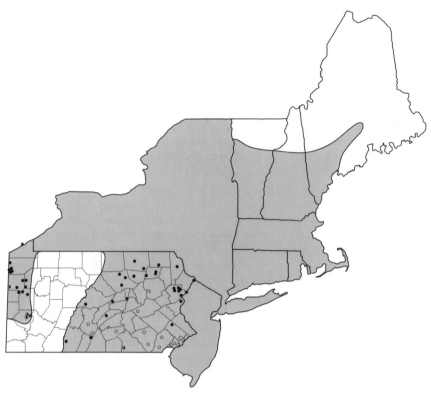

Map 78. Distribution of the eastern ribbon snake *(Thamnophis sauritus)*.

The eastern garter snake (Plate 128) is a medium-sized, fairly heavy-bodied species. Its pattern generally consists of a medial stripe and two lateral stripes (involving scale rows 2 and 3) on a background that varies from dark green to olive-brown to black. The stripes are usually yellow but may occasionally have a greenish or bluish cast to them. Although the dorsal stripe is normally well developed, it may at times be interrupted by dark bars or be absent. The areas between the stripes, especially on neonates and subadults, usually have two alternating rows of dark spots that, when well developed, give the animal a blotched appearance. The spots are highly visible when the body is distended after a large meal. The dorsal surface of the head is a darker shade of the background coloration and is generally without markings, except for two small white or yellow spots that usually occur on the parietal scales near the midline of the head, often giving the appearance of a single spot. The ventral coloration varies from yellow to green, and each side of the venter is marked with a lateral row of small dark spots that may be hidden by the overlapping ventral scales. Both albino (Barton 1947, Hensley 1959) and melanistic individuals have been reported (Blanchard and Blanchard 1940, Gibson and

Falls 1988, King 1988). In addition, Carpenter (1948) reported decidedly red specimens from Michigan.

The dorsal scales are keeled and occur in 19 rows at midbody. The anal scale is entire, and the subcaudals occur in two rows.

The maritime garter snake is smaller, and its pattern of stripes is less distinct (see Remarks).

Eastern garter snakes exhibit significant sexual dimorphism in both body size and body proportions. Males are the smaller sex, as evident in a sample from randomly selected sites around Pennsylvania. Males averaged 337.6 mm (13½ in.) SVL and 444.5 mm (17¾ in.) ToL. Females averaged 439 mm (17½ in.) SVL and 550.3 mm (22 in.) ToL. Those sizes represent the normal range of size in most populations in the Northeast. Larger individuals do exist (1,000–1,100 mm [40–44 in.] ToL), and the record length is 1,238 mm (49½ in.) (Conant and Collins 1991). Males have a significantly longer tail than females. In males, the tail averages 32.1% of SVL and 24.2% of ToL. In females, it is only 27.6% of SVL and 21.6% of ToL.

Confusing Species. The garter snake differs from the eastern ribbon snake in that the lateral stripes are on scale rows 2 and 3 rather than 3 and 4. It differs from the shorthead garter snake in that the head is somewhat distinct from the body and that there are usually distinct blotches between the vertebral and lateral stripes.

Habitat and Habits. The garter snake is the most commonly encountered species of snake in the Northeast and also has the greatest range of habitat utilization of any species in the region. Garter snakes are found in virtually all habitats, from open talus slides and cultivated fields to closed-canopy deciduous and coniferous forests and from swamps, marshes, and bogs to dry upland habitats. They are frequently encountered around human habitations and are the snakes that people most often see.

Eastern garter snakes have been found active every month of the year in Pennsylvania. Normal activity begins between 15 and 25 March and continues until the end of October or the beginning of November. Warm fall weather will often extend the activity season into late November or early December. We have seen as many as seven adults active on a warm afternoon in late November. Annual activity generally increases rapidly from late March through April and reaches a peak in May. Activity then remains high throughout the summer and gradually tapers off in September and October. Daily activity time varies with season. During the spring and fall, eastern garter snakes are primarily diurnal and active in the middle of the day. With increasing daytime temperature in summer, activity patterns change, and most individuals are active either in early morning or in late afternoon and early evening. Some nocturnal activity does occur in the summer. Of all northeastern snakes, this species is the one most likely to be found moving about on roads at night.

We have not observed hibernation in the Northeast, but Carpenter (1953) reported that garter snakes use ant mounds, vole tunnels, and crayfish burrows as hibernation sites in Michigan. Costanzo (1989) reported on a population of garter snakes from Wisconsin that utilized an abandoned farm well. The snakes actually hibernated underwater and obtained oxygen by means of cutaneous rather than pulmonary gas exchange. Indeed, he suggested that survival might be higher than in terrestrial situations owing to the reduced chance of dehydration.

Eastern garter snakes appear to be rather sedentary animals. Several authors (Carpenter 1952, H. Fitch and Shirer 1971, Freedman and Catling 1979) have commented on their tendency to move only very short distances on a daily basis. Garter snakes may, however, travel long distances between their summer activity area and winter hibernation site if suitable hibernacula are scarce.

It is common to find two or more garter snakes sharing a single cover object, and we have found as many as six under a single rock. Neonate garter snakes have a strong tendency to aggregate with conspecifics in the laboratory (Burghardt 1983). Heller and Halpern (1981), in a laboratory experiment using a simple Y maze, showed that snakes preferred areas previously occupied ("conditioned") by large numbers of conspecifics. The environmental cues for site selection in aggregation behavior remain unknown.

A review of the literature indicates that eastern garter snakes are generalized feeders that take a wide variety of both vertebrate and invertebrate prey items. A more careful examination of the literature reveals that, although diet is varied throughout the snake's geographic range, it tends to be more restricted at a regional or local level. For example, E. Brown (1979a) noted that, in the Carolinas, amphibians (both salamanders and frogs) predominated in the diet, with worms being a minor component, but Hamilton (1951) showed that in New York, the majority of food consumed by garter snakes was worms. Fish were virtually absent in both of the above studies, but Lagler and Salyer (1945) showed that, at fish cultural stations in Michigan, fish constituted 42.9% of the diet of garter snakes. In Pennsylvania specimens that we examined, worms accounted for 87% of the diet and salamanders and anurans accounted for the rest. Although fish were never noted in the diet of wild specimens, they were readily consumed by captive individuals. Burghardt (1975) found that ingestively naive neonates showed a marked preference for worm extract. Burghardt and Denny (1983) demonstrated that, although olfaction is important, movement is the main cue that initiates attack behavior.

When first encountered, garter snakes generally attempt to escape. If escape is impossible, then aggressive behavior, varying from individual to individual, is displayed. At one extreme, some remain fairly quiescent and allow themselves to be picked up and will not attempt any defensive behavior. At the other extreme, individuals flatten the head and body, flare the lips to expose the teeth, and strike violently. If they bite, they tend to hold on and chew. The reasons for these differences in behavior remain unknown, but digestive state may influence at least some individual behavior. Hertzog and Bailey (1987) have shown that young individuals are more aggressive shortly after eating a large meal. The reason may be that a large meal adversely affects locomotor activity (Ford and

Shuttlesworth 1986) and as a result reduces the probability of successful escape. No matter how passive or aggressive, most individuals release musk and feces if picked up.

Reproduction.   Courtship and mating occur primarily in April and May, although there may be some mating activity in the fall (September and October). Females release sex pheromones that attract males. It has been shown that males are most effective in trailing and locating females in the spring and have reduced effectiveness in the fall. In midsummer, males do not respond to female sex pheromones (Ford 1981). This variation in the responsiveness of males in the laboratory corresponds to the actual mating activity of males in the wild. Occasionally, more than one male will trail a single female. When this happens a "ball" of snakes may result. This is an intertwined mass of snakes that may comprise 20 or more individuals (Gardner 1955). Balls of snakes have been observed in Pennsylvania in both spring and fall. One particularly large ball of snakes caused a great deal of excitement when it rolled down the side of a hill into a suburban Pittsburgh bus stop during the height of morning rush hour (McCoy, pers. obser.).

It has long been known that after sperm transfer male eastern garter snakes deposit material that produces a copulatory plug (Blanchard and Blanchard 1942). It has been suggested that this is an adaptation to prevent sperm competition by inhibiting the female from future mating. Schwartz and colleagues (1989) demonstrated that multiple paternity is common in garter snakes, suggesting that the copulatory plug is ineffective in preventing sperm competition.

Females exhibit a pattern in which all yolking of follicles occurs in the spring after emergence from hibernation. Follicular growth is fairly rapid, and by the middle of May follicles are of ovulatory size. Eastern garter snakes are viviparous, and the young develop in the oviducts. Eastern garter snakes have an extended parturition season, from early August to the end of September. The litter size from a sample of Pennsylvania animals ranged from 4 to 30 young and was strongly correlated with female body size. Seigel and Fitch (1985) showed dramatic yearly fluctuations in litter size in a Kansas population. Over a 9-year period, the mean clutch size varied from 11.2 to 23.3 young. They found that clutch size was larger in wet years and smaller in dry years. Occasional large litters (up to 85 young) have been reported, but these appear to be exceptions (H. Fitch 1970).

Females mature at between 360 and 380 mm ($14\frac{3}{8}$–$15\frac{1}{4}$ in.) SVL. Males mature at a smaller size. The smallest mature male found in Pennsylvania had a SVL of 270 mm ($10\frac{3}{4}$ in.).

The female reproductive cycle in the Northeast appears to be annual. H. Fitch (1965) noted in Kansas that the frequency of annual, rather than biennial, reproduction increased with age. All animals of a reproductive size that we examined and collected during the reproductive season were gravid. Dunlap and Lang (1990) made an interesting observation concerning maternal size and the sex ratio of neonates. They suggested that small females tend to produce litters in which females predominate and large females produce litters in which males predominate.

Remarks.   The two subspecies of garter snake in the Northeast can be told apart on the basis of color and tail length. The maritime garter snake is smaller than the eastern garter snake. The dorsal stripe may be gray, tan, or yellow when present; however, it is often lacking or developed only anteriorly. The lateral stripes are usually more distinct and white, gray, or tan. The background coloration is cinnamon-brown, olive-gray, or olive-yellow. The ventral color is whitish anteriorly fading to gray posteriorly.

Tail loss frequency is fairly high in eastern garter snakes. Willis and colleagues (1982) noted a tail loss frequency of 6% for males and 13% for females in a Michigan population. The difference between sexes was significant, and tail loss frequency was shown to increase with size. Tail loss frequency is even higher in Pennsylvania garter snakes: 12% in males and 27% in females. As in Michigan, the difference between sexes is significant, and the frequency of tail loss for both sexes increases with increasing body size. Tail loss presumably occurs primarily as a result of unsuccessful predation attempts. If this is the case, it would seem that attack rates are higher in Pennsylvania than in Michigan or that Pennsylvania predators are less effective in capturing prey. Furthermore, it suggests that the probability of being attacked by a predator increases with age and that females are much more susceptible to predatory attack than are males. Females might be at greater risk owing to reduction in locomotor ability when gravid.

Distribution.   The eastern garter snake occurs over much of eastern North America. It ranges from northwestern Quebec and central Ontario southward to the Florida keys and eastern Texas. The maritime garter snake occurs in Maine, New Hampshire, northeastern Massachusetts, and northern Vermont and adjacent Canada.

The maritime garter snake does not occur in Pennsylvania, but the eastern garter snake is widely distributed throughout the entire state.

Virginia
Named after Virginia

The genus *Virginia* contains the earth snakes. There are only two species in the genus, and their range is restricted to the United States. They occur primarily in the southeastern United States and reach the northern limit of their distribution in Pennsylvania.

The earth snakes are small, stocky animals. Their scales are either smooth or slightly keeled. The head is small and pointed, and the eyes are small. They are extremely secretive snakes but may occasionally be found by searching under cover objects soon after rainstorms. They are very docile snakes and make no attempt to bite if captured.

Although they primarily feed on earthworms, they occasionally eat insect larvae. Both species give birth to live young.

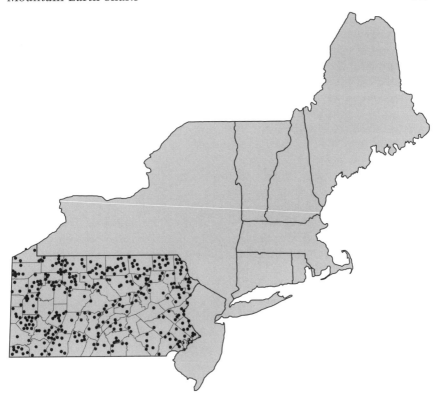

Map 79. Distribution of the eastern garter snake *(Thamnophis sirtalis).*

Mountain Earth Snake *Virginia valeriae pulchra* (Richmond)
Named for Valeria Blaney; L. *pulcher,* beautiful

Description.   The mountain earth snake (Plate 129) is small and stout-bodied and has a short tail. The head is short and pointed and is not distinct from the body. The dorsal background coloration varies from reddish brown to brown or gray. The dorsal pattern, which may be absent, consists of a series of small black dots that form longitudinal rows. These dots occur on scale rows 4 and 5 on each side of the body and medially on scale row 7 on each side. Occasionally, a lighter middorsal stripe is present between the median rows of dots. The ventral coloration is immaculate white to pale yellow, occasionally edged with pink. The dorsal head color is similar to, but generally darker than, the dorsal background coloration and becomes gray or white on the supralabials. The eye is bordered with black. The infralabials and chin are generally immaculate white; however, specimens from the northern part of Pennsylvania occasionally have dark maculations on the anterior portion of the chin and infralabials.

The dorsal scales occur in 17 rows at midbody. The dorsal scales are keeled but not strongly so, and specimens tend to have a smooth polished appearance. Keeling is usually absent from scale rows 1 and 2. The anal plate is divided, and the subcaudals occur in two rows.

Mountain earth snakes exhibit significant sexual dimorphism in size and body proportions. Adult males from Pennsylvania average 199.6 mm (8 in.) SVL and 248.1 mm (9$\frac{7}{8}$ in.) ToL. The smallest mature male found in Pennsylvania had a SVL of 147 mm (5$\frac{7}{8}$ in.), but this is unusual. Females average 240.7 mm (9$\frac{1}{2}$ in.) SVL and 282.5 mm (11$\frac{1}{4}$ in.) ToL.

Males have a significantly longer tail than females. The mean tail length for males is 25.9% of SVL and 20.6% of ToL, and for females it is 18.1% of SVL and 15.3% of ToL.

The young are dull brown to gray above and white below. Richmond (1954) stated that the young are without markings, but we have found the spotted pattern present in neonates.

Confusing Species.   The other subspecies, the eastern earth snake, has smooth scales in 15 rows at midbody. The eastern worm snake has smooth scales, 13 scale rows at midbody, and very small eyes. Northern brown snakes have strongly keeled scales and seven supralabials as opposed to the six supralabials found in mountain earth snakes.

Habitat and Habits.   Mountain earth snakes are primarily inhabitants of hardwood or mixed hardwood-conifer forests in upland regions. They are most commonly found on moderate to steep hillsides where there is an abundance of rocky cover and second-growth vegetation. In these areas, they are almost always found under rocks.

In Pennsylvania, mountain earth snakes begin to emerge from hibernation in late April but do not become common until mid-May. Activity remains fairly constant through July, then increases in August. It begins to taper off in September and ceases by mid-October.

Mountain earth snakes do not appear to have any well-developed daily activity cycle. Richmond (1954) reported them to be most commonly found after periods of heavy rain, but Bothner and Moore (1964) reported collecting a large series in Pennsylvania during fairly dry conditions. It is our experience that, although the activity of mountain earth snakes in a given area is indeed sporadic, it cannot be adequately correlated with specific environmental conditions.

They are usually found singly under cover objects, but pairs have been observed sharing a refuge. In the laboratory, neonates show a strong tendency to aggregate.

Mountain earth snakes feed exclusively on earthworms.

Reproduction.   Nothing is known of the time of mating in this subspecies, but its relatively late emergence in the spring and continued fairly high activity in September suggest the possibility of a fall mating period.

Mountain earth snakes are viviparous. Females emerge from hibernation with moderately large (3–4 mm; $\frac{1}{8}$ in.) ovarian follicles. Females containing enlarged oviducal eggs first appear in early June, and individuals with well-developed embryos are found in late July and August. Parturition occurs later in mountain earth snakes than it does in most viviparous snakes in Pennsylvania. The earliest date for parturition is 19 August

(Richmond 1954), and the latest date for the birth of a litter is 30 September (Bothner and Moore 1964). Most births appear to occur in late August and September.

In a sample of specimens from the Carnegie Museum, litter size varied from 4 to 11 young. Pisani (1971) reported a litter of 14 young born to a 319-mm ($12\frac{3}{4}$-in.) SVL female. Litter size is not correlated with body size.

Neonates have a mean SVL of 85.9 mm ($3\frac{3}{8}$ in.) and a mean ToL of 103.4 mm ($4\frac{1}{8}$ in.). The sex ratio of neonates does not deviate significantly from 1:1.

Males generally become sexually mature at about 170–175 mm ($6\frac{3}{4}$–7 in.) SVL. Females become sexually mature at a SVL of about 220–230 mm ($8\frac{3}{4}$–$9\frac{1}{8}$ in.).

Remarks. Mountain earth snakes are inoffensive animals that do not attempt to bite when handled. Occasionally, they will release musk or will defecate when picked up. Ernst and Barbour (1989) reported on a specimen from Pennsylvania that pretended to be dead when first captured.

Distribution. The mountain earth snake ranges from the Allegheny Mountains and the Allegheny Plateau of northern Pennsylvania southward through extreme western Maryland into adjacent West Virginia.

In Pennsylvania, mountain earth snakes have a disjunct range, with three main centers of occurrence as follows: (1) a long Laurel Ridge in Westmoreland, Somerset, and Fayette counties; (2) the Allegheny Plateau of Warren, Forest, Clarion, and Venango counties; and (3) the Allegheny Mountains of Potter, Cameron, Clinton, and Elk counties. The hiatus in its distribution in northern Pennsylvania may well be an artifact of survey intensity rather than of the biology of the animal, since individuals have recently been found in Clearfield County approximately halfway between the two centers of distribution in the north.

Eastern Earth Snake *Virginia valeriae valeriae* Baird and Girard
Named for Valeria Blaney
Description. The eastern earth snake, like the mountain earth snake, is a small stout-bodied animal with a short tail. The head is short and pointed and is not distinctly separated from the body. The dorsal background coloration varies from dark gray to dark brown. Often, the dorsum has small black dots, generally arranged in four longitudinal rows. The venter and chin are immaculate white. The labial scales are either white or, occasionally, suffused with brown.

The dorsal scales are smooth and polished and occur in 15 scale rows at midbody. The anal plate is divided, and the subcaudals occur in two rows.

In Pennsylvania, adult eastern earth snakes have an average SVL of 182.2 mm ($7\frac{3}{8}$ in.) and an average ToL of 211.6 mm ($8\frac{1}{2}$ in.). The maximum size reported for the subspecies is 294 mm ($11\frac{3}{4}$ in.) ToL (Groves 1961). Males have significantly longer tails than do females. The mean tail length of males is 25.5% of SVL, and that of females is 15.3% of SVL.

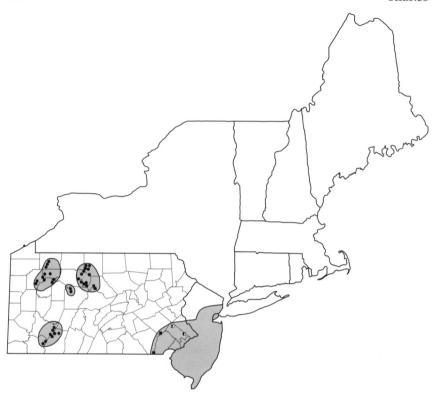

Map 80. Distribution of the earth snakes. Solid circles represent the mountain earth snake *(Virginia valeriae pulchra)*, and solid and half-open squares represent the eastern earth snake *(V. v. valeriae)*.

Confusing Species. The mountain earth snake has slightly keeled scales and 17 scale rows at midbody. The eastern worm snake has 13 scale rows at midbody and very small eyes. The northern brown snake has strongly keeled scales in 17 rows.

Habitat and Habits. Virtually nothing is known of the biology of this subspecies in Pennsylvania. As a result, the following discussion and that on reproduction are based on information gathered in other parts of the animal's range.

The eastern earth snake is primarily an inhabitant of deciduous forests and adjacent open areas (Conant and Collins 1991, Pisani and Collins 1972). They are seldom encountered except after heavy rains, when they may be found under rocks, logs, and other surface debris.

Nothing is known of the seasonal activity of this subspecies. It has been found in Pennsylvania in May, June, and August. Eastern earth snakes feed exclusively on earthworms.

Like the mountain earth snake, the eastern earth snake is an inoffensive animal that never attempts to bite. Blanchard (1923) reported on a specimen that flattened itself dorsoventrally when it was discovered. This behavior has apparently not been observed since its initial mention by Blanchard.

Reproduction.   It is not known when courtship and mating occur. In Virginia, Blem and Blem (1985) noted that follicles began to enlarge in late March and early April and that by mid-May ovulation had occurred. Birth has been reported as occurring from early August (Blem and Blem 1985) to mid-September in Ohio (D. Walker 1963). Litter size appears to vary from 4 to 14 young. Blem and Blem (1985) reported an average litter size of 6.6 young from Virginia. In Ohio, the average size of neonates was 96.6 mm ($3\frac{7}{8}$ in.) ToL (range: 88–103.2 mm; $3\frac{1}{2}$–$4\frac{1}{8}$ in.) (Walker 1963).

Males have been reported to mature at about 125 mm (5 in.) SVL, and females at about 185 mm ($7\frac{3}{8}$ in.) SVL (Blem and Blem 1985).

Remarks.   The present status of this subspecies in Pennsylvania is questionable. No verifiable individuals have been reported since 1942. In addition, most of the historical locations are in areas that have been subjected to significant amounts of development for housing, industry, and agriculture. It is very likely that this subspecies has been extirpated from Pennsylvania.

Distribution.   The eastern earth snake ranges from north-central New Jersey southward to northern Florida. It occurs westward to the Mississippi-Louisiana border and from there northward through central Tennessee and Kentucky to extreme southern Ohio and western West Virginia.

For its distribution in the Northeast, see the previous account (mountain earth snake). In Pennsylvania, its occurrence is restricted to the southeastern Coastal Plain and adjacent Piedmont. Its western limit in the state roughly coincides with the edge of the Valley and Ridge Province. A report by Atkinson (1901) from Allegheny County was undoubtedly based on a misidentified specimen. Roddy (1928) reported an individual from Lancaster County that was a misidentified northern brown snake.

VIPERIDAE (VIPERS AND PIT VIPERS)

The family Viperidae contains poisonous snakes characterized by a highly developed venom delivery system. They possess long hollow fangs through which venom can be injected into prey. The fangs attach to a short maxillary bone and can rotate. As a result, when the mouth is closed the fangs rest against the roof of the mouth, but when the mouth opens to strike the fangs rotate forward, bringing them into an erect position.

The family occurs worldwide except for Australia and Antarctica and contains about 290–300 species. Viperids are stout-bodied snakes with a large triangular head distinctly set off from the neck by its extreme width. All New World viperids are in the subfamily of pit vipers (subfamily Crotalinae). Pit vipers are so named because of cavities located on each side of the head between the nostrils and eyes. The membranes that line the pit are sensitive to changes in temperature and are used by the snakes to locate endothermic prey such as birds and small mammals. The pits are so sensitive and directional that a blindfolded snake can strike unerringly.

Snake venom is a complex mixture of both high- and low-molecular-weight compounds that varies from species to species. As a result, the toxicity of the venom and the effects of envenomation vary from species to species. In general, however, the venom of pit vipers is hemotoxic, acting on the blood and circulatory system of the prey.

With one exception, the bushmaster of Central America and northern South America, all New World viperids give birth to live young rather than lay eggs.

Agkistrodon
Gr. *agkistron*, a fish hook; Gr. *odous*, tooth

The genus *Agkistrodon* contains the copperheads and water moccasins. Ten species are contained in the genus. Members of the genus are found in North America from the northeastern United States to Honduras and in Asia and parts of southeastern Europe.

The copperheads and water moccasins are medium to large, heavy-bodied snakes. As is typical of pit vipers, they have a large triangular head. The body scales are strongly keeled. Members of the genus are found from upland forests to marshes and swamps. When approached, they will often rapidly vibrate their tail and strike at intruders.

Copperheads and water moccasins are dietary generalists. They feed on a wide variety of food items, including frogs, salamanders, other snakes, lizards, fish, small mammals, and the occasional bird. The New World species are viviparous.

Northern Copperhead *Agkistrodon contortrix mokasen* (Daudin)
L. *contortus*, twisted; *mokasen*, a word of Algonquin origin
Description. Northern copperheads (Plate 130) are medium-sized, heavy-bodied snakes. The head is large, flat, and triangular and is distinctly set off from the body by a narrow neck. Copperheads are attractive snakes patterned in rich earth tones. The dorsal background coloration varies from pinkish brown to light tan. Dorsal bands are distributed at regular intervals along the body. The bands are narrowest middorsally and widest at the ventrolateral margins, giving them an hourglass shape. The bands are chestnut-brown, becoming darker near the margins. Dark spots may occur in the lighter lateral portions of the bands and in the background areas between bands. The banding pattern continues onto the tail. Although this is a very bold pattern when viewed out of context, it is exceedingly cryptic in the normal habitat of the animals. In some specimens, the coloration is so dark that the pattern tends to become obscure; however, "black copperheads" have never been reported from Pennsylvania (Gloyd and Conant 1990).

The head is unpatterned and dorsally is bright coppery brown. The lower half of the head is lighter (usually tan). The venter is cream-colored or light brown and has dark, diffuse blotches along the margins of the ventrals.

The dorsal scales are keeled and occur in 21–23 rows at midbody. The anal plate is entire, and the subcaudals occur in a single row.

Copperheads exhibit significant sexual dimorphism in body size but not in tail length. Males average 705.5 mm (28 in.) SVL and 798.9 mm (32 in.) ToL. Mature females average 558.7 mm (22½ in.) SVL and 641.5 mm (25½ in.) ToL. The mean tail length is 14% of ToL. Although tail length is not sexually dimorphic, it is associated with body size. Small snakes have a significantly longer tail than larger individuals. For example, the average tail length of individuals under 500 mm (20 in.) is 15.4% of ToL, whereas the average tail length of individuals over 800 mm (32 in.) is only 11.6% of ToL. Intermediate-sized snakes have an average tail length of 14.6% of ToL. The record size for northern copperheads is 1,346 mm (53¾ in.) ToL (Gloyd and Conant 1990).

In juveniles, the terminal portion of the tail is bright sulfur yellow, but otherwise they resemble adults.

Confusing Species. Because of their banded or blotched pattern and pugnacious behavior the northern water snake and the eastern milk snake are often mistaken for northern copperheads. They both lack facial pits and have round rather than elliptical pupils, and their head is not distinctly set off from the body by a thin neck.

Habitat and Habits. The northern copperhead is primarily an inhabitant of deciduous woodlands and associated open fields and clearings. It is often found near streams, but water is by no means a habitat requirement. Klemens (1993) indicated that, in Connecticut, they are most frequently observed along trap rock ledges. Reinert (1984a, 1984b) demonstrated that, in eastern Pennsylvania, northern copperheads prefer relatively open habitats with abundant rocks and little understory vegetation. He also showed that this preference is most pronounced in gravid females.

On the basis of capture records in Pennsylvania and Connecticut, the annual activity cycle extends from late April through the first half of October and may extend into November in the southeastern portion of Pennsylvania. The activity cycle is unimodal, with activity gradually increasing to a seasonal high in August and then gradually decreasing through September and October as individuals move into hibernacula.

Daily activity appears to vary with season. In Tennessee, northern copperheads are decidedly diurnal in spring and fall but become primarily nocturnal in summer (Sanders and Jacob 1981).

Hibernacula have not been reported from Pennsylvania, but in other parts of their range northern copperheads have been reported to hibernate in caves (Drda, 1968), rodent burrows (Sanders and Jacob 1981), and rocky areas with a southern exposure (H. Fitch 1960). H. Fitch (1960) determined that, in Kansas, they generally return to the same hibernaculum year after year. Peterson and Fritsch (1986) noted that, in Connecticut, they den along the borders of swamps, reservoirs, streams, and rivers in wooded areas. Peterson and Fritsch's observation suggests that the animals might make substantial seasonal movements between these hibernacula sites and the trap rock ridges that they favor in summer.

Northern copperheads tend to be solitary except when they aggregate in the vicinity of communal hibernacula and when they are mating.

All feeding studies of northern copperheads have shown them to eat small mammals, especially voles and white-footed deer mice (H. Fitch 1960, Garton and Dimmick 1969, Hamilton and Pollack 1955). Studies by Garton and Dimmick (1969) and E. Brown (1979a) have shown that insects may constitute an important food source for some populations. Northern copperheads are primarily sit-and-wait predators, capturing suitable prey items when they approach within striking distance. Their cryptic coloration allows them to effectively blend into the background and become virtually invisible to potential prey. Because of this foraging mode, northern copperheads are generally found resting in flat coils, with the head looped in the center of the coil, ready to strike. Young northern copperheads have a bright yellow tail, and it has been suggested that they use it to lure prey within striking distance (Neill 1960).

Male northern copperheads engage in combat. This activity has been reported by several authors (H. Fitch 1960, B. Stewart 1984) and has been intensively studied by Schuett and Gillingham (1989). Combat involves the males' maintaining a vertical position, with the anterior third of their body off the ground. They wrestle with each other—touching, entwining, swaying, and pushing—until one is toppled. They neither bite nor strike during combat. Schuett and Gillingham suggested that the high degree of physical contact is designed to fatigue an opponent. Most aggressive encounters between males are associated with reproduction and occur when the males are courting or defending potential mates. The larger male generally wins the encounter. In all likelihood, this explains the reverse sexual size dimorphism in northern copperheads, since the larger males will enjoy a higher success rate in combat and presumably will have greater reproductive success.

Literature reports of the northern copperhead's degree of aggressiveness are mixed. Some authors regard it as a very aggressive snake (e.g., Atkinson 1901, Surface 1906); others consider it to be mild mannered and inoffensive (H. Fitch 1960, McCauley 1945). We concur with the latter. Their excellent camouflage, however, makes them potentially dangerous, in that it is possible to unknowingly step on or put your hand on a resting individual. In such a situation, it is not surprising that the snake often strikes at the offending member. Such encounters led early authors to consider the snake to be aggressive.

Reproduction.   Northern copperheads, as are all other North American pit vipers, are viviparous. Courtship and mating occur in spring, late summer, and early fall and have been described in detail by Schuett and Gillingham (1988). They also showed that sperm from fall matings remains viable for spring fertilization of ovulated eggs (Schuett and

Gillingham 1986) and further demonstrated that multiple matings with several males can result in litters of mixed paternity.

Females emerge from hibernation with small ovarian follicles that undergo rapid vitellogenesis and are ready to be ovulated by the end of May or the beginning of June. Parturition does not begin until the middle of August and may extend into the first half of October. On that basis, embryonic development appears to be slow in northern copperheads. In Pennsylvania, the majority of neonates have been found from about 17 September to 8 October. Late in the season, food availability is reduced, and neonate foraging success is therefore potentially lower. As a result, the young may enter hibernation with insufficient food reserves, but they usually have significant reserves of egg yolk, which supply sufficient energy for survival through their first winter.

H. Fitch (1960) reported that females in a Kansas population exhibited a biennial reproductive cycle. This has also been reported by Collins (1974). In Pennsylvania, it appears that, although females may not breed every year, they do not follow a strict biennial cycle. In a sample of 25 mature females from the reproductive season, 68% contained either oviducal eggs or developing embryos, while 32% showed no sign of reproductive activity.

The mean litter size in a sample of Pennsylvania northern copperheads was 5.7 young and ranged from 4 to 9 young. Litter size is positively correlated with female body size. Seigel and Fitch (1985) noted that mean litter size within a population varied from year to year, presumably in response to climatic conditions and associated prey availability. Litter size was highest in wet years and lowest in dry years. Throughout the range of the northern copperhead, litter size has been reported to vary from 1 to 10 young (Gloyd and Conant 1990). The average size of neonates in Pennsylvania is 181.8 mm ($7\frac{1}{4}$ in.) SVL and 218.9 mm ($8\frac{3}{4}$ in.) ToL and is similar to the neonate size reported from other parts of the species' range.

Females mature at a SVL of between 460 and 500 mm ($18\frac{1}{2}$–20 in.). The smallest mature male from Pennsylvania was 480 mm ($19\frac{1}{4}$ in.) SVL, and the largest immature male was 408 mm ($16\frac{3}{8}$ in.) SVL. Apparently maturity occurs at some point between these SVLs, but the precise size in the Northeast remains unknown.

Remarks. Northern copperheads are venomous and should be treated with respect, but not fear. As is typical of North American pit vipers, copperheads have hemolytic venom. It causes destruction of red blood cells and small vessels and results in hemorrhage. Symptoms of northern copperhead envenomation may include (but not be restricted to) any or all of the following: pain and swelling, hemorrhage, weakness, increase or decrease in heart rate and pulse, nausea and vomiting, headache, and difficulty in breathing. Fortunately, although the northern copperhead is responsible for a significant percentage of all snake bites reported, fatalities resulting from its envenomation are almost nonexistent. This is not to suggest that a bite should not be treated as a serious medical emergency.

Distribution.   The northern copperhead ranges from southern Massachusetts southward to Georgia and northern Alabama and extreme northeastern Mississippi. It ranges from southern New York west through Pennsylvania to Illinois.

In the Northeast, this species occurs in southeastern and southwestern Connecticut and through the Central Connecticut Lowlands into Massachusetts. An isolated population occurs in eastern Massachusetts. The species is widespread in southeastern New York. In Pennsylvania, northern copperheads are widely distributed throughout the southern two-thirds of the state but are absent from most of the northern-tier counties. One unsubstantiated literature record (A. Smith 1945) exists for a specimen from Sugar Grove, Warren County, but this is in all probability based on a misidentification or a mislabeled specimen. The northern copperhead is probably more common in Pennsylvania than it appears to be, but owing to its secretive nature and cryptic coloration it often is not observed. Some steep, forested ravines in and near cities and towns in western Pennsylvania still support small colonies of these snakes.

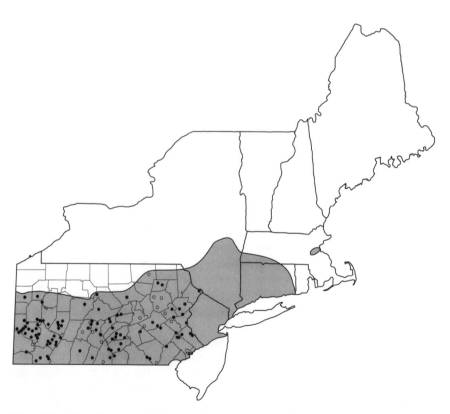

Map 81. Distribution of the northern copperhead *(Agkistrodon contortrix mokasen).*

Crotalus
Gr. *krotalon*, a rattle

The genus *Crotalus* contains the rattlesnakes that have small scales on the top of the head (see *Sistrurus* for the other rattlesnakes). Twenty-six species are found in the genus. In distribution, they range from southern Canada, throughout the United States except for Maine and Delaware, and southward to central Argentina in South America.

Rattlesnakes are small to large, heavy-bodied snakes. The dorsal body scales are strongly keeled. As might be expected from their geographic range, rattlesnakes inhabit a wide variety of environments, from tropical jungle to open prairie and from moist eastern woodlands to arid western deserts. They range in elevation from sea level and below to over 3,700 m (12,200 ft). Although rattlesnakes are venomous, they are not belligerent and will, if at all possible, avoid an encounter with people.

The rattle, the rattlesnake's most notable feature, is composed of a series of loosely connected horny segments that, when shaken, rapidly makes a distinct buzzing or rattling sound. The nature of the sound varies with the size of the snake and the condition of the rattle. A new segment is added every time a snake sheds its skin. Because shedding occurs more than once a year (up to four or five times), it is not possible to determine a snake's age by counting the number of segments in the rattle.

Rattlesnakes incapacitate their prey by the injection of venom. They feed on a wide variety of foods, but mammals constitute the major dietary item for most species. All rattlesnakes are viviparous.

Timber Rattlesnake *Crotalus horridus* Linnaeus
L. *horrens*, creating horror
Description. The timber rattlesnake (Plates 131 and 132) is the largest of the three venomous snakes found in the Northeast. Timber rattlesnakes are heavy-bodied. The head is large, flat, and triangular and is distinctly set off from the body by a narrow neck. The pupils of the eyes are elliptical, and a distinct deep thermal-sensitive pit is situated between the eye and the nostril.

This species is generally boldly patterned with dark brown or black blotches or chevronlike bands. The background color varies from yellowish brown to dark brown. The tail and posterior portion of the body are jet-black. The dark body blotches are usually set off from the background coloration by a narrow edge of pale yellow or beige. Occasionally, entirely black individuals are found. It has been suggested that these all-black animals are males, but this is not the case; both males and females may be black. The ventral surfaces are cream-colored to yellow-brown and usually are mottled with small black maculations. Albinos, including one from Westmoreland County, Pennsylvania, have been reported for this species (Hensley 1959).

The dorsal scales are strongly keeled, giving the snake a very rough appearance. Dorsal scales occur in 21–26 scale rows at midbody (Klauber 1956). The anal plate is entire, and the subcaudal scales occur in a single row.

Reliable data on size in timber rattlesnake populations from Pennsylvania are not available. The lack of small wild-caught individuals in collections may be partly due to the actual biology of the species. Galligan and Dunson (1979) reported that only 32 out of 221 animals that they examined in the field in Pennsylvania were under 600 mm (24 in.) SVL. The largest male that they found was about 1,150 mm (46 in.) SVL, and the largest female was 1,000 mm (39 in.) SVL. These sizes fall far short of the 1,880 mm (74 in.) ToL reported by Klauber (1956) as the maximum size for the species. Most likely, in years past when the snakes were less persecuted larger specimens would have been commonly encountered in Pennsylvania.

Confusing Species.   The only other rattlesnake found in Pennsylvania is the small eastern massasauga, which differs from the timber rattlesnake not only in size but also in having nine large platelike dorsal head scales rather than a large number of smaller scales.

Habitat and Habits.   In the Northeast, timber rattlesnakes primarily inhabit upland forested regions where rocky outcroppings and talus slopes occur. Today, timber rattlesnakes tend to be restricted primarily to inaccessible areas far removed from human habitat and normal human activity.

Reinert and Colleagues (1984) noted that most foraging activity occurred at night but that some animals were still active in the daytime.

The timber rattlesnake is one of the last species of snake in the Northeast to emerge from hibernation. Galligan and Dunson (1979) noted that over a several-year period in central Pennsylvania snakes first emerged from hibernation between 23 and 30 April. Entrance into hibernation generally occurs by early or mid-October. W. Brown and Colleagues (1982) reported that snakes farther north, in New York, do not emerge from hibernation until the beginning or middle of May and return to den sites by the beginning of September.

The preferred hibernation sites are in rocky ledges, in crevices, or in talus slopes with southern exposure. In New York, the body temperature of hibernating snakes varied from a high of 15.7°C (60°F) to a low of 4.3°C (39°F), with a mean of 10.5°C (50°F) (W. Brown 1982). Den sites are usually near open areas or clearings in the forest where it is possible for the snakes to bask.

W. Brown (1982) found that some snakes move as much as 1.4 km (0.9 mi) away from the den site during the summer but that others have very restricted movements. Galligan and Dunson (1979) found that movement patterns can be very sporadic, with an individual remaining in a small area for an extended period of time (several weeks) and then rapidly making a long-distance move before again resuming a sedentary existence.

Snakes have been known to move as much as 2 km (1.2 mi) in less than 2 days (Reinert, pers. comm.). Gravid females are far less mobile than either males or nongravid females.

Individuals using the same hibernacula in Pennsylvania are more closely related to each other than to randomly selected individuals. This finding suggests that local populations of timber rattlesnakes may be composed of individuals from an isolated hibernacula or a small number of hibernacula drawn into association by the common use of basking sites (Bushar et al. 1998).

Timber rattlesnakes are sit-and-wait predators. Reinert and Colleagues (1984) demonstrated that they take up a coiled position along a small mammal runway and wait for the prey. A typical location for foraging is next to a small to medium-sized fallen log. The snake coils with its head resting either on the top of the log or on a body coil facing the log. Most foraging recorded by Reinert and Colleagues (1984) occurred at night, although snakes did occasionally forage during the day. In eastern Pennsylvania (Berks County), the diet of rattlesnakes was composed exclusively of small mammals, with the proportions of prey species in the snakes' diet being similar to the frequency of occurrence of the small mammals in the community. Food items consumed were white-footed deer mice, red-back voles, chipmunks, rabbits, and flying squirrels.

Male timber rattlesnakes are known to engage in combat activity (Sutherland 1958); however, it is not known if this is a common or a rare behavior. When it does occur, it appears to be very similar to that described for northern copperheads.

In general, timber rattlesnakes are considered to be relatively mild-mannered snakes that are far more likely to seek an escape route than to stay and defend themselves if they are encountered in the wild.

Reproduction. Timber rattlesnakes are viviparous. The exact timing of courtship and mating in Pennsylvania is not known. In New York, the mating season occurs between mid-July and late September (Aldridge and Brown 1995, W. Brown 1995). Several other authors have reported that mating occurs from midsummer to early fall (Ernst and Barbour 1989, Keenlyne 1978), but P. Anderson (1965) reported finding snakes in copula in April in Missouri.

The vitellogenic cycle in females is extremely variable. The cycle may be biennial (Galligan and Dunson 1979), triennial (Gibbons 1972), or even quadrennial (W. Brown 1991). These variations in the cycle do not appear to be associated with geography, but rather with the physiological state of the female. A well-nourished individual from Pennsylvania or New York might have a biennial cycle, whereas a less well-fed specimen from South Carolina might reproduce only once every 3 years. In all cases, the eggs are fertilized shortly after they are ovulated in late spring or early summer. Gestation takes most of the summer, and the young are born in very late summer or early fall.

Male timber rattlesnakes from New York that are older than 6 years of age have sperm present in their vas deferens throughout the year (Aldridge and Brown 1995), but mating occurs only in late summer to early fall. Females store sperm through the winter.

Litter size in Pennsylvania varies from 5 to 9 young, which falls within the range generally reported for the species across its range (H. Fitch 1970). Exceptionally large litters (up to 19 young) have been reported (Martof et al. 1980). The size at birth ranges from 271 to 350 mm ($10\frac{7}{8}$–14 in.) ToL (Ernst and Barbour 1989). Neonates lack a rattle but possess a single horny button at the tip of the tail (a segment of rattle is added each time the skin is shed). Young are born with fully functional fangs and venom glands.

In New York, females mature at an average of 8.3 years of age, whereas males mature at an average age of 5.3 years (Aldridge and Brown 1995; W. Brown 1991).

Remarks. Reinert and Rupert (1999) found that translocated snakes exhibited a mortality of 54.5% during the same time period that resident snakes exhibited a mortality of only 11.1%. This difference is probably due to increased movement on the part of translocated animals. Reinert and Rupert found that translocated animals had a mean home range of 600 ha (1,440 acres). The home range size of resident individuals was an order of magnitude smaller, 59.9 ha (140 acres). The translocation of snakes is often discussed as a conservation strategy for rattlesnakes. The above results strongly argue against the translocation of individuals except in the most extreme of situations.

It is our opinion that, at present, timber rattlesnakes are endangered in Pennsylvania primarily owing to exploitation by snake hunters. The species has recently been afforded legal protection as a candidate species and is being managed as a game species, with season, bag limit, minimum size, and areas closed to collecting firmly established and enforced.

Distribution. The timber rattlesnakes' historical range extends from central New England southward to the Florida panhandle and westward through the eastern third of Texas. In the West, their range extends north through eastern Oklahoma, Kansas, and Nebraska and terminates in extreme eastern Minnesota. The species is absent from most of the Great Lakes states.

In the Northeast, the timber rattlesnake is found from southern New Hampshire and the Lake Chaplain region of Vermont through the southern two-thirds of New York and the western half of both Massachusetts and Connecticut. Isolated populations have been recorded from Rhode Island and eastern Massachusetts. In Pennsylvania, the range of the timber rattlesnake extends throughout the Valley and Ridge Province, the Laurel Highlands, and the more mountainous regions of the northern Allegheny Plateau.

The distribution of timber rattlesnakes, both in Pennsylvania and through the entire range of the species, has been dramatically affected by human activity, and the species is now absent from many areas where it was previously abundant.

Sistrurus
L. *sistrum*, rattle

The genus *Sistrurus* contains the massasauga and the pygmy rattlesnakes. There are three species in the genus. The genus ranges from southern Canada southward to the southern tip of Florida and into the Mexican highlands. In the West, it ranges into the grasslands of southeastern Arizona.

These are small to moderate-sized, stout-bodied animals. Their body scales are strongly keeled. Members of the genus may be distinguished from *Crotalus* species by the presence of nine large plates on the top of the head instead of a series of numerous small scales. They are primarily found in boggy or swampy areas and may be found in either open habitat or forests.

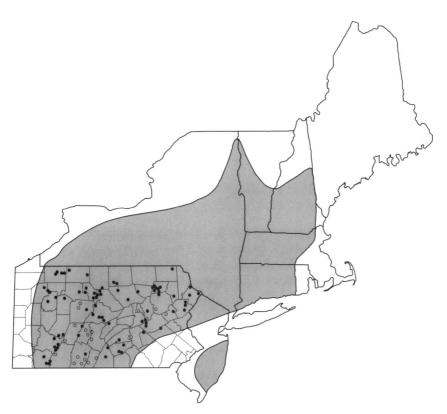

Map 82. Distribution of the timber rattlesnake *(Crotalus horridus).*

Sistrurus feed on frogs, small birds, and mice and other small rodents. All three species give birth to live young.

Eastern Massasauga *Sistrurus catenatus catenatus* (Rafinesque)
L. *caten*, a chain
Description. The eastern massasauga (Plate 133) is a medium-sized, stout-bodied species. The dorsal background coloration varies from gray to grayish brown. The dorsal pattern consists of a row of large irregular middorsal body blotches in conjunction with three (occasionally two) rows of staggered rounded blotches on each side of the body. The body blotches are dark brown, bordered with black and often outlined by a fine white line. Two stripes (on each side) that are bordered with white extend from the neck to the anterior portion of the head. The more dorsal of the stripes extends to the posterior border of the eye, while the lower stripe extends to a point slightly in front of and below the eye. Dark blotches occur on the top of the head. The ventral coloration varies from dark gray to black. The gray phase may be either immaculate or heavily mottled with gray-black or black blotches. The background coloration of the tail is similar to that of the body, but the tail is distinctly ringed rather than blotched.

The head is wider than the neck, and the pupils are elliptical rather than rounded as in nonvenomous species of snake found in the Northeast. A deep thermally sensitive pit lies between the eye and the nostril on each side of the head.

The dorsal scales are strongly keeled and occur in 21–27 rows ($X = 25$ rows). The anal plate is divided, and the subcaudals occur in a single row.

Analysis of a sample of 17 eastern massasauga specimens from Pennsylvania revealed significant sexual size dimorphism, with females being significantly larger than males. Adult males average 441.4 mm ($17\frac{5}{8}$ in.) SVL and 495 mm ($19\frac{3}{4}$ in.) ToL. Adult females average 541 mm (22 in.) SVL and 592.5 mm ($23\frac{5}{8}$ in.) ToL. Seigel (1986), however, found no significant difference in size between males and females in a Missouri population of the western subspecies (*S. catenatus tergeminus*). The larger size of females is also extremely unusual for rattlesnakes in general, where males tend to be significantly larger than females. The record size for the species is 1,003 mm ($40\frac{1}{4}$ in.) ToL (Conant and Collins 1991).

Males have a longer tail than females. Males have a mean tail length of 12% of SVL and 10.7% of ToL. Females have a mean tail length of 9.4% SVL and 8.5% of ToL.

Confusing Species. The presence of a rattle distinguishes the eastern massasauga from all other northeastern snakes except the timber rattlesnake. It can be distinguished from the timber rattlesnake by the dorsal head scales. Nine large platelike scales occur on the dorsal surface on the eastern massasauga, whereas the timber rattlesnake has numerous small granular head scales.

Habitat and Habits. The habitat utilized by eastern massasaugas varies with the season. During spring and fall, they are normally found in low-lying, poorly drained soils that are usually saturated in the spring. During the summer, they are most commonly encountered in dry, open fields, where vegetation is sparse (Reinert and Kodrich 1982). Habitat management studies are under way in New York (G. Johnson and Leopold 1998), but at present the results are inconclusive.

In Pennsylvania, eastern massasaugas are active from early April to mid-October. In a study in Butler County, Reinert and Kodrich (1982) noted that activity gradually increased from early April until a peak was reached in June, after which activity gradually decreased until all snakes finally entered hibernation in mid to late October. It has also been noted that diel activity patterns vary with season. During the relatively cool months of spring and fall snakes are diurnal, but in the heat of the summer they are primarily active in late afternoon and at night.

Eastern massasaugas hibernate in crayfish burrows, mammal burrows, and natural cracks and crevices in swampy lowland areas (Reinert and Kodrich 1982).

Reinert and Kodrich (1982) found that the mean home range size was approximately 1 ha (2.4 acres) for both males and females. They also noted that gravid females moved less than did either males or nongravid females under similar conditions.

Nothing is known of the food habits of eastern massasaugas in Pennsylvania and New York, but it can be assumed that their diet is similar to that in other parts of the country. In Wisconsin (Keenlyne and Beer 1973) and Missouri (Seigel 1986), eastern massasaugas feed almost exclusively on rodents, with these small mammals making up 85.7% and 95.4% of the diet, respectively. The vast majority of rodents identified in the diet were voles. Most of the rest of the diet was composed of other species of snake. It would appear, however, that snakes are utilized as a food item only by young eastern massasaugas. Prey are primarily located by the heat-sensitive pits located on the sides of the head. Once located, the prey item is struck with the fangs and venom is injected.

The disposition of individual snakes varies from mild and sluggish (Klauber 1956) to alert and irritable (Ernst and Barbour 1989).

The venom is mainly hemolytic, as is typical of viper venom, destroying red blood cells and the walls of capillaries. Symptoms of envenomation include, but are not restricted to, the following: pain and swelling in the area of the bite, hemorrhage, nausea, nervousness, and cold sweats. Although fatalities are rare, they have been known to occur (Lyon and Bishop 1936).

Reproduction. Eastern massasaugas are viviparous. Courtship and mating have been observed in Pennsylvania in late July and early August (Reinert 1981) but may occur at other times of the year. In Pennsylvania, the female reproductive cycle is biennial. Oviducal eggs are present as early as the middle of May. The developmental time is long, with birth occurring from the middle of August to the beginning of September. Litter size in Pennsylvania varies from 3 to 9 young and is significantly correlated with female body size (Reinert 1981). Pennsylvania litter size is

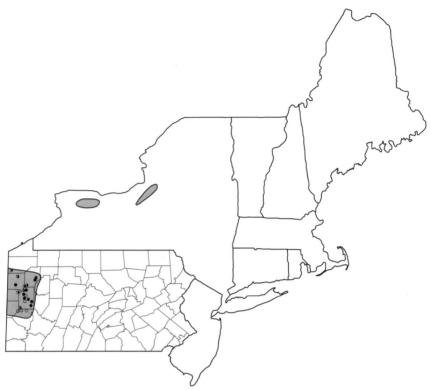

Map 83. Distribution of the eastern massasauga *(Sistrurus catenatus catenatus)*.

similar to that reported for a population from Missouri (Seigel 1986) but is much smaller than the average litter size of 11.1 young reported for a population from along the Chippewa River in southern Wisconsin (Keenlyne 1978). Pennsylvania neonates have a mean ToL of 235.7 mm ($9\frac{3}{8}$ in.) (Reinert 1981), which is similar to neonate size from other parts of the range.

Reinert (1981) reported the smallest mature female to have a ToL of 448 mm ($17\frac{7}{8}$ in.). Males mature at about 350 mm (14 in.) SVL and 385 mm ($15\frac{3}{8}$ in.) ToL. In studies that have reported it, the sex ratio does not vary from 1:1.

Remarks.   The distribution of the eastern massasauga in western Pennsylvania is very spotty. Atkinson and Netting (1927) suggested that massasaugas originally entered Pennsylvania by means of an extension of the moist prairie habitat and then spread out into adjacent marshes. With the subsequent loss of the prairie habitat from most of Pennsylvania owing to climatic change, populations became fragmented and isolated in moist lowland habitat.

This natural fragmentation in conjunction with human-induced habitat destruction has greatly diminished the occurrence of this snake in Pennsylvania. A recent survey has revealed that of 22 historical eastern massasauga localities known in Pennsylvania, at present only six definitely support viable populations of the snake. Four other locations may still harbor populations, but whether they do remains to be determined. The remaining historical localities no longer support populations, primarily because of habitat destruction. As a consequence of this great reduction in habitat, the eastern massasauga has been declared an endangered species in Pennsylvania.

This process of habitat fragmentation and loss due to habitat destruction is not unique to Pennsylvania. For example, only two undisturbed eastern massasauga localities are known to occur in New York, and in Missouri the animals are now restricted to five relatively small isolated locations.

Distribution. The eastern massasauga ranges from southern Ontario, western New York, and western Pennsylvania, through all of the lower peninsula of Michigan, the northern half of Ohio and Indiana, and the northern two-thirds of Illinois, to southern Wisconsin, extreme eastern Iowa, and northeastern Missouri.

In Pennsylvania, its historical range included parts or all of the following counties: Allegheny, Butler, Crawford, Lawrence, Mercer, and Venango. Today, it is known only from Butler, Mercer, and Venango counties. A population may still exist in Crawford County, but its existence has not been confirmed.

Appendix: Pennsylvania Species Mensural and Reproductive Data

Mensural Data

SALAMANDERS

Snout-vent length is abbreviated SVL; total length is abbreviated ToL. The statistic (student t test) is a test for significant differences between adult males and females. Statistically significant t values are indicated by an asterisk. Mensural data do not exist for the following Pennsylvania salamander species: *Ambystoma tigrinum tigrinum, Aneides aeneus, Plethodon wehrlei,* and *Pseudotriton montanus montanus.*

Genus and species	SVL (mm) Mean ± SE	Range, N	ToL (mm) Mean ± SE	Range, N	SVL at maturity (mm)
Cryptobranchus alleganiensis alleganiensis					
male	—	—	427 ± 7.5	290–538, 101	300–330
female	—	—	540 ± 8.1	357–675, 65	370–400
statistic	—		$t = 5.06^*$		
			$p < 0.001$		
Necturus maculosus maculosus					
male	—	—	266 ± 10.9	230–295, 26	130
female	—	—	291 ± 3.6	240–350, 48	150
statistic	—		$t = 4.05^*$		
			$p < 0.001$		
Ambystoma jeffersonianum					
male	65.2 ± 0.7	55–79, 8	129.2 ± 1.6	119–152, 8	55
female	81 ± 0.9	75–90, 7	158.2 ± 1.3	140–174, 7	70–75
statistic	—		—		
Ambystoma maculatum					
male	84.1 ± 1.4	77–104, 24	165.3 ± 3.1	148–200, 24	72
female	93.8 ± 3	77–104, 22	178.4 ± 6.3	148–199, 24	78
statistic	$t = -0.56$		$t = -0.23$		
	$p = 0.57$		$p = 0.81$		
Ambystoma opacum					
male	58.0 ± 1	54–60, 6	97.5 ± 2.5	90–101, 6	58
female	61.5 ± 1.5	54–70, 7	105.7 ± 1.7	93–113, 7	64.4
statistic	$t = -1.43$		$t = -2.45^*$		
	$p = 0.18$		$p = 0.02$		

Genus and species	SVL (mm) Mean ± SE	Range, N	ToL (mm) Mean ± SE	Range, N	SVL at maturity (mm)
Notophthalmus viridescens viridescens					
male	48.2 ± 0.4	41–52, 84	89.7 ± 1.1	80–107, 84	40–42
female	49.3 ± 0.5	42–56, 96	91.8 ± 1.1	80–101, 96	40–42
statistic	$t = 0.38$		$t = 0.75$		
	$p = 0.69$		$p = 0.45$		
Desmognathus fuscus fuscus					
male	51.2 ± 1	38–63, 35	94.0 ± 1.8	72–108, 15	38–40
female	46.2 ± 0.6	42–52, 25	86.3 + 1.1	66–103, 13	42–45
statistic	$t = -3.46^*$		$t = 2.04^*$		
	$p < 0.001$		$p = 0.02$		
Desmognathus monticola					
male	59.1 ± 1	47–73, 50	107.5 ± 3.4	97–130, 20	49
female	57.2 ± 1	49–73, 43	111.2 ± 2.2	97–130, 27	52–53
statistic	$t = 0.68$		$t = -0.91$		
	$p = 0.49$		$p = 0.37$		
Desmognathus ochrophaeus					
male	37.4 ± 0.9	34–42, 27	75.3 ± 1.6	66–83, 23	32
female	39.0 ± 1	31–48, 57	78.9 ± 1.8	64–91, 43	35
statistic	$t = 1.86$		$t = 1.96$		
	$p = 0.06$		$p = 0.06$		
Eurycea bislineata					
male	39.9 ± 0.4	33–45, 29	84.1 ± 1.4	73–98, 22	33
female	41.5 ± 0.5	35–47, 31	86 ± 2.1	64–105, 21	35–36
statistic	$t = 1.98$		$t = 1.06$		
	$p = 0.06$		$p = 0.29$		
Eurycea longicauda longicauda					
male	51.8 ± 0.62	45–62, 53	131.5 ± 3	108–166, 27	45
female	54.9 ± 0.7	47–67, 53	140.0 ± 3	119–170, 35	48
statistic	$t = -3.0^*$		$t = -1.91$		
	$p = 0.001$		$p = 0.2$		
Gyrinophilus porphyriticus porphyriticus					
male	91.0 ± 2.3	77–110, 18	147.2 ± 4.3	124–181, 18	77–80
female	97.4 ± 1.5	85–111, 16	157.1 ± 2.8	142–182, 16	82–85
statistic	$t = -1.98$		$t = -1.86$		
	$p = 0.06$		$p = 0.07$		
Hemidactylium scutatum					
male	27.9 ± 0.4	22–35, 39	61.5 ± 1.2	45–74, 33	22
female	34.5 ± 0.6	29–41, 33	73.6 ± 1.5	56–91, 27	29
statistic	$t = -8.7^*$		$t = 5.7^*$		
	$p < 0.001$		$p < 0.001$		
Plethodon cinereus					
male	42.3 ± 0.6	37–48, 23	80.5 ± 2.0	66–99, 18	35
female	44.0 ± 0.5	40–51, 49	83.0 ± 1.4	76–99, 18	40
statistic	$t = -2.6^*$		$t = 0.96$		
	$p = 0.009$		$p = 0.34$		

Genus and species	SVL (mm)		ToL (mm)		SVL at maturity (mm)
	Mean ± SE	Range, N	Mean ± SE	Range, N	
Plethodon glutinosus					
male	68.6 ± 1.5	56–83, 24	136.4 ± 3.9	114–153, 23	55–56
female	73.5 ± 1	65–85, 22	150.3 ± 2.5	136–166, 20	65
statistic	$t = -2.36^*$		$t = -2.46^*$		
	$p = 0.02$		$p = 0.01$		
Plethodon hoffmani					
male	48.2 ± 0.5	41–53, 40	98.0 ± 1.3	91–109, 28	41
female	51.8 ± 0.3	50–57, 27	106.5 ± 1.2	100–118, 16	50
statistic	$t = 5.16^*$		$t = 4.3^*$		
	$p < 0.001$		$p < 0.001$		
Plethodon richmondi					
male	46.1 ± 2.3	39–54, 18	91.0 ± 4.1	69–116, 16	—
female	—	—	—	—	—
statistic	—		—		
Pseudotriton ruber ruber					
male	77.2 ± 1.5	65–93, 26	124.0 ± 2.5	105–150, 23	60–65
female	83.5 ± 1.4	75–90, 12	131.7 ± 2.5	118–146, 12	75
statistic	$t = 2.46^*$		$t = 1.95^*$		
	$p = 0.009$		$p = 0.02$		

TOADS AND FROGS

Snout-urostyle length is abbreviated SUL. The statistic (student t test) is a test for significant differences between adult males and females. Statistically significant t values are indicated by an asterisk. Mensural data do not exist for Pennsylvania *Scaphiopus holbrookii*.

Genus and species	SUL (mm)	
	Mean ± SE	Range, N
Bufo americanus americanus		
male	59.0 ± 0.8	52–65, 21
female	78.0 ± 2.1	68–90, 11
statistic	$t = -5.91^*$	
	$p < 0.001$	
Bufo woodhousii fowleri		
male	55.7 ± 1.3	48–65, 15
female	71.5 ± 2.6	57–81, 19
statistic	$t = -5.6^*$	
	$p < 0.001$	
Acris crepitans crepitans		
male	21.3 ± 0.3	20–25, 20
female	22.7 ± 0.8	20–26, 7
statistic	$t = 1.55$	
	$p = 0.13$	

Genus and species	SUL (mm)	
	Mean ± SE	Range, N
Hyla versicolor/H. chrysoscelis		
male	43.0 ± 0.7	37–52, 24
female	49.0 ± 1.0	47–52, 4
statistic	$t = -2.64^*$	
	$p = 0.01$	
Pseudacris brachyphona		
male	24.6 ± 0.4	21.3–29, 27
female	30.3 ± 0.5	28.3–33.6, 10
statistic	$t = -6.8^*$	
	$p < 0.001$	
Pseudacris crucifer crucifer		
male	25.2 ± 0.4	21.3–29.5, 27
female	31.8 ± 0.6	29.4–34.4, 11
statistic	$t = -6.8^*$	
	$p < 0.001$	
Pseudacris triseriata		
male	24.9 ± 0.4	21–29, 31
female	28.7 ± 0.5	27–31, 11
statistic	$t = -5.4^*$	
	$p < 0.001$	
Rana catesbeiana		
male	120.5 ± 3.7	85–152, 21
female	117.3 ± 5.0	82–149, 16
statistic	$t = 0.52$	
	$p = 0.60$	
Rana clamitans melanota		
male	86.1± 1	80–95, 24
female	85.5 ± 0.9	80–94, 25
statistic	$t = 0.46$	
	$p = 0.64$	
Rana palustris		
male	53.0 ± 1.4	44–64, 19
female	66.4 ± 1	50–81, 28
statistic	$t = -3.6^*$	
	$p < 0.001$	
Rana pipiens		
male	69.8 ± 0.9	63–81, 25
female	78.6 ± 1.4	66–95, 26
statistic	$t = -3.4^*$	
	$p < 0.001$	
Rana sphenocephala		
male	55.8 ± 0.7	47–67, 39
female	63.7 ± 2.6	55–82, 16
statistic	$t = 4.49^*$	
	$p < 0.001$	

Genus and species	SUL (mm)	
	Mean ± SE	Range, *N*
Rana sylvatica		
male	53.6 ± 3.7	48–56, 15
female	61.1 ± 4.6	54–72, 15
statistic	$t = -2.39^*$	
	$p = 0.02$	

TURTLES

Carapace length is abbreviated CL. The statistic (student *t* test) is a test for significant differences between adult males and females. Statiscally significant *t* values are indicated by an asterisk. Mensural data do not exist for the following Pennsylvania turtle species: *Apalone mutica mutica, Emydoidea blandingii, Kinosternon subrubrum subrubrum,* and *Pseudemys rubriventris.*

Genus and species	CL (mm)	
	Mean ± SE	Range, *N*
Chelydra serpentina serpentina		
male	351 ± 9.6	256–400, 70
female	284 ± 7	208–340, 42
statistic	$t = 5.7^*$	
	$p < 0.001$	
Sternotherus odoratus		
male	107 ± 3.3	82–126, 17
female	98.6 ± 2.7	88–108, 23
statistic	$t = 2.71^*$	
	$p = 0.009$	
Chrysemys picta		
male	119.3 ± 3.3	100–133, 13
female	140.9 ± 4	105–164, 18
statistic	$t = -4.7^*$	
	$p < 0.001$	
Clemmys guttata		
male	105.4 ± 0.9	88–118, 65
female	102.4 ± 1.5	83–126, 33
statistic	$t = 1.75$	
	$p = 0.08$	
Clemmys insculpta		
male	176 ± 2.6	137–208, 35
female	158 ± 2.8	126–195, 54
statistic	$t = 4.56^*$	
	$p < 0.001$	

Genus and species	CL (mm) Mean ± SE	Range, N
Clemmys muhlenbergii		
male	88.7 ± 2.5	80–95, 5
female	87.6 ± 1.4	78–98, 13
statistic	$t = 0.2$	
	$p = 0.83$	
Graptemys geographica		
male	108 ± 2.3	102–118, 7
female	198 ± 5.1	182–217, 7
statistic	$t = -16.1^*$	
	$p < 0.001$	
Terrapene carolina carolina		
male	126.7 ± 1.7	103–150, 17
female	124.6 ± 2	96–148, 20
statistic	$t = 2.1^*$	
	$p = 0.03$	
Apalone spinifera spinifera		
male	156 ± 3.3	145–186, 16
female	362 ± 20.1	305–462, 7
statistic	$t = 6.2^*$	
	$p < 0.001$	

LIZARDS

Snout-vent length is abbreviated SVL; tail length is abbreviated TL. The statistic (student t test) is a test for significant differences between adult males and females. Statiscally significant t values are indicated by an asterisk. Mensural data do not exist for Pennsylvania *Eumeces laticeps*.

Genus and species	SVL (mm) Mean ± SE	Range, N	TL (mm) Mean ± SE	Range, N
Sceloporus undulatus hyacinthinus				
male	63.7 ± 0.8	55–74, 27	—	
female	66 ± 1.1	58–78, 28	—	
statistic	$t = -3.4^*$			
	$p = 0.001$			
neonate	—	—	—	
Eumeces anthracinus anthracinus				
male	54.1 ± 0.9	50–59, 9	—	
female	55.7 ± 0.9	50–60, 11	—	
statistic	$t = -0.94$			
	$p = 0.35$			
neonate	25.2 ± 0.4	23–27, 7	26 ± 0.2	24–28, 7

Genus and species	SVL (mm)		TL (mm)	
	Mean ± SE	Range, N	Mean ± SE	Range, N
Eumeces fasciatus				
male	67.4 ± 1.5	55–75, 16	—	
female	66.0 ± 2.1	56–72, 7	—	
statistic	$t = -1.53$			
	$p = 0.13$			
neonate	25.7 ± 0.27	24–28, 17	—	

SNAKES

Snout-vent length is abbreviated SVL; total length is abbreviated ToL; tail length is abbreviated TL. The statistic (student t test) is a test for significant differences between adult males and females. Statiscally significant t values are indicated by an asterisk. The z statistic is a measure of significance that is used when the data to be analyzed are not normally distributed. Mensural data do not exist for the following Pennsylvania snake species: *Crotalus horridus, Opheodrys aestivus,* and *Virginia valeriae valeriae.*

Genus and species	SVL (mm)		ToL (mm)		TL/SVL		TL/ToL		SVL at maturity (mm)
	Mean ± SE	Range, N	Mean ± SE	Range, N	Mean ± SE	Range, N	Mean ± SE	Range, N	
Carphophis amoenus amoenus									
male	198.5 ± 8.3	146–219, 11	241.7 ± 11	175–268, 11	0.22 ± 0.03	0.165–0.21, 11	0.183 ± 0.02	0.136–0.173, 10	—
female	240.9 ± 5.3	216–276, 10	278.4 ± 6.4	249–319, 10	0.154 ± 0.03	0.198–0.255, 10	0.132 ± 0.01	0.12–0.144, 10	—
statistic	t = 4.46*	p < 0.001	t = 3.01*	p = 0.004	z = 3.63*	p = 0.002	z = 3.63*	p = 0.002	
neonate	—		—		—		—		—
Clonophis kirtlandii									
male	252	228–285, 7	337	304–383, 7	0.333		0.251		—
female	321 ± 4.5	287–356, 5	411	371–451, 5	0.279	—	0.218	—	—
statistic	—		—			—			
neonate	109	100–120, 14	142.7	133–153, 14	—		—		—
Coluber constrictor constrictor									
male	956.8 ± 26.5	741–1,127, 23	1,246.0 ± 44	867–1,498, 18	0.318 = 0.6	0.271–0.36, 17	0.245 ± 3.5	0.213–0.28, 18	700
female	1,000.5 ± 30	749–1,227, 32	1,263.5 ± 48	950–1,517, 17	0.313 ± 0.1	0.263–0.331, 19	0.236 ± 0.5	0.213–0.279, 19	700
statistic	t = 1.1	p = 0.13	t = 0.29	p = 0.67	z = 1.79	p = 0.07	z = 2.5*	p = 0.01	
neonate	209.0 ± 4.8	185–240, 18	275.5 ± 6.2	243–314, 18	—		—		—
Diadophis punctatus edwardsii									
male	272 ± 4.8	210–325, 68	347 ± 6.8	264–430, 66	0.30 ± 0.002	0.29–0.34, 133	0.24 ± 0.001	0.23–0.25, 133	210
female	286 ± 4	217–433, 70	355 ± 5.6	275–533, 67	0.25 ± 0.003	0.2–0.3, 136	0.197 ± 0.001	0.17–0.23, 136	230
statistic	t = 1.7	p = 0.08	t = 0.8	p = 0.4	z = 5.19*	p < 0.001	z = 4.13*	p < 0.001	
neonate	104 ± 1.7	87–120, 25	130 ± 2.0	110–147, 25	—		—		—

Elaphe obsoleta obsoleta									
male	1,078.3 ± 32.4	760–1,625, 19	1,321.8 ± 38.1	919–1,948, 19	0.19 ± 0.2	0.17–0.21, 22	0.16 ± 0.1	0.15–0.178, 22	760
female	1,125.8 ± 30.6	895–1,425, 18	1,344.1 ± 46	1,077–1,710, 18	0.20 ± 0.2	0.18–0.22, 21	0.173 ± 0.2	0.16–0.186, 21	895
statistic	$t = 0.758$ $p = 0.23$		$t = 0.41$ $p = 0.34$		$z = 1.2$ $p = 0.9$		$z = 1.5$ $p < 0.1$		—
neonate	—		—		—		—		—
Heterodon platirhinos platirhinos									
male	435.8 ± 26.5	360–565, 8	546.8 ± 35.8	438–715, 8	0.245 ± 0.04	0.2–0.282, 8	0.196 ± 0.03	0.166–0.22, 8	
female	611.0 ± 35.8	464–770, 14	722.0 ± 34.2	539–904, 14	0.179 ± 0.4	0.136–0.201, 14	0.152 ± 0.03	0.119–0.167, 14	
statistic	$t = 4.13^{*}$ $p < 0.001$		$t = 3.33^{*}$ $p = 0.003$		$z = 3.9^{*}$ $p < 0.001$		$z = 3.9^{*}$ $p < 0.001$		—
neonate	138.1 ± 3.2	105–160, 17	165.3 ± 2.8	129–191, 17	—		—		
Lampropeltis triangulum triangulum									
male	725.8 ± 17.9	454–987, 53	826 ± 21	540–1,141, 47	0.151 ± 0.01	0.128–0.177, 46	0.132 ± 0.01	0.11–0.15, 46	
female	677.3 ± 16.2	535–915, 38	768.2 ± 17.7	598–1,032, 36	0.144 ± 0.02	0.117–0.182, 36	0.127 ± 0.021	0.105–0.21, 36	
statistic	$t = 1.91^{*}$ $p = 0.027$		$t = 2.14^{*}$ $p = 0.016$		$z = 2.7^{*}$ $p = 0.005$		$z = 2.8^{*}$ $p = 0.004$		—
neonate	—		—		—		—		
Nerodia sipedon sipedon									
male	445 ± 13.4	315–620, 44	575 ± 19	421–748, 33	0.35 ± 0.02	0.317–0.385, 33	0.26 ± 0.01	0.24–0.27, 33	
female	700 ± 16.5	514–844, 28	907 ± 22.4	770–1,101, 21	0.277 ± 0.03	0.253–0.304, 22	0.217 ± 0.01	0.202–0.233, 22	
statistic	$t = 11.9^{*}$		$t = 10.9^{*}$		$z = 6.2^{*}$		$z = 6.2^{*}$		
$p < 0.001$	$p < 0.001$		$p < 0.001$		$p < 0.001$		$p < 0.001$		
neonate	—		—		—		—		
Opheodrys vernalis									
male	269.6 ± 6.3	206–318, 32	414.8 ± 10.6	318–515, 30	0.545 ± 0.05	0.464–0.592, 32	0.356 ± 0.04	0.318–0.467, 32	
female	323.8 ± 5.2	242–403, 47	450.3 ± 7.8	323–599, 47	0.434 ± 0.03	0.393–0.486, 47	0.302 ± 0.01	0.282–0.327, 47	

Genus and species	SVL (mm)		ToL (mm)		TL/SVL		TL/ToL		SVL at maturity (mm)
	Mean ± SE	Range, N	Mean ± SE	Range, N	Mean ± SE	Range, N	Mean ± SE	Range, N	
statistic	$t = 6.48^*$ $p < 0.001$		$t = 3.41^*$ $p < 0.001$		$z = 7.4^*$ $p < 0.001$		$z = 7.3^*$ $p < 0.001$		
neonate	—		—		—		—		—
Regina septemvittata									
male	405.5 ± 7.7	318–500, 33	539.6 ± 11.2	420–677, 29	0.336 ± 0.03	0.295–0.376, 30	0.251 ± 0.02	0.228–0.273, 30	
female	490.3 ± 9.7	400–638, 35	630.5 ± 10.7	518–748, 40	0.296 ± 0.02	0.259–0.334, 34	0.227 ± 0.01	0.197–0.25, 30	
statistic	$t = 6.65^*$ $p < 0.001$		$t = 5.73^*$ $p < 0.001$		$z = 6.1^*$ $p < 0.001$		$z = 6.4^*$ $p < 0.001$		
neonate	—		—		—		—		—
Storeria dekayi									
male	210.7 ± 2.2	175–255, 52	277.6 ± 2.7	231–331, 49	0.325 ± 0.04	0.24–0.378, 49	0.241 ± 0.01	0.22–0.265, 49	
female	254 ± 2.7	222–303, 68	315.8 ± 3.5	273–401, 64	0.243 ± 0.01	0.214–0.282, 64	0.195 ± 0.01	0.176–0.221, 64	
statistic	$t = 6.45^*$ $p < 0.001$		$t = 3.41^*$ $p < 0.001$		$z = 7.5^*$ $p < 0.001$		$z = 7.6^*$ $p < 0.001$		
neonate	—		—		—		—		—
Storeria occipitomaculata occipitomaculata									
male	213.1 ± 3.8	170–258, 39	283.3 ± 4.2	211–345, 37	0.317 ± 0.01	0.26–0.36, 37	0.24 ± 0.01	0.22–0.29, 37	170
female	245.9 ± 3.3	185–298, 50	308.5 ± 4.3	227–372, 46	0.259 ± 0.01	0.21–0.26, 46	0.204 ± 0.01	0.18–0.23, 46	185
statistic	$t = 2.59^*$ $p = 0.01$		$t = 2.83^*$ $p = 0.005$		$z = 5.2^*$ $p < 0.001$		$z = 5.2^*$ $p < 0.001$		
neonate	73.8 ± 0.8	65–84, 68	96.7 ± 1.1	86–119, 68					—

Thamnophis brachystoma									
male	273.1 ± 3.7	200–363, 102	366.8 ± 5.3	261–474, 93	0.348 ± 0.01	0.299–0.381, 102	0.256 ± 0.01	0.21–0.284, 93	200
female	325.3 ± 3.6	273–416, 93	418 ± 4.7	349–525, 74	0.297 ± 0.01	0.245–0.346, 93	0.23 ± 0.01	0.2–0.25, 74	273
statistic	t = 9.9*	p < 0.001	t = 6.9*	p < 0.001	z = 7.8*	p < 0.001	z = 7.9*	p < 0.001	—
neonate	111.3 ± 1.5	99±115, 68	148.5 ± 2.4	132–155, 68	—		—		—
Thamnophis sauritus									
male	400.5 ± 11.8	310–480, 15	614.5 ± 24	474–725, 10	0.533 ± 0.09	0.489–0.585, 10	0.342 ± 0.04	0.328–0.369, 10	330
female	459.3 ± 10.5	350–607, 31	682.0 ± 19.3	540–860, 19	0.486 ± 0.08	0.421–0.433, 18	0.326 ± 0.03	0.296–0.348, 18	370
statistic	t = -3.75*	p < 0.001	t = 2.73*	p < 0.001	z = 3.5*	p < 0.001	z = 3.5*	p < 0.001	—
neonate	158.5 ± 1.2	146–167, 18	236 ± 1.7	221–247, 18	—		—		—
Thamnophis sirtalis sirtalis									
male	337.6 ± 5.7	270–462, 58	444.5 ± 8.5	335–607, 51	0.321 ± 0.02	0.285–0.365, 50	0.242 ± 0.01	0.221–0.267, 50	270
female	439 ± 6.3	360–640, 52	550.3 ± 11.1	400–800, 38	0.276 ± 0.02	0.239–0.313, 37	0.216 ± 0.02	0.193–0.245, 37	360–380
statistic	t = 11.2*	p < 0.001	t = 7.8*	p < 0.001	z = 7.5*	p < 0.001	z = 7.2*	p < 0.001	—
neonate		—			—				—
Virginia valeriae pulchra									
male	199.6 ± 3.7	150–270, 38	248.1 ± 4.2	186–285, 38	0.259 ± 0.02	0.225–0.288, 39	0.206 ± 0.02	0.152–0.2, 32	170–175
female	240.7 ± 3.1	200–300, 30	282.5 ± 4.7	237–354, 29	0.181 ± 0.01	0.185–0.224, 38	0.153 ± 0.01	0.132–0.171, 33	220–230
statistic	t = 7.69*	p < 0.001	t = -5.34*	p < 0.001	z = 7.2*	p < 0.001	z = 7.2*	p < 0.001	—
neonate	85.9 ± 1	75–99, 38	103.4 ± 1.1	89–122, 38	—		—		—

Genus and species	SVL (mm)		ToL (mm)		TL/SVL		TL/ToL		SVL at maturity (mm)
	Mean ± SE	Range, N	Mean ± SE	Range, N	Mean ± SE	Range, N	Mean ± SE	Range, N	
Agkistrodon contortrix mokasen									
male	705.5 ± 9.2	500–963, 37	798.9 ± 21	580–1,084, 35	0.14 ± 0.02	0.119–0.178, 37	0.127 ± 0.01	0.106–0.151, 37	480
female	558.7 ± 6.4	520–600, 21	641.5 ± 6.1	580–700, 21	0.14 ± 0.01	0.136–0.167, 21	0.128 ± 1.01	0.118–0.143, 23	460–500
statistic	$t = -5.07^*$		$t = -5.10^*$		$z = 0.31$		$z = 0.07$		
	$p < 0.001$		$p < 0.001$		$p = 0.75$		$p = 0.93$		
neonate	181.8 ± 1.92	160–215, 56	218.9 ± 2.18	190–248, 56	—		—		—
Sistrurus catenatus catenatus									
male	441.4 ± 38.5	345–630, 7	495 ± 43.9	383–710, 9	0.12 ± 0.02	0.11–0.126, 7	0.107 ± 0.02	0.099–0.112, 7	—
female	541 ± 15	460–625, 10	592.5 ± 18.1	497–692, 10	0.94 ± 0.03	0.8–0.115, 10	0.085 ± 0.03	0.074–0.104, 10	—
statistic	$t = 2.71^*$		$t = 2.3^*$		$z = 3.22^*$		$z = 3.22^*$		
	$p = 0.007$		$p = 0.01$		$p < 0.001$		$p = 0.001$		
neonate	—		—		—		—		—

Reproductive Data

SALAMANDERS

The r statistic is used to determine if there is a significant correlation between female body size and clutch size. Statistically significant r values are indicated by an asterisk. Reproductive data are not available for the following Pennsylvania salamander species: *Ambystoma jeffersonianum, A. maculatum, A. opacum, A. tigrinum tigrinum, Aneides aeneus, Desmognathus monticola, Notophthalmus viridescens viridescens, Plethodon richmondi, P. wehrle,* and *Pseudotriton montanus montanus.*

Species	No. of eggs		Statistic
	Mean ± SE	Range, N	
Cryptobranchus alleganiensis alleganiensis	359 ± 81.5	235–478, 11	$r = 0.84^*$ $p < 0.001$
Necturus maculosus maculosus	108.6 ± 4.5	42–182, 59	$r = 0.74^*$ $p < 0.001$
Desmognathus fuscus fuscus	28.6 ± 1.90	18–51, 18	$r = 0.8^*$ $p < 0.001$
Desmognathus ochrophaeus	19.1 ± 0.8	12–24, 26	$r = 0.67^*$ $p < 0.001$
Eurycea bislineata	40.7 ± 2.1	30–74, 21	$r = 0.39$ $p = 0.07$
Eurycea longicauda longicauda	60.5 ± 5.3	33–92, 15	$r = 0.79^*$ $p = 0.003$
Gyrinophilus porphyriticus porphyriticus	78.4 ± 6.5	44–132, 5	—
Hemidactylium scutatum	22.4 ± 3.2	8–38, 10	$r = 0.78^*$ $p = 0.003$
Plethodon cinereus	6.0 ± 0.3	3–11, 34	$r = 0.55^*$ $p < 0.001$
Plethodon glutinosus	25	12–34, 7	$r = 0.83^*$ $p = 0.05$
Plethodon hoffmani	6.1 ± 0.3	4–9, 14	$r = 0.16$ $p = 0.29$
Pseudotriton ruber	78.8 ± 7.7	50–102, 8	—

LIZARDS

The r statistic is used to determine if there is a significant correlation between female body size and clutch size. Statistically significant r values are indicated by an asterisk. Reproductive data do not exist for the following Pennslvania lizard species: *Sceloporus undulatus hyacinthinus* and *Eumeces laticeps*.

| | No. of eggs | | |
Species	Mean ± SE	Range, N	Statistic
Eumeces anthracinus anthracinus	7.4 ± 0.3	5–11, 9	r = 0.87 p = 0.12
Eumeces fasciatus	9.0 ± 0.7	8–11, 4	—

SNAKES

The r statistic is used to determine if there is a significant correlation between female body size and clutch or litter size. Statistically significant r values are indicated by an asterisk. Reproductive data do not exist for the following Pennsylvanis snake species: *Clonophis kirtlandii, Crotalus horridus, Elaphe obsoleta obsoleta, Opheodrys aestivus, Sistrurus catenatus catenatus,* and *Virginia valeriae valeriae.*

| | No. of eggs or young | | |
Species	Mean ± SE	Range, N	Statistic
Carphophis amoenus amoenus	5 ± 0	5, 3	—
Coluber constrictor constrictor	13.7 ± 1.5	6–19, 10	r = 0.95* p < 0.001
Diadophis punctatus edwardsi	3.8 ± 0.1	2–10, 148	r = 0.58* p < 0.001
Heterodon platyrhinos platyrhinos	14.8 ± 2.8	9–25, 8	r = 0.90* p = 0.005
Lampropeltis triangulum triangulum	9.7 ± 0.8	6–14, 10	r = 0.00 p = 1
Nerodia sipedon sipedon	20.6 ± 2.0	11–36, 14	r = 0.78* p < 0.001
Opheodrys vernalis	5.4 ± 0.3	3–7, 19	r = 0.03 p = 0.43
Regina septemvittata	9.7 ± 0.6	4–15, 20	r = 0.84* p < 0.001

| Species | No. of eggs or young | | Statistic |
	Mean ± SE	Range, N	
Storeria *dekayi* *dekayi*	14.2 ± 0.8	5–25, 24	$r = 0.51^*$ $p < 0.001$
Storeria *occipitomaculata* *occipitomaculata*	11.5 ± 0.5	4–21, 45	$r = 0.84^*$ $p < 0.001$
Thamnophis *brachystoma*	9.2 ± 0.4	5–14, 27	$r = 0.66^*$ $p < 0.001$
Thamnophis *sauritus*	11.3 ± 0.5	8–13, 8	$r = 0.52$ $p = 0.09$
Thamnophis *sirtalis* *sirtalis*	22.4 ± 2.6	4–30, 39	$r = 0.76^*$ $p < 0.001$
Virginia *valeriae* *pulchra*	7.2 ± 0.4	4–11, 14	$r = 0.36$ $p = 0.09$
Agkistrodon *contortrix* *mokasen*	5.7 ± 0.4	4–9, 13	$r = 0.66^*$ $p = 0.006$

Glossary

Adpress   To press close. In herpetology, to press the forelimbs backward and the hind limbs forward along the sides of the body, as in the number of costal grooves between adpressed limbs.

Aestivation   A state of inactivity brought about by hot or dry climatic conditions.

Agonistic behavior   Aggressive behavior between members of the same species.

Allometric growth   Changes in the shape or relative proportion of body parts correlated with growth.

Amplexus   The mating embrace of frogs and toads, in which the male grasps the female around the waist or chest with his forelegs; also, the mating embrace of newts, in which the male grasps the female around the neck or head with his hind legs.

Anal plate   The ventral scale directly anterior to the vent; in snakes, it may be divided or entire.

Arboreal   Existing primarily in trees or shrubs.

Arenicolous   Living or occurring in a sandy habitat.

Balancers   Thin, rodlike projections on each side of the head of some early larvae of pond-type salamanders. They function to prevent the larvae from sinking into the substrate and also allow the larvae to maintain a normal position in the water column.

Barbel   Small fleshy projection, usually located on the chin of an animal.

Base   Part of the tail where it is joined to the body.

Benthic   Living on the bottom substrate of a body of water.

Biennial   Refers to an event that occurs every other year, such as biennial reproduction, in which eggs are laid in alternating years.

Bifurcate   Split or divided into two parts or segments.

Bimodal   Having two main peaks (modes) of occurrence within a given time period, usually a year.

Bridge   One of the bony structures that unite the carapace and plastron of a turtle's shell.

Brumation   An inactive state brought about by reduced environmental temperatures; often referred to as hibernation.

Canthus rostralis   A ridge, that runs along the side of the head from the corner of the eye to the nares and that is lighter in color than the rest of the head.

Carapace   The dorsal portion of the shell of a turtle.

Caudal   Referring to the tail or the posterior end of the organism.

Caudal autotomy The ability of an animal to shed its tail, usually in response to an attack from a predator; common to many species of salamanders and lizards.

Cavernicolous Referring to organisms that live in caves.

CL Medial straight-line carapace length of turtles.

Cloaca The chamber just inside the vent that receives reproductive, excretory, and digestive-waste products (e.g., gametes, urine, feces).

Congeneric Referring to species of the same genus.

Conspecific Referring to individuals of the same species.

Constriction A mode of subduing prey in which the snake coils about the potential prey item and slowly tightens its hold until the animal is no longer able to breath. Death, as a consequence, occurs by suffocation.

Costal Referring to the area of the ribs or the side of the body.

Costal grooves Vertical lines present on the sides of some salamanders, at the insertion between the back and the forelimbs and the back and the hind limbs.

Cranial crests Bony ridges located on the head of most toads. The number of crests and their degree of development differ from species to species.

Cruciform Shaped like a cross.

Cryptic behavior Any behavior on the part of an organism that reduces the probability of its being seen or recognized.

Cryptic coloration A pattern of coloration that allows the organism to blend into its environment.

Cycloid scales Circular, highly polished scales.

Diel Referring to a 24-hour (i.e., daily) cycle.

Diploid Possessing two pairs of chromosomes in each body cell.

Direct development The process in which all embyronic development occurs within the confines of the egg. Hence, the emerging young resembles the adult in form.

Disjunct distribution Referring to situation in which the range of a species is not continuous, but rather is restricted to isolated areas. Disjunct distributions often occur at the margins of a species' range.

Diurnal Active during the day.

Dorsal Pertaining to the back.

Dorsolateral fold A thick ridge of skin along the side of the back of some frogs.

Electrophoresis A laboratory technique utilizing an electrical current to separate proteins as they travel through a medium such as a starch gel. Used in genetic and population studies.

Eutrophic Referring to a body of water that is rich in nutrients.

Extirpation The local or regional extinction of a species population or populations; literal meaning, to "pull up by the roots."

Follicle An egg while it is still contained within the ovary.

Fossorial Referring to an underground existence or underground activity.

Gill slit An external opening at the side of the neck through which water flows out of the gill chamber.

Gravid The condition of containing mature eggs or developing young.

Gular scute The most anterior scute or pair of scutes on the plastron of a turtle.

Hectare A metric measure of area, being an area 100 m on a side. Approximately equal to 2.4 acres.

Hedonic gland Glandular structure, usually located on the head, that secretes chemicals used in courtship.

Hibernation A state of inactivity brought about by reduced environmental temperatures. In reptiles and amphibians, the state of inactivity brought about by reduced temperature is more appropriately called brumation, but hibernation has such common usage that it is generally acceptable.

Home range The area in which an animal carries out its normal daily activities.

Hypertrophied Referring to any structure that is overdeveloped or excessively developed.

Infralabial Referring to any scale bordering the lateral margins of the lower lip.

Innate Existing from birth. In biology, behaviors that an animal is born with are innate or instinctive.

Intercalary disc An additional element found in the fingers and toes of treefrogs. It is located between the ultimate and penultimate phalange and allows for greater flexibility in climbing.

Intergrade Referring to the organism that results from a cross between members of different subspecies or species. When such a crossing occurs commonly in a specific geographic area, the area is referred to as a zone of intergradation.

Keeled Possessing a distinct medial ridge, as in the keeled scales of snakes and lizards.

Kinosternid Any member of the family Kinosternidae.

Labial Referring to the lips, as in labial scales.

Larva The gilled immature stage of frogs, toads, and some salamanders.

Lateral Pertaining to the sides of the body.

Littoral zone That area of a lake or pond where rooted aquatic vegetation occurs.

Locus The position that a gene occupies in a chromosome.

Loreal pit A depression between the eye and the nares (in the loreal scale) of rattlesnakes and copperheads that contains heat-sensitive receptors.

Marginals The scutes located along the periphery of the carapace of a turtle's shell.

Mature The condition of being capable of reproduction.

Medial Pertaining to the middle of the body or toward the middle.

Mental scale The medial, unpaired scale at the tip of the chin in snakes and lizards.

Mesic Referring to a moist environment.

Metamorphosis A series of changes that occur when a larva transforms to an adult. The process is more extreme in frogs and toads than it is in salamanders.

Nares The openings to the nasal passages.

Nasolabial groove A moderately deep groove on plethodontid salamanders that runs from the nares to the border of the upper lip.

Neonate A recently born or hatched individual.

Neotenic Retaining larval characteristics in the adult stage.

Nocturnal Active at night.

Nuchal Referring to the back of the neck.

Nuptial excrescences Bumps or tuberosities on the appendages of male amphibians that function in holding onto a female during the process of amplexus.

Ocellus A circular, eyelike spot present in the pattern of some animals.

Oligotrophic Referring to a lake that is low in nutrients and, therefore, plant life and primary productivity.

Omnivorous Feeding on a mixed diet of plant and animal material.

Ontogenetic change Change in the appearance of an organism brought about by the developmental or aging process.

Ophiophagus Feeding on snakes.

Osteoderms Bony elements located in the skin of an animal. Usually associated with and underlying the scales.

Oviparous Referring to the reproductive strategy of laying eggs.

Oviposition The act of laying eggs.

Ovoviviparous Referring to the reproductive strategy of retaining the egg inside the body until ready to hatch.

Parotoid glands Enlarged glands located on the back of the head of toads and some species of frog.

Phalanges The bones of the toes and fingers.

Plastron The ventral portion of the shell of a turtle.

Pond larvae Larvae of salamanders that are adapted to a life in standing water. These generally have large feathery gills, well-developed dorsal and caudal fins, and a fairly heavy cylindrical body.

Polytypic When used in reference to species, the term indicates the existence of two or more subspecies.

Postmental scale The second medial chin scale of a lizard; may be entire or transversely divided in skinks.

Proximal That portion nearest the body.

Release call A call given by either a male or a nonreceptive female frog when clasped in a mating embrace by a male frog.

Rostral scale The unpaired scale at the tip of the nose of snakes and lizards.

Satellite male A noncalling male frog that remains close to a male that is calling.

Scute Ventral body scale of snake or enlarged plates on turtle shell.

Sibling species   Species that are reproductively isolated from each other but are indistinguishable on the basis of external characters of appearance.

Spermatophore   A gelatinous structure produced within the cloacal region of male salamanders that is used to support a mass of sperm.

Spermatotheca   A pocketlike structure in the wall of the cloaca of female salamanders where sperm is stored until needed to fertilize eggs.

Subcaudal scales   The scales that form the ventral surface of the tail of a snake.

Subocular scale   Scales located below the eye.

SUL   Snout-urostyle length, the straight-line distance from the tip of the snout to the end of the body of frogs and toads.

Supracillary scales   Small scales bordering the edge of the upper eyelid in lizards.

Supralabial scale   Any scale bordering the lateral margins of the upper lip of snakes and lizards.

SVL   Snout-vent length, measured from the tip of the snout to the proximal margin of the cloaca of snakes, lizards, and salamanders.

Talus   Large deposits of loose rock found at the base of hills and along hillsides.

Territory   A defended area occupied by an animal.

Tetraploid   Possessing fours pairs of chromosomes in each body cell.

ToL   Total length, measured from the tip of the snout to the tip of the tail of snakes, lizards, salamanders, and tadpoles.

Transformation   *See* Metamorphosis.

Tympanum   A thin, usually circular, tightly stretched membrane that transmits sound waves to the middle ear; on frogs and toads located on the sides of the head, posterior and dorsal to the eye.

Unimodal   Having one main peak (mode) of occurrence within a given time period, usually a year.

Urostyle   The fused caudal (tail) vertebrae of frogs and toads that forms a bony rodlike element.

Vent   Opening to the cloacal chamber.

Venter   The belly of the animal.

Ventral   Pertaining to the belly.

Vitellogenesis   The process of depositing yolk into an ovarian follicle.

Viviparous   A condition in which the embryo develops within the female's reproductive system and receives at least some nutrition directly from the female via a placenta.

Literature Cited

Akin, J.A. 1998a. Fourier series estimation of ground skink population density. Copeia 1998: 519–522.

———. 1998b. Intra- and inter-sexual aggression in the ground skink *(Scincella lateralis)*. Can. J. Zool. 76: 87–93.

Akin, J.A., and V.R. Townsend Jr. 1998. *Scincella lateralis* (ground skink): Aquatic behavior. Herpetol. Rev. 29: 43.

Aldridge, R.D. 1979. Female reproductive cycles of the snakes *Arizona elegans* and *Crotalus viridis*. Herpetologica 35: 256–261.

Aldridge, R.D., and W.S. Brown. 1995. Male reproductive cycle, age at maturity, and cost of reproduction in the timber rattlesnake *(Crotalus horridus)*. J. Herpetol. 29: 399–407.

Allard, H.A. 1945. A color variant of the eastern worm snake. Copeia 1945: 42.

Anderson, J.D., and R.V. Giacosie. 1967. *Ambystoma laterale* in New Jersey. Herpetologica 23: 108–111.

Anderson, J.D., and P.J. Martino. 1966. The life history of *Eurycea longicauda longicauda* associated with ponds. Amer. Midl. Natur. 75: 257–279.

———. 1967. Food habits of *Eurycea longicauda longicauda*. Herpetologica 23: 105–108.

Anderson, J.D., and G.K. Williamson. 1973. The breeding season of *Ambystoma opacum* in the northern and southern parts of its range. J. Herpetol. 7: 320–321.

Anderson, P. 1965. The reptiles of Missouri. Columbia: University of Missouri Press.

Angle, J.P. 1969. The reproductive cycle of the northern ravine salamander, *Plethodon richmondi richmondi*, in the Valley and Ridge Province of Pennsylvania and Maryland. J. Wash. Acad. Sci. 59: 192–202.

Arndt, R.G. 1980. A hibernating eastern hognose snake, *Heterodon platyrhinos*. Herpetol. Rev. 11: 30–32.

Arndt, R.G., and W.A. Potter. 1973. A population of the map turtle, *Graptemys geographica*, in the Delaware River, Pennsylvania. J. Herpetol. 7: 373–375.

Ashton, R.E., Jr. 1975. A study of movement, home range, and winter behavior of *Desmognathus fuscus* (Rafinesque). J. Herpetol. 9: 85–91.

Ashton, R.E., Jr., and P.S. Ashton. 1978. Movements and winter behavior of *Eurycea bislineata* (Amphibia, Urodela, Plethodontidae). J. Herpetol. 12: 295–298.

Atkinson, D.A. 1901. The reptiles of Allegheny County, Pennsylvania. Ann. Carnegie Mus. 1: 145–157.

Atkinson, D.A., and M.G. Netting. 1927. The distribution and habits of the massasauga. Bull. Antivenin Inst. Amer. 1: 40–44.

The Atlas of Pennsylvania. 1989. Philadelphia: Temple University Press.

Attaway, M.B., G.C. Packard, and M.J. Packard. 1998. Hatchling painted turtles *(Chrysemys picta)* survive only brief freezing of their bodily fluids. Comp. Biochem. Physiol. A 120: 405–408.

Babcock, H.L. 1971. Turtles of the northeastern United States. New York: Dover Publications.

Bachman, M.D., R.G. Carlton, J.M. Burkholder, and R.G. Wetzel. 1986. Symbiosis between salamander eggs and green algae: Microelectrode measurements inside eggs demonstrate effect of photosynthesis on oxygen concentration. Can. J. Zool. 64: 1586–1588.

Bailey, R.M. 1948. Winter mortality in the snake *Storeria dekayi*. Copeia 1948: 215.

Baldauf, R.J. 1943. Handlist of Berks County amphibians and reptiles. Mengel Nat. Hist. Soc. Lflt. 1: 1–8.

———. 1952. Climatic factors influencing the breeding migration of the spotted salamander, *Ambystoma maculatum* (Shaw). Copeia 1952: 178–181.

Barbour, R.W. 1950. The reptiles of Big Black Mountain, Harlan County, Kentucky. Copeia 1950: 100–107.

———. 1960. A study of the worm snake, *Carphophis amoenus* Say, in Kentucky. Trans. Ky. Acad. Sci. 21: 10–16.

Barbour, R.W., and E.P. Walters. 1941. Notes on the breeding habits of *Pseudacris brachyphona*. Copeia 1941: 116.

Barbour, R.W., J.W. Hardin, J.P. Schafer, and M.J. Harvey. 1969a. Home range, movements, and activity of the dusky salamander, *Desmognathus fuscus*. Copeia 1969: 293–297.

Barbour, R.W., W.J. Harvey, J.P. Schafer, and J.W. Hardin. 1969b. Home range, movements, and activity of the eastern worm snake *Carphophis amoenus amoenus*. Ecology 50: 470–476.

Barton, A.J. 1947. An albino eastern garter snake from Pennsylvania. Copeia 1947: 140.

———. 1948. Snake litters. Herpetologica 4: 198.

Barton, A.J., and J.W. Price. 1955. Our knowledge of the bog turtle, *Clemmys muhlenbergi*, surveyed and augmented. Copeia 1955: 159–165.

Baumann, W.L., and M. Huels. 1982. Nests of the two-lined salamander, *Eurycea bislineata*. J. Herpetol. 16: 81–83.

Bayless, L.E. 1975. Population parameters for *Chrysemys picta* in a New York pond. Amer. Midl. Natur. 93: 168–176.

Beane, E.D., T.J. Thorp, and D.A. Jackan. 1998. *Heterodon simus* (southern hognose snake): Diet. Herpetol. Rev. 29: 44–45.

Beatson, R.R. 1976. Environmental and genetical correlates of disruptive coloration in the water snake, *Natrix s. sipedon*. Evolution. 30: 241–252.

Beiswenger, R.E. 1975. Structure and function in aggregations of the American toad, *Bufo americanus*. Herpetologica 31: 222–233.

Bell, E.L. 1955. An aggregation of salamanders. Proc. Pa. Acad. Sci. 29: 265–266.

———. 1960. Observations on the amphibians and reptiles of Huntingdon County, Pennsylvania. Proc. Pa. Acad. Sci. 34: 159–161.

Bellis, E.D. 1965. Home range and movements of the wood frog in a northern bog. Ecology 46: 90–98.

Bennett, D.H. 1972. Notes on the terrestrial wintering of mud turtles (*Kinosternon subrubrum*). Herpetologica 28: 245–247.

Berven, K.A. 1988. Factors affecting variation in reproductive traits within a population of wood frogs (*Rana sylvatica*). Copeia 1988: 605–615.

Bishop, S.C. 1926. Notes on the habits and development of the mudpuppy *Necturus maculosus* (Rafinesque). N.Y. State Mus. Bull. 268: 1–38.

———. 1941. The salamanders of New York. N.Y. State Mus. Bull. 324.

Blair, W.F. 1958. Mating call in the speciation of anuran amphibians. Amer. Natur. 42: 27–51.

Blanchard, F.N. 1923. The snakes of the genus *Virginia*. Pap. Mich. Acad. Sci. Arts Lett. 3: 343–365.

———. 1928. Topics from the life history and habits of the red-backed salamander in southern Michigan. Amer. Natur. 62: 156–164.

———. 1930. Further studies of the eggs and young of the eastern ringneck snake, *Diadophis punctatus edwardsii*. Bull. Antivenin Inst. Amer. 4: 4–10.

———. 1931. Secondary sexual characteristics of certain snakes. Bull. Antivenin Inst. Amer. 4: 95–104.

———. 1933a. Eggs and young of the smooth green snake, *Liopeltis vernalis* (Harlan). Pap. Mich. Acad. Sci. Arts Lett. 17: 493–508.

———. 1933b. Late autumn collections and hibernating situations of the salamander *Hemidactylium scutatum* (Schlegel) in southern Michigan. Copeia 1933: 216.

———. 1933c. Spermatophores and the mating season of the salamander *Hemidactylium scutatum* (Schlegel). Copeia 1933: 40.

———. 1934. The relation of the female four-toed salamander to her nest. Copeia 1934: 137–138.

———. 1937. Data on the natural history of the red-bellied snake, *Storeria occipito-maculata* (Storer) in northern Michigan. Copeia 1937: 151–162.

Blanchard, F.N., and F. Blanchard. 1940. The inheritance of melanism in the garter snake *Thamnophis sirtalis sirtalis* (Linnaeus) and some evidence of effective autumn mating. Pap. Mich. Acad. Sci. Arts Lett. 26: 117–193.

———. 1942. Mating of the garter snake *Thamnophis sirtalis sirtalis* (Linnaeus). Pap. Mich. Acad. Sci., Arts Lett. 27: 215–234.

Bleakney, S. 1952. The amphibians and reptiles of Nova Scotia. Can. Field Nat. 66: 125–129.

———. 1958. A zoogeographical study of the amphibians and reptiles of eastern Canada. Nat. Mus. Canada Bull. no. 155. Biol. series no. 54.

Blem, C.R., and L.B. Blem. 1985. Notes on *Virginia* (Reptilia: Colubridae) in Virginia. Brimleyana 11: 87–95.

———. 1989. Tolerance of acidity in a Virginia population of the spotted salamander, *Ambystoma maculatum* (Amphibia: Ambystomatidae). Brimleyana 15: 37–45.

Bogart, J.P., and A.O. Wasserman. 1972. Diploid-polyploid cryptic species pairs: A possible clue to evolution by polyploidization in anuran amphibians. Cytogenetics 11: 7–24.

Bohnsack, K.K. 1951. Temperature data on the terrestrial hibernation of the green frog, *Rana clamitans*. Copeia 1951: 236–239.

Bond, H.D. 1931. Some amphibians and reptiles of Monongalia County, West Virginia. Copeia 1931: 53–54.

Bothner, R.C. 1963. A hibernaculum of the short-headed garter snake, *Thamnophis brachystoma* Cope. Copeia 1963: 572–573.

———. 1976. *Thamnophis brachystoma*. Cat. Amer. Amph. Rept. 190.1–190.2.

Bothner, R.C., and T.C. Moore. 1964. A collection of *Haldea valeriae pulchra* from western Pennsylvania, with notes on some litters of their young. Copeia 1964: 709–710.

Branch, L.C., and R. Altig. 1981. Nocturnal stratification of three species of *Ambystoma* larvae. Copeia 1981: 870–873.

Brandon, R.A., G.M. Labanick, and J.E. Huheey. 1979. Relative palatability, defensive behavior, and mimetic relationships of red salamanders *(Pseudotriton ruber)*, mud salamanders *(Pseudotriton montanus)*, and red efts *(Notophthalmus viridescens)*. Herpetologica 35: 289–303.

Brandt, B.B. 1936. The frogs and toads of eastern North Carolina. Copeia 1936: 215–223.

Branson, B.A., and E.C. Baker. 1974. An ecological study of the queen snake, *Regina septemvittata* (Say) in Kentucky. Tulane Stud. Zool. Bot. 18: 153–171.

Braswell, A.L., and W.M. Palmer. 1984. *Cemophora coccinea copei* (northern scarlet snake) reproduction. Herpetol. Rev. 15: 49.

Breckenridge, W.J. 1944. Reptiles and amphibians of Minnesota. Minneapolis: University of Minnesota Press.

Breden, F., A. Lum, and R. Wassersug. 1982. Body size and orientation in aggregates of toad tadpoles, *Bufo woodhousei*. Copeia 1982: 672–680.

Breder, R.B. 1927. The courtship of the spotted salamander. Zool. Soc. Bull. 30: 50–56.

Breitenbach, G.L. 1982. The frequency of communal nesting and solitary brooding in the salamander *Hemidactylum scutatum*. J. Herpetol. 16: 341–346.

Brodie, E.D., Jr. 1976. Additional comments on the Batesian mimicry of *Notophthalmus viridescens* efts by *Pseudotriton ruber*. Herpetologica 32: 68–70.

———. 1977. Salamander antipredator postures. Copeia 1977: 523–535.

Brodie, E.D., Jr., D. Robert, T. Nowak, and W.R. Harvey. 1979. The effectiveness of antipredator secretions and behavior of selected salamanders against shrews. Copeia 1979: 270–274.

Brooks, G.R. 1964. Food habits of the ground skink. Q. J. Fla. Acad. Sci. 26: 361–367.

———. 1967. Population ecology of the ground skink, *Lygosoma laterale* (Say). Ecol. Monogr. 37: 71–87.

———. 1975. *Scincella lateralis* (Say). Cat. Amer. Amph. Rept. 169.1–169.4.

Brooks, R.J., G.P. Brown, and D.A. Gailbraith. 1991. Effects of a sudden increase in natural mortality of adults on a population of the common snapping turtle *(Chelydra serpentina)*. Can. J. Zool. 69: 1314–1320.

Brooks, R.J., C.M. Shilton, G.P. Brown, and N.W.S. Quinn. 1992. Body size, age distribution, and reproduction in a northern population of wood turtles *(Clemmys insculpta)*. Can. J. Zool. 70: 462–469.

Brown, E.E. 1958. Feeding habits of the northern water snake *Natrix sipedon sipedon* Linnaeus. Zoologica 43: 55–71.

———. 1979a. Some snake food records from the Carolinas. Brimleyana 1: 113–124.

———. 1979b. Stray food records from New York and Michigan snakes. Amer. Midl. Natur. 102: 200–203.

Brown, G.P., and R.J. Brooks. 1994. Characteristics of and fidelity to hibernacula in a northern population of snapping turtles *(Chelydra serpentina)*. Copeia 1994: 222–226.

Brown, G.P., and P.J. Weatherhead. 1997. Effects of reproduction on survival and growth of female northern water snakes, *Nerodia sipedon*. Can. J. Zool. 75: 424–432.

Brown, J.L. 1965. Stability of color phase ratio in populations of *Plethodon cinereus*. Copeia 1965: 95–98.

Brown, L.E., R.S. Funk, D. Moll, and J.K. Tucker. 1975. Distributional notes on reptiles in Illinois. Herpetol. Rev. 6: 78–79.

Brown, P.S., S.A. Hastings, and B.E. Frye. 1977. A comparison of the water balance response in five species of plethodontid salamanders. Physiol. Zool. 50: 203–214.

Brown, W.S. 1982. Overwintering body temperatures of timber rattlesnakes *(Crotalus horridus)* in northeastern New York. J. Herpetol. 16: 145–150.

———. 1991. Female reproductive ecology in a northern population of the timber rattlesnake, *Crotalus horridus*. Herpetologica 47: 101–115.

————. 1995. Heterosexual groups and the mating season in a northern population of timber rattlesnakes, *Crotalus horridus*. Herpetol. Nat. Hist. 3: 127–133.

Brown, W.S., and W.S. Parker. 1976. Movement ecology of *Coluber constrictor* near communal hibernacula. Copeia 1976: 225–242.

Brown, W.S., D.W. Pyle, K.R. Greene, and J.B. Friedlaender. 1982. Movements and temperature relationships of timber rattlesnakes *(Crotalus horridus)* in northeastern New York. J. Herpetol. 16: 151–161.

Browne, R.A., N.A. Haskell, C.R. Griffin, and J.W. Ridgeway. 1996. Genetic variation among populations of the redbelly turtle *(Pseudemys rubriventris)*. Copeia 1996: 192–194.

Bruce, R.C. 1975. Reproductive biology of the mud salamander, *Pseudotriton montanus*, in western South Carolina. Copeia 1975: 129–137.

————. 1978. Reproductive biology of the salamander *Pseudotriton ruber* in the southern Blue Ridge Mountains. Copeia 1978: 417–423.

————. 1980. A model of the larval period of the spring salamander, *Gyrinophilus porphyriticus*, based on size-frequency distributions. Herpetologica 36: 78–86.

————. 1982. Egg-laying, larval period, and metamorphosis of *Eurycea bislineata* and *E. junaluska* at Santeetlah Creek, North Carolina. Copeia 1982: 755–762.

————. 1986. Upstream and downstream movements of *Eurycea bislineata* and other salamanders in a southern Appalachian stream. Herpetologica 42: 149–155.

————. 1989. Life history of the salamander *Desmognathus monticola*, with a comparison of the larval periods of *D. monticola* and *D. ochrophaeus*. Herpetologica 45: 144–155.

————. 1990. An explanation for differences in body size between two desmognathine salamanders. Copeia 1990: 1–9.

Bruce, R.C., and N.G. Hairston. 1990. Life-history correlates of body-size differences between two populations of the salamander, *Desmognathus monticola*. J. Herpetol. 24: 124–134.

Burger, J. 1977. Determinants of hatchling success in diamondback terrapin, *Malaclemys terrapin*. Amer. Midl. Natur. 97: 444–464.

————. 1990. Effects of incubation temperature on behavior of young black racers *(Coluber constrictor)* and kingsnakes *(Lampropeltis getulus)*. J. Herpetol. 24: 158–163.

Burger, J., and W.A. Montevecchi. 1975. Nest site selection in the terrapin, *Malaclemys terrapin*. Copeia 1975: 113–119.

Burger, J., and R.T. Zappalorti. 1986. Nest site selection by pine snakes, *Pituophis melanoleucus*, in the New Jersey Pine Barrens. Copeia 1986: 116–121.

————. 1988. Habitat use in free ranging pine snakes, *Pituophis melanoleucus*, in the New Jersey Pine Barrens. Herpetologica 44: 48–55.

————. 1991. Nesting behavior of pine snakes *(Pituophis melanoleucus)* in the New Jersey Pine Barrens. J. Herpetol. 25: 152–160.

Burger, J., R.T. Zappalorti, M. Gochfeld, W.I. Boarman, M. Caffrey, V. Doig, S.D. Garber, B. Lauro, M. Mikorsky, C. Safina, and J. Silva. 1988. Hibernacula and summer den sites of pine snakes *(Pituophis melanoleucus)* in the New Jersey Pine Barrens. J. Herpetol. 22: 425–433.

Burger, J., R.T. Zappalorti, J. Dowell, T. Georgiadise, J. Hill, and M. Gochfeld. 1992. Subterranean predation on pine snakes *(Pituophis melanoleucus)*. J. Herpetol. 26: 259–263.

Burghardt, G.M. 1968. Chemical preference studies on newborn snakes of three sympatric species of *Natrix*. Copeia 1968: 732–737.

————. 1973. Chemical release of prey attack: Extension to naive newly hatched lizards, *Eumeces fasciatus*. Copeia 1973: 178–181.

388   *Literature Cited*

————. 1975. Chemical prey preference polymorphism in newborn garter snakes *Thamnophis sirtalis*. Behaviour 52: 202–225.

————. 1983. Aggregation and species discrimination in newborn snakes. Z. Tierpsychol. 61: 89–101.

Burghardt, G.M., and D. Denny. 1983. Effects of prey movement and prey odor on feeding in garter snakes. Z. Tierpsychol. 62: 329–347.

Burton, T.M. 1976. An analysis of the feeding ecology of the salamanders (Amphibia, Urodela) of the Hubbard Brook Experimental Forest, New Hampshire. J. Herpetol. 10: 187–204.

Burton, T.M., and G.E. Likens. 1975. Salamander populations and biomass in the Hubbard Brook Experimental Forest, New Hampshire. Copeia 1975: 541–546.

Bury, R.B. 1979. Review of the ecology and conservation of the bog turtle, *Clemmys muhlenbergii*. U.S. Fish. Wildl. Ser. Spec. Sci. Rep.—Wildl. 219.

Bush, F.M., and E.F. Menhinick. 1962. The food of *Bufo woodhousei fowleri* Hinckley. Herpetologica 18: 110–114.

Bushar, L.M., H.K. Reinert, and L. Gelbert. 1998. Genetic variation and gene flow within and between local populations of the timber rattlesnake, *Crotalus horridus*. Copeia 1998: 411–422.

Cagle, F. 1937. Egg laying habits of the slider turtle (*Pseudemys troosti*), the painted turtle (*Chrysemys picta*) and the musk turtle (*Sternotherus odoratus*). J. Tenn. Acad. Sci. 12: 87–95.

Cahn, A.R. 1937. The turtles of Illinois. Ill. Biol. Monogr. 35: 1–218.

Caldwell, J.P. 1986. Selection of egg deposition sites: A seasonal shift in the southern leopard frog, *Rana sphenocephala*. Copeia 1986: 249–253.

Caldwell, R.S. 1975. Observations on the winter activity of the red-backed salamander, *Plethodon cinereus*, in Indiana. Herpetologica 31: 21–22.

Canterbury, R.A., and T.K. Pauley. 1994. Time of mating and egg deposition of West Virginia populations of the salamander *Aneides aeneus*. J. Herpetol. 28: 431–434.

Carpenter, C.C. 1948. An erythristic *Thamnophis sirtalis sirtalis*. Herpetologica 4: 211–212.

————. 1952. Comparative ecology of the common garter snake (*Thamnophis s. sirtalis*), the ribbon snake (*Thamnophis s. sauritus*), and Butler's garter snake (*Thamnophis butleri*) in mixed populations. Ecol. Monogr. 22: 235–258.

————. 1953. A study of hibernacula and hibernating associations of snakes and amphibians in Michigan. Ecology 34: 74–80.

Carr, A. 1952. Handbook of turtles: The turtles of the United States, Canada, and Baja California. Ithaca, N.Y.: Comstock.

Carroll, T.E., and D.W. Ehrenfeld. 1978. Intermediate-range homing in the wood turtle, *Clemmys insculpta*. Copeia 1978: 117–126.

Catling, P.M., and B. Freedman. 1980. Food and feeding behavior of sympatric snakes at Amherstburg, Ontario. Can. Field Natur. 94: 28–33.

Cecil, S.G., and J.J. Just. 1979. Survival rate, population density and development of a naturally occurring anuran larva (*Rana catesbeiana*). Copeia 1979: 447–453.

Chase, J.D., K.R. Dixon, J.E. Gates, D. Jacobs, and G.J. Taylor. 1989. Habitat characteristics, population size, and home range of the bog turtle, *Clemmys muhlenbergii*, in Maryland. J. Herpetol. 23: 356–362.

Christens, E., and J.R. Bider. 1987. Nesting activity and hatching success of the painted turtle (*Chrysemys picta marginata*) in southwestern Quebec. Herpetologica 43: 55–65.

Christman, S.P. 1974. Geographic variation for salt water tolerance in the frog *Rana sphenocephala*. Copeia 1974: 773–778.

Clark, D.R., Jr. 1970. Ecological study of the worm snake *Carphophis vermis* (Kennicott). Univ. Kans. Publ. Mus. Natur. Hist. 19: 85–194.

Clark, D.R., Jr., and R.J. Hall. 1970. Function of the blue tail-coloration of the five-lined skink *(Eumeces fasciatus)*. Herpetologica 26: 271–274.

Clark, K.L. 1986. Responses of spotted salamander, *Ambystoma maculatum*, populations in central Ontario to habitat acidity. Can. Field Natur. 100: 463–469.

Clarke, R.D. 1974a. Activity and movement patterns in a popuation of Fowler's toad, *Bufo woodhousei fowleri*. Amer. Midl. Natur. 92: 257–274.

———. 1974b. Food habits of toads, genus *Bufo* (Amphibia: Bufonidae). Amer. Midl. Natur. 91: 140–147.

———. 1974c. Postmetamorphic growth rates in a natural population of Fowler's toad, *Bufo woodhousei fowleri*. Can. J. Zool. 52: 1489–1498.

———. 1977. Postmetamorphic survivorship of Fowler's toad, *Bufo woodhousei fowleri*. Copeia 1977: 594–597.

Clausen, H.J. 1936. Observations on the brown snake *Storeria dekayi* (Holbrook), with especial reference to the habits and birth of young. Copeia 1936: 98–102.

Clausen, R.T. 1938. Notes on *Eumeces anthracinus* in central New York. Copeia 1938: 3–7.

Claussen, D.L., P.M. Daniel, S. Jiang, and N.A. Adams. 1991. Hibernation in the eastern box turtle, *Terrapene c. carolina*. J. Herpetol. 25: 334–341.

Clay, W.M. 1935. The occurrence of albinos in a brood of the common water snake, *Natrix sipedon sipedon* (L.). Copeia 1935: 115–118.

Cliburn, J.W., and A.B. Porter. 1987. Vertical stratification of the salamanders *Aneides aeneus* and *Plethodon glutinosus* (Caudata: Plethodontidae). J. Ala. Acad. Sci. 58: 18–22.

Cochran, P.A. 1987a. *Graptemys geographica* (map turtle) adult mortality. Herpetol. Rev. 18: 37.

———. 1987b. *Opheodrys vernalis* (smooth green snake) behavior. Herpetol. Rev. 18: 36–37.

Cochran, P.A., and J.D. Lyons. 1985. *Necturus maculosus* (mudpuppy) juvenile ecology. Herpetol. Rev. 16: 53.

Cochran, P.A., and D.R. McConville. 1983. Feeding by *Trionyx spiniferus* in backwaters of the upper Mississippi River. J. Herpetol. 17: 82–86.

Cohen, E. 1948. Emergence of *Coluber constrictor constrictor* from hibernation. Copeia 1948: 137–138.

Collins, J.T. 1974. Amphibians and reptiles in Kans. Univ. Kans. Mus. Natur. Hist. Publ. Educ. Ser. 1.

Conant, R. 1938. On the seasonal occurrence of reptiles in Lucas County, Ohio. Herpetologica 1: 137–144.

———. 1943. Studies on North American water snakes. I. *Natrix kirtlandii* (Kennicott). Amer. Midl. Natur. 29: 313–341.

———. 1950. On the taxonomic status of *Thamnophis butleri* (Cope). Bull. Chic. Acad. Sci. 9: 71–77.

———. 1951. The reptiles of Ohio. Notre Dame, Ind.: University of Notre Dame Press.

———. 1975. A field guide to reptiles and amphibians of eastern and central North America. Boston: Houghton Mifflin.

———. 1978. Distributional patterns of North American snakes: Some examples of the effects of Pleistocene glaciation and subsequent climatic changes. Bull. Md. Herpetol. Soc. 14: 241–259.

Conant, R., and J.T. Collins. 1991. A field guide to reptiles and amphibians: Eastern and central North America. Boston: Houghton Mifflin.

Congdon, J.D., and R.E. Gatten Jr. 1989. Movements and energetics of nesting *Chrysemys picta.* Herpetologica 45: 94–100.

Congdon, J.D., D.W. Tinkle, G.L. Breitenbach, and R.C. van Loben Sels. 1983. Nesting ecology and hatching success in the turtle *Emydoidea blandingi.* Herpetologica 39: 417–429.

Congdon, J.D., G.L. Breitenbach, R.C. van Loben Sels, and D.W. Tinkle. 1987. Reproduction and nesting ecology of snapping turtles *(Chelydra serpentina)* in southeastern Michigan. Herpetologica 43: 39–54.

Cook, F.R. 1964. Communal egg laying in the smooth green snake. Herpetologica 20: 206–207.

Cooper, J.E. 1956. Aquatic hibernation of the red-backed salamander. Herpetologica 12: 165–167.

Cooper, W.E., Jr., and N. Burns. 1987. Social significance of ventrolateral coloration in the fence lizard, *Sceloporus undulatus.* Anim. Behav. 35: 526–532.

Cooper, W.E., Jr., and L.J. Vitt. 1986a. Blue tails and autotomy: Enhancement of predator avoidance in juvenile skinks. Z. Tierpsychol. 70: 265–276.

———. 1986b. Tracking of female conspecific odor trails by male broad-headed skinks *(Eumeces laticeps).* Ethology 71: 242–248.

———. 1987. Ethological isolation, sexual behavior and pheromones in the *fasciatus* species group of the lizard genus *Eumeces.* Ethology 75: 328–336.

Corse, W.A., and D.E. Metter. 1980. Economics, adult feeding and larval growth of *Rana catesbeiana* on a fish hatchery. J. Herpetol. 14: 231–238.

Costanzo, J.P. 1989. A physiological basis for prolonged submergence in hibernating garter snakes *Thamnophis sirtalis*: Evidence for an energy sparing adaptation. Physiol. Zool. 62: 580–592.

Costanzo, J.P., and R.E. Lee Jr. 1993. Cryoprotectant production capacity of the freeze-tolerant wood frog, *Rana sylvatica.* Can. J. Zool. 71: 71–75.

Courtois, D., R. Leclair Jr., S. Lacasse, and P. Magnan. 1995. Habitats préférentiels d'amphibiens ranidés dans des lacs oligotrophes du Bouclier laurentien, Québec. Can. J. Zool. 73: 1744–1753.

Criddle, S. 1937. Snakes from an ant hill. Copeia 1937: 142.

Crocker, D.W. 1960. Mudpuppies in Maine. Maine Field Natur. 16: 14–17.

Crump, M.L. 1984. Intraclutch egg size variability in *Hyla crucifer* (Anura: Hylidae). Copeia 1984: 302–308.

Cupp, P.V., Jr. 1971. Fall courtship of the green salamander, *Aneides aeneus.* Herpetologica 27: 308–310.

Davic, R.D. 1983. Microgeographic body size variation in *Desmognathus fuscus fuscus* salamanders from western Pennsylvania. Copeia 1983: 1101–1104.

Davidson, J.A. 1956. Notes on the food habits of the slimy salamander *Plethodon glutinosus glutinosus.* Herpetologica 12: 129–131.

Dearolf, K. 1956. Survey of North American cave vertebrates. Proc. Pa. Acad. Sci. 30: 201–210.

DeGraaf, R.M., and D.D. Rudis. 1983. Amphibians and reptiles of New England. Amherst: University of Massachusetts Press.

Demagnadier, P.G., and M.L. Hunter Jr. 1998. Effects of silivicultural edges on the distribution and abundance of amphibians in Maine. Conserv. Biol. 12: 340–352.

DePari, J.A., M.H. Linck, and T.E. Graham. 1987. Clutch size of the Blanding's turtle, *Emydoidea blandingi,* in Massachusetts. Can. Field Natur. 101: 440–442.

Dial, B.E., and L.C. Fitzpatrick. 1983. Lizard tail autotomy: Function and energetics of postautotomy tail movement in *Scincella lateralis.* Science 219: 391–393.

———. 1984. Predator escape success in tailed versus tailless *Scincella lateralis* (Sauria: Scincidae). Anim. Behav. 31: 301–302.

Dickerson, M.C. 1920. The frog book. New York: Doubleday.

DiGiovanni, M., and E.D. Brodie Jr. 1981. Efficacy of skin glands in protecting the salamander *Ambystoma opacum* from repeated attacks by the shrew *Blarina brevicauda*. Herpetologica 37: 234–237.

Dodd, C.K., Jr. 1989. Population structure and biomass of *Sternotherus odoratus* (Testudines: Kinosternidae) in a northern Alabama lake. Brimleyana 15: 47–56.

Dole, J.W. 1965. Summer movements of adult leopard frogs, *Rana pipiens* Schreber, in northern Michigan. Ecology 46: 236–255.

Douglas, M.E. 1979. Migration and sexual selection in *Ambystoma jeffersonianum*. Can. J. Zool. 57: 2303–2310.

Drda, W.J. 1968. A study of snakes wintering in a small cave. J. Herpetol. 1: 64–70.

Drivers, E.C. 1936. Observations on *Scaphiopus holbrooki* (Harlan). Copeia 1936: 67–69.

Drymond, J.R., and F.E.J. Fry. 1932. Notes on the breeding habits of the green snake *(Liophis vernalis)*. Copeia 1932: 102.

Duellman, W.E. 1954. The salamander *Plethodon richmondi* in southwestern Ohio. Copeia 1954: 40–45.

Duellman, W.E., and A. Schwartz. 1958. Amphibians and reptiles of southern Florida. Bull. Fla. State Mus. Biol. Sci. 3: 181–324.

Dundee, H.A., and M.C. Miller III. 1968. Aggregative behavior and habitat conditioning by the prairie ringneck snake, *Diadophis punctatus arnyi*. Tulane Stud. Zool. Bot. 15: 41–58.

Dundee, H.A., and D.A. Rossman. 1989. The amphibians and reptiles of Louisiana. Baton Rouge: Louisiana State University Press.

Dunlap, K.D., and J.W. Lang. 1990. Offspring sex ratio varies with maternal size in the common garter snake, *Thamnophis sirtalis*. Copeia 1990: 568–570.

Dyrkacz, S. 1977. The natural history of the eastern milk snake (Reptilia, Serpentes, Colubridae) in a disturbed environment. J. Herpetol. 11: 155–159.

———. 1981. Recent instances of albinism in North American amphibians and reptiles. Herpetol. Circ. 11: 1–31.

Edgren, R.A. 1949. An autumnal concentration of *Ambystoma jeffersonianum*. Herpetologica 5: 137–138.

———. 1955. The natural history of the hog-nosed snakes, genus *Heterodon*: A review. Herpetologica 11: 105–116.

———. 1957. Melanism in hog-nosed snakes. Herpetologica 13: 131–135.

Emery, A.R., A.H. Berst, and K. Kodaira. 1972. Under-ice observations of wintering sites of leopard frogs. Copeia 1972: 123–126.

Emlen, S.T. 1968. Territoriality in the bullfrog, *Rana catesbeiana*. Copeia 1968: 240–243.

———. 1977. "Double clutching" and its possible significance in the bullfrog. Copeia 1977: 749–751.

Ernst, C.H. 1968. Homing ability in the spotted turtle, *Clemmys guttata* (Schneider). Herpetologica 24: 77–78.

———. 1970a. Home range of the spotted turtle, *Clemmys guttata* (Schneider). Copeia 1970: 391–393.

———. 1970b. Reproduction in *Clemmys guttata*. Herpetologica 26: 228–232.

———. 1971. Population dynamics and activity cycles of *Chrysemys picta* in southeastern Pennsylvania. J. Herpetol. 5: 151–160.

———. 1976. Ecology of the spotted turtle, *Clemmys guttata* (Reptilia, Testudines, Testudinidae), in southeastern Pennsylvania. J. Herpetol. 10: 25–33.

———. 1977. Biological notes on the bog turtle, *Clemmys muhlenbergii*. Herpetologica 33: 214–216.

———. 1982. Environmental temperatures and activities in wild spotted turtles, *Clemmys guttata*. J. Herpetol. 16: 112–120.

———. 1983. *Clemmys guttata* (spotted turtle) × *Clemmys muhlenbergii* (bog turtle): Natural hybrid. Herpetol. Rev. 14: 75.

———. 1986a. Ecology of the turtle, *Sternotherus odoratus*, in southeastern Pennsylvania. J. Herpetol. 20: 341–352.

———. 1986b. Environmental temperatures and activities in the wood turtle, *Clemmys insculpta*. J. Herpetol. 20: 222–229.

Ernst, C.H., and R.W. Barbour. 1972. Turtles of the United States. Lexington: University Press of Kentucky.

———. 1989. Snakes of eastern North America. Fairfax, Va.: George Mason University Press.

Ernst, C.H., and E.M. Ernst. 1971. The taxonomic status and zoogeography of the painted turtle, *Chrysemys picta*, in Pennsylvania. Herpetologica 27: 390–396.

Ernst, C.H., R.T. Zappalorti, J.E. Lovich. 1989. Overwintering sites and thermal relations of hibernating bog turtles, *Clemmys muhlenbergii*. Copeia 1989: 761–764.

Ernst, C.H., J.E. Lovich, and R.W. Barbour. 1994. Turtles of the United States and Canada. Washington, D.C.: Smithsonian Institution Press.

Evermann, B.W., and H.W. Clark. 1916. The turtles and batrachians of the Lake Maxinkuckee region. Proc. Ind. Acad. Sci. 1916: 472–518.

Ewing, H.E. 1933. Reproduction in the eastern box turtle, *Terrapene carolina carolina*. Copeia 1933: 95–96.

———. 1943. Continued fertility in female box turtles following mating. Copeia 1943: 112–114.

Farrell, R.F., and T.E. Graham. 1991. Ecological notes on the turtle *Clemmys insculpta* in northwestern New Jersey. J. Herpetol. 25: 1–9.

Fitch, F.W., Jr. 1947. A record *Cryptobranchus alleganiensis*. Copeia 1947: 210.

Fitch, H.S. 1954. Life history and ecology of the five-lined skink, *Eumeces fasciatus*. Univ. Kans. Publ. Mus. Natur. Hist. 8: 1–156.

———. 1960. Autecology of the copperhead. Univ. Kans. Publ. Mus. Natur. Hist. 13: 85–288.

———. 1963a. Natural history of the black rat snake *(Elaphe o. obsoleta)* in Kansas. Copeia 1963: 649–658.

———. 1963b. Natural history of the racer *Coluber constrictor*. Univ. Kans. Publ. Mus. Natur. Hist. 15: 351–468.

———. 1965. An ecological study of the garter snake, *Thamnophis sirtalis*. Univ. Kans. Publ. Mus. Natur. Hist. 15: 493–564.

———. 1970. Reproductive cycles in lizards and snakes. Univ. Kans. Mus. Natur. Hist. Misc. Publ. 52: 1–247.

———. 1975. A demographic study of the ringneck snake *(Diadophis punctatus)* in Kansas. Univ. Kans. Mus. Natur. Hist. Misc. Publ. 62: 1–53.

Fitch, H.S., and H.W. Shirer. 1971. A radiotelemetric study of spatial relationships in some common snakes. Copeia 1971: 118–128.

Foley, G.W. 1971. Perennial communal nesting in the black racer *(Coluber constrictor)*. Herpetol. Rev. 3: 41.

Ford, N.B. 1981. Seasonality of pheromone trailing behavior in two species of garter snake, *Thamnophis* (Colubridae). Southwest. Natur. 26: 385–388.

Ford, N.B., and G.A. Shuttlesworth. 1986. Effects of variation in food intake on locomotory performance of juvenile garter snakes. Copeia 1986: 999–1001.

Forester, D.C. 1977. Comments on the female reproductive cycle and philopatry by *Desmognathus ochrophaeus* (Amphibia, Urodela, Plethodontidae). J. Herpetol. 11: 311–316.

———. 1979. The adaptiveness of parental care in *Desmognathus ochrophaeus* (Urodela: Plethodontidae). Copeia 1979: 332–341.

———. 1981. Parental care in the salamander *Desmognathus ochrophaeus*: Female activity pattern and trophic behavior. J. Herpetol. 15: 29–34.

———. 1984. Brooding behavior by the mountain dusky salamander: Can the female's presence reduce clutch desiccation? Herpetologica 40: 105–109.

Forester, D.C., and D.V. Lykens. 1986. Significance of satellite males in a population of spring peepers *(Hyla crucifer).* Copeia 1986: 719–724.

Fowler, H.W. 1906. The amphibians and reptiles of New Jersey. Annu. Rep. N.J. State Mus. 1906: 29–250.

Fowler, H.W., and E.R. Dunn. 1917. Notes on salamanders. Proc. Acad. Natur. Sci. Phila. 69: 7–28.

Fowler, J.A. 1940. A note on the eggs of *Plethodon glutinosus.* Copeia 1940: 133.

———. 1966. A communal nesting site for the smooth green snake in Michigan. Herpetologica 22: 231.

Fraker, M.A. 1970. Home range and homing in the water snake, *Natrix sipedon sipedon.* Copeia 1970: 665–673.

Franz, R. 1964. The eggs of the long-tailed salamander from a Maryland cave. Herpetologica 20: 216.

Franz, R., and H. Harris. 1965. Mass transformation and movement of larval long-tailed salamanders, *Eurycea longicauda longicauda* (Green). J. Ohio Herpetol. Soc. 5: 32.

Freda, J., and W.A. Dunson. 1986. Effects of low pH and other chemical variables on the local distribution of amphibians. Copeia 1986: 454–466.

Freedman, B., and P.M. Catling. 1979. Movements of sympatric species of snakes at Amherstburg, Ontario. Can. Field. Natur. 93: 399–404.

Freeman, J.R., and C.C. Freeman. 1982. *Diadophis punctatus edwardsi* (northern ringneck snake): Size. Herpetol. Rev. 13: 96.

Freyburger, W.A., Jr. 1941. *Scaphiopus holbrooki holbrooki,* the spadefoot toad, at Lewisburg. Proc. Pa. Acad. Sci. 15: 180–183.

Galligan, J.H., and W.A. Dunson. 1979. Biology and status of timber rattlesnake *(Crotalus horridus)* populations in Pennsylvania. Biol. Conserv. 15: 13–58.

Gardner, J.B. 1955. A ball of gartersnakes. Copeia 1955: 310.

Garton, J.S., and R.W. Dimmick. 1969. Food habits of the copperhead in middle Tennessee. J. Tenn. Acad. Sci. 44: 113–117.

Gehlbach, F.R. 1970. Death-feigning and erratic behavior in leptotyphlopid, colubrid, and elapid snakes. Herpetologica 26: 24–34.

George, C.J., C.W. Bayles, and R.B. Sheldon. 1977. The presence of the red-spotted newt, *Notophthalmus viridescens* Rafinesque (Amphibia, Urodela, Salamandridae) in water exceeding 12 meters in Lake George, New York. J. Herpetol. 11: 87–90.

Gergits, W.F., and R.G. Jaeger. 1990. Site attachment by the red-backed salamander, *Plethodon cinereus.* J. Herpetol. 24: 91–93.

Gibbons, J.W. 1967. Variation in growth rates in three populations of the painted turtle, *Chrysemys picta.* Herpetologica 23: 296–303.

———. 1972. Reproduction, growth, and sexual dimorphism in the canebrake rattlesnake *(Crotalus horridus atricaudatus).* Copeia 1972: 222–226.

———. 1983. Reproductive characteristics and ecology of the mud turtle, *Kinosternon subrubrum* (Lacepede). Herpetologica 39: 254–271.

Gibbons, J.W., and S. Nelson Jr. 1968. Observations on the mudpuppy, *Necturus maculosus* in a Michigan Lake. Amer. Midl. Natur. 80: 562–564.

Gibbons, J.W., and R.D. Semlitsch. 1987. Activity patterns. Pages 396–421 in R.A. Seigel, J.T. Collins, and S.S. Novak, eds., Snakes: Ecology and evolutionary biology. New York: Macmillan.

Gibbs, J.P. 1998. Distribution of woodland amphibians along a forest fragmentation gradient. Landscape Ecol. 13: 263–268.

Gibson, A.R., and J.B. Falls. 1988. Melanism in the common garter snake: A Lake Erie phenomenon. In J.F. Downhower, ed., The biogeography of the island region of western Lake Erie. Columbus: Ohio State University Press.

Gilbert, P.W. 1941. Eggs and nests of *Hemidactylum scutatum* in the Ithaca region. Copeia 1941: 47.

Gilhen, J. 1984. Amphibians and reptiles of Nova Scotia. Halifax: Nova Scotia State Museum.

Gill, D.E. 1978. Effective population size and interdemic migration rates in a metapopulation of the red-spotted newt, *Notophthalmus viridescens* (Rafinesque). Evolution 32: 839–849.

Gillingham, J.C. 1979. Reproductive behavior of the rat snakes of eastern North America, genus *Elaphe*. Copeia 1979: 319–331.

———. 1980. Communication and combat behavior of the black rat snake *(Elaphe obsoleta)*. Herpetologica 36: 120–127.

Gist, D.H., J.A. Michaelson, and J.M. Jones. 1990. Autumn mating in the painted turtle, *Chrysemys picta*. Herpetologica 46: 331–336.

Given, M.F. 1987. Vocalization and acoustic interactions of the carpenter frog, *Rana virgatipes*. Herpetologica 43: 467–481.

———. 1988. Territoriality and aggressive interactions of male carpenter frogs, *Rana virgatipes*. Copeia 1988: 411–421.

———. 1990. Spatial distribution and vocal interactions in *Rana clamitans* and *Rana virgatipes*. J. Herpetol. 24: 377–382.

———. 1993. Male response to female vocalizations in the carpenter frog, *Rana virgatipes*. Anim. Behav. 46: 1139–1149.

Gloyd, H.K., and R. Conant. 1990. Snakes of the *Agkistrodon* complex: A monographic review. Society for the Study of Amphibians and Reptiles Contrib. Herp. 6.

Godley, J.S., R.W. McDiarmid, and N.N. Rojas. 1984. Estimating prey size and number in crayfish-eating snakes, genus *Regina*. Herpetologica 40: 82–88.

Goin, O.B., and C.J. Goin. 1951. Notes on the natural history of the lizard, *Eumeces laticeps*, in northern Florida. Q. J. Fla. Acad. Sci. 14: 29–33.

Goldsmith, S.K. 1984. Aspects of the natural history of the rough green snake, *Opheodrys aestivus* (Colubridae). Southwest. Natur. 29: 445–452.

Gordon, D.M., and R.D. MacCulloch. 1980. An investigation of the ecology of the map turtle, *Graptemys geographica* (LeSueur), in the northern part of its range. Can. J. Zool. 58: 2210–2219.

Gordon, R.E. 1952. A contribution to the life history and ecology of the plethodontid salamander *Aneides aeneus* (Cope and Packard). Amer. Midl. Natur. 47: 666–701.

———. 1967. *Aenides aeneus*. Cat. Amer. Amph. Rept. 30.1–30.2.

Gosner, K.L., and I.H. Black. 1957. The effects of acidity on the development and hatching of New Jersey frogs. Ecology 38: 256–262.

———. 1967. *Hyla andersonii* Baird. Cat. Amer. Amphib. Rept. 54.1–54.2.

———. 1968. *Rana virgatipes* Cope. Cat. Amer. Amphib. Rept. 67.1–67.2.

Graham, T.E., and T.S. Doyle. 1978. Dimorphism, courtship, eggs and hatchlings of the Blanding's turtle, *Emydoidea blandingii* (Reptilia, Testudines, Emydidae) in Massachusetts. J. Herpetol. 13: 125–127.

Graham, T.E., and A.A. Graham. 1997. Ecology of the eastern spiny softshell, *Apalone spinifera spinifera*, in the Lamoille River, Vermont. Chelonian Conserv. Biol. 2: 363–369.

Graham, T.E., R.A. Saumure, and B. Ericson. 1997. Map turtle winter leech loads. J. Parisitol. 83: 1185–1186.

Gray, R.H. 1971. Fall activity and overwintering of the cricket frog *(Acris crepitans)* in central Illinois. Copeia 1971: 748–750.

———. 1983. Seasonal, annual and geographic variation in color morph frequencies of the cricket frog, *Acris crepitans*, in Illinois. Copeia 1983: 300–311.

Green, N.B. 1938. The breeding habits of *Pseudacris brachyphona* (Cope) with a description of the eggs and tadpole. Copeia 1938: 79–82.

Green, N.B., and T.K. Pauley. 1987. Amphibians and reptiles in West Virginia. Pittsburgh: University of Pittsburgh Press.

Gregory, P.T. 1977. Life history observations of three species of snakes in Manitoba. Can. Field Natur. 91: 19–27.

Grizzell, R.A. 1949. The hibernation site of three snakes and a salamander. Copeia 1949: 231–232.

Grobman, A.B. 1989. Clutch size and female length in *Opheodrys vernalis*. Herpetol. Rev. 20: 84.

Grogan, W.L., Jr. 1974. Effects of accidental envenomation from the saliva of the eastern hognose snake, *Heterodon platyrhinos*. Herpetologica 30: 248–249.

Groves, F. 1961. Notes on two large broods of *Haldea v. valeriae* (Baird and Girard). Herpetologica 17: 71.

———. 1984. *Storeria dekayi dekayi* (northern brown snake): Coloration. Herpetol. Rev. 15: 19.

Guidry, E.V. 1953. Herpetological notes from southeastern Texas. Herpetologica 9: 49–56.

Halk, J.H. 1986. *Trionyx spiniferus* (spiny softshell turtle): Size. Herpetol. Rev. 17: 91.

Hall, R.J. 1976. Summer foods of the salamander, *Plethodon wehrlei* (Amphibia, Urodela, Plethodontidae). J. Herpetol. 10: 129–131.

———. 1977. A population analysis of two species of streamside salamanders, genus *Desmognathus*. Herpetologica 33: 109–113.

Hall, R.J., and D.P. Stafford. 1972. Studies in the life history of Wehrle's salamander, *Plethodon wehrlei*. Herpetologica 28: 300–309.

Hamilton, W.J., Jr. 1930. Notes on the food of the American toad. Copeia 1930: 45.

———. 1940. The feeding habits of larval newts with reference to availability and predilection of food items. Ecology 21: 351–356.

———. 1943. Winter habits of the dusky salamander in central New York. Copeia 1943: 192.

———. 1948. The food and feeding behavior of the green frog, *Rana clamitans* Latreille, in New York state. Copeia 1948: 203–207.

———. 1951. The food and feeding behavior of the garter snake in New York State. Amer. Midl. Natur. 46: 385–390.

Hamilton, W.J., Jr., and J.A. Pollack. 1955. The food of some crotalid snakes from Fort Benning, Georgia. Natur. Hist. Misc. 140: 1–4.

———. 1956. The food of some colubrid snakes from Fort Benning, Georgia. Ecology 37: 519–526.

————. 1961. The food of some lizards from Fort Benning, Georgia. Herpetologica 17: 99–106.

Hardy, J.D., and Y. Mork. 1950. A giant red salamander from Maryland. Herpetologica 6: 74.

Hardy, L.M., and M.C. Lucas. 1991. A crystalline protein is responsible for dimorphic egg jellies in the spotted salamander, *Ambystoma maculatum* (Shaw) (Caudata: Ambystomatidae). Comp. Biochem. Physiol. 100A: 653–660.

Harris, J.P., Jr. 1959. The natural history of *Necturus:* III. Food and feeding. Field Lab. 28: 105–111.

Harris, R.N., and D.E. Gill. 1980. Communal nesting, brooding behavior, and embryonic survival of the four-toed salamander *Hemidactylium scutatum.* Herpetologica 36: 141–144.

Harris, R.N., W.W. Knight, I.T. Carreno, and T.J. Vess. 1995. An experimental analysis of joint nesting in the salamander *Hemidactylium scutatum* (Caudata: Plethodontidae): The effects of population density. Anim. Behav. 50: 1309–1316.

Hassinger, D.D., J.D. Anderson, and G.H. Dalrymple. 1970. The early life history and ecology of *Ambystoma tigrinum* and *Ambystoma opacum* in New Jersey. Amer. Midl. Natur. 84: 474–495.

Healy, W.R. 1974. Population consequences of alternative life histories in *Notophthalmus v. viridescens.* Copeia 1974: 221–229.

Heatwole, H. 1962. Environmental factors influencing local distribution and activity of the salamander, *Plethodon cinereus.* Ecology 43: 460–472.

Hecnar, S.J. 1994. Nest distribution, site selection and brooding in the five-lined skink *(Eumeces fasciatus).* Can. J. Zool. 72: 1510–1516.

Hecnar, S.J., and R.J. M'Closkey. 1997. Changes in the composition of a ranid frog community following bullfrog extinction. Amer. Midl. Natur. 137: 145–150.

————. 1998. Effects of human disturbance on five-lined skinks, *Eumeces fasciatus,* abundance and distribution. Biol. Conserv. 85: 213–222.

Hedeen, S.E. 1972. Postmetamorphic growth and reproduction of the mink frog, *Rana septentrionalis.* Copeia 1972: 169–175.

————. 1986. The southern geographic limit of the mink frog, *Rana septentrionalis.* Copeia 1986: 239–244.

Hedges, S.B. 1986. An electrophoretic analysis of holarctic hylid frog evolution. Syst. Zool. 35: 1–21.

Heinen, J.T. 1985. Cryptic behavior in juvenile toads. J. Herpetol. 19: 524–527.

Heller, S., and M. Halpern. 1981. Laboratory observations on conspecific and congeneric scent trailing in garter snakes *(Thamnophis).* Behav. Neur. Biol. 33: 372–377.

Henderson, R.W., and M.A. Nickerson. 1975. Observations on the feeding behavior and movements of the snakes *Oxybelis aeneus* and *O. fulgidus.* Br. J. Herpetol. 5: 663–667.

Hensley, M.M. 1959. Albinism in North American amphibians and reptiles. Publ. Mus. Mich. State Univ. Biol. Ser. 1: 133–159.

Hertzog, H.A., Jr., and B.D. Bailey. 1987. Development of antipredator responses in snakes: II. Effects of recent feeding on defensive behaviors of juvenile garter snakes *(Thamnophis sirtalis).* J. Comp. Psychol. 101: 387–389.

Highton, R. 1962. Geographic variation in the life history of the slimy salamander. Copeia 1962: 597–613.

————. 1971. Distributional interactions among eastern North American salamanders of the genus *Plethodon.* Pages 139–188 in P.C. Holt, ed., The distributional history of the biota of the southern Appalachians. Virginia Poly. Inst. State Univ. Res. Div. Monogr. 4.

———. 1989. Biochemical evolution in the slimy salamanders of the *Plethodon glutinosus* complex in the eastern United States. Part 1. Geographic protein variation. Ill. Biol. Monogr. 57: 1–78.

———. 1999. Geographic protein variation and speciation in the salamanders of the *Plethodon cinereus* group with the description of two new species. Herpetologica 55: 43–90.

Highton, R., and T. Savage. 1961. Functions of the brooding behavior in the female red-backed salamander, *Plethodon cinereus*. Copeia 1961: 95–98.

Hillis, R.E., and E.D. Bellis. 1971. Some aspects of the ecology of the hellbender, *Cryptobranchus alleganiensis alleganiensis* in a Pennsylvania stream. J. Herpetol. 5: 121–126.

Hoff, J.G. 1977. A Massachusetts hibernation site of the red-backed salamander, *Plethodon cinereus*. Herpetol. Rev. 8: 33.

Holomuzki, J.R. 1982. Homing behavior of *Desmognathus ochrophaeus* along a stream. J. Herpetol. 16: 307–309.

Hom, C.L. 1987. Reproductive ecology of female dusky salamanders, *Desmognathus fuscus* (Plethodontidae), in the southern Appalachians. Copeia 1987: 768–777.

Horne, M.T., and W.A. Dunson. 1994. Exclusion of the Jefferson salamander, *Ambystoma jeffersonianum*, from some potential breeding ponds in Pennsylvania: Effects of pH, temperature, and metals on embryonic development. Arch. Environ. Contam. Toxicol. 27: 323–330.

Houtcooper, W.C. 1981. Life history notes: *Desmognathus monticola* (seal salamander): Coloration. Herpetol. Rev. 12: 78.

Howard, R.D. 1978. The influence of male-defended oviposition sites on early embryo mortality in bullfrogs. Ecology 59: 789–798.

Hudson, R.G. 1949. A record length milk snake. Herpetologica 5: 47.

———. 1955. Observations on the larvae of the salamander *Eurycea bislineata bislineata*. Herpetologica 11: 202–204.

———. 1956. The leopard frog *Rana pipiens sphenocephala* in southeastern Pennsylvania. Herpetologica 12: 182–183.

Huheey, J.E. 1958. Some feeding habits of the eastern hog-nosed snake. Herpetologica 14: 68.

Huheey, J.E., and R.A. Brandon. 1973. Rock-face populations of the mountain dusky salamander, *Desmognathus ochrophaeus*, in North Carolina. Ecol. Monogr. 43: 59–77.

Hunter, M.L., Jr., J. Albright, and J. Arbuckle. 1992. The amphibians and reptiles of Maine. Maine Agr. Exp. Sta. Bull. 838.

Ingram, W.M., and E.C. Raney. 1943. Additional studies on the movement of tagged bullfrogs, *Rana catesbeiana* Shaw. Amer. Midl. Natur. 29: 239–241.

Ireland, P.H. 1989. Larval survivorship in two populations of *Ambystoma maculatum*. J. Herpetol. 23: 209–215.

Iverson, J.B. 1979. Reproduction and growth of the mud turtle, *Kinosternon subrubrum* (Reptilia, Testudines, Kinosternidae), in Arkansas. J. Herpetol. 13: 105–111.

———. 1986. A checklist with distribution maps of the turtles of the world. Richmond, Ind: Paust Printing.

Iverson, J.B., and T.E. Graham. 1990. Geographic variation in the redbelly turtle, *Pseudemys rubriventris* (Reptilia: Testudines). Ann. Carnegie Mus. 59: 1–13.

Iverson, J.B., and G.R. Smith. 1993. Reproductive ecology of the painted turtle (*Chrysemys picta*) in the Nebraska sandhills and across its range. Copeia 1993: 1–21.

Jackson, J.F., W. Ingram III, and H.W. Campbell. 1976. The dorsal pigmentation pattern of snakes as an antipredator strategy: A multivariate approach. Amer. Natur. 110: 1029–1053.

Jackson, M.E., D.E. Scott, and R.E. Estes. 1989. Determinants of nest success in the marbled salamander *(Ambystoma opacum)*. Can. J. Zool. 67: 2277–2281.

Jaeger, R.G. 1978. Plant climbing by salamanders: Periodic availability of plant-dwelling prey. Copeia 1978: 686–691.

———. 1980. Microhabitats of a terrestrial forest salamander. Copeia 1980: 265–268.

———. 1981. Dear Enemy recognition and the costs of aggression between salamanders. Amer. Natur. 117: 926–974.

Jaeger, R.G., D. Kalvarsky, and N. Shimizu. 1982. Territorial behaviour of the red-backed salamander: Expulsion of intruders. Anim. Behav. 30: 490–496.

Janzen, F.J. 1994. Vegetational cover predicts the sex ratio of hatchling turtles in natural nests. Ecology 75: 1593–1599.

Jenssen, T.A., and W.D. Klimstra. 1966. Food habits of the green frog, *Rana clamitans*, in southern Illinois. Amer. Midl. Natur. 76: 169–182.

Johnson, G., and D.J. Leopold. 1998. Habitat management for the eastern massasauga in a central New York peatland. J. Wildl. Manage. 62: 84–97.

Johnson, J.E., and A.S. Goldberg. 1975. Movement of larval two-lined salamanders *(Eurycea bislineata)* in the Mill River, Massachusetts. Copeia 1975: 588–589.

Johnson, T.R. 1987. The amphibians and reptiles of Missouri. Jefferson City: Conservation Commission of the State of Missouri.

Jones, J.M. 1973. Effects of thirty years hybridization on the toads *Bufo americanus* and *Bufo woodhousei fowleri* at Bloomington, Indiana. Evolution 27: 435–448.

Jones, S.M., and D.L. Droge. 1980. Home range size and spatial distributions of two sympatric lizard species *(Sceloporus undulatus, Holbrookia maculata)*. Herpetologica 36: 127–132.

Jordan, R., Jr. 1970. Death-feigning in a captive red-bellied snake, *Storeria occipitomaculata* (Storer). Herpetologica 26: 466–468.

Judd, W.W. 1954. Observations on the food of the little brown snake, *Storeria dekayi*, at London, Ontario. Copeia 1954: 62–64.

———. 1957. The food of Jefferson's salamander, *Ambystoma jeffersonianum*, in Rondeau Park, Ontario. Ecology 38: 77–81.

Juterbock, J.E. 1987. The nesting behavior of the dusky salamander, *Desmognathus fuscus*. II. Nest site tenacity and disturbance. Herpetologica 43: 361–368.

———. 1990. Variation in larval growth and metamorphosis in the salamander *Desmognathus fuscus*. Herpetologica 46: 291–303.

Kaplan, R.H., and M.L. Crump. 1978. The non-cost of brooding in *Ambystoma opacum*. Copeia 1978: 99–103.

Karlin, A.A., and S.I. Guttman. 1981. Hybridization between *Desmognathus fuscus* and *Desmognathus ochrophaeus* (Amphibia: Urodela: Plethodontidae) in northeastern Ohio and northwestern Pennsylvania. Copcia 1981: 371–377.

Kats, L.B., and R.G. Van Dragt. 1986. Background color-matching in the spring peeper, *Hyla crucifer*. Copeia 1986: 109–115.

Kauffeld, C.F. 1957. Snakes and snake hunting. Garden City, N.Y.: Hanover House.

Kaufmann, J.H. 1991. *Clemmys insculpta* (wood turtle): Cleaning symbiosis. Herpetol. Rev. 22: 98.

———. 1992a. Habitat use by wood turtles in central Pennsylvania. J. Herpetol. 26: 315–321.

———. 1992b. The social behavior of wood turtles *(Clemmys insculpta)*, in central Pennsylvania. Herpetol. Monogr. 6: 1–25.

————. 1995. Home ranges and movements of wood turtles, *Clemmys insculpta*, in Central Pennsylvania. Copeia 1995: 22–27.

Keen, W.H. 1979. Feeding and activity patterns in the salamander *Desmognathus ochrophaeus* (Amphibia, Urodela, Plethodontidae). J. Herpetol. 13: 461–467.

Keen, W.H., and L.P. Orr. 1980. Reproductive cycle, growth, and maturation of northern female *Desmognathus ochrophaeus*. J. Herpetol. 14: 7–10.

Keen, W.H., and R.W. Reed. 1985. Territorial defence of space and feeding sites by a plethodontid salamander. Anim. Behav. 33: 1119–1123.

Keen, W.H., and S. Sharp. 1984. Responses of a plethodontid salamander to conspecific and congeneric intruders. Anim. Behav. 32: 58–65.

Keenlyne, K.D. 1978. Reproductive cycles in two species of rattlesnakes. Amer. Midl. Natur. 100: 368–375.

Keenlyne, K.D., and J.R. Beer. 1973. Food habits of *Sistrurus catenatus catenatus*. J. Herpetol. 7: 382–384.

King, R.B. 1986. Population ecology of the Lake Erie water snake, *Nerodia sipedon insularum*. Copeia 1986: 757–772.

————. 1988. Polymorphic populations of the garter snake *Thamnophis sirtalis* near Lake Erie. Herpetologica 44: 451–458.

King, R.B., and B. King. 1991. Sexual differences in color and color change in wood frogs. Can. J. Zool. 69: 1963–1968.

King, W. 1935. Ecological observations on *Ambystoma opacum*. Ohio J. Sci. 35: 4–15.

Kivat, E., and J. Stapleton. 1983. *Bufo americanus*, estuarine habitat. Herpetol. Rev. 14: 46.

Klauber, L.M. 1956. Rattlesnakes. Berkeley: University of California Press.

Kleeberger, S.R. 1985. Influence of intraspecific density and cover on home range of a plethodontid salamander. Oecologia 66: 404–410.

Klemens, M.K. 1993. Amphibians and reptiles of Connecticut and adjacent regions. State Geological and Natural History Survey of Connecticut, Bulletin No. 112.

Klimstra, W.D. 1959. Foods of the racer, *Coluber constrictor* in southern Illinois. Copeia 1959: 210–214.

Knight, A.W., and J.W. Gibbons. 1968. Food of the painted turtle, *Chrysemys picta*, in a polluted river. Amer. Midl. Natur. 80: 558–562.

Kofron, C.P. 1979. Female reproductive biology of the brown snake, *Storeria dekayi*, in Louisiana. Copeia 1979: 463–466.

Korschgen, L.J., and T.S. Baskett. 1963. Foods of impoundment- and stream-dwelling bullfrogs in Missouri. Herpetologica 19: 89–99.

Kramek, W.C. 1972. Food of the frog *Rana septentrionalis* in New York. Copeia 1972: 390–392.

————. 1976. Feeding behavior of *Rana septentrionalis* (Amphibia, Anura, Ranidae). J. Herpetol. 10: 251–252.

Kramek, W.C., and M.M. Stewart. 1980. Ontogenetic and sexual differences in the pattern of *Rana septentrionalis*. J. Herpetol. 14: 369–375.

Kramer, D.C. 1974. Home range of the western chorus frog *Pseudacris triseriata triseriata*. J. Herpetol. 8: 245–246.

Kroll, J.C. 1976. Feeding adaptations of hognose snakes. Southwest. Natur. 20: 537–557.

Krzysik, A.J. 1979. Resource allocation, coexistence, and the niche structure of a streambank salamander community. Ecol. Monogr. 49: 173–194.

Kuchler, A.W. 1964. Potential natural vegetation of the conterminous United States. Amer. Geograph. Soc. Special Publication.

Kumpf, K.E., and S.C. Yeaton Jr. 1932. Observations on the courtship behavior of *Ambystoma jeffersonianum*. Amer. Mus. Novit. 546: 1–7.

Labanick, G.M. 1976. Prey availability, consumption and selection in the cricket frog, *Acris crepitans* (Amphibia, Anura, Hylidae). J. Herpetol. 10: 293–298.

Labanick, G.M., and R.A. Schlueter. 1976. Growth rates of recently transformed *Bufo woodhousei fowleri*. Copeia 1976: 824–826.

Lachner, E.A. 1942. An aggregation of snakes and salamanders during hibernation. Copeia 1942: 262–263.

Lagler, K.F. 1943. Food habits and economic relations of the turtles of Michigan with special reference to fish management. Amer. Midl. Natur. 29: 257–312.

Lagler, K.F., and C. Salyer II. 1945. Influence of availability on the feeding habits of the common garter snake. Copeia 1945: 159–162.

Landre, E. 1980. The blue-spotted salamander. Sanctuary Bull. Mass. Audubon Soc. 20: 6–7.

Lang, J.W. 1969. Hibernation and movements of *Storeria occipitomaculata* in northern Minnesota. J. Herpetol. 3: 196–197.

Lawler, S.P. 1989. Behavioral responses to predators and predation risk in four species of larval anurans. Anim. Behav. 38: 1039–1047.

Layne, J.R., Jr. 1995. Seasonal variation in the cryobiology of *Rana sylvatica* from Pennsylvania. J. Therm. Biol. 20: 349–353.

Layne, J.R., Jr., and N.B. Ford. 1984. Flight distance of the queen snake, *Regina septemvittata*. J. Herpetol. 1984: 496–498.

Layne, J.R., Jr., and J. Kefauver. 1997. Freeze tolerance and postfreeze recovery in the frog *Pseudacris crucifer*. Copeia 1997: 260–264.

Layne, J.R., Jr., and R.E. Lee Jr. 1989. Seasonal variation in freeze tolerance and ice content of the tree frog *Hyla versicolor*. J. Exp. Zool. 249: 133–137.

Lazell, J.D., Jr. 1976a. Geographic distribution note: *Desmognathus ochrophaeus*. Herpetol. Rev. 7: 122.

———. 1976b. This broken archipelago: Cape Cod and the islands, amphibians and reptiles. New York: Demeter Press.

———. 1979. Diamondback terrapins at Sandy Neck. Aquasphere, J. New Eng. Aquarium 13: 28–31.

Leclair, R., Jr., and J. Castanet. 1987. A skeletochronological assessment of age and growth in the frog *Rana pipiens* Schreber (Amphibia, Anura) from southwestern Quebec. Copeia 1987: 361–369.

Lee, D.S., and A.W. Norden. 1973. A food study of the green salamander, *Aneides aeneus*. J. Herpetol. 7: 53–54.

Linck, M.H., J.A. DePari, B.O. Butler, and T. E Graham. 1989. Nesting behavior of the turtle *Emydoidea blandingi*, in Massachussetts. J. Herpetol. 23: 442–444.

Linsdale, J.M. 1927. Amphibians and reptiles of Doniphan County, Kansas. Copeia 164: 75–81.

Linzey, D.W. 1967. Food of the leopard frog, *Rana p. pipiens*, in central New York. Herpetologica 23: 11–17.

Little, M.L., B.L. Monroe Jr., and J.E. Wiley. 1989. The distribution of the *Hyla versicolor* complex in the northern Appalachian highlands. J. Herpetol. 23: 299–303.

Litzgus, J.B., and R.J. Brooks. 1998a. Growth in a cold environment: Body size and sexual maturity in a northern population of spotted turtles, *Clemmys guttata*. Can. J. Zool. 76: 773–782.

———. 1998b. Reproduction in a northern populatin of *Clemmys guttata*. J. Herpetol. 32: 252–259.

Logier, E.B.S. 1952. The frogs, toads, and salamanders of eastern Canada. Toronto: Clarke, Irwin and Co.

Lotter, F. 1978. Reproductive ecology of the salamander *Plethodon cinereus* (Amphibia, Urodela, Plethodontidae) in Connecticut. J. Herpetol. 12: 231–236.

Lotter, F., and N.J. Scott Jr. 1977. Correlation between climate and distribution of the color morphs of the salamander *Plethodon cinereus*. Copeia 1977: 681–690.

Lovich, J. 1988. Aggressive basking behavior in eastern painted turtles *(Chrysemys picta picta)*. Herpetologica 44: 197–202.

Lovich, J., E.H. Ernst, R.T. Zappalorti, and D.W. Herman. 1998. Geographic variation in growth and sexual size dimorphism of bog turtles *(Clemmys muhlenbergi)*. Amer. Midl. Natur. 139: 69–78.

Lowcock, L.A. 1985. An albino yellow spotted salamander, *Ambystoma maculatum*, from Oak Bay, Quebec. Can. Field Natur. 99: 105–106.

Lykens, D.V., and D.C. Forester. 1987. Age structure in the spring peeper: Do males advertise longevity? Herpetologica 43: 216–223.

Lynch, J.D. 1966. Communal egg laying in the pilot blacksnake, *Elaphe obsoleta obsoleta*. Herpetologica 22: 305.

Lynn, W.G., and T. Von Brand. 1945. Studies on the oxygen consumption and water metabolism of turtle embryos. Biol. Bull. 88: 112–125.

Lyon, M.W., Jr., and C.A. Bishop. 1936. Bite of the prairie rattlesnake *Sistrurus catenatus* Raf. Proc. Ind. Acad. Sci. 45: 253–256.

MacCulloch, R.D., and W.F. Weller. 1988. Some aspects of reproduction in a Lake Erie population of Blanding's turtle, *Emydoidea blandingii*. Can. J. Zool. 66: 2317–2319.

Mahmoud, I.Y. 1969. Comparative ecology of the kinosternid turtles of Oklahoma. Southwest. Natur. 14: 31–66.

Major, P.D. 1975. Density of snapping turtles, *Chelydra serpentina* in western West Virginia. Herpetologica 31: 332–335.

Martof, B.S. 1956. Growth and development of the green frog, *Rana clamitans*, under natural conditions. Amer. Midl. Natur. 55: 101–117.

———. 1975. *Pseudotriton ruber*. Cat. Amer. Amph. Rept. 167.1–167.3.

Martof, B.S., W.M. Palmer, J.R. Bailey, and J.R. Harrison III. 1980. Amphibians and reptiles of the Carolinas and Virginia. Chapel Hill: University of North Carolina Press.

McAlister, W.H. 1963. Evidence of mild toxicity in the saliva of the hognose snake *(Heterodon)*. Herpetologica 19: 132–137.

McCauley, R.H., Jr. 1945. The reptiles of Maryland and the District of Columbia. Privately printed, Hagerstown, Md.

McCoy, C.J. 1982. Amphibians and reptiles in Pennsylvania: Checklist, bibliography, and atlas of distribution. Spec. Publ. Carnegie Mus. Natur. Hist. 6: 1–91.

———. 1992. Rediscovery of the mud salamander *(Pseudotriton montanus*, Amphibia, Plethondontidae) in Pennsylvania, with restriction of the type locality. J. Pa. Acad. Sci. 66: 92–93.

McCoy, C.J., Jr., and A.V. Bianculli. 1966. The distribution and dispersal of *Heterodon platyrhinos* in Pennsylvania. J. Ohio Herpetol. Soc. 5: 153–158.

McDowell, S.B. 1987. Systematics. Pages 3–50 in R.A. Seigel, J.T. Collins, and S.S. Novak, eds., Snakes: Ecology and evolutionary biology. New York: McGraw-Hill.

McGregor, J.H., and W.R. Teska. 1989. Olfaction as an orientation mechanism in migrating *Ambystoma maculatum*. Copeia 1989: 779–781.

McKinstry, D.M. 1987. Herpetology of Presque Isle State Park, Erie, Pennsylvania. Bull. Md. Herpetol. Soc. 23: 58–64.

McLeod, R.F., and J.E. Gates. 1998. Response of herpetofaunal communities to forest cutting and burning at Chesapeake Farms, Maryland. Amer. Midl. Natur. 139: 164–177.

Meeks, D.E., and J.W. Nagel. 1973. Reproduction and development of the wood frog, *Rana sylvatica*, in eastern Tennessee. Herpetologica 29: 188–191.

Meeks, R.L., and G.R. Ultsch. 1990. Overwintering behavior of snapping turtles. Copeia 1990: 880–884.

Merchant, H. 1972. Estimated population size and home range of the salamanders *Plethodon jordani* and *Plethodon glutinosus*. J. Wash. Acad. Sci. 62: 248–257.

Merkle, D.A., S.I. Guttman, and M.A. Nickerson. 1977. Genetic uniformity throughout the range of the hellbender *Cryptobranchus alleganiensis*. Copeia 1977: 549–553.

Merrell, D.J. 1977. Life history of the leopard frog, *Rana pipiens*, in Minnesota, Occ. Pap. Bell Mus. Natur. Hist. Univ. Minn. 15: 1–23.

Messere, M., and P.K. Ducey. 1998. Forest Floor distribution of northern red back salamanders, *Plethodon cinereus*, in relation to canopy gaps, first year following selective logging. Forest Ecol. Managment 107: 319–324.

Minton, S.A., Jr. 1954. Salamanders of the *Ambystoma jeffersonianum* complex in Indiana. Herpetologica 16: 173–179.

———. 1972. Amphibians and reptiles of Indiana. Ind. Acad. Sci. Monogr. 3.

Mitchell, J.C. 1974. Statistics of *Chrysemys rubriventris* hatchlings from Middlesex County, Virginia. Herpetol. Rev. 5: 71.

———. 1988. Population ecology and life histories of the freshwater turtles *Chrysemys picta* and *Sternotherus odoratus* in an urban lake. Herpetol. Monogr. 2: 40–61.

———. 1994. The reptiles of Virginia. Washington, D.C.: Smithsonian Institution Press.

Mohr, C.E. 1943. The eggs of the long-tailed salamander *Eurycea longicauda longicauda* (Green). Proc. Pa. Acad. Sci. 27: 86.

Moll, D. 1976. A review of supposed insect catching by basking *Graptemys geographica*. Trans. Ill. State Acad. Sci. 69: 302–303.

Montague, J.R. 1987. Yolk absorption and early larval growth in desmognathine salamanders. J. Herpetol. 21: 226–228.

Montevecchi, W.A., and J. Burger. 1975. Aspects of the reproductive biology of the northern diamondback terrapin, *Malaclemys terrapin terrapin*. Amer. Midl. Natur. 94: 166–178.

Moore, J.A. 1952. An analytical study of the geographic distribution of *Rana septentrionalis*. Amer. Natur. 86: 5–22.

Moreno, G. 1989. Behavioral and physiological differentiation between the color morphs of the salamander, *Plethodon cinereus*. J. Herpetol. 23: 335–341.

Morgan, A.H., and M.C. Grierson. 1932. Winter habits and yearly food consumption of adult spotted newts, *Triturus viridescens*. Ecology 13: 54–62.

Morin, P.J., S.P. Lawler, and E.A. Johnson. 1990. Ecology and breeding phenology of larval *Hyla andersonii:* The disadvantages of breeding late. Ecology 71: 1590–1598.

Mount, R.H. 1975. The reptiles and amphibians of Alabama. Auburn University Experiment Station.

Mushinsky, H.R. 1976. Ontogenetic development of microhabitat preference in salamanders: The influence of early experience. Copeia 1976: 755–758.

———. 1979. Mating behavior of the common water snake, *Nerodia sipedon sipedon* (Reptilia, Serpentes, Colubridae) in eastern Pennsylvania. J. Herpetol. 13: 125–127.

Myers, C.W. 1965. Biology of the ringneck snake, *Diadophis punctatus*, in Florida. Bull. Fla. State Mus. Biol. Sci. 10: 43–90.

Nagel, J.W. 1977. Life history of the red-backed salamander, *Plethodon cinereus*, in northeastern Tennessee. Herpetologica 33: 13–18.

———. 1979. Life history of the ravine salamander *(Plethodon richmondi)* in northeastern Tennessee. Herpetologica 35: 38–43.

Neill, W.T. 1948. Hibernation of amphibians and reptiles in Richmond County, Georgia. Herpetologica 4: 107–114.

———. 1960. The caudal lure of various juvenile snakes. Q. J. Fla. Acad. Sci. 23: 173–200.

Nelson, D.H., and J.W. Gibbons. 1972. Ecology, abundance, and seasonal activity of the scarlet snake, *Cemophora coccinea*. Copeia 1972: 582–584.

Netting, M.G. 1932. Blanding's turtle, *Emys blandingii* (Holbrook) in Pennsylvania. Copeia 1932: 173–174.

———. 1935. A nontechnical key to the amphibians and reptiles of western Pennsylvania. Nawakwa Fireside 3–4: 34–49.

———. 1936. The chain snake, *Lampropeltis getulus getulus* (L.), in West Virginia and Pennsylvania. Ann. Carnegie Mus. 25: 77–82.

———. 1938. The occurrence of the eastern tiger salamander, *Ambystoma t. tigrinum* (Green) in Pennsylvania and near-by states. Ann. Carnegie Mus. 27: 159–166.

Netting, M.G., and N. Richmond. 1932. The green salamander, *Aneides aeneus*, in northern West Virginia. Copeia 1932: 101–102.

Neuman, N.H. 1906. The habits of certain tortoises. J. Comp. Neurol. Psychol. 16: 126–152.

Nichols, J.T. 1947. Notes on the mud turtle. Herpetologica 3: 147–148.

———. 1982. Courtship and copulatory behavior of captive eastern hognose snakes, *Heterodon platyrhinos*. Herpetol. Rev. 13: 16–17.

Noble, G.K. 1926. The Long Island newt: A contribution to the life history of *Triturus viridescens*. Amer. Mus. Novit. 228: 1–11.

Noble, G.K., and M.K. Brady. 1930. The courtship of plethodontid salamanders. Copeia 1930: 52–54.

———. 1933. Observations on the life history of the marbled salamander, *Ambystoma opacum* Gravenhorst. Zoologica 11: 89–132.

Noble, G.K., and H.J. Clausen. 1936. The aggregation behavior of *Storeria dekayi* and other snakes, with especial reference to the sense organs involved. Ecol. Monogr. 6: 269–316.

Noble, G.K., and B.C. Marshall. 1929. The breeding habits of two salamanders. Amer. Mus. Novit. 347: 1–11.

Noble, G.K., and R.C. Noble. 1923. The Anderson tree frog *(Hyla andersonii* Baird): Observations on its habits and life history. Zoologica 11: 416–455.

Nunes, V.S., and R.G. Jaeger. 1989. Salamander aggressiveness increases with length of territorial ownership. Copeia 1989: 712–718.

Nyman, S. 1987. Life history notes: *Ambystoma maculatum* reproduction. Herpetol. Rev. 18: 14–15.

Nyman, S., M.J. Ryan, and J.D. Anderson. 1988. The distribution of the *Ambystoma jeffersonianum* complex in New Jersey. J. Herpetol. 22: 224–228.

Obbard, M.E., and R.J. Brooks. 1981. A radio-telemetry and mark-recapture study of activity in the common snapping turtle, *Chelydra serpentina*. Copeia 1981: 630–637.

———. 1987. Prediction of the onset of the annual nesting season of the common snapping turtle, *Chelydra serpentina*. Herpetologica 43: 324–328.

Oplinger, C.S. 1966. Sex ratio, reproductive cycles, and time of ovulation in *Hyla crucifer crucifer* Wied. Herpetologica 22: 276–283.

―――. 1967. Food habits and feeding activity of recently transformed and adult *Hyla crucifer crucifer* Wied. Herpetologica 23: 209–217.

Organ, J.A. 1960. The courtship and spermatophore of the salamander *Plethodon glutinosus*. Copeia 1960: 34–40.

―――. 1961a. The eggs and young of the spring salamander, *Pseudotriton porphyriticus*. Herpetologica 17: 53–56.

―――. 1961b. Studies of the local distribution, life history, and population dynamics of the salamander genus *Desmognathus* in Virginia. Ecol. Monogr. 31: 189–220.

Organ, J.A., and D.J. Organ. 1968. Courtship behavior of the red salamander, *Pseudotriton ruber*. Copeia 1968: 217–223.

Orser, P.M., and D.J. Shure. 1975. Population cycles and activity patterns of the dusky salamander, *Desmognathus fuscus fuscus*. Amer. Midl. Natur. 93: 403–410.

Pace, A.E. 1974. Systematic and biological studies of the leopard frogs (*Rana pipiens* complex) of the United States. Misc. Publ. Mus. Zool., Univ. Mich. 148: 1–140.

Packard, G.C., M.J. Packard, P.L. McDaniel, and L.L. McDaniel. 1989. Tolerance of hatchling painted turtles to subzero temperatures. Can. J. Zool. 67: 828–830.

Palmer, W.M., and A.L. Braswell. 1976. Communal egg laying and hatchlings of the rough green snake, *Opheodrys aestivus* (Linnaeus) (Reptilia, Serpentes, Colubridae). J. Herpetol. 10: 257–259.

―――. 1995. Reptiles of North Carolina. Chapel Hill: University of North Carolina Press.

Palmer, W.M., and G. Tregembo. 1970. Notes on the natural history of the scarlet snake *Cemophora coccinea copei* Jan in North Carolina. Herpetologica 26: 300–302.

Pappas, M.J., and B.J. Brecke. 1992. Habitat selection of juvenile Blanding's turtles, *Emydoidea blandingii*. J. Herpetol. 26: 233–234.

Pauktis, G.L., R.D. Shuman, and F.J. Janzen. 1989. Supercooling and freeze tolerance in hatchling painted turtles (*Chrysemys picta*). Can. J. Zool. 67: 1082–1084.

Pauley, T.K. 1978a. Food types and distribution as a *Plethodon* habitat partitioning factor. Bull. Md. Herpetol. Soc. 14: 79–82.

―――. 1978b. Moisture as a factor regulating habitat partitioning between two sympatric *Plethodon* (Amphibia, Urodela, Plethodontidae) species. J. Herpetol. 12: 491–493.

―――. 1992. Report on amphibian and reptile roadkills in West Virginia. Proc. West Virginia Acad. Sci. 64: 32.

Pauley, T.K., and W.H. England. 1969. Time of mating and egg deposition in the salamander, *Plethodon wehrlei* Fowler and Dunn, in West Virginia. Proc. W. Va. Acad. Sci. 41: 155–160.

Pawling, R.O. 1939. The amphibians and reptiles of Union County, Pennsylvania. Herpetologica 1: 165–169.

Pearson, P.G. 1955. Population ecology of the spadefoot toad, *Scaphiopus h. holbrooki* (Harlan). Ecol. Monogr. 25: 233–267.

Pechmann, J.H.K., and R.D. Semlitsch. 1986. Diel activity patterns in the breeding migrations of winter-breeding anurans. Can. J. Zool. 64: 1116–1120.

Perrill, S.A., and M. Magier. 1988. Male mating behavior in *Acris crepitans*. Copeia 1988: 245–248.

Perrill, S.A., and W.J. Shepherd. 1989. Spatial distribution and male-male communication in the northern cricket frog, *Acris crepitans blanchardi*. J. Herpetol. 23: 237–243.

Peterson, R.C., and R.W. Fritsch. 1986. Connecticut's venomous snakes: The timber rattlesnake and northern copperhead. Bull. State Geol. Natur. Hist. Sur. of Conn. 111: 1–48.

Petranka, J.W. 1979. The effects of severe winter weather on *Plethodon dorsalis* and *P. richmondi* (Amphibia, Urodela, Pelthodontidae) populations in central Kentucky. J. Herpetol. 13: 369–371.

Petranka, J.W., and J.G. Petranka. 1980. Selected aspects of the larval ecology of the marbled salamander *Ambystoma opacum* in the southern portion of its range. Amer. Midl. Natur. 104: 352–363.

———. 1981a. On the evolution of nest site selection in the marbled salamander, *Ambystoma opacum*. Copeia 1981: 387–391.

———. 1981b. Notes on the nesting biology of the marbled salamander, *Ambystoma opacum*, in the southern portion of its range. J. Ala. Acad. Sci. 52: 20–24.

Petranka, J.W., and D.A.G. Thomas. 1995. Explosive breeding reduces egg and tadpole cannibalism in the wood frog, *Rana sylvatica*. Anim. Behav. 50: 731–735.

Petranka, J.W., L.B. Kats, and A. Sih. 1987. Predator-prey interactions among fish and larval amphibians: Use of chemical cues to detect predatory fish. Anim. Behav. 35: 420–425.

Pfingsten, R.A., and F.L. Downs. 1989. Salamanders of Ohio. Bull. Ohio Biol. Sur. 7.

Pfingsten, R.A., and C.F. Walker. 1978. Some nearly all black populations of *Plethodon cinereus* (Amphibia, Urodela, Plethodontidae) in northern Ohio. J. Herpetol. 12: 163–167.

Piatt, J. 1931. An albino salamander. Copeia 1931: 29.

Pinder, A.W., and S.C. Friel. 1994. Oxygen transport in egg masses of the amphibians *Rana sylvatica* and *Ambystoma maculatum:* Convection, diffusion, and oxygen production by algae. J. Exp. Biol. 197: 17–30.

Pisani, G.R. 1971. An unusually large litter of *Virginia valeriae pulchra*. J. Herpetol. 5: 207–208.

Pisani, G.R., and R.C. Bothner. 1970. The annual reproductive cycle of *Thamnophis brachystoma*. Sci. Stud. 26: 15–34.

Pisani, G.R., and J.T. Collins. 1972. The smooth earth snake, *Virginia valeriae* (Baird and Girard), in Kentucky. Trans. Ky. Acad. Sci. 32: 16–25.

Platt, D.R. 1969. Natural history of the hognose snakes *Heterodon platyrhinos* and *Heterodon nasicus*. Univ. Kans. Publ. Mus. Natur. Hist. 18: 253–420.

Platz, J.E. 1989. Speciation within the chorus frog *Pseudacris triseriata*: Morphometric and mating call analyses of the boreal and western subspecies. Copeia 1989: 704–712.

Platz, J.E., and D.C. Forester. 1988. Geographic variation in mating call among the four subspecies of the chorus frog *Pseudacris triseriata* (Wied). Copeia 1988: 1062–1066.

Plummer, M.V. 1976. Some aspects of nesting success in the turtle *Trionyx muticus*. Herpetologica 32: 353–359.

———. 1977a. Activity, habitat and population structure in the turtle, *Trionyx muticus*. Copeia 1977: 431–440.

———. 1977b. Notes on the courtship and mating behavior of the softshell turtle, *Trionyx muticus* (Reptilia, Testudines, Trionychidae). J. Herpetol. 11: 90–92

———. 1977c. Reproduction and growth in the turtle *Trionyx muticus*. Copeia 1977: 440–447.

———. 1981. Habitat utilization, diet and movements of a temperate arboreal snake *(Opheodrys aestivus)*. J. Herpetol. 15: 425–432.

——. 1985a. Demography of green snakes *(Opheodrys aestivus)*. Herpetologica 41: 373–381.

——. 1985b. Growth and maturity in green snakes *(Opheodrys aestivus)*. Herpetologica 41: 28–33.

——. 1987. Geographic variation in body size of green snakes *(Opheodrys aestivus)*. Copeia 1987: 483–485.

——. 1989. Observations on the nesting ecology of green snakes *(Opheodrys aestivus)*. Herpetol. Rev. 20: 87–89.

——. 1990. Nesting movements, nesting behavior, and nest sites of green snakes *(Opheodrys aestivus)* revealed by radiotelemetry. Herpetologica 46: 190–195.

Plummer, M.V., and D.B. Farrar. 1981. Sexual dietary differences in a population of *Trionyx muticus*. J. Herpetol. 15: 175–179.

Plummer, M.V., and H.L. Snell. 1988. Nest site selection and water relations of eggs in the snake, *Opheodrys aestivus*. Copeia 1988: 58–64.

Pluto, T.G., and E.D. Bellis. 1986. Habitat utilization by the turtle, *Graptemys geographica*, along a river. J. Herpetol. 20: 22–31.

——. 1988. Seasonal and annual movements of riverine map turtles, *Graptemys geographica*. J. Herpetol. 22: 152–158.

Pope, C.H. 1928. Some plethodontid salamanders from North Carolina and Kentucky with the description of a new race of *Leurognathus*. Amer. Mus. Novit. 306: 1–19.

——. 1944. Amphibians and reptiles of the Chicago area. Chicago: Chicago Museum of Natural History Press.

Portnoy, J.W. 1990. Breeding biology of the spotted salamander *Ambystoma maculatum* (Shaw) in acidic temporary ponds at Cape Cod, USA. Biol. Cons. 53: 61–75.

Pough, F.H. 1971. Leech-repellent property of eastern red-spotted newts, *Notophthalmus viridescens*. Science 174: 1144–1146.

——. 1974. Comments on the presumed mimicry of red efts *(Notophthalmus)* by red salamanders *(Pseudotriton)*. Herpetologica 30: 24–27.

Pough, F.H., E.M. Smith, D.H. Rhodes, and A. Collazo. 1987. The abundance of salamanders in forest stands with different histories of disturbance. For. Ecol. Manage. 20: 1–9.

Powders, V.N., and W.L. Tietjen. 1974. The comparative food habits of sympatric and allopatric salamanders, *Plethodon glutinosus* and *Plethodon jordani* in eastern Tennessee and adjacent areas. Herpetologica 30: 167–175.

Prieto, A.A. 1975. Reproductive cycle of the northern ring-necked snake, *Diadophis punctatus edwardsi* (Merrem) in New Jersey. Bull. N.J. Acad. Sci. 20: 14–17.

Pritchard, P.C.H. 1989. The alligator snapping turtle: Biology and conservation. Milwaukee: Milwaukee Public Museum.

Punzo, F. 1992. Dietary overlap and activity patterns in sympatric populations of *Scaphiopus holbrooki* (Pelobatidae) and *Bufo terrestris* (Bufonidae). Florida Scientist. 55: 38–44.

Quinn, N.W.S., and D.P. Tate. 1991. Seasonal movements and habitat of wood turtles *(Clemmys insculpta)* in Algonquin Park, Canada. J. Herpetol. 25: 217–220.

Ralin, D.B. 1968. Ecological and reproductive differentiation in the cryptic species of the *Hyla versicolor* complex (Hylidae). Southwest. Natur. 13: 283–300.

Rand, A.S. 1954. A defense display in the salamander *Ambystoma jeffersonianum*. Copeia 1954: 223–224.

Raney, E.C. 1940. Summer movements of the bullfrog, *Rana catesbeiana* Shaw, as determined by the jaw-tag method. Amer. Midl. Natur. 23: 733–745.

Raney, E.C., and W.M. Ingram. 1941. Growth of tagged frogs (*Rana catesbeiana* Shaw and *Rana clamitans* Daudin) under natural conditions. Amer. Midl. Natur. 26: 201–206.

Raney, E.C., and E.A. Lachner. 1942. Summer food of *Chrysemys picta marginata*, in Chautauqua Lake, New York. Copeia 1942: 83–85.

Raney, E.C., and R.M. Roecker. 1947. Food and growth of two species of water-snakes from western New York. Copeia 1947: 171–174.

Reinert, H.K. 1981. Reproduction by the massasauga (*Sistrurus catenatus catenatus*). Amer. Midl. Natur. 105: 393–395.

———. 1984a. Habitat separation between sympatric snake populations. Ecology 65: 478–486.

———. 1984b. Habitat variation within sympatric snake populations. Ecology 65: 1673–1682.

Reinert, H.K., and W.R. Kodrich. 1982. Movements and habitat utilization by the massasauga, *Sistrurus catenatus catenatus*. J. Herpetol. 16: 162–171.

Reinert, H.K., and R.R. Rupert Jr. 1999. Impact of translocation on behavior and survival of timber rattlesnakes, *Crotalus horridus*. J. Herpetol. 33: 45–61.

Reinert, H.K., D. Cundall, and L.M. Bushar. 1984. Foraging behavior of the timber rattlesnake, *Crotalus horridus*. Copeia 1984: 976–981.

Richmond, N.D. 1947. Life history of *Scaphiopus holbrookii holbrookii* (Harlan). Part I: Larval development and behavior. Ecology 28: 53–67.

———. 1952. First record of the green salamander in Pennsylvania, and other range extensions in Pennsylvania, Virginia, and West Virginia. Ann. Carnegie Mus. 32: 313–318.

———. 1954. The ground snake, *Haldea valeriae* in Pennsylvania and West Virginia with description of new subspecies. Ann. Carnegie Mus. 33: 251–260.

Rigley, L. 1971. "Combat dance" of the black rat snake, *Elaphe o. obsoleta*. J. Herpetol. 5: 65–66.

Ritke, M.E., J.G. Babb, and M.K. Ritke. 1990. Life history of the gray treefrog (*Hyla chrysoscelis*) in western Tennessee. J. Herpetol. 24: 135–141.

Robb, L., and D. Toews. 1977. Effects of low ambient pH on perivitelline fluid of *Ambystoma maculatum* (Shaw) eggs. Environ. Pollut. 44: 101–107.

Robinson, C., and J.R. Bider. 1988. Nesting synchrony—A strategy to decrease predation of snapping turtle (*Chelydra serpentina*) nests. J. Herpetol. 22: 470–473.

Robinson, G.D., and W.A. Dunson. 1976. Water and sodium balance in the estuarine diamondback terrapin (*Malaclemys*). J. Comp. Physiol. 105: 129–152.

Robinson, K.M., and G.G. Murphy. 1978. The reproductive cycle of the eastern spiny softshell turtle (*Trionyx spiniferus spiniferus*). Herpetologica 34: 137–140.

Robinson, T.S., and K.T. Reichard. 1965. Notes on the breeding biology of the midland mud salamander, *Pseudotriton montanus diastictus*. J. Ohio Herpetol. Soc. 5: 29.

Roble, S.M. 1985. Observations on satellite males in *Hyla chrysoscelis, Hyla picta* and *Pseudacris triseriata*. J. Herpetol. 19: 432–436.

Roddy, H.J. 1928. Reptiles of Lancaster County and the state of Pennsylvania. Lancaster, Pa.: Science Press.

Rosen, M., and R.E. Lemon. 1974. The vocal behavior of spring peepers, *Hyla crucifer*. Copeia 1974: 940–950.

Rosen, P.C. 1991. Comparative ecology and life history of the racer (*Coluber constrictor*) in Michigan. Copeia 1991: 897–909.

Ross, D.A., and R.K. Anderson. 1990. Habitat use, movements, and nesting of *Emydoidea blandingi* in central Wisconsin. J. Herpetol. 24: 6–12.

Ross, D.A., K.N. Brewster, R.K. Anderson, N. Ratner, and C.M. Brewster. 1991. Aspects of the ecology of wood turtles, *Clemmys insculpta*, in Wisconsin. Can. Field Nat. 105: 363–367.

Rossman, D.A. 1963. The colubrid snake genus *Thamnophis*: A revision of the *sauritus* group. Bull. Fla. State Mus. 7: 99–178.

———. 1970. *Thamnophis sauritus* (Linnaeus). Cat. Amer. Amph. Rept. 99.1–99.2.

Rossman, D.A., and P.A. Myer. 1990. Behavioral and morphological adaptations for snail extraction in the North American brown snakes (genus *Storeria*). J. Herpetol. 24: 434–438.

Rossman, D.A., and R. Powell. 1985. *Clonophis* Cope. Cat. Amer. Amph. Rept. 364.1–364.2.

Routman, E., R. Wu, and A.R. Templeton. 1994. Parsimony, molecular evolution, and biogeography: The case of the North American giant salamander. Evolution 48: 1799–1809.

Row, C.L., and W.A. Dunson. 1993. Relationship among abiotic parameters and breeding effort by three amphibians in temporary wetlands of central Pennsylvania. Wetlands 13: 237–246.

Rowe, J.W. 1992. Dietary habits of the Blanding's turtle *(Emydoidea blandingi)* in northeastern Illinois. J. Herpetol. 26: 111–114.

Rowe, J.W., and E.O. Moll. 1991. A radiotelemetric study of activity and movements of the Blanding's turtle *(Emydoidea blandingi)* in northeastern Illinois. J. Herpetol. 25: 178–185.

Rubin, D. 1963. An albino two-lined salamander. Herpetologica 19: 72.

———. 1965. Occurrence of the spadefoot toad, *Scaphiopus holbrooki* (Harlan) in Vigo County, Indiana. Herpetologica 21: 153–154.

Ryan, M.J. 1978. A thermal property of the *Rana catesbeiana* (Amphibia, Anura, Ranidae) egg mass. J. Herpetol. 12: 247–248.

———. 1980. The reproductive behavior of the bullfrog *(Rana catesbeiana)*. Copeia 1980: 108–114.

Sanders, J.S., and J.S. Jacob. 1981. Thermal ecology of the copperhead *(Agkistrodon contortrix)*. Herpetologica 37: 264–270.

Saumure, R.A., and J.R. Bider. 1998. Impact of agricultural development on a population of wood turtle *(Clemmys insculpta)* in southern Quebec, Canada. Chelonian Conserv. Biol. 3: 37–45.

Sayler, A. 1966. The reproductive ecology of the red-backed salamander, *Plethodon cinereus*, in Maryland. Copeia 1966: 183–193.

Schoener, T.W. 1979. Inferring the properties of predation and other injury-producing agents from injury frequencies. Ecology 60: 1110–1115.

Schueler, F.W. 1975. Geographic variation in the size of *Rana septentrionalis* in Quebec, Ontario, and Manitoba. J. Herpetol. 9: 177–186.

———. 1987. *Rana septentrionalis*: Terrestrial activity. Herpetol Rev. 18: 72.

Schuett, G.W., and J.C. Gillingham. 1986. Sperm storage and multiple paternity in the copperhead, *Agkistrodon contortrix*. Copeia 1986: 807–811.

———. 1988. Courtship and mating of the copperhead, *Agkistrodon contortrix*. Copeia 1988: 374–381.

———. 1989. Male-male agonistic behaviour of the copperhead, *Agkistrodon contortrix*. Amph. Rept. 10: 243–266.

Schwartz, J.M., G.F. McCracken, and G.M. Burghardt. 1989. Multiple paternity in wild populations of the garter snake, *Thamnophis sirtalis*. Behav. Ecol. Sociobiol. 25: 269–273.

Schwartzkopf, L., and R.J. Brooks. 1985. Sex determination in northern painted turtles: Effect of incubation at constant and fluctuating temperatures. Can. J. Zool. 63: 2543–2547.

Seale, D.B. 1982. Physical factors influencing oviposition by the woodfrog, *Rana sylvatica*, in Pennsylvania. Copeia 1982: 627–635.

Seibert, H.C., and C.W. Hagen Jr. 1947. Studies on a population of snakes in Illinois. Copeia 1947: 6–22.

Seigel, R.A. 1980. Nesting habits of diamondback terrapins *(Malaclemys terrapin)* on the Atlantic coast of Florida. Trans. Kans. Acad. Sci. 83: 239–246.

———. 1984. Parameters of two populations of diamondback terrapins *(Malaclemys terrapin)* on the Atlantic coast of Florida. Pages 77–87 in R.A. Seigel, L.E. Hunt, J.L. Knight, L. Malaret, and N.L. Zuschlag, eds., Vertebrate ecology and systematics: A tribute to Henry S. Fitch. University of Kansas Museum of Natural History Special Publication 10.

———. 1986. Ecology and conservation of an endangered rattlesnake, *Sistrurus catenatus*, in Missouri, USA. Biol. Conserv. 35: 333–346.

Siegel, R.A., and H.S. Fitch. 1985. Annual variation in reproduction in snakes in a fluctuating environment. J. Anim. Ecol. 54: 497–505.

Seigel, R.A., and J.W. Gibbons. 1995. Workshop on the ecology, status, and management of the diamondback terrapin *(Malaclemys terrapin)*, Savannah River Ecology Laboratory, 2 August 1994: Final results and recommendations. Chelonian Conserv. Biol. 1: 240–243.

Semlitsch, R.D. 1980. Geographic and local variation in population parameters of the slimy salamander *Plethodon glutinosus*. Herpetologica 36: 6–16.

Semlitsch, R.D., and G.B. Moran. 1984. Ecology of the redbelly snake *(Storeria occipitomaculata)* using mesic habitats in South Carolina. Amer. Midl. Natur. 111: 33–40.

Sexton, O.J., and L. Claypool. 1978. Nest sites of a northern population of an oviparous snake, *Opheodrys vernalis* (Serpentes, Colubridae). J. Natur. Hist. 12: 365–370.

Sexton, O.J., and S.R. Hunt. 1980. Temperature relationships and movements of snakes *(Elaphe obsoleta, Coluber constrictor)* in a cave hibernaculum. Herpetologica 36: 20–26.

Sexton, O.J., and K.R. Marion. 1974. Duration of incubation of *Sceloporus undulatus* eggs at constant temperature. Physiol. Zool. 47: 91–98.

Sexton, O.J., J. Bizer, D.C. Gayou, P. Freiling, and M. Moutseous. 1986. Field studies of breeding spotted salamanders, *Ambystoma maculatum* in eastern Missouri, USA. Milw. Public Mus. Contr. Biol. Geol. 67: 1–19.

Shirose, L.J., and R.J. Brooks. 1995. Growth rate and age at maturity in syntopic populations of *Rana clamitans* and *Rana septentrionalis* in central Ontario. Can. J. Zool. 73: 1468–1473.

Shoop, C.R. 1965. Aspects of reproduction in Louisiana *Necturus* populations. Amer. Midl. Natur. 74: 357–367.

———. 1987. Sea turtles. Pages 357–358 in R.H. Bachus, ed., Georges Bank. Cambridge, Mass.: MIT Press.

Simmons, R.S., and C.J. Stine. 1961. Ankylosis and xanthism in the eastern worm snake. Herpetologica 17: 206–208.

Skorepa, A.C., and J.E. Ozment. 1968. Habitat, habits, and variation of *Kinosternon subrubrum* in southern Illinois. Trans. Ill. State Acad. Sci. 61: 247–251.

Smith, A.G. 1945. *Agkistrodon mokeson mokeson* (Daudin) in Pennsylvania. Proc. Pa. Acad. Sci. 19: 69–79.

Smith, C.K., and J.W. Petranka. 1987. Prey size distribution and size specific foraging success of *Ambystoma* larvae. Oecologica 71: 239–244.

Smith, D.C. 1983. Factors controlling tadpole populations of the chorus frog *(Pseudacris triseriata)* on Isle Royale, Michigan. Ecology 64: 501–510.

Smith, D.G. 1998. Ecological factors influencing the antipredator behaviors of the ground skink, *Scincella lateralis.* Behav. Ecol. 8: 622–629.

Smith, H.M. 1967. The handbook of lizards, 4th ed. Binghamton, N.Y.: Comstock Publishing.

Smith, H.M., and F.N. White. 1955. Adrenal enlargement and its significance in the hognose snakes *(Heterodon).* Herpetologica 11: 137–144.

Smith, P.W. 1961. The amphibians and reptiles of Illinois. Ill. Natur. Hist. Sur. Bull. 28: 1–298.

Southerland, M.T. 1986. The effects of variation in streamside habitats on the composition of mountain salamander communities. Copeia 1984: 731–741.

Stangel, P.W. 1988. Premetamorphic survival of the salamander, *Ambystoma maculatum* in eastern Massachussetts. J. Herpetol. 22: 345–347.

Stenhouse, S.L., N.G. Hairston, and A.E. Cobey. 1983. Predation and competition in *Ambystoma* larvae: Field and laboratory experiments. J. Herpetol. 17: 210–220.

Stewart, B.G. 1984. *Agkistrodon contortrix laticinctus* (broad-banded copperhead): Combat. Herpetol. Rev. 15: 17.

Stewart, M.M. 1968. Population dynamics of *Eurycea bislineata* in New York. J. Herpetol. 2: 176–177.

Stickel, L.F. 1950. Populations and home range relationships of the box turtle, *Terrapene c. carolina* (Linnaeus). Ecol. Monogr. 20: 351–378.

———. 1978. Changes in a box turtle population during three decades. Copeia 1978: 221–225.

———. 1989. Home range behavior among box turtles *(Terrapene c. carolina)* of a bottomland forest in Maryland. J. Herpetol. 23: 40–44.

Stickel, L.F., W.H. Stickel, and F.C. Schmid. 1980. Ecology of a Maryland population of black rat snakes *(Elaphe o. obsoleta).* Amer. Midl. Natur. 103: 1–14.

Stille, W.T. 1954. Eggs of the salamander *Ambystoma jeffersonianum* in the Chicago area. Copeia 1954: 300.

Stinner, J., N. Zarlinger, and S. Orcutt. 1994. Overwintering behavior of adult bullfrogs, *Rana catesbeiana,* in northeastern Ohio. Ohio J. Sci. 94: 8–13.

Stokes, G.D., and W.A. Dunson. 1982. Permeability and chemical structure of reptile skin. Amer. J. Physiol. 242: F681–F689.

Stoneburner, D.L. 1978. Salamander drift: Observations on the two-lined salamander *(Eurycea bislineata).* Freshwater Biol. 8: 291–293.

Storey, K.B., and J.M. Storey. 1987. Persistence of freeze tolerance in terrestrially hibernating frogs after spring emergence. Copeia 1987: 720–726.

Surface, H.A. 1906. The serpents of Pennsylvania. Monthly Bull. Div. Zool. Pa. Dept. Agr. 4: 114–202.

———. 1908. First report on the economic features of the turtles of Pennsylvania. Zool. Bull. Div. Zool. Pa. Dept. Agr. 6: 107–195.

———. 1913. First report on the economic features of the amphibians of Pennsylvania. Zool. Bull. Div. Zool. Pa. Dept. Agr. 3: 68–153.

Sutherland, I.D.W. 1958. The "combat dance" of the timber rattlesnake. Herpetologica 14: 23–24.

Swain, T.A., and H.M. Smith. 1978. Communal nesting in *Coluber constrictor* in Colorado (Reptilia: Serpentes). Herpetologica 34: 175–177.

Swanson, P.L. 1948. Notes on the amphibians of Venango County, Pennsylvania. Amer. Midl. Natur. 40: 362–371.

———. 1952. The reptiles of Venango County, Pennsylvania. Amer. Midl. Natur. 47: 161–182.

Taylor, E.H. 1935. A taxonomic study of the cosmopolitan scincoid lizards of the genus *Eumeces* with an account of the distribution and relationships of its species. Bull. Univ. Kans. 36: 1–643.

Test, F.H., and H. Heatwole. 1962. Nesting sites of the red-backed salamander, *Plethodon cinereus*, in Michigan. Copeia 1962: 206–207.

Thomas, E.S., and M.B. Trautman. 1937. Segregated hibernation of *Sternotherus odoratus* (Latreille). Copeia 1937: 231.

Thompson, E.L., and G.J. Taylor. 1985. Notes on the green salamander, *Aneides aeneus* in Maryland. Bull. Md. Herpetol. Soc. 21: 107–114.

Thompson, E.L., J.E. Gates, and G.J. Taylor. 1980. Distribution and breeding habitat selection of the Jefferson salamander, *Ambystoma jeffersonianum*, in Maryland. J. Herpetol. 14: 113–120.

Tiebout, H.M., III, and J.R. Cary. 1987. Dynamic spatial ecology of the water snake, *Nerodia sipedon*. Copeia 1987: 1–18.

Tilley, S.G. 1973. Observations on the larval period and female reproductive ecology of *Desmognathus ochrophaeus* (Amphibia: Plethodontidae) in western North Carolina. Amer. Midl. Natur. 89: 394–407.

Tilley, S.G., and M.J. Mahoney. 1996. Patterns of genetic differentiation in salamanders of the *Desmognathus ochrophaeus* complex (Amphibia: Plethodontidae). Herpetol. Monogr. 10: 1–42.

Tilley, S.G., B.L. Lundrigan, and L.P. Brower. 1982. Erythrism and mimicry in the salamander *Plethodon cinereus*. Herpetologica 38: 409–417.

Tinkle, D.W. 1961. Geographic variation in reproduction, size, sex ratio and maturity of *Sternothaerus odoratus* (Testudinata: Chelydridae). Ecology 42: 68–76.

Tinkle, D.W., and R.E. Ballinger. 1972. *Sceloporus undulatus:* A study of the intraspecific comparative demography of a lizard. Ecology 53: 570–584.

Topping, M.S., and C.A. Ingersol. 1981. Fecundity in the hellbender, *Cryptobranchus alleganiensis*. Copeia 1981: 873–876.

Trapido, H. 1940. Mating time and sperm viability in *Storeria*. Copeia 1940: 107–109.

———. 1944. The snakes of the genus *Storeria*. Amer. Midl. Natur. 31: 1–84.

Trauth, S.E. 1982. *Cemophora coccinea* (scarlet snake) reproduction. Herpetol. Rev. 13: 126.

Tryon, B.W. 1984. Additional instances of multiple egg clutch production in snakes. Trans. Kans. Acad. Sci. 87: 98–104.

Tucker, J.K. 1976. Observations on the birth of a brood of Kirtland's water snake, *Clonophis kirtlandi* (Kennicott) (Reptilia, Serpentes, Colubridae). J. Herpetol. 10: 53–54.

———. 1977. Notes on the food habits of Kirtland's water snake, *Clonophis kirtlandii*. Bull. Md. Herpetol. Soc. 13: 193–195.

Turner, F.B. 1960. Estimation of a Louisiana population of the skink, *Lygosoma laterale*. Ecology 41: 574–577.

Tuttle, S.E., and D.M. Carroll. 1997. Ecology and natural history of the wood turtle (*Clemmys insculpta*) in southern New Hampshire. Chelonian Conserv. Biol. 2: 447–449.

Tyning, T.F. 1977. A yellow albino *Desmognathus fuscus* from western Massachussetts. Herpetol. Rev. 8: 118.

Ultsch, G.R., and J.T. Duke. 1990. Gas exchange and habitat selection in the aquatic salamanders *Necturus maculosus* and *Cryptobranchus alleganiensis*. Oecologia 83: 250–258.

Uzzell, T. 1967. *Ambystoma laterale*. Cat. Amer. Amph. Rept. 48.1–48.2.

Vinegar, A., and M. Friedman. 1967. *Necturus* in Rhode Island. Herpetologica 23: 51.

Vitt, L.J., and W.E. Cooper Jr. 1985. The evolution of sexual dimorphism in the skink *Eumeces laticeps*: An example of sexual selection. Can. J. Zool. 63: 995–1002.

———. 1986a. Foraging and diet of a diurnal predator *(Eumeces laticeps)* feeding on hidden prey. J. Herpetol. 20: 408–415.

———. 1986b. Skink reproduction and sexual dimorphism: *Eumeces fasciatus* in the southeastern United States, with notes on *Eumeces inexpectatus*. J. Herpetol. 20: 65–76.

———. 1986c. Tail loss, tail color, and predator escape in *Eumeces* (Lacertilia: Scincidae): Age-specific differences in costs and benefits. Can. J. Zool. 64: 583–592.

Vogt, R.C. 1981a. Food partitioning in three sympatric species of map turtle, genus *Graptemys* (Testudinata, Emydidae). Amer. Midl. Natur. 105: 102–111.

———. 1981b. Natural history of amphibians and reptiles of Wisconsin. Milwaukee: Milwaukee Museum Press.

Vogt, R.C., and J.J. Bull. 1984. Ecology of hatchling sex ratio in map turtles. Ecology 65: 582–587.

Waldman, B. 1982. Adaptive significance of communal oviposition in wood frogs *(Rana sylvatica)*. Behav. Ecol. Sociobiol. 10: 169–174.

Waldman, B., and M.J. Ryan. 1983. Thermal advantages of communal egg mass deposition in wood frogs *(Rana sylvatica)*. J. Herpetol. 17: 70–72.

Walker, C.F. 1946. The amphibians of Ohio. Part 1: The frogs and toads (order Salientia). Ohio State Mus. Sci. Bull. 1: 1–109.

Walker, C.F., and W. Goodpaster. 1941. The green salamander, *Aneides aeneus*, in Ohio. Copeia 1941: 178.

Walker, D.J. 1963. Notes on broods of *Virginia valeriae* Barid and Girard in Ohio. J. Ohio Herpetol. Soc. 4: 54.

Wallace, J.T., and R.W. Barbour. 1957. Observations on the eggs and young of *Plethodon richmondi*. Copeia 1957: 48.

Walls, S.C., and R. Altig. 1986. Female reproductive biology and larval life history of *Ambystoma* salamanders: A comparison of egg size, hatchling size, and larval growth. Herpetologica 42: 334–345.

Ward, F.P., C.J. Hohmann, J.F. Ulrich, and S.E. Hill. 1976. Seasonal microhabitat selection of spotted turtles *(Clemmys guttata)* in Maryland elucidated by radioisotope tracking. Herpetologica 32: 60–64.

Warkentin, K.M. 1992. Microhabitat use and feeding rate variation in green frog tadpoles *(Rana clamitans)*. Copeia 1992: 731–740.

Weatherhead, P.J. 1989. Temporal and thermal aspects of hibernation of black rat snakes *(Elaphe obsoleta)* in Ontario. Can. J. Zool. 67: 2332–2335.

Weatherhead, P.J., and M.B. Charland. 1985. Habitat selection in an Ontario population of the snake, *Elaphe obsoleta*. J. Herpetol. 19: 12–19.

Weatherhead, P.J., and D.J. Hoysak. 1989. Spatial and activity patterns of black rat snakes *(Elaphe obsoleta)* from radiotelemetry and recapture data. Can. J. Zool. 67: 463–468.

Weaver, W.G., Jr. 1965. The cranial anatomy of the hog-nosed snakes *(Heterodon)*. Bull. Fla. State Mus. Biol. Sci. 9: 275–304.

Webb, R.G. 1962. North American recent soft-shelled turtles *(family Trionychidae)*. Univ. Kans. Publ. Mus. Natur. Hist. 13: 429–611.

Wells, K.D. 1976. Multiple egg clutches in the green frog *(Rana clamitans)*. Herpetologica 32: 85–87.

———. 1977. Territoriality and male mating success in the green frog *(Rana clamitans)*. Ecology 58: 750–762.

———. 1980. Spatial associations among individuals in a population of slimy salamanders *(Plethodon glutinosus)*. Herpetologica 36: 271–275.

Wells, K.D., and R.A. Wells. 1976. Patterns of movement in a population of the slimy salamander, *Plethodon glutinosus*, with observations on aggregation. Herpetologica 32: 156–162.

Werner, E.E., G.A. Wellborn, and M.A. Peek. 1995. Diet composition in postmetamorphic bullfrogs and green frogs: Implication for interspecific predation and competition. J. Herpetol. 29: 600–607.

Werner, J.K. 1971. Notes on the reproductive cycle of *Plethodon cinereus* in Michigan. Copeia 1971: 161–162.

Whitaker, J.O., Jr. 1971. A study of the western chorus frog, *Pseudacris triseriata*, in Vigo County, Indiana. J. Herpetol. 5: 127–150.

Whitaker, J.O., Jr., D. Rubin, and J.R. Munsee. 1977. Observations on food habits of four species of spadefoot toads, genus *Scaphiopus*. Herpetologica 33: 468–475.

White, D., Jr., and D. Moll. 1991. Clutch size and annual reproductive potential of the turtle *Graptemys geographica* in a Missouri stream. J. Herpetol. 25: 493–494.

Whitford, W.G., and A. Vinegar. 1966. Homing, survivorship, and overwintering of larvae in spotted salamanders, *Ambystoma maculatum*. Copeia 1966: 515–519.

Wilder, I.W. 1924. The developmental history of *Eurycea bislineata* in western Massachussetts. Copeia 1924: 77–80.

Williams, D.R., J.E. Gates, C.H. Hocutt, and G.J. Taylor. 1981. The hellbender: A nongame species in need of management. Wildl. Soc. Bull. 9: 94–100.

Williams, E.C., Jr., and W.S. Parker. 1987. A long-term study of a box turtle *(Terrapene carolina)* population at Allee Memorial Woods, Indiana, with emphasis on survivorship. Herpetologica 43: 328–335.

Williams, K.L. 1978. Systematics and natural history of the American milk snake, *Lampropeltis triangulum*. Milw. Public Mus. Publ. Biol. Geol. 2: 1–258.

Williams, T.A., and J.L. Christiansen. 1981. The niches of two sympatric softshell turtles, *Trionyx muticus* and *Trionyx spiniferus*, in Iowa. J. Herpetol. 15: 303–308.

Willis, L., S.T. Threlkeld, and C.C. Carpenter. 1982. Tail loss patterns in *Thamnophis* (Reptilia: Colubridae) and the probable fate of injured individuals. Copeia 1982: 98–101.

Wilson, V. 1951. Some notes on a captive scarlet snake. Herpetologica 7: 172.

Wood, J.T. 1944. Fall aggregation of the queen snake. Copeia 1944: 253.

———. 1945. Ovarian eggs in *Plethodon richmondi*. Herpetologica 2: 206–209.

Wood, J.T., and W.E. Duellman. 1951. Ovarian egg complements in the salamander *Eurycea bislineata rivicola* Mittleman. Copeia 1951: 181.

Woodward, B.D. 1982. Local intraspecific variation in clutch parameters in the spotted salamander *(Ambystoma maculatum)*. Copeia 1982: 157–160.

———. 1987. Interactions between Woodhouse's toad tadpoles *(Bufo woodhousei)* of mixed sizes. Copeia 1987: 380–386.

Woolcott, W.L. 1959. Notes on the eggs and young of the scarlet snake, *Cemophora coccinea* Blumenbach. Copeia 1959: 263.

Wright, A.H. 1932. Life-histories of the frogs of Okefinokee swamp, Georgia. New York: Macmillan.

Wright, A.H., and A.A. Wright. 1949. Handbook of frogs and toads. Ithaca, N.Y.: Comstock.

———. 1957. Handbook of snakes of the United States and Canada. 2 vols. Ithaca. N.Y.: Comstock.

Wyman, R.L., and D.S. Hawksley-Lescault. 1987. Soil acidity affects distribution, behavior, and physiology of the salamander *Plethodon cinereus*. Ecology 68: 1819–1827.

Yearicks, E.F., R.C. Wood, and W.S. Johnson. 1981. Hibernation of the northern diamondback terrapin, *Malaclemys terrapin*.

Yoder, H.D. 1940. The amphibians of Blair County. Proc. Pa. Acad. Sci. 14: 90–92.

Zappalorti, R.T., E.W. Johnson, and Z. Leszczynski. 1983. The ecology of the northern pine snake, *Pituophis melanoleucus melanoleucus* (Daudin) (Reptilia, Serpentes, Colubridae), in southern New Jersey, with special notes on habitat and nesting behavior. Bull. Chic. Herpetol. Soc. 18: 57–72.

Index

Note: Page numbers with an m indicate maps.